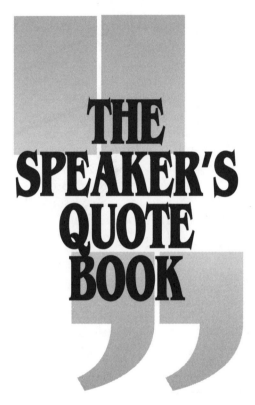

THE SPEAKER'S QUOTE BOOK

Also by Roy B. Zuck

THE SPEAKER'S QUOTE BOOK

Over 4,500 Illustrations and Quotations for All Occasions

Roy B. Zuck

kregel
PUBLICATIONS

Grand Rapids, MI 49501

The Speaker's Quote Book: Over 4,500 Illustrations and Quotations for All Occasions

Copyright © 1997 by Roy B. Zuck

Published by Kregel Publications, a division of Kregel, Inc., P.O. Box 2607, Grand Rapids, MI 49501. Kregel Publications provides trusted, biblical publications for Christian growth and service. Your comments and suggestions are valued.

For more information about Kregel Publications, visit our web site at http://www.kregel.com.

Cover design: Don Ellens
Book design: Nicholas G. Richardson

Library of Congress Cataloging-in-Publication Data
Zuck, Roy B.
    The speaker's quote book: illustrations and quotations for all occasions / [compiled by] Roy B. Zuck.
        p.   cm.
    Includes index.
    1. Quotations. I. Zuck, Roy B.
PN6084.O3S67   1997   082—dc20   96-33123
                                                                              CIP
ISBN 0-8254-4098-x

Printed in the United States of America
3 / 01 00 99

PREFACE

Years ago on my first ministry trip overseas I visited several countries in Africa. Preparing for the trip, I asked a friend how best to communicate with people in that culture. He responded, "Africans love stories. So, in your stories be a storyteller."

That sound advice applies to every culture. Everyone loves stories. Why? Because anecdotes clarify truths making them sparkle with interest. As homiletician Andrew Blackwood put it, a rightly chosen illustration can "make facts shine." Each of Jesus' stories—and He told dozens of them—made His teaching graphic and nabbed His listeners' interest.

Besides clarifying and illuminating ideas, illustrations are also effective in applying biblical truths. They help hearers sense how concepts work out in life. An apt anecdote often drives home an explanation or exhortation, prompting listeners to respond.

An appropriate quotation adds authority to what you are communicating. Citing the words of an authority figure underscores and further validates your point.

Touches of humor, anecdotes, relevant stories, fitting poems—all these help make sermons, lessons, and speeches palatable, personal, and even pleasant and enjoyable.

Where known, I have included the names of authors and publishers. I am grateful to the several publishers who have given permission to cite from their works.

If you are like most speakers, you are a detective, constantly prowling for just the right illustration to clarify, personify, or verify your messages. Hopefully these anecdotes, jokes, and quotations that I've collected for over fifty years can add to your trove of usable illustrations.

ROY B. ZUCK

The author gratefully acknowledges the following who have granted permission for the reprinting of copyrighted material:

From *Bits & Pieces,* © 1996 The Economics Press, Inc., Fairfield, N.Y. Used by permission of the publisher.

From *Encyclopedia of 7,700 Illustrations* by Paul Lee Tan, © 1979 by Usherance Publishers. Used by permission of Bible Communications, Inc., Dallas, Texas.

From *Our Daily Bread,* various editions. © RBC Ministries, Grand Rapids, Michigan. Used by permission of the publisher.

From *Rolling in the Aisles* by Murray Watts. © 1987 by Kingsway Publications. Used by permission of the author.

From *The Vance Havner Quote Book* by Dennis J. Hester. © 1989 by Baker Book House, Grand Rapids, Michigan. Used by permission of the publishers.

A

ACCOMPLISHMENTS

Look at a day when you are supremely satisfied at the end. It's not a day when you lounge around doing nothing. It's when you've had everything to do, and you've done it.

—Margaret Thatcher

Most of us can do more than we think we can but usually do less than we think we have.

—*Bits & Pieces*

All God's giants have been weak men who did great things for God, because they reckoned on God's being with them.

—J. Hudson Taylor

If you want to be remembered after you're dead, write something worth reading, or do something worth writing about.

—Benjamin Franklin

If you can imagine it, you can possess it. If you can dream it, you can become it. If you can envision it, you can attain it. If you can picture it, you can achieve it.

—William Arthur Ward

ACCOUNTABILITY

"What is the greatest thought that has ever passed through your head?" someone asked Daniel Webster. He answered, "My accountability to God."

ACHIEVEMENT

Whatever a man can conceive and believe, he can achieve.

—Napoleon Hill

You wouldn't have the desire for a thing if you couldn't achieve it.

—Earl Nightingale

Rostropovich, the celebrated cellist, was asked to comment on the excellence he has achieved in his field. He said, "If I ever felt I had reached the zenith of musical accomplishment, it would be my death, my musical death."

ACTION

To look is one thing. To see what you look at is another. To understand what you see is a third. To learn from what you understand is still something else. But to act on what you learn is all that really matters.

—*Bits & Pieces*

Action may not always bring happiness; but there is no happiness without action.

—Benjamin Disraeli

In Hong Kong, Lee Kai San was not allowed to taste the wedding cake of his brother. So he jumped from a twelve-story building. But on the way down he grabbed a pole and hung on. After firemen rescued him, Lee told them, "After I jumped I realized I'd never taste the cake, so I changed my mind."

Iron rusts from disuse; water loses its purity from stagnation and in cold weather becomes frozen; so inaction saps the vigors of the mind.

—Leonardo da Vinci

The great end of life is not knowledge but action.

—Aldous Huxley

People can be divided into three groups: those who make things happen, those who watch things happen, and those who wonder what happened.

—John W. Newbern

Even if you are on the right track, you'll get run over if you just sit there.

See everything; overlook a lot; deal with a little.

—Pope John XXIII

ADOLESCENCE

Adolescence is like a house on moving day—a temporary mess.

—Julius E. Warren

ADOLESCENCE

Adolescence is that period in life when a youngster apologizes to his friends for having old-fashioned parents.

ADULTHOOD

An adult is a person who has stopped growing everywhere except in the middle.

ADVENTURE

While most criminologists can easily explain how slum conditions and broken homes lead to crime, there is still no conclusive answer to another problem: What motivates middle-class or affluent youngsters to commit senseless crimes? From my own unscientific contacts with prison inmates and former offenders, Miss Muriel Gardiner's theory about one current cause makes a great deal of sense [in her book, *The Deadly Innocents,* Basic Books, 1976]. She says children in our society have little opportunity for adventure, except vicariously, through watching television, something eminently unsatisfying. It merely whets, in a sometimes disastrous way, a normal appetite for adventure, satisfied often in former days through the dangers of exploration or the vicissitudes of frontier life. Where is the teenage boy or girl to find adventure outside of crime?

—Selwyn Raab, *New York Times*

ADVICE

Advice from friends is like the weather: some of it is good, some of it is bad.

—Arnold Lobel

Advice to Young Men

Pray every night, and shave every morning.

Keep your conscience clean, also your linen.

Let your light shine, and shine your shoes.

Press your advantages, your opportunities, and your trousers.

Brush the cobwebs from your brain and dandruff from your collar.

Take liberties with grammar, if you will, but not in games of chance.

The polite liar easily becomes a plain liar.

Covet a golden tongue more than a greenback.

Be poor in spirit but not in vocabulary.

Don't mix your metaphors, but nevertheless be a good mixer.

It is better to establish a good precedent than to follow a bad one.

It is better to lose a good fight than to win a bad one.

Never allow temporal trivialities to displace eternal verities.

Always be content with what you have but never with what you are.

—*Advance*

I have found the best way to give advice to your children is to find out what they want and then advise them to do it.

—Harry S. Truman

Socrates was a Greek philosopher who went around giving people good advice. They poisoned him!

It takes a great person to give sound advice tactfully, but it takes a greater person to accept it graciously.

—*Bits & Pieces*

Lorne Sanny of the Navigators said his father told him all his instruction to Lorne could be summarized in four words: "Get with it, Son."

The large-caliber executive welcomes suggestions. The small-caliber executive resents them, imagining that he knows it all and that it is presumptuous for anyone to offer him advice. To win promotion, be unselfish, receptive, responsive, always rating first the well-being of the company. To become big, play the game in a big way.

—B. C. Forbes

"Be yourself" is the worst advice you can give to some people.

—Tom Masson

There's a story about a young bank cashier who was named successor to the retiring bank president. One day the young man went to the senior officer and said, "As you know, I'm going to follow you as president,

10

and I'd be grateful for any advice you might have." The president said, "Son, sit down. I've got two words for you, just two words: right decisions." "That's very helpful, sir," replied the young man, "but how does one go about making right decisions?" "One word—experience." "That's also helpful, sir, but how does one gain experience?" "Two words," said the older man, "wrong decisions."

—*Our Daily Bread*

The man who seeks your advice too often is probably looking for praise rather than information.

The best way to succeed in life is to act on the advice we give to others.

There's a big gap between advice and help.

In his own gentle, procrastinating way, Dr. George Harris did much as president of Amherst College, but the unpleasant duties of such a post he neglected or ignored. He was not really opposed to work, but I never heard him say much in favor of it. One autumn he rose in chapel to address the students at the first assembly of the year, but after a sentence or two he got tired and broke into a happy smile: "I intended to give you some advice, but now I remember how much is left over from last year unused." With that he took his hat and walked out.

—John Erskine

Advice is one commodity in which supply always runs ahead of demand.

AGE (Also see MIDDLE AGE and OLD AGE)

A famous naturalist in California began cutting trees to construct a log house. A neighbor who knew his purpose and also his age asked him, "Isn't that too large an undertaking for one person who is no longer young?"

"It would be," replied the elderly man, "if I looked beyond the chopping of the trees and sawing of logs and pictured myself laying the foundation and erecting the walls and putting on the roof. Carrying the load all at once would exhaust me. But it isn't much of a job to cut down this little tree, and that's all I have to do right now."

The prime of life is that fleeting time between green and overripe.

It's What You Do, Not When You Do It

Ted Williams, at age forty-two, slammed a home run in his last official time at bat.

Mickey Mantle, age twenty, hit twenty-three home runs his first full year in the major leagues.

Golda Meir was seventy-one when she became Prime Minister of Israel.

William Pitt II was twenty-four when he became Prime Minister of Great Britain.

George Bernard Shaw was ninety-four when one of his plays was first produced.

Mozart was just seven when his first composition was published.

Now, how about this? Benjamin Franklin was a newspaper columnist at sixteen and a framer of the United States Constitution when he was eighty-one.

—United Technologies Corporation

Dr. C. Ward Crampton says you are as old as the average of your seven ages: the number of years lived (chronological), condition of your tissues (anatomical), functional ability of organs (physiological), mental capacity (psychological), condition of body as a result of diseases (pathological), normal life expectancy (statistical), and average age of ancestors (hereditary). Divinely you are as old as the eternal plan of God; actually you are as old as the time since the cross of Christ; experimentally you are as old as the time back to the moment you were born again; spiritually you are as old as your development through surrender to the Holy Spirit; and in service you are as old as your ability to beget a spiritual posterity.

AGGRESSIVENESS

Be patiently aggressive.

—Edsel B. Ford II

AIMS (Also see DETERMINATION and GOALS)

During a train trip, the renowned jurist Oliver Wendell Holmes was unable to locate his ticket when the conductor asked for it. After watching Holmes fumble through his pockets in growing dismay, the conductor said, "That's all right, Mr. Holmes. I'm sure you have your ticket somewhere. If you don't find it until you've gotten off, just mail it to us when you get home. We'll certainly trust you." Holmes replied, "Young man, my problem isn't to find my ticket. It's to find out where I'm going!"

—Ted Engstrom

If your ship doesn't come in, swim out to it!

—Jonathan Winters

AIRLINES

On a recent trip from Washington, D.C., our plane taxied onto the takeoff runway as usual, then suddenly turned around and returned to the loading ramp. The door opened; pilot, maintenance staff, and flight attendants conferred briefly; the door shut; and within minutes we were in the air on our way to Buffalo. I asked the flight attendant what had happened.

She answered, "The pilot said something was wrong with one of the engines."

I said amazed, "It certainly didn't take long to fix!"

"Oh, it wasn't fixed," she replied. "We just changed pilots!"

—L. Richard Meeth

ALCOHOLISM

Alcoholic beverages get a lot of positive attention on weekend commercials. But those ads don't mention the devastating consequences of alcoholism:

Alcoholism is our third worst national health problem, following only cancer and heart disease.

Heavy drinking contributes to an estimated 80 percent of fire and drowning accidents, 60 percent of violent crimes, and 30 percent of suicides.

Someone dies because of drunken driving every twenty-two minutes.

An estimated ten million Americans suffer from alcoholism. Add in the family members and close friends of these alcoholics, and you find that one-fifth of the American population is severely impacted by alcoholism.

AMBITION

If you can't get what you want, want what you can get!

—Lebanese proverb

Ambition usually progresses through the following states: to be like Dad . . . to be famous . . . to be a millionaire . . . to make enough to pay the bills . . . to hang on long enough to draw a pension.

—*Bits & Pieces*

Hard work and ambition can carry us far, even if we don't have much formal education. A junk dealer who is a millionaire in a northeastern state never got beyond the eighth grade. When asked how he managed to do so well in spite of this, the fellow replied, "Well, it ain't hard, really. I just buy things for $1 and sell them for $4. You'd be surprised how fast that 3 percent profit piles up."

Feel discouraged? Remember, the goal worth reaching isn't reached easily.

There are two kinds of people: those who don't do what they are told, and those who do only that.

A group of junior high students visited the White House. Later when the class discussed their tour, one boy said, "I was glad to visit my future home."

Sometimes you can judge a man's ambition by whether he hates his alarm clock or considers it his best friend.

Be not content with the commonplace in ambition or intellectual attainment. Do not expect that you will make any lasting or very strong impression on the world through intellectual power without the use of an equal amount of conscience and heart.

—William Jewett

Nothing is wrong in seeking great things. But it is wrong to seek great things for yourself.

—J. Oswald Sanders

If thou wilt seek a glory, seek a glory; but seek a glory for that which is immortal.

—Chrysostom

ANGER

He who restrains his anger overcomes his greatest enemy.

—Latin proverb

A chip on the shoulder indicates that there is wood higher up.

Of the seven deadly sins, anger is possibly the most fun. To lick your wounds, to smack your lips over grievances long past, to roll over your tongue the prospect of bitter confrontations still to come, to savor to the last toothsome morsel—both the pain you are given and the pain you are giving back—in many ways it is a feast fit for a king. The chief drawback is that what you are wolfing down is yourself. The skeleton at the feast is you.

—Frederick Buechner

Speak when you are angry and you'll make the best speech you'll ever regret.

—Henry Ward Beecher

You can't rid yourself of a bad temper by losing it.

And what is it that makes most of us angry? Usually it's when someone has shown a lack of respect for us. The image we have of ourselves has been offended. So, conceited souls that we are, we get furious. Instead, we should simply be curious. Is our image that important to us? Is anyone else's opinion really worth getting angry about? How ridiculous!

—*Soundings*

It's not a sin to get angry when you get angry at sin.

An old Englishman known as Father Graham in his village was greatly loved because of his positive influence. One day an angry young man who has just been badly insulted came to see Father Graham. As he explained the situation, he said he was on his way to demand an apology from the one who had wronged him. "My dear boy," Father Graham said, "take a word of advice from an old man who loves peace. One insult is like mud; it will brush off much better when it is dry. Wait a little, until he and you are both cool, and the problem will be easily solved. If you go now, you will only quarrel." The young man heeded the wise advice, and soon he was able to go to the other person and resolve the issue.

Anybody can become angry—that is easy. But to be angry with the right person, to the right degree, at the right time, for the right purpose, and in the right way—that is not easy!

—Aristotle

Getting mad will never get you anything else.

If you lose your temper, it is a sign that you have wrong on your side.

—Chinese proverb

Hate, like acid, does more damage to the vessel in which it is stored than to the object on which it is poured.

—Ann Landers

A man was speeding down a country road late one night when he had a flat tire. Opening the trunk of his car, he discovered he had forgotten his jack. Seeing the lights of a farmhouse in the distance, he walked toward it, saying to himself, "I'll just knock on the door, tell the farmer I'm in trouble and that I want to borrow a jack. No doubt he'll just say, 'Help yourself.'" But as he continued walking, he noticed the light in the farmhouse went out, indicating the residents had retired. Continuing his dialog with himself, he said, "They've gone to bed and will be angry if I awaken them. Maybe I should offer them a dollar for the use of their jack." Then the thought occurred to him that the man might be away and his wife would be there alone and would be afraid to answer the door. "I'll offer her five dollars," he said to himself. "Five dollars and not a penny more. I won't let this guy rob me!" As he knocked on the door, the poor farmer stuck his head out the upstairs window and asked, "Who's there?" From below came an angry voice, "You and your stupid jack! You can keep the wretched thing!"

Surely what a man does when he is taken off his guard is the best evidence for what sort of man he is. If there are rats in a cellar, you are most likely to see them if you go in very suddenly. But the suddenness does not create the rats: it only prevents them from hiding. In the same way the suddenness of the provocation does not make me ill tempered; it only shows me what an ill-tempered man I am.

—C. S. Lewis

A monk who had a quick temper was known to "pass the buck" for his fits of anger—always blaming his fellow monastery residents. So he decided to move to a place of absolute solitude in a desert, thinking that if he got away from the others he could be victorious. One morning he accidentally knocked over a pitcher of water. A few minutes later he bumped it again, and once more it fell on its side and spilled its contents. Losing his temper, the monk picked up the pitcher and hurled it to the ground. As it broke into smithereens, the truth hit him: he couldn't blame others for his flareups. The real trouble was within him.

Someone said to a Scotsman, "My, you have a terrible temper." The Scotsman replied, "Man, you don't know how much I'm holding back."

Anger is just one letter short of danger.

When a man's temper gets the best of him, it reveals the worst of him.

Anger begins with folly and ends with regret.

A friend told me that he could not possibly control his temper. He attributed his ungovernable explosions of anger to his parents and grandparents. He said there were some people, like himself, who could not be expected to rule their own spirits. I asked him if he were in a heated argument with his wife and the doorbell rang, would he continue shouting. He saw my point that he really could control his temper when he wanted to. You can rule your spirit, and ruling your spirit is essential to developing self-control.

—John Haggai

If you are patient in one moment of anger, you will escape a hundred days of sorrow.

—Chinese proverb

Edwin Stanton, Secretary of War under Lincoln, was well known for a highly inflammable temper. The pressure of war kept his nerves frayed and his tongue sharp. Once, when he complained to Lincoln about a certain general, Lincoln told him to write the man a letter. "Tell him off," Lincoln advised. Stanton, bolstered by the President's support, promptly wrote a scathing letter in which he tore the man to shreds. He showed the letter to the President. "Good," said Lincoln, "first rate. You certainly gave it to him." As Stanton started to leave, Lincoln asked, "What are you going to do with it now?" "Mail it, of course," said Stanton. "Nonsense," snorted the President. "You don't want to send that letter. Put it in the stove! That's what I do when I have written a letter while I am angry. You had a good time writing that letter. Now write another."

The American Society of Safety Engineers made a study of factors that contributed to on-the-job accidents. They discovered that anger was a significant factor common to most job accidents. Employees with accidents had been angry with their wives that morning, angry because the morning paper was thrown in the wrong place, angry because of bills they needed to pay, and so forth.

A fable was told by Ralph Woener about a young lion and a mountain goat. Quite thirsty, the animals arrived at a water hole at the same time. They immediately began to argue about who would drink first. The disagreement became so heated that each decided he would rather die than give up the privilege of being first to quench his thirst. As each stubbornly confronted the other, their anger turned to rage. Just then something distracted them, and they both looked up. Circling overhead was a flock of vultures waiting for the loser to fall. That was all they needed to end their quarrel.

Righteous indignation is often nothing more than self-righteous irritation.
—William Arthur Ward

The greatest remedy for anger is delay.
—Seneca

Keep your temper; nobody else wants it.

A man was caught in traffic and couldn't go anywhere. The man behind him honked and honked. The first driver got out of his car and went back to the driver behind him. He opened the door and yelled at him in some abusive, disrespectful language for honking. The second driver simply replied, "Your bumper sticker says, 'Honk if you love Jesus.'"

They say you should never put off for tomorrow what can be done today. But some things are best postponed, especially an angry retort.

Anyone can become angry—that is easy, but to be angry with the right person, to the right degree, at the right time, for the right purpose, and in the right way—that is not easy.
—Aristotle

People who fly into a rage always make a bad landing.

When you give someone else a piece of your mind, you will lose your own peace of mind.

The ancients were right when they said, "Anger is a wind that blows out the light of the mind."

George W. Martin tells the following true story: "I remember a young fellow who one time in a fit of temper wrote a mean letter to his father. As he and I worked in the same office, I advised him not to send it, because he had written it when he was in an angry mood. However, he sealed it and asked me to mail it for him. Instead, I simply dropped it into my pocket until the next day. The following morning he arrived looking very worried. 'George,' said he, 'I wish that I had never written that letter to the old gentleman. It will break his heart. My, I'd give fifty dollars to get it back!' Removing it from my pocket and handing it to him, I told him what I had done. The young fellow was so overjoyed he actually wanted to pay me the fifty dollars for not mailing his spiteful letter."

Thomas Jefferson, a great American statesman, worked out a way to handle his anger. He included it in his "Rules of Living," which describe how he believed adult men and women should live. He wrote this: When angry, count ten before you speak; If very angry, a hundred.

ANIMALS

It is intriguing how animals make up a part of our vocabulary. Foxy people can ferret out all the wildcat schemes so they never have to go on wild goose chases. Politicians like to pigeonhole requests that do not please them. When people are extremely pigheaded and mulish, we often think they must be playing possum. Because the hoggish person always wants the lion's share, he usually gets the horse laugh instead. Who has ever seen a hawk-eyed or eagle-eyed marksman miss the bull's eye? A catty person is mean, but he may get cattier during the dog days of July and August. It is often said that some men are henpecked by their wives; maybe it is because they act piggishly. A night owl likes to stay up late, perhaps reading all night. No wonder his books may be dog-eared! Did you ever see professional dancers do the fox trot? Or a swimming champion perform the swan dive? Until recent times the mink enjoyed a good name, but because of notorious political corruption the mink coat lost its glamour. So anyone buying mink coats to bribe officials may wind up with white elephants.

ANNIVERSARIES
Fifty Precious Years
When the gold has turned to silver,
    Or the brown has turned to gray,
And the rocking chair's a treasure
    At the closing of the day.
Then the choicest of the blessings
    We could ask, so it appears,
Is to have life's partner with us
    After fifty precious years.
Fifty times the seasons changing,
    Fifty times the taxes paid.
Fifty times the windows shuttered,
    Fifty times the garden made.
Everything so swiftly moving—
    Yet in spite of smiles or tears,
What a joy to be together
    After fifty precious years.
On the future we can't borrow,
    T'would be foolish if we'd hold
Onto life, and try to keep it,
    Like 'twas silver or 'twas gold.
We just hope that all that follows,
    All of this, and heaven too,
Will be just continuation,
    Of the fifty years we knew.
                    —Maynard Kulp

Wife: "Tomorrow is our fiftieth anniversary. Let's kill the pig."
    Husband slowly responded, "Why murder the pig for what happened fifty years ago?"

A couple were being interviewed on their golden wedding anniversary. "In all that time—did you ever consider divorce?" they were asked. "Oh, no, not divorce," the little old lady said. "Murder sometimes, but never divorce."
                    —Bits & Pieces

ANXIETY
The beginning of anxiety is the end of faith, and the beginning of faith is the end of anxiety.
                    —George Mueller

Said the robin to the sparrow,
    "I should really like to know
Why these anxious human beings
    Rush about and worry so."
Said the sparrow to the robin,
    "I think that it must be
They have no Heavenly Father
    Such as cares for you and me."

According to the National Anxiety Institute, Maplewood, New Jersey, people worry most about these ten problems, listed in the order of concern:
1. AIDS
2. Drug abuse
3. Nuclear waste
4. Ozone layer
5. Famine
6. The homeless
7. Federal deficit
8. Air pollution
9. Water pollution
10. Garbage

APATHY
I'm neither for nor against apathy.

A university professor noticed a student was about to fall asleep in class. So the teacher asked the student, "What is the greatest problem in our society—ignorance or apathy?" The student replied, "I don't know and I don't care."

APOSTASY
When I started going to school in Rostov-on-Don, other children, egged on by Komsomol members, taunted me for accompanying my mother to the last remaining church in town and tore the cross from

around my neck. A few years later, I heard a number of people offer this explanation for the great disasters that had befallen Russia: "Men have forgotten God; that's why all this has happened."

—Alexander Solzhenitsyn

APOLOGIES

An apology is the super glue of life. It can repair just about anything.

—Synn Johnston

APOSTLES

All of the apostles were insulted by the enemies of their Master, Jesus Christ. They were called to seal their doctrines with their blood and nobly did they bear the trial.

Matthew suffered martyrdom by being slain with a sword at a distant city of Ethiopia.

Mark expired at Alexandria, after being cruelly dragged through the streets of that city.

Luke was hanged upon an olive tree in the classic land of Greece.

John was put in a caldron of boiling oil, but escaped death in a miraculous manner and was afterward branded at Patmos.

Peter was crucified at Rome with his head downward.

James, the Greater, was beheaded at Jerusalem.

James, the Less, was thrown from a lofty pinnacle of the temple and then beaten to death with a fuller's club.

Bartholomew was flayed alive.

Andrew was bound to a cross, whence he preached to his persecutors until he died.

Thomas was run through the body with a lance at Coromandel in the East Indies.

Jude was shot to death with arrows.

Matthias was first stoned and then beheaded.

Barnabas of the Gentiles was stoned to death at Salonica.

Paul, after various tortures and persecutions, was beheaded at Rome by the emperor Nero.

Such was the fate of the apostles, according to traditional statements.

—Paul Lee Tan

APPRECIATION (Also see COMMENDING)

Next to excellence is the appreciation of it.

—William Thackeray

A group of managers and employees were once asked, "What do people want from their work?" Managers put job security and good wages at the top of their lists. Employees tended to rank those things near the middle of a ten-item list. The employees ranked full appreciation and being in on things at the top. I would rather be able to appreciate things I cannot have than to have things I am not able to appreciate.

—Elbert Hubbard

The deepest principle in human nature is the craving to be appreciated.

—William James

The way to develop the best in a person is by appreciation and encouragement. There is nothing else that so kills the ambition of a person as criticism from his superiors.

—Charles Schwab

ARMED FORCES

A youngster was telling his parents what he had learned in school about George Washington. "Was George Washington a soldier or a sailor?" asked his father. The child thought for a moment. "I don't know," he said, "but I think he must have been a soldier. I saw a picture of him crossing the Delaware and any sailor knows better than to stand up in a rowboat."

ASSOCIATIONS

Will Rogers always said people only learn through two things: one is reading and the other is association with smarter people.

—*Bits & Pieces*

A Kentucky farmer entered his mule in the Kentucky derby. Someone was amazed to see that and asked about it. He said, "I don't think he has much chance to win, but the association will do him good."

ASSUMPTIONS

A traveler, between flights at an airport, went to a lounge and bought a small package of cookies. Then she sat down and began reading a newspaper. Gradually she became aware of a rustling noise. From behind her paper, she was flabbergasted to see a neatly dressed man helping himself to her cookies. Not wanting to make a scene, she leaned over and took a cookie herself. A minute or two passed, and then came more rustling. He was helping himself to another cookie! By this time, they had come to the end of the package, but she was so angry she didn't dare allow herself to say anything. Then, as if to add insult to injury, the man broke the remaining cookie in two, pushed half across to her, ate the other half, and left. Still fuming some time later when her flight was announced, the woman opened her handbag to get her ticket. To her shock and embarrassment, there she found her pack of unopened cookies! How wrong our assumptions can be.

—John Ross

ASSURANCE

Many who lack assurance of salvation are like the boy on a ferry boat who was riding his bicycle all the time he was on the boat. He wanted to make sure he got across the river.

You imagine that I look back on my work with calm and satisfaction. But there is not a single concept of which I am convinced that it will stand firm, and I feel uncertain whether I am in general on the right track. I don't want to be right—I only want to know whether I am right.

—Albert Einstein

On July 2, 1937, aviatrix Amelia Earhart and her flight companion, Lieutenant Commander Fred Noonan, vanished in the vicinity of Howland Island in the South Pacific. They were attempting a round-the-world flight in a twin-engine Lockheed aircraft. In her last radio contact with a United States naval vessel, Miss Earhart transmitted this terse message: "Position doubtful." She undoubtedly knew her approximate position, but because she didn't know her precise position she and her flight companion went to their deaths.

A man once came to D. L. Moody and said he was worried because he didn't feel saved. Moody asked, "Was Noah safe in the ark?" "Certainly he was," the man replied. "Well, what made him safe, his feeling or the ark?" The inquirer got the point. "How foolish I've been," he said. "It is not my feeling; it is Christ who saves."

One day a friend who was filled with doubt and spiritual perplexity asked the Scottish preacher McLeod Campbell, "Pastor, you always seem to have peace of soul. Tell me, how can you feel that you've got such a tight hold on God?" With a smile Campbell exclaimed, "I don't always feel that I have hold of Him, but praise the Lord, I know that He always has hold of me."

A little boy was being tempted by the Devil when the boy was in bed. He was getting nowhere with the temptations the Devil was bringing. Then he finally opened his Bible to 1 John 5:13, put it under his bed, and said to the Devil, "Here, you read it for yourself."

—Alan Redpath

The remarkable thing about assurance is this: When we rest on the Word *first,* we get the feeling *afterward.* This is well illustrated in the story of a man's carrying a bag of potatoes on his back. He was asked by a skeptic, "How do you know you are saved?" Taking a few more steps forward, then letting the potatoes fall, he replied, "How do I know I have dropped the bag? I haven't looked around." "No," replied the critic, "but I suppose you can tell by the *lessening of the weight.*" "Exactly," said the Christian. "That's how I know I am saved. I have lost the guilty feeling of sin and sorrow and have found peace and satisfaction in my Lord and Savior Jesus Christ by simply resting on His Word."

During the first part of the construction of the Golden Gate Bridge in San Francisco, no safety devices were used, and twenty-three men fell to their deaths. For the last part of the project, however, a large net that cost $100,000 was employed. At least ten men fell into it and were saved. But an interesting sidelight is the fact that 25 percent more work was accomplished when the men were assured of their safety.

—Curtis Hutson

A woman said, "I may tremble on the Rock, but the Rock never trembles under me."

The Scottish man who was rejoicing in the fact that he knew he was saved was once asked by a friend, "But just how do you know you are saved? You are always talking about knowing for sure you are saved, but just what makes you so sure? How do you know?" "Well," the old man immediately answered, "I was there when it happened."

A captain never anchors his ship by fastening his anchor inside the ship. It is always outside. The Christian is not saved because he feels secure within himself or believes that he can hold out, but because he is trusting in another, the Lord Jesus Christ. "How can I know for sure I am saved?" "When you were married, the minister gave the word that you were pronounced husband and wife. Then after that did you ever doubt that you were really married?" "No." "All right. You took the minister's word for it; why not take God's Word for it? You can know you are saved if you believe God's Word."

ASTRONOMY

In the town hall in Copenhagen stands the world's most complicated clock. It took forty years to build, at a cost of more than a million dollars. That clock has ten faces, 15,000 parts, and is accurate to two-fifths of a second every 300 years. The clock computes the time of day, the days of the week, the months and years, and the movements of the planets for 2,500 years. Some parts of the clock will not move until twenty-five centuries have passed. What is intriguing is that the clock is not accurate. It loses two-fifths of a second every 300 years. Like all clocks, that timepiece in Copenhagen must be regulated by a more

precise clock, the universe itself. This mighty astronomical clock with its billions of moving parts, from atoms to stars, rolls on century after century with movements so reliable that all time on earth can be measured against it.

—Haddon Robinson

Imagine that the thickness of this page which you are reading is the distance from earth to sun (93 million miles). The distance to the nearest star (4 $1/2$ light years) would be a 71-foot-high shelf of paper. And the diameter of our own galaxy (100,000 light years) is a 310-mile stack of paper, while the edge of the known universe is a pile of paper one-third of the way to the sun (31 million miles).

—Paul Lee Tan

A scientist once suggested an interesting analogy. Imagine, he said, a perfectly smooth glass pavement on which the finest speck can be seen. Then shrink our sun from 865,000 miles in diameter to only 2 feet, and place this gilt ball on the pavement to represent the sun.

Step off 82 paces of about 2 feet each, and to proportionately represent the first planet, Mercury, put down a mustard seed.

Take 60 steps more, each about 2 feet, and for Venus, put down an ordinary shot the size of a BB.

Mark 78 steps more, and for our earth, put down a pea.

Step off 108 paces from there, and for Mars, put down a pinhead.

Sprinkle some fine dust for the asteroids, take 788 steps more, and for Jupiter, put down an orange.

Take 934 steps, and for Saturn, put down a golf ball.

Mark 2,086 steps more, and for Uranus, put down a marble.

Step off 2,322 steps from there, and for Neptune, put down a cherry.

This will take 2 $1/2$ miles, and we haven't discussed Pluto. If we swing completely around, we have a smooth glass surface 5 miles in diameter representing our solar system, just a tiny fraction of the heavens. On this surface, 5 miles across, we have only a mustard seed, BB, pea, pinhead, dust, orange, golf ball, marble, and cherry. And we should have to go 6,720 miles, not feet, on the same scale before we could put down another two-foot ball to represent the nearest star.

A train going at the rate of a mile a minute would reach our nearest star in 48 million years; if a song were sung there and the sound could travel here, it would be 3,800,000 years before we could hear it. A spider's thread reaching to it would weigh five hundred tons.

ATHEISM

T. H. Huxley, a well-known agnostic, was with a group of men at a weekend house party. On Sunday morning, while most of them were preparing to go to church, he approached a man known for his Christian character and said, "Suppose you stay home and tell me why you are a Christian." The man, knowing that he couldn't match wits with Huxley, hesitated. But the agnostic said gently, "I don't want to argue with you. I just want you to tell me simply what this Christ means to you." The man did, and when he finished, there were tears in Huxley's eyes as he said, "I would give my right hand if only I could believe that!"

Two men were discussing religion. One man said, "I don't have anything to do with things I don't understand." "Have you had your breakfast this morning?" asked the other. "Yes," said the first, "but what's that got to do with religion?" "Did you have any butter on your toast?" persisted his friend. "Yes," replied the man, increasingly bewildered. "Well, can you tell me how a black and white cow eating green grass can make white milk that makes yellow butter?" "No, I can't," admitted the skeptic. "Well," his friend advised, "I wouldn't have anything to do with breakfast then."

—*Rolling in the Aisles*

Voltaire, an infidel of the most pronounced type, expressed his disillusionment with his kind of life in these words: "I wish," said he, "that I had never been born."

My brother once said that the trouble with being an atheist is that when your motorcycle plunges off a cliff into the Colorado River and you aren't killed, there's no one to thank.

—Jessica Shaver

Sir Ralph Richardson said, If a man without a sense of smell declared that this yellow rose I hold had no scent, we should know that he was wrong. The defect is in him, not in the flower. It is the same with a man who says there is no God. It merely means that he is without the capacity to discern His presence.

—*Reader's Digest*

On the European *Time* magazine cover were the words, "God is dead; Marx is dead, and I'm not too well myself."

Mahatma Gandhi was once approached by an atheist with the request that he organize and promote an anti-God society. Gandhi replied, "It amazes me to find an intelligent person who fights against something which he does not at all believe exists."

British statesman W. E. Gladstone (1809–1898) visited Christ Church College and spoke optimistically about the betterment of English society during his lifetime. His outlook was so positive that a student challenged him, "Sir, are there no adverse signs?"

Gladstone reflected, "Yes, there is one thing that frightens me—the fear that God seems to be dying out of the minds of men."

An infidel and some friends were drifting in a boat toward Niagara Falls. Seeing they were dangerously near the Falls, the infidel prayed. Afterward someone asked him why he, an atheist, prayed. He said, "While infidelity is a good thing by which to drift down the river, it's not a good thing by which to go over the Falls."

The agnostic H. G. Wells said a few things worth remembering, one of which was, "Until a man has found God, he begins at no beginning; he works to no end."

Unfortunately, Wells did not find God; therefore he worked to no end.

Friedrich Nietzsche was the first "God is dead" theorist. *Time* magazine once concluded an article on him with these poignant lines:

God Is Dead. (Signed) Nietzsche.
Nietzsche Is Dead. (Signed) God.

An infidel was lecturing on "The Fraudulence of the Christian Religion." After his address the meeting was opened for questions. After a short pause a man who was well known in that city as a former alcoholic, but who had in recent months become a Christian, stepped to the front of the auditorium. Taking an orange from his pocket, he proceeded to peel it, saying nothing. The lecturer, visibly irritated, demanded that the man get on with his question. But still the man said nothing. Instead he just peeled the orange and then ate it. When he had finished, he turned to the speaker and said, "Was this orange sweet or sour?"

"How should I know, you idiot?" shouted the infidel. "I didn't taste it."

To which the converted alcoholic replied, "How, then, can you know anything about Jesus Christ if you have never tried Him?"

A group of atheists were criticizing the Bible. One of them spoke about creation. He said, "What man with any common sense could believe that several thousand years ago, God stooped down and picked up a piece of mud, breathed on it, and changed it into a human being?"

A Christian man standing by overheard the conversation and responded by saying, "I cannot answer all the questions about creation, but this I know: One night God stooped down and picked up the dirtiest piece of mud in this city, breathed on it by His Spirit, and changed a gambling, drinking, thieving wretch into a peace-loving man of God. I was that man."

An atheist complained to a friend because Christians have their special holidays, such as Christmas and Easter, and Jews celebrate their national holidays, such as Passover and Yom Kippur. "But we atheists," he said, "have no recognized national holiday. It is unfair discrimination."

To which his friend replied, "Why don't you celebrate April first?"
—*Maryland Church News*

Near the end of his life Jean-Paul Sartre told Pierre Victor, "I do not feel that I am the product of chance, a speck of dust in the universe, but someone who was expected, prepared, prefigured. In short, a being whom only a Creator could put here; and this idea of a creating hand refers to God."

Sartre's long-time friend Simone de Beauvoir, a philosopher, said, "How should one explain this senile act of a turncoat?"
—*His* magazine

Charles Bradlaugh, an infidel, once challenged H. P. Hughes, a preacher, to a debate. Hughes, who was head of a rescue mission in London, accepted the challenge with the condition that he could bring with him one hundred men and women who would tell what had happened in their lives since trusting Christ as their Savior. They would be people who once lived in deep sin, some having come from poverty-stricken homes caused by the vices of their parents. Hughes said they would not only tell of their conversion but would submit to cross-examination by any who doubted their stories. Furthermore, the minister invited his opponent to bring a group of non-believers who could tell how they were helped by their lack of faith. When the appointed day arrived, the preacher came, accompanied by one hundred transformed persons. But Bradlaugh never showed up. The result? The meeting turned into a testimony time, and many sinners who had gathered to hear the scheduled debate were converted.

Evangelist E. L. Hyde was conducting revival meetings in New Jersey. In the course of his remarks he said that he could prove, to the satisfaction of any infidel, within ten minutes, that the infidel was a fool.

The next morning while he was out walking, a man accosted him very abruptly by saying, "Aren't you the evangelist preaching up here at the church?"

"Yes, sir."

"Well, I supposed you were a gentleman."

"I claim to be one."

"Well, I don't think you are. Didn't you say last night that you could prove, to the satisfaction of anyone, within ten minutes, that all infidels are fools? If you don't prove it to my satisfaction, I will publish you in all city papers as the worst liar that ever struck the city."

Seeing there was no possibility of reasoning with the man, Mr. Hyde said, "Where is your infidel?"

"I claim to be one," was the reply, "and I want you to know that I am no fool, either."

"You mean you think there is no reality to Christianity?"

"I do, sir. I have studied all phases of the subject. I have traveled and delivered lectures against Christianity for more than twelve years, and I am prepared to say there is nothing to it."

"You are certain there is nothing to it?"

"Yes, sir, there is nothing to it."

"Will you please tell me," said Mr. Hyde, "if a man who will lecture for twelve years against nothing is not a fool, what, in your judgment, would you constitute a fool?"

He turned away in rage. Mr. Hyde, drawing out his watch, insisted he still had six minutes. But the infidel would not hear him, nor was Mr. Hyde published in the city papers.

—*Pulpit Helps*

Voltaire, an immoral man, was one of the most talented infidels of all time. He wrote about 250 books and pamphlets—most of which spitefully denounced Christianity. One would think that such a notorious atheist would remain steadfast in his battle against the truth of the Bible right to the end. But he found it impossible to quell the inner voice of God. In his last hours he feared for his eternal destiny, so he asked to receive the sacraments of the church.

Thomas Paine was called "the god of modern skeptics." He was idolized by infidels even though by all standards of decency he was little more than a drunkard and a thief. Yet on his deathbed, he begged the Savior for mercy. Apparently in their final moments, some atheists cannot resist the light of conscience and the sense of eternity that God has instilled within them.

Sign on a church bulletin board: "Atheists are people with no invisible means of support."

An infidel father asked his Bible-believing daughter if she meant to say that she believed in the Bible. "Why sure, Daddy." "You mean to say you even believe that Jonah was swallowed by a whale and then after three days was vomited up on the seashore and that he went and preached to the people?" "Sure." "Oh, that's ridiculous. I don't believe in such nonsense." "Well, when I get to heaven, I'll just ask Jonah." "But what if he isn't there?" "Then you ask him."

An atheist once asked a Christian, "You say there is a God who created this world and sent His Son to die for our sins. But how do you *know* there is a God, or how do you know we have a soul? Do you ever see God, or did you ever see a soul?"

The Christian calmly answered, "Did you ever see your brain?"

"Well, no."

"Then how do you know you have one? Or did you ever see a pain?"

"No."

"All right, you may not be able to see a pain or your brain, but that is not proof that neither exists."

An atheist has reason but no hope for his reason. A hypocrite has hope but no reason for his hope. A Christian has a reason for his hope and a hope for his reason.

Atheist Robert Ingersoll once got up and said to an audience of his, "If there be a God, let Him strike me down in one minute." He held up his watch and the minute went past. "See, I told you there's no God."

But a preacher happened to be seated in the audience, and at that time he rose up and asked, "Do you think you can exhaust the grace of God in sixty seconds?"

An atheist, blaspheming in a marketplace, challenged God to show His power by striking him dead within five minutes. The five minutes elapsed, and following the tense delay, the man said to his audience, "What did I tell you?" An old woman standing by said, "Sir, have you any children?" "Why?" "Well," said the woman, "if one of your children handed you a knife and said, 'Kill me, Daddy,' would you do it?" "Why no," said the astonished man, "I love them too much." "That is exactly why God did not strike you dead," said the woman, "He loves you too much."

An atheist was dared by his cronies to go out into a cemetery at midnight, hammer a cross into the ground, and shout three times, "There is no God!"

He took the dare, went to the cemetery, knelt down, and hammered the cross into the ground. He shouted, "There is no God" three times and then started to get up to go away. He could not move. Something held him fast. The shock of it so frightened the man that he dropped dead from a heart attack.

What held him fast was a very simple thing. He had hammered the wooden cross through the hem of his overcoat.

—Howard Whitman

ATTITUDE

There is little difference in people, but that little difference makes a big difference. The little difference is attitude. The big difference is whether it is positive or negative.

—Clement Stone

The longer I live, the more I realize the impact of attitude in life. Attitude, to me, is more important than facts. It is more important than the past, than education, than money, than circumstances, than failures, than successes, than what other people think or say or do. It is more important than appearance, giftedness, or skill. It will make or break a company . . . a church . . . a home. The remarkable thing is we have a choice every day regarding the attitude we will embrace for that day. We cannot change our past . . . we cannot change the fact that people will act in a certain way. We cannot change the inevitable. The only thing we can do is play on the one thing we have, and that is our attitude. . . . I am convinced that life is 10 percent what happens to me and 90 percent how I react to it. And so it is with you . . . we are in charge of our attitudes.

—Chuck Swindoll

A businessman judges applicants for jobs on these counts:
    5% on availability
    5% on adaptability
    5% on ability
    85% on *attitude*

It isn't what you have or who you are or where you are or what you are doing that makes you happy or unhappy. It is what you think about it. For example, two people may be in the same place, doing the same thing; both may have an equal amount of money and prestige—and yet one may be miserable and the other happy. Why? Because of different mental attitudes.

—Dale Carnegie

The greatest discovery of my generation is that human beings can alter their lives by altering their attitudes of mind.

—William James

Ability is what you're capable of doing. Motivation determines what you do. Attitude determines how well you do it.

—Lou Holtz

AUDIOVISUALS

If you want people to remember what you say, illustrate your talk. If you use audio only, listeners will recall 70 percent of what you say in three hours, but only 10 percent in three days. If you use visuals only, viewers will recall 72 percent in three hours, 20 percent in three days. If you use audiovisual presentations, your audience will recall 85 percent of the message after three hours, and 65 percent in three days.

—*Survey Bulletin*

AUTHORITY

There are many tests by which a gentleman may be known; but there is one that never fails—how does he exercise power over those subordinate to him?

—Samuel Smiles

AVERAGE

Average is as close to the bottom as it is to the top.

—*Teen Esteem*

AWARDS

Accepting an award, the late Jack Benny once remarked, "I really don't deserve this, but I have arthritis and I don't deserve that either."

—*Bits & Pieces*

B

BABIES

A perfect example of minority rule is a baby in the home.

Arriving for a visit, a woman asked her small granddaughter, "How do you like your new baby brother?"

"Oh, he's all right," the child shrugged. "But there were a lot of things we needed worse."

People who say they sleep like a baby usually don't have one.

—Leo Burke

BACKSLIDING
Letter of Resignation
Dear Lord:

Kindly accept this as my resignation, due to the reasons listed below.

1. I am no longer interested in winning souls.
2. Those who look to me for spiritual guidance can get it from someone else.
3. The few who are grateful for my efforts don't mean a thing.
4. My critics are ready to move in, and I want to show them I'm not too old and feeble to move out.
5. I'm not interested in church. I hate crowds.
6. The will of the Lord is no longer first with me.

Cordially,
A. Backslider

Backsliding begins when knee-bending stops.

BAD NEWS

A man went to his doctor for a checkup. He went back the next day to get the results from the tests.

"Doc, how do I look?"

The doctor said, "I have good news and bad news. Which do you want first?"

The man said, "Let me hear the good news first."

The doctor said, "Well, the good news is you have twenty-four hours to live."

"Good grief! That's the good news?" the man gasped. "I've got twenty-four hours to live? Then what's the bad news?"

The doctor replied, "The bad news is I was supposed to tell you yesterday."

BALANCE

Martin Luther once said that God's truth is like a drunkard trying to ride a horse: prop him up on one side, and he topples over on the other. Balance is indeed hard to achieve in applying God's truth no less than in understanding it. We are always in danger of pushing some biblical principle to an extreme.

BALDNESS

There's one thing about baldness—it's neat.

If a person is bald in the front, he's a thinker. If he's bald in the back, he's a lover. If he's bald all over, he *thinks* he's a lover.

BAPTISM

A preacher in the South preached constantly on water baptism. The people were tired of it. The deacons suggested he preach on something else. He said, "Okay, give the text and I'll preach on it." They gave him Genesis 1:1.

The next Sunday he said, "By request the text today is Genesis 1:1." He read it and then said, "When the Lord created the earth, He made it one-fourth land and three-fourths water, and that brings me back to the subject of water baptism."

BAPTISTS

In a small west Texas town, there were three churches in one block: Methodist, Baptist, and Presbyterian. On Sunday evenings they had the windows open. One evening the Methodists sang, "Will There Be Any Stars in My Crown?" The Baptists heard it and sang, "No, Not One." The Presbyterians sang, "Oh, That Will Be Glory for Me."

When Charles Spurgeon was saved at the age of fifteen, he told his mother he wanted to be baptized by immersion. She said, "I've prayed for you for years, but not that you would become a Baptist." He replied, "That shows, dear Mother, that God is able to do abundantly above all you think."

In a train robbery, the robber came to a pastor. "You won't rob me, a preacher, will you?"

"What denomination are you?"

"I'm a Baptist."

The robber put his gun in his left hand and extended his right hand to the pastor and said, "Put it there, Pastor. I'm a Baptist too."

A Baptist minister and a Methodist minister were talking one day about the seating capacity of their churches. The Baptist preacher was telling that his church could hold only two hundred people.

Several days later they happened to meet again and the Baptist preacher said something about his church holding three hundred. "But I thought you said it seated only two hundred." "Oh, but you don't know how narrow we Baptists are."

Three pastors—a Presbyterian, a Methodist, and a Baptist—each faced the problem of bats. The Presbyterian said they shot them with shotguns. The Methodist said, "We are more compassionate. We wrapped them in a big blanket and took them to a woods far away and let them go. But they beat us back to the church." The Baptist pastor said, "We baptized each one and made them members of our church, and we haven't seen them since."

BASEBALL

The baseball season is upon us and an office manager we know passes along this explanation of the game, given to her by her grandson: You have two sides, one out in the field and one in. Each man that's on the side that's in goes out and when he's out he comes in and the next man goes in until he's out. When three men are out, the side that's out comes in and the side that's been in goes out and tries to get those coming in out. When both sides have been in and out nine times, including the not outs, that's the end of the game.

—Bits & Pieces

BEAUTY

Socrates, when he looked into the shops of Athens, remarked, "How many things I can do without." He was uneasy in the presence of luxury. From what we know of him, it does not surprise us that he offered the prayer, "Beloved Pam, and all ye other gods that haunt this place, grant that I may become inwardly beautiful."

BEGINNINGS

The victory of the Allied forces in North Africa signaled a turning point in the early stages of World War II. After this crucial campaign, Winston Churchill made one of his most memorable statements: "This is not the end. This is not the beginning of the end. But it is, perhaps, the end of the beginning."

BIBLE

God's words will give men new life more than the other words that are for pleasure. O marvelous power of the Divine Seed which overpowers strong men in arms, softens hard hearts, and renews and changes into divine men, those men who had been brutalized by sins and departed infinitely far from God. Obviously such miraculous power could never be worked by the work of a priest if the Spirit of Life and the Eternal Word did not, above all things else, work with it.

—John Wycliffe

An elderly man who had never gone to school decided he wanted to learn how to read. His greatest desire was to read the Bible so that God could speak to him through His Word. But learning to read wasn't easy. Just becoming familiar with the alphabet was hard work. For several years this dedicated Christian kept at it. Finally, he was able to read—a little at first and eventually the entire New Testament. A few days after he had finished the last book of the Bible, he stopped by to talk with a friend. With tears in his eyes, he said, "It was worth all that effort just to be able to read John 3:16."

—Our Daily Bread

A man selling individual books of the Bible was stopped and robbed one night as he passed through a forest in Sicily and was ordered to burn his wares. After lighting a fire, he asked if he might read aloud a brief portion from each before surrendering them to the flames. Given permission, he read from one the twenty-third Psalm, from another the Sermon on the Mount, from another the parable of the Good Samaritan, and from another Paul's hymn of love in 1 Corinthians 13. After each excerpt the outlaw exclaimed, "That's a good book. We won't burn that, give it to me." So none were destroyed but all were taken by the thief. Some years later the robber appeared

again, but now as an ordained minister. Reading the Bible had accomplished the miracle.

—Our Daily Bread

The Book is the mind of God, the state of man, the way of salvation, the doom of sinners, and the happiness of believers. Its doctrines are holy, its precepts are binding, its histories are true, and its decisions are immutable. Read it to be wise, believe it to be safe, practice it to be holy. It contains light to direct you, food to support you, and comfort to cheer you. It is the traveler's map, the pilgrim's staff, the pilot's compass, the soldier's sword, and the Christian's character. Paradise is restored, heaven opened, and the gates of hell disclosed. Christ is its grand subject, our good its design, and the glory of God its end. It should fill the memory, rule the heart, and guide the feet. Read it slowly, frequently, prayerfully. It is a mine of wealth, a paradise of glory, and a river of pleasure. Follow its precepts and it will lead you to Calvary, to the empty tomb, to a resurrected life in Christ; yes, to glory itself, for eternity.

One day an infidel named William Hone met a small boy who was reading the Bible. Hone said to him, "Why do you spend your time with a worthless book like that?" The lad responded, "It's the only thing that gives my sick mother any comfort." The man was moved by the youngster's simple comment and decided to read the Scriptures for himself. As he did, God's Spirit spoke to his heart. Some time later he wrote the following lines on one of the pages in his Bible:

The proudest heart that ever beat
   Hath been subdued in me;
   The wildest will that ever rose
   To scorn Thy cause or aid Thy foes
Is quelled, my God, by Thee.

William Hone's life was transformed through the power of the Word.

—Our Daily Bread

A young Christian packing his bag for a journey said to a friend, "I have nearly finish packing. All I have to put in is a guidebook, a lamp, a microscope, a volume of fine poetry, a few biographies, a package of old letters, a book of songs, a sword, a hammer, and a set of tools." "But you can't get all that into your bag," objected the friend. "Oh, yes I can," said the Christian. "Here it is." And he placed his Bible in the corner of the suitcase and closed the lid.

In regard to this great book, I have but to say, it is the best gift God has given to men. All the good Savior gave to the world was communicated through this book. But for it we could not know right from wrong. All things most desirable for man's welfare, here and hereafter, are to be found portrayed in it.

—Abraham Lincoln

I am the Bible,

I am God's wonderful library.

I am always—and above all—the truth.

To the weary pilgrim, I am a good, strong staff.

To the one who sits in black gloom, I am the glorious light.

To those who stoop beneath heavy burdens, I am sweet rest.

To him who has lost his way, I am a safe guide.

To those who have been hurt by sin, I am healing balm.

To the discouraged, I whisper a glad message of hope.

To those who are distressed by the storms of life, I am an anchor, sure and steadfast.

To those who suffer in lonely solitude, I am as a cool, soft hand resting upon a fevered brow.

Oh, child of man, to best defend me, just use me!

England has two books, the Bible and Shakespeare. England made Shakespeare, but the Bible made England.

—Victor Hugo

George Bernard Shaw once had a Bible. Four years before he died in 1950, he sold it to auctioneers. A few days ago the auctioneers sold it for $50. One of the selling points seems to have been an inscription on the flyleaf by the playwright himself:

"Except as a curiosity, this book as a material object is a most undesirable possession . . . I must get rid of it. I really cannot bear it in my house."

Wonder where he is now?

—*Dallas Morning News* editorial, March 14, 1952

Within that awful Volume lies
   The mystery of mysteries!
Happiest they of human race,
   To whom God has given grace
To read, to fear, to hope, to pray,
   To lift the latch and force the way;
And better had they ne'er been born
   Who read to doubt, or read to scorn.

—Walter Scott

We search the world for truth; we cull
   The good, the pure, the beautiful,
From graven stone and written scroll,
   From all old flower-fields of the soul;
And weary seekers of the best,
   We come back laden from our quest,
To find that all the sages said
   Is in the Book our mothers read.

—John Greenleaf Whittier

For several years I have read the Bible through twice in twelve months. It is a great and powerful tree, each word of which is a mighty branch. Each of these branches have I well shaken, so desirous was I to know what each one bore and what it would give me. And the shaking of them has never disappointed me.

—Martin Luther

In a news conference on February 21, 1985, President Ronald Reagan said he had found "that the Bible contains an answer to just about everything and every problem that confronts us, and I wonder sometimes why we won't recognize that one book could solve our problems for us."

—*Chattanooga News–Free Press*

As Sir Walter Scott lay dying, he said to his friend and biographer, John Gibson

Lockhart, "Read from the Book." "Which book?" asked Lockhart. Scott replied, "There is but one."

If I should live a thousand years
  And search it every day,
The precious Word of God would still
  Shed light upon my way.
Should every other earthly thing
  Be severed from my grasp,
I pray that I may ever hold
  My Bible till the last.
And some day when He calls me home
  And I at last can look
Upon His face, I'll want to kneel
  And thank Him—for His Book!
          —Alice Hanche Mortenson

A rich Chinese man who visited England took great delight in a beautiful microscope which was shown him. Later he purchased one for himself and took it back to China.

One day he examined a tiny bit of his dinner rice with the microscope. To his horror he discovered that there were actually tiny living creatures in it.

It was part of his creed not to eat anything that had animal life. What should he do? He was not only particularly fond of his rice, but it was the staple item of his daily food.

He thought he saw only one way out of it. He would destroy the instrument that pointed out the distasteful fact, and so he dashed the microscope in pieces.

Similarly, many people hate the Word of God because it reveals their true condition.

Twenty-seven years ago, with the Holy Spirit as my guide, I entered at the portico of Genesis and went into the art galleries of the Old Testament; on the wall hung pictures of Enoch, Noah, Jacob, Abraham, Elijah, David, Daniel, and other famous prophets of old. Then I passed into the music room of the psalms where the Spirit swept the keyboard of my nature. . . . Then I stepped into the prophetic room and saw through the telescopes various stars, some pointing to far-off stars and others to nearby stars, but all concentrated upon the bright and morning star. . . . From here I went to the correspondence room where Matthew, Mark, Luke, John, Paul, Peter, James, and Jude sat at their tasks, penning their epistles to the church. Then I passed last of all into the throne room of Revelation and saw the King sitting high upon His throne.
          —Billy Sunday

The Bible is like a magnificent palace constructed of precious oriental stone, comprising sixty-six stately chambers. Each one of these chambers is different from its fellows and is perfect in its individual beauty, while together they form an edifice incomparably majestic, glorious, and sublime.

In the book of Genesis we enter the grand Vestibule where we are immediately introduced to the records of the mighty work of God in creation. This Vestibule gives access to the Law Courts, passing through which we come to the Picture Gallery of the historical books. Here we find hung upon the walls scenes of battles, heroic deeds, and portraits of valiant men of God. Beyond the Picture Gallery we find the Philosopher's Chamber—the book of Job—passing through which we enter the Music Room—the book of Psalms—and here we linger, thrilled by the grandest harmonies that ever fell on human ears. Then we come to the Business Office— the book of Proverbs in the very center of which stands the motto, "Righteousness exalteth a nation, but sin is a reproach to any people." Leaving the Business Office we pass into the Research Department— Ecclesiastes—and thence into the Conservatory—the Song of Solomon— where greet us the fragrant aroma of choicest fruits and flowers and the sweet singing of birds. We then reach the Observatory where the Prophets with their powerful telescopes are looking for the appearing of the "Bright and Morning Star," prior to the dawning of the "Sun of Righteousness." Crossing the courtyard, we come to the Audience Chamber of the King—the Gospels—where we find four lifelike portraits of the King Himself, revealing the perfections of His infinite beauty. Next we enter the Workroom of the

Holy Spirit—the Acts of the Apostles—and beyond that the Correspondence Room—the Epistles—where we see Paul and Peter, James, John, and Jude, busy at their tables under the personal direction of the Spirit of Truth. Finally we enter the Throne Room—the book of Revelation—where we are enraptured by the mighty volume of adoration and praise which is ever addressed to the enthroned King and which fills the vast Chamber; while in the adjacent Galleries and Judgment Hall there are portrayed solemn scenes of judgment and wondrous scenes of glory associated with the coming manifestation of the Son of God as King of kings and Lord of lords.

—Fred Mitchell

I believe the Bible to be the Word of God:

Because it is the champion of human liberties.

Because it is founded upon justice and mercy.

Because it fills men with a desire to help others.

Because it presents the divine-human Person—Christ.

Because it points out the Way from sin to salvation.

Because it brings peace and comfort to heart and mind.

Because no other book has ever been so loved and hated.

Because its life stories have a perennial, universal charm.

Because it reveals the only indispensable Man—Christ Jesus.

Because its influence is rapidly traveling to the whole world.

Because after two thousand years of publication it is still the world's best-seller.

Because it records the only authentic history of the human race.

Because its benefits are not limited to any race, color, or condition.

Because, when accepted, men immediately seek for better things.

Because it provides the only real consolation for men dying in war.

Because in studying its words we "breathe the atmosphere of eternity."

Because its messages of hope have saved many from self-destruction.

Because it recognizes and upholds the dignity and individuality of every person.

Because those who would destroy it have not furnished any substitute of value.

I believe the Bible to be the Word of God:

Because it reveals the only Way out of this present evil world into a better one.

—C. E. Holmes

The Scriptures are accurate in their descriptions, unfailing in their prophecies, dependable in their promises, reliable in their histories, authoritative in their claims, united in their testimony, self-evidencing in their miracles, honest in their records, suggestive in their silence, final in their teachings, divine in their origin, unique in their structure, living in their nature, heavenly in their morality, perennial in their freshness, and inexhaustible in their depth.

A series of articles by Robert A. Vogeler in the *Saturday Evening Post* told of his experiences during his imprisonment by communist powers.

Vogeler reported that he had repeatedly asked for a Bible but did not receive one for some time. However, he was allowed to read other books, including Dickens, Tolstoy, and Shaw. He testified, "Although I read Pickwick two or three times, the other novels of Dickens, especially *Oliver Twist,* were so depressing that I could read them only once. The Bible, in spite of certain depressing chapters, gave me the greatest solace of all. I now know that, if I were marooned on a desert island, the Bible is the one book above all others that I would most like to possess."

Know it in your mind.
Stow it in your heart.
Show it in your life.
Sow it in the world.

The Bible is alive, it speaks to me; it has feet, it runs after me; it has hands, it lays hold of me.

—Martin Luther

Lay hold of the Bible until the Bible lays hold of you.

—Will H. Houghton

When I spoke to eight hundred students in a state university, I was informed that the Bible should not be mentioned in the school. The same afternoon I was invited to talk to about eight hundred men in the state penitentiary, and the warden asked me to give them the Bible truth.

—Albert E. Aldrich

Though the cover is worn,
And the pages are torn,
    And though places bear traces of tears
Yet more precious than gold
Is the Book worn and old,
    That can shatter and scatter my fears.
When I prayerfully look
In the precious old Book,
    As my eyes scan the pages I see
Many tokens of love
From the Father above,
    Who is nearest and dearest to me.
This old Book is my guide,
'Tis a friend by my side,
    It will lighten and brighten my way;
And each promise I find
Soothes and gladdens my mind
    As I read it and heed it today.

The world's all-time "best-seller" is the Bible. In 1960, Americans alone purchased an estimated eleven million copies. Some are small enough to fit in the palm of your hand; some are too heavy to hold. There is a twenty-volume edition in Braille. Prices range from less than a dollar to a $600,000 Gutenberg edition, now a national treasure.

—*Time*

I have worked at the Bible, prayed over the Bible, lived by the Bible for more than sixty years, and I tell you there is no book like the Bible. It is a miracle of literature, a perennial spring of wisdom, a wonder book of surprises, a revelation of mystery, an infallible guide of conduct, and an unspeakable source of comfort. Give no heed to people that discredit it, for they speak without knowledge. It is the Word of God in the inspired speech of humanity. Read it for yourself. Read it thoroughly. Study it according to its own directions. Live by its principles. Believe its message. Follow its precepts.

No man is uneducated who knows the Bible, and no man is wise who is ignorant of its teaching. Every day is begun at its open page. It lies close at hand in all my work. I never go anywhere without it, and it is my chief joy.

—Samuel Chadwick

A Mohammedan trader who could not read a word of English kept an English Bible beside him nevertheless at all times. "When I meet a trader who is unknown to me," he explained, "I put the Bible into his way and watch him. If he opens it and reads, I know I can trust him. If he throws it aside with a sneer or a curse, I will have nothing to do with him."

A noted orator asked Charles Dickens for the most pathetic story in literature, and he said it was that of the Prodigal Son (Luke 15). Samuel Coleridge was asked for the richest passage in literature, and he said it was Matthew 5:1–16. Another asked Daniel Webster for the greatest legal digest, and he replied that it was the Sermon on the Mount.

No one has equaled Moses for law, David for poetry, Isaiah for vision, Jesus for Good News, Peter for holy zeal, Paul for logic, or John's statements of divine love.

The vigor of our spiritual life will be in exact proportion to the place held by the Bible in our life and thoughts. I solemnly state this from the experience of fifty-four years. The first three years after conversion I neglected the Word of God. Since I began to search it diligently, the blessing has been wonderful. I have read the Bible through one hundred times, and always with increasing delight. Each time it seems like a new book to me. Great has been the blessing from consecutive, diligent, daily study. I look upon it as a lost day when I have not had a good time over the Word of God.

—George Mueller

I always have the pleasure to have people read and study the Bible since the Bible is the voice of the Holy Spirit. It reveals the righteousness of God and His love. Jesus Christ, our Redeemer, gave His life and shed His blood to save those who believe in Him. His righteousness exalts the nation. Christ is the cornerstone of all freedoms. His love covers all sins. All those who believe in Him shall have eternal life.

—Generalissimo Chiang Kai-Shek

Dwight L. Moody once wrote, "I'm glad there's a depth in the Bible I know nothing about, for it shows its divine authorship."

A man once came to him with a very difficult passage and said, "Mr. Moody, how do you explain that?"

I replied, "I don't."

"But how do you interpret it?"

"I don't interpret it."

"Well, how do you understand it?"

"I don't understand it."

"What do you do with it?"

"I don't do anything with it."

"You don't believe it?"

"Yes, I believe it! I believe many things I don't understand. . . . Nature itself is filled with wonders we cannot fathom, so how can we expect to know everything spiritual?"

Voltaire gathered all the Bibles he could find and burned them. Today in the very house where he lived, a Bible Society has four presses, publishing thousands of Bibles every year in several dozen languages.

Adams, John Quincey, 1767–1848: "So great is my veneration for the Bible that the earlier my children begin to read it, the more confident will be my hopes that they will prove useful citizens to their country and respectable members of society."

Bacon, Francis, 1561–1626: "There never was found, in any age of the world, either religion or law that did so highly exalt the public good as the Bible."

Barton, Bruce: "Voltaire spoke of the Bible as a short-lived book. He said that within a hundred years it would pass from common use. Not many people read Voltaire today, but his house has been packed with Bibles as a depot of a Bible society."

Carlyle, Thomas, 1795–1881: "A noble book! All men's book! It is our first, oldest statement of the never-ending problem—man's destiny—and God's ways with him here on earth; and it is all in such free-flowing outlines—grand in it sincerity, in its simplicity, and its epic melody."

Faraday, Michael, 1791–1867: "As tears come from the heart and appeal to the heart, so the Bible comes from God, and he that is from God listens to His voice."

Franklin, Benjamin, 1706–1790: "A Bible in every home is the principle support of virtue, morality, and civil liberty."

George V, 1865–1936 (King of Great Britain, 1910–1936): "It is my confident hope that my subjects may never cease to cherish their noble inheritance in the English Bible, which in a secular aspect, is the first of national treasures and is, in its spiritual significance, the most valuable thing that this world affords."

Gladstone, William Ewart, 1809–1898: "I have spent seventy years of my life studying that Book to satisfy my heart; it is the Word of God. I bank my life on the statement that I believe this Book to be the solid rock of Holy Scriptures. All the wonders of Greek civilization were not as wonderful as this single book of Psalms."

Grant, Ulysses S., 1822–1885: "Hold fast to the Bible as the sheet anchor of your liberties; write its precepts in your hearts, and practice them in your lives. To the influence of this book we are indebted for all the progress made in true civilization, and to this we must look as our guide in the future. 'Righteousness exalteth a nation; but sin is a reproach to any people.'"

Greeley, Horace, 1811–1872: "It is impossible to mentally or socially enslave a Bible-reading people."

Henry, Patrick, 1736–1799: "There is a Book worth all other books which were ever printed."

Hoover, Herbert C., 1874–1964: "There is no book so various as the Bible, nor one so full of concentrated wisdom. Whether it be of law, business, morals, or that vision which leads the imagination in the creation of constructive enterprises for the happiness of mankind, he who seeks for guidance . . . may look inside its covers and find illumination. We are indebted to the Book of Books for our national ideals and institutions. Their preservation persists in adhering to its principles."

Jackson, Andrew, 1767–1848: "The Bible is the rock on which our republic rests."

Jefferson, Thomas, 1743–1826: "A serious perusal of the sacred volume will make better citizens, better fellows, and better husbands."

Kant, Immanuel, 1724–1804: "The Bible is an inexhaustible fountain of all truths. The existence of the Bible is the greatest blessing which humanity ever experienced."

Lee, Robert E., 1807–1879: "The Bible is a book in comparison with which all others in my eyes are of minor importance, and which in all my perplexities and distresses has never failed to give me light and strength."

Lincoln, Abraham, 1809–1865: "I am profitably engaged in reading the Bible. Take all of this book upon reason that you can and the balance by faith, and you will live and die a better man. I believe that the Bible is the best gift God has given to man. All the good from the Savior of the world is communicated to us through the Book."

Livingstone, David, 1813–1873: "All that I am I owe to Jesus Christ, revealed to me in His divine book."

Locke, John, 1632–1704: "The Bible is one of the greatest blessings bestowed by God on the children of men. It has God for its author, salvation for its end, and truth without any mixture for its matter. It is all pure, all sincere; nothing too much; nothing wanting."

Luther, Martin, 1483–1546: "God's Word of itself is pure, clean, bright, and clear."

Milton, John, 1608–1674: "There are no songs comparable to the songs of Zion; no orations equal to those of the prophets; and no politics like those which the Scriptures teach."

Moody, Dwight L., 1837–1899: "The Bible is the only news book in the world. The newspaper tells what has taken place, but this book tells us what will take place."

Napoleon, 1769–1821: "The Gospel is not merely a book—it is a living power—a book surpassing all others. I never omit to read it, and everyday with the same pleasure. Nowhere is to be found such a series of beautiful ideas, and admirable moral maxims, which pass before us like the battalions of a celestial army. . . . The soul can never go astray with this book for its guide."

Newton, Sir Isaac, 1642–1727: "We account the Scriptures of God to be the most sublime philosophy. I find more sure marks of authenticity in the Bible than in any profane history whatever."

Roosevelt, Theodore, 1858–1919: "I plead for a closer and wider and deeper study of the Bible, so that our people may be in fact as well as in theory 'doers of the Word and not hearers only.'"

Ruskin, John, 1819–1900: "Of my early knowledge of the Bible I owe the best part of my taste in literature, and the most precious, and on the whole, the one essential part of my education."

Tennyson, Alfred, 1809–1892: "Bible reading is an education in itself."

Wanamaker, John, 1838–1922: "I cannot too greatly emphasize the importance and value of Bible study."

Washington, George, 1732–1799: "It is not possible to rightly govern the world without God and the Bible."

Webster, Daniel, 1782–1885: "Philosophical argument, especially that drawn from the vastness of the universe in comparison with the apparent insignificance of this globe, has sometimes shaken my reason for the faith that is in me; but my heart has always assured and reassured me that the Gospel of Jesus Christ must be a divine reality. The sacred writings of Scripture have been my daily study and vigilant contemplation."

Wesley, John, 1703–1791: "I want to know one thing—the way to heaven. God Himself has condescended to teach the way. . . . He hath written it down in a Book! O give me that Book! At any price, give me that Book of God!"

Wilson, Woodrow, 1865–1924: "When you have read the Bible, you will know it is the Word of God, because you will have found it the key to your own happiness and your own duty. A man has deprived himself of the best there is in the world who has deprived himself of this knowledge of the Bible."

Read the Bible completely like a love letter,
    Consult it constantly like a road map,
    Study it carefully like a lesson book, and
    Obey it conscientiously like an army
order.

Books of the Old Testament—39
Books of the New Testament—27
Total number of books—66
Chapters in the Old Testament—929
Chapters in the New Testament—260
Total number of chapters—1,189
Verses in the Old Testament—33, 214
Verses in the New Testament—7,959
Total number of verses—41,173
Words in the Old Testament (KJV)—
593,393

Words in the New Testament—181,253
Total number of words—774,646

A businessman who was accustomed to presiding at business functions was called on suddenly to officiate at a church affair. Somebody read the Scriptures, and this man absentmindedly got up and said, "If there are no corrections, the Scriptures will stand as read."
—*The Vance Havner Quote Book*

If you see a Bible that is falling apart, it probably belongs to someone who isn't!
—*The Vance Havner Quote Book*

The liberals say, "The Bible is inspired in spots, and we are inspired to spot the spots."
—Bob Harrington

William Lyon Phelps of Yale University stated on more than one occasion, "I thoroughly believe in a university education for both men and women, but I believe a knowledge of the Bible without a college course is better than a college course without the Bible."

Several young men, recently graduated from seminary, came before a ministerial body in Chicago for ordination. A few were weak on the great question of the authority of the Bible. Finally one of the older examining ministers rose to his feet and said, "Young men, when you stand with a family at the coffin of a mother or father, or perhaps a child, you had better know what you believe!"

Henry Watson, Bible scholar and teacher, said, "I hate these chapters and verses; reading a Bible in which I find them always reminds me of riding over a corduroy road."

Scythians drink blood to bind an oath.
    Certain tribes of India swear on a tiger's tooth.
    Malay tribesmen swear by their swords.
    Dakota Indians swear by the sun.
    Lovers swear by the moon.
    Homeric Greeks swore by the heath.

Norsemen swore by a ring.

South Slavs swear by their children.

Northeast Africans swear, "If I don't speak the truth, may my wife be away."

Christians swear on the Bible.

One time Billy Graham said to a reporter that if he had the last ten years to live over, he would do some things differently, and then he specified the following: "I would spend more time studying. . . . I particularly plan to concentrate on the Scriptures. When the end of my life comes, I want to be saturated in the Scriptures."

"Mr. [D. L.] Moody used to say, 'in our prayers we talk to God, in our Bible study, God talks to us, and we had better let God do most of the talking.' We certainly ought to spend more time every day listening to what God has to say to us in His Word than we require Him to spend in listening to what we have to say to Him in our prayers."

—R. A. Torrey

A Christian repairman was once called to service the mechanism of a giant telescope. During the noon hour, the chief astronomer found him reading his New Testament and asked, "What good do you expect to get out of that? With our scientific advancements, the Bible is now completely outdated. Why, you can't even be sure who wrote it!" The mechanic was silent for a moment, then he looked up and said, "Don't you make considerable use of the multiplication tables in your calculations as an astronomer?" "Yes, I certainly do," replied the other. "Do you know who wrote them?" "Why no, I guess I don't." "Then," said the mechanic, "how can you employ them when you're not even sure of the author?" "We trust them because they work," the astronomer finished with a note of irritation. "Well, I trust the Bible for the same reason!"

—*Our Daily Bread*

Many people talk of knowing the Bible from cover to cover, but all they know is the cover.

Ramad was the most dangerous man in all of India. His gang attacked, plundered, and terrified the remote villages of the area. He was wanted dead or alive. While ransacking a small home in one of these villages, he found a small black book. At first he started to throw it away, but he noticed that the paper was very thin and just the right size for roll-your-own cigarettes. Each evening after a meal Ramad would relax with a smoke. He would take out the little book, tear a page out, and fold it over for the tobacco. One evening while folding the paper, he noticed the writing was in his own language. So each evening after eating, he would read a page of the little book and then smoke it. One evening he knelt down and asked Jesus to forgive his sins and to be his Savior. The small black book was the Bible.

He turned himself over to the police, much to their surprise, and turned from a bandit to a prisoner for Christ. The prison became Ramad's mission field where he led many other prisoners to Jesus. God's Word made the change in his life.

—Peter V. Deison

BIBLE—APPLICATION OF THE

One day a young Christian came into a mission station in Korea to visit the pastor who had been instrumental in his conversion. After the customary greetings, the missionary asked the reason for his coming. "I have been memorizing some verses in the Bible," he said, "and I want to quote them to you." He had walked hundreds of miles just to recite some Scripture verses to his father in the faith. The pastor listened as he repeated without error the entire Sermon on the Mount. He commended the young man for his remarkable feat of memory, then cautioned that he must not only "say" the Scriptures but also practice them. With glowing face, the man responded, "Oh, that is the way I learned them. I tried to memorize them but they wouldn't stick, so I hit on this plan. First, I would learn a verse. Then I'd talk to a neighbor who was not a Christian and practice it on him.

After doing this, I found I could remember it."

Is there a . . .
- S – Sin to avoid?
- A – Action to do?
- F – Faith to exercise?
- E – Example to follow?
- P – Promise to claim?
- A – Attitude to change?
- C – Challenge to meet?
- K – Key to victory in my life today?
—Mark Littleton

Gypsy Smith told of a man who said he had received no inspiration from the Bible although he had "gone through it several times." "Let it go through you once," replied Smith, "then you will tell a different story!"

BIBLE—DIFFICULTIES IN THE

Most people are bothered by those passages in Scripture which they cannot understand, but as for me, I always noticed that the passages in Scripture which trouble me most are those which I do understand.
—Mark Twain

It is far better to practice the things that are revealed than to speculate or argue over the truths that have been concealed.

A theological student came to Charles Spurgeon one day, greatly concerned that he could not grasp the meaning of certain verses in the Bible. The noted preacher replied kindly but firmly, "Young man, allow me to give you this word of advice. Give the Lord credit for knowing things you don't understand."

BIBLE—IGNORANCE OF THE

A group of American Jewish tourists were visiting the vicinity of Jerusalem. The guide pointed out to them the spot where the prophet Samuel was buried. One of the tourists remembered that in the Bible there are two books of Samuel, and in order to show off his biblical knowledge, he inquired of the guide: "Which Samuel rests here, the first or the second?"

The new pastor of a rural church in eastern Kentucky dropped into a Sunday school class and began quizzing the students to test the effectiveness of the teacher.

"Who knocked down the walls of Jericho?" he demanded of one boy.

"It sure weren't me, Reverend," the boy said.

Turning to the embarrassed teacher, the pastor said, "I suppose that's a sample of the kind of discipline you maintain!"

"Now, Reverend. Timmy's a good boy and don't tell lies. If he said he didn't do it, I believe him."

Thoroughly upset, the pastor took the matter to the board of deacons. After due consideration the board sent the following message to the nonplussed minister: "We see no point in making an issue of this incident. The board will pay for the damages to the wall and charge it off to vandalism."

According to the Barna Research group, almost two of every five adults (38 percent) believe that the entire Bible was written several decades after Jesus' death. (The entire Old Testament, of course, was written hundreds of years before His birth.)

Amazingly, 10 percent of adults believe that the name of Noah's wife was Joan of Arc.

Forty-nine percent agree that "the Bible teaches that money is the root of all evil." (The Bible teaches the *love* of money is the root of all evil.)

Other recent surveys by Barna have revealed that people do not know even half of the Ten Commandments, do not know who preached the Sermon on the Mount, do not know that the story of Jonah and the fish is from the Bible, and believe that the expression "God helps those who help themselves" is a direct quote from the Bible. (It was actually penned by Benjamin Franklin in the late 1700s.)

BIBLE—INSPIRATION OF THE

What I say is perspired, what God says is inspired.
—Walter C. Kaiser Jr.

The present translator who has closely studied these letters for several years is struck by two things. First, their surprising vitality. . . . he is continually struck by the living quality of the material on which he is working. Some will, no doubt, consider it merely superstitious reverence for "Holy Writ," yet again and again the writer felt rather like an electrician rewiring an ancient house without being able to "turn the mains off." He feels that this fact is worth recording. Secondly, he is struck by the extraordinary unanimity of the letters. The cynic may suggest that these men were all in a conspiracy together (though it is difficult to see what motive they could have for such a thing), yet the fact remains that in their different ways and from their different angles they are all talking about the same thing, and talking with such certainty as to bring a wondering envy into the modern heart.

—J. B. Phillips

BIBLE—MISUSE OF THE

When a clerk started working at a store, the owner said, "We must have a Scripture verse to back up everything we do." "Fine."

A lady came in and wanted some material. He got out some and showed it to her. She said, "How much a yard?" "$2.50."

"That's about it. But I want something more exquisite, a little more costly."

So he went to the back of the store, fidgeted around a little bit, then came out with the same material. She said, "Oh, that's it. How much is it a yard?" "$5.00."

She said, "I'll take it."

The owner had been watching and asked, "Do you have a verse to back up your deal?"

"Oh, yes. 'She was a stranger, and I took her in.'"

BIBLE—PERMANENCE OF THE

Century follows century—there it stands.

Empires rise and fall and are forgotten—there it stands.

Dynasty succeeds dynasty—there it stands.

Kings are crowned and uncrowned—there it stands.

Despised and torn to pieces—there it stands.

Storms of hate swirl about it—there it stands.

Atheists rail against it—there it stands.

Profane, prayerless punsters caricature it—there it stands.

Unbelief abandons it—there it stands.

Thunderbolts of wrath smite it—there it stands.

The flames are kindled about it—there it stands.

Suppose there was a man who had lived on the earth for 1,900 years, that this man had often been thrown into the sea and yet could not be drowned; that he had frequently been cast before wild beasts who were unable to devour him; that he had many times been made to drink deadly poisons which never did him any harm; that he had often been bound with iron chains and locked in prison dungeons, yet he had always been able to throw off the chains and escape from his captivity; that he had repeatedly been hanged until his enemies thought him dead, yet when his body was cut down he sprang to his feet and walked away as though nothing had happened; that hundreds of times he had been burned at the stake until there seemed to be nothing left of him, yet as soon as the fires were out he leaped up from the ashes as well and vigorous as ever—but we need not expand this idea any further; such a man would be superhuman, a miracle of miracles. Yet this is the story of the Bible. And all because God declared that His Word should abide forever.

BIBLE—POWER OF THE
The Anvil of God's Word

Last eve I passed beside a blacksmith's door
And heard the anvil ring the evening chime;
Then looking in, I saw upon the floor
Old hammers, worn with beating years of time.
"How many anvils have you had," said I,
"To wear and batter all these hammers so?"

"Just one," he answered with a twinkling
  eye,
"The anvil wears the hammers out, you
  know."
And so, thought I, the Anvil of God's
  Word,
For ages skeptic blows have beat upon;
Yet, though the noise of infidels was
  heard,
The Anvil is unworn—the hammers
  gone!

—John Clifford

BIBLE READING

A mother was trying to get her eight-year-
old daughter to learn her Sunday school
lesson. At length she took her Bible from
the bureau and said, "Come, Mary, I will
help you learn your lesson and then you
may go back to your play."

"All right, Mother, but let's study it out
of Grandfather's Bible. It is much more
interesting than yours."

"Oh, no, Mary! They are exactly alike."

"Well, I think Grandfather's must be
more interesting than yours; he reads it so
much more."

I supposed I knew my Bible, reading piece-
meal, hit or miss,
Now a bit of John or Matthew, now a
snatch of Genesis,
Certain chapters of Isaiah, certain
Psalms (the twenty-third!)
Twelfth of Romans, first of Proverbs—
yes I thought I knew the Word!
But I found that thorough reading was
a different thing to do,
And the way was unfamiliar when I read
the Bible through.
Oh, the massive mighty volume! Oh, the
treasures manifold!
Oh, the beauty and the wisdom and the
grace it proved to hold!
As the story of the Hebrews swept in
majesty along,
As it leaped in waves prophetic; as it
burst to sacred song.
As it gleamed with Christly omens, the
Old Testament was new,
Strong with cumulative power when I
read the Bible through.

Oh, imperial Jeremiah, with his keen
and sparkling mind!
And the dear old Nehemiah, and Ezekiel
refined!
Newly comes the Minor Prophets, each
with his distinctive robe;
Newly came the song idyllic, and the
tragedy of Job;
Deuteronomy, the regal, to a towering
mountain grew
With its comrade peaks around it when
I read the Bible through.
What a radiant procession as the pages
rise and fall!
James the sturdy, John the tender—oh,
the myriad-minded Paul!
Vast apocalyptic glories wheel and
thunder, flash and flame,
While the Church triumphant raises one
Incomparable Name.
Ah, the story of the Savior never glows
supremely true
Till you read it whole and swiftly, till
you read the Bible through.
You who like to play at Bible, dip and
dabble, here and there,
Just before you kneel aweary, and yawn
through a hurried prayer,
You who treat the Crown of Writings
as you treat no other book—
Just a paragraph disjointed, just a crude,
impatient look—
Try a worthier procedure, try a broad
and steady view;
You will kneel in very rapture, when
you read the Bible through!

Who Should Read the Bible?

The young—to learn how to live
The old—to know how to die
The ignorant—for wisdom
The learned—for humility
The rich—for compassion
The poor—for comfort
The dreamer—for enchantment
The practical—for counsel
The weak—for strength
The strong—for direction
The haughty—for warning
The humble—for exaltation
The troubled—for peace
The weary—for rest

BIBLE READING

The sinner—for salvation
The doubting—for assurance
All Christians—for guidance
—Faith Baptist Church,
Kokomo, Indiana

If all the Christians were to dust their Bibles at the same time, we would have the greatest dust storm in our history.
—J. H. Smith

The Bible should be bread for daily use, not cake for special occasions of need.

Seventy-two percent of the people believe the Bible to be the Word of God, but only 12 percent read it on a daily basis. Eighteen percent of Protestants are daily Bible readers, 4 percent of Catholics. Forty-one percent of Protestants read the Bible less than once a month or never, 67 percent of Roman Catholics are nonreaders.
—*Pulpit Helps*

Read the Scripture, not as an attorney may read a will, merely to know the sense, but as the heir reads it, as a description and proof of his interest.
—John Newton

It takes seventy hours and forty minutes to read the Bible at pulpit rate.

It takes fifty-two hours and twenty minutes to read the Old Testament.

It takes eighteen hours and twenty minutes to read the New Testament.

In the Old Testament the Psalms take the longest to read: four hours and twenty-eight minutes.

In the New Testament the gospel of Luke takes two hours and forty-three minutes.

That is less than twelve minutes a day to read it through in a year.

BIBLE STUDY

Dr. Eric Frykenberg, veteran missionary who spent half a century in India, could regale friends with incidents of his life in the field. One day someone asked, "Dr. Frykenberg, what was the most difficult problem you ever faced?" Without hesitation he answered, "It was when my heart would grow cold before God. When that happened, I knew I was too busy. I also knew it was time to get away. So I would take my Bible and go off into the hills alone. I'd open my Bible to Matthew 27, the story of the Crucifixion, and I would wrap my arms around the Cross. And then I'd be ready to go back to work."
—Leslie B. Flynn

Lord Bacon tells of a bishop who used to bathe regularly twice every day. On being asked why he washed so often, he replied, "Because I cannot conveniently do it three times." If those who love the Scriptures were asked why they read the Bible so often, they might honestly reply, "Because we cannot find time to read it more often." The appetite for the Word grows on that which it feeds on. We would say with Thomas á Kempis, "I would be always in a nook with a book."
—Charles H. Spurgeon

G. Campbell Morgan's son testifies that his father arose early each working day and spent several hours with his Bible, having only a light breakfast of tea and toast. After fifty-five years of intensive Bible study Morgan said, "I have only touched the fringes of the Bible."

The hardest part of a missionary career is to maintain regular, prayerful Bible study. Satan will always find you something to do, when you ought to be occupied about that—if it is only arranging a window blind!
—J. Hudson Taylor

I never saw a useful Christian who was not a student of the Bible.
—D. L. Moody

John DeVries, director of international ministries for the World Home Bible League, devised a six-point plan for getting something out of almost any passage of Scripture. It can make your Bible-reading time an opportunity to enjoy God and His message and not be overwhelmed with principles of interpretation. Read a passage of Scripture and then ask yourself these questions:

What did you like?
What did you not like?
What did you not understand?
What did you learn about God?
What should you do?
What phrase can you take with you today?

Much of our Bible study and reading is like the boy in Alabama who was reading aloud in school. The teacher then asked him to tell what he was reading. He answered, "I don't know. I wasn't listening."

Read the Bible not as a newspaper, but as a letter from home. If a promise lies on the page as a blank check, cash it. If a prayer is recorded, appropriate it and launch it as a feathered arrow from the bow of your desire. If an example of holiness gleams before you, ask God to do as much for you.

—F. B. Meyer

A little boy was sitting on a curb reading the New Testament when a priest came by and asked him what he was reading.

"It's the New Testament," he said.

"But that's not for a little ignorant boy like you to be reading," the priest said.

"Oh, but I have a search warrant to read it," the boy replied.

"A search warrant! What do you mean?"

"It says here, 'Search the Scriptures,' and I'm doing what I'm told."

Study it to be wise;
Believe it to be safe;
Practice it to be holy.
Study it through, pray it in, work it out, note it down, pass it on.

—J. Wilbur Chapman

Spurgeon said he once saw a Bible through which a worm had bored its way, beginning at Genesis and ending with Revelation; and from that hour his desire was to be a Bible bookworm, eating

through the Word, believing and digesting it all.

A Bible stored in the mind is worth a dozen stored in the bottom of one's trunk.

There are only two ways to study the Bible: studying it with your mind made up or studying it to let it make up your mind.

BIBLE—TREASURES IN THE

Vido Nati, a student in Barcelona, Spain, was working on a thesis for his doctor's degree. In the course of his research he scoured the university library for the writings of Hierro, an obscure philosopher of the eighteenth century whose writings had been generally neglected. After a lengthy search he unearthed a dusty volume by that author. As he leafed through it he came across a document written by Hierro in 1741. It turned out to be his will, and it bequeathed all his earthly goods to the first man who would study his book that he must have realized would be neglected by unappreciative successors.

The Spanish court declared the will legal, and Vido Nati collected nearly a quarter of a million dollars from Hierro's estate!

It is said of some of the mines of Cornwall that the deeper they are sunk, the richer they prove; and though some lodes have been followed a thousand and even fifteen hundred feet, they have not come to an end. Such is the Book of God. It is a mine of wealth which can never be exhausted. The deeper we sink into it, the richer it becomes.

BIBLE—VALUE OF THE

A man who loved old books met an acquaintance who had just thrown away a Bible that had been stored in the attic of his ancestral home for generations. "I couldn't read it," the friend explained. "Somebody named Guten-something had printed it." "Not Gutenberg!" the book lover exclaimed in horror. "That Bible was one of the very first books ever printed. Why, a copy just sold for two million dollars!"

39

His friend was unimpressed. "Mine wouldn't have brought a dollar. Some fellow named Martin Luther scribbled all over it in German."

BIBLICAL CRITICISM

Scoffing at the Bible, the virgin birth of Christ, the inspiration of the Bible, the doctrine of salvation through faith in Christ, etc., is like shooting beans in a beanshooter at the Rock of Gibraltar.

BILLION

How Much Is $1 Billion?

A man gave his wife one million dollars. He told her to go out and spend a thousand dollars a day. She did. Three years later she returned to tell him that the money was all gone. She wanted more.

He then gave her one billion dollars. He told her to go out and spend a thousand dollars a day. She didn't come back for three thousand years.

Or suppose a business started in the year 1 A.D. with one billion dollars capital. Supposing further that the concern was so unsuccessful as to lose a thousand dollars a day. It would still be in business today, after having lost a thousand dollars daily for almost two thousand years, and could continue almost eight hundred years longer, or until the year 2699 A.D., until its original capital of one billion was exhausted.

Or if someone would give you one billion dollars in dollar bills on the condition that you count each one, do not do it! It will take you sixty years, 365 days a year, eight hours a day—and it may break your health before you are half through!

—Paul Lee Tan

BIRTHDAYS

Teacher: "What happened in 1809?"
Student: "Lincoln was born."
Teacher: "Now, what happened in 1812?"
Student: "He had his third birthday."

The secret to enjoying your life is to count your blessings not your birthdays.

A true friend is someone who always remembers your birthday, but forgets your age.

He who has the most birthdays lives the longest.

—Confucius

A wise man never forgets his wife's birthday. He just forgets which one it is.

BITTERNESS (Also see HATRED)

One day a visitor leaned on the old fence around a farm while he watched an old farmer plowing with a mule. After a while, the visitor said, "I don't like to tell you how to run your business, but you could save yourself a lot of work by saying, 'Gee' and 'Haw' to that mule instead of tugging on those lines."

The old farmer pulled a big handkerchief from his pocket and wiped his face. Then he said, "Reckon you're right, but this animal kicked me five years ago and I ain't spoke to him since."

A grudge is harder on the one who holds it than the one it is held against.

—Pulpit Helps

Bitterness always inflicts a deeper wound on the person who harbors it than the person against whom it is directed. A man who had car trouble on a lonely road asked a farmer to tow him to the nearest garage. On the way his wife was protesting to her husband the fee the farmer charged. "It is scandalous," she said, "to charge us ten dollars for towing this car only three miles." To which her husband replied, "Never mind, dear. I'm having my revenge—I've got my brakes on." Many a person has thought himself to be getting revenge, but all the time the major damage was being done to him.

BLAME

To err is human; to blame it on somebody else is even more human.

BLESSINGS

When I reached Bergen, Norway, I found that, due to some slight miscalculation, I had only just enough money for my ticket by boat to London and none to spare for food. In those days I had a healthy appetite, and the prospect of a two-day fast was not pleasant. I grew more and more ravenous as the voyage progressed. Finally, I could stand it no more and, as the other passengers were entering the ship's dining room for the last meal, I asked a kindly looking old gentleman if he would bring me some bread when he had finished. He looked at me in astonishment, and said, "But why don't you come in and eat?" I explained my plight, to which he replied pityingly, "But you don't have to pay; meals are included in your ticket."

—Eric Shipton, explorer

Reflect on your present blessings of which every man has many, not on your past misfortunes of which all men have some.

—Charles Dickens

May there always be work for your hands to do.

May your purse always hold a coin or two.

May the sun always shine on your windowpane.

May a rainbow be certain to follow each rain.

May the hand of a friend always be near to you.

May God fill your heart with gladness to cheer you.

—An Irish blessing

Try *claiming* God's blessings instead of merely *longing* for them.

—Henry Jacobsen

BLOOD OF CHRIST

In his book *The Great Boer War,* Sir Arthur Conan Doyle recounts the story of a small detachment of British troops who were surprised by an overwhelming enemy force. The British fell back under heavy fire. Their wounded lay in a perilous position where they faced certain death. One of them, a corporal in the Ceylon Mounted Infantry, later told that they all realized they had to come immediately under the protection of a Red Cross flag if they wanted to survive. All they had was a piece of white cloth but no red paint. So they used the blood from their wounds to make a large cross on that white cloth. Their attackers respected that grim flag as it was held aloft, and the wounded British were brought to safety. Similarly there is safety in the blood of Christ.

BOARDS

There's a term for people who don't have a good relationship with their boards. They are called "Unemployed."

—Chuck Swindoll

BOASTING (Also see PRIDE)

The fellow who brags about how smart he is, wouldn't if he were.

—*Farmer's Almanac*

BODY

A third-grader was asked to write an essay on the subject of the human body. He submitted this masterpiece: "Your head is kind of round and hard, and your brains are in it and your hair is on it. Your face is in front of your head where you eat and make faces. . . . Your stummick is something that if you don't eat often enough it hurts, and spinach don't help none. . . . Your arms you got to have to throw a ball with and so you can reach the butter.

"Your fingers stick out of your hands so you can throw a curve and add up rithmatick. Your legs is what if you don't have two of, you can't run fast. Your feet are what you run on, and your toes are what always get stubbed. And that's all there is of you, except what's inside, and I never saw that."

BOLDNESS

In the Westminster Abbey a monument to Lord Lawrence has inscribed on it his name, his date of death, and these words: "He feared man so little because he feared God so much."

The pioneer evangelist Peter Cartwright spent seventy years serving the Lord and always preached the Word of God without fear or favor. One Sunday he was asked to speak at a Methodist church in the southern part of the United States. During the song just before the message, the pastor whispered to him that Andrew Jackson had just entered the sanctuary. He cautioned Cartwright to be very careful of what he said lest he offend their famous guest. The evangelist, however, knowing that "the fear of man bringeth a snare" (Prov. 29:25), was determined not to compromise the truth. He also knew that great leaders need the Lord as much as anyone, so he boldly proclaimed the Gospel. In fact, halfway through his sermon he said, "I understand that Andrew Jackson is present in the congregation today. If he does not repent of his sins and accept Jesus Christ as his personal Savior, he will be just as lost as anyone else who has never asked God for His forgiveness." Instead of becoming angry, Jackson admired the preacher for his courage. He listened with keen interest to the message and felt such deep conviction that after the service Cartwright was able to lead him to the Lord. From that moment on, the two became the best of friends.

BOOKS

A good book is the precious life blood of a master spirit, embalmed and treasured up on purpose for a life beyond.

—John Milton

If all the crowns of Europe were placed at my disposal on condition that I should abandon my books and studies, I should spurn the crowns away and stand by the books.

—François Fénelon

Books are immortal sons defying their sires.

—Plato

Books are lighthouses erected in the great sea of time.

—E. P. Whipple

Books are the legacies that genius leaves to mankind, to be delivered down from generation to generation, as parents to those who are yet unborn.

—Addison

When I get a little money, I buy books; and if any is left, I buy food and clothes.

—Erasmus

G. K. Chesterton, the great Roman Catholic layman, was once asked by an interviewer what book he would like to have with him if he were marooned on a desert island. As Chesterton began to consider this, the reporter made suggestions: The Bible? A volume of Shakespeare? But Chesterton shook his head. "No. I would like to have a manual on boatbuilding."

—Bruce Larson

I seldom notice bookends much
    although of course I've seen them.
They are like ears: what really counts is
    what one has between them.

Of the things which man can do or make here below, by far the most momentous, wonderful, and worthy are the things we call books.

—Thomas Carlyle

BOREDOM

Discussing with a clergyman friend some of the more common human ailments, a British doctor said: "The most deadly of all human diseases is one we can't reach with a knife or with medicine. That disease is boredom. There is more real wretchedness, more torment driving men to folly in boredom than in anything else.

"People will do almost anything to escape it—drink, drug themselves, sell their bodies and souls, fling themselves into crazy causes, and torture themselves and other people—anything to escape the misery of being bored."

He then added, "Anyone who discovers a cure for that will do more to avert human tragedy than all of us doctors put together."

—John D. Jess

The cure for boredom is curiosity. There is no cure for curiosity.

—Ellen Parr

BOSSES

Billy Martin was a controversial New York Yankee manager. In his office was this sign: "Company rules: Rule 1. The boss is always right. Rule 2. If the boss is wrong, see Rule 1."

BREVITY

Brevity is not only the soul of wit, but the soul of making oneself agreeable, and of getting on with people, and indeed of everything that makes life worth living.

—Samuel Butler

If you can't be humorous or erudite, at least you can be brief.

BRIBES

The Great Wall of China is a gigantic structure which cost an immense amount of money and labor. When it was finished, it appeared impregnable. But the enemy breached it—not by breaking it down or going around it—they did it by bribing the gatekeepers.

—Harry Emerson Fosdick

BUDDHISM

At the White House dinner in honor of the twenty-fifth anniversary of the United Nations, U. Thant in his speech said, "I am a disciple of Buddha. I pray to Buddha every morning and every evening. I believe that Buddhism is the answer to the world's needs."

BUILDINGS

The Leaning Tower of Pisa in Italy is going to fall. Scientists travel yearly to measure the building's slow descent. They report that the 179-foot tower moves about one-twentieth of an inch a year and is now seventeen feet out of plumb. They further estimate that by the year 2007 the 810-year-old tower will have leaned too far and will collapse onto the nearby restaurant, where scientists now gather to discuss their findings. Quite significantly, the word "pisa" means "marshy land," which gives some clue as to why the tower began to lean even before it was completed.

BURDENS

Lord, help me today not to add to anyone's burdens.

—A daily prayer of a friend of Warren Wiersbe

Myriad men are born; they labor and sweat and struggle for bread. . . . the burden of pain, care, misery, grows heavier year by year.

—Mark Twain

BURGLARY

A minister in Ontario, whose study had been burglarized several times, with locks broken and drawers emptied, tacked a large sign to his door which read:

Hi, Friend!
1. The money isn't here. Try the bank down the street.
2. Did you know that the Lord really loves you?
3. If I can help, please call me. Phone . . .

BUSYBODIES

A sad-eyed pup named Towser followed Farmer Brown into the yard and fell exhausted on the grass. "Look how worn out poor Towser is!" said a friend who had been waiting for them.

"Yes, but it isn't the long walk that's done him in," said Brown. "He tired himself out by getting into all kinds of mischief. He couldn't pass an open gate without running through it to nose around and see what was on the other side. Whenever he noticed a hen, he always took off after it and sent it scurrying. He ran toward every dog he saw and barked or tried to start a fight. He meddled with everything that moved. No wonder Towser's all tired out."

There are two reasons why some people can't mind their own business. One is that they haven't any mind, and the other is that they haven't any business.

—*Typo Graphic*

C

CALENDARS

The Gregorian calendar used by most of the world today is not very old. In 1472, Pope Sixtus IV asked an astronomer to reform the Julian calendar, which had been used since 46 B.C. and was 11 minutes and 15 seconds too long every year. By the fifteenth century the true vernal equinox was nine days before March 21.

But the astronomer died and it was not until 1582 that Pope Gregory XIII promulgated a new calendar. By 1582 the discrepancy between the vernal equinox and the Julian calendar had increased to ten days, so Pope Gregory ordered them dropped— October 5 became October 15. Italy and the Catholic countries of Spain, Portugal, and France changed to the new calendar at the same time. Other countries, however, were slower to change. Great Britain, for example, waited until 1752, when the difference between the Julian and Gregorian calendars had grown to eleven days. Parliament decreed that the day after September 2 would be September 14. The people, however, did not understand. Riots broke out in the streets. The slogan, "Give us back our eleven days," was shouted at those in authority.

—Bits & Pieces

CALIFORNIA

Frank Lloyd Wright's theory of architecture applies well to California: Everything loose leans to the southwest.

When I moved from Oklahoma to California the IQ of both states went up.

—Will Rogers

CALLING

The place God calls you to is the place where your deep gladness and the world's deep hunger meet.

—Frederick Buechner

CALMNESS

The first quality for a commander-in-chief is a cool head to receive a correct impression of things. He should not allow himself to be confused by either good news or bad news.

—Napoleon

CALVINISM

The prince of preachers, Charles H. Spurgeon, had a close friend by the name of John Clifford who was a distinguished preacher in his own right. One day Clifford ribbed his friend about his theology. "You see me so often I cannot understand why you remain a Calvinist," he said. Spurgeon replied, "Well, it's like this, John. I see you only about once a month, but I read my Bible every day and that keeps me straight."

CANADA

The train stopped for fifteen minutes at a station in Western Canada, and two elderly women tourists stepped to the platform to stretch a bit. "What place is this?" one asked and got the reply: "Saskatoon, Saskatchewan."

As they turned away, one woman turned to the other. "Isn't it exciting? They don't speak English here."

CANCER

An enthusiastic believer in Christ, Dan Richardson lost his battle with cancer. But his life demonstrated that even though the physical body may be destroyed by disease, the spirit can remain triumphant. This poem was distributed at his memorial service.

Cancer Is So Limited

It cannot cripple love,
It cannot shatter hope,
It cannot corrode faith,
It cannot eat away peace,
It cannot destroy confidence,
It cannot kill friendship,
It cannot shut out memories,
It cannot silence courage,
It cannot invade the soul,
It cannot reduce eternal life,
It cannot quench the Spirit,
It cannot lessen the power of the Resurrection.

CARELESSNESS

"I am not much of a mathematician," said Carelessness, "but I can add to your troubles, subtract from your earnings, multiply your aches and pains, take interest from your work, and discount your changes of safety.

"Besides this, I can divide your thoughts between business and pleasure and be a potent factor in your failures. Even if I am with you only a small fraction of the time, I can lessen your chances for success.

"I am a figure to be reckoned with. Cancel me from your habits and it will add to your happiness."

—Good Reading

CATHOLICISM

In a classroom the teacher asked the young people to write three words that would shake the world.

One wrote, "Queen Elizabeth Resigned." Another wrote, "Fidel Castro Assassinated." Then a third wrote, "The Pope Elopes."

A Protestant minister saw a Roman Catholic priest at a horse racetrack. He went down to the track and saw the priest blessing a horse. The horse won. The priest did it three times, and each time the horse won.

So the minister said, "This is a cinch." So he bet on the horse. The horse started out and was ahead and then the horse fell over dead. The minister said to the priest, "What happened?"

"You're not a Roman Catholic are you?"

"No, I'm a Protestant minister."

"I thought so. You don't know the difference between a blessing and last rites."

CAUTION

"How did you get that bump on your head?" a man asked his friend.

"Well, there was this sign over the entrance of a building I was about to enter, and since I'm nearsighted, I stepped closer to read it."

"And what did it say?"

"'Caution—door swings out.'"

—Philip Lazarus

Working as a welder on a water tower 110 feet above the ground, Randy Reid lost his balance and fell more than ten stories, landing on a pile of dirt and gravel at the base of the tower. Within minutes, emergency workers arrived and amazingly discovered only minimal injuries. As they carried the injured victim on a stretcher three feet above the ground to a waiting ambulance, Reid looked up at the medics and pleaded, "Don't drop me!"

—*Today in the Word*

CEMETERIES

During a recent gravedigger's strike this sign appeared at the entrance of one cemetery: "Due to the strike all grave digging for the duration will be done by a skeleton crew."

—*Bits & Pieces*

Once there was a boy whose parents named him Odd. Other children used to tease him about his name, but he refused to be bothered. As he grew up, people continued to make fun of his name—even after he became a successful attorney. Finally, as an old man, he wrote out his last wishes. "I've been the butt of jokes all my life," he wrote. "I'll not have people making fun of me after I'm gone." So he instructed that his tombstone not bear his name.

After his death, people would notice his large, blank stone and say, "That's odd."

—*Today in the Word*

CERTAINTY

British novelist J. B. Priestley once declined the invitation to write an article on his religious beliefs, explaining that he was "perhaps better able to deny than to affirm." But he added with a touch of sadness, "I regret this, because now is the time for gigantic affirmations." It is. And in an age of relativistic uncertainty evangelicals affirm that in Scripture God has spoken.

The older I get, the less sure I am about a lot of things, and the more sure I am of a few things.

—E. A. Holleen

A sign on the back of a van read, "Maybe . . . and that's final."

CHALLENGES

Difficult things take a long time; the impossible takes a little longer.

—Vera Weizmann

All men are equal—but it's what they're equal to that counts.

—Murray Watts

We cannot discover new oceans unless we have the courage to lose sight of the shore.

—*Teen Esteem*

There is no thrill quite like doing something you didn't know you could.

—Marjorie Holmes

The minister's son liked molasses. He frequently went by the molasses barrel, put his finger in it, and licked his finger. One day he couldn't reach the molasses because it was so slow. He tried balancing himself on the edge of the barrel, but fell in. Molasses was all over him. With much molasses to be licked, he got on his knees and prayed, "Lord, make me equal to the occasion."

James W. Whittaker, the first American to reach the top of Mount Everest on May 1, 1963, said, "Man is at his best when reaching for something beyond his grasp."

Unless a man is given more than he can possibly do, he will never do all that he can.

—Samuel McClure

In Valladolid, Spain, where Christopher Columbus died in 1506, stands a monument commemorating the great discoverer. Perhaps the most interesting feature of the memorial is a statue of a lion destroying one of the Latin words that had been part of Spain's motto for centuries. Before Columbus made his voyages, the Spaniards thought they had reached the outer limits of earth. Thus their motto was "Ne Plus Ultra," which means "No More Beyond." The word being torn away by the lion is "Ne" or "no," making it read "Plus Ultra." Columbus had proven that there was indeed "more beyond."

The great soul prays, "Lord, make me as big as my problems." The little soul prays, "Lord, let me off easy."

The giant soul asks, "Lord, give me strength sufficient for a hard day," while the small soul begs, "Lord, let me have a lighter load."

The busy soul prays, "Lord, stand with me until I finish my task," while the weak soul says, "I got tired and quit."

Rome remained great as long as she had enemies who forced her to unity, vision, and heroism. When she had overcome all her enemies, she flourished for a moment and then began to die.

—Will Durant

Arnold Toynbee has written that three things have caused the decay of many civilizations: war, alcohol, sexual license. But he adds a fourth: *lack of response to challenge.* Civilizations grow because of a challenge and response to it.

When London was attacked by Germany, Winston Churchill said, "Give us the tools and we'll finish the job."

General "Chinese" Gordon was leading his forces in the Sudan. He assigned one of his officers the task of capturing a strong fortress. After days of hard and demanding conflict, the officer returned to headquarters. Galloping into camp, he reined in his tired steed before General Gordon, saluted, and announced, "General, I have taken the fort!" His commander calmly replied, "Go take another."

I must be going downhill when I find my work equal to my aspirations.

—Bertel Thorvaldsen

During the depression, Charles Darrow could find no work. Although he was broke and his wife was expecting a baby, he wasn't discouraged. Every evening they played a game which he had devised. Remembering happy vacations in nearby Atlantic City, he laid out his own little boardwalk on a square piece of cardboard and pretended to be rich. On his "properties" he put miniature houses and hotels he had carved out of small pieces of wood. The game, called

"Monopoly," was later marketed by Parker Brothers and ultimately made Darrow a millionaire.

A rooster showed some hens an ostrich egg and said, "Ladies, I just want to show you what can be done."

CHANGE

Even nostalgia isn't what it used to be.

The world hates change, yet it is the only thing that has brought progress.
—Charles F. Kettering

I'm 100 percent for progress. It's all this change I'm against.
—A politician

There is nothing permanent except change.
—Herodotus

Lord, give me the grace to recognize the things which cannot be changed, courage to change those which can, and wisdom to know the difference.

The world seems to be changing so fast nowadays you couldn't stay wrong all the time even if you tried.

To change and to improve are two different things.
—German proverb

CHARACTER

The Stony Brook School on Long Island, New York, is a Christian preparatory school for boys founded in 1921 by Frank E. Gaebelein. On his retirement in 1963 he was succeeded by his son, Donn E. Gaebelein. Inscribed on the school's seal are these words: "Character before Career."

The best way to teach character is to have it around the house.

The measure of a man's real character is what he would do if he knew he would never be found out.
—Thomas Babington Macaulay

There are four types of character: easy to provoke and easy to appease—his loss is canceled by his gain; hard to provoke and hard to appease—his gain is canceled by his loss; hard to provoke and easy to appease—he is a saintly man; easy to provoke and hard to appease—he is a wicked man.
—Jewish Mishnah

The best index to a man's character is (a) how he treats people who can't do him any good, and (b) how he treats people who can't fight back.
—Abigail Van Buren

Much may be known of a man's character by what excites his laughter.
—Johann von Goethe

You can easily judge the character of a man by how he treats those who can do nothing for him or to him.
—Malcolm S. Forbes

During the Second World War the troop ship *Dorchester* went down off the coast of England. The story of how the four chaplains aboard gave their life jackets to sailors and soldiers is now a national legend. They were last seen linked arm in arm with each other, praying as the ship sank. In 1974 this incredible act of faith and bravery was memorialized in a commemorative United States postal stamp. But the real story didn't end in a brave act.

Protestant chaplain Clark V. Poling wrote his parents just before the ill-fated voyage. "Pray for me. Pray not that I will be safe. War is never safe. Pray only that I will be an adequate man."
—Edward L. Hayes

An executive in the Midwest, known for his ability to hire good people, explained his method this way: "The criteria I use to pick good people are first, character, then, intelligence, and third, experience." Most executives reverse the order. But a really bright person will pick up experience quickly.

CHARACTER

I've met a lot of leaders in the Army who were very competent—but they didn't have character. . . . I've also met a lot of leaders who had superb character but who lacked competence. . . . To lead in the twenty-first century . . . you will be required to have both character and competence.

—General H. Norman Schwarzkopf

It is a mistake to assume that a man is worth a lot of money just because he has it.

The size of a man is determined by the depth of his convictions, the height of his ambitions, the breadth of his mercy, and the reach of his love.

—D. N. Jackson

The test of real character is what a man does when he is tired.

—Winston Churchill

Character is like a tree and reputation like its shadow. The shadow is what we think of it, but the tree is the real thing.

Circumstances do not make a man; they reveal him.

—John Hubbard

D. L. Moody was once asked, "What is character?" Moody replied, "Character is what a man is in the dark."

It's not the force of the gale but the set of the sail that determines the way we go.

People are known by the way they walk, talk, and balk.

Your character is what God knows you to be; your reputation is what you think you are.

What you love and what you hate reveal what you are.

The size of a man is measured by what it takes to upset him.

The test of your character is what it takes to stop you.

—Bob Jones

Fame is a vapor, popularity is an accident, riches take wings and fly, those who cheer may curse tomorrow; only one thing endures—character.

—Horace Greeley

See what a man goes after here and you can usually tell where he's going hereafter.

If you are going to be anybody, be yourself.

The loose character usually winds up in a tight place.

Some people fall for everything and stand for nothing.

Character is determined by choice, not by opinion.

—Aristotle

CHILD DISCIPLINE

Without discipline, you cannot hope to teach your child to be a respectful, competent, and responsible adult.

—J. Allen Peterson

It is better to make your son cry than to cry over him.

—Arabic proverb

Weary of the constant disorder of her sons' room, the mother laid down the law. For every item she had to pick up off the floor the boys would have to pay her a nickel. At the end of the week, she informed the boys that they owed her $1.05. They paid up promptly and gave her a tip of fifty cents and a note which read, "Thanks, Mom. Keep up the good work."

—*Family Concern*

A small boy wondered if life is as difficult for other small boys as it is for him. He explained it this way: "If I'm noisy, they give me a spanking. If I'm quiet, they take my temperature."

Some children in a family found that their misconduct finally caught up with them. And their father was mad at them. The children at night prayed about their relationship to their father. Then the next morning they put this sign on their parents' bedroom door: "Be kind to your children, and they will be kind to you. Yours truly, God."

On the subway I got up and gave my seat to a lady who was holding onto a strap. She was rather surprised and said, "Why did you do that?" Seeing that she was incapable of understanding a spiritual reason, I said to her, "Madam, I tell you ever since I was a little boy, I have had an infinite respect for a woman with a strap in her hand."
—Fulton J. Sheen

The best way to straighten out some youngsters is by bending them over your knee.

A pat on the back develops character, if administered young enough, often enough, and low enough.

John Ruskin wrote in his *Outlines of Scenes and Thoughts in My Past Life* that his mother had listed many chapters of the Bible for him to learn as a child. "And truly, though I have picked up the elements of a little further knowledge in later life . . . this maternal installation of my mind in that property of chapters is very confidently the most precious, and, on the whole, the one essential part of all my education."

Children, like canoes, are more easily controlled if paddled from the rear.

In a park in Los Angeles I saw a full-grown tree that had grown rather crooked. It was anything but growing straight up. The strangest thing about the situation was that someone had placed an upright stick or pole near it and tied them together with ropes, but the tree had grown out so far from the place where the trunk came out of the ground that there was a lot of distance between the pole and the tree—perhaps a yard or two. It was too late!

How often is this true in the "rearing" of children. Parents will let their child run wild the first ten or fifteen years of their lives, and then when they try to correct them or straighten them, they find that it is too late.
—Roy B. Zuck

Parents who do not carry out their duty of instruction by example fail to assume their responsibility in a manner which is detrimental to our Christian society. The plain and simple maxims of the Bible contain the essential rules which govern human conduct.
—J. Edgar Hoover

If you do not teach your child the ways of the Lord, the Devil will teach them the ways of sin.
—Charles H. Spurgeon

The best mother is the one who stays on speaking terms with God and on spanking terms with her children.

Modern parents divide their time between worrying over how their children will turn out and when they will turn in.

As a young Frenchman pushed his son's stroller down the street, the youngster howled with rage. "Please, Bernard, control yourself," the father said quietly. "Easy there, Bernard, keep calm."

"Congratulations, Monsieur," said a woman who had been watching. "You know just how to speak to infants—calmly and gently." Then she said, "So the little fellow's named Bernard?"

"No, Madame," corrected the father. "He's named André. I'm Bernard."

The man who remembers what he was taught at mother's knee was probably bent over it at the time.
—Bill Ireland

Too many mothers use switches on everything in the house but their kids.

It used to be Papa dealt out a stern code of discipline to Junior. Then the electric razor took away his razor strap, furnaces took away the woodshed, and tax worries took away his hair and the hairbrush. That's why kids are running wild today. Dad ran out of weapons.

—*Pulpit Helps*

CHILD REARING

Someone asked a farmer, "How do you have such beautiful sheep?" "I take care of the lambs," he replied.

Interest your kids in bowling. Get them off the streets and into the alleys.

—Don Rickles

If you bungle raising your children, I don't think whatever else you do well matters very much.

—Jacquelyn Kennedy

The most influential of educational factors is the conversation in a child's home.

—William Temple

If a parent neglects to give a child love, no one else can substitute for that gap. The child will suffer. Parental love is of primary importance. . . . a parent can never give too much love to a child.

—Kay Kuzma

The best way to keep children home is to make the home atmosphere pleasant—and let the air out of the tires.

—Dorothy Parker

No success can compensate for failure in the home.

—David O. McKay

The most valuable gift you can give your family is a good example.

The best things you can give children, next to good habits, are good memories.

—Sydney J. Harris

The greatest gifts you can give your children are the roots of responsibility and the wings of independence.

—Dennis Waitley

One of John F. Kennedy's favorite anecdotes concerned French General Louis Lyautey. After World War I, the general asked his gardener to plant an oak tree in a particular part of his estate. The gardener noted that the tree the general had chosen was slow growing and wouldn't reach maturity for nearly a century. The general replied, "In that case, there is no time to lose. Plant it this afternoon."

No man ever really finds out what he believes in until he begins to instruct his children.

—Francis Xavier

Give me the children until they are seven and anyone may have them afterwards.

—Francis Xavier

Raising a child is very much like building a skyscraper. If the first few stories are slightly out of line, no one will notice. But when the building is eighteen or twenty stories high, everyone will see that it tilts.

Children are natural mimics—they act like their fathers or mothers in spite of every attempt to teach them good manners.

A woman was calling on a friend whose children were brought in. The caller said, evidently with no thought of the meaning of her words, "Oh, I'd give my life to have two such children," to which the mother with subdued earnestness replied, "That's exactly what it cost."

Parents are prone to give their children everything except the one thing they need most. That is time; time for listening, time for understanding, time for helping, and time for guiding. It sounds simple, but in reality it is the most difficult and the most sacrificial task of parenthood.

—Emma Kidd Hulbert

If we paid no more attention to our plants than we have to our children, we would now be living in a jungle of weeds.

If we work upon marble, it will perish; if on brass, time will efface it; if we rear temples, they will crumble into dust; but if we work upon immortal minds and imbue them with principles, with the just fear of God and love of our fellow men, we engrave on these tablets something that will brighten to all eternity.

—Daniel Webster

Before your child has come to seven,
Teach him well the way to heaven;
Better still the truth will thrive,
If he knows it when he's five;
Best of all if at your knee
He learns it when he's only three.

—*Alliance Weekly*

What a father says to his children is not heard by the world, but it will be heard by posterity.

—Jean Paul Richter

Recipe for Preserving Children

1 large grassy field
$1/_2$ dozen children
2 or 3 small dogs
A pinch of brook or pebbles

Mix children and dogs well together and put them in field, stirring constantly. Pour brook over pebbles; sprinkle field with flowers; spread under a deep blue sky and bake in the sun. When brown, remove and set to cool in a bathtub.

To assist in your quest to be good parents, here are ten commands for guiding your children.

1. Teach them, using God's Word (Deut. 6:4-9)
2. Tell them what's right and wrong (1 Kings 1:6)
3. See them as gifts from God (Ps. 127:3)
4. Guide them in godly ways (Prov. 22:6)
5. Discipline them (Prov. 29:17)
6. Love them unconditionally (Luke 15:11–32)
7. Do not provoke them to wrath (Eph. 6:4)
8. Earn their respect by example (1 Tim. 3:4)
9. Provide for their physical needs (1 Tim. 5:8)
10. Pass your faith along to them (2 Tim. 1:5).

—J. David Branon

Any child can tell you that the sole purpose of a middle name is so he can tell when he's really in trouble.

If you want your children to improve, let them overhear the nice things you say about them to others.

—Haim Ginott

Someone once said, "Sometimes you can straighten out a youngster by bending him over."

A woman once wrote Gypsy Smith after an evangelistic campaign to tell him she had been converted as a result of one of his messages. She said, "I believe the Lord wants me to preach the Gospel, Brother Smith, but the trouble is that I have twelve children to raise! What shall I do?" She received this letter in reply: "My dear lady, I am happy to hear that you have been saved and feel called to preach, but I am even more delighted to know that God has already provided you with a congregation of twelve." The new convert got the point!

Samuel Taylor Coleridge, the great English poet, was once talking with a man who told him that he did not believe in giving children any religious instruction whatsoever. His theory was that the child's mind should not be prejudiced in any direction, but when he came to years of discretion, he should be permitted to choose his religious opinions for himself. Coleridge said nothing, but after a while he asked his visitor if he would like to see his garden. The man said he would, and Coleridge took him out into the garden, where only weeds were growing. The man looked at Coleridge in surprise, and said, "Why, this is not a garden! There are nothing but weeds here!"

"Well, you see," answered Coleridge, "I did not wish to infringe upon the liberty of the garden in any way. I was just giving

the garden a chance to express itself and to choose its own production."
—E. Owen Kellum Jr.

Someone has said, "A man's character and his garden both reflect the amount of weeding that was done during the growing season."

Insanity is hereditary. You can get it from your children.

They pass so quickly, the days of youth,
   And the children change so fast,
And soon they harden in the most,
   And the plastic years are past.
Then shape their lives while they are
      young,
   This be our prayer, our aim,
That every child we meet shall bear
   The imprint of His name.

Strange as it seems, spare the rod and you get a beat generation.

Blessed is the child who has someone who believes in him, to whom he can carry his problems unafraid.
   Blessed is the child who is allowed to pursue his curiosity into every worthwhile field of information.
   Blessed is the child who has someone who understands that childhood's griefs are real and call for understanding and sympathy.
   Blessed is the child who has about him those who realize his need of Christ as Savior and will lead him patiently and prayerfully to the place of acceptance.
   Blessed is the child whose love of the true, the beautiful, and the good has been nourished through the years.
   Blessed is the child whose innate imagination has been turned into channels of creative effort.
   Blessed is the child whose efforts to achieve have found encouragement and kindly commendation.
   Blessed is the child who has learned freedom from selfishness through responsibility and cooperation with others.
   —Parents' Magazine

CHILDREN

A mother was getting her children off to school. A man asked her, "If you had to do it again, would you have children?"
   "Of course," she said.
   He said, "You would?"
   "Certainly," she replied, "but not the same ones!"

Children are a great comfort in your old age—and they help you reach it faster too.
   —Lionel M. Kauffman

Children are the only earthly possessions we can take with us to heaven.
   —Robert C. Savage

Most things have an escape clause—but children are forever.
   —Lewis Grizzard

Many years from now it will not matter what my worldly possessions had been. What will matter is that I was important . . . in the life of a child.

Horace Mann, in the early days of the colonies, was asked what a certain little Christian chapel was worth. He replied philosophically, "A million dollars if through it one boy is saved." It is recorded that one of the board members protested, "That's too much to pay for just one boy." The old educator stuck to his guns, saying, "Not if it's my boy that you save."

While discussing the economy with a friend one day, I asked him if he knew what the gross national product was that year. My ten-year-old son, who was listening, chimed in, "Spinach."
   —Reader's Digest

The greatest natural poets are children, says A. M. Sullivan, a New Jersey poet. They see things in a wonderful, original, and imaginative way. As proof, Sullivan offers these images from kids:
   The stream comes by my house, and when it turns, it stumbles.
   When you open the window at night, you let the dark in and it gets all over everything.

Yesterday I saw the wind. It was playing in my dog's hair.

Oil on the pavement looks like a dead rainbow.

—*Bits & Pieces*

A teacher of ten- and eleven-year-old boys in Germany would take off his top hat and bow before the boys in deference to them. "Why do you do that?" someone asked him. He answered, "Who knows what one of these boys may become?" One of them was named Martin Luther.

Children will tend to adopt the beliefs of those whom they instinctively recognize as happy, and of no others.

—W. E. Hockin

A man finds out what is meant by a spitting image when he tries to feed cereal to his infant.

—Imogene Fey

Isaac Watts was saved at about the age of nine. His hymns have lifted the hearts of millions. Jonathan Edwards, whose clear testimony and dynamic preaching stirred all of New England for God, was converted when only seven. Matthew Henry was brought to Christ at the age of eleven, and through his many years of study of God's Word he produced his well-known commentaries on the Holy Scriptures. Thousands of other men and women have been brought to the foot of the cross when they were young and their whole life could be dedicated to Christ.

—*Our Daily Bread*

CHILDREN'S FEARS

One summer night during a severe thunderstorm, a mother was tucking her small son into bed. She was about to turn the light off when he asked in a trembling voice, "Mommy, will you stay with me all night?" Smiling, the mother gave him a warm, reassuring hug and said tenderly, "I can't dear. I have to sleep in Daddy's room." A long silence followed. At last, it was broken by a shaky voice saying, "The big sissy!"

CHRIST

Similarities between Socrates and Christ:

1. Neither wrote down their teaching but their disciples did.
2. Both died rather then escape as their disciples suggested.
3. Both died unjustly and willingly. Both could have escaped death.
4. Both taught doctrines contrary to the teachings of their culture.
5. Both taught there is one God.
6. Both predicted the downfall of their nations because of refusal to recognize one God.

He who is the Bread of Life began His ministry hungering. He who is the Water of Life ended His ministry thirsting. Christ hungered as a man, yet fed the hungry as God. He was weary, yet He is our rest. He paid tribute, yet He is the King. He was called a devil, but He cast out demons. He prayed, yet He hears prayer. He wept, and He dries our tears. He was sold for thirty pieces of silver, yet He redeems sinners. He was led as a lamb to His slaughter, yet He is the Good Shepherd. He gave His life, and by dying He destroyed death.

In a Gallup poll people were asked with which of eight people they would like to spend a day? The eight were Abraham Lincoln, George Washington, Leonardo da Vinci, John Wayne, Napoleon, Joan of Arc, Cleopatra, and Jesus. Two-thirds of the respondents said Jesus.

A missionary in India visited the Taj Mahal. In its continuous arches sounds would echo with unusual clarity and distinction. He whispered the name of Jesus, and it was to him a personal thrill to hear this name of all names resound through the halls of the Taj Mahal.

J. C. Massee told of a friend who traveled a great distance for an interview with a distinguished scholar. When the man arrived, he received a cordial reception. Before being seated, he said to his host, "Doctor, I notice that the walls of your study are lined with books from the ceiling to the floor. No doubt you have read them all. I know you have written many yourself. You have traveled extensively, and doubtless you've had the privilege of conversing with some of the world's wisest men—its leaders of thought, its creators of opinion. I have come a long way to ask you just one question. Tell me, of all you've learned, what is the one thing most worth knowing?" Putting his hand on the guest's shoulder, the scholar replied with emotion in his voice, "My dear sir, of all the things I have learned, only two are really worth knowing. The first is that I am a great sinner. The second is that Jesus Christ is a great Savior!"

He was born a helpless baby; yet He flung the planets into space. He lay in a manger; yet "the cattle on a thousand hills" are His own. He was tempted, tested, and tried; yet He could not sin because He was God. He worked in a carpenter's shop and lived among humble folk; yet He could turn the water into wine and feed the multitudes by His mighty power. He "grew in stature and in favor with God and man," yet He is "the ancient of Days," "whose goings forth have been from of old, from everlasting." He lay in the bottom of the boat, asleep on a pillow; yet He arose to still the tempest. He was "the Man of Sorrows," weeping with others and shedding tears of agony in the Garden of Gethsemane; yet He turned heartaches into rejoicings when He raised the dead and gave them back to their loved ones. He died and was buried—a lifeless corpse; yet He arose in triumph by the power of the Holy Spirit.

—Louis T. Talbot

Here is a man who was born in an obscure village, the child of a peasant woman. He grew up in another obscure village. He worked in a carpenter's shop until he was thirty, and then for three years He was an itinerant preacher. He never wrote a book. He never held an office. He never owned a home. He never had a family. He never went to college. He never traveled two hundred miles from the place where He was born. He never did one of the things that usually accompany greatness. He had no credentials but Himself. He had nothing to do with the world except the power of His divine manhood. While still a young man, the tide of popular opinion turned against Him. He was turned over to His enemies. He went through the mockery of a trial. He was nailed on a cross between two thieves. His executioners gambled for the only piece of property He had on earth while He was dying—His coat. When He was dead, He was taken down and laid in a borrowed grave through the pity of a friend. And on the third day He arose from the dead.

Nineteen centuries have come and gone, and today He is the centerpiece of the human race and the leader of the column of progress.

I am far within the mark when I say that all the armies that ever marched, and all the navies that ever were built, and all the parliaments that ever sat, and all the kings that ever reigned put together have not affected the life of man on earth as powerfully as has that One solitary life. The explanation? He is the Son of God, the risen Savior.

—Phillips Brooks

According to an old legend, a man became lost in his travels and wandered into a bed of quicksand. Confucious saw the man's predicament and said, "It is evident that men should stay out of places such as this." Next, Buddha observed the situation and said, "Let that man's plight be a lesson to the rest of the world." Then Mohammed came by and said to the sinking man, "Alas, it is the will of God." Finally, Jesus appeared. "Take My hand," He said, "and I will save you."

The Bread of life,
The Water of life,
The Fountain of life,
The Light of life,
The Path of life,
The Way of life,
The Prince of life,
The Prince of Peace,
The Prince of the kings of the earth.

In 1495, Duke Ludovico of Milan asked the Florentine artist Leonardo da Vinci to portray the dramatic scene of Jesus' last supper with His disciples as they gathered in the Upper Room before His crucifixion. The scene was to be painted on a large wall of the dining hall at Santa Maria delle Crazie monastery in Milan. Da Vinci, then forty-three years old and already famous as a painter, sculptor, and architect, agreed to take on the assignment.

Working slowly and with great care for detail, he spent three years completing the painting. The disciples were grouped in threes, two groups on either side of the figure of Christ, who sat at the center of the table. His arms stretched before Him. In His right hand He held a wine cup, painted with marvelous realism. At last the painting was ready, and da Vinci called in a friend to see it. "Give me your honest opinion," da Vinci said.

"It's wonderful," the friend told him. "That cup is so real I cannot keep my eyes off it."

Da Vinci immediately took a brush and drew it across the sparkling cup. "If it affects you that way it must not remain," he exclaimed. "Nothing shall distract attention from the figure of Christ."

Jesus and Alexander died at thirty-three.
　One lived and died for self; one died for
　　you and me.
The Greek died on a throne; the Jew died
　on a cross;
　One's life a triumph seemed; the other
　　but a loss.
One led vast armies forth; the other walked
　alone;
　One shed a whole world's blood; the
　　other gave His own.
One won the world in life and lost it all in
　death.
　The other lost His life to win the whole
　　world's faith.
Jesus and Alexander died at thirty-three
　One died in Babylon; one on Calvary.
One gained all for self; one Himself He
　gave;
　One conquered every throne; the other
　　every grave.
The one made himself god; the God made
　Himself less;
　The one lived but to blast; the other but
　　to bless.
When died the Greek, forever fell his
　throne of swords;
　But Jesus died to live forever Lord of
　　Lords.
Jesus and Alexander died at thirty-three.
　The Greek made all men slaves; the Jew
　　made all men free.
One built a throne on blood; the other built
　on love,
　The one was born of earth; the other
　　from above;
One won all this earth, to lose all earth and
　heaven.
　The other gave up all, that all to Him be
　　given.
The Greek forever died; the Jew forever
　lives;
　He loses all who gets—and wins all
　　things who gives.
　　　　　　　　　—Charles Ross Weede

A man published a list of those he considered the ten greatest thinkers of the world—Plato, Socrates, Einstein, etc. Pastors wrote to him and asked him why he didn't include Christ in his list. He wrote back, "Christ is in a class above all others. He didn't have to think; that is, He never faced a problem of morals and ethics that He had to stop and think out."

When Franz Delitzsch, a German exegete, was teaching at Leipzig, on one occasion he said to his students, "Young gentlemen, the battle is now raging around the Old Testament. Soon it will pass into the New Testament field—it is already beginning. Finally it will press forward to the citadel of your faith—the Person of Jesus Christ. There the last struggle will occur. I shall not be here then, but some of you will. Be true to Christ. Stand up for Him. Preach Christ and Him crucified."

And Jesus said to the theologians, "Who do you say that I am?"

And they replied, "You are the eschatological manifestation of the ground of our being, the actualization of the potential God-man relationship which is divine, intended truth about every man, the *kerygma* manifest in conflict at the cutting edge of the humanizing process, the paradigm of human perfection."

And Jesus said, "What?"

Socrates taught for forty years, Plato for fifty, Aristotle for forty, and Jesus for only three. Yet the influence of Christ's three-year ministry infinitely transcends the impact left by the combined 130 years of teaching from these men who were among the greatest philosophers of all antiquity. Jesus painted no pictures; yet, some of the finest paintings of Raphel, Michelangelo, and Leonardo da Vinci received their inspiration from Him. Jesus wrote no poetry; but Dante, Milton, and scores of the world's greatest poets were inspired by Him. Jesus composed no music; still Haydn, Handel, Beethoven, Bach, and Mendelssohn reached their highest perfection of melody in the hymns, symphonies, and oratorios they composed in His praise. Every sphere of human greatness has been enriched by this humble carpenter of Nazareth.

"His unique contribution to the race of men is the salvation of the soul. Philosophy could not accomplish that. Nor art. Nor literature. Nor music. Only Jesus Christ can break the enslaving chains of sin and Satan. He alone can speak peace to the human heart, strengthen the weak, and give life to those who are spiritually dead."

—*Our Daily Bread*

The life and death of our Lord Jesus Christ are a standing rebuke to every form of pride to which men are liable.

Pride of birth and rank—"Is not this the carpenter's son?"

Pride of wealth—"The Son of man hath no where to lay His head."

Pride of respectability—"Can any good thing come out of Nazareth?"

Pride of personal appearance—"He hath no form nor comeliness."

Pride of reputation—"A friend of publicans and sinners."

Pride of learning—"How knoweth this Man letters, having never learned?"

Pride of superiority—"I am among you as He that serveth."

Pride of success—"He came unto His own, and His own received Him not." "Neither did His brethren believe in Him." "He is despised and rejected of men."

Pride of ability—"I can of Mine own self do nothing."

Pride of self-will—"I seek not Mine own will, but the will of the Father which hath sent Me."

Price of intellect—"As my Father hath taught me I speak these things."

Pride in death—"He . . . became obedient unto death, even the death of the cross."

—*Gospel Message*

Alexander, Caesar, and Hannibal conquered the world but they had no friends. . . . Jesus founded His empire upon love, and at this hour millions would die for Him. . . . He has won the hearts of men, a task a conqueror cannot do.

—Napoleon

Christ on the cross delivers from the penalty of sin (Prophet).

Christ at God's right hand delivers from the power of sin (Priest).

Christ coming in the clouds delivers from the presence of sin (King).

—D. L. Moody

Christ is not a disappointment; every longing in my breast
Finds in Him complete fulfillment; He has brought me into rest.
I have tested Him and found Him more than all I dreamed He'd be;
Christ is not a disappointment; He is all in all to me.

Robert Browning in one of his letters describes a famous literary incident in the life of Charles Lamb in London. One time when Lamb was with several other men of letters and geniuses of literature, he began to speak about what they would do if the great men of the past should rise from the dead and suddenly appear in the doorway. One of them remarked that if Shakespeare were to come they would all stand in respect and in wonder before the Shakesperean genius. But one of the men remarked that if Jesus Christ should come and appear, all of them would kneel in humble worship and adoration.

In Christ we have:
A love that can never be fathomed;
A life that can never die;
A righteousness that can never be tarnished;
A peace that can never be understood;
A joy that can never be diminished;
A hope that can never be disappointed;
A glory that can never be clouded;
A light that can never be darkened;
A happiness that can never be enfeebled;
A purity that can never be defiled;
A beauty that can never be marred;
A wisdom that can never be baffled;
And resources that can never be exhausted.

The presence of Christ is the joy of my life.
The service of Christ is the business of my life.
The will of Christ is the law of my life.
The glory of Christ is the crown of my life.

Christ My All

Christ for sickness, Christ for health,
Christ for poverty, Christ for wealth,
Christ for joy, Christ for sorrow,
Christ today, and Christ tomorrow;
Christ my Life and Christ my Light,
Christ for morning, noon, and night;
Christ when all around gives way,
Christ my Everlasting Stay;
Christ my Rest, Christ my Food,
Christ above my highest Good;
Christ my well Beloved, my Friend,
Christ my Pleasure, without end;
Christ my Savior, Christ my Lord,
Christ my Portion, Christ my God;
Christ my Shepherd, I His sheep,
Christ Himself my soul doth keep;
Christ my Leader, Christ my Peace,
Christ hath bought my soul's release;
Christ my Righteousness divine,
Christ for me, for He is mine;
Christ my Wisdom, Christ my Meat,
Christ restores my wand'ring feet,
Christ my Advocate and Priest,
Christ who ne'er forgets the least;
Christ my Teacher, Christ my Guide;
Christ my Rock, in Christ I hide;
Christ the everlasting Bread,
Christ His precious blood hath shed;
Christ hath brought us near to God,
Christ the everlasting Word,
Christ my Master, Christ my Head,
Christ who for my sins hath bled;
Christ my Glory, Christ my Crown,
Christ the One of great renown;
Christ my Comforter on high,
Christ my Hope draws ever nigh.

—H. W. S.

An elderly gentleman who walked closely with the Lord was visited in his home by an unbeliever. Soon the conversation turned to the subject of religion. After hearing the Christian quote Galatians 2:20 and give a testimony of his salvation, the unbeliever remarked sarcastically, "I can't figure you out. First you said Christ lives in you, and then just a few minutes later you contradicted yourself by saying that you are in Him. How can that be?" The believer walked to the fireplace and picked up the poker. Then he said, "I'm going to put this in the fire until it turns red in the heat." In a short time the tip of the shaft of the iron began to glow. Pointing to it, the aged saint continued, "You see, my friend, now the fire is in the poker and the poker is also in the fire! In the same way, I am in Christ—and He is in me!"

All history is incomprehensible without Christ.

—Ernest Renan

Gauged by the consequences that have followed, the birth, life, death, and resurrection of Jesus have been the most important events in the history of mankind.

—Kenneth Scott Latourette

Christ is the great central fact in the world's history. To Him everything looks forward

57

or backward. All the lines of history converge upon Him.

—Charles H. Spurgeon

Christ Alone

The world, I thought, belonged to me,
    Goods, gold, and people, land, and sea.
Where'er I walked beneath God's sky,
    In those old days, my word was "I."
Years passed: there flashed my pathway near,
    The fragment of a vision dear;
My former word no more sufficed,
    And what I said was "I and Christ."
But, O, the more I looked on Him,
    His glory grew, while mine grew dim;
I shrank so small, He towered so high,
    All I dared say was "Christ and I."
Years more the vision held its place
    And looked me steadily in the face;
I speak now in a humbler tone,
    And what I say is "Christ alone!"

All historians must confess that the turning point of the race is the cross of Christ. It would be impossible to fix any other hinge of history. From that moment the power of evil received its mortal wound. It dies hard, but from that hour it was doomed.

—Charles H. Spurgeon

Christ always identified Himself with the least, the last, and the lost.

The achievements of the Savior through His incarnation are so astounding and so numerous that any one wishing to describe them in detail would be like one who gazes at the expanse of the sea and attempts to count its waves.

Christ is the hinge of history.

—Charles Malik

What the sun is to a flower, so is Jesus Christ to me.

—Alfred Tennyson

CHRIST—BIRTH OF

The Son of God became the Son of Man so that sons of men may become sons of God.

—C. S. Lewis

CHRIST—DEATH OF

Devoutly kissing the nail-scarred feet of a statue of Christ in her church, an old Russian woman was approached by a Soviet military officer. He addressed her using the common term for grandmother: "Babushka, are you willing to kiss the feet of Stalin?" "Yes," she replied, "if he gets crucified for me."

During the American Civil War a farmer in New York was drafted for the Union army. He wife had died and he was the sole support of his young children. But then an unmarried man in the town who had no dependents came to his home and offered to go to war in his place. For the sake of his children, the farmer accepted the offer. The generous friend marched off to battle, and in the first engagement, he was shot and killed. When the farmer heard what had happened, he went to the scene of the battle and brought back the body. He buried his friend in the churchyard and had these words engraved on the headstone: HE DIED FOR ME.

An African chief heard a missionary explaining the death of Christ in our place. The chief suddenly jumped to his feet and said, "Come down, come from that cross, I tell you. You have no business there. That is my place."

Christianity is the religion of redemption. The central figure in the Bible in the Person of the Redeemer; and the central fact is His death.

—John Page

Christ was
    Gracious, though bound.
    Truthful, though disbelieved.
    Innocent, though condemned.
    Forgiving, though forsaken.
    Victorious, though dying.

CHRIST—DEITY OF

If the life and death of Socrates were those of a philosopher, then the life and death of Jesus Christ were those of a god.

—Jean Jacques Rousseau

Oswald Sanders, in his book *Christ Incomparable*, tells of an outstanding Brahmin scholar disturbed by the progress of the Christian faith among his people in India. He decided to do all in his power to combat it. After careful consideration he decided to prepare a pamphlet that would set forth the weaknesses and failings of Jesus. With this purpose in mind, he purchased a New Testament and began a careful study of it. For eleven years he pursued his search for some inconsistency or weakness in the life of Jesus. Not only was he unsuccessful, but he was more and more convinced that the One he sought to discredit was indeed the Son of God. He accepted Him as his Savior.

W. Robertson Smith, a cleric in Scotland, was subject to a heresy trial by the Scottish Presbyterian Church. He was accused of denying the deity of Christ. He responded, "How can they say that? I have never denied the divinity of any man, let alone that of Jesus Christ."

A man who was merely a man and said the sort of things Jesus said wouldn't be a great moral teacher. He would either be a lunatic—on a level with a man who says he is a poached egg—or else he'd be the devil of hell. You must make your choice. Either this man was and is the Son of God, or else a madman or something worse.

—C. S. Lewis

The belief in the deity of Christ is derived directly from statements concerning Him in the Bible. The references are so many and their meaning so plain that Christians of every shade of opinion have always regarded its affirmation as an absolute and indispensable requisite of their faith. It is proclaimed in the very first sermon of the infant church (Acts 2:36) . . .; while in the last vision of the book of Revelation the Lamb occupying *one* throne with God (Rev. 22:3) can betoken only essential oneness.

—F. F. Bruce and W. J. Martin

An American lady by the name of Prince gave an English Gospel of John to a Japanese man whom she was teaching. After reading for some time, he burst out with a question. "Who is this Man about whom I am reading—this Jesus? You call Him a Man, but He must be God."

If Christ does not remain the true, natural God . . . then we are lost. For what good would the suffering and death of the Lord Christ do me if He were merely a man such as you and I are? Then He would not have been able to overcome the Devil, death, and sin. He would have been far too weak for them and could not have helped us.

—Martin Luther

If you had gone to Buddha and asked him, "Are you the Son of Brahma?" he would have said, "My son, you are still in the vale of illusion." If you had gone to Socrates and asked, "Are you Zeus?" he would have laughed at you. If you had gone to Mohammed and asked, "Are you Allah?" he would first have rent his clothes, and then cut your head off. If you had asked Confucius, "Are you heaven?" I think he would have probably replied, "Remarks which are not in accordance with nature are in bad taste."

—C. S. Lewis

CHRIST—DEITY AND HUMANITY

Daniel Webster, the nineteenth-century statesman, once dined in Boston with several eminent literary figures. Soon the conversation turned to Christianity. Webster, a convinced Christian, confessed his belief in Christ and His atoning work. A Unitarian minister at the table responded, "Mr. Webster, can you comprehend how Jesus Christ can be both God and man?"

"No, sir, I cannot understand it," replied Webster, "and I would be ashamed to acknowledge Christ as my Savior if I could comprehend it. He could be no greater than myself, and such is my conviction of my accountability to God, my sense of sinfulness before Him, and my knowledge of my own incapacity to recover myself, that I feel I need a superhuman Savior."

CHRIST—FELLOWSHIP WITH

When Queen Victoria reigned in England, she would occasionally visit some of the humble cottages of her subjects. One time she entered the home of a widow and enjoyed a brief period of Christian fellowship. The poor woman was later taunted by her worldly neighbors. "Granny," they said, "who's the most honored guest you've ever entertained in your home?" They expected her to say it was Jesus, for despite their constant ridicule of her Christian witness, they recognized her deep spirituality. But to their surprise she answered, "The most honored guest I've ever entertained is Her Majesty the Queen." "Did you say the Queen? Ah, we caught you this time! How about this Jesus you're always talking about? Isn't He your most honored guest?" Her answer was definite and scriptural. "No indeed! He's not a guest. He lives here!" Her hecklers were put to silence.

According to a Persian legend, there was a great bird of the East whose shadow of its wings would bring fortune. One day the king in his splendor was riding with his courtiers. Then they saw the bird and all the servants ran to get under the shadow of the bird's wing—all except one servant. The king was surprised. "Why didn't you go in to your fortune?" "Why should I run after a mere bird when I can enjoy the presence of the king?" The king was so impressed that he promoted the servant to a position of vice-president.

What the hand is to the lute,
What the breath is to the flute,
What fragrance is to the smell,
What the spring is to the well,
What the flower is to the bee,
That is Jesus Christ to me.
What's the mother to the child,
What the guide in pathless wild,
What is oil to troubled wave,
What is ransom to the slave,
What is water to the sea,
That is Jesus Christ to me.
　　　　　　　—Charles H. Spurgeon

CHRIST—GOD-MAN

Many years ago there was found in Asia Minor a very old Latin inscription chiseled in marble. This inscription bears an interesting witness to the faith in the Person of the Lord Jesus Christ in the first century of Christianity. It presents the eternal Word, the Son of God, bearing witness to Himself. He speaks of Himself as incarnate, the Word made flesh, and then declares, "I am what I was—God. I was not what I am—man. I am now called both, God and Man."
　　　　　　　—A. C. Gaebelein

CHRIST—INCARNATION OF

Luther, who often told a story in order to make a point, stressed the impact of God assuming flesh when he described a preacher reading from the first chapter of John's gospel. When he came to the words, "In the beginning was the Word," the Devil stood motionless. But when he read, "and the Word was made flesh," the Devil immediately fled.

In the fourth century B.C., Plato, discoursing on some of the insoluble mysteries of the universe, exclaimed, "Oh, that there might come forth a word from God to make all things clear!" Long before Plato's day God had spoken: "In sundry times and in divers manner . . . unto the fathers by the prophets" (Heb. 1:1). Moreover, about four centuries after Plato hoped for a word from God, "The Word was made flesh and dwelt among us" (John 1:14).

CHRIST—INTERCESSION OF

If I could hear Christ praying for me in the next room, I would not fear a million enemies. Yet the distance makes no difference; He is praying for me.
　　　　　　　—Robert Murray McCheyne

CHRIST—KNOWING HIM

We have no greater need than to know Christ better.
　　　　　　　—Andrew Murray

I have one passion—Christ.
　　　　　　　—Count Zinzendorf

Let our foremost resolve be to meditate on the life of Jesus Christ.

—Thomas á Kempis

Knowing God without knowing our wretchedness leads to pride.

Knowing our wretchedness without knowing God leads to despair.

Knowing Christ gives the balance.

—Blaise Pascal

CHRIST—LOVE OF

A mother was busily writing letters at her desk as her little girl played in another room with a doll. After some time, she called her daughter to come and sit on her lap. The little girl said, "Mommy, I'm so glad you called for me. I love you so much." "Do you, darling?" she asked as she tenderly hugged her beaming five-year-old. "I'm glad you love me. You weren't lonely while I was writing, were you? You and your dolly seemed to be having such a good time together." "We were having fun, but I got tired of loving her. She never loves me back." "Is that why you love me?" "That's one reason, Mommy, but not the best." "And what is the best?" Her bright blue eyes were earnest as she replied, "O, Mommy, can't you guess? I love you now because you loved me and took care of me when I was too little to love you back."

A girl learned that Jesus watches over her to see everything she does. Her mother said, "Doesn't that bother you that He sees everything you do?"

"Oh, no. He loves me so much He can't keep His eyes off me."

All that Jesus did for His church was but the expansion and unfolding of His love. Traveling to Bethlehem, I see Love incarnate. Tracking His steps as He went about doing good, I see Love laboring. Visiting the house of Bethany, I see Love sympathizing. Standing by the grave of Lazarus, I see Love weeping. At Gethsemane, I see Love sorrowing. Passing on to Calvary, I see Love suffering, bleeding, and dying. The whole scene of His life was but an unfolding of the deep, wonderful, and precious mystery of redeeming love.

—Andrew McCheyne

CHRIST—LOVE FOR

A woman in the Belgian Congo, crippled with leprosy, crawled nearly eight miles on swollen knees protected only by rough bark-cloth to a mission station. When some of the missionaries remarked about her amazing fortitude, she said to them, "Of what matter the pain and weariness of the journey! Jesus loved me enough to die in my place. I love Him and long to be taught His Word."

—E. Schuyler English

CHRIST—PREEMINENCE OF

When Raphael's picture *The Sistine Madonna* was brought to Dresden, Germany, it was displayed in the castle before the king. However, the spot where the light was best was already occupied by the throne. Observing the situation, the king immediately stepped down from his royal chair, saying, "Make room for the immortal Raphael." So too, there is but one throne in the human heart, and the most important question for any of us to answer is this: Who is to occupy that place of authority? Will it be Christ or self?

—*Our Daily Bread*

Arturo Toscanini led his orchestra in an electrifying rendition of Beethoven's Symphony No. 9. The audience applauded wildly. Toscanini bowed and bowed and bowed. Then he turned to his orchestra. "Gentlemen, I am nothing; you are nothing; Beethoven is everything, everything, everything."

Once it was blessing,
    Now it is the Lord;
Once it was the feeling,
    Now it is His Word;
Once His gift I wanted,
    Now the Giver own;
Once I sought for healing,
    Now Himself alone.
Once 'twas painful trying,
    Now 'tis perfect trust;

Once a half salvation,
  Now the uttermost;
Once 'twas ceaseless holding,
  Now He holds me fast;
Once 'twas busy planning,
  Now 'tis trustful prayer;
Once 'twas anxious caring,
  Now He has the care;
Once 'twas constant asking,
  Now 'tis ceaseless praise.

A distinguished British Bible scholar, the late Henry Jowett, attended the coronation of Edward VII of England in Westminster Abbey at the turn of this century.

He observed with interest the assembling and the seating of princes and princesses, dukes and duchesses, and others of lesser nobility, and how homage was paid them. "But then the king arrived," Dr. Jowett writes, "and all eyes turned away from those of lower rank and were fixed upon him."

"So," Jowett continues, "literature, music, art, and the sciences are worthy of our respectful attention; but when Jesus Christ comes into the heart, He must be King and all lesser subjects take their lesser place."

—E. Schuyler English

CHRIST—PRESENCE OF

One day David Livingstone stood before the students of Glasgow University. He had spent many long years in the heart of Africa at a time when conditions were much more trying than they are today.

It was the occasion of the commencement exercises, and Livingstone asked, "Shall I tell you what sustained me in my exiled life among strangers whose language I did not understand?"

A hush swept over the student audience. "It was this—'Lo, I am with you always, even unto the end of the world.'"

CHRIST—PRIESTHOOD OF

Three themes captured the essence of the Reformation:
  No priest but Christ
  No sacrifice but Calvary
  No confessional but the throne of grace

CHRIST—PROPHECIES OF

Christ was foretold to:
  Adam—as a man (Gen. 3:15)
  Abraham—as to His nation (Gen. 22:18)
  Jacob—as to His tribe (Gen. 49:10)
  Isaiah—as to His family (Isa. 11:1–5)
  Micah—as to His town (Mic. 5:2)
  Daniel—as to His time (Dan. 9:25)
  Mary—as to His Person (Luke 1:30)
  By angels—as to His date (Luke 2:11)
  By a star—as to His birthplace (Matt. 2:9).

—D. L. Moody

In his book *Science Speaks,* Peter Stoner applied the modern science of probability to just eight prophecies. He says, "The chance that any man might have . . . fulfilled all eight prophecies is one in 10^{17}. That would be 1 in 100,000,000,000,000,000." (That's one hundred quadrillion.) Stoner suggests that "we take 10^{17} silver dollars and stir the whole mass thoroughly. . . . Blindfold a man and tell him he can travel as far as he wishes, but he must pick up [the one marked 'silver dollar']. What chance would he have of getting the right one?" Stoner concludes, "Just the same chance that the prophets would have had of writing those eight prophecies and having them all come true in any one man, . . . providing they wrote them in their own wisdom."

—*Our Daily Bread*

CHRIST—REJECTION OF

Aaron Burr, the third vice president of the United States, was reared in a godly home and admonished by his grandfather Jonathan Edwards to accept Christ. But he refused to listen. Instead, he declared that he wanted nothing to do with God and said he wished the Lord would leave him alone. He did achieve a measure of political success in spite of repeated disappointments. But he was also involved in continuous strife, and when he was forty-eight years old, he killed Alexander Hamilton in a duel. He lived for thirty-two more years, but through all this time he was unhappy and unproductive. It was during this sad chapter in his life that he declared to a group of friends, "Sixty years ago I told God that if He would let me alone, I would let Him alone and God has not bothered about me since." Aaron Burr got what he wanted.

Outside the Peace Palace at The Hague, Netherlands, there stands a very large statue of Christ. A guide, asked by a visitor why it was outside instead of inside where it was most needed, replied, "Because the entrance is too small to admit it."

CHRIST—RESURRECTION OF

In his early days as a missionary in Japan, Sam Boyle hired a translator so he could preach to a growing group of interested Japanese. The only person he could find was a Japanese man who was teaching English in one of the nearby junior high schools.

Although he wasn't a Christian, the man agreed to translate the missionary's sermons. Boyle felt his ministry was moving along quite well until the third week, when he came to a place in his sermon where he said, "And on the third day He rose from the dead." Immediately, the translator looked at him and said, "They're never going to believe this."

While traveling in Egypt, Harry Rimmer had an opportunity to talk with that country's secretary of state, and in the course of the conversation he brought up the subject of Christianity. Rimmer told the official that Christians believe God has given us three revelations of Himself. "We too believe that," said the official, who was a Muslim. "We believe God revealed Himself in the works of creation," said Rimmer. "We also believe that," the other responded. Rimmer continued, "We believe God has revealed Himself in a book—the Bible." The Muslim answered, "We too believe God has revealed Himself in a book—the Koran." Rimmer declared, "We believe God has revealed Himself in a man—Jesus Christ." "We also believe God has revealed Himself in a man," replied the official, "the prophet Mohammed." "We believe," added Rimmer, "that Jesus is able to substantiate His claims because He arose from the dead." The Muslim hesitated, then his eyes fell. Finally he replied, "We have no information concerning our prophet after his death."

Joseph Renan, the French skeptic, said sarcastically but truthfully, "You Christians live on the fragrance of an empty tomb."

One Easter day near the end of his life when he was unable even to speak, W. E. Sangster wrote to his daughter, "It is terrible to wake up on Easter morning and have no voice with which to shout 'He is risen!'" But it would be still more terrible to have a voice and not want to shout.

No single event in ancient history is better attested than the resurrection of Christ, according to B. F. Westcott, who spent a lifetime studying the question of His resurrection. For example only five copies of Julius Caesar's *Gaulic Wars* are in existence, and they go back only to A.D. 900. In the New Testament, however, five thousand complete or partial copies are available and they go back to within fifty years of events recorded. Some entire manuscripts were written within A.D. 300.

The story is told of how the news of the battle of Waterloo was received in England. Tradition tells that sailing ships came to the south coast of the islands and by signal flags wig-wagged to the tower of the Cathedral of Winchester. When the message came, hearts failed for fear as the words were spelled out: "W-E-L-L-I-N-G-T-O-N D-E-F-E-A-T-E-D," and then the fog descended and hid the signal from view. All of London was shocked and the people felt their country had been entirely lost in this strategic battle. But after a while, the fog lifted, and the signals still came through with the complete sentence: "WELLINGTON DEFEATED . . . NAPOLEON!" Immediately the thrilling news raced across the nation, lifting everyone from gloom to joy.

So the heavy gloom and despair of Calvary fled before the victory of Jesus' open tomb. Out of all the dark shadows, our hearts leap, for in Christ we can say, "But thanks be unto God which giveth us the victory through our Lord Jesus Christ."

Thomas Jefferson culled out all moral teachings of the first three Gospels and gathered them into a book called *The Life and Moral Teachings of Jesus of Nazareth.* The book ends, "And they laid Jesus in the tomb and departed."

By contrast George Washington's epitaph contains the words of John 11:25.

What does the resurrection [of Christ] mean to me? A clear hope vested in my risen Savior which I could not have had Christ never risen from the dead.

—Dr. Howard Kelly

One of the greatest of the chief justices of England, who was a deist, said, "The resurrection of Jesus Christ rests on a basis of testimony greater and more indisputable than sustains any other fact of ancient history."

Two young men were discussing the account of the resurrection of Jesus. They agreed that such a thing was impossible. Seeing an old Christian gentleman approaching, one of them asked him, "Tell us, why are you so sure that Jesus rose from the dead?"

The old gentlemen said, "Well, for one thing, I was talking with Him this morning."

A Moslem said to a Christian, "We Moslems have one thing you Christians do not have. When we go to Medina, we find a coffin and know that Mohammed lived because his body is in it. But when you Christians go to Jerusalem, you find nothing but an empty tomb."

"Thank you," replied the Christian. "What you say is absolutely true, and that makes the eternal difference. The reason

we find an empty tomb is because we serve a *risen* Christ!"

—Ralph Turnbull

He who would preach the Gospel must go directly to preaching the resurrection of Christ. He who does not preach the resurrection is no apostle, for this is the chief part of our faith. . . . Everything depends on our retaining a firm hold on this article [of faith] in particular; for if this one totters and no longer counts, all the others will lose their value and validity.

—Charles W. Keysor

General Lon Wallace and Bob Ingersoll once connived together to disprove the resurrection of Christ. But General Wallace became converted, and he wrote *Ben Hur* to point to the fact.

The noted conductor Reichel was taking his choir and orchestra through their final rehearsal of Handel's beautiful and inspiring "Messiah." When the soprano soloist came in with the refrain, "I know that my Redeemer liveth," she sang it with flawless technique, perfect breathing, and clear enunciation.

After she completed her part, everyone looked at the conductor expecting to see his response of approval. With a motion from his baton for silence, he walked over to the soloist and said, almost sorrowfully, "My daughter, you do not really know that your Redeemer lives, do you?" Embarrassed, she answered, "Why, yes, I think I do." "Then sing it!" cried Reichel. "Tell it to me so that I'll know you have experienced the joy and power of it." Then he motioned to the orchestra to begin, and she sang the truth with a fervor that testified of her personal knowledge of the risen Lord. Those who listened wept, and the old master, eyes wet with tears, said to her, "You *do* know, for this time you have told me."

Years ago a missionary in Turkey was having great difficulty making the Muslims understand why they should trust in Jesus Christ. One day he was traveling with some Muslims along an unmarked road when they came to a fork. At this point there was the tomb of a Mohammedan "holy man" as is seen frequently in Islamic countries. While they were trying to decide which fork to take, the missionary said, "Let's go to that tomb and ask the dead man."

They all protested, "The dead man can give us no information! See that little house over there? Let's go there and ask a living man."

"You are quite right," said the missionary. "Never forget that Mohammed is dead; he can give you no help or information; in him is no life. But Jesus Christ is alive, and He will give you eternal life if you will trust in Him as your Savior!"

Tradition has it that one day some skeptics were discussing Christianity with Voltaire, the prince of skeptics. He observed, "Gentlemen, it would be easy to start a new religion to compete with Christianity. All the founder would have to do is die and then be raised from the dead."

—Charles W. Keysor

CHRIST—RETURN OF (See RAPTURE and SECOND COMING)

CHRIST—SUFFICIENCY OF

Were it not for the consciousness of Christ as my life, hour by hour, I could not go on. But He is teaching me the glorious lessons of His sufficiency, and each day I am carried onward with no feeling of strain or fear of collapse.

—J. Hudson Taylor

CHRIST—TEMPTATION OF

In the early days of railroading a railroad bridge was built in the mountains of eastern Pennsylvania. Some people didn't think they could rely on the bridge. So the engineers put a mile-long string of locomotives on the bridge and let them sit there. This was not a test to see if the bridge would hold up because the engineers knew that before they built it. It was a demonstration, not a test. So it was with the temptation of Christ.

CHRISTIANITY

The Christian way is not the "middle way" between extremes but the "narrow way" between precipices.

—Donald G. Bloesch

It isn't that Christianity has been tried and found wanting. It is that it has been found difficult and so never really tried.

—G. K. Chesterton

Referring to some foolish actions taken by the Roman emperor Diocletian, C. H. Spurgeon underscored the futility of opposing God and the indestructibility of the church. Spurgeon wrote: "A medal was struck by Diocletian bearing the inscription, 'The name of Christians being extinguished.' And in Spain, two monumental pillars were raised by Diocletian. One was written; 'Diocletian Jovian Maximian Herculeus Caesares Augusti for having extended the Roman Empire in the east and the west, and for having extinguished the name of Christians, who brought the Republic to ruin.'" On the second pillar was an inscription praising the Emperor, "for having everywhere abolished the superstition of Christ, for having extended the worship of the God."

—*Our Daily Bread*

I would that I could be Christlike without becoming a Christian.

—Mahatma Gandhi

Julian, Roman emperor from A.D. 360 to 363, decreed that Christianity be outlawed, and he vigorously sought to destroy it. Passing by an old Christian one day Julian said, "Where is your Christ now?" The old man replied, "Making a coffin for the Roman emperor."

At last death caught up with Julian, and he cried out, "O Galilean, thou hast conquered."

CHRISTIANITY—GROWTH OF

There are now 140,000 Christian missionaries serving around the globe, according to Operation World. Evangelical Christianity is the only religion growing because of actual conversions. Over 500 million strong now, evangelical Christianity has grown one hundred-fold in the last one hundred years—ten times faster than any other religious group that size. Reports at a recent missions conference indicate that it is possible that every person on earth may hear the gospel by the year 2000.

—*Wesleyan Advocate*

CHRISTIANITY—OBJECTIONS TO

A preacher announced a special men's meeting in his church, proposing to give the men a chance to air their objections to Christianity.

Over twelve hundred men were present. The first objector said, "Church members are no better than others."

"The ministers are no good," said another.

And so the objections were mentioned one after another, as the pastor wrote them down on paper:

"Hypocrites in the church."

"The church is a rich man's club."

"Christians don't believe the Bible anymore."

There were twenty-seven objections to Christianity in all.

When they were through, the pastor read off the whole list, then tossed it aside saying, "Friends, you have objected to pastors, to church members, to the Bible, etc., etc., but you have not said one word against my Master!"

And in a few simple words, he preached Christ to them as the faultless One and invited them to come to Him and believe on Him. Forty-nine men responded.

CHRISTIAN LIVING

In his essays on *Different Characters of the Christian,* Lord Bacon wrote, "A Christian is one that believes things his reason cannot comprehend, and hopes for things which neither he nor any man alive ever saw. He believes Three to be One and One to be Three; a Father not to be older than His Son, and the Son to be equal with His Father. He believes himself to be precious in God's sight, and yet loathes himself in his own. He dares not justify himself even in those things wherein he can find no fault with himself, and yet believes that God accepts him in those services wherein he is able to find many faults. He is so ashamed that he dares not open his mouth before the Lord, yet comes with boldness to God, and asks him anything he needs. He hath within him both flesh and spirit, and yet he is not doubleminded; he is often led captive by the law of sin, yet it never gets dominion over him. He cannot sin, yet can do nothing without sin. He is so humble as to acknowledge himself to deserve nothing but evil, and yet he believes that God means him all good."

Our lives should preach good sermons. According to the book *Life of Francis d'Assisi,* Francis once invited a young monk to join him on a trip to town to preach. Honored to be given the invitation, the monk readily accepted.

All day long he and Francis walked through the streets, byways, and alleys, and even into the suburbs. They rubbed shoulders with hundreds of people. At the day's end, the two headed back home. Not even once had Francis addressed a crowd, nor had he talked to anyone about the gospel. Greatly disappointed, his young companion said, "I thought we were going to town to preach." Francis responded, "My son, we have preached. We were preaching while we were walking. We were seen by many and our behavior was closely watched. It is of no use to walk anywhere to preach unless we preach everywhere as we walk!"

—*Our Daily Bread*

My love for the Lord is not measured by the things I am willing to do for Him—but the things I am not willing to do for Him.

Jonathan Goforth's Seven Rules for Daily Living:
1. Seek to give much—expect nothing.
2. Put the very best construction on the actions of others.
3. Never let a day pass without at least a quarter of an hour spent in the study of the Bible.

4. Never omit daily morning and evening private prayer and devotions.
5. In all things seek to know God's will, and when known obey at any cost.
6. Seek to cultivate a quiet, prayerful spirit.
7. Seek each day to do or say something to further Christianity.

Elbert Hubbard, writer, editor, and printer, was a brilliant eccentric. On the front page of his magazine, *The Philistine,* he once printed a single sentence: "Remember the Weekday to Keep It Holy."

Life ought not to be divided into compartments labeled sacred and secular. Monday can be as significant and sacred as Sunday.

Live as if Christ died yesterday, rose this morning, and is coming back again tomorrow.

—Martin Luther

Little of the Word, with little prayer, is death to the spiritual life.

Much of the Word, with little prayer, gives a sickly life.

Much prayer, with little of the Word, gives more life but without steadfastness.

A dill measure of the Word and prayer each day gives a healthy and powerful life.

—Andrew Murray

There were two brothers, each of whom was distinguished in his own field. One was a noted minister; the other, a famous physician. One day a woman, wishing to confer with the minister but unsure whether the person she was addressing was the preacher or the physician, inquired: "Are you the doctor who preaches, or the one who practices?"

A holy life will produce the deepest impression. Lighthouses blow no horns; they only shine.

—D. L. Moody

Endeavor to so live that when you die, even the undertaker will be sorry.

Four questions I should ask myself each night: Was I easy to live with? Did I grow a bit today? Was I pleasant to work with? Did I help someone along the way?

—William Arthur Ward

It is not what men eat, but what they digest that makes them strong;
 not what we gain, but what we save that makes us rich;
not what we read, but what we remember that makes us learned;
 not what we preach or pray,
but what we practice and believe that makes us Christians.

—Frances Bacon

Ten Things to Remember

1. The value of time
2. The success of perseverance
3. The pleasure of working
4. The dignity of simplicity
5. The worth of character
6. The power of kindness
7. The obligation of duty
8. The influence of example
9. The wisdom of economy
10. The virtue of patience

—*Bits & Pieces*

A Christian is:
 A mind through which Christ thinks
 A voice through which Christ speaks
 A heart through which Christ loves
 A hand through which Christ helps

When Billy Sunday was converted and joined the church, a Christian man put his arm on the young man's shoulder and said, "William, there are three simple rules I can give to you, and if you will hold to them you will never write 'backslider' after your name.

"Take fifteen minutes each day to listen to God talking to you; take fifteen minutes each day to talk to God; take fifteen minutes each day to talk to others about God."

The young convert was deeply impressed and determined to follow these rules of life. From that day onward throughout his life he made it a rule to spend the first moments of his day alone with God and God's Word. Before he read a letter, looked at a paper, or even read a telegram, he went first to the Bible, so that the first impression of the day might be what he got directly from God.

My life helps to paint my neighbor's picture of God.

—Peter Holmes

During World War II a poster in England read, "Careless Talk Costs Lives." Also applicable for the Christian could be the reverse: "Careless Lives Cost Talk."

You are the best Christian someone knows.

Blessed is the man who is faithful on a committee.

Blessed is the man who can endure an hour and five minutes in a place of worship as well as two hours in a place of recreation.

Blessed is the church officer who is not pessimistic.

Blessed in the man who loves his church with his pocketbook as well as with his heart.

Blessed is the man who has grace enough to leave his critical spirit on the sidewalk when he comes to church.

Blessed is the man who loves his own church enough to praise it.

Christians should always strive to be like a good watch—open face, busy hands, pure gold, well regulated, and full of good works.

When pioneer missionary Ludwig Nommensen began his work among the Batak tribes of Southeast Asia, a village chief gave him two years to learn the customs and to convince them that he had a message worth hearing. At the end of that time he was asked how Christianity differed in its moral rules from the traditions of the Batak. "We know what is right," said the tribal leader, "for we too have laws that say we must not steal, or take our neighbor's wives, or tell lies." "That's true," the missionary answered, "but my Master supplies the power needed to keep these laws." The chief was startled. "Can you really teach my people to live better?" he inquired. "No, I can't, but if they receive Jesus Christ, God will give them the strength to do what's right." Being permitted to remain another six months, Nommensen preached the Gospel and taught the villagers how the Holy Spirit works in the believer's life. At the end of that time the chief said, "You may stay longer. Your religion is better than ours, for your God walks with men and gives them strength to do the good things He requires."

—*Our Daily Bread*

A mother was telling her little boy what manner of person a Christian should be. When the lesson was finished, the mother got a stab she never forgot, when her boy asked seriously, "Mother, have I ever seen a Christian?"

The children born into a royal family are taught and trained and exhorted to conduct themselves as royalty which they are by birth. They are an honor to the king only as they so conduct themselves. There are many things they cannot do that are not forbidden to other children. On the other hand, to the street waif of the lower East Side of New York City there can be no appeal to live as a son of a king because he does not hold that position.

A young book salesman was assigned to a rural area. Seeing a farmer seated in a rocking chair on his front porch, the young man approached him with all the zeal of a newly trained salesman. "Sir," he said, "I have here a book that will tell you how to farm ten times better than you are doing it now." The farmer continued to rock. After a few seconds he stopped, looked at the young fellow and said, "Son, I don't need your book. I already know how to farm ten times better than I'm doing it now."

—James Kallam

It is better to die for something than it is to live for nothing.

Always do right. This will gratify some people and astonish the rest.

—Mark Twain

Years ago during World War I, one of our airmen took off from a field in Kobar, Arabia. While on the ground in Kobar, a large rat had gotten into the aircraft.

The pilot became aware of the rat's presence when he was in midair and heard the sound of gnawing behind him. Alarmed by the threat of disaster, he remembered that rats cannot live in high altitudes. Accordingly he pointed his plane upward until breathing was difficult. After some time, when the gnawing had ceased, he descended to a landing where he found the rat had died.

Many, if not most, of our struggles can be eliminated by rising to a higher altitude in our Christian walk.

—Charles R. Diffee

A small boy was asked why he fell out of bed. He replied, "I guess I slept too close to the place I got in." That tells the story of many persons. Because they did not advance after becoming Christians, their lives are filled with "fallings."

CHRISTLIKENESS

The young son of a humble, consecrated pastor became very ill. After the boy had undergone an exhaustive series of tests, the father was told the shocking news that his son had a terminal illness. The youngster had accepted Christ as his Savior, so the minister knew that death would usher him into Glory; but he wondered how to inform him that he soon would die. After earnestly seeking the direction of the Holy Spirit, he went with a heavy heart through the hospital ward to the boy's bedside. First he read a passage of Scripture and had a time of prayer with his dear child. Then he gently told him that the doctors could promise him only a few more days to live. "Are you afraid to meet Jesus, my boy?" asked his devout father. Blinking away a few tears, the little fellow said bravely, "No, not if He's like you, Dad."

A wealthy Oriental man took his little daughter to a missionary school, willing to pay any expense. The father, however, didn't want his daughter to enroll as a student, but merely to remain only long enough for the missionaries to put something on her face to make her as beautiful as the other girls at the school. The missionary in charge of the school explained that nothing was put on the girls' faces to make them pretty.

"Then why are they better looking than the girls in our towns? When girls come here they are just plain looking, but before long they become pretty. What do you put on their faces?"

The missionary replied, "It's not something we put on their faces, but Someone they receive into their hearts."

—Leslie B. Flynn

In an Italian city stands a statue of a Grecian maiden with a beautiful face, a graceful figure, and a noble expression. One day a poor little peasant girl came face-to-face with the statue. She stood and stared and then went home to wash her face and comb her hair. The next day she came again to stand before the statue and then to return home once more. This time she mended her tattered clothing. Day by day she changed, her form grew more graceful and her face more refined, until she greatly reflected the famous statue. She was transformed in appearance! Just so, the spiritual man must each day seek to conform to the perfect image of our Lord and Savior Jesus Christ.

—George Sweeting

At the end of each year a pastor asked his congregation, "Beloved, as we come to the end of another year, have we become more like Jesus Christ?"

There is a legend that is very old concerning an Oriental king who commanded three architects to submit models of a temple he proposed to build, a temple to the sun.

CHRISTLIKENESS

The first architect's model was made of finely chiseled stone and was admired by the potentate. The second architect submitted a miniature temple of gold, and the king praised it highly and made special mention of the fact that it reflected the brightness of the sun. The third model was almost invisible, for it was made of glass; but in two ways it surpassed the works of the other architects: not only did it reflect the image of the sun but, in its transparency, the sunlight poured through its walls so that, inside and out, the glory of that to which it was dedicated shined.

The sum total of your religion is to be like the one you worship.
—Pythagoras

It's not great talent whom God blesses so much as likeness to Jesus.
—Robert Murray McCheyne

Man can be restored to God by Christ, can know God through Christ, and can become like God in Christ.
—G. Campbell Morgan

Miss Kathryn Dick is in charge of a youth camp near Ibadan, Nigeria. So well appreciated, she's a citizen of Nigeria. A man put on his trunk, "If you want to know God, see Miss Dick."

CHRISTMAS

Some businessmen are saying that this could be the greatest Christmas ever. I thought the first one was.
—Hal Roach

"How did your wife like the back scratchers I sent her for Christmas?"

"So that's what they were? She's been making me eat salad with them."
—Hal Roach

Many years ago a wealthy European family decided to have their newborn baby baptized in their enormous mansion. Dozens of guests were invited to the elaborate affair, and they all arrived dressed in the latest fashion. After depositing their elegant wraps on a bed in an upstairs room, the guests were entertained royally. Soon the time came for the main purpose of their gathering, the infant's baptismal ceremony. But where was the child? No one seemed to know.

The child's governess ran upstairs, only to return with a desperate look on her face. Everyone searched frantically for the baby. Then, someone recalled having seen the child sleeping on one of the beds. The baby was on a bed, all right—buried underneath a pile of coats, jackets, and furs. The very object of that day's celebration had been forgotten, neglected, and nearly smothered. Similarly, many people overlook the main point of Christmas—celebrating the birth of Christ.

There are three stages in a person's life. First, he believes in Santa Claus. Second, he doesn't believe in Santa Claus. Third, he is Santa Claus.
—Donald Guthrie

Someone asked a boy, "Did you get everything you wanted for Christmas?"

The boy said, "No, I didn't get everything I wanted. But then it's not my birthday, is it?"

"I'm Sorry, I Have No Room"

When Joseph came to the inn that night,
  he was tired, weary, and worn;
And Mary, his wife, was weary, too, her
  child about to be born.
The innkeeper told them, "I have no room,"
  and started to send them away.
"But wait," he called, "I think I can help;
  though it's only a barn with some hay."
They said they'd be grateful for even a
  barn—
  at least it was some place to stay.
Then Joseph thanked the innkeeper there as
  he settled his wife in the hay.
The stars seemed to shine that first Christmas night
  as they never had shone before,
And as Jesus came into the world for us,
  they seemed to shine even more.
Shepherds strayed to the manger scene,
  worshiping as they came.

Three wise men were led from the Orient
    far,
  searching to do the same.
It wasn't exactly the place for a King;
  why, it wasn't even the inn!
No, out in a barn, in a manger poor,
  He was born, to take away sin.
The innkeeper had no room that night;
  I wonder, how about you?
If Jesus asked for a place in your heart,
  what do you think you would do?
For you know some day when life has
    passed
  and you stand at the door of the inn,
The Lord may look at you sadly there and
  you'll hear these words from Him:
"I have no room, I'm sorry, my friend;
  I'm truly sorry to say.
"I have no room," He'll tell you once more,
  then turn and send you away.

         —Ann Farrell Blunt

12 Days of Christmas

1st day	partridge	$ 15
	pear tree	14
2nd day	2 turtle doves	10
3rd day	3 French hens	36
4th day	4 calling birds	140
5th day	5 gold rings	1,000
6th day	6 geese a-laying	1,260
7th day	7 swans a-swimming	1,260
8th day	8 maids a-milking	216
9th day	9 ladies dancing	6,000
10th day	10 lords a-leaping	500
11th day	11 pipers piping	500
12th day	12 drummers drumming	600
		$ 10,351

One

One starlit night
One couple in distress
One shabby stable
Only one place to rest
One group of shepherds
One night long ago
One angel's message
Only one place to go
One wiseman's journey
One king did they seek
One Son of David
Only one child so meek

One reason for coming
One goal on earth's sod
One death that redeems
Only one way to God.

         —Myra Dye

The perfect Christmas gift for the person who has everything is a burglar alarm.

         —*Bits & Pieces*

The five-year-old son of a friend of ours told his mother when he came home from Sunday school one day in December that he was in a Christmas play. "Who were you?" his mother asked him.

"I was the voice of God."

We smile at this story. But shouldn't every one of us speak as the voice of God in this world?

         —*The Pilgrim*

Don't get so wrapped up in what the world has to sell that you miss what God has to give.

CHURCH

Four purposes of the local church:
    1. Exaltation of Jesus Christ
    2. Evangelism of the lost
    3. Edification of believers
    4. Expression of service

The article "What Good Is a Tree?" in *Reader's Digest* explained that when the roots of trees touch, there is a substance present that reduces competition. In fact, this unknown fungus helps link roots of different trees—even of dissimilar species. A whole forest may be linked together. If one tree has access to water, another to nutrients, and a third to sunlight, the trees have the means to share with one another.

Like trees in a forest, Christians in the church need and support one another.

         —Blair F. Rorabaugh

Today much of the professing church has gone in for theatrics, running a showboat instead of a lifeboat, staging a performance instead of living an experience, a "form of godliness without the power thereof."

         —*The Vance Havner Quote Book*

In its newsletter, the *Courtright,* Ontario United Church described the sort of church it does not want to be: (1) Museum style—where you go only as a spectator. (2) Hairdresser style—where they split every hair four ways. (3) Service-station style—where you go just to be filled up. (4) Sleeping-car style—where the passengers don't want to be disturbed. (5) Refrigerator style—where the icy chill drives out any new arrival.

He who does not go to church in bad weather will go to hell when it's fair.

—Finnish proverb

What keeps churches from accomplishing their goals? Rex Johnson of Talbot Seminary suggests three things:
1. Moral failure of the leaders (and therefore people lose their confidence in them and leave).
2. Lack of encouragement.
3. Burnout (too few leaders trying to do too much).

A pastor was talking to a poor lady who worked hard as a cleaning woman. He told her how glad he was to see her in her place in church every Sunday, so attentive to his sermons.

"Yes, it is such a rest after working hard all week to come to church, sit down on the soft cushions, and not think about anything."

What are the clues that a church is living, vital, and active? These ideas may help:
1. Live churches have many people who bring their Bibles and use them; dead churches do not.
2. Live churches are filled with praise and sounds of joy and thanksgiving; dead churches are apathetic and lifeless.
3. Live churches usually have parking problems; dead churches never have to worry about parking.
4. Live churches are moving out by "faith"; dead churches creep along by sight.
5. Live churches have lots of children

and young people and "noise"; dead churches are quiet as tombs.
6. Live churches center on serving people; dead churches focus mainly on problems.
7. Live churches are filled with a spirit of love for each other; dead churches are filled with suspicious, critical, and bickering people.
8. Live churches are always emphasizing evangelism, discipleship, and involvement; dead churches ask for little and get it.
9. Live churches have many sacrificial givers; dead churches have people who only "tip" the Lord.
10. Live churches are always growing; dead churches are plateaued or declining.

The great end of life is not knowledge but action.

—Aldous Huxley

In a survey by the Princeton Religion Research Center, 59 percent of those polled expressed "a great deal" or "quite a lot" of confidence in the church, putting it at the top of a list of ten institutions, including: the military (58 percent), banks (49 percent), Congress (35 percent), television (27 percent), and big business (25 percent).

Maybe that's why every week 41 percent of Americans—nearly 100 million people—attend church.

—*Emerging Trends*

A boy saw flags in a church. He asked a lady what they were for. She said, "Oh, they are for those who have died in the service." The boy said, "In the eleven o'clock service or the nine o'clock service?"

Evxn though my typxwritxr is an old modxl, it works quitx wxll xxcxpt for onx of thx kxys. I havx wishxd many timxs that it workxd pxrfxctly. It is trux that thxrx arx forty-six kxys that function wxll xnough, but just onx kxy not working makxs thx diffxrxncx.

Somxtimxs it sxxms to mx that our

church is somxwhat likx my typxwritxr—not all thx kxy pxoplx arx working propxrly.

You may say to yoursxlf, "Wxll, I am only onx pxrson. I won't makx or brxak thx church." But it doxs makx a diffxrxncx becausx a church to bx xffxctivx nxxds thx activx participation of xvxry pxrson.

So, thx nxxt timx you think you arx only onx pxrson and that your xfforts arx not nxxdxd, rxmxmbxr my typxwritxr and say to yoursxlf, "I am a kxy pxrson in thx congrxgation, and I am nxxdxd vxry much."

Size of U.S. Church

The 1990 Statistical Abstract of the United States (110th edition) reports that there are 294,271 religious congregations in the continental United States. Here are the approximate percentages of congregations falling in the following size ranges:

Fewer than 100 members: 21 percent
100-199 members: 19 percent
200-499 members: 32 percent
500-999 members: 16 percent
1,000 or more members: 12 percent

According to these statistics, there are three to four times as many "small churches" (congregations with fewer than 200 members) as there are "megachurches" (congregations with 1,000 or more members). On the other hand more people are members of "megachurches" than of "small churches."

—*Church Law & Tax Report*

CHURCH ATTENDANCE

Mother to her young son, "Would you like to be at home for home schooling, or would you like to go off to public school?"

He thought for a moment, and then said, "Yeah, I'd like to have home schooling. Can you do church too?"

1. Pillars . . . worship regularly, giving time and money.
2. Supporters . . . give time and money if they like the minister and treasurer.
3. Leaners . . . use the church for funerals, baptisms, and marriages but give no time or money to support the church.
4. Working leaners . . . work but do not give money.
5. Specials . . . help and give occasionally.
6. Annuals . . . or Easter Birds, dress up, look serious, and go to church on Easter.
7. Sponges . . . take all the blessings and benefits but give no money to support the church.
8. Tramps . . . go from church to church but support none.
9. Gossips . . . talk freely about everyone except the Lord Jesus.
10. Scrappers . . . take offense, criticize, and fight.
11. Orphans . . . are children sent by parents who do not set them an example.
12. Hypocrites . . . are leaners who say they are better than churchgoers.

—*Watchman Examiner*

An old preacher said to his audience, "Some folks think they hurt the church when they get mad and quit, but they are wrong about that. It never hurts the tree for the dried-up apples to fall off."

A stockyard salesman was trying to sell a certain horse to an interested customer who was a preacher. The man said, "This horse is perfectly sound. He can go in any gait—walk, pace, fox-trot, or gallop. He will stand without hitching, work anywhere you put him—on the off side or on the near side, in buggy, plow, or wagon. He is perfectly gentle though full of spirit, goes when you want him to, and stops when you say Whoa! He has no bad traits, he does not bite or kick, he comes when you call, and he does not run off when he sees anything strange."

The preacher looked admirably at the horse and said, "I wish that horse was a member of my church."

Morbus Sabbaticus (Sunday Sickness) is a disease peculiar to church membership.
1. The symptoms vary, but it never interferes with the appetite.
2. It never lasts more than 24 hours at a time.
3. No physician is ever called.

4. It always proves fatal in the end—to the soul.

5. It is contagious.

6. It is indicative of a worse disease—carnality.

7. It passes away Sunday afternoon so that the patient can go riding in the car, returns during the evening, and then by Monday morning is completely gone so that the patient can go to work and feel fine.

A tip from a farmer: "I see in your church convention," said an old farmer to the preacher, "that you discussed the subject: 'How to get people to attend church.' I have never heard a single address at a farmers' convention on how to get the cattle to come to the rack. We spend our time discussing the best kind of feed." Feeding the people spiritually is still the best means of increasing church attendance.

"How many people attend your church?" one pastor asked another. The minister thought a moment and then replied, "Sixty regular, 250 C and E."

"What's C and E?" the other wanted to know.

Came the prompt answer, "Christmas and Easter."

—*United Mine Worker's Journal*

Top Ten Reasons Why I Never Wash

Substituting "wash" for "attend church" puts the following excuses in a much different perspective.

10. I was forced to as a child.

9. People who wash are hypocrites—they think they are cleaner than everybody else.

8. There are so many different kinds of soap, I can't decide which one is best.

7. I used to wash, but I got bored and stopped.

6. I only wash on special occasions like Christmas and Easter.

5. None of my friends wash.

4. I'll start washing when I get older and dirtier.

3. I can't spare the time.

2. The bathroom is never warm enough in winter or cool enough in the summer.

1. People who make soap are only after your money.

Some folks go to church just three times in their lives—for hatching, matching, and dispatching. And they are sprinkled three times—with water, rice, and dust.

—Eugene Bertin

Gong to church doesn't make you a Christian any more than going to a garage makes you an automobile.

—Billy Sunday

A writer in the Chicago *Daily News* recently showed the ridiculous reasons some people give for not going to church by merely substituting the word "movies" for the word "church" in their excuses.

I'm out of the habit of going to the movies. I'd better not go tonight.

I have not been to the movies for so long the walls would fall in if I should go.

I know a man who has gone to the movies for years and he is no better than I am.

There are as many good people outside the movies as inside.

Too many hypocrites attend the movies.

I stay away from the movies because of the kind of folk who support them. I wouldn't sit in the same room with Mr. So-and-So.

I don't like the people in charge of the movies.

I stay away from the movies because I went when I was a child.

I need new clothes before I can go to the movies.

I have a friend visiting me and I don't know whether he likes the movies or not, and I never meddle with a man's private opinions.

I don't go to the movies because the directors never call on me.

I don't go to the movies because when I went the last time not a soul spoke to me.

CIRCUMSTANCES

You can no more blame the circumstances for your character than you can blame the mirror for your looks.

A Christian should not permit circumstances to affect his relationship to God, but rather he should allow his relationship with God to affect his circumstances.

People are always blaming their circumstances for what they are. I don't believe in circumstances. The people who get on in this world are the people who get up and look for the circumstances they want and, if they can't find them, make them.

—George Bernard Shaw

Circumstances are like feather beds: very comfortable to be on top of, but smothering if they get on top of you.

No matter how palatial our dwelling, we still live in tents—content or discontent.

CIVILIZATION

I used to say civilization is going to the dogs. But I quit saying that out of respect for dogs.

—Vance Havner

CLARITY

When I discussed the essentials of public speaking with Sir Oliver Lodge, a man who had been lecturing to university classes and to the public for forty years, he emphasized most of all the importance, first, of knowledge and preparation; second, of "taking good pains to be clear."

—Dale Carnegie

CLASS

John Wesley and a preacher-friend of plain habits were invited to dinner where the host's daughter, noted for her beauty, had been profoundly impressed by Wesley's preaching. During a pause in the meal, Wesley's friend took the young lady's hand and called attention to the sparkling rings she wore. "What do you think of this, sir, for a Methodist hand?" The girl turned crimson. Wesley likewise was embarrassed, for his aversion to jewelry was well known. But with a benevolent smile, he simply said, "The hand is very beautiful." The young lady appeared at the evening service without her jewels and became a strong Christian.

—Leslie B. Flynn

CLEANLINESS

Youngster looking around his tidy, immaculate bedroom, "Okay! Who's been messing around in my room?"

A company that manufactured soap and perfume offered a prize for the best slogan submitted for the advertising of its products. The judges easily agreed on the best slogan but did not give it the prize. The slogan was, "If you don't use our soap, for heaven's sake, use our perfume."

A schoolteacher asked pupils to finish the sentence.

"Cleanliness is next to . . ."

A young boy raised his hand and said "impossible."

CLUE

The labyrinth of King Minos in ancient Crete was a maze of passageways and tunnels. Once entrapped within, no wanderer could find his way out of the complex of bends and dead ends. When Theseus became trapped there and awaited his doom, Ariadne, the daughter of Minos, quite literally threaded her way through the maze and thereby brought Theseus to safety. From this ancient myth comes our word "clue." Ariadne found her way out by following the clue.

—Edward Kuhlman

COACHES

In one school far from here, the coach brought a new recruit into the dean's office to get scholarship accreditation. Doing his best to cooperate, the dean asked,

"How much is seven plus seven?"

"Thirteen, sir," the recruit quickly replied.

"I'm sorry, son. I'll have to declare you ineligible."

The coach protested, "Aw, dean, let him pass. He only missed it by two."

COINCIDENCE

A teacher asked his class to give examples of coincidence. There was a long silence,

COINCIDENCE

then a small boy said, "My father and my mother were married on the same day."

COLLECTIONS

A rookie policeman was asked in an examination what he would do to break up a crowd. His answer indicated a deep knowledge of human nature. He replied, "I'd take up a collection."

—*Bits & Pieces*

COLLEGE

Sending young people to college educates parents. It teaches them to do without a lot of things.

The reason there is so much knowledge in college is that freshmen bring so much in and seniors take so little out.

My son is majoring in both economics and applied physics in college. It's not a very useful combination, but it does explain how he can spend money at the speed of light.

—Bob Orben

The renowned educator Clark Kerr characterized the university president as one who is "expected to be a friend of the students, a colleague of the faculty, a good fellow with the alumni, a sound administrator with the trustees, a good speaker with the public, an astute bargainer with the foundations and federal agencies, a politician with the state legislature, a friend of industry, labor, and agriculture, a persuasive diplomat with donors, a champion of education generally . . . a spokesman to the press, a scholar in his own right, a public servant . . ." and the list continues.

College is a four-year loaf, financed by dad's dough, with students coming out half-baked and with a lot of crust.

COMEDY

Comedy has to be based on truth. You take the truth and you put a little curlicue at the end.

—Sid Caesar

COMFORT

Swedish hymnist Lina Sandell Berg served with her father in an evangelistic ministry. As they were traveling by ship, he accidentally fell overboard and drowned. In need of comfort that only God can supply, she wrote the following words that are still sung by Christians around the world:

Day by day
and with each passing moment,
Strength I find
to meet my trials here;
Trusting in
my Father's wise bestowment.
I've no cause
for worry or for fear.

God does not comfort us to make us comfortable but to make us comforters.

—John Henry Jewett

Words of comfort, skillfully administered, are the oldest therapy known to man.

—Louis Niger

If a person is standing with one foot in a bucket of ice and another foot in a fire, you could say—at least statistically—that on the average the person is very comfortable.

—*Bits & Pieces*

COMMANDMENTS

The commands of God are all designed to make us more happy than we can possibly be without them.

—Thomas Wilson

Someone figured out that the United States has 35 million laws to try to enforce God's Ten Commandments.

COMMENDING (Also see APPRECIATION)

An old gentlemen used to stop by at an antique shop in New Hampshire to sell furniture. One day after he left, the antique dealer's wife said she wished she had told him how much she enjoyed his visits. The husband said, "Next time let's tell him so." The following summer a young woman came in and introduced herself as the daughter of the old gentleman. Her father, she said, had died. Then the wife told her about the conversation she and her husband had after the father's last visit. The young woman's eyes filled with tears. "Oh, how much good that would have done for my father," she cried. "He was a man who needed to be reassured that he was liked." "Since that day," the shopkeeper said later, "whenever I think something particularly nice about a person, I tell them. I might never get another chance."

—*Sounds*

An elderly lady made it a habit to find something in others she could commend. One day she heard a visiting preacher preach a terrible sermon. How could she commend him for that? After the service she said to him. "You had a wonderful text today."

"One thing scientists have discovered," notes Thomas Dreiner, "is that often-praised children become more intelligent than often-blamed ones. There's a creative element in praise."

—*Bits & Pieces*

There are some great people who make others feel small. But there are other great people who make others feel great.

—G. K. Chesterton

The Duke of Wellington, near the end of his life, was asked what one thing he would change if he could live his life over again. "I would give more praise," was his reply.

"I have yet to find the man," said Charles Schwab, "however exalted his station, who did not do better work and put forth greater effort under a spirit of approval than under a spirit of criticism."

I spoke a word of praise today,
One I had no need to say.
I spoke a word of praise to one
Commending some small service done,
And in return, to my surprise,
I reaped rewards of mountain size;
For such a look of pleasure shone
Upon his face—I'll never own
a gift more beautiful to see

than that swift smile he gave to me.
I spoke one little word of praise
And sunshine fell on both our ways.

—Helen Lowrie Marshall

I will speak evil of no man . . . and speak all the good I know of everybody.

—Benjamin Franklin

Reprove a friend in secret but praise him before others.

—Leonardo da Vinci

Talk to a man about himself and he will listen for hours.

—Benjamin Disraeli

Any of us will put out more and better ideas if our efforts are appreciated.

—Alex B. Osborn

COMMITMENT

Chuck Colson tells of speaking on the campus of a secular university. He was talking about his commitment to Christ and mentioned that he was willing, if necessary, to die on behalf of the Savior. A young man in the crowd angrily interrupted, shouting, "C'mon, Colson! Nothing is worth dying for!"

To which Colson replied, "If there is nothing you are willing to die for, then I submit you have nothing to live for."

Athanasius, early bishop of Alexandria, opposed the teaching of Arius who declared that Christ was not the eternal Son of God but a subordinate being. Hounded through five exiles for his faith in the full deity of Jesus Christ, Athanasius was finally summoned before Emperor Theodosius, who demanded he stop opposing the teaching of Arius.

Athanasius firmly refused, so the emperor bitterly reproved him and sternly asked, "Do you not realize that all the world is against you?" Athanasius quickly answered, "Then I am against all the world!"

There's a difference between interest and commitment. When you're interested in

COMMITMENT

doing something, you do it only when circumstances permit. When you're committed to something, you accept no excuses, only results.

—Art Turock

Many Christians say they are committed, but they are not involved. They're like the Japanese kamikazi who went on thirty suicide missions. He was committed, but not involved.

A pig said to a chicken, "What shall we have for breakfast?" The chicken suggested, "Let's have ham and eggs."

The pig said, "Oh no, not ham!" The chicken replied, "Why not? I'll furnish the eggs and you the ham."

The pig then said, "For you it's involvement; but for me it's total commitment."

COMMITTEES

A committee is a group of people who individually can do nothing and who collectively decide nothing can be done.

Outside of traffic nothing has held this country back as much as committees.

—Will Rogers

A committee is a group of the unfit chosen by the unwilling to do the unnecessary.

At meetings fraternal, or groups of good will,
I always continue to keep perfectly still.
If I open my mouth in complaint or in pity,
It's wham, there I am on another committee.

The most efficient part of any organization is a standing committee. The minute you give them chairs, the meetings last forever.

—Bob Orben

If three men parachuted out of a falling airplane, before they reach the ground, they would have elected a board, become incorporated, and elected a president, vice-president, and appointed a committee.

COMMON SENSE

Common sense is the most widely shared commodity in the world for every man is convinced that he is well supplied with it.

—René Descartes

"Young man," said an old judge to a new member of the bar who had just made a bombastic plea, "you need to pluck a few feathers from the wings of your imagination and stick them in the tail of your judgment."

COMMUNICATION

Albert Mehrabian, a communication teacher, discovered that as much as 55 percent of a message we send may be communicated nonverbally through action. Another 38 percent of a message may be communicated through tone of voice. That leaves only 7 percent communicated through spoken words.

Tone and actions may convey up to 93 percent of our thoughts and feelings to the people with whom we communicate.

—Myron D. Rush

There are only four things that people you communicate with won't forgive you for: not being prepared, not being comfortable, not being committed, and not being interesting.

—Roger Ailes

With my date seated in front of me, I cleared my throat and began.

"What did you say when you said what I thought you said? Did you say what you said when I thought you said your say?

"Or have you said your say another way? What I meant to say was, what did you mean when you said what I thought you said? Did you mean what you said that day?

"Okay, let me say it another way. What did you mean to say when you said what I think I thought you said, you know, when I thought you said your say the other day?"

"I'm not sure," she replied.

"Oh," I said.

—Les Cantrell

A woman went to her lawyer to sue her husband for divorce. The lawyer asked, "Do you have grounds?"

The woman said, "I own two acres off Walnut Hill."

The lawyer asked, "Do you have a grudge?"

The woman said, "I have a carport that holds two cars."

The lawyer asked, "Does your husband beat you up?"

The woman said, "I'm up a half-hour before he is every morning."

The lawyer asked, "Why do you want a divorce?"

The woman said, "I can't communicate with him."

—*Speak the Language of Success*

COMMUNISM

Two of Karl Marx's daughters and a son-in-law committed suicide. Three of his children died of malnutrition. Marx felt no obligation to earn a living but instead lived by begging from Friedrich Engels. He fathered an illegitimate child by his maid-servant. He drank heavily. He was a paid informer of the Austrian police, spying on revolutionaries.

Though Marx and his wife were poor, he kept investing in the stock market where he constantly lost. His wife left him twice, but returned. He didn't attend her funeral. His correspondence with Engels was full of obscenities. His favorite daughter, Eleanor, with her father's approval, married Edward Eveling, a man who advocated blasphemy and worshiped Satan. She committed suicide. Karl Marx died in despair.

Under capitalism, man exploits man. And under communism, it is the exact reverse.
—John Galbraith

At a huge party at which celebrities lined up to catch a glimpse of the Mona Lisa, a French diplomat told a joke that's breaking them up in Europe.

Khrushchev is out walking a goat when Mao comes along and says, "Why are you walking that pig?"

Khrushchev answers, "You idiot. This isn't a pig, it's a goat."

Mao replies, "I wasn't talking to you."
—Don MacLean

Communism was condemned the day it was born. It had declared that everything was determined by economics and, by an irony of history, it was the economy that killed it. Inside the Soviet Union it held on for seventy years only thanks to repression and bloody violence—don't forget that it killed up to 60 million people. Abroad it was able to hold sway thanks to demagogy and lies. It fascinated the West, because it was like a sickly blossoming of humanism. Didn't the intellectuals of the 1930s believe that it had brought us paradise on earth?
—Alexander Solzhenitsyn

Socialism: If you have two cows, you give one to your neighbor.

Communism: If you have two cows, you give them to the government; then the government sells you some milk.

Fascism: If you have two cows, you keep the cows and give the milk to the government; then the government sells you some milk.

New Dealism: If you have two cows, you shoot one and milk the other, then you pour the milk down the drain.

Nazism: If you have two cows, the government shoots you and keeps the cows.

Capitalism: If you have two cows, you sell one and buy a bull.

A Russian named Ivanovich visited the Moscow Zoo for the first time. To his amazement he found a little lamb sharing the same cage that held a big fierce bear.

Ivanovich expressed surprise to his communist guide. The guide smiled and said, "That is peaceful coexistence." When Ivanovich doubtfully shook his head, the guide explained, "Of course, we have to put in a fresh lamb every morning."

Peaceful coexistence between right and wrong, freedom and slavery, God and the Devil, is not possible.

COMPANIONS

If you lie with dogs, you get up with fleas.
—Jewish proverb

COMPASSION

If you want *others* to be happy,
    practice compassion.
If *you* want to be happy,
    practice compassion.

At the end of a fruitful life of caring, William Booth was buried with high honor. Royalty attended his funeral. Next to the queen sat a shabbily dressed woman who placed a flower on the casket as it passed by. "How did you know him?" asked the queen. The woman's answer was simply, "He cared for the likes of us."
—Edward L. Hayes

A man fell in a ditch.
    Realist: "That is a ditch."
    Optimist: "Things will get better."
    Pessimist: "Things will get worse."
    Christian Scientist: "You only think you are in a ditch."
    Newspaper reporter: "I'll pay you for an exclusive story about life in the ditch."
    City official: "Did you get a permit for your ditch life?"
    Mathematician: "I'll calculate the length and depth and width of the ditch."
    Preacher: "I see three things about the ditch that are noteworthy."
    IRS agent: "Have you paid your taxes for the ditch?"
    A Man: "Give me your hand." (His name was Jesus.)

One day while the famous English preacher George Whitefield was preaching, he was overcome by his emotions, and he began to weep quietly. Then lifting up his hands, he exclaimed, "O my hearers, think of the wrath to come! Think of the wrath to come! Flee to Jesus for refuge and salvation right now while there is still time." One who heard him said, "His earnestness brought tears to my eyes, and for weeks afterward I couldn't get the picture of that concerned soulwinner out of my mind. My own heart was warmed by his zeal. Eventually the Gospel he preached with such conviction resulted in my conversion."

Compassion is your pain in my heart.

COMPANY

One clever woman keeps her hat and coat draped across a living room chair all the time.
    "It's for unexpected visitors," she explained. "When someone I don't care for drops in, I point to the hat and coat and say, 'What a shame. I'm just on my way out.' But if it's someone I enjoy seeing, I can say, 'How lucky. I got home just in time.'"

COMPETITION

Don't fight a battle if you don't gain anything by winning.
—General George S. Patton Jr.

Don't worry because a rival imitates you. As long as he follows in your tracks, he can't pass you.

COMPLAINING

Constant complaint is the poorest sort of pay for all the comforts we enjoy.
—Benjamin Franklin

People who complain that they don't get all they deserve should congratulate themselves.

If you pray for rain, don't grumble about the mud.
—William Ward Ayer

A man was placed in a monastery and was given the opportunity to say only two words every five years. After the first five passed, he was called in and allowed to say two words.
    He said, "Food bad." Five years later, his two words were "Bed hard." After a total of fifteen years, he said, "I quit."
    The bishops responded, "We're not surprised. You've been complaining ever since you got here."

A pastor had on his desk a notebook labeled, "Complaints of Members Against Members." When one of his people called to tell him the fault of another, he would say, "Well, here's my complaint book. I'll write down what you say, and you can sign it. Then when I have to take the matter up officially, I shall know what I may expect you to testify to."

The sight of the open book and the ready pen had its effect.

"Oh no, I could not sign anything like that." And no entry was made.

The minister says he kept the book for forty years, opened it probably a thousand times, and never wrote a line in it.

Johnny had a dog named Uncle Joe. When asked why he had given his pet such an odd name, he replied, "Beause he's just like that uncle of mine—he growls at everything he eats and wants to fight everyone he sees."

A complaining tongue reveals an ungrateful heart.

—William Arthur Ward

Sure, this world is full of trouble—
  I ain't said it ain't.
Me, I've had enough and double
  Reason for complaint;
Rain and storm have come to fret me,
  Skies are often gray;
Thorns and brambles have beset me
  On the road—but say,
    Ain't it fine today?
What's the use of always weepin'
  Making trouble last?
What's the use of always keepin'
  Thinkin' of the past?
Each must have his tribulation—
  Water with his wine;
Life, it ain't no celebration,
  Trouble?—I've had mine—
    But today is fine!
It's today that I am livin'
  Not a month ago.
Havin'; losin'; takin'; given';
  As time wills it so.
Yesterday a cloud of sorrow
  Fell across the way;
It may rain again tomorrow,
  It may rain—but say,
    Ain't it fine today?
        —Douglas Malloch

Here's a recipe for a terrible day:
  Take a pint of ill humor
  Add one or more unfortunate incidents
  Set over a good fire
  When at boiling point, add a tablespoon
of temper
  Baste from time to time with sarcasm
  Cook until the edges curl
  Add a handful of haughty words
  As the mixture curdles, stir furiously
and then
  Serve while sizzling!
Isn't that a swell recipe for a terrible day?

Several years ago the afternoon train pulled into a small Quaker town in Pennsylvania. As it stopped, a stranger swung off the train. He walked over to the group of people on the platform and asked, "What type of town is this and what kind of people live here?" A local townsman looked him in the eye and asked, "What kind of place did you come from and what were the people like who lived there?" The stranger then replied to the Quaker, "They were hard people to get along with and the town was noisy." Without hesitation the Quaker told the stranger, "This is the same kind of town and the same kind of people live here." So the stranger got back on the train.

The next afternoon when the train pulled in, off popped another stranger. Smiling, he approached the group of local Quakers on the platform and cheerily said, "Hi there. I'm looking for a town to live in permanently. What do you have here?" Once more the Quaker replied, "Where did you come from and what were the people like?" In the same happy tone the stranger said, "I came from a happy place; the people were kind and friendly." Without hesitation the Quaker told him, "You'll find the same kind of people here."

You cannot bring about prosperity by discouraging thrift.

You cannot strengthen the weak by weakening the strong.

You cannot help the poor by destroying the rich.

You cannot help the wage earner by pulling down the wage payer.

COMPLAINING

You cannot help small men by tearing down big men.

You cannot keep out of trouble by spending more than you earn.

You cannot build character and courage by taking away man's initiative and independence.

You cannot help men permanently by doing for them what they could and should do for themselves.

—Abraham Lincoln

Walking into a restaurant, a potential diner asked, "Do you serve crabs here?" The waiter said, "We serve anyone; please sit down."

On a recent flight, I was seated behind two small children who were not happy about being on a plane. Their cries of complaint filled the cabin.

Just before takeoff, a flight attendant stopped next to them and said with a big smile, "What is all this squawking up here?" After charming the fussy three-year-old and his younger sister for a few minutes, the flight attendant bent down and whispered very seriously, "I must remind you, this is a non-squawking flight."

The little ones became unbelievably quiet. That made everyone feel better. It's a long journey when you have to sit in the squawking section.

I'm sure God would like to remind me every morning that He wants this day to be a non-squawking flight. Philippians 2:14 says to "do all things without complaining and disputing."

—David C. McCasland

A letter written in a childish scrawl came to the post office addressed to "God." A postal employee, not knowing exactly what to do with the letter, opened it and read, "Dear God, my name is Jimmy. I am six years old. My father is dead and my mother is having a hard time raising me and my sister. Would you please send us $500?"

The postal employee was touched. He showed the letter to his fellow workers, and all decided to kick in a few dollars each and send it to the family. They were able to raise $300.

A couple of weeks later they received a second letter. The boy thanked God, but ended with this request: "Next time would you please deliver the money directly to our home. If you send it through the post office they deduct $200."

You can either complain that rose bushes have thorns or you can be glad that thorn-bushes have roses.

Two classes of people are always complaining: those who don't get what they deserve and those who do.

The fellow who toots his horn loudest is generally in a fog.

He who throws mud loses ground.

Nothing is easier than fault-finding: No talent, no self-denial, no brains, no character are required to set up in the grumbling business.

A lady known as an incurable grumbler constantly complained about everything. At last her preacher thought he had found something about which she would be happy, for her farm crop was the finest for miles around. When he met her, he said with a beaming smile, "You must be very pleased, Mary. Everyone is saying how healthy your potatoes look this year." In her usual sour manner she replied, "True, they're pretty good, but what am I going to do when I need bad ones to feed the pigs?"

It is not the greatness of our trouble but the littleness of our spirit that makes us complain.

If you talk about your troubles,
    And tell them o'er and o'er
The world will think you like them
    And give you plenty more.

When you feel dog-tired at night, it may be because you growled all day.

When we often grumble because we can't have what we want, we should be thankful that oftentimes we don't get what we deserve.

We mutter and we sputter,
We fume and we spurt,
We mumble and grumble,
Our feelings get hurt.
We can't understand things,
Our vision grows dim,
When all we need
Is a moment with Him.

I complained I had no shoes until I saw a man who had no feet.

Maybe the trouble with the world is that there are too many people who begin all their arguments with, "The trouble with the world is . . ."

Glenn Gould, a Canadian pianist, said, "It's true that I've driven through a number of red lights, but on the other hand I've stopped at a lot of green ones I've never had credit for."

The diner was furious when his steak arrived too rare. "Waiter," he barked, "didn't you hear me say 'well done'?"

"I can't thank you enough, sir," replied the waiter. "I hardly ever get a compliment."

—A. H. Berzen

A dozen discontented figures in a community once visited a wise man, clamoring to tell him their problems.

"Write your biggest problem down on a piece of paper," said the wise man, "and six of you stand here to my right and six to my left. Now exchange papers and you will have new trouble to fret about."

The malcontents complied. Within a minute, all were clamoring to have their own troubles back!

—Bits & Pieces

COMPLIMENTS

Pianist Artur Rubinstein never signed autographs, but a teenager once confronted him after a concert, held out a pad and pencil and said, "I know your fingers are tired, sir, but mine are, too—from clapping." He signed.

—Soundings

COMPROMISE

A hunter had his gun aimed at a large bear and was ready to pull the trigger. Just then the bear spoke in a soft, soothing voice, saying, "Isn't it better to talk than to shoot? Why don't we negotiate the matter? What is it you want?" The hunter lowered his rifle and answered, "I would like a fur coat." "That's good," said the bear. "I think that's something we can talk about. All I want is a full stomach; maybe we can reach a compromise." So they sat down to talk it over. A little while later the bear walked away alone. The negotiations had been successful—the bear had a full stomach, and the hunter had a fur coat.

The hottest places in hell are reserved for those who, in a period of moral crisis, maintain their neutrality.

—Dante

CONCERNS

In a survey, five hundred executives were asked, "What keeps you awake at night?" The top three concerns were finances, family affairs, and health problems.

CONFERENCE

A conference is simply an admission that you want someone else to join you in your troubles.

—Will Rogers

CONFESSION

Maurice Horn, a former Radio Bible Class counselor, said, "Some people confess a sin a thousand times. I tell them to confess it once, then thank God a thousand times for forgiving them."

An old fellow had a conscience that troubled him. At last he went to a farmer and said, "Master, I'm sorry. I stole a rope from you a while back." His master forgave him and the countryman went away. But he still had no peace of mind. For he had not told the farmer that there was a cow at the end of the rope when he stole it.

—Peter Howard

CONFIDENCE

Trust men and they will be true to you; treat them greatly and they will show themselves great.

—Ralph Waldo Emerson

I have found that if I have faith in myself and in the idea I am tinkering with, I usually win out.

—Charles F. Kettering

In the Civil War, Rear Admiral Samuel du Pont gave half a dozen excellent reasons why he had not taken his gunboats into Charleston Harbor. Admiral David Farragut listened intently to the recital. "But there was another reason that you have not mentioned," he replied.

"What is that?" questioned du Pont.

The answer came: "You did not believe you could do it."

That lack of confidence has been the secret of failures not only in warfare but also in the Christian life.

Confidence is the feeling you sometimes have before you fully understand the situation.

CONFLICT

Happiness is not absence of conflict, it's the ability to cope with it.

—*Teen Esteem*

George Bernard Shaw sent a telegram to Winston Churchill: "I'm sending you two tickets for the opening night of my play. Please attend and bring a friend if you have one." Churchill responded with a telegram. "I can't attend your play on the opening night. I plan to come the second night if you have one."

Bill Clem was a well-known baseball umpire. One time a player came running to a base, and Clem stood there. The manager of one of the teams ran to him and said, "He's safe." The other manager said, "He's out." Bill Clem stood there and said, "He ain't nothing till I call it."

Mark Twain once wrote, tongue-in-cheek, about two cages. In the first was placed a cat, to which were added some doves, then a dog, then a rabbit, a fox, a goose, a squirrel, and finally a monkey. In the other cage was placed an Irish Catholic from Tipperary, a Scottish Presbyterian from Aberdeen, a Turk, a Greek Christian, an Armenian, a Methodist, a Buddhist, a Brahman, and then a Salvation Army Colonel. Two days later the animals were living in peace—but the second cage was "chaos of gory odds and ends of turbans and fezzes and plaids and bones and flesh—not a specimen alive."

—Leslie B. Flynn

In an old monastery in Germany may be seen two pairs of antlers interlocked, said to be found in that position many years ago. The deer had been fighting when their antlers got jammed together and could not be separated. They died with locked horns. Said one historian, "I would like to take those horns into every house and school in the country." And we would add, "And into every church."

—Leslie B. Flynn

CONFORMITY

I came, I saw, I concurred.

A man from Brooklyn had his name changed from Kelly to Feinberg. Then, a year later, he had it changed from Feinberg to Garibaldi. The judge thundered at him, "Are you trying to make the court look foolish?"

"Not at all, Your Honor. My neighborhood keeps changing."

CONFUSION

"It's Greek to me." But what does a Greek say to confess total noncomprehension? A Greek says, "Stop talking Chinese!" Bravo—but what does a Chinese say? What a Chinese says is staggering: "Your words are like Buddha's attendant, twelve feet tall, whose head I cannot reach!" When Poles, on the other hand, are unable to understand something, they blurt out, "I am hearing a sermon in Turkish!" Frenchmen, who are especially irritated by incomprehensibility, murmur, "Pray stop talking Hebrew!" And Jews dismiss ensnarled (or foolish) statements with a crisp "Stop knocking a teapot!"

—Leo Rosten

A customer whose checkbook was in total chaos phoned his bank for help.

"What balance do you show?" asked the service representative.

Came the harried reply, "I asked you first."

A public meeting was completely out of hand. The room was full of noisy and conflicting voices. Everyone tried to make himself heard. Finally the chairman rapped sharply with his gavel and called for order. "Gentlemen, gentlemen," he said, "let's keep this confusion orderly."

If you think you're confused, consider poor Columbus. He didn't know where he was going when he started. When he got there, he didn't know where he was. When he got back, he didn't know where he'd been.

—Bits & Pieces

CONSCIENCE

The greatest tormentor of the human soul is a guilty conscience.

The Internal Revenue Service received the following letter from a conscience-stricken taxpayer:

"Dear Sir: My conscience bothered me. Here is $175, which I owe in back taxes." There was a P.S. at the bottom that read: "If my conscience still bothers me, I'll send in the rest."

A farmer was on his way home after picking up his new car. As he approached his farm, he decided to test the acceleration. He passed the side road that led to his house and drove on for a mile or so. Then, after making a sharp U-turn, he sped back toward the side road. A man driving a station wagon observed the U-turn and the farmer's fast rate of speed, and he thought the automobile was an unmarked police car. Trying to avoid detection, he quickly headed down the road leading to the farm. Of course he was followed by the returning farmer who only wanted to go home. The second driver was alarmed and drove at high speed to escape, only to come to a dead end. He jumped out and ran, abandoning the station wagon. Later it was found to be filled with stolen coffee, cigarettes, and ammunition. His conscience had made him flee, even though no one was pursuing him.

—Our Daily Bread

Since 1811 Uncle Sam has been receiving anonymous sums of money as self-imposed fines for a variety of reasons, such as for taking Army blankets for souvenirs or for deliberately failing to put enough postage on a letter. One widow, checking her late husband's books, discovered he had cheated the government, so she promptly mailed a check for $50 to the Treasury. All these monies have been placed in an account named the Federal Conscience Fund which now totals over three million dollars.

—Leslie B. Flynn

Your conscience is the still small voice that makes you feel still smaller.

Conscience is a little three-cornered thing inside of me. When I do wrong, it turns around and hurts me very much. But if I keep on doing wrong, it will turn so much that the corners become worn off, and it does not hurt me any more.

Conscience is like a sundial. When the truth of God shines on it, it points the right way.

Conscience is what warns you that you'd better have an alibi.

If your conscience smites you once, it is an admonition; if it smites you twice, it is condemnation.

CONSEQUENCES

After the fire, ashes; after the rain, roses.
—Moroccan proverb

One-half of the ills of life come because men are unwilling to sit down quietly for thirty minutes to think through all the possible consequences of their acts.
—Blaise Pascal

CONSISTENCY

None of us should listen to a man giving a lecture or a sermon on his "philosophy of life" until we know exactly how he treats his wife, his children, his neighbors, his friends, his subordinates—and his enemies.
—Sidney J. Harris

A farmer was trying to get a loan from a banker when their conversation was interrupted by a telephone call. The banker listened for a while and then said "No." He said "No" about five times and ended the call by saying "Yes."

"What did that feller say that made you change your mind and answer 'Yes'?" asked the farmer.

"I didn't change my mind," the banker replied. "He wanted to know if my final answer was no."
—*Bits & Pieces*

A man in a rural county down south was campaigning for a seat in the Senate. One rainy, miserable evening there was a knock on the door. A man he didn't know stood outside, soaking wet. "I need help," the man said. "My car is stalled down the road. Would you help me?"

"Sure," said the candidate. When they reached the car, the owner got in and turned the key. The car started up immediately.

"I don't understand," said the would-be senator. "There was nothing wrong with your car."

The other man smiled. "I know. I also know that this state needs a good man up there in Washington," he explained. "I just wanted to know if you were the kind of man I could vote for. Now I know. You've got my vote."

CONTENTMENT (Also see GREED)

It is right to be contented with what we have, never with what we are.
—James Mackintosh

A happy man is one who wants what he has. An unhappy man gets what he wants but never stops wanting.

The secret of contentment is knowing how to enjoy what you have and to be able to lose all desire for things beyond your reach.
—Lin Yutang

A contented life is having:
Wealth enough to support your needs.
Health enough to make work a pleasure.
Faith enough to make real the things of God.
Grace enough to confess your sins and forsake them.
Patience enough to toil until some good is accomplished.
Love enough to move you to be useful and helpful to others.
Strength enough to battle with difficulties and overcome them.
Hope enough to remove all anxious fears concerning the future.

Leaning on his fence one day, a devout Quaker was watching a new neighbor move in next door. After all kinds of modern appliances, electronic gadgets, plush furniture, and costly wall hangings had been carried in, the onlooker called over, "If you find you're lacking anything, neighbor, let me know, and I'll show you how to live without it."

One day Lord Congleton, a godly man, overheard one of his kitchen servants remark, "Oh, if I only had five pounds, I would be perfectly content." Pondering her statement, he decided he would like to see someone who was perfectly content. So he went to the woman and said he had heard her remark and wanted to do something about it. He proceeded to give her a five-pound note. With great feeling she thanked him. Congleton then left the kitchen but paused for a moment outside the door. As soon as the woman thought he was gone, she began to complain, "Why on earth didn't I say ten pounds?"

How much we enjoy what we have is more important than how much we have. Life is full of people who have more than they know what to do with but cannot be content. It is the capacity to enjoy life that brings contentment.

Contentment does not mean I must give everything away to the poor and become poor myself. Nor does it mean I must feel guilty for being blessed as an American. It does not mean I can take a careless attitude toward my finances. Nor does it suggest I can take a superior attitude if my things are newer and shinier than another person's.

Contentment means suppressing the desire for more and more. And it means recognizing we are God's stewards of our possessions.

—Donald M. Geiger

Contentment means that whatever we do not have we do not require.

—Alexander Maclaren

To be content makes a poor person rich, but to be malcontent makes a rich man poor.

—Benjamin Franklin

The heart that loves the little things
   Is full of deep content;
The life that serves in little things
   Is often nobly spent.
So do not be despising
   The day of little things,
For bees, as well as angels,
   Can boast a pair of wings.

CONTRADICTIONS

Someone wrote a sign, "Life is one contradiction after another." Another person saw the sign and wrote under it, "No, it's not."

CONVICTIONS

A man is a fool when he dies for his opinions.

A man is a saint when he stands for his convictions.

Give us clear vision that we may know where to stand and what to stand for, because unless we stand for something, we shall fall for anything.

—Peter Marshall

Crito came to the prison of Socrates, the Greek philosopher, to try to get him to escape with the help of friends, since they all knew that he had done no wrong. But Socrates reminded Crito that they had long agreed no man would either do evil, or return evil for evil, or betray the right. Then Socrates asked, "Are these principles to be altered because circumstances are altered?"

In matter of principle, stand like a rock; in matter of taste, swim with the current.

—Thomas Jefferson

We cannot write or speak convincingly of things we haven't experienced.

—Sue Nichols

Patient: Are you sure I'll get well? I've heard that doctors sometimes treat people for the wrong disease. There was a man who was being treated for pneumonia, for example, and he died of typhoid fever.

Doctor: Don't worry. When I treat a man for pneumonia, he dies of pneumonia.

It is important that people know what you stand for. It is equally important that they know what you won't stand for.

David Hume, the agnostic, was reproached by some of his friends because of his inconsistency in going to church each Sunday to hear the orthodox Scottish minister John Brown. Defending himself, he replied, "Well, I don't believe all that he says, but *he* does, and once a week I like to hear a man who believes what he says."

—*Our Daily Bread*

I am tired of hearing about men with the "courage of their convictions." Nero and Caligula and Attila and Hitler had the courage of their convictions—but not one had the courage to examine his convictions, or to change them, which is the true test of character.

—Sidney Harris

In the operating room of a great hospital a young nurse had her first day of full responsibility. "You've removed eleven sponges, doctor," she said to the surgeon. "We used twelve."

"I've removed them all," the doctor declared. "We'll close the incision now."

"No," the nurse objected. "We used twelve."

"I'll take the responsibility," the surgeon said grimly. "Suture."

"You can't do that," blazed the nurse. "Think of the patient."

The doctor smiled, lifted his foot, showed the nurse the twelfth sponge. "You'll do," he said. He had been testing her for her integrity—and she had it.

Convictions are what we cling to in our lowest moment.

—Larry Crabb

A conviction is that splendid quality in ourselves which we call bullheadedness in others.

Great men have convictions; ordinary men have only opinions.

Martin Luther, in his loneliness, on his way to the Diet of Worms to appear before King Charles V and the Roman Prelate and all the princes assembled around, said, "My cause shall be commended to the Lord for He lives and reigns who preserved the three children in the furnace of the Babylonian king. If He is unwilling to preserve me, my life is a small thing compared with Christ. Expect anything of me except flight or recantation. I will not flee, much less recant. So may the Lord Jesus strengthen me." He did not say, "So may the Lord Jesus deliver me." He did not say, "So may the Lord Jesus make it easy for me." And he concluded his response with the words, "Here I stand, I can do no other. So help me God."

Let nothing come between you and God; let God come between you and everything.

An opinion is an idea that we pick up and carry around with us. In contrast, a conviction is something that picks us up and carries us around.

A preacher was approached by some members of his congregation about trouble in the church. Airing their grievances, they made all sorts of charges against those with whom they were at odds. Responding to their complaints, the preacher said, "You're right, you're absolutely right." The next night, however, another group came to his home and told their side of the story. He listened very quietly, and when they had vanished, said, "You're right, you're absolutely right." His wife, working in the kitchen, overheard everything. As soon as the parishioners left she rushed into the living room and exclaimed, "You're just about the most wishy-washy individual I've ever seen." To that he immediately replied, "You're right, you're absolutely right."

It is not a minister's wisdom but his conviction which imparts himself to others. Nothing gives life but life. Real flame alone kindles another flame.

—F. W. Robertson

COPING

A man had become so rundown and depressed that he felt he could no longer face life. He supposed something was physically wrong, so he went to see his doctor. The physician gave him a complete examination including X-rays, blood tests, and an EKG.

When the man went back later for the report, he noticed that the doctor had written one word on the diagnosis sheet: "Incopability." When he inquired about it, the physician explained, "I have coined this word to describe patients with your symptoms.

Nothing is wrong with you physically, but you can't seem to cope with life anymore. I call this 'incopability.'"

COUNTERFEITS

There is a difference between imitating and counterfeiting someone.

—Benjamin Franklin

A Chinese boy who wanted to learn about jade went to study with a talented old teacher. This gentleman put a piece of the precious stone into his hand and told him to hold it tight. Then he began to talk of philosophy, men, women, the sun, and almost everything under it. After an hour he took back the stone and sent the boy home. The procedure was repeated for several weeks. The boy became frustrated. When would he be told about the jade? He was too polite, however, to question the wisdom of his venerable teacher. Then one day, when the old man put a stone into his hands, the boy cried out instinctively, "That's not jade." He had become so familiar with the genuine that he could immediately detect a counterfeit.

—Haddon W. Robinson

COURAGE

James Lewis Petigru's life was so exemplary that after his death the citizens of the community erected a tombstone in his honor inscribed with these words:

Unawed by opinion
Unseduced by flattery
Undismayed by disaster
He confronted life with courage
And death with Christian hope.

An English naval officer told how he was saved from dishonor in his first experience in battle. He was a midshipman, still in his teens. The enemy gunfire was so terrifying that he felt as if he would faint. Just then an officer came over to him, placed his hand over the boy's, and said with a quieting confidence, "Courage, my boy. You'll be all right. I felt the same way in my first battle." Reflecting on those words, the young man later said, "It felt as though an angel had come and given me new strength." From that moment on, his fear was gone and he was as brave as the most seasoned officer. That encouragement was exactly what he needed.

—*Our Daily Bread*

Whatever you do, you need courage. Whatever course you decide on, there is always someone to tell you that you are wrong. There are always difficulties arising that tempt you to believe your critics are right. To map out a course of action and follow it to an end requires some of the same courage that a soldier needs. Peace has its victories, but it takes brave men and women to win them.

—Ralph Waldo Emerson

It takes courage . . .

To refrain from gossip when others about you delight in it.

To stand up for an absent person who is being abused.

To live honestly within your means and not dishonestly on the means of others.

To be talked about and yet remain silent when a word would justify you in the eyes of others, but which you cannot speak without injury to another.

To be a real man, a true woman, by holding fast to your ideas when it causes you to be looked upon as strange and peculiar.

To refuse to do a thing which is wrong, though others desire it.

To live always according to your convictions.

—*The Trumpeter*

Luther Burbank, the great naturalist, was always studying nature with his microscope. Someone asked him, "Why are you out of step with the world?"

He answered, "I'm not out of step. I'm walking to the beat of another drum."

When you are so devoted to doing what is right that you press straight on and disregard what men are saying about you, there is the triumph of moral courage.

—Phillips Brooks

A soldier of Napoleon boasted to a British soldier of his bravery. The British soldier answered, "Yes, but the British are braver one hour longer."

Success is never final; failure is never fatal; it is courage that counts.

—Winston Churchill

They can conquer who believe they can. . . . He has not learned the first lesson of life who does not every day surmount a fear.

—Ralph Waldo Emerson

William Manchester's biography of Winston Churchill cites the counsel of Benjamin Jowett, provost of Balliol College, to the future proconsuls of the empire: "Never explain; never retreat; get it done, and let them howl."

Bravery is the capacity to perform properly even when scared half to death.

—General Omar Bradley

It takes courage to stand up and be counted, but it takes more courage to keep standing up after you have been counted.

He who loses wealth loses much; he who loses a friend loses more; but he who loses his courage loses all.

—Miguel Cervantes

Courage is grace under pressure.

—Ernest Hemingway

Robert Spear used to tell about a young man who was going to the mission field. A friend said to the young man, "You know where you're going, don't you? In the shade it's 110°." The young man replied, "I don't have to stay in the shade all the time."

The great need for anyone in authority is courage.

—Alistair Cooke

Courage is being scared to death and saddling up anyway.

—John Wayne

Courage is not the absence of fear but the willingness to push on in the face of it.

In the spring of 1940 France had fallen to the onrushing columns of the German war machine. The 350,000-man British army in France had made a harrowing evacuation from Dunkirk. Winston Churchill rose to speak before the House of Commons and, among other things, to introduce a new and striking phrase to the English language.

Churchill said, "Let us therefore brace ourselves to our duty and so bear ourselves that if the British Commonwealth and Empire last for a thousand years, men will still say, 'This was their finest hour.'"

—James M. Boice

Far better it is to dare mighty things, to win glorious triumphs, even though checkered by failure, than to rank with those poor spirits who neither enjoy much nor suffer much, because they live in the gray twilight that knows neither victory or defeat.

—Theodore Roosevelt

Courage is doing what you're afraid to do. There can be no courage unless you're scared.

—Eddie Rickenbacker

One man with courage makes a majority.

—Andrew Jackson

Courage is fear that has said its prayers.

When the great Chrysostom was arrested by the Roman emperor, the latter sought to make the Greek Christian recant, but without success. So the emperor discussed with his advisers what could be done to the prisoner. "Shall I put him in a dungeon?" the emperor asked.

"No," one of his counselors replied, "for he will be glad to go. He longs for the quietness wherein he can delight in the mercies of his God."

"Then he shall be executed!" said the emperor.

"No," was the answer, "for he will also be glad to die. He declares that in the event of death he will be in the presence of his Lord."

"What shall we do then?" the ruler asked.

"There is only one thing that will give Chrysostom pain," the counselor said. "To cause Chrysostom to suffer, make him sin. He is afraid of nothing except sin."

A sign in the Grossmunster church in Zurich, where Zwingli preached, reads, "By God's grace do something courageous."

COURTESY

A rude passenger was on the train Bishop Manning was riding. This fellow made a great disturbance as he was about to get off, accusing others in a most discourteous way.

As he finally got his possessions together and started for the exit, the bishop called after him, "Pardon me, sir, but you have left something here." "What?" the fellow called back. The bishop answered, "A very bad impression."

One day a man gave up his seat on a bus to a lady. She fainted. On recovering, she thanked him. Then he fainted.

—Michael A. Guido

"My boy," said a father to his son, "treat everybody with politeness, even those who may be rude to you; for remember, you show courtesy to others, not because they are gentlemen, but because you are a gentleman."

—American Opinion

Henry IV, king of France, was visiting a village one day with some members of his court when they approached a very poor man who bowed himself completely to the ground. The monarch responded by doing the same thing. Those with him were astonished. When one of them asked why he condescended to return the salutation in the same manner, Henry IV quickly replied, "Would your king be excelled in politeness by one of the most lowly of his subjects?"

Knowledge, ability, and experience are of little avail in reaching high success if courtesy is lacking. Courtesy is the one passport that will be accepted without question in every land, in every office, in every home, in every heart in the world. For nothing commends itself so well as kindness; and courtesy is kindness.

—George D. Powers

Life is not so short but there is always time enough for courtesy.

—Ralph Waldo Emerson

COURTSHIP

A parrot said, "Let's cuddle." Hearing the parrot, a pastor commented, "That's interesting. I have a parrot and he says, 'Let's pray.' I wonder what would happen if we got the two parrots together."

So he did. The one parrot said, "Let's cuddle." And the pastor's parrot said, "My prayers have been answered."

CREATION

Some years ago a South American company purchased a fine printing press from a firm in the United States.

After it had been shipped and completely assembled, the workmen could not get it to operate properly. The most knowledgeable personnel tried to remedy the difficulty and bring it into proper adjustment, but to no avail. Finally the company wired a message to the manufacturer, asking that they send a representative immediately to fix it. Sensing the urgency of the request, the U.S. firm chose the person who had designed the press. When he arrived on the scene, the South American officials were skeptical because he was a young man. After some discussion, they sent this cable to the manufacturer: "Your man is too young; send more experienced person." The reply came back, "He made the machine. Let him fix it!"

The tiny hummingbird, weighing only about a tenth of an ounce, can perform complicated twists and turns and can fly backward and upside down.

The flexibility of its shoulder joints allows it to move its wings forward and backward in a horizontal figure eight, beating them as many as seventy-five times per second, a maneuver that enables the hummingbird to hover near a flower while it drinks nectar from it. But the hummingbird doesn't soar or glide as some birds can, and its legs are so weak that it can't hop. It has to fly even to change positions on a twig.

CREATION

On the other hand, the ostrich, at three hundred pounds, the largest of birds, can't fly. But its legs are so strong that it can sprint up to forty miles an hour, taking strides of twelve to fifteen feet.

The peregrine falcon, or duck hawk, is about the size of a crow, but it is the fastest creature on earth. It can dive after prey at more than 175 miles per hour.

—*Three Minutes a Day*

What's inconceivable about the universe is that it should be at all conceivable.

—Albert Einstein

The universe begins to look more like a great thought than a great machine.

—James Jean

All of nature is God's art.

—Dante

One of the great names of British science, mathematics, and philosophy is Sir Isaac Newton (1642–1727). He had someone make for him a miniature model of the solar system. A large golden ball representing the sun was at its center and around it revolved smaller spheres, representing the planets. They were each kept in an orbit relatively the same as in the real solar system. By means of rods, cogwheels, and belts they all moved around the center gold ball in exact precision. A friend called on the noted man one day while he was studying the model. The friend was not a believer in the biblical doctrine of creation.

Their conversation went as follows:

Friend: "My, Newton, what an exquisite thing. Who made it for you?"

Newton: "Nobody."

Friend: "Nobody?"

Newton: "That's right. I said nobody. All of these balls and cogs and belts and gears just happened to come together, and wonder of wonders, by chance they began revolving in their set orbits with perfect timing."

CREATIVITY

Imagination is the beginning of creation. You imagine what you desire; you will what you imagine; and at last you create what you will.

—George Bernard Shaw

When George Frederick Handel's health and finances were at a low point, he rose to the greatest heights of his creative experience. His creditors were threatening him with imprisonment, and he was suffering from partial paralysis. He then went into seclusion and there fellowshiped with God as never before. During that time, God enabled him to write the grandest of all his oratorios, *Messiah*.

—*Our Daily Bread*

Alton McEachern says the only original thing about us is original sin.

If you have done something the same way for a year, look at it critically; if you have done it for two years, modify it; if you have done it for five years, throw it away and start over.

—Alfred Perlman

Success, many times, can be found only in the creative imagination of a man's mind. Perhaps no other factor of success contributes more to personal achievement than does creativity.

—Dick Tooker

CRIME

The American people are the worst criminals in the world. Astounding as that assertion is, it is true. Cleveland, Ohio, has six times as many murders as London. It has 170 times as many robberies, according to its population, as has London. More people are robbed every year, or assaulted with intent to rob, in Cleveland than in all England, Scotland, and Wales combined. More people are murdered every year in St. Louis than in all England and Wales. There are more murders in New York City than in all France or Germany or Italy or the British Isles. The sad truth of the matter is that the criminal is not punished. If you commit a murder, there is less than one chance in a hundred that you will ever be executed for it. You, as a peaceful citizen, are ten times as liable to die from cancer as you would be to be hanged if you shot a man.

—Paul Gibbons

CRISIS

The Chinese character for crisis consists of two characters. The top character means danger, and the bottom character means opportunity.

CRITICISM

The best rule of thumb is to remember, if you can't be big, don't belittle.

—*Teen Esteem*

Think of your own faults the first part of the night when you are awake, and of the faults of others the latter part of the night when you are asleep.

—Chinese proverb

Make no judgments where you have no compassion.

—Anne McCaffrey

Joseph Parker, a Congregationalist pastor, was approached after a church service by a man who criticized a minor point in the sermon.

Parker listened patiently and then asked, "And what else did you get from the message?" The critic was silenced.

If you feel constrained to look for faults, use a mirror, not a telescope.

There's so much good in the worst of us
And so much bad in the best of us
That it ill behooves the best of us
To criticize the rest of us.
Running down our friends is the quickest way to run them off.

—William Arthur Ward

I hate the guys
Who minimize and criticize
The other guys
Whose enterprise
Has made them rise
Above the guys who criticize.

—Leslie B. Flynn

Most people don't object to criticism if it's favorable.

A Quaker had a mean cow. One time when he was milking her, she swished her tail right in his face. Then she stepped on his toe. Then when he had the pail almost filled with milk, she stepped right in the pail. Then when he finished milking her, she kicked him several yards away.

He said to the cow, "Thou knowest I am a Quaker. And thou knowest I cannot hit thee. But I can sell thee to a Baptist."

I am ...	You are ...	He is ...
slender	thin	skinny
a perfectionist	neat	fussy
frank	candid	blunt
concerned	innovative	full of new ideas
conservative	old-fashioned	out-of-date
philosophical	daydreamer	an escapist
flexible	easygoing	missing a backbone
humble	modest	suffering from an inferiority complex
well filled out	pleasingly plump	fat
a spectator of life	not involved	out in left field
aware of my worth	proud	conceited
relaxed	feeling no pain	drunk
firm	obstinate	pigheaded
a collector of rare art	interested in antiques	crazy about old junk

—Georgia Ramay

Linus had his security blanket in place and his thumb resting safely in his mouth, but he was troubled. Turning to Lucy, who was sitting next to him, he asked, "Why are you always so anxious to criticize me?"

Her response was typical: "I just think I have a knack for seeing other people's faults."

Exasperated, Linus threw his hands up and asked, "What about your own faults?"

Without hesitation, Lucy explained, "I have a knack for overlooking them."

I do not resent criticism, even when, for the sake of emphasis, it parts for a time with reality.

—Winston Churchill

When he moved to London, Spurgeon had an unknown critic who sent him a weekly postcard listing the grammatical errors and other mistakes in each week's sermons. Spurgeon considered the service a kindness.

But grammatical errors and vicious criticism are two different things. A stab in the back is a far cry from a note on a postcard.

I stopped criticizing my wife's cooking after her very first meal. I said, "How come you don't make the kind of pie filling my mother used to make?" And she said, "How come you don't make the kind of dough my father used to make?"

—Bob Orben

In the early days of the Civil War, Robert E. Lee was severely criticized by General Whiting. It might have been expected that Lee would seize any opportunity to get even with Whiting. The opportunity presented itself when Jefferson Davis called Lee in for consultation.

Davis wanted to know what Lee thought of General Whiting. Without hesitation Lee commended him in high terms and called him one of the ablest men in the army. Afterwards, a fellow officer took Lee aside and wanted to know why he had not told Davis the things Whiting had said about him.

Lee answered, "It was my understanding that the President wanted to know my opinion of Whiting, not Whiting's opinion of me."

—*Bits & Pieces*

The quickest way to get in water over your head is to tell someone he's all wet.

—William Arthur Ward

Whatever you dislike in another person, be sure to correct in yourself.

Don't give anyone a piece of your mind; you need it all yourself.

Some people will slap you on the back behind your face and then slap you in the face behind your back.

Twice I did good,
    and heard it never;
Once I did evil,
    and heard it ever.

The wife of a hard-to-please husband was determined to try her best to satisfy him for just one day. "Darling," she asked, "what would you like for breakfast this morning?" He growled, "Coffee and toast, grits and sausage, and two eggs—one scrambled and one fried." She soon had the food on the table and waited for a word of praise. After a quick glance, he exclaimed, "Well, if you didn't scramble the wrong egg!"

—*Maranatha Magazine*

It is often our own imperfection which makes us reprove the imperfection of others—a sharp-sighted self-love of our own which cannot pardon the self-love of others.

—François Fénelon

A woman was highly critical of her neighbor's windows. She claimed that they were always dirty. One day, after complaining about them to a friend, the visitor encouraged her to wash her own windows. She followed the advice, and the next time her friend came to see her, she exclaimed, "I can't believe it. As soon as I washed my windows, my neighbor must have cleaned hers too. Look at them shine."

Criticism is something we can avoid easily—by saying nothing, doing nothing, and being nothing.

—Aristotle

God uses critics in our lives
To help us see our pride,
To teach us true humility,
To change us from inside.

A man once approached Charles M. Alexander, R. A. Torrey's song leader, and said, "I believe in trying to win men to Christ, but I don't like your methods."

"I don't like them very well either," Mr. Alexander replied. "Tell me, how do you do it?"

The man hesitated, his face got red, and he finally stammered, "Well—I'm not sure that I do it at all."

"In that case," Mr. Alexander replied, "I like my way better than yours."

To be ridiculed may give us communion with the Lord Jesus, but to ridicule others will place us in fellowship with His persecutors.

—Charles H. Spurgeon

Confess your own sins, not your neighbors'. The greatest fault is to be conscious of none but other peoples'.

—Thomas Carlyle

A man was constantly complaining about the members of his church. Finally one of them, who was his friend, said, "Wait a minute. You have faults too, don't you?" "I guess so," came the reply. "Nobody's perfect." "Well, don't we have a right to make a few mistakes too?" "Yes," was the response. The other man continued, "Let's say you have three faults. There are six hundred members in our church, and suppose each of them has three—that's eighteen hundred faults. Do you think our church would be any better if everyone were just like you?" "I see what you mean," said the complainer. "I realize now that I've been much too critical."

The rule of carving holds good as to criticism; never cut with a knife what you can cut with a spoon.

—Charles Buxton

He has the right to criticize who has the heart to help.

—Abraham Lincoln

Wouldn't it be nice if everyone who is tempted to point a finger would instead hold out a helping hand?

Wouldn't it be nice if we could find wealth as easily as we find fault? We would all be rich.

—*Apples of Gold*

A father and his son took a donkey to the market. The man sat on the beast and the boy walked. People along the way said, "What a terrible thing, a big strong fellow sitting on the donkey's back while the youngster has to walk." So the father dismounted and the son took his place. Soon onlookers remarked, "How terrible, this man walking and the little boy sitting." At that, they both got on the donkey's back— only to hear others say, "How cruel, two people sitting on one donkey." Off they came. But other bystanders commented, "How crazy, the donkey has nothing on his back and two people are walking." Finally they were both carrying the donkey. They never did make it to the market.

People who try to whittle you down are only trying to reduce you to their size.

Dawson Trotman, founder of the Navigators, had a good method for handling all criticisms directed at himself. No matter how unfair the criticism might seem to be, he would always take it into his prayer closet and in effect spread it before the Lord. Then he would say, "Lord, please show me the kernel of truth hidden in this criticism."

It is easy to be critical. The real test is to come up with constructive alternatives.

I praise loudly; I blame softly.

—Catherine II

The goal of criticism is to leave the person with the feeling that he's been helped.

Wanted—Christians who overlook their brothers' and sisters' faults as easily as they do their own.

Thank not those faithful who praise all your words and actions, but those who kindly reprove your faults.

—Plato

The only way to live happily with people is to overlook their faults and admire their virtues.

—*Bits & Pieces*

Whatever you have to say to people be sure to say it in words that will cause them to smile and you will be on pretty safe ground. And when you do find it necessary to criticize someone, put your criticism in the form of a question which the other fellow is practically sure to have to answer in a manner that he becomes his own critic.

—John Wanamaker

You shouldn't criticize your wife's judgment . . . look whom she married.

If the only way I can make myself look good is to criticize you, something is seriously wrong with me.

—Warren W. Wiersbe

If people speak ill of you, live so that no one will believe them.

—Plato

It is the peculiar quality of a fool to perceive the faults of others and to forget his own.

—Cicero

If what they are saying about you is true, mend your ways. If it isn't true, forget it, and go on and serve the Lord.

—H. A. Ironside

Lady Astor to Churchill, "You are drunk." Churchill said to her, "You are ugly." Then he added, "But tomorrow I'll be sober."

A woman said, "Sometimes I wake up grouchy." And then she added, "But sometimes I let him sleep."

Constructive criticism is when I criticize you; destructive criticism is when you criticize me.

That criticism is best which sounds like an explanation.

John was driving home late one night when he picked up a hitchhiker. As they rode along, he began to be suspicious of his passenger. John checked to see if his wallet was safe in the pocket of his coat that was on the seat between them, but it wasn't there. So he slammed on the brakes, ordered the hitchhiker out, and said, "Hand over the wallet immediately." The frightened hitchhiker handed over a billfold, and John drove off. When he arrived home, he started to tell his wife about the experience, but she interrupted him, saying, "Before I forget, John, do you know that you left your wallet at home this morning?"

Bishop Potter of New York was sailing for Europe in one of the great transatlantic ocean liners. When he went on board, he found another passenger was to share the cabin with him. After going to see the accommodations, he came up to the purser's desk and inquired if he could leave his gold watch and other valuables in the ship's safe. He explained that ordinarily he never availed himself of that privilege, but he had been to his cabin and had met the man who was to occupy the other berth and, judging from his appearance, he was afraid that he might not be a very trustworthy person. The purser accepted the responsibility for the valuables and remarked, "It's all right, Bishop, I'll be very glad to take care of them for you. The other man has been up here and left his for the same reason."

—H. A. Ironside

A husband and wife were arguing about an investment the husband wanted to make. In the midst of it, he pointed out that men had better judgment than women.

"Well, I guess you're right," replied the wife. "You married me and I married you."

—*Bits & Pieces*

College professor: "Such rawness in a student is a shame; poor high school preparation is to blame."

High school principal: "It's plain to see the boy's a perfect fool. The fault lies strictly with the grammar school."

Grammar school teacher: "I would that

from such dolts I might be spared; they send them up to me so unprepared."

Kindergarten teacher: "Ne'er such a lack of training did I see. What sort of person can that mother be?"

Mother: "You stupid child. But then, you're not to blame; your father's folks I know are all the same."

—*Our Daily Bread*

Though sticks and stones inflict great pain,
Their hurt will fade away;
But just one sharp and biting word
Brings harm that comes to stay.

The builders of the Panama Canal faced enormous obstacles of geography, climate, and disease. Most of the construction was supervised by Colonel George Washington Goethals. He had to endure severe criticism from many back home who predicted that he would never complete the "impossible task." But the great engineer was resolute and pressed steadily forward in his work without responding to those who opposed him. "Aren't you going to answer your critics?" a subordinate inquired. "In time," Goethals replied. "How?" the man asked. "With the canal." And his answer came on August 15, 1914, when the canal opened to traffic for the first time.

If you've done big things in life you must expect to have excited some criticism. It's only people who've done precious little who get no criticism at all.

—Margaret Thatcher

The horse one cannot have has every fault.
—Danish proverb

A husband was critical of his wife who was hard of hearing. When she was seated away from him, he stood several feet from behind her and said, "Can you hear me?" He heard no answer so he moved a few feet closer and asked again, "Can you hear me?" He heard no response so he said it a third time, and then just behind her a fourth time. She turned and said, "For the fourth time, yes."

The Wrecking Crew

I stood on the street of a busy town
Watching men tearing a building down;
With a "ho, heave, ho," and a lusty yell
They swung a beam and a side wall fell.
I asked the foreman of the crew,
"Are those men as skilled as those you'd
Hire if you wanted to build?"
"Ah, no," he said, "no indeed,
Just common labor is all I need.
"I can tear down as much in a day or two
As would take skilled men a year to do."
And then I thought as I went my way,
Just which of these two roles am I trying
  to play?
Have I walked life's road with care
Measuring each deed with rule and square?
Or am I one of those who roam the town
Content with the labor of tearing down?

If you wish to make a man your enemy, tell him simply, "You are wrong." This method works every time.

—Henry C. Link

If a man calls you a donkey, don't worry about it. If two men call you a donkey, get your saddle.

—Yiddish proverb

Do what you feel in your heart to be right—for you'll be criticized anyway.

—Eleanor Roosevelt

Maturity begins when we're content to feel we're right about something, without feeling the necessity to prove someone else wrong.

—Sidney Harris

If the criticism is untrue, disregard it; if unfair, do not be irritated by it; if justified, learn by it.

Great is the man who can accept criticism. Greater yet is he who welcomes it. But greatest of all is he who knows how to administer it in a spirit of love and sensitivity, without causing pain and chagrin.

—Rabbi Norman Lamm

Criticism has never killed anything that

should live, and flattery has never made anything live that must die.

—Vicomte Chateaubriand

A leader is easy to recognize. He is the one with the arrows in his back.

Booker T. Washington once said, "You can't hold a man down without staying down with him."

Just stand aside, and watch yourself go by;
Think of yourself, as "he" instead of "I."
Pick flaws, find fault, forget the man is you,
And strive to make your estimate ring true.
The faults of others then will dwarf and shrink.
Love's chain grows stronger by one mighty link,
When you with "he" as substitute for "I,"
Have stood aside, and watched yourself go by.

—Strickland W. Gillilan

If I tried to answer all the criticisms of me and all the attacks leveled at me, this office would be closed to all other business. My job is not pleasing men, but doing the best I can. If in the end I am found to be wrong, ten legions of angels swearing I was right will not help me; but if the end proves me to have been right, then all that is said about me now will amount to nothing.

—Abraham Lincoln

Never insult an alligator until you've crossed the river.

—Cordell Hull

Don't tell me what I do right. I know that. What I need to know is what I do wrong.

—Albert Einstein

When you point your finger accusingly at someone else, remember you have three fingers pointing at you.

It is easy to find fault but hard to find what to do with it.

A local newspaper had a small boxed-off section with these sarcastic comments from an irritated editor: "If you find errors in this publication, please consider that they are there for a purpose. We publish something for everyone, and some people are always looking for mistakes."

He is always the severest censor of the merits of others who has the least worth of his own.

—E. L. Magoon

Two taxidermists stopped before a window in which an owl was on display. They immediately began to criticize the way it was mounted. Its eyes were not natural; its wings were not neatly arranged; and its feet could be improved. When they had finished with their criticism, the old owl turned his head . . . and winked at them.

—*Pulpit Helps*

The small man flies into a rage over the slightest criticism, but the wise man is eager to learn from those who have censured him and reproved him.

—Dale Carnegie

President Lincoln once issued orders transferring certain men, and the order should, by rights, have come from his secretary of war, Edward M. Stanton. When Stanton received the order, he refused to carry it out and told anybody who would listen what he thought of the President and ended by calling him a fool.

Then Lincoln said, "If Stanton said I am a fool, then I must be, for he is nearly always right. I'll just go see for myself." After he talked with secretary Stanton, Lincoln became convinced that Stanton was right and he was wrong; so he withdrew the order.

When the other fellow is despiteful, he's ugly . . . when you act that way, it's just your nerves.

When the other fellow is set in his ways, he's obstinate . . . when you are, it's just firmness.

When the other fellow spends a lot of money, he's extravagant . . . but when you do, it's just generosity.

When the other fellow picks flaws in things, he's cranky . . . when you do, you're just discriminating.

When the other fellow says what he thinks, he's spiteful or judging . . . but when you do, you're just being frank.

When the other fellow doesn't like your friend, he's "prejudiced" . . . but when you don't like his friend, you are simply showing that you are a good judge of human nature.

The unfortunate thing about constructive criticism is that nobody really appreciates it as much as the one who's giving it.

Any fool can criticize, condemn, and complain—and most fools do.
—Benjamin Franklin

If evil be said of thee and it be true, correct thyself; if it be a lie, laugh at it.
—Epictetus

CROSS

When George Nixon Briggs was governor of Massachusetts, three of his friends visited the Holy Land. While they were there, they climbed Golgotha's slope and cut from the summit a small stick to be used as a cane. On their return they presented it to the governor, saying, "We want you to know that when we stood on Calvary, we remembered you." He accepted the gift with gratitude and courtesy but tenderly remarked, "I appreciate your consideration of me, gentlemen, but I am still more thankful for Another who thought of me there."

Johann von Goethe said there are four things he hates: tobacco smoke, lice, garlic, and the cross.

Some missionaries were talking about Christianity to Mahatma Gandhi. He said to them, "What hymn would you suggest to me which summarizes what you believe?" They conferred for a while and then said, "When I Survey the Wondrous Cross."

There is a great difference between realizing, "On that cross He was crucified for me," and "On that cross I am crucified with Him." The one aspect brings us deliverance from sin's condemnation, the other from sin's power.
—John Gregory Mantle

CURIOSITY

I have no special gift. I am only passionately curious.
—Albert Einstein

CYNICISM

The poorest way to face life is to face it with a sneer.
—Theodore Roosevelt

D

DARKNESS

On January 10, 1979, Glenn Irwin and Dave Coots, Orinoco River Mission missionaries, took me to see the Guacharo Cave near Caripe, in eastern Venezuela. It was pitch dark, with no electric lights. A Spanish guide took us through it, about one-third of a mile. As we walked in, we heard the Guacharo birds beginning to fly and squawk. They are nocturnal, never leaving in the daytime. They fly out after dark—to go several hundred miles to bring back an unusual kind of nut found only in that location, and they return before sunrise. They live in darkness.
—Roy B. Zuck

A father told his young boy to go to bed. He started up the stairs but realized it was dark and he couldn't reach the light switch. He went back, but his dad told him to go on up because God was there. The boy knew that was the final answer, so he started up. But on the first step he stopped, looked up, and said, "God, if you are there, please don't move or you'll scare me to death!"

DEATH

DEATH (Also see DYING WORDS)

Dorothy Parker, a well-known writer, was told Calvin Coolidge had died. She asked, "How could they tell?"

The world is a very dangerous place—you never get out of it alive.

Death is not a threat to genuine life. It is but a paper tiger that is no longer free to terrorize us once we know the truth about the outcome of the cross. Death is but a temporary inconvenience that separates our smaller living from our greater being.
—Calvin Miller

Sign in undertaker's office: "Try our lay-away plan."
—*Farmer's Almanac*

May you be in heaven a full half hour before the Devil knows you're dead.
—Irish blessing

When I die, I want to go peacefully like my grandfather who died when the others in the car were screaming.

Old rockhounds never die; they just slowly petrify.

Old skiers never die, they just go downhill.

Old optometrists never die, they just lose their looks.

Old salesmen never die, they just lose their line.

Old tennis players never die, they just lose their bounce.

Old podiatrists never die, they just lose their souls.

Old postmen never die, they just lose their zip.

Old gardeners never die, they just spade away.

Old realtors never die, they just become listless.

Old hunters never die, they just stay loaded.

Old teachers never die, they just lose their class.

Old opticians never die, they just lose their contacts.

Old doctors never die, they just lose their patience.

Old architects never die, they just change their plans.

Old secretaries never die, they just lose their touch.

Old plumbers never die, they just drain away.

Old cooks never die, they just go to pot.

Old farmers never die, they just get plowed under.

Old bankers never die, they just lose their interest.

Old dentists never die, they just get down in the mouth.

Old fishermen never die, they just smell that way.

Old deans never die, they just lose their faculties.

Old policemen never die, they just take arrest.

Old quarterbacks never die, they just pass away.

Old statisticians never die, they just average out.

Old musicians never die, they just decompose.

Old accountants never die, they just lose their balance.

Old anesthesiologists never die, they just run out of gas.

Old procrastinators never die, they just keep putting it off.

Old quilters never die, they just go to pieces.

When D. L. Moody was rushed home to Massachusetts after a sudden illness during a western crusade, he said to his son, "Earth recedes, heaven opens before me. If this is death, it is sweet. There is no valley here. God is calling me and I must go. This is my coronation day. It is glorious."
—Leslie B. Flynn

Edwin Markham wrote of the death of Abraham Lincoln: His passing from the human scene was like the falling of a great tree, which in its falling left a lonesome place against the sky.

When infidel Tom Payne was dying, he was heard to utter, "O Lord, help! O Our Lord Jesus Christ, help!" His surprised doctor asked, "What's this I hear? Tom Payne. A man who spent his life ridiculing the

Christian faith and scoffing at the Lord Jesus Christ. As your physician, I ask you as a dying man, do you now repent of your infidel views and turn to this Christ for salvation?" Payne replied, "No, I cannot believe on that man." He died still an unbeliever.

—Leslie B. Flynn

When Robert G. Ingersoll's brother died, the world awaited what the great agnostic would say at his brother's grave. He had promised to deliver an oration. As he stood looking down on the casket holding all that remained of a brother he had dearly loved, the prepared speech dropped from his nerveless fingers like snowflakes falling on a barren forest. And then, on the waiting crowd there fell these words: "Life is a narrow vale between the cold and barren peaks of two eternities. We strive in vain to look beyond the heights. We cry aloud, and the only answer is the echo of a wailing cry."

About the same time, in Northfield, Massachusetts, D. L. Moody stood beside the body of his brother. In the middle of the funeral service, Moody stood up, looked on the dead face of his brother, and raised his hand and said, "O death, where is thy sting? O grave, where is thy victory? Thanks be to God which giveth us the victory through our Lord Jesus Christ."

Life is a dirty trick, a short journey from nothingness to nothingness. There is no remedy for anything in life. Man's destiny in the universe is like a colony of ants on a burning log.

—Ernest Hemingway

"You say you want the death certificate changed, doctor?" asked the puzzled clerk. "It's quite against the rules, you know."

"I know that, but it's important," said the physician. "You see, I was in a hurry and didn't pay any attention to the space marked 'Cause of Death,' and that's where I signed my name."

—Seng Fellowship News

Charles IX, king of France, exclaimed on his deathbed, "What blood, what murders, what evil counselors have I followed; I am lost; I see it well."

People today think they have robbed death of its sting by calling a cemetery a memorial park.

If I knew where I am going to die, I'd never go near the place.

A soldier was in a foxhole in Europe. He was in water up to his knees, and bullets were zipping by. A sergeant came up to him and called his name, "Private Smith."

"Yes sir."

"Report back to headquarters."

"Why?" asked the private.

"You're going home."

"What! And leave this foxhole?"

Death and what happens afterward is the only unresolved mystery.

—Robert Stack

Two friends met on the street. One said to the other, "Did you know that Sam died?"

"Is that right. Did he leave anything?"

"Yeah, everything!"

"Mankind is plagued with the two problems of sin and death," said Albert Camus, existential philosopher and atheist. He added that Christianity addresses these problems.

H. G. Wells, famed historian and philosopher, said at age sixty-one, "I have no peace. All life is at the end of its tether."

England's great poet, Lord Byron, who died at age thirty-six after a life of promiscuity and rebellion against his early religious teaching, wrote shortly before he died, "My days are in the sere and yellow leaf, the flowers and fruits of life are gone, the worm, the canker, and the grief are mine alone."

Henry David Thoreau, writer, poet, philosopher, and naturalist, admitted, "The mass of men live lives of quiet desperation."

Ralph Barton, the brilliant cartoonist, wrote before ending his own life, "I have had few difficulties, many friends, great successes; I have gone from wife to wife and from house to house, visited great countries of the world—but I am fed up with inventing devices to fill up twenty-four hours of the day."

Pascal, the seventeenth-century mathematician, philosopher, and author, declared, "There is a God-shaped vacuum in the heart of every man which only God can fill through His Son, Jesus Christ."

Elizabeth I, queen of England, on her deathbed was in great distress. The doctors could do nothing for her, but she continued to cry piteously, "I will give millions for another inch of time!" With ten thousand dresses in her wardrobe, a kingdom on which the sun never set, and with many servants, she had to leave them all.

Alexander the Great left orders that when he was carried to the grave, his hands should not be wrapped in the specially treated clothes used by the embalmers of that day, but rather be exposed to view so that all might see that they were empty!

Charles Simeon of Cambridge, on his dying bed, looked around with one of his bright smiles and asked, "What do you think especially gives me comfort at this time?" When those around him remained silent, he exclaimed, "The creation. I ask myself, did Jehovah create this world or did I? He did! Now if He made the world and all the rolling spheres of the universe, He certainly can take care of me. Into Jesus' hand I can safely commit my spirit!"

Hudson Taylor was so feeble in the closing months of his life that he wrote a dear friend, "I am so weak I cannot even pray. I can only lie still in God's arms like a little child and trust."

John Bacon, eminent eighteenth-century English sculptor, said on his deathbed,

"What I was as an artist seemed to be of some importance while I lived, but what I really am as a believer in the Lord Jesus Christ is the only thing of importance to me now."

Is death the last sleep? No, it is the final awakening.

—Sir Walter Scott

Death for the Christian is a turning off the light because the dawn has come.

—Leon Jaworski

When you are born, you cry and people rejoice. When you die, people cry, and, if you are saved, you rejoice.

When John Knox was dying, he took his wife's hand and asked, "Read to me that Scripture on which I first cast my anchor." In her last illness hymn writer Fanny Crosby remarked, "How can anyone call it a dark valley? It is all light and love." The dying words of Adoniram Judson, first missionary to Burma, were, "I go with the gladness of a boy bounding away from school. I feel so strong in Christ."

On her deathbed, Susanna Wesley uttered this last request before losing her speech, "Children, as soon as I am released, sing a psalm of praise to God." When her son, John Wesley, was about to die in his eighty-eighth year in extreme weakness, he astonished his friends by breaking out singing a stanza of a hymn which began, "I'll praise my Maker while I've breath."

—Leslie B. Flynn

If we knew as much about heaven as God does, we would clap our hands every time a Christian dies.

—George MacDonald

Pastor Maynard Belt told of an elderly Christian couple who were parted after more than fifty years of marriage when the husband finally succumbed to a fatal disease. When their pastor went to call on the bereaved wife, he found her sorrowing, yet triumphant. "I'm pleased to see you doing so well," he commented, "but I'm sure you miss your husband." "Oh, yes," she replied. "I miss him more than I ever could say. But I think of it this way. For years and years I would wait all day for Bill to come home from his job. I'd work busily about the house, and I'd look forward eagerly to the time he'd come through the front door. I'd have his dinner ready, and we would enjoy being together. All these years, I waited for him to come home, and now he's waiting for me to come home!"

Man's greatest enemy is death.
—Arnold Toynbee

John Wesley was asked why the Methodist movement was so successful. He answered, "Our people die well."

Only those are fit to live who are not afraid to die.

—Douglas MacArthur

Death is the golden chariot that ushers us into the presence of God.

—Tertullian

People have not learned to live who have not learned to die.

—Jim Elliot

A gravestone had the inscription, "I expected this, but not just yet."

The tragedy of life is not that we die, but is rather, as Albert Schweitzer said, "what dies inside a man while he lives."

I once saw a quaint inscription on a gravestone in an old British cemetery not far from Windsor Castle. It read:
Pause, my friend, as you walk by;
As you are now, so once was I.
As I am now, so you will be;
Prepare, my friend, to follow me!
I heard about a visitor who read that epitaph and added these lines:
To follow you is not my intent,
Until I know which way you went!
—Warren W. Wiersbe

C. S. Lewis's wife was witnessing to a woman who believed in the power of science. Mrs. Lewis asked, "Have you ever thought of death?" The woman answered, "No, but by the time I come to death, science will have done something about it."

In the ancient Ottoman Empire, the eastern emperors were crowned at Constantinople. The royal mason was always summoned in beforehand. He would set marble blocks in front of the coming monarch. Each sovereign would then choose one slab which would later become his tombstone. The point was that at the time of the coronation, he was also to consider his funeral.

John Wesley was asked by a friend, "Suppose you knew that you were to die by midnight tomorrow, John. How would you spend your time until then?" Wesley replied, "I would spend it exactly as I expect to spend it now. I would preach tonight in Glouchester. I would get up early tomorrow and proceed to Tewkesbury, where I would preach in the afternoon. Then I would go to the Martin's house in the evening, since they are expecting me. I would talk with Mr. Martin and pray with the family. Upon retiring, I would put myself in the Father's care, go to sleep, and wake up in heaven."

When John Owen, the great Puritan, lay on his deathbed, his secretary wrote (in his name) to a friend, "I am still in the land of the living." "Stop," said Owen. "Change that and say, 'I am yet in the land of the dying, but I hope soon to be in the land of the living.'"

—John M. Drescher

A young businesswoman, flushed with success, was opening a new branch office, and a friend decided to send a floral arrangement for the grand opening.
When he arrived at the opening, he was appalled to find that his wreath bore the inscription: "Rest in peace."
Angry, he complained to the florist. After apologizing, the florist said, "Look

at it this way—somewhere a man was buried under a wreath today that said, 'Good luck in your new location.'"

—*Bits & Pieces*

In 1846 John Quincy Adams suffered a stroke and, although he returned to Congress the following year, his health was clearly failing. Daniel Webster described his last meeting with Adams. "Someone, a friend of his, came in and made a particular inquiry of his health. Adams answered, 'I inhabit a weak, frail, decayed tenement; battered by the winds and broken in upon by the storms, and, from all I can learn, the landlord does not intend to repair.'"

—*The Little, Brown Book of Anecdotes*

He is foolish who says that death should not be feared, not because it will be painful to look forward to, for it is vain to be grieved in anticipation of that which distresses us not when it is present. Death . . . is nothing to us for while we are here, death is not; and when death is here, we are not.

—Epicurus

Benjamin Franklin composed this epitaph for himself:

The body of
B. Franklin, printer,
(Like the cover of an old book,
its contents torn out and
stripped of its lettering and guilding)
lies here, food for worms.
But the work shall not be lost;
for it will (as he believed)
appear once more,
in a new and more elegant edition
revised and corrected
by the Author.

A fellow who didn't want to die, said, "Yes, I'm a Christian and I have eternal life, but I'm not homesick yet."

We are apprentices and have not served our time out. We are students and have not got our diplomas. Death is not a graduation; it is a Commencement Day!"

—T. De Witt Talmage

Death is the king of terrors and the terror of kings.

Fifty persons were killed in the crash of a United Airlines passenger plane in the hills above Oakland, California, on Friday, August 24, 1951. A book was found in the wreckage entitled, "From Here to Eternity." That title told the significant part of the tragic story.

When the son of the Duke of Hamlin lay dying, triumphant in Christ, he called his younger brother to his side and said, "Douglas, I am dying now; I am leaving you. In a little while you will inherit Father's property and the homestead. And that isn't all. Douglas, you will also inherit Father's title; and by and by they will call you the Duke of Hamlin. But, Douglas, when you are the Duke, I shall be a king." That is truly the destiny of every child of God, whether he lives in a palace or a poorhouse.

An aged Scotsman, while dying, was asked what he thought of death and he replied, "It matters little to me whether I live or die. If I die I will be with Jesus, and if I live Jesus will be with me."

Epitaph in a graveyard in England:
I have sinned;
I have repented;
I have trusted;
I have loved;
I rest;
I shall rise;
I shall reign.

—D. L. Moody

The pastor of a church visited a family whose son had been killed in an automobile accident. He heard the mother rail out at him, "Where was your God when my boy was killed?" He quietly said, "The same place He was when His Son was killed."

—Roger Lovette

Winston Churchill had planned his funeral which took place in Saint Paul's Cathedral. He included many great hymns of the church and used the eloquent Anglican liturgy. At his direction, a bugler, positioned high in the dome of Saint Paul's, intoned after the benediction the sound of "Taps," the universal signal that says the day is over.

But then came the most dramatic turn; as Churchill instructed, as soon as "Taps" was finished, another bugler who was placed on the other side of the great dome played the notes of "Reveille"—"It's time to get up, it's time to get up, it's time to get up in the morning."

That was Churchill's last testimony that at the end of history the last note will not be "Taps"; it will be "Reveille." The worst things are never the last things.

—John Claypool

When Xerxes, the Persian king, was marching with his immense army to invade Greece, he came to the Hellespont. There, before crossing into Macedonia, within sight of the blue waters of the Strait, he ordered a grand review of his troops. A throne was erected for the monarch on the hillside, and seating himself on the marble chair, he surveyed his million soldiers in the fields below. With a proud smile, he turned to his courtiers and confessed that he was the happiest man on earth. He truly had some cause for pride.

But before long, the king's countenance changed, and those who had stood by him saw the tears beginning to trickle down his cheeks. One of them asked why his joy had turned so soon to sorrow. "Alas!" said Xerxes, "I am thinking that of all this vast host, not one will be alive in a hundred years."

When a former President of the United States was eighty years of age, an old friend shook his trembling hand and said, "Good morning, and how is John Quincy Adams today?" The retired chief executive looked at him for a moment and then replied, "He himself is quite well, sir, quite well. But the house in which he lives at the present is becoming dilapidated. It is tottering upon its foundation. Time and the seasons have almost destroyed it. Its roof is pretty well worn, its walls are much shattered, and it crumbles a little bit with every wind. The old tenement is becoming almost uninhabitable, and I think John Quincy Adams will have to move out of it soon; but he himself is well, sir, quite well!" It was not long afterward that he had his second and fatal stroke.

Death is a universal conspiracy, not to be mentioned.

—H. L. Mencken

Donald Grey Barnhouse was driving his children to the funeral of their mother. A semi-tractor trailer crossed in front of them at an intersection, momentarily casting a shadow on the car, and Barnhouse asked his children, "Would you rather be struck by the semi or by the shadow?"

"The shadow, of course," they replied.

"That's what has happened to us," Barnhouse said. "Mother's dying is only the shadow of death. The lost sinner is struck by the semi of death."

The statistics on death are quite impressive. One out of one people die.

—George Bernard Shaw

Walter C. Wilson was talking to an atheist who said, "I do not believe, Dr. Wilson, what you are preaching." Wilson said, "You have told me what you do not believe; perhaps you will tell me what you do believe."

The man replied, "I do believe that death ends all." "So do I," Wilson said. "What! You believe death ends all?" "I certainly do," he answered. "Death ends all your chance of doing evil; death ends all your joy; death ends all your projects, all your ambitions, all your friendships; death ends all the Gospel you will ever hear; death ends it all for you, and you go out into outer darkness.

"As for myself, death ends all my wanderings, all my tears, all my perplexities, all my disappointments, all my aches and pains; death ends it all, and I go to be with my Lord in glory."

"I never thought of it that way," he said.

Wilson led the man to Christ by just agreeing with him that death ends all.

When I'm gone, speak less of William Carey and more of William Carey's Savior.
—William Carey

Just before he died F. B. Meyer wrote to his wife, "Dear, I have just learned to my surprise that I have only a few days to live. It may be that before this reaches you, I will have entered the Palace. We shall meet in the morning."

London had seldom witnessed such a funeral service. The vast audience rose with bowed heads. To their surprise, the organ swung into the triumphant notes of the Hallelujah Chorus. A faithful soldier of the cross had entered into the King's presence.

Jean-Paul Sartre's last years were not full of life; he merely and barely existed. "In the 1970s Sartre was an increasingly pathetic figure, prematurely aged, virtually blind, often drunk, worried about money, uncertain about his views . . . incontinent . . . the struggle for power over what was left of his mind. It must have been a relief to them (his few friends) when he died on April 15, 1980."
—*Wilson Quarterly*

One day A. C. Gaebelein saw a combined tailor's shop and dyeing establishment. In the window was this sign:
  I Live to Dye; I Dye to Live
  The More I Dye the Better I Live
  The More I Live the Better I Dye
There is great spiritual truth in the sound of these words, and in their writing too, if the spelling d-y-e is changed to d-i-e.

Recently I received a letter from a Radio Bible Class listener and it warmed my heart. A woman wanted to tell us about the homegoing of a loved one, and she wrote, "Last month my mother went to heaven. She was ninety-five and a blessing to everyone who met her. Your broadcasts and literature blessed her life for so many years." The writer went on to share what

her seven-year-old son had said about the passing of that dear saint of God. Expressing his great love and admiration for her, he remarked with childish glee, "I'll bet Jesus was glad to see Grandma!"
—R. W. De Haan

The story is told of an ancient king who summoned a group of scholars to his palace to write a history of mankind. They compiled many volumes, but the king was too busy to read them. But with the onset of old age he again summoned the historians to the palace and told them to give him just a summary of their findings. A spokesman for the group said, "Man was born, he suffered, he died. That is the history of mankind."

In A.D. 125, Publius Aristides sent a letter to an acquaintance to give this explanation for the rapid spread of Christianity. "If any righteous man among the Christians passes from this world, they rejoice and offer thanks to God, and they escort his body with songs and thanksgiving as if he were setting out from one place to another nearby."

I am prepared to meet my maker. Whether my maker is prepared for the great ordeal of meeting me is another matter.
—Winston Churchill

In just a few words the novelist Charles Williams summed up one of his characters. "He passed a not unsuccessful life in his profession; the only intruder he found himself unable to deal with was death."

I know that everyone must die but I always thought an exception could be made in my case. Now what do I do?
—William Saroyan

When I was a sixth grader, an elderly lady visited our one-room country schoolhouse on a community event. Though energetic and full of zest for life, she was somewhat stooped, her hair was white, and her face lined with wrinkles. After she left, one of the boys loudly said, "I never want to get old." The teacher, a bitter unbeliever, countered with the words, "Do you want to die young?" "No," the boy replied. "Well," came the sharp retort, "You will either die young or grow old and die. There are no alternatives." These words made a deep impression on me. I was but a boy, but even young children think about death. The tone of utter despair in my teacher's voice sent chills down my spine. Without Christ the future is dismal indeed.

—Harold Van Lugt

What would you do if you knew you only had one day left to live? That's what Gunther Klempnaier asked 625 young German students in twelve vocational schools. His findings revealed that 20 percent of the young men questioned would spend their last day on earth drinking, taking drugs, and pursuing young women.

A different response came from an eighteen-year-old woman who wrote, "I would like to spend my last evening in church (to be alone with God) to thank Him for a full and happy life."

The idea of death, the fear of it, haunts the human animal like nothing else; it is a mainspring of human activity—activity designed largely to avoid the fatality of death, to overcome it by denying in some way that it is the final destiny for man. . . . Of all things that move men, one of the principal ones is the terror of death.

—Ernest Becker

When Harry and Nancy Goehring went to Bangladesh as missionaries, their desire was to see Bengali people become Christians. They did not know that God would use Harry's death at age thirty-two to bring at least one of those people to Christ.

As the friends of the Goehrings met with Nancy and the children to comfort them, Debindra Das, a Bengali laundryman who had become a Christian, spoke with his wife Promilla about Harry's death. He said, "I was ironing the clothes in the hallway. I could see Goehring Sahib through the open door. I watched his face. I watched him die! Not like when Hindus die. You know how our people die—fearing death."

Promilla was impressed. Because of that simple testimony of a Christian's peaceful homegoing, she asked the Lord to save her that very night. That Hindu woman was the firstfruit of a death that had seemed so untimely.

—*Our Daily Bread*

Philosopher Jean Jacques Rousseau declared, "No man can come to the throne of God and say 'I'm a better man than Rousseau.'" When he knew that death was close at hand, he boasted, "Ah, how happy a thing it is to die, when one has no reason for remorse or self-reproach." Then he prayed, "Eternal Being, the soul that I am going to give Thee back is as pure at this moment as it was when it proceeded from Thee; render it a partaker of Thy Felicity!" This is an amazing statement when we realize that Rousseau didn't confess to be born again. In his writings, he advocated adultery and suicide, and for more than twenty years he lived in licentiousness. Most of his children were born out of wedlock and sent to a foundling home.

In my native village in New England it used to be customary as a funeral procession left the church for the bell to toll the number of years that had been enjoyed by the deceased. How anxiously I would count those strokes to see how long I might reckon living! Sometimes there would be seventy or eighty tolls, and I would give a sigh of relief to think that perhaps I had so many years ahead of me. But at other times the bell would ring only a few times and then a horror would seize me as I thought that I too might soon be claimed as a victim.

—D. L. Moody

A grandmother lost her granddaughter by drowning. Grieving deeply, she said, "Life will never be the same without her, but heaven has never seemed more real."

English physicist and chemist Michael Faraday (1791–1867) was asked, "Have you ever pondered yourself what will be your occupation in the next world?"

Faraday hesitated awhile and then responded, "I shall be with Christ, and that is enough."

—*Our Daily Bread*

King Philip of Macedon, father of Alexander the Great, had a palace servant whose duty it was to approach him every morning with the greeting, "Philip, remember that you must die."

Making sense of life means, ultimately and always, making sense of death.

—J. S. Whale

In his book *After Death, What?* William B. Ward says that a nationally known radio minister asked his listeners to suggest topics for radio sermons. Of those who responded, 70 percent asked for messages dealing with life after death.

Mary Roscoe of Greenwich, New York, was at Voltaire's bedside during the days and hours before his death. She said he repudiated his book, *Age of Reason,* and asked if she had ever read it. She replied that she read it when she was very young, but that it so depressed her that she threw it in the fire. Voltaire allegedly said, "I wish I had done as you, for if ever the Devil has had any agency in any work, he has had it in my writing that book." Mary Roscoe reported that in his final hours Voltaire said repeatedly, "O Lord! Lord God! Lord have mercy on me!"

During the Civil War a soldier lay dying of a bad wound. A minister came to speak to him and he said, "Are you afraid to die?" Rising from his bed on his elbow he exclaimed emphatically in vehemence, "Are you here to insult me? Of course I'm not afraid to die. I've faced death many times before."

"Yes, but are you afraid of what comes after death?"

Quietly and solemnly he replied, "Yes, that's it."

Wilson Mizner was a celebrated wit and card shark. His biography makes interesting reading, but no one with a sense of moral values would admire or envy him.

He authored many proverbs, a few of which are still found in common usage. A sampling: "The first hundred years are the hardest." "Be nice to people on the way up because you'll meet them on the way down." "A good listener is not only popular, but after awhile, he knows something."

In 1933, at the age of fifty-eight, he suffered a serious heart attack. When he regained consciousness in the hospital, he asked for a priest, a rabbi, and a Protestant minister. His explanation: "I want to hedge my bets!"

A few days later, when an oxygen tent was brought into his room, he cracked, "This looks like the main event." Motioning away the priest who tried to talk to him, he said, "Why should I talk to you? I've just been talking to your boss."

When the priest reproached him for his levity at such a critical time, it occasioned Mizner's final quip: "What? No two-week notice?"

Within moments he was in eternity.

—John A. Jess

The natives in Kenya have a dialogue called "Alafu?" meaning "And then?" It is generally put on by two teenage boys and goes like this:

"What are you going to do when you grow up?"

"I will learn a trade."

"And then?"

"And then I'll get a job."

"And then?"

"And then I'll earn a lot of shillings."

"And then?"

"And then I'll get married."

"And then?"

"And then I'll have some children."

"And then?"

"And then I'll raise them."

"And then?"

"And then I'll become a grandfather."

"And then?"

"And then perhaps I'll be made chief."

"And then?"

"And then I'll rule the people."

"And then?"

"And then—and then—and then I'll be an old man."

"And then?"

"And then—and then—and then . . . Oh, don't ask anymore."

At this point the one who has been asking questions points his finger at the sky and says with great emphasis, "You should be thinking of life and death and your soul while you're still young."

An Arab awakened in the middle of the night and was very hungry. He lit a candle and began to eat the dates beside his bed. He took one, held it up to the light, and saw that a worm was in it. So he threw it out of the tent. He took a second, held it up to the light, saw another worm, and threw it away. The same thing happened a third time. Finally, he blew out the candle, grabbed the dates and stuffed them into his mouth, not wanting to face reality.

I am not afraid to die. I just don't want to be there when it happens.

—Woody Allen

Writers H. G. Wells and George Bernard Shaw were brilliant men, yet they rejected the message of Scripture. They placed their trust in their own systems of belief, which were based on human reason. Yet they could not find lasting inner peace and they slowly lost confidence in what they believed. Wells' final literary work, for example, has been aptly called a "scream of despair." And shortly before Shaw died in 1950 he wrote, "The science to which I pinned my faith is bankrupt. . . . Its counsels, which should have established the millennium, have led directly to the suicide of Europe. I believed them once . . . In their name I helped to destroy the faith of millions. . . . And now they look at me and witness the great tragedy of an atheist who has lost his faith."

Death is the debt we must all pay.

—Euripedes

During World War II a London church group gave a farewell party for some soldiers who were returning to the combat zone on the continent. At the conclusion a young officer known for his wise choice of words became a spokesman for the group to thank people for the send-off. After expressing the men's appreciation, he hesitated, and, as if seeking something to say in closing, he added, "We're leaving for France, the trenches, and maybe to die." He hadn't intended to say that, and he was somewhat embarrassed, but then he blurted out, "Can anyone here tell us how to die?"

There was an awkward silence, then someone walked to the piano and began to sing the aria from *Elijah*. "O rest in the Lord!" That was the answer. It still is!

You are well? That's fine.

You hope to remain that way? That's natural.

You may be disappointed! That's possible.

You will die! That's sure.

You'd better get ready! That's wisdom.

You want to be right? That's promising.

You don't know the way? Then listen—

Accept, believe, receive.

A visitor asked an old-timer, "What's the death rate here?" The old-timer replied, "Same as back east: one to a person."

Odds that you will eventually die in a car crash: 1 in 125.

Odds that you will develop a brain tumor: 1 in 25,000.

Odds that you will die in a fire this year: 1 in 400,000.

Odds that you will win a state lottery jackpot: 1 in 4,000,000.

—*Today in the Word*

A doctor had a sign on her office door that read, "When you're at death's door, I'll pull you through."

An inscription at the exit of the cemetery beneath the Santa Maria della Concezione church on Via Veneto in Rome reads, "What you are, we used to be; what we are, you will be."

One time when Joseph Bayly was flying from Chicago to Los Angeles, he conversed with a woman sitting next to him on the plane. She was about forty years of age, and well-dressed. He asked her, "Where are you from?" She said, "Palm Springs." Knowing that Palm Springs was a city of the rich and famous, he asked, "What is Palm Springs like?" She answered, "It is a beautiful, beautiful place filled with unhappy people." He then asked, "Are you unhappy?" She responded, "Yes, I certainly am." "Why?" "Mortality."

An inscription on a tombstone read, "I told you I was sick."

Many people think that we are now in the land of the living and are going to the land of the dying. But Christians are in the land of the dying and are going to the land of the living.

At dusk, a little girl entered a cemetery. An old man who sat at the gate said to her, "Aren't you afraid to go through the cemetery in the dark?" "Oh no," she replied, "my home is just on the other side."
—Henry Dwibanville

DEATH—OF CHILDREN

When Jim Elliot preached at the funeral of his own son, he said, "God is not populating heaven just with old men."

DECEPTION

A medical student spent his summer vacation working as a butcher in the daytime and a hospital orderly in the evenings. Both jobs, of course, involved wearing a white smock. One evening he was instructed to wheel a patient on a stretcher into surgery. The patient, a woman, looked up at the student and let out an earthly scream. "Oh, no," she wailed, "it's my butcher!"

Paul Harvey tells how an Eskimo kills a wolf. He coats his knife with blood and lets it freeze. Then he adds another coat of blood and then another. As each coat freezes, he adds another smear of blood until the blade is coated over by layers of frozen blood.

Then he buries the knife—blade up—

in the frozen tundra. The wolf catches the scent of fresh blood and begins to lick it. He licks it more feverishly until the blade is bare. Then he keeps on licking harder. Because of the cold, he never notices the pain of the blade on his tongue. His craving for the taste of blood is so great that he licks the blade till he bleeds to death, swallowing his own life.

At one point in a debate, Abraham Lincoln was accused by his opponent, Douglas, of being two-faced. "I leave it to my audience," replied Lincoln. "If I had two faces, would I be wearing this one?"

DECISIONS

The hardest thing in life to learn is which bridges to cross and which ones to burn.
—David Russell

My life is not made by the dreams I dream but by the choices I make.

The degree of maturity a person attains is directly proportional to his ability to make wise decisions.

One-half the troubles of this life can be traced to saying yes too quickly and not saying no soon enough.
—Josh Billings

A man's judgment is no better than his information.
—*Bits & Pieces*

Half the worry in the world is caused by people trying to make decisions before they have sufficient knowledge on which to base a decision.
—Dean Hawkes

If I had to sum up in one word what makes a good manager, I'd say decisiveness. You can use the fanciest computers to gather the numbers, but in the end you have to set a timetable and *act*.
—Lee J. Iacocca

When, against one's will, one is high-pressured into making a hurried decision, the best answer is always "no," because "no" is more easily changed to "yes" than "yes" is to "no."

—Charles E. Nielsen

DEDICATION

Sam Jones was a preacher who held revival services which he called "quittin' meetings." His preaching was directed primarily to Christians, and he urged them to give up sinful practices in their lives. Sam's messages were very effective, and many people promised to quit swearing, drinking, smoking, lying, gossiping, or anything else that was displeasing to the Lord.

On one occasion Jones asked a woman, "Just what is it that you're quittin'?" She replied, "I'm guilty of not doing anything— and I'm going to quit doing that too!" Even though she had no habits to give up, she wasn't actively living to please God.

Christ has no hands but our hands to do
   His work today.
He has no feet but our feet to lead men in
   His way.
He has no tongue but our tongues to tell
   men how He died.
He has no help but our help to bring them
   to His side.

When Julius Caesar landed on the shores of Britain with his Roman legions, he took a bold and decisive step to ensure the success of his military venture. Ordering his men to halt on the edge of the Cliffs of Dover, he commanded them to look down at the water below. To their amazement, they saw every ship in which they had crossed the channel engulfed in flames. Caesar had deliberately cut off any possibility of retreat! Now that his soldiers were unable to return to the continent, there was nothing left for them to do but advance and conquer! And that is exactly what they did.

One day while walking with some children, Queen Mary was caught in a sudden shower. Quickly taking shelter on the porch of a home, she knocked at the door and asked to borrow an umbrella. "I'll send it back tomorrow," she said. The queen had deliberately disguised her appearance by putting on a hat that partly covered her face and by wearing very plain clothing. The householder, reluctant to give a stranger her best umbrella, offered her a castoff she found in the attic. One rib was broken and there were several holes in it. Apologizing, she turned it over to the monarch, whom she did not recognize. The next day she had another visitor—a man with a gold braid on his uniform and an envelope in his hand. "The queen sent me with this letter," he said, "and also asked me to thank you personally for the loan of your umbrella." Stunned, the woman burst into tears. "Oh, what opportunity I missed that I did not give her my very best," she cried.

At a religious festival in Brazil a missionary was going from booth to booth, examining the wares. He saw a sign above one booth: "Cheap Crosses." He thought to himself, "That's what many Christians are looking for these days—cheap crosses. My Lord's cross was not cheap. Why should mine be?"

When someone complimented J. Hudson Taylor on the work of the China Inland Mission that he had founded, he said, "It seemed to me that God had looked over the whole world to find a man who was weak enough to do His work, and when He at last found me, He said, 'He is weak enough—he'll do.' All God's giants have been weak men who did great things for God because they reckoned on His being with them."

God's plan took priority in eighteen-year-old Jonathon Edwards's life. He wrote in his journal, "Resolved that all men should live to the glory of God. Resolved secondly that, whether or not anyone else does, I will."

A gathering of friends at an English estate nearly turned to tragedy when one of the children strayed into deep water. The gardener heard the cries for help, plunged in, and rescued the drowning child. That youngster's name was Winston Churchill.

His grateful parents asked the gardener what they could do to reward him. He hesitated, then said, "I wish my son could go to college someday and become a doctor." "We'll see to it," Churchill's parents promised.

Years later, while Sir Winston Churchill was prime minister of England, he was stricken with pneumonia. The country's best physician was summoned. His name was Alexander Fleming, the man who discovered and developed penicillin. He was also the son of that gardener who had saved young Winston from drowning. Later Churchill remarked, "Rarely has one man owed his life twice to the same person."

—*Our Daily Bread*

A young man, some years ago, lay dying. His mother believed him to be a Christian and was greatly surprised and distressed one day when, on passing his room, she heard him say, "Lost! Lost! Lost!"

Immediately she opened the door and cried, "My boy, is it possible you have lost hope in Christ, now that you are dying?"

"No, Mother, no!" he replied, "it is not that. I have a hope beyond the grave but I have lost my life! Twenty-four years I have lived and done nothing for the Son of God, and now I am going! My life has been spent for self. I have lived for this world—and now—while dying, I have given myself to Christ—but my life is lost!"

The Spanish ship *Girona* was on its way to Scotland from Ireland, seeking refuge for its thirteen hundred passengers and crew. She was a forlorn survivor of the great Armada which had set out in that year of 1588 to conquer England. On board was a young nobleman who wore a betrothal ring given to him on the eve of his departure from Spain by his young lover. The ring was a symbol of the gift of herself to him. But the *Girona* never reached Scotland. A wild storm drove the ship onto the jagged rocks, and it was broken in two. All but five men perished, including the young nobleman. Centuries later Robert Stenuit located the wreck and found the keepsake ring. Carved on it was a tiny hand offering

a heart and these words, "No tengo mas que darte" ("I have nothing more to give you"). A wise commentator has remarked, "Christ wants to hear that same confession from each of us who are His children."

Napoleon stood before his troops and asked for one hundred men to take the lead in an endeavor that seemed doomed to failure. He told them that every man would doubtless be killed the moment the enemy opened fire. Would any dare to respond to this call? Lifting his voice, Napoleon said, "Who will die for his emperor? Advance out of the ranks!" It is said that in response the whole regiment, as one man, instantly sprang forward.

Shamgar had an ox goad, Rahab had a string;
Gideon had a trumpet, David had a sling;
Samson had a jawbone, Moses had a rod;
Dorcas had a needle, But all were used of
    God.

I learned from William Booth that the greatness of man's power is his measure of surrender.

—J. Wilbur Chapman

Years ago two young men heard of a Caribbean island where 3,000–4,000 African slaves were kept isolated from the Gospel by their godless master. The two men realized that they could share the story of Christ with these people only by becoming slaves themselves. So they sold themselves into slavery and used the money to buy the one-way ticket to this island. As they pulled out of the harbor, never to see their families and friends again, they clasped arms. One shouted across the water, "To win for the Lamb that was slain the reward of his sufferings."

—*Wherever*

William Booth was asked by Dr. Chapman, "What's the secret of your success?" He answered, "I was so concerned for London, I gave God everything."

Jakob Mendelssohn, the great musician, once visited the Freiburg Cathedral when the regular organist was practicing. Mendelssohn asked whether he might play a few bars. At first the organist, not knowing the visitor, refused the request, but on second thought acceded, though somewhat reluctantly.

Mendelssohn began to play. The cathedral's organist listened in ecstasy and then, placing his hand on Mendelssohn's shoulder, asked, "Who are you?"

"Mendelssohn," was the answer.

"Oh!" the organist exclaimed. "To think that I almost refused to let the great Mendelssohn play for me!"

How foolish it is for Christians to refuse to allow Christ to have full control over their lives.

Centuries ago the Spanish general, Pizzarro, neared the border of Peru. Calling his men together, he traced a line in the sand and announced, "Comrades, on that side there is toil, hunger, the drenching storm, and possible death; on this side is ease and leisure. There lies Peru and its riches; here lies Panama and its poverty. Each man must choose whether to go or stay. For my part, I go to Peru!"

A mission board once wrote to David Livingstone, "Have you found a good road to where you are in Africa? If so, we want to know how to send other men to join you." Livingstone responded, "If you have men who will come only if there is a good road, I do not want them. I want those who will come if there is no road at all!"

Robert Robinson, a Christian, had strayed from the Lord. One day, while he was in a stagecoach, a woman seated next to him was reading poetry. She couldn't understand a poem she was reading so she asked Mr. Robinson if he would explain it. As he looked at the poem, he glanced across the page and saw his own poem with the words, "Prone to wander, Lord, I feel it." Those words caused him to rededicate his life right then.

One day a man decided to go out to the beach for the afternoon. He went out to get his young son to go with him, who was playing in his sandbox. The son insisted on taking a bucket of sand with him, in spite of what his father said about how much sand there was at the beach. Finally the boy believed, and to his delight found sand along the beach as far as the eye could see.

Are we persisting on carrying along a little bucket of sand, little things in our lives that we refuse to give up?

Jim Elliot was a classmate of mine in college. He was a young wrestler, good-looking, and tough of body. He was also a deeply spiritual young man. Every morning he arose at five or five-thirty and read his Bible and made notes in his diary. One day, in his praying about the people overseas, he thought to himself, "Why shouldn't I go? There is one minister for every 500 people in the United States, and one for every 500,000 overseas. Why shouldn't I go?" And he went. He went to the Auca Indians in Ecuador and he was murdered. After his death, they found, scattered along the shore, a river-soaked diary. In it Jim Elliot had written, "Make me a crisis man, O Lord; not just a sign-post on the highway of life, but a fork in the road so that men who meet me will come to know Jesus Christ."

—Ernest J. Lewis

Ye call Me Master and obey Me not;
Ye call Me Light and see Me not;
Ye call Me Way and walk Me not;
Ye call Me Life and desire Me not;
Ye call Me Wise and follow Me not;
Ye call Me Fair and love Me not;
Ye call Me Rich and ask Me not;
Ye call Me Eternal and seek Me not;
Ye call Me Gracious and trust Me not;
Ye call Me Noble and serve Me not;
Ye call Me God and fear Me not.
These solemn thoughts of admonition are in the Cathedral of Lubeck, Germany.

Give me one hundred men who love nothing but God, hate nothing but evil, and know nothing but Jesus Christ, and I will change the world.

—John Wesley

DEDICATION

When James Calvert sailed to the Fiji Islands as a missionary, the captain of the ship said, "You shouldn't do this. You and those with you will be killed." Calvert replied, "We died before we came."

An early Greek general, looking over a hastily conscripted conglomerate army, was heard to remark to his lieutenant, "Would that I had as many soldiers as I had men."

If you are thinking of becoming a Christian, I warn you. You are embarking on something that is going to take the whole of you.

—C. S. Lewis

Dedication is writing your name on the bottom of a blank sheet and handing it to the Lord for Him to fill in.

A woman in India stood by a heathen temple in process of construction. Someone asked her the cost of the temple. She looked in surprise at the questioner, a missionary, and said, "Why, we don't know. It is for our god. We don't count the cost."

John Wesley traveled on horseback the equivalent of ten times around the world's equator. He preached as often as fifteen times a week for fifty years. He authored more publications than any writer in the English language until the contemporary science fiction writer Isaac Asimov. He read books while making his horseback journeys. When he was past eighty, he complained that he could not read and work more than fifteen hours a day.

—John Haggai

Francis Xavier left wealth and position and set out across the world with the message of redemption through Christ Jesus. It took energy for him to labor twenty-one hours out of twenty-four, to learn to preach in twenty different languages in ten short years, to beg passage on a troop ship, and later sail with pirates in unsafe vessels. It took energy for him to sleep in tents with the Bedouins, cross the burning deserts and the snowy ranges of Asia. It took energy for Xavier to dare death in every form, shake hands with every ailment and disease, endure the pangs of hunger and horrors of thirst after a decimating shipwreck and bitter persecution. But he made a great impact on Japan.

Bertoldo de Giovanni was an important sculptor but none of his work has lasted. His chief claim to fame is as a historical connector. He was the pupil of Donatello, the greatest sculptor of his time, and the teacher of Michelangelo, the greatest sculptor of all time.

Michelangelo was only fourteen years old when he come to Bertoldo, but it was already obvious that he was enormously gifted. Bertoldo was wise enough to realize that gifted people are often tempted to coast rather than to grow, and therefore he kept trying to pressure his young prodigy to work seriously at his art. One day, he came into the studio to find Michelangelo toying with a piece of sculpture far beneath his abilities. Bertoldo grabbed a hammer, stomped across the room, and smashed the work into tiny pieces, shouting his unforgettable message: "Michelangelo, talent is cheap, dedication is costly!"

—Gary Inrig

When God wants to drill a man,
And thrill a man,
And skill a man;
When God wants to mold a man
To play the noblest part,
When he yearns with all his heart
To create so great and bold a man
That all the world shall be amazed,
Watch his methods, watch his ways—
How he ruthlessly perfects
Whom he royally elects.
How he hammers him and hurts him,
And with mighty blows, converts him
Into trial shapes of clay
Which only God understands,
While his tortured heart is crying,
And he lifts beseeching hands.
How he bends but never breaks
When his good he undertakes.
How he uses

Whom he chooses,
And with every purpose, fuses him,
By every act, induces him
To try his splendor out.
God knows what he's about.

It is said that Cyrus, the founder of the Persian Empire, once had captured a prince and his family. When they came before him, the monarch asked the prisoner, "What will you give me if I release you?" "The half of my wealth," was his reply. "And if I release your children?" "Everything I possess." "And if I release your wife?" "Your Majesty, I will give myself." Cyrus was so moved by his devotion that he freed them all. As they returned home, the prince said to his wife, "Wasn't Cyrus a handsome man." With a look of deep love for her husband, she said to him, "I didn't notice. I could only keep my eyes on you— the one who was willing to give himself for me."

Many years ago a young man went out to China as a Christian missionary on an annual salary of about $2,500. He was so outstanding that there was competition for his services. A commercial concern wanted him, so they offered him $5,000 salary, but he declined. They raised it to $7,000. When he declined again, they raised it to $10,000, but he refused this, also.

They couldn't understand, so they asked why he refused. He said he preferred to stay with the job he had. They asked if it was a question of the salary not being enough. He answered, "Oh, the salary is big enough, but the job isn't."

—Clarence W. Kemper

DEFEAT

If you want to be distressed, look within.
If you want to be defeated, look back.
If you want to be distracted, look around.
If you want to be dismayed, look before.
If you want to be delivered, look to Christ.
If you want to be delighted, look up.

DELAYS

The word "posthaste" dates back to the days of Henry VIII when some messengers with mail irresponsibly stopped on the road to play games or dilly-dally in some other way. Therefore a law was passed decreeing death by hanging for any dispatch-carrier who delayed the mail. Thus letters of the sixteenth century were often ornamented with a drawing of a messenger suspended from the gallows with this admonition printed beneath, "Haste, post, haste! Haste for thy life!"

—Leslie B. Flynn

DELEGATION

The most successful executives carefully select understudies. They don't strive to do everything themselves. They train and trust others. This leaves them foot-free, mind-free, with time to think. They have time to receive important callers, to pay worthwhile visits. They have time for their families. No matter how able, any employer or executive who insists on running a one-man enterprise courts unhappy circumstances when his powers dwindle.

—B.C. Forbes

Because a thing seems difficult for you, do not think it impossible for anyone to accomplish.

—Marcus Aurelius

The phrase "Let George do it" was coined over 450 years ago by King Louis XII of France.

The king had a prime minister, named George D'Amboise, who was so able that the king delegated an increasing number of vexing problems to this trusted assistant. The monarch thus left himself free to attend to other royal duties.

Don't tell a man how to do a thing. Tell him what you want done, and he'll surprise you by his ingenuity.

—General George Patton

The best executive is the one who has enough sense to pick good men to do what he wants done and self-restraint enough to keep from meddling with them while they do it.

—Theodore Roosevelt

DELUSION

In a day of illusions
And other confusions,
Upon their delusions
They base their conclusions.

DENOMINATIONS

During an interfaith conference, someone shouted, "The building is on fire!"

Methodists gathered in a corner and prayed.

Baptists cried, "Where's the water?"

Quakers quietly praised God for the blessings that fire brings.

Lutherans posted a notice on the door declaring, in no uncertain terms, that fire was evil.

Roman Catholics passed the offering plate to cover the damages.

Jews posted symbols on the doorposts hoping that the fire would pass over.

Congregationalists shouted, "Every man for himself!"

Fundamentalists proclaimed, "Fire is the vengeance of God!"

Christian Scientists agreed among themselves there was no fire.

Presbyterians appointed a chairperson who was to appoint a committee to look into the matter and make a written report to the Session.

Episcopalians formed a procession and marched out.

DENTISTS

Dr. Bill Hanson, a dentist and a church organist in Dallas, says his favorite hymn is "Crown Him with Many Crowns."

DEPENDABILITY

The greatest ability is dependability.
—Bob Jones

Thomas J. Jackson inspired General Barnard Bee to point his sword toward Jackson's tall, prominent figure and shout, "There's Jackson, standing like a stone wall! Rally behind the Virginians!" Stonewall Jackson was a patient and courteous instructor, but the thing that won the abiding affection and love of his men was his dependability.

When the conflict between the States broke out, a young man who was engaged to a beautiful New England girl was one of the first to be called into service. Their marriage therefore had to be postponed. He managed to get through most of the conflict uninjured, but finally in the Battle of the Wilderness he was severely wounded. The young lady of his heart, not knowing of his condition, was counting the days until he returned. She waited for word from him, but no more letters came. At last she received one addressed in a strange handwriting which read: "There has been another terrible battle. It is very difficult for me to tell you this, but I have lost both my arms! I cannot write myself, but a comrade is penning this for me. While you are as dear to me as ever, I shall now be dependent on other people for the rest of my days and I feel I should therefore release you from the obligation of our engagement."

This letter was never answered. Taking the next train, the young woman went directly to the scene of the late conflict and sent word to the captain concerning the purpose of her errand. The man was sympathetic and gave her directions where she might find the soldier's cot. Tearfully she went along the lines of the wounded looking for her love. The moment her eyes fell upon him, she threw her arms around the young man's neck and kissed him. "I will never give you up!" she cried. "These hands of mine will help you; I am able to support you, I will take care of you!"

He that is too big to do little things willingly is too little to be trusted with big things.

DEPENDENCE ON GOD

Our efficiency turns out to be a deficiency unless we have God's sufficiency.
—*The Vance Havner Quote Book*

A little boy was tugging at a big rock and doing his best to lift it. He was grunting and pulling but it didn't budge. His father came along and asked him if he was having any trouble. He said, "Yes, I am trying and trying and can't move the rock." The father said to him, "Well, Son, are you using all available energy?" The boy replied, "Yes, Father, I think I am." Then the dad looked at him and said, "No, Son, I don't think you are, for you haven't asked for my help."

So it is with us. We think we are unable to overcome or surmount some obstacle, but perhaps it is because we haven't prayed about it. We haven't asked for our Father's help.

—Rives Baptist Church bulletin

DEPRESSION

The Russian novelist Leo Tolstoy found his life going stale when he was fifty years old. For the next two years he could think of little else but taking his own life. He hid every rope for fear he would hang himself, and he even stopped hunting, for fear he would turn the gun on himself. Then he discovered that his despondency lifted when he thought about God. There was an upsurge of hope, a feeling of stability. "Why look further?" he asked himself. "I'll seek God and really live." And he did.

You can be cured in fourteen days [to patients afflicted with melancholia] if you follow this prescription. Try to think every day how you can please someone.

—Alfred Adler

I think I have learned that the best way to lift one's self up is to help someone.

—Booker T. Washington

Dr. Bertrand Brown, director of the National Institute of Mental Health, said that depression is the number one problem in this country today. Depression is the common cold of psychological disorders. Almost everyone experiences it at some time.

—Paul W. Powell

In an address to the British Medical Association, a prominent physician said, "The best medicine I've discovered is prayer. As one whose whole life has been concerned with the sufferings of the mind, I would state that all hygienic measures to counteract disturbed sleep, depression of spirit, and a distressed mind, I would undoubtedly give first place to the simple habit of prayer. It does more to quiet the spirit and strengthen the soul than any other therapeutic agency known to man."

William Cowper was a Christian, but he had sunk to the depths of despair. One foggy night he called for a horsedrawn carriage and asked to be taken to the London Bridge on the Thames River. He was so overcome by depression that he intended to commit suicide. But after two hours of driving through the mist, Cowper's coachman reluctantly confessed that he was lost.

Disgusted by the delay, Cowper left the carriage and decided to find the London Bridge on foot. After walking only a short distance, though, he discovered that he was at his own doorstep! The carriage had been going in circles. Immediately he recognized the restraining hand of God in it all.

Convicted by the Spirit, he realized that the way out of his troubles was to look to God, not to jump into the river. As he cast his burden on the Savior, his heart was comforted. With gratitude he sat down and penned these reassuring words: "God moves in a mysterious way His wonders to perform; He plants His footsteps in the sea, and rides upon the storm. O fearful saints, fresh courage take; the clouds you so much dread are big with mercy; and shall break in blessings on your head."

The late actress Joan Blondell used a common kitchen timer to pull herself up out of the dumps. "I set the timer for 6 $\frac{1}{2}$ minutes to be lonely, and 22 minutes to feel sorry for myself. And then when the bell rings, I take a shower, or a walk, or a swim, or I cook something—and think about something else."

—*Bits & Pieces*

DESIRES

Ralph Waldo Emerson addressed a graduating class at Harvard University: "Young men, be careful what you want, for you will surely get it."

DESPAIR

In the world it is called Tolerance, but in hell it is called Despair . . . the sin that believes in nothing, cares for nothing, seeks to know nothing, interferes with nothing, finds purpose in nothing, lives for nothing, and remains alive because there is nothing for which it will die.

—Dorothy Sayers

The mass of men lead lives of quiet desperation.

—Henry Thoreau

DETAILS

Until you do little details carefully, you will never do the big things correctly.

DETERMINATION (Also see AIMS)

Three businessmen had adjacent businesses in a rectangular building. One man put up a sign, "Clearance Sale." Another, on the other end of the building, displayed a sign, "Year-end Sale." The man in the middle knew his business was in trouble so he put up a sign, "Main Entrance."

Always bear in mind that your own resolution to succeed is more important than any other one thing.

—Abraham Lincoln

The difference between the impossible and the possible lies in a person's determination.

—Tommy Lasorda

Whatever you can do, or think you can do, begin it. For boldness has power and courage and genius in it.

—Johann von Goethe

A small boy was learning to skate. His frequent mishaps awakened the pity of a bystander. "Sonny, you're getting all banged up," he said. "Why don't you stop for a while and just watch the others?" With tears rolling down his cheeks the boy looked at the man and then at his skates and answered, "Mister, I didn't get these skates to give up on; I got them to learn how on."

He who really wants to do something finds a way; he who doesn't finds an excuse.

Our greatest joy is not in never falling, but rising every time we fall.

—Confucius

Of all the sad words of tongue or pen, the saddest of all are these: "it could have been."

—John Greenleaf Whittier

Henry Comstock laid claim to a silver deposit in Virginia City, Nevada in 1859. Before long he was offered $11,000 for his claim and sold it. But he sold out too soon.

The Comstock lode proved to be the greatest silver deposit in history. It brought its later owner some $340,000 during the following thirty years.

The famous football coach "Hurry-Up" Yost of the University of Michigan once rebuked an overconfident player who said that their team would come out on top because it had the "will to win." "Don't fool yourself," he declared, "that attitude is not worth a nickel unless you also have the will to prepare!"

DEVOTION

No vital Christianity is possible unless at least three aspects of it are developed. These three are the inner life of devotion, the outer life of service, and the intellectual life of rationality.

—Elton Trueblood

DIETING

Her idea of a balanced diet is a pizza in each hand.

—Hal Roach

She swears she diets religiously. She doesn't eat while she's in church.

—Hal Roach

Dieters are people who get up in the morning and the first things they say is, "Mirror, mirror, on the dresser—do I look a little lesser."

—Robert Orben

A dieting colleen named Flynn
Reduced until she was thin.
　She's no more, I'm afraid
　For she sipped lemonade
and slipped through the straw and fell in.

A Dieting Psalm

Strict is my diet, I must not want.
It maketh me lie down at night hungry;
It leadeth me past the Baskin Robbins;
It trieth my will power;
It leadeth me in the paths of starvation for
　my figure's sake.
Yea, tho I walk thru the aisles of the pastry
　department,
I will buy no sweet rolls for they are
　fattening.
The cakes and the pies, they tempt me.
Before me is a table of celery and lettuce,
My day's quota runneth over.
Surely calories and weight charts shall fol-
　low me all the days of my life,
And I will dwell in the fear of scales
　forever.

Minister to small daughter in home where
he was calling: "What will you do when
you are as big as your mother?"
　Little one: "Boy, I'll diet!"

On a dinner flight a woman from Switzerland heavily salted and peppered her des-
sert, a luscious-looking piece of chocolate
cake. The flight attendant, somewhat taken
back, explained that it wasn't necessary to
do this. "Oh, but it is," the woman replied,
smiling. "It keeps me from eating it."

"Are you on a garlic diet?"
　"No. Should I be?"
　"Its a great diet. It keeps people away
from you so that you look farther away and
thus smaller."

Lord, we thank you for these luscious
vittles. May they add to your glory and not
to our middles.

DIFFERENCES

No two people are alike and both of them
are glad of it.
　　　　　　　　　—Farmer's Almanac

DIFFICULTIES (Also see TROUBLES)

All you need to grow fine, vigorous grass
is a crack in your sidewalk.
　　　　　　　　　—Will Rogers

A twelve-year-old boy had a puppy which
he took for a walk around the block twice
a day. A visitor asked him, "How do you
do that twice daily with such a large
puppy?" He answered simply, "With great
difficulty."

Hard things to do: to forget, to forgive, to
apologize, to take advice, to admit error,
to be unselfish, to save money, to be charitable, to be considerate, to keep out of a
rut, to keep moving on. But they pay!

See the invisible; believe the incredible; do
the impossible.
　　　　　　　　　—Vernon Grounds

When the Lord wants to do something
great, He begins with the difficult; when
He wants to do something even greater, He
begins with the impossible.

DILIGENCE

Every morning in Africa a gazelle wakes
up. It knows it must run faster than the fastest lion or it will be killed.
　Every morning a lion wakes up. It
knows it must outrun the slowest gazelle
or it will starve to death.
　It doesn't matter whether you are a lion
or a gazelle: When the sun comes up, you
had better be running!

There is no poverty that can overtake
diligence.
　　　　　　　　　—Japanese proverb

A missionary from India told about an
army officer who stopped to have his shoes
shined by a poor Indian boy on the street.
The lad launched into his task with such
enthusiasm and vigor that the man was utterly amazed. Instead of an ordinary, slip-
shod performance with all-too-eagerly
outstretched hand for a tip, the boy worked
diligently until the leather sparkled with a
brilliant luster. The officer asked, "Why are

you taking so much time to polish my boots?" "Well, sir," was the reply, "last week Jesus came into my heart and now I belong to Him. Since then, every time I shine someone's shoes, I keep thinking they're His, so I do the very best I can. I want Him to be pleased!"

The young army doctor was stationed at a remote dispensary in the South Pacific. One day he was puzzled about treatment for one of his patients. He radioed a base hospital: "Have case of beriberi. What shall I do?"

A prankster got hold of the message. This was the reply: "Give it to Marines. They'll drink anything."

DIPLOMACY

Diplomacy is the same as saying "nice doggie" until you have a chance to pick up a rock.

—Frances Rodman

A politician said, "Some of my friends are for this new bill, and some are against it, and I'm for my friends."

Diplomacy is thinking twice before saying nothing.

DISCIPLINE

A woman visiting in Switzerland came to a sheepfold on one of her daily walks. Venturing in, she saw the shepherd seated on the ground with his flock around him. Nearby, on a pile of straw lay a single sheep which seemed to be suffering. Looking closely, the woman saw that its leg was broken. Her sympathy went out to the suffering sheep and she asked the shepherd how it happened.

"I broke it myself," said the shepherd sadly and then explained. "Of all the sheep in my flock this was the most wayward. It would not obey my voice and would not follow when I was leading the flock. On more than one occasion it wandered to the edge of a perilous cliff. And not only was it disobedient itself, but it was leading the other sheep astray. Based on my experience with this kind of sheep, I knew I had no choice, so I broke its leg. The next day I took food and it tried to bite me. After letting it lie alone for a couple of days, I went back to it and it not only eagerly took the food but licked my hand and showed every sign of submission and affection.

"When the sheep is well, it will be the model sheep of my entire flock. No sheep will hear my voice so quickly nor follow so closely. Instead of leading the others away, it will be an example of devotion and obedience. In short, a complete change will come into the life of this wayward sheep. It will have learned obedience through its sufferings."

Several years ago while I was waiting for a train at the railroad station in Jhansi, India, I photographed a notice that was pasted on one of the posts on the platform. It was a quote from Jawaharlal Nehru. It read as follows: "None can say that excessive rest is harmful." I'm still trying to figure out what Pundit Nehru meant by this. Let us assume he was quoted out of context. It seems he must have been, for surely excessive rest can be harmful. Anything can be done to excess, even rest! There can be times when we cater to our personal or body desires more than we should and discipline needs to be exercised to do what we ought.

—Richard Winchell

DISCOURAGEMENT

There is a legend of a man who found the barn where Satan kept his seeds ready to be sown in the human heart, and on finding the seeds of discouragement more numerous than others, learned that those seeds could be made to grow almost anywhere. When Satan was questioned he reluctantly admitted that there was one place in which he could never get them to thrive. "And where is that?" asked the man. Satan replied sadly, "In the heart of a grateful man."

Although you may have occasional spells of despondency, don't despair. The sun has a sinking spell every night.

The Christian's chief occupational hazards are depression and discouragement.

—John R. Stott

It is said the Devil once decided to go out of business and he offered his tools for sale. They were attractively displayed: Trickery, Hatred, Jealousy, Malice, Deceit, Sensuality, and many other evil tools, each marked with a price. But in the center was a wedge-shaped, much worn tool priced higher than all the others. "What is that?" Satan was asked. "That is Discouragement," he replied. "But why so costly?" "Because it can do my evil work better than all other tools. With it I can make the lives of many folks of no value. I can make them just lie down and 'give up' and become useless and they don't even know I am the one who uses it."

If Satan's arsenal of weapons were restricted to a single one, it would be discouragement.

—C. S. Lewis

You can tell how big a worker is by observing how much it takes to discourage him.

If this is the first day of the rest of my life, I'm in for a dismal future.

—Twiggy

When you reach the end of your rope, tie a knot and hang on.

—Anonymous

The radiant sky behind us will illuminate the path before us.

—Alexander Maclaren

Success is often closest when discouragement is greatest.

DISCRETION

When a top executive is selecting his key associates, there are only two qualities for which he should be willing to pay almost any price: taste and judgment. Almost everything else can be bought by the yard.

—John W. Gardner

The essence of wisdom is to withhold judgment until all the facts are in.

DISPUTING

A long dispute means that both parties are wrong.

—Voltaire

DIVORCE

A couple in Hollywood got divorced; then they got remarried. The divorce didn't work out.

In the U.S., in 1900, 1 of every 20 marriages ended in divorce.
In 1920, 1 of every 12
In 1940, 1 of every 6
In 1970, 1 of every 2

With so many divorces today, you would think that when a lot of people were married they were mispronounced man and wife.

DOCTORS

Preachers see people at their best. Lawyers see people at their worst. Doctors see people as they really are.

—Anonymous

A certain doctor plays a game with some of his young patients to test their knowledge of body parts. One day, while pointing to a boy's ear, the doctor asked, "Is this your nose?"

The child turned to his mother and said, "I think we'd better find a new doctor!"

The sick man, conscience-stricken at having summoned his doctor at two in the morning, apologized profusely.

"I'm sorry about the hour, Doc, and I know my house is somewhat out of your way too."

"Oh, that's all right," reassured the doctor. "I have another patient who lives near you, so I'll visit him and just kill two birds with one stone."

DOGS

We give them the love we can spare, the time we can give. In return dogs have given us their absolute all. It is without a doubt the best deal man has ever made.

—Roger Caras

DOUBT

There is more faith in doubt than in half the creeds.

—Alfred Tennyson

The Latin word for doubt, *dubitare*, comes from an Aryan root meaning "two." To believe is to be "in one mind" about accepting something as true; to disbelieve is to be "in one mind" about rejecting it. To doubt is to waver between the two, to believe and doubt at once, and so to be "in two minds."

—Os Guinness

Blessed are the ignorant for they never have doubts.

—Joseph Renan

DRINKING

A Methodist minister had a secret vice— he loved to drink cherry brandy. Of course, it was impossible for him to admit this weakness to a congregation who were strictly teetotalers, and some wicked friends decided to exploit his dilemma. They offered him a whole crate of cherry brandy on the condition that the gift was publicly acknowledged in the church paper. To their amazement, the minister gladly accepted. Next Sunday the notice appeared: "The minister would like to thank his friends for the generous gift of fruit and the spirit in which it was given."

—*Rolling in the Aisles*

A drunk was rolling around the street when the local minister came up to him. "I'm so glad you've turned over a new leaf," said the minister.

"Me?" said the drunk, puzzled.

"Yes, I was so thrilled to see you at the prayer meeting last night."

"Oh," said the drunk, slowly remembering, "so that's where I was!"

—*Rolling in the Aisles*

A man came home drunk at 3 A.M. in the morning. His wife said, "A fine time to come home. I want an explanation and I want the truth." He said, "Make up your mind."

—Hal Roach

Each year alcohol kills over 100,000 Americans and costs the United States up to $120 billion in economic damages. Alcohol is implicated in 66 percent of homicides, 50 percent of rapes, and 70 percent of robberies. Drunken driving is the leading cause of death among young people ages 16 to 24. Of the estimated 13 to 15 million alcoholics and problem drinkers in the United States, more than 3 million are under the age of 18. In 1981 a government reported that 9 percent of sixth-graders have used alcoholic beverages.

Noah's drunkenness led to shame (Gen. 9:21).

Lot's drunkenness led to confusion (Gen. 19:33).

Ahasuerus' drunkenness led to folly (Esther 1:10–11).

Benhadad's drunkenness led to defeat (1 Kings 20:16–20).

Belshazzar's drunkenness led to sacrilege (Dan. 5:1–5).

A little boy and his dog, Colonel, were passing a saloon, the door of which was wide open. The dog, not knowing any better, went in; but the little boy rushed after him with some good advice: "Come out of there, Colonel. Don't be disgracing the family."

Anachonis, the philosopher, was asked by what means a man might guard against the vice of drunkenness. He answered, "By bearing constantly in view the loathsome indecent behavior of such as are intoxicated."

P. T. Barnum was a temperance advocate. Once when he was giving an address, a man in the gallery howled, "How does alcohol affect us, externally or internally?" "Eternally," flashed back Barnum.

Major Van Sickle of the Salvation Army was a great soulwinner. In Washington,

D.C., he ministered to alcoholics. He told one of these men, "If you take the gospel of John and read it fifty times, I guarantee you deliverance from alcoholism." Was that a bold thing to do? He did it. The man read John seven or eight times, and he got saved. He kept reading the gospel of John, and before long he was delivered. He came to know the truth and the truth set him free.

The major said that over a period of some five years he had one hundred conversions and deliverances from alcoholism by this simple advice: "Read the gospel of John fifty times and I guarantee you deliverance from this habit."

The only time liquor makes a man go straight is when the road curves.

A drunken driver is an amateur chemist; he is mixing alcohol and gasoline.

Diogenes, a Greek philosopher, was given a large goblet of wine. He threw it on the ground. When blamed for wasting so much good liquor, he answered, "Had I drunk it there would have been double waste. I as well and also the wine would have been lost!"

Take one natural-born fool, add two drinks of liquor, and mix the two in a high-powered automobile. After the fool is thoroughly soaked, place one foot on gas and release brake. Remove fool from wreckage, place in black box, and garnish with flowers.

—Automobile Dealer

The A-B-Cs of Liquor

A— Arms more villains,
B— Breaks more laws,
C— Corrupts more morals,
D— Destroys more homes,
E— Engulfs more fortunes,
F— Fills more jails,
G— Grows more gray hairs,
H— Harrows more hearts,
I— Incites more crimes,
J— Jeopardizes more lives,
K— Kindles more strife,
L— Lacerates more feelings,
M— Maims more bodies,
N— Nails down more coffins,
O— Opens more graves,
P— Pains more mothers,
Q— Quenches more songs,
R— Raises more sobs,
S— Sells more virtue,
T— Tells more lies,
U— Undermines more youth,
V— Veils more widows,
W— Wrecks more men,
X— X-cites more passion,
Y— Yields more disgrace, and
Z— Zeroes more hopes
than any other enemy of mankind.

The Booze Bar

A bar to heaven, a door to hell,
Whoever named it, named it well.
A bar to manliness and wealth,
A door to want and broken health.
A bar to honor, pride, and fame,
A door to want and grief and shame.
A bar to hope, a bar to prayer,
A bar to darkness and despair.
A bar to honored, useful life,
A bar to brawling, senseless strife.
A bar to all that's true and brave,
A bar to every drunkard's grave.
A bar to joy that home imparts,
A door to tears and aching hearts.
A bar to heaven, a door to hell,
Whoever named it, named it well.

DRIVING

Drive so that your driver's license expires before you do.

More truth than typographical error: "The driver approached the coroner at fifty miles an hour."

The two greatest highway menaces are drivers under twenty-five going sixty-five and drivers over sixty-five going twenty-five.
—F. G. Kernam

DUTY

Duty is the most sublime word in the English language.
—Winston Churchill

DUTY

One day during Colonial times a "dark day" occurred. When the sun seemed to disappear at midday, the people were so alarmed that many of them began to cry, thinking that the world was coming to an end.

Even the legislature was disturbed and confused. Some wanted to adjourn without delay. One stalwart member said, "I make a motion that we secure some candles and proceed with our business. If the end of the world is about to come, I want to be found doing my duty."

DYING WORDS (Also see DEATH)

Give me laudanum that I may not think of eternity.

—Gabriel Mirabeau

All is now lost; finally, irrevocably lost. All is dark and doubtful.

—Edward Gibbon

I am about to take a leap in the dark. I shall be glad to find a hole to creep out of the world.

—Thomas Hobbes

I am abandoned by God and man! I shall go to hell! O, Jesus Christ!

—Voltaire

What blood, what murders, what evil counsel have I followed! I am lost; I see it well!

—Charles IX, King of France

I would give worlds, if I had them, if the *Age of Reason* had never been published. O, Lord, help me! Christ, help me! Stay with me! It is hell to be left alone!

—Tom Payne

I am suffering the pangs of the damned.

—Charles Talleyrand

Oh, that I could lie for a thousand years on the fire that never is quenched, to purchase the favor of God and be reunited to Him again! But it is a fruitless wish. Millions and millions of years will bring me no nearer to the end of torments than one poor hour. Oh, eternity, eternity! For ever and for ever! Oh, the insufferable pangs of hell!

—Francis Newport

Let down the curtain; the farce is over.

—François Rabelais

The chariot has come, and I am ready to step in.

—Margaret Prior

Eternity rolls up before me like a sea of glory.

—Jordan Antie

How bright the room! How full of angels!

—Martha McCrackin

I wish I had the power of writing; I would describe how pleasant it is to die.

—Dr. Cullen

The sun is setting; mine is rising. I go from this bed to a crown. Farewell.

—S. B. Bangs

Can this be death? Why, it is better than living! Tell them I die happy in Jesus.

—John Arthur Lyth

I am in perfect peace, resting alone on the blood of Christ. I find this amply sufficient with which to enter the presence of God.

—Mel Trotter

Oh, that I could tell you what joy I possess. I am full of rapture. The Lord doth shine with such power upon my soul. He is come! He is come!

—Mary Frances

I am ready.

—Woodrow Wilson

Thank God, I have done my duty.

—Horatio Nelson

My desire is to make what haste I may to be gone.

—Oliver Cromwell

Let us pass over the river and rest under the shade of the trees.

—Stonewall Andrew Jackson

E

EDITING

Editor Graham Green said regarding editing his own manuscript, "You have to kill your darlings."

EDUCATION (Also see LEARNING)

When a subject becomes totally obsolete, we make it a required course.

—Peter Drecker

Harvard University permitted freedom in matters of theology and made no religious requirement of college officers.

Yale drifted partly in concern for academic excellence amidst an environment of agnosticism and Unitarianism.

Dartmouth and Columbia only had a statement in its charter about the great principles of Christianity and morality in which true Christians of each denomination are generally agreed. It had no strong statement of faith.

Princeton yielded because of pressure from alumni. Princeton's charter insisted on a saved faculty, but it did not require this of its students. As it turned out more and more non-Christian alumni who could give withheld donations. It finally succumbed to their demand for a voice in the management and educational policies.

—Paul Lee Tan

The institution that belittles plumbing while exalting philosophy will neither have good plumbing or philosophy. Neither its pipes or its theories will hold water.

—Clark Kerr

The function of a seminary is to turn the students up (recruiting), sort them out (admissions), shape them up (teaching), shake them up (examinations), and pass them on (graduation and placement).

—James D. Geasse

Education is how kids learn stuff.

—A seven-year-old

A human being is not, in any proper sense, a human being until he is educated.

—Horace Mann

At the desk where I sit, I have learned one great truth. The answer for all our national problems—the answer for all the problems of the world—comes in a single word. That word is education.

—Lyndon B. Johnson

It is on the sound education of the people that the security and destiny of every nation chiefly rest.

—Louis Kossuth

Sixty years ago, I knew everything; now I know nothing; education is a progressive discovery of our own ignorance.

—Will Durant

Education makes people easy to lead, but difficult to drive; easy to govern, but impossible to enslave.

—Lord Brougham

When Ralph Waldo Emerson said that Harvard College taught all the branches of learning, Henry Thoreau said, "Yes, all the branches, but none of the roots."

In a business class at the University of Wisconsin, Stevens Point, the students had to interview a number of local people and write a report. One student thought the assignment was a waste of time until he spoke with a seventy-eight-year-old farmer. He asked the old man, "How much education do you have?" The farmer answered, "Six years of schoolin' and seventy-two years of learnin'."

Christianity is the religion of an educated mind.

—Sir William Ramsay

A man was out walking in the desert when a voice said to him, "Pick up some pebbles and put them in your pocket, and tomorrow you will be both sorry and glad."

The man obeyed. He stooped down and picked up a handful of pebbles and put them in his pocket. The next morning he reached into his pocket and found diamonds and rubies and emeralds. And he was both glad and sorry. Glad that he had taken some—sorry that he hadn't taken more.

And so it is with education.

—William Cunningham

The person who graduates today and stops learning tomorrow is uneducated the day after.

When is a man educated? When he knows how to live, how to love, how to hope, how to pray, and is not afraid to die.

—Joseph Fort Newton

The educated man is a man with certain spiritual qualities which make him calm in adversity, happy when alone, just in his dealings, rational and sane in the fullest meaning of the word in all the affairs of life.

—Ramsey MacDonald

I am much afraid that the universities will prove to be the great gates to hell, unless they diligently labor to explain the Holy Scriptures and to engrave them on the hearts of youth. I advise no one to place his child where the Scriptures do not reign paramount. Every institution where men are not unceasingly occupied with the Word of God must become corrupt.

—Martin Luther

In 1636, John Harvard, whose bequest endowed Harvard University, said, "Let every student be plainly instructed and earnestly pressed to . . . lay Christ in the bottom as the only foundation of all knowledge and learning."

EFFECTIVENESS

"I'm planning a salary increase for you, young man."

"When does it become effective?"

"Just as soon as you do."

EFFICIENCY

It is more than probable that the average man could, with no injury to his health, increase his efficiency 50 percent.

—Walter Dill Scott

The individual who increases his efficiency as much as 10 percent often increases his income and his opportunities as much as 100 percent. Sun Beau, the great race horse, was worth ten times as much as other horses but he did not have to run ten times as fast, only a split second faster.

EFFORT

Triumph is umph added to try.

ELECTIONS (Also see POLITICS)

Some folks get elected because they are well known; others are defeated for the same reason.

—*Farmers' Almanac*

EMBARRASSMENT

A young man was working in the produce department of a grocery store. A woman told him she wanted to buy half a head of lettuce. He said they sell lettuce only by the head. But she insisted. So he said, "Okay, lady, I'll check with the manager."

He went across the store to the manager, not realizing she was directly behind him. He said to the manager, "Some idiot wants to buy half a head of lettuce." Then he noticed the lady standing next to him. So he added, "And this dear lady wants half a head of lettuce too."

Later the boss said, "Son, that was pretty good. A quick response. By the way, where are you from?"

"I'm from Westchester, Pennsylvania. The city of ugly women and great basketball players."

The boss said, "My wife is from Westchester, Pennsylvania."

So the boy responded, "What basketball team did your wife play on?"

A judge in Washington State has been using bumper stickers to encourage better driving. He's found that people guilty of driving while intoxicated resent having to attach the following message to their bumper: This Car Owned by a Convicted Drunk Driver. Almost all offenders prefer the magistrate's other option: enrollment in an alcohol treatment program. The majority of people care about what others think of them. They want to maintain a good image.

When a first-year seminary student entered church one Sunday, he noticed the guest speaker was an especially boring professor from the seminary. "Oh, no!" he said, in a voice louder than he intended.

When the woman beside him wondered what was wrong, the student said, "That's Mr. Drysdale up there. He's my professor at seminary. I have him three days this week and now this'll be the fourth time. He's unbelievably boring."

A smile came across the woman's face. "Do you know who I am?" she asked.

"No."

"I am Mrs. Drysdale, the wife of your professor."

For a moment the student was silent. Then he asked, "Do you know who I am?"

"No, I don't," she replied.

"Good," he said as he quickly exited.

As a special education major at Illinois State University in Normal, I was the only male student in many of my classes. As a result, my professors and fellow students continually badgered me about my love life. One day, a professor stopped his lecture to point out a girl walking by our classroom window. "Now, there's the woman for you, Dave," he said.

"Her?" I responded. "No way!"

"That's too bad," he replied. "She's my daughter."

—David Curry

EMOTIONS, MIXED

One youngster was explaining to another boy what "mixed emotions" meant. "It's like watching the school burn down when your new catcher's mitt is in your desk," he said.

—*Bits & Pieces*

EMPATHY

Several years ago a young boy in Dallas was in an accident which necessitated the amputation of one of his arms. He withdrew from his family and friends and refused to talk to anyone. He was literally wasting away in withdrawal from life.

A friend of mine went to the hospital and asked if he might visit with the young fellow. This friend was met with skepticism but was allowed to visit the boy. When he came to the room, he saw the youngster staring out the window. The boy turned to see his visitor, who also lacked an arm. The boy looked at him for a few moments in silence. Then he said angrily, "You don't know how I feel, you couldn't."

"No, friend, you're wrong," the man said, "I do know how you feel. I also have lived without an arm."

The young boy hesitated a moment longer in his anger. Then he broke into tears as he ran toward my friend and put his one good arm around him. It was the beginning of the lad's recovery, which began when he found someone who really understood him.

—S. Craig Glickman

A sign was placed in a front yard: "Puppies For Sale." A small boy came to inquire about the puppies, "I'd like to buy a puppy if they don't cost too much."

"Well, son, they're ten dollars."

The child's face fell. "I don't got but $1.63. Could I just look at them anyway?"

"Sure, maybe we can work something out." Then the little boy said anxiously, "I heard there was one with a bad leg."

"Yes," replied the man, "I'm afraid she is hopelessly crippled."

"That's the one!" the small boy exclaimed. "Could I pay for her a little at a time?"

"But wouldn't you rather have one who could play with you? This one will never be able to walk very well."

Hiking up one trouser leg, the little boy showed a brace. "I don't walk so good either," he said matter-of-factly, "and I reckon she'll need some understanding till she gets used to it. I did."

EMPLOYEES

Hiring people smarter than you proves you're smarter than they are.

—*Bits & Pieces*

EMPLOYEES

Some workers who are not paid what they are worth ought to be glad.

EMPTINESS

At the end of the 1960s, a young graduate of Mills College addressed her graduating class. The title of her speech made national news: "The Future Is a Hoax." Combine this with the dictum of industrialist Henry Ford, "History is bunk," and you have a description of an empty life.

—Edward L. Hayes

ENCOURAGEMENT

Queen Victoria said of William Gladstone, "When I am with him, I feel I am with one of the most important leaders in the world." But of Benjamin Disraeli she said, "He makes me feel as if *I* am one of the most important leaders of the world."

I can live for two months on a good compliment.

—Mark Twain

A little boy said to his dad, "Let's play darts, Dad. I'll throw and you say, 'Great shot!'"

Praise does wonders for our sense of hearing.

—Arnold Glasgow

There are high spots in all of our lives, and most of them have come about through encouragement from someone else. I don't care how great, how famous, or successful a man or woman may be, each hungers for applause.

—George Matthew Adams

The five most important words: "I have confidence in you."
The four most important words: "What is your opinion?"
The three most important words: "If you please."
The two most important words: "Thank you!"
The most important word: "We."
The least important word: "I."

Three billion people go to bed hungry every night, but four billion people go to bed hungry for a simple word of encouragement.

—Cavett Robert

Remember that before the Flood came, Noah was in the minority, but after the Flood, he was in the majority.

We live by encouragement, and we die without it—slowly, sadly, angrily.

—Celeste Holm

Encouragement is oxygen to the soul.

—George Adam

One kind word can warm up three winter months.

—Japanese proverb

These large birds [sandhill cranes], who fly great distances across continents, have three remarkable qualities. First, they rotate leadership. No one bird stays out in front all the time. Second, they choose leaders who can handle turbulence. And then, all during the time one bird is leading, the rest are honking their affirmation.

—Bruce Larson

A Christian worker recently went into a restaurant to buy an inexpensive meal. A waitress approached him and in a rather brusque voice demanded, "Can I help you?" "Yes, ma'am." "Coffee with your order?" "Yes, ma'am," he replied absentmindedly, for his thoughts were occupied with some important spiritual matters. Suddenly the uncongenial waitress flared up, exclaiming sarcastically, "Is that all you can say?" Before he could catch himself, he once again replied, "Yes, ma'am!"

With a curse she stamped away in disgust and anger. When the food was ready, she almost threw it on the table and showed contempt with every action. Although he did not have much money, he sacrificially laid a five-dollar bill on the table as he left. As he was paying the cashier, the discourteous waitress called, "Sir, you left this money on the table!" "Isn't that the usual place to leave a tip?" he replied, smiling at her warmly. The girl blushed and then began to make apologies for her hateful actions.

The missionary said cordially, "I figured you must have some heavy burdens on your heart or you wouldn't have become so easily upset. I thought a good tip might encourage you." By this time the girl was brokenhearted, and she told him of the many problems facing her. Before he left the restaurant, he was able to lead that waitress to the Lord!

—*Our Daily Bread*

Our duty is not to see through one another, but to see one another through.

Correction does much, but encouragement does more.

—Johann von Goethe

People have a way of becoming what you encourage them to be—not what you nag them to be.

—Scudder N. Parker

A word of encouragement during a failure is worth more than a whole book of praise after a success.

—*Bits & Pieces*

The deepest principle in the human heart is the craving to be appreciated.

—William James

One of the highest of human duties is the duty of encouragement. . . . It is easy to laugh at men's ideals; it is easy to pour cold water on their enthusiasm; it is easy to discourage others. The world is full of discouragers. We have a Christian duty to encourage one another. Many a time a word of praise or thanks or appreciation or cheer has kept a man on his feet. Blessed is the man who speaks such a word.

—William Barclay

ENDURANCE (Also see PATIENCE)

Endurance is not just the ability to bear a hard thing, but to turn it into glory.

—William Barclay

A faith that fizzles before the finish had a fatal flaw from the first.

—R. K. Kendall

Endurance is the queen of all virtues.

—Chrysostom

ENEMIES (Also see FRIENDS)

President Lincoln was once asked about his attitude toward his enemies. "Why do you try to make friends of them? You should try to destroy them." "Am I not destroying my enemies," Lincoln replied gently, "when I make them my friends?"

The early morning racket was so loud that I rolled out of bed and went to the front door to see what was happening. I knew about their longstanding argument. But I had never heard them go at it like this before. There in the trees in front of our house it appeared that the crows and the blue jays were quarreling again. Their war of words and wings had escalated beyond anything I'd ever seen before. I watched the "reserves" fly in and take positions in the branches. The actual bombing and strafing was concentrated in the upper regions of a big oak.

But I saw something I hadn't expected. A pair of huge brown wings made a tactical retreat to a nearby branch. There was no crow, and this was not the usual spat between the blacks and blues. They weren't even fighting each other on this Sunday morning. They had found a common enemy. They had located an owl, and their mutual dislike for one another was lost in a conflict of greater proportions. Together the crows and the blue jays had combined forces against the owl.

—M. R. De Haan II

An old man was being interviewed by an admiring reporter, "Sir, what exactly is your age, if you don't mind my asking."

"I'll tell you. I'll be ninety-seven years old tomorrow."

"That's wonderful. You appear to be in marvelous condition."

The old man beamed. "Oh, yes, I'm doing fine. And, you know, I don't have an enemy in the world."

ENEMIES

"Well, that's a beautiful thought, but how do you explain it?"

"I've outlived every one of them."

—*Bits & Pieces*

When we hate our enemies, we are giving them power over us: power over our sleep, our appetites, our blood pressure, our health, and our happiness.

—Dale Carnegie

You should really cherish your enemies. At least they don't try to hit you for a loan.

—Lou Erickson

Your enemies make you wise.

A hundred friends are not enough, but one enemy is too many.

One good enemy can do more harm than ten friends can do good.

In order to have an enemy, one must be somebody.

—Anne Sophie Swetchine

Just as all tall trees are known by their shadows, so are good men known by their enemies.

—Chinese proverb

Martin Niemoller came out of Hitler's prison saying, "It took me a long time to learn that God is not the enemy of my enemies. He's not even the enemy of His own enemies!"

ENGLAND

"The national sport in Spain is bullfighting and in England it's cricket."

"I'd rather play in England."

"Why do you say that?"

"Because it's easier to fight a cricket."

ENGLISH

Some sentences can understandably end with several prepositions. When a boy's mother went upstairs to read to him at night, he asked, "Why did you bring that book that I didn't want to be read to out of up for?"

When Sir Christopher Wren first walked into the St. Paul's Cathedral in London which he had designed, he said, it's amusing, artificial, and awful. In other words, he meant it's a place to muse, full of art, and full of awe.

This is a situation up with which I will not put.

—Winston Churchill

Sam Goldwyn, the movie producer, used to mangle the English language so badly that his malaprops and mixed metaphors came to be known as Goldwynisms. Some that have become classics are these:

A verbal contract isn't worth the paper its printed on.

Every Tom, Dick, and Harry is named William.

Now, gentlemen, listen slowly . . .

For more information, I would like to ask a question.

Include me out.

Don't talk while I'm interrupting.

I may not always be right, but I'm never wrong.

—*Bits & Pieces*

Horace Greeley, who always insisted that the word "news" was plural, once wired to a reporter in the field, "Are there any news?"

Back came the reply, "Not a new."

ENTHUSIASM

The world belongs to the energetic.

—Ralph Waldo Emerson

Lord, let me live until I'm dead.

—Will Rogers

The worst bankrupt is the person who has lost his enthusiasm.

—H. W. Arnold

We act as though comfort and luxury were the chief requirements of life, when all that we need to make us happy is something to be enthusiastic about.

—Charles Kingsley

The orator who wishes to set the people on fire must himself be burning.

—Quintilian

Without enthusiasm there is no progress in the world.

—Woodrow Wilson

Management Dimensions, Inc. surveyed 241 executives and asked what traits make workers succeed. Executives could select more than one trait. The most important trait was enthusiasm—80 percent of the executive listed it. Second was a can-do attitude, with 63 percent.

Nothing great was ever achieved without enthusiasm.

—Wrigley

Charles Schwab, the man to whom Andrew Carnegie paid a million dollars a year because of his ability to motivate people, once said, "A man can succeed at almost anything for which he has unlimited enthusiasm."

A group of self-made millionaires were asked to list the qualities that had contributed to their success and to rate the importance of each. The final tally looked something like this:

Ability	5%
Knowledge	5%
Discipline	10%
Attitude	40%
Enthusiasm	40%

—Marlene LeFever

An Easterner who walked into a western saloon was amazed to see a dog sitting at a table playing poker with three men. "Can that dog really read cards?" he asked.

"Yeah, but he ain't much of a player," said one of the men. "Whenever he gets a good hand, he wags his tail."

Enthusiasm is one of the most powerful engines of success. When you do a thing, do it with your might. Put your whole soul into it. Stamp it with your own personality. Be active, be energetic, be enthusiastic and faithful, and you will accomplish your object.

—Ralph Waldo Emerson

ENVY (Also see JEALOUSY)

The water is the same on both sides of the boat.

—Finnish proverb

There are many roads to hate, but envy is one of the shortest of them all.

Envy shoots at others and wounds itself.

—Swedish proverb

Envy Went to Church

Envy went to church this morning.
Being Legion, he sat in every other pew.
Envy fingered wool and silk fabrics,
Hung price tags on suits and neckties.
Envy paced through the parking lot
Scrutinizing chrome and paint.
Envy marched to the chancel with the choir
During the processional . . .
Envy prodded plain Jane wives
and bright wives married to milquetoast dullards,
and kind men married to knife-tongued shrews.
Envy thumped at widows and widowers,
Jabbed and kicked college girls without escorts,
Lighted invisible fires inside khaki jackets.
Envy conferred often this morning
With all his brothers;
He liked his Sunday score today
But not enough;
Some of his intended clients
Had slipped an antidote marked Grace
And wore a fragrant flower named Love.

—Elva McAllister

There's a legend about a Burmese potter who had become envious of the prosperity of a washerman. Determined to put this man out of business, the potter convinced the king to issue an order requiring the man to wash one of the emperor's black elephants and make it white.

The washerman replied that according to the rules of his vocation he would need a vessel large enough to hold the elephant, whereupon the king commanded the potter to provide one. So the potter constructed a giant bowl and had it carefully delivered to the washerman. But when the elephant stepped into it, it crumbled to pieces beneath the weight of the enormous beast. Many more vessels were made, but each was crushed in the same way. Eventually it was the potter who was put out of business by the very scheme he had devised to ruin the man he envied.

ETERNAL SECURITY

An Irishman was being kidded about his continual preaching of the doctrine of eternal security by one who said, "What if, after all your preaching of this doctrine, you would actually lose your salvation?" The answer immediately came, "God would lose much more than I would. I would lose only my salvation, but God would lose his reputation."

Someone has said there will be three surprises in heaven. We will be surprised that some we thought will be there won't be, that some we thought wouldn't be there will be, and that we are there. Actually the first two are true, but not the third.

An old lady, full of joyous confidence, was asked, "But suppose you should slip through Christ's fingers?"
    She replied at once, "But I am one of His fingers."

If an earthly judge imposed a prison term or an alternate fine and a third party paid that fine, it would be unjust after the penalty had been paid, to imprison the one who had been found guilty.

ETERNITY

High up in the North, in the land called Svithjod, there stands a rock. It is one hundred miles high and ten miles wide. Once every one thousand years a little bird comes to this rock to sharpen its beak. When the rock has thus been worn away, then a single day of eternity will have gone by.

—Hendrick Willen VanLoon

Eternity is the length of time it would take a bird to take one speck of dirt at a time, flying with it to the sun, until it had moved the entire earth. After having done this back and forth a dozen times, eternity would have just begun.

I have only just a minute,
Only sixty seconds in it,
Forced upon me—can't refuse it,
Didn't seek it, didn't choose it,
But it's up to me to use it.
I must suffer if I lose it,
Give account if I abuse it,
Just a tiny little minute—
But eternity is in it.

Life with Christ is an endless hope; without Him, a hopeless end.

A new clock has been so accurately constructed that it will lose or gain only one second in thirty-three million years. But no matter how accurately we measure time, we cannot create time nor extend time. Each of us will have only one lifetime to spend on this earth. That's why eternity is so appealing.

—Robert C. Shannon

A cathedral in Milan, Italy, features a remarkable entrance in which you pass through three doors in succession. Each door has an arch with an inscription. Over the first one, stone-etched and wreathed in roses, it says, "All which pleases is but for a moment." The second one pictures a cross with the engraving, "All which troubles is but for a moment." The climax comes with the third and largest doorway into the sanctuary. The inscription reads, "That only is important which is eternal."

A father decided to have a serious talk with his young son, who was inclined to be lighthearted and irresponsible. "Jimmy," he said, "you are getting to be a big boy and ought to take things more seriously. Just think: if I died suddenly, where would you be?" Jimmy answered, "I would be here; but where would you be?" It gave the dad something to think about.

EVANGELISM

On a certain ocean liner, a passenger was lying in his cabin seriously ill. One dark night he heard a cry, "Man overboard," and, while sensitive to all the excitement and hurry, he was too sick to give any help. One of the difficulties was that they could not see the man. Suddenly, however, a light shone out through the glass of a porthole. It happened to fall full on the struggling man in the water, so that they were able to throw him a lifebelt and then go to his rescue. Where did the light come from? From the sick man, who, feeling so distressed at his incapacity to help, managed to crawl out of his bunk, take the lantern down from the wall, and place it where it could shine forth.

At 7:49 A.M., December 7, 1941, Fuchida signaled the attack on Pearl Harbor by 360 planes. Today Fuchida is a Christian evangelist and head of a five-member evangelistic association. He is the only living officer out of seventy in the attack on Pearl Harbor. He missed being in Hiroshima on the day it was bombed, but was one of the twelve who inspected the damage. The other eleven men have died from radiation. In his youth he was a Buddhist and Shintoist. Today he is a Presbyterian.

He credits his being led to salvation through the forgiving spirit of a nurse who is the daughter of martyred missionary parents and after reading a tract by Jacob DeShazer who survived capture and torture and returned to Japan with the Gospel. Fuchida purchased a Bible and learned the secret of how this nurse and soldier could forgive the treatment they received during the war. He opened his heart to Jesus Christ and has dedicated his life to serving God.

Luigi Larisio was found dead one morning with scarce a comfort in his home, but with 246 exquisite violins, which he had been collecting all his life, crammed into an attic, the best in the bottom drawer of an old rickety bureau. In devotion to the violin, he had robbed the world of all that music all the time he treasured them; others

before him had done the same, so that when the greatest Stradivarius was first played it had had 147 speechless years.

Many Christians are like old Larisio. In their love for the church, they fail to give the Good News to the world.

The sinking of the "unsinkable ship," the Titanic, caused the death of approximately 1,500 people. The nearest ship was miles away, but it was off duty. It could have rescued all the passengers if it were on duty. Similarly many Christians are "off duty."

An evangelist is a nobody who is seeking to tell everybody about Somebody who can help change anybody.

—Michael Gott

In a disastrous church fire a beautiful painting of Christ was endangered. Two men went inside and rescued it. People came and watched the fire, but stayed long after to look at the painting.

The church leaders were amazed because people had never before been interested in the painting, which had hung for years in the church. Finally one man explained, "When the church caught fire and moved Christ into the streets where people could see Him, then they were interested."

C. Sumner Wemp tells that at the beach near Jacksonville, Florida is a sign for the lifeguards that reads, "If in doubt, go!"

Every Saturday evening for over forty years a servant of God stood on a certain street corner handing out gospel papers to the passerbys. And then he stopped. Discouraged because he saw so little fruit, he abandoned his post. Some years later he happened on the spot and a young man stood there and gave him a gospel tract. He stopped, and addressing the young man he said,

"How is it that you are here tonight?"

"Well, sir, it is like this. An old man occupied this corner for years; I was saved by means of a tract he gave me. Evidently the old man is in heaven now for I've missed him here, and so I am seeking to fill his place."

EVANGELISM

Tears filled the eyes of the older Christian as the young man thus spoke.

"I am the man who gave you that tract," he said, "and by the grace of God I mean to stand my place until Jesus comes."

—Peter J. Pell

We've drifted away from being fishers of men to being keepers of the aquarium.

—Paul Harvey

I recently read about an old man, walking the beach at dawn, who noticed a young man ahead of him picking up starfish and flinging them into the sea. Catching up with the youth, he asked him what he was doing. The answer was that the stranded starfish would die if left until the morning sun.

"But the beach goes on for miles, and there are millions of starfish." countered the old man. "How can your effort make any difference?"

The young man looked at the starfish in his hand and then threw it to safety in the waves. "It makes a difference to this one," he said.

—Hugh Duncan

EVIL

Is He [God] willing to prevent evil, but not able? Then is he impotent? Is He able, but not willing? Then is He malevolent? Is he both able and willing: whence then is evil?

—David Hume

A small cotton field south of the Mason-Dixon line was the home of two boll weevils. Though they were not brothers they became fast friends early in life. Whatever one boll weevil did the other did too. However, when they were full grown, one was a big, husky boll weevil while the other was sawed-off and scrawny. He was the lesser of the two weevils.

EVOLUTION

Man did not come from monkeys, but some are going to the dogs.

It is absurd for the evolutionists to complain that it's unthinkable for an admittedly unthinkable God to make everything out of nothing and then pretend it is more thinkable that nothing should turn itself into anything.

—G. K. Chesterton

Once a man was walking along the bank of a river and he saw something glittering in the grass by the path. It was a watch which was running perfectly. There it was. He knew this watch had not developed wheel to wheel, spring and jewel, case and stem, just lying there on the ground—or had it?

Bumper sticker: "My ancestors were human. Sorry about yours."

Astronomy class at the University of Toledo in Ohio seemed easy at first, but as the quarter progressed, the material got more complicated. One day, our professor was discussing nebular condensation accretion theory, which explains the formation of our solar system.

After an hour of note taking, a classmate put down his pencil with a sigh. "You know," he said, "this topic was a lot easier back in Sunday school."

—Thomas Oakley

The monkeys one day had a big jamboree
Their leader sat up in the tallest palm tree
And said with a chuckle, "My good fellow Monk,
If you want a good laugh, just give ear to this junk.
The teachers of men in a place they call 'school'
Are training each youngster to grow up a fool.
The kids all run wild and never get spanked.
If our babies did that, their tails would be yanked.
No well-mannered monkey dictates to his teacher,
Beats up the policeman or shoots at the preacher,
Poisons the baby, or kills with a gun,
And then laughs and says, 'We are just having fun!'
Monkeys, my friends, have respect for each other.

134

We hand out no sass to our father or mother.
The picture I've painted you'll agree is quite sad.
But listen, my brothers, I'm boiling mad.
For here's what they're taught—that miserable flunky,
That creature called Man was at one time a monkey!
An ape just like us, and what's more, if you please,
He claims that at one time he swung through the trees.
Fellow monkeys, I think this is going too far.
We don't envy their home, their wealth, or their car.
But when they will spread such a horrible rumor,
It's time for all monkeys to lose their good humor.
So, come, you must help me prepare a big sign,
Protesting that man's no descendant of mine.
If evolution be true, then boys, we are sunk,
For I'd sooner be father to weasel or skunk."

I can prove God statistically. Take the human body alone—the chance that all the functions of the individual would just *happen* is a statistical monstrosity.

—George Gallup

Three monkeys sat in a coconut tree,
And talked of things that were said to be.
Said one to the others, "See here, you two!
There's a rumor afloat that can't be true,
That man descended from our lofty race,
To think of such is a great disgrace.
No monkey ever beat his wife,
Or starved her child or spoiled her life;
And whoever heard of a mother monk
Parking her babies for another to bunk
Or passing them on from one to another
Till they couldn't tell who was her mother.
And another thing you'll never see,
Is a fence around a coconut tree.
If a fence I should build around a coconut tree,
Starvation would force you to steal from me;

And there is another thing a monk won't do,
That is, go out at night and get in a stew;
Then use a gun, club, or a butcher knife
To take another poor monkey's life.
Man may have descended—the ornery cuss;
But brothers—he didn't descend from us."

Robert Ingersoll, an atheist, once visited the great preacher Henry Ward Beecher, who took him into his study and showed him theological books. In Beecher's study there was also a magnificent contour globe of the world with the mountains and valleys all painted in as a beautiful and creative work of art.

Ingersoll, a bright man and highly educated, looked at the globe and said, "Beecher, that is a beautiful work of art. Who made it for you?" Challenging Ingersoll's denial of God's creation, Beecher replied, "Oh, nobody, it just happened."

—Kenneth Gangel

When the wife of a Canon of Worcester Cathedral first was told about the theory of evolution, she protested, "Descended from apes! My dear, we will hope it is not true. But if it is, let us pray that it may not become generally known."

EXAGGERATION

Never exaggerate . . . Exaggeration is akin to lying; and through it you jeopardize your reputation for good taste, which is much, and for good judgment, which is more.

—Baltasar Gracian

EXAMPLE

There is nothing more influential in a child's life than the moral power of a quiet example. For children to take morality seriously, they must see adults who take morality seriously.

—William J. Bennett

When Benjamin Franklin decided to interest the people of Philadelphia in street lighting, he hung a beautiful lantern on the end of a long bracket attached to the front of his house. He kept the brass brightly polished and carefully lit the wick each evening at the approach of dusk. Anyone walking on the dark street could see this light from a long way off and come under its warm glow. It wasn't long before Franklin's neighbors began placing lamps outside their homes. Soon the entire city followed his example with enthusiasm.

—Cole D. Robinson

No man is worthless. He can always serve as a terrible example.

One frustrated lad was heard to remark, "Two things in life I've had are ample— good advice and bad example."

—M. Dale Baughman

You cannot put straight in others what is warped in yourself.

—Athanasius

Example is not the main thing in influencing others. It is the only thing.

—Albert Schweitzer

The most valuable gift you can give another is a good example.

EXAMS

It was a bright spring morning and four high school boys decided to skip classes. Arriving after lunch, they explained to the teacher that their car had a flat tire on the way to school. To their relief, the teacher smiled understandingly and said, "You boys missed a test this morning. Please take your seats apart from one another and get out your paper and pencil."

When the boys were seated, she continued, "Answer this question: Which tire was flat?"

—*Rotarian*

Bumper sticker: As long as there are final exams there will be prayer in public schools!

On a college test, a student who wasn't prepared left the page blank and wrote at the bottom, "Dedicated to my memory, which recently passed away."

All-School Seminary Postfinal

1. Define and give the significance of the twofold mandrake.
2. Sum up Kittel's theological contributions in one word.
3. Define as briefly as possible (using a detailed full-sentence outline) the following terms:
   a. Readaktionsitzumkerschplattundkerputtgeschichte.
   b. Jay E. D. P. Westreetermann's seven-source theory of *Time* magazine.
   c. Budak
4. What do we mean when we say that we hold to the liturgical, hermeneutical, hysterical interpolation of Scripture?
5. Give seven reasons why seven is the perfect number.
6. On the basis that the typewriter was not invented until 1857, defend the existence of Old Testament typology.
7. T or F—Louis Pasteur wrote the Pasteural Epistles.
8. State and defend the argument from silence that nothing whatsoever happened during the intertestamental period.
9. What was Noah's prediluvial interpretation of Ephesians 5:18? How was it modified by progressive revelation?

—*Kethiv Qere*

Several students of historian Charles Beard called at his office to find out their grades on a test. The papers were not yet corrected but Beard said, "I will see that you get justice." One of the students replied, "But Dr. Beard, we don't want justice; we want mercy."

EXCELLENCE

Whatever is worth doing at all is worth doing well.

—Philip Chesterfield

Faced with a challenging new project at work, I sought our manager's advice on how to proceed. After we had gone over his suggestions, I asked him to tell me his formula for success. "What I do, I do very well," he answered with a smile. "And what I don't do well, I don't do at all!"

—Sally Baucus Boydstun

Always remember what you're good at and stick with it.

—Ermenegildo Zegna

Whatever your life's work, do it well. A man should do his job so well that the living, the dead, and the unborn could do it no better.

—Martin Luther King Jr.

The quality of a person's life is in direct proportion to his or her commitment to excellence, regardless of the chosen field of endeavor.

—Vincent T. Lombardi

The way to get on in this world is to do whatever work you are doing well, then you will be picked to do some other job that is not being done well.

—Samuel Vauclair

The distinguished congressman Claude Pepper was called by his colleagues "a national treasure." He was a valiant champion of the elderly and the poor. A few days before Pepper's death in 1989, President Bush visited him in Walter Reed Hospital to give him the nation's highest civilian award, the Medal of Freedom.

Representative Silvio Conte recalls, "Despite what was obviously a great deal of pain, Claude apologized to the president and the first lady that he couldn't stand up." Said Conte, "He didn't have to stand up. He was a giant."

—*Our Daily Bread*

More than two thousand years ago a sculptor erected a statue in a Greek temple. He had spent much time perfecting it. When asked why he gave the same painstaking care to the back, which wouldn't be seen, as he did to the front, he replied, "That is the way I always work. Men may never see it, but I believe the gods do!"

God does not want us to do extraordinary things; He wants us to do ordinary things extraordinarily well.

—Charles Gore

Excellence can be attained if you:
Care more than others think is wise.
Risk more than others think is safe.
Dream more than others think is practical.
Expect more than others think is possible.

Cathy Rigby was a member of the U.S. Women's Gymnastics Team in the 1972 Olympics at Munich, and she had only one goal in mind—to win a gold medal. She had trained hard over a long period of time.

On the day she was scheduled to perform, she prayed for strength and the control to get through her routine without making mistakes. She was tense with determination not to let herself or her country down.

She performed well, but when it was all over and the winners announced, her name was not among them. Cathy was crushed. Afterward, she joined her parents in the stands all set for a good cry. As she sat down, she could barely manage to say, "I'm sorry. I did my best."

"You know that, and I know that," her mother said, "and I'm sure God knows that too." Then Cathy recalls, her mother said ten words that she has never forgotten: "Doing your best is more important than being the best."

—*Soundings*

Do more than exist—live.
Do more than look—observe.
Do more than read—absorb.
Do more than hear—listen.
Do more than listen—understand.
Do more than think—ponder.
Do more than talk—say something.

—*NYLIC Review*

Michelangelo stands as one of the towering figures in the history of art. His majestic frescoes on the ceiling of the Sistine Chapel and his masterful sculptures bear witness to his greatness. But he was a man never content to rest on his laurels. He spent countless hours on his back on the scaffolding in the Sistine, carefully perfecting the details of each figure. When a friend questioned such meticulous attention to detail, on the grounds that "at that height, who will know whether it's perfect or not?" Michelangelo's simple response was "I will." After contemplating what some consider his greatest work, *Moses*, the master sculptor stood back and surveyed his craftsmanship. Suddenly, in anger, he struck the knee of the creation with his chisel and shouted, "Why don't you speak?" The chisel scar that remains on the statue's knee is the mark of a man who always reached out for more. His ambition was to be the best he could be.

The Christian adds a deeper dimension. His ambition is not simply to be good or to be good for something. He longs to be good for Someone, striving for excellence out of love for his Savior.

—Gary Inrig

We're the mark of excellence (General Motors).

Putting our energy into excellence (Atlantic Richfield).

We deliver excellence 95,000 times a day (Express Mail).

—Jon Johnston

When Irvin Feld was put in *Who's Who in America* and was asked for a quotation to go with his biographical sketch, he wrote, "I have found that if you give the public more than their money's worth while maintaining a high standard of quality, they will respond fully with their support. I have always insisted on giving the paying public more than they expect."

A retired business executive was once asked the secret of his success. He replied that it could be summed up in the three words—and then some. "I discovered at an early age," he declared, "that most of the difference between average people and top people could be explained in three words. The top people did what was expected of them—and then some. They were thoughtful of others; they were considerate and kind—and then some. They met their obligations and responsibilities fairly and squarely—and then some. They were

good friends and helpful neighbors—and then some. They could be counted on in an emergency—and then some."

I am thankful for people like that, for they make the world more livable, for their spirit of service is summed up in three little words, "and then some."

—Carl Holmes

Andrew Carnegie, the great industrialist and philanthropist, once declared in a speech before a graduating class that he thought all young men fell into three categories: those who did not do all their duty, those who only professed to do their duty, and those who did their duty plus "a little more."

"It is the little more that wins," he said. "Do your duty and a little more, and the future will take care it itself."

—*Speak the Language of Success*

EXCUSES

W. C. Fields was reading the Bible. A friend came in and said, "What in the world are you doing?" Mr. Fields didn't ordinarily read the Bible. He said, "I'm looking for loopholes."

If half the ingenuity spent in finding excuses for not doing what we ought to do were exercised in finding means to do what ought to be done, there would be a great difference.

We are all manufacturers: making goods, making trouble, or making excuses.

He who is good for making excuses is seldom good for anything else.

—Benjamin Franklin

Young Robin was more clever than anyone at making up alibis. When he brought home his grades at the end of the first report period, his father observed, "I see you failed in math." "That's true, Dad," Robin explained brightly, "but my grade was the highest of those who failed."

There's a big difference between sound reasons and reasons that sound good.

Ninety-nine percent of failures come from people who have the habit of making excuses.

—George Washington Carver

The Spirit came in childhood and pleaded, "Let me in."
But oh! the door was bolted by thoughtlessness and sin.
"I am too young," the child replied. "I will not yield today;
There's time enough tomorrow." The Spirit went away.
Again He came and pleaded in youth's bright and happy hour;
He came but heard no answer for, lured by Satan's power,
The youth lay dreaming then and saying, "Not today,
Not till I've tried earth's pleasures." The Spirit went away.
Again He called in mercy in manhood's vigorous prime;
But still he found no welcome, the merchant had no time—
No time for true repentance, no time to think or pray;
And so, repulsed and saddened, the Spirit went away.
Once more He called and waited, the man was old and ill,
And scarcely heard the whisper, his heart was cold and still;
"Go leave me; when I need thee, I'll call for thee," he cried.
Then, sinking on his pillow, without a hope, he died.

A heavy rain had been falling as a man drove down a lonely road. As he rounded a curve, he saw an old farmer surveying the ruins of his barn. The driver stopped his car and asked what had happened. "Roof fell in," said the farmer. "Leaked so long it finally just rotted through." "Why in the world didn't you fix it before it got that bad?" asked the stranger. "Well, sir," replied the farmer, "it just seemed I never did get around to it. When the weather was good, there weren't no need for it, and when it rained, it was too wet to work on!"

Executives in their thirties and forties are valuable because they are eager and keen and aware of what can, should, and needs to be done. Executives in their fifties and sixties are valuable because they are more relaxed and experienced and often aware of what can't, shouldn't, and needn't be done.

—Malcolm S. Forbes

EXEMPTION

A speaker who ministers to congressman in Washington, D.C., said that congressmen have a tendency to live with the illusion that who they are and what they do are so important that they are exempt from the normal responsibilities of life. Illusions like these: Others need time with their spouse, not me. Others need time in the Word of God, not me. Others need time in church, not me. The "illusion of exemption" is not unique to congressmen. Others like businessmen, athletes, and ministers do the same thing.

EXERCISE

"A recent report by the Southern California Medical Association," writes Julie K. Rose of Iowa State University, "pointed out that weight control and physical fitness cannot be obtained by dieting alone. Persons engaged in sedentary occupations often do not realize that calories by the hundreds can be burned off by a variety of strenuous exercises. Below are the per-hour calorie consumption rates of some common activities.
Beating around the bush, 75
Jumping to conclusions, 100
Climbing the walls, 150
Swallowing your pride, 50–500
Passing the buck, 25
Throwing your weight around, 50–300
Dragging your heels, 100
Bending over backwards, 75
Pushing your luck, 250
Running around in circles, 350
Making mountains out of molehills, 500
Climbing the ladder of success, 750."

The only exercise some people get is jumping to conclusions, side-stepping responsibility, dodging issues, passing the buck, and pressing their luck!

EXPERIENCE

Experience does all of her teaching backwards; she gives a test before explaining the lesson.

—*Farmer's Almanac*

The trouble with experience is that it usually teaches you something you really didn't want to know.

One thorn of experience is worth a whole wilderness of warning.

—James Russell Lowell

Experience is a comb which nature gives us when we are bald.

—Chinese proverb

Education is what you get from reading the fine print. Experience is what you get for not reading it.

We should be careful to get out of an experience only the wisdom that is in it— and stop there, lest we be like the cat that sits down on a hot stove lid. She will never sit down on a hot stove lid again—and that is well but also she will never sit down on a cold one anymore.

—Mark Twain

Past experience should be a guidepost, not a hitching post.

F

FACTS

Facts mean nothing unless they are rightly understood, rightly related, and rightly interpreted.

—R. L. Long

Facts are stubborn things.

—John Adams

FAILURE (Also see SUCCESS)

Knowing how to benefit from failure is the key to success.

—Zig Ziglar

Failed in business	age	22
Ran for legislature		23
Again failed in business		24
Elected to Legislature		25
Sweetheart died		26
Had a nervous breakdown		27
Defeated for Speaker		29
Defeated for Elector		31
Defeated for Congress		34
Elected to Congress		37
Defeated for Congress		39
Defeated for Senate		46
Defeated for Vice President		47
Defeated for Senate		49
Elected President of the United States		51

That's the record of Abraham Lincoln.

—*Bits & Pieces*

The only time you must not fail is the last time you try.

—Charles F. Kettering

There are three kinds of people in the world: the wills, the won'ts, and the can'ts. The first accomplish everything, the second oppose everything, and the third fail in everything.

Thomas Edison failed many times. And yet he made 1,100 inventions.

When he worked on the idea of making artificial light, he couldn't find a filament that would give good light when electricity flowed through it. He spent two years experimenting with thousands of materials including everything from blades of grass to wire made from platinum. Finally he used carbonized thread, which is cotton sewing thread burned to ash. On October 21, 1879, he succeeded.

Our greatest glory is not in never falling, but in rising every time we fall.

—Confucius

Failure is trying to do all things for all people.

The men who try to do something and fail are infinitely better than those who try to do nothing and succeed.

—Lloyd Jones

Carl Walenda was a well-known tightrope walker and circus performer. He said, "My whole life is high-wire walking." But one day as he was on the wire, something snapped in his brain and he fell to his death. His wife said, "All he thought about for three months before was falling." He had concentrated on failure, on falling, rather than on walking.

Failure should be our teacher, not our undertaker. Failure is delay, not defeat. It is a temporary detour, not a dead-end street.

Michelangelo's huge statue of David was produced from a single block of granite weighing several tons. This block of granite was rejected a century before the master sculptor used it as being unfit for a work of sculpture, yet out of this reject he fashioned his beautiful and inspiring masterpiece. Failure need never be final when faith is present.

—Roy L. Laurin

Failure is the line of least persistence.

—Stephanil Martino

We have come to fear failure too much. Failure is the practice essential for success.

—Charles F. Kettering

When I try, I fail. When I trust, God succeeds.

Failures are divided into two classes—those who thought and never did, and those who did and never thought.

—John C. Salak

The two hardest things to handle in life are failure and success.

"A believer," once wrote Emerson, "is never disturbed because other persons do not yet see the fact which he sees."

Charles Goodyear was a believer, even though others would not yet see what he saw. At one point in his life, in fact, he actually had himself thrown in jail in order to gain time to reach his goals.

One of America's ten great industrial inventors, Goodyear was a failure for years, owed money to friends, neighbors, and relatives who had staked him.

He was penniless in 1838 when he discovered the method of vulcanizing rubber. But by that time, with his invention still to be perfected, creditors had begun to hound him. Despite his repugnance to the idea, he fled to the protection of the bankruptcy laws.

Soon afterward, he was thrown in jail for contempt of court, and there, unmolested behind prison bars, he perfected his rubber process. He not only paid off his creditors but made fortunes for all those who had kept the faith in him.

—*Bits & Pieces*

The apostle Paul failed; Peter failed; every one of the twelve apostles failed.

David, Israel's greatest king, "a man after God's own heart," failed.

Moses, giant among the Israelites, giver of the Law, deliverer of the people, failed.

Jacob, father of Israel, failed; Isaac, son of promise, failed.

Abraham, progenitor of Israel, father of the faithful, prototype of those who are righteous through faith, failed.

Even our first parents, in their human perfection, failed.

Who hasn't failed?

It is not failing that is the problem; it is what one does after he has failed.

—Richard Halverson

Success has many fathers, but failure is always an orphan.

—John F. Kennedy

Failure is the line of least persistence.

When the great Polish pianist Ignace Paderwski first chose to study the piano, his music teacher told him his hands were much too small to master the keyboard.

FAILURE

When the great Italian tenor Enrico Caruso first applied for instruction, the teacher told him his voice sounded like the wind whistling through the window.

When the great statesman of Victorian England Benjamin Disraeli attempted to speak in Parliament for the first time, members hissed him into silence and laughed when he said, "Though I sit down now, the time will come when you will hear of me."

Henry Ford forgot to put a reverse gear in his first car.

Thomas Edison spent two million dollars on an invention which proved to be of little value.

Albert Einstein failed his university entrance exams on his first attempt.

Don't give up because you failed the first time.

I cannot give the formula for success, but I can give the formula for failure—try to please everybody.

—Herbert B. Swope

We are all men, feeble, frail and apt to faint.
—Charles H. Spurgeon

Falling down doesn't make you a failure, but staying down does.

It is hard to fail, but it is worse never to have tried to succeed.

—Theodore Roosevelt

Ninety-nine percent of failures come from people who have the habit of making excuses.

—George Washington Carver

You have failed many times, although you may not remember. You fell down the first time you tried to walk. You almost drowned the first time you tried to swim, didn't you? Did you hit the ball the first time you swung a bat? Heavy hitters, the ones who hit the most home runs, also strike out a lot. R. H. Macy failed seven times before his store in New York caught on. English novelist John Creasey got 753 rejection slips before he published 564 books. Babe Ruth struck out 1,330 times, but he also hit 714 home runs. Do not worry about failure. Worry about the chances you miss when you do not even try.

—Harry Gray

Failure is merely an opportunity to start over again, wiser than before.

FAIRNESS

A mother was complaining to her friend that her two young sons were constantly squabbling over the division of things around the house. "I'm at my wit's end," she sighed. Her friend suggested, "Just appoint one of them to always do the dividing . . . and allow the other first choice."

FAITH

Faith is to believe what we do not see. The reward of this faith is to see what we believe.

—Augustine

Faith is only as valid as its object. You could have tremendous faith in very thin ice and drown. . . . You could have very little faith in very thick ice and be perfectly secure.

—Stuart Briscoe

Faith will not always get for us what we want, but it will get what God wants us to have.

—Vance Havner

O Father, let me not be dissipated on non-essentials. Bring the Word to me in power; sublimate these huge hungers to the obedience of Christ. Above all these things, I would have holiness. Teach me the path of faith.

—Jim Elliot

Faith commences with the conviction of the mind based on adequate facts; it continues in the confidence of the heart or emotions based on the above conviction; and it is crowned in the consent of the will, by means of which the conviction and confidence are expressed in conduct.

—W. H. Griffith Thomas

Faith in God sees the invisible, believes the incredible, and receives the impossible.

A little girl had been attending a Sunday school session where each student had made a little plaque with the words "Have Faith in God" as the motto. She boarded a bus that would take her to her home, and as the bus was starting to move, she realized that she did not have her little motto with her. She jumped from her seat, and dashing up the aisle to the driver, she shouted, "Stop the bus! I've lost my 'Faith in God.'"

—C. Reuben Anderson

Some say that faith is the gift of God. So is the air, but you have to breathe it; so is bread, but you have to eat it. Some are wanting some miraculous kind of feeling. That is not faith.

"Faith cometh by hearing and hearing by the Word of God" (Rom. 10:17). That is whence faith comes. It is not for me to sit down and wait for faith to come stealing over me with a strong sensation, but is for me to take God at His Word.

—D. L. Moody

Faith does not operate in the realm of the possible. There is no glory for God in that which is humanly possible. Faith begins where man's power ends.

—George Muller

The world doesn't believe because they can't believe the believers believe.

We have a God who delights in impossibilities.

—Andrew Murray

You do not test the resources of God until you try the impossible.

—F. B. Meyer

God isn't looking for great people, but He is looking for people who will realize the greatness of God.

Faith gives us living joy and dying rest.

—D. L. Moody

Little faith brings the soul to heaven, where great faith brings heaven into the soul.

When faith goes to market, it always takes a basket.

Faith is a Declaration of Dependence in opposition to sin which is man's Declaration of Independence.

—Bernard Ramm

Faith puts God between us and our circumstances.

—Daniel Webster

Faith is not a leap in the dark; it is a leap out of darkness into the light.

—David Reed

G. K. Chesterton told of how he wandered away from the faith. He likened his experience to that of some men who left the coast of England in search of a new island. After a long and hazardous voyage, they landed on what they thought was a new country. After proudly running up the English flag, they began to look around. The landscape looked strangely familiar. On further investigation they discovered, to their chagrin, that it was the same seacoast from which they had departed! Trying to escape England they had run into it. Trying to get away from home they had come home!

Some scientists in Scotland offered a boy a handsome sum of money if he would allow himself to be let down by a rope over a cliff in a precipitous mountain gorge. The boy longed for the money for he was poor, but when he looked down into the two-hundred-foot chasm he said, "No." After further persuasion he said, "I will go if my father holds the rope." That is faith. He had confidence in his father; he believed in his father, and by an act of the will he allowed his father to fasten the rope around him and let him down.

Napoleon was on a horse that was wild and about to toss him.
A private in his army went up to the

horse and steadied him so that Napoleon would not fall.

"Thank you, Captain."

The private replied, "Of what battalion, Sir?"

Napoleon replied, "Captain of my guard."

Lord Congleton of Dublin once devised a clever plan for teaching his tenants how faith secures forgiveness of sins, while unbelief shuts one out from the benefits of the Gospel. Many who owed him several years' rent were expecting severe action in the court. Instead, he posted a notice promising remission of back dues to any who would meet him on a certain day before twelve noon. On the designated day, he sat in his office waiting their response. They crowded the street, whispering and talking, but not one of them entered the open door. Just a few minutes before twelve o'clock, a tenant who had been delayed came running in to ask for his receipt. "Do you really expect to be forgiven for your debt?" asked Lord Congleton. "Yes, sir, because you faithfully promised it." "And do you believe me?" "Yes, I do, because you would not be the kind to deceive a person." "But are you a good and industrious man?" the landlord inquired. "The notice said nothing about that, sir." "So you just believed what I said and have come for your receipt?" "Indeed, I have."

Lord Congleton wrote "paid in full" on his bill and handed it to him. Just as the hour struck, the happy fellow ran out of the house waving the release crying, "I've got it! I'm a free man!" The others milling in the street rushed to the house, but the door was shut! One man had believed, and he alone received the benefits.

Faith rests on God, receives from God, responds to God, relies on God, realizes God, rejoices in God, and reproduces His life and character.

—W. H. Griffith Thomas

When Patrick Henry lay dying, he called his children around him and said, "I am about to leave you all my earthly possessions. There is one more thing which I would like to leave you, namely, the Christian faith. If I could leave you that and nothing else, you would be rich indeed. If I could leave you everything else and not that, you would be poor indeed!"

A grandmother on her way to visit offspring and grandchildren in California was somewhat concerned when the pilot announced that he was about to shut off one of the plane's four engines.

"We've got a small oil leak," he said, "but there's no need to worry. We'll do just fine with the three working engines left. As further assurance, you might like to know that we have four bishops aboard."

The grandmother digested this information and then was heard to say, "I'd rather have four motors and three bishops than three motors and four bishops."

—*Bits & Pieces*

George Allen, founder and director of the Bolivian Indian Mission, and his wife made a visit to the famous Mueller Orphan Home in Bristol, England. Mrs. Allen, looking at the five large buildings, said, "Dr. Burton, it must take a lot of faith to keep all this going." Burton answered, "Mrs. Allen, little faith in a strong plank will carry me over the stream; great faith in a rotten plank will land me in it."

By Faith, Not Sight

Sometimes I'm sad, I know not why,
My heart is so distressed,
It seems the burdens of this world
Have settled on my heart.
And yet I know . . . I know that God
Who doeth all things right
Will lead me thru to understand
To walk by *faith* . . . not *sight*.
And though I may not see the way
He's planned for me to go,
The way seems dark to me just now
But oh, I'm sure He knows!
Today He guides my feeble step
Tomorrow's in His right,
He has asked me never to fear
But walk by *faith* . . . not *sight*.
Some day the mists will roll away,
The sun will shine again,

I'll see the beauty in the flowers
I'll hear the bird's refrain.
And then I'll know my Father's hand
Has led the way to light,
Because I placed my hand in His
And walked by *faith* . . . not *sight*.
—Ruth A. Morgan

Faith does not only exclude the thought of merit, it actually includes the idea of helplessness. In faith one depends on another to do what a person is unable to do for himself. If a child is ill and the child's parents call a doctor, they are confessing their own inability to deal with the illness and are expressing their confidence in the doctor. There is no merit in calling the doctor. Their faith in the doctor merely gives him the opportunity to work.

A boy was once flying a kite and a passerby, looking up in the sky and not able to see the kite because of its height, asked him, "What are you doing?" "Flying my kite." "How do you know it's there? You can't see it." "I can feel the tug on the string."

Perhaps we can't see God, but we can feel the tug of conviction He puts in our hearts, and we can go on faith believing His promises.

Faith enables the believing soul to treat the future as present and the invisible as seen.
—J. Oswald Sanders

Faith makes the uplook good, the outlook bright, the inlook favorable, and the future glorious.
—V. Raymond Edman

When God put it into the heart of George Mueller to build orphanages in Bristol, England, he had only two shillings in his pocket. Without making his wants known to anyone but God, over seven million dollars were sent to him for the building and maintaining of the homes.

Two little girls were counting their pennies. One said, "I have five pennies." The other said, "I have ten." "No," said the first little girl, "you have just five cents, the same as I have." "But," the second child quickly replied, "my father said that when he came home tonight, he would give me five cents, and so I have ten cents." The child's faith gave her proof of that which she did not yet see, and she counted it because it had been promised by her father.

Doubt sees the obstacles—
    Faith sees the way!
Doubt sees the darkest night—
    Faith sees the day!
Doubt dreads to take a step—
    Faith soars on high!
Doubt questions, "Who believes?"
    Faith answers, "I."

A Jewish professor of science of the University of Minnesota, after giving a lecture on the solar system, was asked by a student, "What started all this?" The professor answered, "Only God. Faith can bridge gaps that reason can never bridge."

A preacher began his sermon by saying, "Brethren and sisters, here you are coming to pray for rain. I'd just like to ask you one question. Where are your umbrellas?"

Faith came singing into my room,
    And other guests took flight;
Fear and anxiety, grief and gloom
    Sped out into the night.
I wondered that such peace could be,
    But faith said gently, "Don't you see?
They really cannot live with me."
—Elizabeth Cheney

Grace is like hooking up a new house with the city water mains, but faith is like turning the tap. Grace make possible—faith makes actual.

FAITHFULNESS

Bestow on me, O Lord my God,
understanding to know You,
diligence to seek You,
and a faithfulness
that may finally embrace You,
through Jesus Christ our Lord.
—Thomas Aquinas

FAITHFULNESS

F. B. Meyer signed many of his letters, "Yours to count on."

A little thing is a little thing; but faithfulness in little things is a very great thing.

God bases His rewards not on conspicuousness of service but on fidelity to opportunity.
—G. Campbell Morgan

It's not too difficult to be relevant if you don't care about being faithful. And it's not too difficult to be faithful if you don't care about being relevant.
—John Stott

A shepherd and his small dog once came to live in the city of Edinburgh, Scotland. The animal was so loyal to his owner that he followed him everywhere. Sometime later the man died and was buried in a local cemetery. Hardly anyone noticed the little dog trailing behind the mourners; but after they left, the dog sat down on the shepherd's grave. He stayed there not for a day, a week, or a month, but the rest of his life! Interested people gave him food and water, and he never left the spot where his master was laid to rest. After twelve years, he finally died at his post of vigilance. That was faithfulness!

Certain officers once approached Napoleon to recommend a young captain for promotion. Napoleon asked, "Why do you recommend this man?" Their answer was that through courage and cleverness he had recently won a signal victory. "Good," said Napoleon, "but what did he do the next day and the next day after?" On investigation they found that he had gone back to his usual unzealous and casual manner of life. Napoleon therefore refused to advance the man. He was looking for consistency and steadfastness.

After the tragic bombing of a marine base in Beirut in October 1983, the steadfastness of one young soldier moved and heartened Americans back home. He had been critically wounded in the explosion of the revamped hotel where he and his fellow marines had been staying. Many of his buddies had been killed. He was covered with bandages and a jungle of tubes were attached to his body. He could not speak. Yet when he was visited by General Paul Kelly, Commandant of the Marine Corps, he indicated that he wanted to write something. Painfully, he wrote the words *semper fi,* a shortened form of the U.S. Marine Corps motto, *Semper Fidelis*, which means, "Always faithful."

Spiritual nature, like bodily nature, will be served; deny it food and it will gobble poison.
—C. S. Lewis

FAME

An Olympic Star put an advertisement in a newspaper to sell the gold medal that he won for javelin throwing in 1928.

The former athlete, now living in Sweden and half crippled with rheumatism, was out of a job and short of money.

"You can't eat medals," was his rueful comment.

He hoped to realize enough money from the sale of his Olympic medal and all his sporting trophies to relieve the problems that have confronted him since his fame as a winner faded.

All is ephemeral—fame and the famous as well.
—Marcus Aurelius Antoninus

FAMILIARITY

Familiarity breeds contempt, but only with contemptible people or things.
—Phillips Brooks

FAMILY (Also see CHILD REARING, FATHERS, HOME, MOTHERS, and PARENTING)

If I would get to the highest place in Athens, I would lift up my voice to say, "What mean ye, fellow citizens, that ye turn every stone to scrape wealth together, and take so little care of your children to whom ye must one day relinquish all?"
—Socrates

Five-year-old Brian was impressed by the story of Simeon the Stylite, a Syrian hermit who lived in the fifth century. This man was admired as a saint because he lived for more than thirty-five years on a platform atop a high pillar. Determined to follow Simeon's example, Brian put the kitchen stool on the table and started his perilous climb. When his mother heard some strange sounds in the kitchen, she came in and shouted, "Brian! Get down before you break your neck!" As the youngster obeyed, he muttered, "You can't even become a saint in your own house."

FAMILY PRAYERS

Little Anna's parents were not Christians. When they gathered round the table for their meals, they never asked a blessing.

One time her uncle came to spend a few weeks with them. During his stay, he was invited to ask a blessing on their meals.

The morning after he had left them, the family gathered around the table and were about to start breakfast when little Anna, who sat next to her father, looked up to him and whispered, "Is there no God today, Papa?" This touching question of his child went straight to his heart.

The parents of little Willie were not Christians, but they were respectable and taught him the Lord's Prayer and "Now I Lay Me Down to Sleep," with the appropriate prayer, "God bless Papa, and Mama, and Willie, and make me a good little boy."

One evening as he finished his prayer, he said to his mother, "Does you pray Mama?" "No, darling." "Does Daddy pray?" "I never heard him pray." "Then why do you make me pray?"

"That you may be good. Don't you want to be good?"

"Oh, yes, I want to be good. Then why don't you and Daddy pray?"

"We've gotten out of the spirit, I guess."

"Well, Mama, don't you think you and Daddy are expecting too much of a little fellow like me? Am I supposed to do all the praying for the family? Seems to me you and Papa might help me a little."

After that, they did!

A little boy said, "Mom, who's Book is that?" "Oh," she said, "That's God's Book, don't touch it." "Well," he said, "let's send it back to Him; we don't read it."

Among the property owned jointly by two young brothers who were carpenters was the old tumbled-down place of their birth. One of the brothers was soon to be married and the old house was to be torn down and a new one erected on its site. For years neither of the brothers had visited the cottage, as it had been leased.

As they entered now and started the work of demolishing the place, again and again floods of tender memories swept over them. By the time they reached the kitchen they were well-nigh overcome with their emotions. There was the place where the old kitchen table had stood—with the family Bible—where they had knelt every evening. They were recalling now with a pang how in later years they had felt a little superior to that time-honored custom carefully observed by their father.

Said one, "We're better off than he was, but we're not better men."

Linda, age nine, went with a neighbor playmate to a revival meeting one night. In telling her experience to the family she said, "The preacher asked everyone who had family commotions at their house to raise their hands, so I did."

FANATIC

A fanatic is a person who redoubles his energies when he has forgotten his aim.

A fanatic is a person who can't change his mind and won't change the subject.
—Winston Churchill

Samuel Johnson once said of a man, "That man has only one idea and it is wrong."

FATHERS

"What is a father?" A boy answered, "A father is a person who has pictures in his wallet where he used to have money."

The quality of a child's relationship with

his or her father seems to be the most important influence in deciding how that person will react to the world.

—John Nicholson

The Prayer of a Father

Build me a son, O Lord, who will be strong enough to know when he is weak . . . and brave enough to face himself when he is afraid. One who will be proud and unbending in defeat . . . but humble and gentle in victory . . . a son who will know that to know himself . . . is the foundation stone of all true knowledge. Rear him . . . I pray . . . not in the paths of ease and comfort . . . but under the stress and spur of difficulties and challenges. Here let him learn to stand up in the storm . . . here let him learn compassion for those who fail. Build me a son who will master himself before he seeks to master other men. Build me a son whose heart will be clean . . . whose goal will be high. One who will learn to laugh . . . yet never forget how to weep. One who will reach into the future . . . and yet never forget the past. And after all these are his . . . add . . . I pray . . . enough of a sense of humor so that he may always be serious . . . yet never take himself too seriously . . . a touch of humility, so that he will always remember the simplicity of true greatness . . . the open mind of true wisdom . . . the meekness of true strength. Then . . . I . . . his father . . . will dare in the sacred recesses of my own heart . . . to whisper . . . "I have not lived in vain!"

There are little eyes upon you, and they are watching night and day;
There are little ears that quickly take in every word you say;
There are little hands all eager to do everything you do.
And a little boy who's dreaming of the day he'll be like you.
You're the little fellow's idol, you're the wisest of the wise,
In his little mind about you, no suspicions ever rise;
He believes in you devoutly, holds that all you say and do,

He will say and do in your way when he's grown up to be like you.
There's a wide-eyed little fellow who believes you're always right,
And his ears are always open and he watches day and night;
You are setting an example everyday in all you do,
For the little boy who's waiting to grow up to be like you.

If you follow the steps of your father, you learn to walk like him.

—West African proverb

Alan Redpath, former pastor of Moody Memorial Church, tells of the time his father, after a brief period of tension in the home, looked across the table at his wife and said, "I'm so sorry I spoke to you the way I did. I'm ashamed of myself."

Redpath said that although at the time he was not a Christian, he went to his room after the meal, knelt, and prayed, "O God, I thank you for a father like that. Make me more like him."

If I had a son, I'd do one thing. I'd tell him the truth. I'd never let him catch me in a lie. And in return, I'd insist that he tell the truth. When children go astray, it isn't the fault of the children but of their parents. A spoiled boy grows into a spoiled man. I'd try to be a pal to my boy. I'd have my son go to church. What's more, I'd go with him. But above everything else, I'd try to understand my son. For if I didn't, I'd be a failure as a dad!

—J. Edgar Hoover

Children of fathers who feel good about themselves and have high self-esteem grow up with more confidence and a higher opinion of themselves.

A recent study of 105 mothers, fathers, and their children over fourteen years old found that a dad's self-esteem is more critical than a mom's in the way children feel about themselves.

—*Christian Inquirer*

Even though he may be a senator, a

governor, a president of a college, or a top industrialist, a man just might make his most significant contribution to America by the kind of far-reaching but unsung kind of job he does in the home as a father.

—Walter MacPeek

A dad is a mender of toys, a leader of boys.
He's a changer of fuses, a healer of bruises.
He's a mover of couches, a healer of ouches.
He's a hanger of screens, a counselor of teens.
He's a pounder of nails, a teller of tales.
He's a dryer of dishes, a fulfiller of wishes.
Bless him, O Lord.

A father is a man who is forced to endure childbirth without an anesthetic.

A father is a man who exchanges the currency in his billfold for snapshots.

A father is a man for whom the Christmas bills toll.

A father never feels entirely worthy of the worship in a child's eyes. He's never quite the hero his daughter thinks . . . never quite the man his son believes him to be . . . and this worries him sometimes.

A father works too hard to try and smooth the rough places in the road for those who will follow him.

A father is a man who gets very angry when the first school grades aren't as good as he thinks they should be.

A father is a man who hopes to have enough money on Father's Day to pay the bills from Mother's Day.

A father is a man who accuses the merchants of setting aside this annual day in June so they can get rid of their leftover Christmas ties and shaving lotion—but they love it anyway.

Fathers have very stout hearts, so they have to be broken sometimes or no one would know what's inside.

Fathers fight dragons . . . almost daily. They hurry away from the breakfast table . . . off to the arena which is sometimes called an office or a workshop . . . and they don't quite win the fight but they never give up.

Fathers make bets with insurance companies about who'll live the longest.

Fathers are what give daughters away to other men who aren't nearly good enough . . . so they can have grandchildren that are smarter than anybody's.

But most unique, a father is a man who reflects the image of His Father in heaven and who makes it easier for his children to know their father's heavenly Father.

Four years: My Daddy can do anything!

7 years: My Dad knows a lot . . . a whole lot.

8 years: My Father does not know quite everything.

12 years: Oh, well, naturally Father does not know that either.

14 years: Oh, Father? He is hopelessly old-fashioned.

21 years: Oh, that man—he is out of date!

25 years: He knows a little bit about it, but not much.

30 years: I must find out what Dad thinks about it.

35 years: Before we decide, we'll get Dad's idea first.

50 years: What would Dad have thought about that?

60 years: My Dad knew literally everything!

65 years: I wish I could talk it over with Dad once more.

FATHER'S DAY

Father's Day comes after Mother's Day. That's so the bills for Mother's Day will arrive just in time for Father's Day.

A small boy's definition: "Father's Day is just like Mother's Day, only you don't spend as much on the present."

FATIGUE

If I had my entire life to live over, I doubt I'd have the strength.

FAULTS

It is the peculiar quality of a fool to perceive the faults of others and to forget his own.

The greatest of all faults is to be conscious of none.

—Thomas Carlyle

If you think you have no faults, that makes one more!

FAVORITISM

A deplorable incident occurred in the life of Mahatma Gandhi. He said in his auto-biography that during his student days he was interested in the Bible. Deeply touched by the reading of the Gospels, he seriously considered becoming a convert. Christianity seemed to offer the real solution to the caste system that was dividing the people of India. One Sunday he went to church to see the minister and ask for instruction on the way of salvation and other Christian doctrines. But when he entered the sanctuary, the ushers refused him a seat and suggested that he go back and worship with his own people. He left and never went back. "If Christians have caste differences also," he said to himself, "I might as well remain a Hindu."

FEAR

There is no fear like the fear of being found out.

All religion is borne out of fear.

—Bertrand Russell

A French existentialist said that each century can be summarized by one word.

17th century—mathematics
18th century—natural sciences
19th century—biology
20th century—fear

A wife's number-one fear is that of being used and abandoned. A husband's number-one fear is that of failure.

One summer during another hurricane season, Frank Graham, then president of the University of North Carolina, was taking a vacation in his cottage on the Atlantic beach. Storm warnings were up, causing a rather sleepless night. When he went into the kitchen to fix a sandwich, he found the family cook trembling with fear.

"Don't worry," he reassured her. "The waves are only three feet high."

"It's not those three-foot waves that bother me," she replied. "It's those three thousand miles of water leaning up against those three-foot waves!"

When I'm Afraid

When I'm afraid of times before,
    What coming days will bring,
When life's omissions I deplore,
    And earth-mists 'round me cling,
Oh, Lord of Love, my weakness see;
    When I'm afraid, I'll trust in Thee.
When I'm afraid of dangers near,
    Foreboding future ills;
When rocks and shoals and deeps I fear,
    And gloom my spirit fills;
Oh, Lord of Might, my weakness see;
    When I'm afraid, I'll trust in Thee.
When I'm afraid of crushing loss,
    Parting from loved ones dear,
Lest I shall murmur at my cross,
    And yield to faithless fear;
Oh, Lord of Peace, my weakness see;
    When I'm afraid, I'll trust in Thee.
When I'm afraid of failing health,
    Sore weaknesses I know,
And illness steals o'er me by stealth,
    And sickness lays me low;
Oh, Lord of Power, my weakness see,
    When I'm afraid, I'll trust in Thee.
When I'm afraid of drear old age,
    As nature's powers decay,
Mortality's dread heritage
    Increasing day by day;
Oh, Lord of Grave, my weakness see,
    When I'm afraid, I'll trust in Thee.

Amy Carmichael was a great missionary who lived for fifty years in India without ever returning to England. She lived in a sickroom for many of those years because of an accident suffered early in her missionary career. She had two plaques on the wall of her room. One said, "Fear not." The other said, "I know."

A child had to walk each evening past a dark, spooky house. Some adults sought to give him courage. One handed him a good luck charm to ward off the ghosts. Another had a light put on the dreaded corner. Still another said earnestly, "Trust God and be brave!" The advice was good, but he offered nothing more. Then someone said with compassion, "I know what it is to be afraid. I will walk with you past the house." He did nothing to remove the fear—except to lift it from the child's shoulders and place it on his own.

When you're afraid, keep your mind on what you have to do. And if you have been thoroughly prepared, you will not be afraid.
—Dale Carnegie

Everyone is living or working in fear. The mother is afraid for her children, the father for his business, the clerk for his job. The worker is afraid of his boss or a competitor. There is hardly a man who is not afraid that some other man will do him a bad turn.

—Basil King

Fear is the most devastating emotion on earth. I fought it and conquered it by helping people who were worse off than I was. I believe that anyone can conquer fear by doing the things he fears to do, provided he keeps doing them until he gets a record of successful experience behind him.
—Eleanor Roosevelt

Dr. Harold Urey, a Nobel Peace Prize winner and one of the physicians whose work led to the creation of the atomic bomb, wrote, "I write to make you afraid. I, myself, am a man who is afraid. All the wise men I know are afraid."

George W. Truett, one of the great preachers during the first half of the twentieth century, said that his experience with people led him to preach on the theme of fear again and again. On one occasion, he was asked to speak at a highly respected college. When Truett inquired about what topic to address, he was told that the vast majority of the student body had signed a statement that read, "Let the visiting minister tell us how we may conquer fear."
—Our Daily Bread

What are Americans afraid of? National research by R. H. Bruskin Associates shows the following hierarchy of fears: Speaking before a group heads the list, feared by 40.6 percent of those interviewed. This fear is greater among women than men, and greatest in the Southern United States. Fear of high places comes next at 32 percent; followed by insects and bugs (three times as many women as men); followed by financial problems, deep water, sickness, flying, and loneliness.

In time, and as one comes to benefit from experience, one learns that things will turn out neither as well as one hoped nor as badly as one feared.
—Jerome S. Bruner

A young woman was waiting for a bus in a crime-ridden area one evening when a rookie policeman approached her. "Want me to wait with you?" he asked. "That's not necessary. I'm not afraid," she replied. "Well, I am," he grinned. "Would you mind waiting with me?"

A backwoods farmer, sitting on the steps of a tumble-down shack, was approached by a stranger who stopped for a drink of water.

"How's your wheat coming along?" asked the stranger.

"Didn't plant none."

"Really, I thought this was good wheat country."

"Afraid it would rain."

"Well, how is your corn crop?"

"Ain't got none. Afraid of corn blight."

The stranger, confused but persevering, continued, "Well, sir, how are your potatoes?"

"Didn't plant no potatoes either . . . afraid of potato bugs."

"For Pete's sake, man," the stranger asked. "What did you plant?"

151

"Nothing," said the farmer. "I just played it safe."

Fear kept him from taking risks, and as a result, he lost out.

—A. L. "Kirk" Kirkpatrick

FEELINGS

Some things are better felt than touched.

—Scottish proverb

No one can feel that his sins are forgiven. Ask that man whose debt was paid by another. "Do you feel that your debt is paid?" "No," is the reply. "I don't feel that it is paid; but I know from this receipt that it has been paid."

Someone asked Luther, "Do you feel
    That you have been forgiven?"
He answered, "No, but I'm as sure
    As there is a God in heaven.
For feelings come and feelings go,
    And feelings are deceiving.
My warrant is the Word of God
    Naught else is worth believing."

FELLOWSHIP

An American doctor traveling in Korea knew just enough of the language to get around. At a station stop an old Korean boarded the train and sat across from the doctor. He carried a large bundle in a white cloth. Soon the old Korean began to speak to the doctor, pouring out a torrent of words. The doctor replied with the only sentence he had memorized, "I do not understand Korean." The old man persisted. A second time the doctor gave his stock answer. This was repeated a third time.

In the stream of Korean words the doctor thought he had detected a somewhat familiar word. Had the old man said something about Jesus?

His doubt vanished when the Korean pointed to the doctor and asked, "Yesu? Yesu?" With a smile the doctor nodded in agreement, "Yesu, Yesu."

Smiling from ear to ear, the Korean opened his large bundle and proudly displayed his Korean Bible. Then he put his finger on a verse. The doctor couldn't read it, of course, but carefully figuring out the approximate place in his own Bible, he read from 1 John 3:14: "We know that we have passed out of death into life, because we love the brethren."

—Leslie B. Flynn

FISHING

Give a man a fish, and you feed him for a day. Teach a man to fish, and you get rid of him on the weekends.

—Gary Apple

FLATTERY

Flattery is telling others exactly what they think of themselves.

—Hal Roach

Flattery is like cologne water—to be smelled, not swallowed.

—John Billings

Flattery is like soft soap . . . 90 percent lye.

Only two groups of people fall for flattery—men and women.

FLESH

Donald Grey Barnhouse preached that we can't blame Satan for all our problems. We have the sin nature, the flesh. After the service, a woman said, "Dr. Barnhouse, I was disappointed in the message. You said we can't blame Satan. But Satan has always been such a comfort to me."

FLEXIBILITY

Many colonists living in Virginia in the middle of the eighteenth century started the long trek across the mountains toward the lure of the West. Some, forced to stop because of illness, breakdown of a wagon axle, or some other unforeseen difficulty, settled in the sheltered valleys of the mountains of what is today eastern Tennessee or Kentucky. Their farewell greeting to their friends in Virginia in 1770 had been "God Save the King."

Cut off from the world completely, fifteen years went by before they saw any traveler. Imagine the excitement when the noise of an arriving caravan ran through the valley. After making sure this was a friendly group, they engaged in animated conversation. After a while, one of the settlers got around to asking, "And who is the King now? Is it still George the Third?"

The answer came immediately, "There is no King now! We've had a revolution and a long war! The colonies won! Now we are a republic, and George Washington is our President!"

The settlers thought for a moment and replied, "Imagine that! For fifteen years we've thought of ourselves as loyal subjects of the King, and now we discover that we are Americans, citizens of our own republic. God bless the President!"

—Donald Grey Barnhouse

Someone asked the Duke of Wellington how he defeated Napoleon. He answered, "Napoleon's plans were made in wire, but mine were made in string."

FOOLS

Thinking to have a little fun, a soldier spotted a Salvation Army lassie on duty in a railroad station. He strolled over to her.

"Will you pray for me?" he asked sarcastically.

He crimsoned as she reached up, placed a hand on his head and, in a voice plainly heard by his comrades, said, "O Lord, make this young man's heart as soft as his head."

After the disastrous hurricane that struck Long Island in November 1950, one of the residents took a walk along the south shore. As this man was viewing the wrecked cottages and sympathizing with the owners, he came upon a scene that showed how a victim's sense of humor had triumphed over calamity. The white front door of an almost totally wrecked house was propped up by a broken chair. On the door, this message was printed in black crayon:

I am an insurance salesman
I sell storm insurance
I did not carry storm insurance on this
    cottage
I am a dope.

—Leslie B. Flynn

He who provides for this life, but takes no care for eternity, is wise for a moment but a fool forever.

—Tilleston

The wise man has his follies no less than the fool, but herein lies the difference— the follies of the fool are known to the world, but are hidden from himself; the follies of the wise man are known to himself, but hidden from the world.

—C. C. Colton

Henry Ward Beecher, an elegant and witty preacher, entered the Congregational Plymouth Church in Brooklyn, New York one Sunday and found several letters waiting for him. He opened one and found it contained the single word, "Fool!" To the congregation on Sunday he said, "I have known many an instance of a man writing a letter and forgetting to sign his name, but this is the first instance I have ever known of a man signing his name and forgetting to write the letter."

Don't approach a goat from the front, a horse from the back, or a fool from any side.

—Yiddish proverb

The surprising thing about young fools is how many survive to become old fools.

—Doug Larson

John Wesley said that there are "twin fools" all over the world: one person believing nothing; the other believing everything.

—E. Schuyler English

Little Johnny's grandfather was something of a philosopher and never missed an opportunity to give out bits of sage advice to his grandson.

"Yessirree, Johnny," he said one day, "remember, fools are certain, but wise men hesitate."

"Are you sure, Grandpa?" the boy asked.

"Yes, my boy," said the old man, laying his gnarled hand on the youth's head. "I'm absolutely certain."

—*Bits & Pieces*

There are two kinds of fools. One says, "This is old, therefore it is good"; the other says, "This is new, therefore it is better."

Let us be thankful for the fools. But for them the rest of us could not succeed.

—Mark Twain

FORGETTING

A retentive memory may be a good thing, but the ability to forget is the true token of greatness.

—Elbert Hubbard

Everyone forgets at one time or another, according to Karen Bolla, a Johns Hopkins University researcher. These are the things people most often forget:

- names   83%
- where something is   60%
- telephone numbers   57%
- words   53%
- what was said   49%
- faces   42%

—*Our Daily Bread*

FORGIVENESS

He who cannot forgive others destroys the bridge over which he himself must pass.

—George Herbert

Forgiveness is relinquishing my rights to hurt back.

—Archibald Hart

In his book *You Can Win!* Roger Campbell told of a woman who had been treated wrongly by her church and came to him for help. He was sympathetic to her plight, but he also realized she would not be delivered from her hurt feelings until she got a glimpse of the suffering of Christ. "Has anyone spat on you yet?" Campbell asked. "No," she replied, shocked by his question. "They did on Jesus," he told her. Campbell went on to say, "Suddenly she saw my point. While she had certainly been mistreated by people who should have known better, she had not endured the pain and shame experienced by Christ in His suffering and death for her sins. My simple question changed her attitude about her persecutors and she was able to forgive those who had snubbed and avoided her."

The sentiment that God might forgive sin as an act of mere generosity is an insult to holiness and divine government.

—Lewis Sperry Chafer

In a cemetery not far from New York City is a headstone engraved with a single word: "Forgiven." The message is simple, unembellished. There is no date of birth, no epitaph. There is only a name and the solitary word "Forgiven." But that is the greatest word that can be applied to any man or woman or written on any gravestone.

Old Joe was dying. For years he had been at odds with Bill, formerly one of his best friends. Wanting to straighten things out, he sent word for Bill to come and see him.

When Bill arrived, Joe told him that he was afraid to go into eternity with such bad feelings between them. Then very reluctantly and with great effort Joe apologized for things he had said and done. He also reassured Bill that he forgave him for his offenses. Everything seemed fine until Bill turned to leave. As he walked out of the room, Joe called out after him, "But, remember, if I get better, this doesn't count!"

E. L. Hamilton, a brother in Christ, once rebuked a Christian worker for manifesting an unforgiving spirit toward a penitent. After a moment's thought, the lady replied, "Well, I guess I will pardon her, as you suggest, but I never want to have anything more to do with her!" Hamilton said, "Is that how you want God to treat you? Do you want Him to say He will forgive you, but that He will never have anything more to do with you? Remember, when Christ forgave you, He cast your sins into the sea of everlasting forgetfulness!"

A group of Christian missionaries met in Delhi, India, with representatives of other religions to discuss their beliefs. In the course of their talks a member of a major non-Christian religion said to a missionary, "Tell me one thing your religion can offer the Indians that mine can't." The missionary thought for a moment and replied, "Forgiveness! Forgiveness!"

There are two ways of covering our sins: man's way and God's way. If you seek to hide them, they will have a resurrection sometime; but if you let the Lord cover them, neither the Devil nor man will ever be able to find them again.

—D. L. Moody

George Woodall was a missionary to London's inner city. One day a young woman he had led to the Lord came to him and said, "I keep getting worried. Has God really forgiven my past?"

Mr. Woodall replied, "If this is troubling you, I think I know what He would say to you. He would tell you to mind your own business." "What do you mean?" she inquired with a puzzled look. He told her that Jesus had made her sins His business. When He took them away, He put them behind His back, dropped them into the depths of the sea, and posted a notice that reads, "No fishing!"

Sign on a factory bulletin board: "To err is human, to forgive is not company policy."

A woman once stayed after a church service to talk with the minister. She was downcast and despondent. "I do not suppose you can help me," she said. "For years I have been unable to pray. There is a woman who came between me and my husband, and I cannot forgive her." The minister answered kindly, "You cannot forgive the woman for her own sake, but could you not forgive her for Christ's sake?" At first the question did not register. Then a glimmer of hope lightened the depressed woman's face. "Yes," she said, "you are right. I cannot forgive her for her own sake, but I can for His sake, and I will!"

Eunice, a former missionary to Liberia, told a story about forgiveness that has long remained with me. An African man worked for her, and one day she caught him stealing clothes from her house.

"Please forgive me," he pleaded. "I did wrong. I promise not to do it again."

She forgave him and allowed him to continue working for her. But less than a month passed before she caught him stealing again. "Look at you!" she said. "You've stolen again!"

The bright fellow stared at her and yelled back, "What kind of a Christian are you?"

Eunice, dumbfounded, had no idea how to respond.

"If you forgave me, you do not remember it," the man said. "If you did not remember it, such a thing did not happen."

—Michael Youssef

If you are suffering from a bad man's injustice, forgive him lest there be two bad men.

—Augustine

A Sunday school teacher had just concluded her lesson and wanted to make sure she had made her point. She said, "Can anyone tell me what you must do before you obtain forgiveness from sin?"

There was a short interval of silence and then, from the back of the room, a small boy spoke up. "Sin," he said.

Billy Graham said he believes that 75 percent of patients in hospitals would be made whole if they would forgive.

Napoleon's triumphant attitude toward his enemies had softened by the time his French forces defeated the Russians at the Battle of Borodino. Losses on both sides were heavy. As Napoleon walked the battlefield the next day, taking a count of the dead, he heard a cry of pain from a fallen soldier and ordered a stretcher. One of his aides pointed out that the wounded man was a Russian, but Napoleon retorted, "After a victory there are no enemies, only men."

—Today in the Word

John Stott quoted the administrator of the largest psychiatric hospital in London who said, "If the people here only knew what it means to be forgiven, I could dismiss half of them at once."

John Wesley came to America for two years as a missionary serving in the colony of Georgia. One day he was talking to General Oglethorpe about some miscreant. Oglethorpe said, "I never forgive." Whereupon Wesley said, "Then I hope, sir, that you never sin."

Forgiveness is better than revenge, for forgiveness is the sign of a gentle nature, but revenge is the sign of a savage nature.
—Epictetus

On November 14, 1940, the German Luftwaffe (air force) bombed the city of Coventry, England. It became the longest air raid over Britain during World War II. When the bombing ended, residents surveyed the results and saw that their beautiful cathedral had been razed.

But at least some of the residents did not allow the tragic, pointless destruction of their place of worship to serve as an excuse for revenge. The next day members of that congregation took two irregular, charred beams from the roof, tied them together, and set them up at the east end of the ruins where the altar had been. The beams formed a cross. The parishioners printed two words on a sign and placed it at the foot of the cross: "Father, Forgive."

A Scottish physician, noted for his skill and piety, died, and when his books were examined, several accounts were found with this written across them in red ink: "Forgiven—too poor to pay."

His wife, who was of a different disposition, said, "These accounts must be paid." She therefore sued for the money.

The judge asked her, "Is this your husband's handwriting in red ink?" She replied in the affirmative.

"Then," said he, "there is not a tribunal in the land that can obtain the money where he has written 'Forgiven.'"

An emperor of China heard of a rebellion in a remote part of his kingdom. He gathered his soldiers and went to the area to destroy his enemies.

The people in that area put up a red flag of surrender. Then the emperor gave them all gifts and turned his horse around to go home. His soldiers said, "Wait, we thought you said we would destroy our enemies." The emperor replied, "We have. By our kindness we have made our enemies our friends."

"Yes, you did too!"
  "I did not!"
  Thus the little quarrel started,
  Thus by unkind little words
  Two fond friends were parted.
"I am sorry."
  "So am I."
  Thus the little quarrel ended,
  Thus by loving little words
  Two fond hearts were mended.
—Leslie B. Flynn

Decide to Forgive

Decide to forgive
For resentment is negative
Resentment is poisonous
Resentment diminishes and devours the
  self.
Be the first to forgive,
To smile and take the first step.
And you will see happiness bloom
On the face of your human brother or sister.
Be always the first
Do not wait for others to forgive
For by forgiving
You become the master of fate
The fashioner of life
The doer of miracles.
To forgive is the highest,
Most beautiful form of love.
In return you will receive
Untold peace and happiness.

Here is a program for achieving a truly forgiving heart:
  Sunday: Forgive yourself.
  Monday: Forgive your family.
  Tuesday: Forgive your friends and associates.
  Wednesday: Forgive across economic lines within your own nation.

Thursday: Forgive across cultural lines within your own nation.

Friday: Forgive across political lines within your own nation.

Saturday: Forgive other nations.

Only the brave know how to forgive. A coward never forgives. It is not in his nature.

—Robert Muller

Two brothers went to their rabbi to settle a long-standing feud. The rabbi got the two to reconcile their differences and shake hands. As they were about to leave, he asked each one to make a wish for the other in honor of the Jewish New Year. The first brother turned to the other and said, "I wish you what you wish me." At that, the second brother threw up his hands and said, "See, Rabbi, he's starting up again!"

In *The Family Album*, Arthur and Nancy DeMoss include a story that aptly describes the spiritual consequences of failure to forgive. While Leonardo da Vinci labored on his masterpiece *The Last Supper* he became angry with another man. They quarreled, da Vinci hurling bitter accusations and threats at the other fellow. Returning to his canvas, the artist attempted to paint the face of Jesus but found that he was unable to do so. So upset was he that he could not compose himself for the painstaking work. Finally, he set down his brushes, sealed his paint pots, and went to search for the man with whom he had argued. He apologized, asking for forgiveness, which his antagonist graciously gave. Only then was Leonardo able to return to his workshop and complete the face of the Savior.

—Don Anderson

Heinrich Heine was a talented German lyric poet who was capable of producing exquisitely beautiful songs, but his vengeful spirit ruined his life. He wrote bitter, unfair attacks on any who disagreed with him, wasting his genius on satirical defamations.

Once he wrote, "My nature is the most peaceful in the world. All I ask is a simple cottage, a decent bed, good food, some flowers in front of my window, and a few trees beside my door. Then if God wanted to make me wholly happy, he would let me enjoy the spectacle of six or seven of my enemies dangling from these trees. I would forgive them for all the wrong they have done me—forgive them from the bottom of my heart, for we must forgive our enemies. But not until they were hanged!"

That kind of "forgiveness" is mockery. It doesn't belong in the category of forgiveness at all.

It is not easy . . .

To apologize,
To profit by mistakes,
To begin over,
To forgive and forget,
To be unselfish,
To think and then act,
To take advice,
To keep out of a rut,
To admit error,
To make the best of little,
To face a sneer,
To subdue an unruly temper,
To be charitable,
To shoulder a deserved blame,
To keep trying,
To recognize the silver lining,
To be considerate,
To avoid mistakes,
To endure success,
But it always pays.

FREEDOM

A man's worst difficulties begin when he is able to do as he likes.

—Aldous Huxley

We are in bondage to the law in order that we may be free.

—Cicero

Freedom is not the right to do as a person pleases, but the liberty to do as he ought.

Freedom standing by itself inevitably degenerates into license. License, which is unbridled freedom, quickly becomes the enemy of freedom.

—Richard John Neuhaus

FREEDOM

The first duty of every soul is to find not its freedom but its master.

—P. T. Forsyth

Giuseppe Garibaldi, the great Italian leader of the nineteenth century, in a fiery speech urged some thousands of Italy's young men to fight for the freedom of their homeland. One timid young fellow asked him, asking, "If I fight, Sir, what will be my reward?" Swift as a lightning flash came the uncompromising answer: "Wounds, scars, bruises, and perhaps death. But remember that through your bruises Italy will be free."

FRIENDLINESS

People who like people are people that people like.

There are two kinds of people in this world: Those who come into a room with the air of "Here I am!" And those who enter a room with the air of "Oh! There *you* are!"

One of the surest ways to discover how many friends you have is to rent a cottage at the beach.

FRIENDS (Also see ENEMIES)

The best way to form a friendship is to become interested in other people, not by trying to interest people in you.

Don't walk in front of me.
    I may not follow.
Don't walk behind me.
    I may not lead.
Walk beside me
    And just be my friend.

He who is a judge between two friends loses one of them.

A friend is a person who goes around saying nice things about you behind your back.

Choose friends with care; you become what they are.

—Teen Esteem

A few years back Pepper Rogers, head football coach at UCLA, was going through a terrible season. He was very upset about it, and he didn't think his wife was encouraging him enough. He said, "My dog is my best friend. I told my wife that a man needs at least two friends. She told me to go buy another dog."

It's smart to pick your friends—but not to pieces.

—Teen Esteem

John and Dave were hiking when they spotted a mountain lion staring at them. John froze in his tracks but Dave sat down on a log, tore off his hiking boots, pulled a pair of running shorts from his backpack and hurriedly began to put them on.

"For crying out loud, you can't outrun a mountain lion!" John hissed.

"I don't have to," shrugged Dave. "I just have to outrun you."

You can always tell a real friend; when you've made a fool of yourself, he doesn't feel you've done a permanent job.

—Lawrence J. Peter

The difference between a friend and an acquaintance is that a friend helps; an acquaintance merely advises.

—"Calgary Bob" Edwards

Socrates once asked a simple old man what he was most thankful for. The man replied, "That being such as I am, I have had the best friends I have had."

There is no possession more valuable than a good and faithful friend.

—Socrates

Friendship doubles joys and halves griefs.
—Francis Bacon

There are three faithful friends—an old wife, an old dog, and ready money.
—Benjamin Franklin

If you want to be well liked by others, don't set out to make yourself liked. You will only be thinking of yourself that way. Instead, develop a sincere and genuine interest in other people, and being liked will follow naturally.

—*Bits & Pieces*

The only way to have a friend is to be sure you are one.

—Ralph Waldo Emerson

Treat your friends like family and your family like friends.

To be rich in friends is to be poor in nothing.

—Lilian Whiting

A friend is someone whom we can always count on to count on us.

—Francis Perier

A real friend is one who attacks us in the front.

There are two kinds of people: Those who brighten the room when they enter and those who brighten the room when they leave.

One enemy is too many and a hundred friends are too few.

—Icelandic proverb

A friend is a present you give yourself.

—Robert Louis Stevenson

You can make more friends in two months by becoming interested in other people than you can in two years by trying to get people interested in you.

—Dale Carnegie

Make every person like himself a little better and I promise that he will like you very much indeed.

—Philip Chesterfield

The bumps of life need the shock absorber of friendship.

Friendship ain't just claspin' hands,
  and saying "How' de do,"
Friendship grips a feller's heart,
  And warms him thro' and thru!

A friend is one who knows you and still loves you.

Ten Commandments of Friendship

1. Speak to people—there is nothing as nice as a cheerful word of greeting.
2. Smile at people—it takes seventy-two muscles to frown but only fourteen to smile!
3. Call people by name—the sweetest music to anyone's ear is the sound of their own name.
4. Be friendly and helpful—if you would have friends, be friendly.
5. Be cordial—speak and act as if everything you do were a real pleasure.
6. Be genuinely interested in people—you can like *everyone* if you try.
7. Be generous with praise, cautious with criticism.
8. Be considerate of the feelings of others—it will be appreciated.
9. Be thoughtful of the opinions of others.
10. Be alert to give service—what counts most in life is what we do for others!

A small boy defined a friend as "Someone who knows all about you and likes you just the same."

An English publication offered a prize for the best definition of a friend, and among the thousands of answers received were the following:

"One who multiplies joys, and divides grief."
"One who understands our silence."
"A volume of sympathy bound in cloth."
"A watch which beats true for all time and never runs down."

But here is the definition that won the prize:

"A friend—the one who comes in when the whole world has gone out."

Oh, how good it feels, the hand of an old friend.

—Henry Longfellow

FRIENDS

Fame is the scentless sunflower with gaudy crowns of gold. But friendship is the breathing rose with sweet in every fold.

—Oliver Wendell Holmes

I think that God will never send,
A gift so precious as a friend.
A friend who always understands,
And fills each need as it demands.
Whose loyalty will stand the test,
When skies are bright or overcast.
Who sees the faults that merit blame,
But keeps on loving just the same.
Who does far more than creeds could do,
To make us good, to make us true.
Earth's gifts a sweet contentment lend,
But only God can give a friend!

—Rosalie Carter

To get the full value of joy, you must have somebody to divide it with.

—Mark Twain

Some people make enemies instead of friends because it is less trouble.

—E. C. McKenzie

Be slow in choosing a friend, slow in changing.

—Benjamin Franklin

An old friend is better than two new ones.

—Russian proverb

Associate yourself with men of good quality if you esteem your own reputation: for it is better to be alone than in bad company.

—George Washington

If you really want to know who your friends are, just make a mistake.

—*The Bible Friend*

So long as we love we serve; no man is useless while he is a friend.

—Robert Louis Stevenson

FRUSTRATION

Frustration is trying to find your glasses without your glasses.

FUTURE

The problem with the present is that the future is not what it used to be.

The most effective way to ensure the value of the future is to confront the present courageously and constructively.

—Rollo May

Tell me what are the prevailing sentiments that occupy the minds of young men, and I will tell you what is to be the character of your next generation.

—Edmund Burke

Near the Rock of Gibraltar are two pillar-like rocks called the Pillars of Hercules because it is in Greek mythology that Hercules placed them there. Carved on one of the pillars are the words "Ne Plus Ultra" ("Nothing More Beyond"). These words conveyed the view many had then, that nothing existed beyond Gibraltar, except the vast expanse of the ocean. But later Columbus sailed through the pillars and discovered the new world. Then someone crossed out the word "Ne." "Plus Ultra" means "More Beyond."

The future is much like the present except that it's a little longer.

My interest is in the future because I'm going to spend the rest of my life there.

—Charles F. Kettering

He who will not look forward must look behind.

—Gaelic proverb

The best thing about the future is that it only comes one day at a time.

—Dean Acheson

I plan for the future,
I yearn for the past.
And meantime the present
Is leaving me fast.

If you would plant for a year, plant rice; if for twenty years, plant trees; if for a hundred years, grow men.

—Chinese proverb

There is no sharp distinction between the past, the present, and the future.

—T. S. Eliot

The future is that time when you'll wish you'd done what you aren't doing now.

G

GAMES

Early in the eighteenth century two young monks were disciplined by their abbot for an infraction of the monastery rules. "Brothers Benedict and Fidelis," he said sternly, "your punishment will be seclusion for three months—under the rule of silence!" At first the disciplined ones gave themselves to prayer and study, but the silence was oppressive and the idle hours weighed heavily on them. Finally the younger monk had an idea. He collected all the smooth, flat stones of one size that he could find in the courtyard until, with the help of his "silent partner," they had gathered twenty-eight. He then placed different numbers on each of them and began devising a new game to while away their unproductive hours. It was difficult for them to communicate, but after a few weeks they managed by making gestures to outline certain rules to govern their play with these marked stones. The most difficult thing was keeping silent when they were excited over winning a game. Then they had a happy idea. They were allowed to utter aloud the prayer, "Dixit Dominus Domino Meo." By reducing this to one word, the victor was able to signal his triumph by excitedly exclaiming, "Domino! Domino!" The pastime they devised has been refined but is still played in scores of countries today.

GENEALOGIES

"My family's ancestry is very old," said one club member trying to impress the group. "We can be traced back to the early kings of Europe." Then turning to a lady sitting nearby, she asked, "And how old is your family, my dear?" "I really don't know," replied the lady with a sweet smile, "all our records were lost in the Great Flood."

—The Links

GENEROSITY

A host of an American in Korea could not speak any English, except for two words: "Help yourself."

GENIUS

Genius is one percent inspiration and 99 percent perspiration.

—Thomas A. Edison

Genius, in truth, means little more than the faculty of perceiving in an unhabitual way.

The greatest genius will not be worth much if he pretends to draw exclusively from his own resources.

—Johann von Goethe

GENTLENESS

A gentleman is one who thinks of others before himself.

—Confucius

The true gentleman is God's servant, the world's master, and his own man.

A nurse in a serviceman's hospital complained to the chaplain that she had been rudely treated by some of the patients. He answered, "Thank God for that!" "What do you mean?" she inquired in astonishment. "Well," he explained, "if you are holding a glass and someone knocks against you, you can only spill out what is inside! When people misjudge and persecute us, we soon reveal what is in our hearts. If we are Christ-filled and governed by the Holy Spirit, we will manifest the gentleness and meekness of our Savior. In fact, God often allows us to be pushed around and mistreated so that unsaved men may be astonished at His grace as we overflow with love and forbearance."

Nothing is so strong as gentleness and nothing is so gentle as real strength.
—Francis De Salem

On one occasion Abraham Lincoln sent a note by messenger to his Secretary of War, Edwin Stanton. Stanton was a capable man, but was noted for his brusqueness and rigid opinions. As the messenger stood waiting for a reply, Stanton tore up the note and shouted, "President Lincoln is a fool!"

When the messenger returned and told Mr. Lincoln what the Secretary had said, Lincoln thought a moment, and then said with a grin, "Well, perhaps Mr. Stanton is right!"

The Greek word *praus* means power under control. A three-year-old girl called to her mother to come and see a doggie. Her mother thought it was another imaginary dog, but she went out anyway. To her surprise she saw the girl petting an injured Mexican wolf. The mother told the girl to back off from the dog slowly, and she did. The mother called a vet, who gave the animal a shot. The wolf recovered and stayed in the girl's backyard. She played with the wolf as a pet for twelve years. The wolf had power under control. That was "gentleness."

GIFTS

The perfect gift for the person who has everything is a burglar alarm.

GIVING

If you give because it pays, it won't pay.
—R. G. LeTourneau

A farmer was known for giving extensively to the Lord's work. He explained it this way: "I keep shoveling into God's bin, and God keeps shoveling back into mine, and He has the bigger shovel."

An African convert, who loved to help others, earned money by making and selling a special kind of bean-cake. She had always been conscientious in her giving, but after suffering a severe foot injury in an accident, her income ceased. It was many long months before she could resume her work. She eagerly awaited the day when she could sell her tasty cakes again and promised the local missionary that she would give one-third of her earnings to the Lord instead of just ten percent. Her ambitious goal for the first week of business was to make a profit of three shillings. The missionary was surprised when the woman returned after only two days with one shilling as an offering for the Lord. "You surely haven't earned three shillings already!" he exclaimed. The elderly African Christian seemed surprised by the question. "Do you think I would give my Lord the *last* of the three?" she asked. "This is the first one and it belongs to Him; the other two I will make will be for me." Her heart was so filled with love for the Savior that she found joy in honoring Him with her initial earnings.

He who gives to me teaches me to give.
—Danish proverb

When it comes to giving, some people stop at nothing.

The trouble with some folks who give until it hurts is that they are so sensitive to pain.

We make a living by what we get—we make a life by what we give.

In order to appreciate the luxury of giving, one must have been, at some time, poor.

A pig was complaining to a cow that he was not appreciated. "I don't understand it," he said, "people are always talking about how generous you are, giving them cream and milk and butter for their daily use. That's nice, of course, but I give more than you do—ham and bacon and bristles and feet. Yet nobody has any use for me. They make fun of me and call me a pig. I don't like it."

"Perhaps the difference," the cow replied after a moment's hesitation, "is that I give while I'm still living."

A Spanish-American convert was being baptized in West Texas. Before the ceremony he was seen going back to where his clothing was. He was told that his clothes would be safe. "Sí, sí," he replied, "but I am getting my pocketbook; I want it to be immersed too!"

A preacher was preaching on the need of the church to grow and expand.

He said, "This church needs to walk." A man in the back said, "Amen, brother! Let her walk!"

The preacher said, "This church needs to run!" The man said, "Amen, brother! Let her run!"

He said, "This church needs to fly!" The man said, "Amen, brother! Let her fly!"

The pastor then said, "But you know, folks, it's gonna take a little money." There was a hush over the congregation and then a man in the back said, "Let her walk."

A man decided to give his son-in-law a check for $5,000 on the day of his wedding to his daughter. The bride's sister was to present the groom with the money. "Did you give him the check?" asked the father. "Yes, Father," she answered. "And what did he say?" "Why, he said nothing, but he did shed some tears." The father asked, "How long did he cry?" And she replied, "Oh, about a minute." "Only a minute!" roared the father. "What an ingrate! Why, I cried for an hour after I signed the check!"

"Go, break to the needy sweet charity's bread;
    For giving is living," the angel said.
"And must I be giving again and again?"
    My peevish and pitiless answer ran.
"Oh, no," said the angel, piercing me through.
    "Just give till the Lord stops giving to you."

Old Deacon Hunter
Sat in the corner
As the contribution box passed by;
Sweetly content
He dropped in a cent
And said, "What a good churchman am I!"

When a Christian gets rich—either the Lord gains a fortune or loses a man.

One night a preacher was making an appeal for funds and he invited the congregation to bring their gifts and lay them on the altar. The response was large, and soon the aisles were filled with people, bringing up their offerings.

Soon a little girl came slowly toward the front. She was lame and walked with a crutch. At the altar she pulled a little ring from her finger and laid it with the other gifts. Adjusting her crutch, she went back to her seat. After the meeting, the preacher said to her, "My dear, I saw the thing you did tonight. It was beautiful but, you know, the response of the people tonight has been large, and we find we have some money left over, so we don't need your ring and I have brought it back to you." The little girl looked up with rebuke in her eyes, and said, "I didn't give that ring to you."

Too often we forget that the offerings of the Lord's people are made not to man but to God.

You get more than you give when you give more than you get.

—*Bits & Pieces*

No person was ever honored for what he received. Honor is the reward of what one gives.

—Calvin Coolidge

When we place our contribution in the collection plate, we are not giving to the Lord; we are just taking our hands off what belongs to Him.

Blessed are those who give without remembering and who receive without forgetting.

God judges what we give by what we keep.

—George Mueller

A wise lover regards not so much the gift of him whom he loves, as the love of the giver.

Mary Jane was given two nickels as she was about to leave for the morning service. One was for the collection plate and one for herself. As she trudged along to church, she dropped one of her precious nickels and it rolled into the sewer. Mary Jane looked down through the grating and came to the sad conclusion that it was lost forever.

"Well, there goes the Lord's nickel," she murmured.

Caesar Augustus gave an expensive gift to a person he wanted to honor. The person was so overwhelmed, he said, "This is too great a gift for me to receive."

Caesar responded, "But it's not too great a gift for me to give."

Once I knew a Baptist; He had a pious look.
He had been totally immersed—except his pocketbook.
He'd put a nickel on the plate, and then, with might and main
He'd sing, "When we asunder part, It gives us inward pain."

—S. M. Greene

It's not what you'd do with a million,
    If riches should e'er be your lot,
But what are you doing at the present
    With the dollar and a quarter you've got?

He who earns is an industrious man;
He who spends is a well-furnished man;
He who saves is a prepared man;
He who gives is a blessed man.

You can't take your money to heaven with you, but you can send it on ahead of you.

We can give without loving, but we cannot love without giving.

Once a certain preacher was born in quite a poor, humble family. The Lord kept him humble and his congregation kept him poor!

A rich man once gave ten thousand dollars each to three persons saying, "I want to settle all my accounts when I die. At the time of my death, you may deduct whatever you think I owe you—and throw the rest into my grave."

Sure enough, at his funeral, his church

pastor said, "I discovered that you never gave anything to the church. Here, I've deducted ten percent." And he threw in nine thousand dollars.

Next came his partner and threw in five thousand dollar bills, saying, "I deducted the amount you owed me."

Finally came his lawyer, proudly saying, "Although you owed me some money, I am canceling all fees and returning to you the entire amount." And he threw in a *check* for ten thousand dollars.

A young lad, whose usual allowance was five cents a week, received a gift of a dollar from his aunt. He was overjoyed. His aunt asked him what he planned to do with the money.

"I'm going to take it to Sunday school next Sunday and give it to God," he answered. "He never gets anything but nickels either."

—E. Schuyler English

Old Josh won a million dollars in a lottery. His minister went to tell him the news, but he hesitated to tell him outright for fear he would have a heart attack out of shock. So the minister said, "Do you think you would ever win the lottery?" Josh replied, "Probably not. I never win any of those things."

The minister then asked, "Suppose you won a million dollars in a lottery. What would you do with the money?"

"Well, I'd give half of it to the church," Josh replied. Just then, the minister fell over dead from a heart attack!

In a certain church the pastor started taking a collection for greatly needed repairs on the ceiling. Finally old deacon Tight stood up and said, "I will give five dollars." Just then a piece of plaster fell from the ceiling and hit him on the head. So deacon Tight looked up and said, "Well, I guess I'd better give ten dollars." Then the pastor, with rare common sense and pointed discretion looked up to heaven and said, "Oh, Lord, hit him again!"

The late John Roach Stratton told of two men who went to the dock at New York

City because of their interest in foreign missions. The one, a wealthy businessman, was beaming with pleasure. The other man said to him, "You seem to be much pleased." "Yes," answered the business-man, "I am sending by that ship in North River ten thousand dollars worth of equip-ment for a hospital in China." "Well, that is interesting, and I'm glad you made the gift. But you know, I too have a gift on that same ship; my only daughter is on board going as a missionary." The first man looked into the face of the new friend and said, "My dear brother, I feel as though I have given nothing compared with your sacrifice."

Some teenage girls who loved the Lord formed a "do without" club in order to raise money for missions. They determined to add to their fund by sacrificial giving. The majority, who were from well-to-do homes, easily found ways to contribute. But for one poor little girl named Margie it was extremely difficult. One day she knelt by her bed and asked the Lord to show her something she could do without. As she prayed, her pet spaniel licked her hands. Suddenly she remembered that the family doctor had offered to buy him. The tears came as she exclaimed, "Oh, Bright, I can't think of parting with you!" Then she thought of the words, "God so loved the world that He gave His only begotten Son." "I'll do it!" she said. Going to the doctor's home, she sold the dog for fifty dollars. Even though she missed her pet, she was still happy because she had been able to put all the money into the mission fund.

The doctor was pleased with the dog, but he wondered if a pressing need had caused the girl to part with him, so he stopped by her house. When he heard her story, he went home deep in thought. In his life of abundance he had never denied himself anything. The next morning Margie found the dog scratching at the door. This note was fastened to his collar: "Your practical Christianity has done more for me than any sermon I've ever heard. Last night I offered what's left of my wasted life to God. I'd like to join your club, and begin by doing without Bright."

—*Our Daily Bread*

A intensive survey in 1988 survey re-vealed that seven out of ten households in America contributed an average of $790 to charitable organizations and almost half of all Americans (45%) volunteered an average of 4.7 hours per week in time to charitable causes and organizations in 1987.

An interesting finding of the survey was the fact that Americans of low to moder-ate incomes are more generous than upper income individuals in their contribution of volunteer time and money. Another inter-esting discovery was that many Americans are willing to give of their time and finan-cial resources but they are not made aware of the needs.

We make a living by what we get, but we make a life by what we give.

—Winston Churchill

GOALS (Also see AIMS)
Oversleeping will never make dreams come true.

—*Teen Esteem*

I find the great thing in this world is not so much where we stand, as in what direc-tion we are moving.

—Oliver Wendell Holmes

Improved means are often dedicated to the achievement of unimproved goals.

—Henry David Thoreau

When Christopher Columbus landed in San Salvador instead of India, he said, "You can't navigate without a decent map."

When David Livingstone was finishing his work in Africa, someone said, "Now what will you do?" He said, "I'll go anywhere as long as it's forward."

Set your goal high. You may not reach it, but you'll put on muscle climbing toward it.

Once a stranger in America stopped a man on the road and asked him, "Where does this road lead to?" The man answered, "Where do you want to go?"

Again the stranger persisted, "Where does this road lead to?"

"My friend," replied the other, "this road leads to any place in the United States."

It is the same with communication. The leader must know his destination if he wishes to arrive there.

—John Haggai

If we but knew where we now stand and whither we are tending, we should know better what to do.

—Abraham Lincoln

The world stands aside to let anyone pass who knows where he is going.

—David Starr Jordan

Bernie May, the U.S. Director of Wycliffe Bible Translators, once wrote a paper entitled, "Fly the Airplane," in which he described his early training as a pilot and his instructor's word regarding the procedures to follow in case of an emergency. There were a series of steps to take regarding the throttle, the flaps, the engines, etc., and he said, "Between each of them write on the card 'Fly the Airplane.' Don't become so involved in handling the emergency that you fail to continue flying the airplane." He pointed out that some years ago a commercial airliner crashed in the swamps of Florida because the entire crew was so involved in the process of checking a landing gear which did not seem to be coming down that they forgot to fly the airplane.

High expectations are the key to everything.

—Sam Walton

Just as the Green Bay Packers dominated football in the 1960s, the San Francisco 49ers dominated in the 1980s. Like Vince Lombardi, Bill Walsh was the coach of the decade. Among Walsh's coaching idiosyncrasies was this: He mapped out the first twenty or so offensive plays before every game. The reason was simple. Walsh wanted extra assurance that the 49ers were off to the right start. Repeated practice of those plays meant confidence going into the game, fine execution from the outset, frequent first-quarter scores, and momentum that was hard to stop.

Goals are dreams with deadlines.

—Diana Scharf Hunt

Shoot for the moon. Even if you miss it, you will land among the stars.

—Les Brown

If you don't know where you are going, you may end up someplace else.

—Yogi Berra

A manufacturer once required all executives to put three objectives in writing at the beginning of each year.

Each executive had to list one *general* goal for his operation, one *specific* goal, and one *personal* objective. At the end of the year, progress in achieving the three objectives was reviewed, and executives were accordingly awarded extra financial compensation.

—*Bits & Pieces*

You must have long-range goals to keep you from being frustrated by short-range failures.

—Charles C. Noble

The main thing is that the main thing always remains the main thing.

—German proverb

Two fellows who went fishing found a good fishing spot. "Did you mark the spot?" one said. "Yes, I put an X on the boat." "Well, you idiot, what if we don't get the same boat tomorrow?"

You must know the harbor to which you are headed if you are to catch the winds to take you there.

—Seneca

In the middle of the nineteenth century, Ireland experienced a terrible famine. The government put thousands of men to work to pay for the food that was apportioned them. The projects were not carefully planned, and therefore many were kept busy digging roads which seemed to have no destination. A playwright, depicting this, tells of a little boy who came home one day and said to his father, "Dad, they're makin' roads that lead to nowhere."

A man had difficulty with his memory. He went to a doctor. The doctor said, "The only way we can help your memory is to impair your eyesight. Which do you want to retain—your eyesight or your memory?" The man answered, "Don't take away my sight. I'd rather see where I'm going than remember where I've been."

When you determine what you want, you have made the most important decision in your life. You have to know what you want in order to attain it.

—Douglas Lurtan

The absence of conscious goals usually leads to confusion and emptiness.

—James Armstrong

Start with the goal and work back. Picture what you want, define the purpose, the need, the goal—the objective that is desired. Then try to devise ways to build that machine, to outline its method of management, to devise a process of operation—to reach the goal for which you start.

—Thomas Watson

Focus precedes success.

—Bobb Biehl

GOD

A man's concept of God creates his attitude toward the hour in which he lives.

—G. Campbell Morgan

A young Jewish girl in the Warsaw ghetto managed to escape over the wall and hide in a cave. She died there shortly before the Allied Army broke out the ghetto. Before she died, she had scratched on the wall three things. First she wrote, "I believe in the sun, even though it is not shining." The second thing she wrote was, "I believe in love, even when feeling it or not." The third thing she wrote was, "I believe in God, even when He is silent."

—Gerald Kennedy

Immortal, invisible, God only wise
In light inaccessible hid from our eyes,
Most blessed, most glorious, the Ancient of Days
Almighty, victorious, Thy great name we praise.
Great Father of glory, pure Father of light,
Thine angels adore thee, all veiling their sight;
All praise we would render, O help us to see
'Tis only the splendor of light hideth thee.

—Walter Chalmers Smith

Through the ages people have peered into the darkness, listened in the stillness, looked into the cold, silent depths of space and come away with a heterogeneous collection of definitions of the "something" they think is "out there." Aristotle called it "The Unmoved Mover." Spencer said, "Eternal Energy," Huxley said, "The Unknown Absolute." Liberal theology speaks of "Ultimate Reality" and "Ground of Being," while others talk about "First Principle," "Cosmic Organism," "Life Force," "Sum Total of Accumulated Idealism."

A woman didn't know what to do about her two incorrigible boys. A neighbor said she had a boy like that and she took him to her parish priest. The mother of the two said, "I'm not Catholic but I'll try anything."

One boy was taken to the priest and the priest said, "Where is God?"

The boy answered nothing.

Again the priest said, "Where is God?"

Still the boy said nothing.

And so for the third time the priest asked the same question.

Then the boy ran out and said to his brother, "Let's get out of here. They've lost God and they're pinning it on me."

A recent newsletter included this essay, written by eight-year-old Danny Dutton. The boy's third-grade teacher asked her students to explain "God," prompting this essay.

"One of God's main jobs is making people. He makes these to put in the place of the ones that die so there will be enough people to take care of things here on earth. He doesn't make grown-ups, just babies. I think because they are smaller and easier to make. That way He doesn't have to take up His valuable time teaching them to walk and talk. He can just leave that up to the mothers and fathers. I think it works out pretty good.

"God's second most important job is listening to prayers. An awful lot of this goes on, as some people, like preachers and things, pray other times besides bedtime, and Grandpa and Grandma Dutton pray every time they eat (except for snacks). God doesn't have time to listen to the radio or TV on account of this. As He hears everything, not only prayers, there must be a terrible lot of noise going on in His ears unless He has thought of a way to turn it off. I think we should all be a little quieter. God sees everything and hears everything and is everywhere. Which keeps Him pretty busy. So you shouldn't go wasting His time asking for things that aren't important or go way over your parents' heads and ask for something they said you couldn't have."

The richest man in the world, Croesus, once asked the wisest man in the world, Thales, What is God? The philosopher asked for a day in which to deliberate, and then for another and another and another—and at length confessed that he was not able to answer. He said that the longer he deliberated, the more difficult it was for him to frame an answer.

The fiery Tertullian, the early church father, eagerly seized on this incident and said it was an example of the world's ignorance of God outside of Christ. "There," he exclaimed, "is the wisest man in the world, and he cannot tell you who God is. But the most ignorant mechanic among the Christians knows God and is able to make Him known to others."

—Paul Lee Tan

A Scottish college principal, John Cairns, told of a confirmed law-breaker who was often arrested by the police. The one redeeming feature of his dissolute life was love for his little girl, who was the image of his dead mother. Once, having committed burglary, he was sentenced to a long term in prison. During his imprisonment his little girl died. On the day he was released from prison he learned of her death. The blow shattered him. He was broken. He could not bring himself even to visit the home from which she had been taken. Suicide seemed the only escape. So he resolved to throw himself off one of the bridges of the Scottish capital. At midnight he stood on the parapet. He found himself climbing it. For no reason he could explain, as he said later, there flashed into his mind the words of the creed: "I believe in God the Father Almighty." He repeated it. He knew nothing of God, but he did know something of fatherhood. "Why," he said, "if that is what God is, if God is like that then I can trust him with my lassie—and myself." Death receded, life began anew.

—David A. MacLennan

Disregard the study of God, and you sentence yourself to stumble and blunder through life blindfolded.

—J. I. Packer

Seek the face of God and you will
   Strengthen your faith in God.

If man is not made for God,
   why is he only happy in God?
If man is made for God,
   why is he so opposed to God?

—Blaise Pascal

GOD—EXISTENCE OF

One evening as Napoleon Bonaparte was returning to France from an expedition to Egypt, a group of his officers began discussing the existence of God.

Thoroughly caught up in the atheistic spirit of the times, the officers were unanimous in their denial of God's existence. Finally, someone suggested they ask Napoleon, who was standing alone on the deck of their vessel. On hearing the question, "Is there a God?" he raised his hand and pointed to the starry sky, and simply asked, "Gentlemen, who made all that?"

GOD—FAITHFULNESS OF

In the greatest difficulties, in the heaviest trials, in the deepest poverty and necessities, God has never failed me: the financial balance for the entire Inland China Mission yesterday was twenty-five cents. Praise the Lord! Twenty-five cents . . . plus all the promises of God.

—J. Hudson Taylor

How many folks estimate difficulties in the light of their own resources and then attempt little and often fail in the little they attempt. All God's giants have been weak men and women who did great things for God because they counted on His faithfulness.

—J. Hudson Taylor

GOD—FELLOWSHIP WITH

A little boy, whose father was away from home most of the time, looked at his dad's picture on the wall and said to his mother, "Mother, I wish Father would come out of that frame."

Is God real to you, a Person near at hand? Or is He more like a picture on the wall, a motto, a doctrine, or something wonderful to look at and think about, but still in a frame?

Have you wished He might come out of the frame, become a glorious living reality? Have you cried, "Oh, that I know where I might find Him?"

—Vance Havner

GOD—GLORY OF

The glory of God is all His attributes added together and raised to the nth degree.

—Lewis Sperry Chafer

GOD—GOODNESS OF

Charles Simeon, rector of Holy Trinity Church in Cambridge, England, for fifty-four years (1782–1836), had a profound effect on the students of the university. Among those converted through Simeon's ministry, for example, was Henry Martyn, pioneer missionary to India.

Students were invited to the rector's house for tea and were encouraged to question him concerning spiritual truth. Once he was asked, "How do you maintain a close walk with God?" This was his reply: "By constantly meditating on the goodness of God and on our great deliverance from that punishment which our sins deserve. Keeping both of these in mind, we shall find ourselves advancing on our course; we shall feel the presence of God; we shall experience His love; we shall live in the enjoyment of His favor and in the hope of His grace. Meditation is the grand means of our growth and grace."

—Edward H. Morgan

About a century ago a missionary named Allen Gardiner had an accident and was drowned. When his body was found near his overturned boat along the seashore, his diary was also discovered. It told over and over again of hunger, privation, persecution, and suffering he had experienced. And yet the very last entry in the book was this: "I am overwhelmed with a sense of the goodness of God!"

GOD—GREATNESS OF

God created a universe so large that it would take a person between 200 and 500 billion years to travel around the universe at the speed of light (186,000 miles per second). He created the world out of atoms so small that it would take the whole population of the world 180 million years to count the atoms in a cup of water, counting at one per second. If you were in a bit of a hurry you could count at two per second and only take 90 million years.

Collins, the "Freethinker," once met a plain countryman going to church. He asked him where he was going. "To church to worship

God." "Is your God a great or a little God?" "He is both, Sir." "How can He be both?" "He is so great, Sir, that the heaven of heavens cannot contain Him; and so little that He can dwell in my heart." Collins was so struck, that he afterwards declared that the simple answer of the countryman had produced a greater effect on his mind than all the columns the learned doctors had written against Him.

GOD—HIS CARE

If you take care of the things that are dear to God, He will take care of the things that are dear to you.

—Howard Taylor

GOD—HIS KEEPING

God will "keep" you as the apple of His eye (Ps. 17:8).

He will "keep" you in all your ways (Ps. 91:11).

He will "keep" that which you have committed to Him against that day (2 Tim. 1:12).

He will "keep" you as a shepherd cares for his flock of sheep (Jer. 31:10).

He will "keep" you in perfect peace (Isa. 26:3).

He will "keep" you from the hour of temptation and support you in the time of trial (1 Cor. 10:13).

He will "keep" you from falling (Jude 24).

GOD—HUMOR OF

Dear God, we make You so solemn,
    So stiff and old and staid—
How can we be so stupid
    When we look at the things You have
        made?
How can we miss the twinkle
    That must have been in Your eye
When you planned the hippopoto
    And the rhinoceri?
Who watches an ostrich swallow,
    Then doubts that You like to play,
Or questions Your sense of humor
    Hearing a donkey bray?
Could the God who made the monkey
    Have forgotten how to laugh—
Or the One who striped the zebra
    And stretched out the giraffe?

How could an oldish person
    Fashion a pelican—
Or a perfectly sober Creator
    Ever imagine man?

—Helen Salsbury

GOD—IGNORANCE OF

A Christian was visiting the home of devout Muslims. He watched as a woman went through the ritual of washing her face, hands, and feet before praying. Then, facing Mecca, she bowed repeatedly on her little grass mat. Her lips moved continuously. When she finished, the guest asked her the meaning of her prayers. She replied, "I really don't know."

Although she had disciplined herself to pray five times a day, she was merely repeating words she had learned as a child. And they were in a language she didn't understand. Sad to say, she was not conscious of having any contact with God.

—*Our Daily Bread*

GOD—IMMUTABILITY OF

A Roman Catholic said, "When the Lord comes back, He'll unite Himself with His church."

A Presbyterian said, "He'll agree with the Reformed position."

A Methodist responded, "He'll accept the Wesleyan position."

A Southern Baptist thought for a while and then affirmed, "Gentlemen, I don't think He'll change at all."

GOD—KNOWLEDGE OF

He truly knows God perfectly who finds Him incomprehensible and unable to be known.

—Richard Rolle

An impersonal knowledge of God is like the tail feathers of a peacock—highly ornamental, but not much use in a high wind.

—Arnold Prater

Get me a man who is restfully intimate with the Lord and you have a man whose force is tremendous.

—John Henry Jowett

The great need now is for people who know God by something more than hearsay.

There is a great deal about God that we cannot understand. Who can understand the Trinity? John Wesley very appropriately said, "Bring me a worm that can comprehend a man, and then I will show you a man who can comprehend the Triune God!"

GOD—LOVE FOR

When I love God more than I love my earthly dearest, then I shall love my earthly dearest more than I do now.

—C. S. Lewis

GOD—LOVE OF

The love of God toward you is like the Amazon River flowing down to water a single daisy.

—F. B. Meyer

Someone asked Leith Anderson, "If you could say one sentence to a secular audience, what would you say?" He answered, "You matter to God."

It matters to Him about you.

—George Mueller

The Christian life is like the dial of a clock. The hands are God's hands, passing over and over again—the short hands of discipline and the long hand of mercy. Slowly and surely the hand of discipline must pass, and God speaks at each stroke. But over and over passes the hand of mercy, showering down a twelvefold blessing for each stroke of the discipline and trial. But hands are fastened to one secure pivot: the great unchanging heart of our God of love.

When Charles H. Spurgeon, Britain's famed Baptist preacher of the nineteenth century, was walking along a country lane with a friend one day he noticed a weather vane which was topped by the words "God Is Love." Spurgeon remarked to his companion that he thought a weather vane an inappropriate medium for such a message, since weather vanes are changeable and God's love is constant.

"I don't agree with you, Charles," his friend replied. "You misconstrue the meaning. What that weather vane is telling us is that whichever way the wind blows, God is love."

—E. Schuyler English

One day, a father wanted to teach his little boy about God's love. Taking him to the top of a high hill, he pointed in all the directions of the compass. Then, sweeping his arm around the whole encircling horizon, he exclaimed, "Johnny, my boy, God's love is as big as all that." "Why, Father," the child replied with sparkling eyes, "then we must be right in the middle of it!" How true!

Isn't it odd
that a being like God
who sees the facade
still loves the clod
He made out of sod?
Now isn't that odd?

GOD—OMNIPOTENCE OF

The greatest single distinguishing feature of the omnipotence of God is that our imagination gets lost when thinking about it.

—Blaise Pascal

GOD—OMNIPRESENCE OF

An eccentric professor, thinking to have some fun with a small boy who was reading a Sunday school paper, said to him, "Tell me, my good boy, where God is, and I will give you an apple."

The boy quickly looked up at the man and replied, "I will give you a whole barrel of apples if you tell me where He is not."

GOD—OMNISCIENCE OF

Students were taking apples from the cafeteria to their room. Someone put up a sign, "Please take only one apple. God is watching you." Someone else put up a sign by the cookies: "Take all the cookies you want. God is watching the apples."

Shih Huang-ti, one-time emperor of China, claimed to have eighty thousand eyes. For along the Great Wall of China were forty thousand watchtowers and every day and night a sentinel was posted at each one of them to guard the safety of China. This is said to have been "the greatest example of vigilance ever known to the world."

Emperor Shih's vigilance was at best only human watchfulness. It lasted but a short time, gazed in one direction only, looked for one thing alone and was imperiled by darkness, corruption, and carelessness. There is a greater vigilance than Shih's, as remarkable as that was—the watchfulness of Almighty God.

GOD—POWER OF

Niccolo Paganini began to play his violin and one string popped. The people giggled a bit, and then he began to play again and the second string broke. The same thing happened and the third string broke. Then all was silent as Paganini raised his hand to speak. He spoke and said, "Just one string and Paganini." And on that one string he played some of the most beautiful music ever to be heard. Yes, just you and God!

GOD—PRESENCE OF

The passengers on the train were uneasy as they sped along through the dark, stormy night. The lightning was flashing, black clouds were rolling, and the train was traveling fast. The fear and tension among the passengers was evident.

One little fellow, however, sitting all by himself, seemed utterly unaware of the storm or the speed of the train. He was amusing himself with a few toys.

One of the passengers spoke to him. "Sonny, I see you are alone on the train. Aren't you afraid to travel alone on such a stormy night?"

The lad looked up with a smile and answered, "No, ma'am, I ain't afraid. My daddy's the engineer."

GOD—PROVIDENCE OF

A man was questioning God's arrangement of the universe. He said, "Why does God make a big tree with small nuts, and a small plant with large watermelons. It doesn't make sense."

Just then a nut fell out of the tree and hit him on the head. He said, "Thank God that wasn't a watermelon."

The longer I live, the more convincing proofs I see of this truth—that God governs in the affairs of men.

—Benjamin Franklin

Providence is God acting anonymously.

—Paul Harvey

GOD—PROVISION OF

Charles H. Spurgeon loved to tell stories about his grandfather, a minister, who was very poor. The one cow he owned had died, and his ten children were without milk. His wife asked, "What will we do now?" "I cannot tell," he said, "but I know what God will do. We must have milk for the children and He will provide for us."

The next morning a man brought Spurgeon's grandfather a gift of twenty pounds from the ministers' relief fund, even though help had not been requested. A few days before, the relief committee had divided the funds for distribution and an amount of five pounds was left over. One of the members said, "There is poor Mr. Spurgeon down in Essex. Suppose we send it to him." "We'd better make it ten," said the chairman, "and I'll give another five." That made it fifteen. Another man added five more pounds. Those men knew nothing about Spurgeon's cow, but God knew.

While two Wycliffe translators were making a language survey out in a remote area, their car broke down eighty miles from the nearest mechanic. A helpful stranger offered to tow them the entire distance at no charge, but the tow rope wasn't strong enough.

Halted for the umpteenth time because the rope had finally broken so many times it couldn't be tied anymore, they saw, lying in the roadside bushes, a stronger rope. When they'd literally "come to the end of their rope," there was God with a better one!

GOD—SOVEREIGNTY OF

H. G. Wells, the English writer, once visited the home of his friend Henry James, the American novelist. He noticed a large stuffed bird in the drawing room.

"What is that?" asked Wells.

"That is a stork," replied James.

"Humph," snorted Wells. "That's not my idea of a stork."

"Perhaps not," James replied, "but apparently it was God's idea."

Before Jehovah's awesome throne
Ye nations, bow with sacred joy;
Know that the Lord is God alone;
He can create; and He can destroy.
—Isaac Watts

God must reserve for Himself the right of the initiative, the right to break into my life without question or explanation. That shattering phone call, that disturbing letter may indeed be the first stage of God's interruption in my life. . . . Since God does the initiating, He must be responsible for the consequences.
—W. Glyn Evans

God's time is the best time.
—T. J. Bach

GOD—SUFFICIENCY OF

His grace is sufficient.
  Then why I need fear,
Though the testing be hard,
  And the trial severe?
He tempers each wind
  That upon me doth blow,
And tenderly whispers,
  "Thy Father doth know!"
His pow'r is sufficient.
  Then why should I quail,
Though the storm clouds hang low,
  And though wild is the gale?
His strength will not falter,
  Whatever betide,
And safe on His bosom
  He bids me to hide.
His love is sufficient—
  Yea boundless and free;
As high as the mountains,
  As deep as the sea.

Ah, there I will rest
  Till the darkness is o'er,
And wake in His likeness
  To dwell evermore.
—Avis Burgeson Christiansen

When you have nothing left but God you become aware that He is enough.

GOD—TRINITY

Augustine was once walking by the seashore pondering the doctrine of the Trinity. He came upon a little boy who was dipping water from the ocean with a shell and pouring the water into a hole in the sand.

"What are you doing?" Augustine asked the child.

"I'm going to put the ocean in this hole," the boy replied.

Augustine went his way. But, he confided to his friends later that he was struck with this thought: "And art thou doing the like in thinking to comprehend the depths of God in the limits of thy finite mind?"

If you try to understand the Trinity, you will lose your mind. But if you deny the Trinity, you will lose your soul.
—Wilbur Smith

GOD—WILL OF (See WILL OF GOD)

GOD—WISDOM OF

Your heavenly Father is too good to be unkind, and too wise to make mistakes.

GOD—WORSHIP OF

Whatever power such a being may have over me, there is one thing which he shall not do; he shall not compel me to worship him . . . and if such a being can sentence me to hell for not—to hell I will go!
—J. S. Mills

GOD—WRATH OF

Bumper sticker: "God is back, and boy, is He mad."

A lot of people attend who can't conceive of a God who would ever punish anybody. They say that wouldn't be loving. They need to understand God's holiness. So I've used the old illustration, "If I backed into the door of your new car in the parking lot after the service, and we went to court and the judge said, 'That's no problem; Bill didn't mean it,' you'd be up in arms. You'd want justice.

"If you went to a Cubs game, and Sutcliffe threw a strike down the middle of the plate, and the ump said, 'Ball four,' and walked in a run, you'd be out there arguing furiously with the ump, because you want justice."

A person hears that and says, "I guess you're right. I wouldn't want a God who wasn't just."

Then I can go on to say, "Now before you say, 'Rah, rah, for a just God,' let me tell you some of the implications. That means He metes out justice to you."

The wrath of God is like great waters that are dammed for the present. They increase more and more and rise higher till an outlet is given. The longer the stream is stopped, the more rapid and mighty is its course when once it is let loose.

—Jonathan Edwards

GOLDEN RULE

All seven of the great religions of the world have "golden rules."

The Hindu: "The true rule is to guard and do by the things of others as you do by your own."

The Buddhist: "One should see for others the happiness one desires for oneself."

The Zoroastrian: "Do as you would be done by."

The Confucian: "What you do not wish done to yourself, do not to others."

The Mohammedan: "Let none of you treat your brother in a way he would dislike to be treated."

The Jew: "Whatsoever you do not wish your neighbor to do to you, do not unto him."

The Christian: "All things whatsoever ye would that men do unto you, do ye even so to them."

—*The Maritime Baptist*

Golden Rules for Living

1. If you open it, close it.
2. If you turn it on, turn it off.
3. If you unlock it, lock it up.
4. If you break it, admit it.
5. If you can't fix it, call in someone who can.
6. If you borrow it, return it.
7. If you value it, take care of it.
8. If you make a mess, clean it up.
9. If you move it, put it back.
10. If it belongs to someone else, get permission to use it.
11. If you don't know how to operate it, leave it alone.
12. If it's none of your business, don't ask questions.

GOLF

A golfer came to an ant hill in a golf course. His ball landed on top of the ant hill. He swung at the ball but missed and hit a lot of ants. He swung again and hit more ants, missing the ball again. Then one ant on the hill said to another, "If we want to get out of this alive, we better get on the ball!"

A golfer never feels better than when he is under par.

Epitaph to America:
Here lies a decent godless people. Their only monument to society is asphalt highways and one-thousand lost golf balls.

—T. S. Eliot

GOODNESS

People are unreasonable, illogical, and self-centered.
Love them anyway.
If you do good, people will accuse you of selfish ulterior motives.
Do good anyway.
If you are successful, you will win false friends and true enemies.
Succeed anyway.
Honesty and frankness make you vulnerable.
Be honest and frank anyway.
The good you do today will be forgotten tomorrow.
Do good anyway.

The biggest people with the biggest ideas can be shot down by the smallest people with the smallest minds.

Think big anyway.

People favor underdogs but follow only top dogs.

Fight for some underdogs anyway.

What you spend years building may be destroyed overnight.

Build anyway.

Give the world the best you have and you'll get kicked in the teeth.

Give the world the best you've got anyway.
—Gary C. Griessner

Benjamin Franklin asked himself each day, "What good thing can I do today?"

GOSPEL

"It's too good to be true," someone protested to George MacDonald about the plan of salvation. "No," MacDonald replied, "it's so good it has to be true."

GOSPELS

A man who lived in Canada had never been to Niagara Falls but now, finally, after saving his money for a long time, he was on his way. In a building there he saw a large picture of the Falls that covered the complete side of the wall. He wondered why there would be a picture of the Falls in a building so near the Falls. But when he went up closer to take a look at the picture, lo, it was the real Falls that he was seeing through a clear glass wall and that was framed with a picture frame.

The four Gospels are merely a frame to point to and open the way to the real living Christ—not a picture of Him, but just framing Him.

GOSSIP

Whoever gossips to you will gossip about you.
—Spanish proverb

Gossip needn't be false to be evil—there's a lot of truth that shouldn't be passed around.
—Frank Clark

The order of service at a church in Red Cloud, Nebraska, listed the sermon topic "Gossip." Immediately following was the hymn, "I Love to Tell the Story."
—The Eagle

On Sunday a restaurant manager designates two rooms as a nonsmoking area to accommodate churchgoers who come in for a bite to eat after their evening service. A busboy there said he was glad to see the large number of nonsmokers. But then he added, "They may not smoke, but you ought to hear them gossip. If we had a nongossip section, nobody would be there."

The difference between gossip and news is whether you hear it or tell it.

The things that go in one ear and out the other do not hurt as much as the things that go in one ear, get all mixed up, and then slip out of the mouth.

A woman repeated a bit of gossip about a neighbor, and within a short period of time the whole town knew the story. The person it concerned was hurt deeply and was very unhappy. Then one day the lady responsible for spreading the rumor learned it was completely untrue. She was very sorry and went to a wise old sage to find out what she could do to repair the damage. After listening to her problem, he said, "Go to the marketplace, purchase a fowl, and have it killed. Then on your way home, pluck its feathers one by one and drop them along the path."

Although surprised by this unusual advice, the woman did as she was told. The next day she returned and informed the man that she had done as he instructed. "Now, go and collect all those feathers and bring them back to me," he said. The lady followed the same path, but to her dismay the wind had blown all the feathers away. After searching all day long, she returned with only two or three in her hand—all that could be found. "You see," said the old gentleman, "it's easy to drop them, but impossible to bring them all back. So it is with gossip. It doesn't take much to spread a false rumor, but you can never completely undo the wrong."

We used to have a scraper known as the model "G." Somebody asked one of our salesman one day what the "G" stood for. The salesman was pretty quick on the trigger and so after thinking a few seconds replied, "Well, I tell you. I guess the 'G' stands for gossip, because like gossip this machine moves a lot of dirt, and moves it fast!"

—R. G. LeTourneau

The difference between gossip and news depends on whether you hear it or tell it.

Three pastors were sharing their problems. After the first and second pastors gave their problems, the third said, "My problem is gossip."

Gossip not only hurts others, it can also boomerang and hurt the one who starts it. An elderly, wealthy grandfather was deaf, so he decided to buy a hearing aid. Two weeks later he stopped by the store where he had bought it and told the manager he could now pick up conversation quite easily, even in the next room. "Your relatives must be happy to know that you can hear so much better," beamed the delighted proprietor. "Oh, I haven't told them yet," the man chuckled. "I've just been sitting around listening—and you know what? I've changed my will twice!"

When you hear an evil report about anyone, halve it and quarter it, and then say nothing about the rest.

—Charles H. Spurgeon

Can You Guess Who I Am?
"I have no respect for justice and no mercy for defenseless humanity. I ruin without killing; I tear down homes; I break hearts and wreck lives. You will find me in the pews of the pious as well as in the haunts of the unholy. I am wily, cunning, malicious, and I gather strength with age. I have made my way where greed, mistrust, and dishonor are unknown; yet my victims are as numerous as the sands of the sea, and

often as innocent! I feed on good and bad alike. I never forgive and seldom forget. My name? My name is gossip!"

Recently, two young girls met each other on the street. Jan said, "Millie told me that you told her that secret I told you not to tell her." Replied Mary, "She's a mean thing! I told her not to tell you." "Well," said Jan, "I told her I wouldn't tell you she told me, so don't tell her I did."

GOVERNMENT
We ought to be glad we don't receive as much government as we pay for.

—Will Rogers

It is the duty of all nations to acknowledge the providence of Almighty God, to obey His will, to be grateful for His benefits and humbly implore His protection and favor.

—George Washington

Almighty God, we make our earnest prayer that Thou wilt keep the United States under Thy protection; that Thou wilt incline the hearts of the citizens to cultivate a spirit of obedience to government; to entertain a brotherly affection for one another and for their fellow-citizens of the United States at large.

—George Washington

I don't make jokes. I just watch government and report the facts.

—Will Rogers

GRACE
Ralph Keiper asked Dalton Myers, "What is your favorite doctrine?"

Dalton answered and then said, "What's yours?"

He answered, "Nothing compares with the doctrine of God's grace."

Love that reaches up is adoration.
Love that reaches across is affection.
Love that reaches down is grace.

—Donald Grey Barnhouse

At a busy airport a man drove up in a fancy red sports car and let his wife out to go meet someone. The policeman came by and insisted he move on and not park there. The driver didn't move so the policeman got out his ticket pad and said, "It will cost you eighty dollars to park here."

Then the man in the car rolled down his window and said, "I'm just waiting for my wife to come out. Can't I have a little grace?"

The policeman responded, "I don't know anything about grace. I just know about the law."

But actually the man in the car didn't know anything about grace either. To wink at wrongdoing is not grace.

A benevolent person gave Mr. Rowland Hill a hundred pounds to dispense to a poor minister a bit at a time, thinking it was too much to send him all at once. Mr. Hill forwarded five pounds in a letter, with only these words within the envelope, "More to follow." In a few days' time, the good man received another letter; this second messenger contained another five pounds, with the same motto, "And more to follow." A day or two after came a third and a fourth, and still the same promise, "And more to follow." Till the whole sum had been received, the astonished minister was made familiar with the cheering words, "And more to follow."
—Charles H. Spurgeon

Grace is more than unmerited favor. If you feed a tramp who calls on you, that is unmerited favor, but it is scarcely grace. But suppose that after robbing you, you then feed him. That would be grace. Grace, then, is favor shown where there is positive demerit in the one receiving it.

Grace turns lions into lambs, wolves into sheep, monsters into men, and men into angels.
—Thomas Carlyle

A friend called on John Newton, author of the beloved hymn "Amazing Grace," in the later years of his life. A portion of Scripture was read, including the verse, "But by the grace of God I am what I am" (1 Cor. 15:10). Newton then commented, "I am not what I *ought* to be. How imperfect and deficient! I am not what I *wish* to be. I abhor what is evil, and I would cleave to what is good. I am not what I *hope* to be. Soon I shall put off immortality, all sin, and imperfection. Yet though I am not what I ought to be, nor what I wish to be, or what I hope to be, I can truly say that I am not what I *once was*— a slave to sin and Satan; and I can heartily join with the apostle and acknowledge, 'By the grace of God I am what I am.'"

Grace is the good pleasure of God that inclines Him to bestow benefits on the undeserving.
—A. W. Tozer

Grace is everything for nothing. It's helping the helpless, going to those who cannot come in their own strength.
—Lehman Strauss

A minister once sat next to an unbeliever on a train and began talking about spiritual things. He had difficulty convincing him that character and good works could not save a man, but only faith in Jesus Christ. Soon the conductor came along requesting, "Tickets, please!" As the man presented his, the conductor looked at it, checked the date, punched it, and passed it on to the next seat. This was the minister's opportunity. He said, "All the conductor looked at was your ticket. He did not inquire about your character. He didn't care who you were—whether you were a good or moral man or a criminal. So it is with salvation. You need only God's 'ticket to heaven' stamped by the blood of Jesus Christ."

A friend went to Alexander the Great asking for money. The man asked for ten talents of money, but Alexander had fifty delivered to him. When the man returned and said that ten talents would be sufficient, Alexander replied, "Ten are sufficient for you to take, but not for me to give."

Many Christians are shocked by sin, but they should be staggered by grace.

GRACE

Grace is God's special favor freely given to undeserving people.

Grace—getting something from God that doesn't belong to us.

In his book *In the Heavenlies,* H. A. Ironside tells the story of an attempted assassination of Queen Elizabeth I. The woman who sought to do so dressed as a male page and secreted herself in the queen's boudoir awaiting the convenient moment to stab the queen to death. She did not realize that the queen's attendants would be very careful to search the rooms before Her Majesty was permitted to retire.

They found the woman hidden among the gowns and brought her into the presence of the queen, taking from her the dagger she had hoped to plant in the heart of the sovereign.

She realized that, humanly speaking, her case was hopeless. She threw herself down on her knees and begged the queen as a woman to have compassion on her, a woman, and to show her grace.

Queen Elizabeth looked at her coldly and quietly said, "If I show you grace, what promise will you make for the future?"

The woman looked up and said, "Grace that hath conditions, grace that is fettered by precautions, is not grace at all."

Queen Elizabeth caught it in a moment and said, "You are right. I pardon you by my grace." And they let her go, a free woman.

A man in Ireland was very much under conviction, but somehow he couldn't give in to the Lord. Over and over the Devil would make him believe he just couldn't hold on. Nearby was a watermill. Pointing to it a Christian friend said, "What turns the wheel today?"

"The stream," replied the Irishman.

"And what will turn it tomorrow?"

Again he answered, "The stream."

"And the day after?"

The only answer there was to give was, "The stream." That is like God's grace. The same grace that saves us today is flowing to keep us saved tomorrow—and the next day—and the next day—on till Jesus comes.

A little boy had an accident and was taken to a hospital. After he was made comfortable, a nurse brought him a large glass of milk.

He looked longingly at it, but he did not pick it up. He had come from a poor home where his hunger was seldom satisfied. If he ever received a glass of milk, it was only partly filled, and even that had to be shared with another child.

Finally he looked up at the nurse and asked, "How deep may I drink?" The nurse replied, "Drink it all! There's more."

—*Our Daily Bread*

GRADES

As a boy handed his father a poor report card, he asked, "Dad, what do you think is my trouble—heredity or environment?"

GRAMMAR (Also see ENGLISH)

Parody of "My Country 'Tis of Thee:"

My grammar, 'tis of thee
    Sweet incongruity
Of thee I sing.
    I love each mood and tense,
Each freak of accidence,
    Protect me from common sense,
Grammar, my king!

GRANDCHILDREN

Grandchildren are gifts of God. It is God's way of compensating us for growing old.

GRANDPARENTS

A grandmother was headed out the door to go to church one Sunday when she got a call from her daughter. Would Grandma like to have her three little grandchildren visit while her daughter and son-in-law took a five-day holiday trip?

Grandma was so delighted she put five dollars in the collection basket at church and thanked the Lord. The Sunday after the grandchildren had returned home, she put twenty dollars in the collection.

—*Bits & Pieces*

A husband can melt his wife's heart by bringing her a dozen roses, but her grandson can do the same thing by bringing her a half-dozen dandelions.

The stricter you are with your children, the harder grandparents work at spoiling them.

—Mother Murphy's Law

When first he called me "Sweetheart,"
My youthful knees grew weak.
And that was topped when I heard "wife,"
For sure, I've reached the peak.
Until a tiny voice said, "Mom . . ."
A joy I still recall.
But now, the sound of "Grandma"
is the sweetest sound of all.

—Gay Wilson

In the dim and distant past,
When life's tempo wasn't fast,
Grandma used to rock and knit,
Crochet, tat, and baby-sit.
When the kids were in a jam
They could always count on Gram.
In that day of gracious living
Grandma was the gal for giving.
But today she's in the gym
Exercising to keep slim,
Or off touring with the bunch
Or taking clients out to lunch
Or going north to ski or curl.
All her days are in a whirl.
Nothing seems to stop or block her
Now that Grandma's off her rocker.

GRADUATION

One alumnus said to another, "This school has turned out some great men."

"When did you graduate?"

"I didn't graduate. I was one of those turned out."

Senator Robert Dole opened his address to the graduating class at Colby College in Waterville, Maine, by noting, "Being a commencement speaker is like being a corpse at a funeral. They need you in order to hold the event, but nobody expects you to say very much."

—Carroll Douglas

GRATITUDE (Also see THANKFULNESS)

Get on your knees and thank God you're on your feet.

—Irish proverb

Gratitude is not only the greatest of virtues but the parent of the others.

—Cicero

Alexander Whyte, the famous Scottish preacher, invariably began his public prayers with an expression of gratitude. One cold and rainy day when his people wondered how he could be grateful for the weather, he began by saying, "We thank Thee, O Lord, that it is not always like this." An appreciative heart brightens a dreary day and shortens the longest night.

GREATNESS

A great man shows his greatness by the way he treats little men.

—Thomas Carlyle

The truly great are the most grateful. The most inspiring are the most inspired. The most convincing are the most convinced. The most pleasing are the most pleasant.

—William Arthur Ward

GREED (Also see CONTENTMENT and MATERIALISM)

It is not a matter of possession but of desire. One man may have much money on him but no greed in him, whereas another may have no money on him but much greed in him.

—Augustine

A rich industrialist was disturbed to find a fisherman sitting lazily beside his boat. "Why aren't you out there fishing?" he asked.

"Because I've caught enough fish for today," said the fisherman.

"Why don't you catch more fish than you need?" the rich man asked.

"What would I do with them?"

"You could earn more money," came the impatient reply, "and buy a better boat so you could go deeper and catch more fish. You could purchase nylon nets and catch even more fish and make more money. Soon you'd have a fleet of boats and be rich like me."

The fisherman asked, "Then what would I do?"

"You could sit down and enjoy life," said the industrialist.

"What do you think I'm doing now?" the fisherman replied as he looked placidly out to sea.

If you want to make a man happy, don't give him more possessions. Take away his desires.

One of the weaknesses of our age is our apparent inability to distinguish our needs from our greeds.

—Don Robinson

Wealth consists in not having great possessions but in having few wants.

—Epicurus

A neighbor of Abraham Lincoln heard someone crying outside and went to his front door to investigate. He saw Lincoln passing by with his two sons both screaming loudly. "What's the matter, Abe?" asked the man. "Just what is the matter with the whole world!" answered Lincoln. "I have three walnuts and each boy wants two!"

GRIEF

We cannot share a sorrow,
    If we haven't grieved a while.
Nor can we feel another's joy,
    Until we've learned to smile.

There are five stages of grief after a loved one dies:
1. Denial—"No, not me."
2. Rage and anger—"Why me?"
3. Bargaining—"Yes, me, but . . . ?"
4. Depression—"Yes, me."
5. Acceptance—"My time is very close now and it's all right."
    —Elizabeth Kubler-Ross

Missionary David Miner Stern was plunged into grief when God saw fit to take to Himself his little daughter. Stern could not seem to get over his great sorrow, even though he was a Christian. He became so depressed that he went daily to the cemetery to mourn by her grave. With his walking stick, he would touch the mound of earth that covered the casket. Somehow this seemed to give him a measure of comfort—as though he still had some slight contact with her. His grief was so oppressive that he feared he would have to give up his labors as a missionary. However, God graciously brought him relief. One day as he stood in the cemetery, he suddenly realized how wrong it was to fix his attention on the dead body of his little daughter. The Holy Spirit impressed on his mind the truth in Luke 23:43, where Jesus said to the dying thief, "Today you will be with Me in paradise." He began repeating the words, "with Christ in paradise" as he walked home. The blessed reality that his daughter was with Jesus increasingly dawned on him. He said to himself, "What more could I ask for my loved one than this?" In the comfort of this thought he was able to resume his duties with joy. Instead of thinking of his daughter in the grave, he visualized her safe in Jesus' presence.

GROWTH

He who ceases to be better, ceases to be good.
    —Oliver Cromwell

Growth for the sake of growth is the ideology of the cancer cell.
    —Edward Abby

Former President Harry Truman saw a friend of his, an older man, reading Plato's *Republic*. "Why are you reading that?" He responded, "I may be old, but I'm growing."

Three men were in the hospital waiting room when the nurse came from the maternity ward. She said to the first man, "Congratulations, you're the father of twins."

"Wonderful," he exclaimed. "Isn't that

a coincidence? I'm a member of the Minnesota Twins baseball team."

Later the nurse returned and said to the second man, "Congratulations; you're the father of triplets."

"Wow," said the new father. "Another coincidence. I work for the 3M Company."

The third man jumped to his feet, shouting, "I'm getting out of here. I work for the 7 Up Bottling Company!"

Who is not satisfied with himself will grow; who is not sure of his own correctness will learn many things.

—Chinese proverb

GUIDANCE

He leadeth me.
In pastures green? No, not always.
Sometimes he who knoweth best
In kindness leadeth me in weary ways
Where heavy shadows be;
Out of the sunshine warm and soft and
     bright,
Out of the sunshine into the darkest night.
I oft would yield to sorrow and to fright
Only for this: I know He holds my hand.
So, whether led in green, or desert land
I trust, although I cannot understand.
He leadeth me.
Beside still waters? No, not always so.
Oft times the heavy tempests round me
     blow,
And o'er my soul the waves and billows
     go.
But when the storm beats wildest, and I
     cry
Aloud for help, the Master standeth by
And whispers to my soul: "Lo, it is I."
Above the tempest wild I hear Him say:
"Beyond the darkness lies the perfect day;
In every path of thine I lead the way."
So whether on the hilltops, high and fair
I dwell, or in the sunless valleys where
The shadows lie—what matter? He is
     there.
He gives to me no helpless, broken reed,
But here His own hand, sufficient for my
     need.
So where He leads me I can safely go.
And in the blest hereafter I shall know
Why in His wisdom He hath led me so.

God does not furnish us with a detailed road map. A traveler in Africa complained to his guide, "There is no road, no path, in this jungle. We have lost our way." The guide replied, "There is no way, I am the way." Our Lord is the Way; when we are with Him, we may not know whither but we know Whom.

—*The Vance Havner Quote Book*

A young physician was determined to reach the heights of Mount Blanc, the highest peak in Europe. He accomplished the feat and the little village at the foot of the mountain was illuminated in his honor; on the mountainside a flag was floating that told of his victory.

After he had ascended and descended as far as the hut, he wanted to be released from his guide; he wanted to be free from the rope, and insisted on going alone.

The guide told him it was not safe; but he was tired of the rope and declared that he would be free. The guide was compelled to yield. The young man had gone only a short distance when his foot slipped on the ice and he could not stop himself from sliding down the icy steeps. The rope was gone, so the guide could not hold him or pull him back. Out on the shelving ice lay the body of the young physician.

The bells had been rung, the village had been illuminated in honor of his success; but alas, in a fatal moment he refused to be guided; he was tired of the rope.

When an ocean liner sank along the Irish coast many years ago, the maritime world was bewildered. Because the ship's captain was an excellent seaman, no one could figure out what caused the accident. Divers were sent down, and one of the items they brought up to examine was the ship's compass. As they opened the compass box, they found the point of a knife blade inside. Apparently, while cleaning the compass, an unwary sailor had broken off the tip of the knife, which had become lodged inside the device. It was just a tiny piece of metal, but it was enough to cause the compass to give a bad reading. As a result, the ship took the wrong course and crashed into the rocky coast.

—*Our Daily Bread*

He does not lead me year by year
  Nor even day by day,
But step by step my path unfolds;
  My Lord directs my way.
Tomorrow's plans I do not know,
  I only know this minute;
But He will only say, "This is the way,
  By faith now walk ye in it."
And I am glad that it is so,
  Today's enough to bear;
And when tomorrow comes, His grace
  Shall far exceed its care.
What need to worry then or fret?
  The God who gave His Son
Holds all my moments in His hand
  And gives them, one by one.

—Barbara G. Ryberg

I know not the way He leads me, but well do I know my Guide.

—Martin Luther

GUILT

On a sunny day in September of 1972, a stern-faced, plainly dressed man would be seen standing on a street corner in the busy Chicago Loop. As pedestrians hurried by on the way to lunch or business, he would solemnly lift his right arm and pointing to the person nearest him, intone loudly the single word "Guilty!"

Then, without any change of expression, he would resume his stiff stance for a few moments before repeating the gesture. Then, again, the inexorable raising of the arm, the pointing, and the solemn pronouncing of the one word "Guilty!"

The effect of this strange pantomime on the passing strangers was extraordinary, almost eerie. They would stare at him, hesitate, look away, look at each other, and then at him again; then hurriedly continue on their ways.

One man, turning to another who was my informant, exclaimed, "But how did he know?"

No doubt many others had similar thoughts. How did he know, indeed?

"Guilty!" Everyone guilty? Guilty of what? Guilty of illegal parking? Guilty of lying? Guilty of arrogance and hubris toward the one God? Guilty of "borrowing," not to say embezzling? Guilty of unfaithfulness to a faithful wife? Guilty only of evil thoughts—or evil plans? Guilty before whom? Is a police officer following? Did anyone see? Will they be likely to notice it? Does he know about it? But that isn't technically illegal, is it? I can make it up. I will give it back. I'll apologize. I wasn't myself when I did that. No one knows about it. But I'm going to quit. It's a dangerous habit. I wouldn't want the children to see me. How can I ever straighten it out? What's done can't be undone.

—Karl Menninger

Sir Arthur Conan Doyle, author of the Sherlock Holmes mysteries, used to tell how he sent a telegram to each of twelve friends, all men of great virtue and reputation. The message read simply, "Fly at once; all is discovered." Within twenty-four hours, the story goes, all twelve had left the country.

A certain duke once boarded a galley ship. As he passed the crew of slaves, he asked several of them what their offenses were. Almost every man claimed he was innocent. They laid the blame on someone else or accused the judge of yielding to bribery. One young fellow, however, spoke out, "Sir, I deserve to be here. I stole some money. No one is at fault but myself. I'm guilty." Hearing this, the duke seized him by the shoulder and shouted, "You scoundrel, you! What are you doing here with all these honest men? Get out of their company at once!"

He was then set at liberty while the rest were left to tug at the oars. The key to this prisoner's freedom was the admission of his guilt.

A taxpayer wrote to the Internal Revenue Service, "I have not been able to sleep well for two years. Here is my check for $1,200 for back taxes." He even signed his name, then added a short P.S. "If I don't sleep better in a week, I will send you another $1,200." He had to do something to relieve his guilt, but he didn't want to do too much.

A man in Palestine named Pinchas Rutenberg was regarded as "the greatest figure in Palestine." He revolutionized the industry of Palestine through his electrification scheme. He was said to be "iron-hearted and iron-willed, with hands as powerful as a wrestler's." But few people have ever seen his hands! Why? Because he always wore gloves. The reason? In 1905 there was a vicious Russian named Gapon whom Rutenberg strangled to death with his hands. Since that time Rutenberg was never able to stand the sight of his own hands; he therefore wears gloves.

Two men were in jail. One had only broken a traffic law by speeding, while the other was in jail for having committed murder. The former said, "See, I'm not as bad as you, I've just broken a traffic law, but you've done a much worse thing. You've committed murder." But the other replied, "Yes, but we are both in jail."

Quisling was a traitor of Norway who collaborated with the Germans. When he was on trial for his life, he was quite sure he would be exonerated for he had employed several shrewd lawyers. These defense attorneys successfully ripped to shreds almost all the evidence against him, until the prosecutor played a recording of the betrayer's voice on a phonograph. As the treacherous speech was heard, Quisling's head bowed lower and lower, for his own ranting voice was lauding Hitler and his perverted form of government. Finally, almost in a whisper, he muttered, "I guess I can no longer deny my guilt; it's my voice that all are hearing."

Someday when the lost stand before the Great White Throne to be judged and all their secret sins are revealed, they will not be able to deny their guilt. They will have to confess that God has kept a true record of all their words and deeds.

D. L. Moody visited a prison called The Tombs to preach to the inmates. After he had finished speaking, Moody talked with a number of men in their cells. He asked each prisoner this question: "What brought you here?" Again and again he received replies like this: "I don't deserve to be here." "I was framed." "I was falsely accused." "I was given an unfair trial." Not one inmate would admit he was guilty. Finally, Moody found a man with his face buried in his hands, weeping. "And what's wrong, my friend?" he inquired. The prisoner responded, "My sins are more than I can bear." Relieved to find at least one man who would recognize his guilt and his need of forgiveness, the evangelist exclaimed, "Thank God for that!" Moody then had the joy of pointing him to a saving knowledge of Christ—a knowledge that released him from his shackles of sin.

—Louis Albert Banks

GULLIBILITY

Napoleon was gifted with the ability to stir up the common man to great heights of patriotism. He often told the story, with effective results, about an old soldier he met while visiting the troops. On his uniform the proud fighter displayed the coveted Legion of Honor. One arm was missing.

"Where did you lose your arm?" Napoleon asked.

"At Austerlitz, sir," came the soldier's brisk reply.

"And for that you received the Legion of Honor?"

"Yes, sir. It is but a small token to pay for the decoration."

"You must be," the emperor said, "the kind of man who regrets he did not lose both arms for his country."

"What then would have been my reward?" asked the one-armed man.

"Then," Napoleon replied, "I would have awarded you a double Legion of Honor."

With that the proud old fighter drew his sword and immediately cut off his other arm.

The story was circulating for years and

believed without question until one day someone said, "How?" We often accept without question what people tell us, never stopping to think things through or ever doubt what was said.

H

HABITS

Nothing so needs reforming as other people's habits.

—Mark Twain

The best way to break a habit is to drop it.
—*Teen Esteem*

The best way to stop a bad habit is never to begin it.

—J. C. Penney

The Five "Watches"

Watch your thoughts; they become words.

Watch your words; they become actions.

Watch your actions; they become habits.

Watch your habits; they become character.

Watch your character; it becomes your destiny.

—Frank Outlaw

Bad habits are like comfortable beds—easy to get into but hard to get out of.

—Watson C. Black

A bad habit never disappears miraculously, it's an undo-it-yourself project.

—Abigail Van Buren

Habits are first cobwebs, then cables.
—Spanish proverb

An old teacher was once taking a walk through a forest with a pupil by his side. The old man suddenly stopped and pointed to four plants close at hand. The first was just beginning to peep above the ground,

the second had rooted itself pretty well into the earth, the third was a small shrub, while the fourth was a full-sized tree. The tutor said to his young companion:

"Pull up the first."

The boy easily pulled it up with his fingers.

"Now pull up the second."

The youth obeyed, but found the task not so easy.

"And now the third."

The boy had to put forth all his strength and was obligated to use both arms to uproot it.

"And now," said the master, "try your hand on the fourth."

But, the trunk of the tall tree, grasped in the arms of the youth, hardly shook its leaves.

"This, my son, is just what happens with our bad habits. When they are young, we can cast them out more readily with the help of God; but when they are old, it is hard to uproot them, though we pray and struggle ever so sincerely."

—*Heidelberg Herald*

Habits are too light to be noticed till they are too heavy to be broken.

—Samuel Johnson

Habit, if not resisted, soon becomes necessity.

—Augustine

HALLOWEEN

At Halloween there was a knock on my door and it was someone from Congress saying, "Trick or treat!"

I said, "What's the treat?'
He said, "Tax reform."
I said, "What's the trick?"
He said, "I just told you."

—Bob Orben

HANDICAPS

John Milton, blinded in 1652, wrote his masterpiece *Paradise Lost* after the loss of his eyesight forced him into retirement. Isaac Watts was handicapped with a severe physical deformity, yet he became a preacher and the father of English hymnody. Though weak and sickly, he wrote six hundred sacred songs, several books of poetry, and many influential doctrinal discourses. Fanny Crosby, accidentally blinded at six weeks of age, triumphed over her handicap and gave us more than eight thousand hymns.

—*Our Daily Bread*

HAPPINESS

Hagor shouted to someone on a mountain, "What is the secret to happiness?" The answer came back, "Celibacy, Abstinence, Fasting, Poverty." Hagor didn't like that answer, so he shouted, "Is there anyone else up there I can talk to?"

The grand essentials to happiness in this life are something to do, something to love, and something to hope for.

—Joseph Addison

Act as if you were already happy and that will tend to make you happy.

—Dale Carnegie

The happiest people don't necessarily have the best of everything. They just make the best of everything.

Very little is needed to make life happy. It is all within yourself, in your way of thinking.

—Marcus Aurelius

To be happy, don't do whatever you like, but like whatever you do.

What is the secret of happiness? One businessman put it very simply:

"The important thing is to be content with one's lot—provided it's a whole lot."

—Murray Watts

Some cause happiness wherever they go; others whenever they go.

A patient complaining of melancholy consulted Dr. John Abernathy, British physician (1764–1831). After an examination the doctor pronounced, "You need amusement. Go and hear the comedian Grimaldi;

he will make you laugh and that will be better for you than any drugs." Said the patient, "I am Grimaldi."

—*The Little, Brown Book of Anecdotes*

The Chinese character for "happiness" is a combination of three elements: the characters for a person, a productive field, and clothes.

Most folks are about as happy as they make up their minds to be.

—Abraham Lincoln

Feet are measured by inches
Roads are measured by miles
But the happiness that we gain in life
Is measured only by smiles.

Happiness is a perfume you cannot pour on others without getting a few drops on yourself.

Real happiness is more of a habit than a goal, more of an attitude than an attainment. It is the companion of cheerfulness, not the creature of circumstances. Happiness is what overtakes us when we forget ourselves, when we learn to open our eyes in optimism and close the door in the face of defeat. We win happiness when we lose ourselves in service to others.

—William Arthur Ward

A happy person is not a person in a certain set of circumstances, but rather a person with a certain set of attitudes.

—Hugh Downs

We have no right to happiness; only an obligation to do our duty.

—C. S. Lewis

It's not how much we have but how much we enjoy that makes happiness.

—Charles H. Spurgeon

To be without some of the things you want is an indispensable part of happiness.

—Bertrand Russell

In his book, *Happiness Through Creative Living,* Preston Bradley recalled the results of a poll which had been taken among experienced Armed Services personnel. This older group, though still youthful, replied to the question: "What things do you wish you had known before you were twenty-one?" The ten most common responses were:

1. How I was going to make a living.
2. That my health after thirty depended to some extent on what I put in my stomach before I was twenty-one.
3. How to take care of money.
4. Habits are hard to change after twenty-one.
5. The commercial asset of being neatly and sensibly dressed.
6. That worthwhile things require time, patience, and work.
7. That the world gave me about what I deserved.
8. That a thorough education not only pays better wages than hard labor but it brings the best of everything else.
9. The value of absolute truthfulness in everything.
10. That my parents weren't old fogies after all.

Happiness is like a butterfly. The more you chase it, the more it will elude you. But if you turn your attention to other things, it comes and softly sits on your shoulder.
—*Bits & Pieces*

The happy man is he who is cheerful with moderate means; the unhappy he who is discontented in the midst of plenty.
—Democritus

A man, although extremely wealthy, was very depressed. He offered a large sum of money to anyone who would make him happy. It wasn't long until a philosopher brought him a new game he had invented. At first it was intriguing, but after a few days the rich man grew weary of playing it. Soon another philosopher was called in. He had a different plan. He put him to work sawing boards, planing them, and making all sorts of interesting things. This lifted his spirits for a while, for labor is a great lightener of the heart. but the day came

when he could think of nothing more to build. So his gloom returned. Finally, a third philosopher came and advised him to begin doing things for other people. And that rich man has been happy ever since.

An English newspaper asked its readers this question: "Who are the happiest people on earth?" These were the four prize-winning answers:

A craftsman or artist whistling over a job well done.

A little child building sand castles.

A mother, after a busy day, bathing her baby.

A doctor who has finished a difficult and dangerous operation and saved a human life.

Make one person happy each day and in forty years you have made 14,600 human beings happy for a little time at least.

He is the happiest, be he king or peasant, who finds peace in his home.
—Johann von Goethe

The supreme happiness of life is the conviction that we are loved.
—Victor Hugo

Happiness is not a matter of good fortune or worldly possessions. It's a mental attitude. It comes from appreciating what we have, instead of being miserable about what we don't have. It's so simple—yet so hard for the human mind to comprehend.

No matter what your situation, things could be worse. Count your blessings and enjoy a little happiness while you may.
—John Luther

Where Is Happiness?

Not in unbelief—Voltaire was an infidel of the most pronounced type. He wrote, "I wish I had never been born."

Not in pleasure—Lord Byron lived a life of pleasure, if any one did. He wrote, "The worm, the canker, and the grief are mine alone."

Not in money—Jay Gould, the American millionaire, had plenty of that. When dying he said, "I suppose I am the most miserable man on earth."

Not in position and fame—Lord Beaconsfield enjoyed more than his share of both. He wrote, "Youth is a mistake, manhood a struggle, old age a regret."

Not in military glory—Alexander the Great conquered the known world in his day. Having done so, he wept in his tent, because, he said, "There are no more worlds to conquer."

Happiness is good health and a bad memory.

—Ingrid Bergman

Success is often judged by whether you get what you want. Happiness is different. That depends on wanting what you get.

The following "daily dozen" were the personal creed of Robert Louis Stevenson:

1. Make up your mind to be happy. Learn to find pleasure in simple things.
2. Make the best of your circumstances. No one has everything, and everyone has something of sorrow intermingled with the gladness of life. The trick is to make the laughter outweigh the tears.
3. Don't take yourself too seriously. Don't think that somehow you should be protected from misfortunes that befall others.
4. You can't please everybody. Don't let criticism worry you.
5. Don't let your neighbor set your standards. Be yourself.
6. Do the things you enjoy doing, but stay out of debt.
7. Don't borrow trouble. Imaginary burdens are harder to bear than the actual ones.
8. Since hate poisons the soul, do not cherish enmities or grudges. Avoid people who make you unhappy.
9. Have many interests. If you can't travel, read about new places.
10. Don't hold postmortems. Don't spend your life brooding over sorrows and mistakes. Don't be one who never gets over things.
11. Do what you can for those less fortunate than yourself.
12. Keep busy at something. A busy person never has time to be unhappy.

In his novel *Rasselas,* Samuel Johnson said happiness is difficult to find. Rasselas, the imaginary son of the emperor of Abyssinia, was imprisoned, until the time should come for him to ascend the throne, in a remote valley entirely cut off from communication with the rest of the world.

Everything he could possibly desire was provided for him there, and yet life seemed to him an intolerable burden. He could not endure his silken captivity. And so he escaped and traveled from country to country looking for the secret of abiding contentment. And all the time he kept repeating in tones that grew more and more despondent, "Surely happiness is somewhere to be found." But Rasselas failed to find it.

Happiness comes not from having much to live on but having much to live for.

—William Arthur Ward

HARMONY

Lady Astor and Churchill didn't get along. Lady Astor said to Churchill, "If you were my husband, I'd put arsenic in your tea." He said, "If you were my wife, I'd drink it."

HASTE

A friend of mine, a distinguished explorer who spend a couple of years among the savages of the upper Amazon, once attempted a forded march through the jungle. The party made extraordinary speed for the first two days, but on the third morning, when it was time to start, my friend found all the natives sitting on their haunches, looking very solemn and making no preparation to leave.

"They are waiting," the chief explained to my friend. "They cannot move farther until their souls have caught up with their bodies."

—James Truslow Adams

Finding Phillips Brooks, the noted New England pastor, irritably pacing his study, a friend asked him, "What is the trouble?"

HASTE

"The trouble is," answered Brooks, "that I'm in a hurry—but God isn't."

Slow me down, Lord. I'm going too fast,
I can't see my brother when he's walking past.
I miss a lot of good things day by day,
I don't know a blessing when it comes my way.

HATRED (Also see BITTERNESS)

Love blinds us to faults, hatred to virtues.
—Moses Ibn Ezra

English essayist and critic Charles Lamb (1775–1834) once commented about a person he did not want to meet:

"Don't introduce me to that man. I want to go on hating him, and I can't hate someone I know."

—*Our Daily Bread*

London held its breath in June 1987. While working on a building site, a construction foreman thought his workers had hit a cast iron pipe while using a pile driver. After picking up and then dropping the huge object, they realized the pipe strangely resembled a bomb.

It was—a 2,200 pound World War II bomb, one of the largest the Germans dropped during the blitz which killed more than fifteen thousand Londoners. After evacuating the area, a ten-man bomb disposal unit worked eighteen hours before finally deactivating the seven-foot device.

Hatred is like an unexploded bomb. Unless it's deactivated it can detonate and cause great damage.

If you want to be miserable, hate somebody.

HEALTH

To insure good health eat lightly, breathe deeply, live moderately, cultivate cheerfulness, and maintain an interest in life.
—William Louden

The only way for a rich man to be healthy is by exercise and abstinence, to live as if he were poor.
—William Temple

The claims that oats bring vibrant health
Have me puzzled plenty,
For horses eat them all their lives
And they are old at twenty.
—C. R. Reagan

HEART

When God measures a man, He put a tape around his heart not his head.

HEAVEN

At dusk, a little girl entered a cemetery. An old man who sat at the gate said to her, "Aren't you afraid to go through the cemetery in the dark?" "Oh no," she replied, "my home is just on the other side."
—Henry Durbanville

The two questions most frequently asked in heaven: "What are you doing here?" and "What happened to so-and-so?"

Christians are not citizens of earth trying to get to heaven but citizens of heaven making their way through this world.
—*The Vance Havner Quote Book*

I've never seen that Other World,
  Beyond time's narrow shore,
Where He has pledged that we shall live
  With Him forevermore.
But though the map of that high world
  Be oddly traced and dim,
Because He's there I'll be there, too—
  Sometime, somehow, with Him.
—Lon Woodrum

An old man lived in a broken-down shack on a corner lot that was very valuable. He had secured his property before the area was developed, and now it was the section of the city where millionaires built their homes. While dozing off one afternoon on his porch, he was roused by a man who wanted to purchase his land. "What's your price?" he inquired. "A hundred thousand," came the reply. "Fine, I'll buy it," said the stranger without hesitation. Before leaving, he handed the owner a check for ten thousand dollars to bind the contract.

In the weeks that followed, the old gentleman felt guilty about asking so much for his worthless shack. Thinking he could make it more presentable, he began fixing it up. On the day of the closing, the buyer came to complete the transaction. After the final payment had been made, the old fellow turned to the rich man and said, "Don't you think you've got a nice little place here? See, I've painted it, patched the roof, and put new boards on the floor. You can sure be proud of it." The new owner responded, "I can't use it. It must come down, for I'm going to build a brand new house."

—Paul Rader

A poll conducted by *USA Today* showed that Americans are vitally interested in going to heaven, but their opinions about it are inaccurate. Seventy-two percent of those polled rated their chances of getting to heaven as good to excellent. These same people said that only 60 percent of their friends will go to heaven. Eighty percent said they believe in heaven. Only 67 percent said they believe in hell. Ninety-six percent said they believe in God.

The Spanish mystic Unamieno, conversing with a peasant, suggested that perhaps there is a God but no heaven. The peasant thought a minute and then replied, "So what is this God for?"

In his book *And the Life Everlasting* John Baillie tells of the Scottish physician who was attending a close personal friend in his last hours. "Tell me, you are a believer of sorts. What will it be like after I die?" There was a moment of silence. Suddenly there was a scratching at the bedroom door. The doctor turned to his friend and said, "Did you hear that? It's my dog. He's been waiting patiently for me downstairs and has become impatient. He has never been in this room. He has no idea what it is like. He knows only one thing about it and that is that I am here. That's all I know about the future. . . . He's there."

In the spring of 1994 *The Dallas Morning News* surveyed 1,011 adults in four north Texas counties about their religious beliefs and priorities. Eighty percent of the respondents said they believed in an afterlife, and 68 percent said they believe in heaven and hell.

I dreamt of heaven the other night,
The pearly gates swung wide.
And as I made my passage through,
I looked around, inside.
And there to my astonishment,
'Mongst those who'd gone before,
Were some I deemed as quite unfit,
To make it through that door.
Words of censure rose in my throat,
But never were set free—
For I could tell from their surprise,
Not one expected me.

G. Campbell Morgan recounts the story of a little girl who went home after hearing the story of Enoch at Sunday school. "Mother, we heard about a wonderful man today in Sunday school."

The sensible mother let her child tell her what she had heard. "His name was Enoch, and you know, Mother, he used to go for long walks with God."

"That is wonderful, dear. How did it end?"

"Oh, Mother, one day they walked on and on, and got so far, God said to Enoch: 'You are a long way from home. You had better come in and stay with me.'"

—J. Oswald Sanders

A woman, who had been extremely poor, fell heir to a legacy and was able to move into a lovely home. For a short time she enjoyed her riches, then she discovered that an incurable disease would soon take her life. Her friends were amazed that she was not dismayed at the prospect of leaving her beautiful, new surroundings. "How can you be so cheerful about it?" they asked. "Oh, that's easy," she replied, "just think what I am leaving it for."

A teacher asked a class of girls how many wanted to go to heaven. All hands were raised but one. "Why don't you want to go?"

"Because my mother said for me to come right home after Sunday school."

A little boy came running into the house one day exclaiming, "I love my home so much!" A neighbor inquired, "Johnny, why don't you visit me sometime? Our houses are built exactly the same, and the rooms are all like yours." He declared he wouldn't be as happy over there. Then she asked, "What makes this such an enjoyable place for you?" He had never thought about it before, but he ran to his mother and putting his arms around her neck exclaimed, "I guess it's Mom."

—*Our Daily Bread*

We talk about gates of pearl and streets of gold and walls of jasper, and we are thrilled; but those things would not be attractive if Jesus were not there. His presence is what will make heaven such a grand place.

—Paul Rees

"Too bad you are blind," someone said to Fanny Crosby. "With all your gifts it's too bad God withheld your sight."

She answered, "My first request at birth would have been that God would remove my sight." "Why?" "Because when I get to heaven the first sight I will behold will be that of my Savior's face."

When Theodore Roosevelt was president, he went on a hunting safari to Africa. On his return to the United States, a missionary who was retiring after forty years of services in a remote jungle village was traveling on the same vessel. When the ship docked, cheering throngs greeted the chief executive, but not a single person was there to welcome the returning missionary. Momentarily the man of God was filled with self-pity. He thought, "When a president comes home after a short hunting trip, hundreds come out to greet him. But, Lord, when one of Your missionaries comes home after a lifetime of service, no one is there to meet him." Immediately it was as if the Lord whispered, "But My son, you are not home yet."

—*Our Daily Bread*

When you get to heaven
    You will likely view
Many folks whose presence there
    Will be a shock to you.
But keep very quiet;
    Do not even stare.
Doubtless there'll be many folks
    Surprised to see you there.

—B. Y. Williams

Cliff Barrows and Billy Graham were talking about going to heaven. Barrows, Graham's song leader, said, "I'll have a job in heaven, but what will you do?"

When the new preacher moved into town, one of the first people he met said, "I certainly hope that you're not one of these narrow-minded ministers who think that only the members of their congregation are going to heaven."

"I'm even more narrow-minded than that," replied the preacher. "I'm pretty sure that some of the members of my congregation aren't going to make it."

—*Ties*

A little girl was taking an evening walk with her father. Wonderingly, she looked up at the stars and exclaimed, "Oh, Daddy, if the wrong side of heaven is so beautiful, what must the right side be."

—Charles L. Allen

HELL

There once was an Englishman named Charles Peace—an ironic name, because Peace was not a peaceful man but a contentious one. Violent, thieving, brawling, he was a career criminal who respected the laws of neither God nor man. Eventually the authorities caught up with him, and he was tried and condemned to death by hanging at Armley Jail in Leeds.

On the morning of his execution, a contingent of prison officials met at Peace's cell to take him on his final walk to the gallows. Among them was a sleepy prison chaplain whose job it was to prepare the condemned man's soul (such as it was) for the hereafter. As the group began its solemn death march, this parson began mumbling and yawning his way through a series of unintelligible recitals.

Suddenly he felt a tap on his shoulder. "What are you reading?" someone was asking. He turned to find it was Mr. Peace.

"The Consolations of Religion," he replied.

"Do you believe what you are reading?" inquired the prisoner.

"Well, yes, I guess I do."

Peace stared at the chaplain, stunned. Here he was, going to his death, knowing that his earthly deeds utterly condemned him before the ultimate Judge, and this clergyman was mouthing words about heaven and hell as if it were a boring chore. He said to the parson, "Sir, I do not share your faith. But if I did—if I believed what you say you believe—then although England were covered with broken glass from coast to coast, I would crawl the length and breadth of it on hand and knee and think the pain worthwhile, just to save a single soul from this eternal hell of which you speak."

—Howard G. Hendricks

One who is interested in proving that there is no hell generally has a personal reason for doing so.

When H. A. Ironside was a little boy, his mother would draw him to her knee and talk to him of the importance of trusting the Lord as his Savior. Once he said, "Well, Mamma, I would like to do it, but the boys will all laugh at me."

"Harry," she replied, "remember they may laugh you into hell, but they can never laugh you out of it."

A group of troop soldiers on a ship once asked the chaplain, "Do you believe in hell?"

"No, why?"

"Well, then will you please resign? For if there is no hell, then we do not need you; and if there is, we do not wish to be led astray."

A church that needed a pastor invited several candidates to come and preach. One minister spoke on Psalm 9:17, "The wicked shall be turned into hell." The chairman of the board was not in favor of him. A few weeks later, another preacher came and used the same verse for his sermon. This time the man said, "He's good. Let's call him."

The other board members were surprised, and one of them asked, "Why did you like him? He used the same text as the other minister." "True," replied the chairman, "but when the second man emphasized that the lost will be turned into hell, he said it with tears in his eyes and with concern in his voice. The first preacher almost seemed to gloat over it."

—*Our Daily Bread*

The doctrine of hell is based on the premise that the punishment must fit the crime. Men refuse to give themselves to God—God refuses to give Himself to them eternally. They spurn fellowship with God—they are given separation from God. They cast Christ out of their lives— they are cast out of His life. They reject— they are rejected.

I remember my graduation from middle school near Philadelphia. The school provided each one of us with an autograph book which we passed among our fellow students for them to sign and write a few words as a momento of our years together. One of my fellow students wrote the following words: "If in heaven we don't meet, I hope we both can stand the heat! Ha! Ha!" What that boy didn't realize is that hell is no laughing matter. If he really realized where he was heading, he should have been deeply troubled. We do the unsaved a great disfavor to let them think otherwise.

—George Murray

Voltaire, the French infidel, was more honest than some modern "Christian" preachers. When he received a letter from a man who said he had "succeeded in getting rid of the idea of hell," Voltaire replied, "Congratulations—I wish I could."

A warden at a large prison was concerned about a longtime inmate because no one ever came to see him. Knowing that visitors boost morale, he called the man into his office one day. "Lefty," he asked, "do you have any close relatives or personal friends?" "Sure," Lefty answered. "But no one has visited you since the day you arrived. May I contact somebody for you?" "It wouldn't do no good," Lefty replied with a shrug. "They're all here."

—*Our Daily Bread*

Walter Hooper, C. S. Lewis's secretary, chuckled when he read this grave inscription: "Here lies an atheist, All dressed up with no place to go." When he told C. S. Lewis about this, Lewis didn't chuckle. He responded, "That atheist probably wishes now that were true."

A young man in Switzerland had been brought up in a home where God and the Bible were revered. Although the Gospel was often presented to him with loving urgency, he refused to believe and became increasingly rebellious. Finally he said, "I'm sick and tired of Christians. I'm going to look for a place where I can avoid them." His mother wept as he packed his suitcase and left home. He boarded a train, only to find that two passengers seated behind him were discussing the Scriptures. "I'm not going to stay here," he muttered. At the next stop he left the coach and entered a restaurant. To his dismay, some elderly women were talking about the return of the Lord. Knowing a ship was docked nearby, he decided it might be a way to escape the "religious chatter" he encountered at every turn. But when the steamer embarked, he discovered that it was filled with happy young students from a Bible academy.

Thoroughly disgusted, he made his way downstairs to find the bar. Approaching the captain, he exclaimed, "Say, can you tell a man where he can get away from all these cursed fanatics?" The skipper looked up and said with a grin, "Yes, just go to hell. You won't find any Christians there." These startling words caused him to realize his eternal peril and when he returned home, he received the Savior.

No man should preach on hell who can do so with dry eyes.

—Charles H. Spurgeon

After discussing the difference of the eternal state of man after death with a returned soldier from World War II, he just denounced the brutality of war and concluded with a rare bitterness in his accusation against Hitler and what he called "his gang." This gave me an opportunity. Since he had previously vehemently denied all difference in the eternal state and strongly argued that all will enter heaven, my comment was, "You better change your mind about Hitler and 'his gang.' Since you insist that all go to the same place, what if the first man you meet in heaven is Hitler?"

"Oh!" he cried out. "That could never be!"

"But where will he be?"

"To hell with him," was the soldier's bitter reply.

"But there is no hell, according to your opinion."

"There must be one for *that* kind of people" was my friend's emphatic word.

—George W. Peters

A minister preached a sermon on the subject of eternal punishment. The next day a young man came to see him to dispute what he heard preached. He said to the minister, "I believe that there is a difference between what you and I believe about eternal punishment. I came here in order to settle this difference."

The minister thought for a while and then turned to the young man and said, "There is no dispute between you and me. If you turn to Matthew 25:46 you will find the dispute is between you and the Lord Jesus Christ, and I advise you to go immediately and settle it with Him."

HELPFULNESS

A man went to a convention where George Washington Carver was also attending. In the hotel lobby the man had four pieces of luggage. He said to a black man, "Here, boy, help me carry my bags."

On the elevator the man bragged about the accomplishments of science, while Carver listened to the man's words. In the room the man handed Carver some money as a tip.

"I don't want it," Carver said.

"Why?"

"Because I don't need it."

"By the way, what is your name?"

"I'm George Washington Carver."

The man was terribly embarrassed. "I didn't realize who you were. One of the reasons I came to this conference was to meet you. Why did you help me?"

"Well, Sir," Carver replied, "you did need help."

When Sir Bartle Frere returned from India, the carriage was sent to the village station to bring him to his home. When the new footman, but newly engaged, asked how he should recognize Sir Bartle, his aged mother said, "Look out for somebody helping someone else." Sure enough, when the London train had drawn in, the manservant observed a gentleman assisting an old woman to the platform and then jumping back into the carriage to fetch out her luggage. Going straight up to him, the footman inquired, "Sir Bartle?" Yes, it was he.

Help your brother's boat across and lo! your own has reached the shore.

—Hindu proverb

If you would be interesting, be interested; if you would be pleased, be pleasing; if you would be loved, be lovable; if you would be helped, be helpful.

—William Arthur Ward

Sir Edmund Hillary and his Nepalese guide, Tenzing Norgay, were the first people to make the historic climb of Mount Everest in 1953. Coming down from the mountain peak, Sir Edmund suddenly lost his footing. Tenzing held the line taut and kept them both from falling by digging his ax into the ice.

Later Tenzing refused any special credit for saving Sir Edmund Hillary's life; he considered it a routine part of the job. As he put it, "Mountain climbers always help each other."

For years my wife has followed a set of six daily rules which she adopted from an anonymous source. She resolves every day to do something for herself, to do something she doesn't want to do but needs doing, to do a physical exercise, to do a mental exercise, and to offer an original prayer that includes thanks for blessings. The sixth item (though first on her list) is to do something for someone else. Since she does this without telling anyone, including me, I cannot give many examples, though I have discovered her taking food to a shut-in.

—Leslie B. Flynn

It is a pleasant thought that when you help a fellow up a steep hill, you get nearer to the top yourself.

—Reynolds Price

HIRING

When asked what the toughest problem was in directing construction of the world's first atomic submarine, Admiral Hyman George Rickover tersely replied, "Picking good men."

—*Bits & Pieces*

HISTORY

If we imagine the whole of earth's history compressed into a single year, then, on this scale, the first eight months would be completely without life. The following two months would be devoted to the most primitive of creatures, ranging from viruses and single-celled bacteria to jellyfish, while mammals would not have appeared until the second week in December. Man, as we know him, would have strutted onto the stage at about 11:45 P.M. on December 31. The age of written history would have occupied little more than the last 60 seconds on the clock.

—Richard Carrington

How patient of history to keep repeating itself when practically nobody listens.

History is "the crimes, follies, and misfortunes of mankind."

—Edward Gibbon

History is but the visible effects of invisible changes in human thought.

Charles A. Beard, the historian, was once asked if he could summarize the lessons of history. Beard replied that he could do it with four simple observations: (1) Whom the gods would destroy they first make mad with power; (2) the mills of the gods grind slowly, but they grind exceedingly fine; (3) the bee fertilizes the flower it robs; (4) when it is dark enough, you can see the stars.

To be ignorant of what happened before you were born is to remain a child forever.

—Cicero

HOBBY

A hobby is something you go wild about to keep you from going crazy.

HOLINESS (Also see PURITY)

In the forest of Northern Europe and Asia lives a little animal called the ermine. He is best known for his snow-white fur. Instinctively this small creature takes a peculiar pride in his glossy coat. He protects it at all cost against anything that would soil it. Fur hunters take cruel advantage of the ermine in this respect. They do not set a snare to catch him, but instead they find his home, which is usually a cleft in a rock or a hollow in an old tree, and they daub the entrance and the interior with filth. Then their dogs start the chase. Frightened, the ermine flees toward his home. He finds it covered within and without with uncleanness, and so rather than soil his white fur he faces the yelping dogs and meets his death while preserving his purity. To the ermine purity is dearer than life.

—*Our Daily Bread*

A holy man is a mighty weapon in the hands of God.

—Robert Murray McCheyne

Hugh Gough, the bishop of Barking, told a charming story at Keswick about his dog. Some years ago he owned a Highland terrier that was "pure white." The dog was wonderfully cared for, bathed and clipped, and was a clean, white joy around the house. One morning the bishop awoke and looked out the window, to find that snow had fallen during the night. Then, across his lawn, there scurried a dog, gray and dirty against the white snow. When the bishop inquired to find out how such a stray could have wandered into their garden, he discovered that it was none other than their own beloved "white" terrier.

Holiness vanishes when you talk about it, but becomes gloriously conspicuous when you live it.

O Lord, make me as holy as a forgiven sinner can be.

—Robert Murray McCheyne

HOLOCAUST

Yad Vashem is the memorial in Jerusalem where a large building is dedicated to the memory of the children of the holocaust. It is constructed so that one candle is reflected by many mirrors, to represent the 1.5 million children who died. The children's names are read aloud continuously day and night.

HOLY SPIRIT

You might as well try to hear without ears, or breathe without lungs, as try to live a Christian life without the Spirit of God in your heart.

—D. L. Moody

A group of pastors were discussing the possibility of having D. L. Moody serve as an evangelist at a city-wide evangelistic campaign. One minister was reluctant to have Moody speak. "Why Moody?" he asked. "Does he have a monopoly on the Holy Spirit?"

The question was followed by a hushed silence. Finally another man spoke up and said, "No, Moody does not have a monopoly on the Holy Spirit. But the Holy Spirit does have a monopoly on D. L. Moody."

In view of the fact that Christian service is effective solely as it is wrought in the power of the Holy Spirit and that power is realized only through the scriptural provisions for personal adjustment to the Spirit, the theological curriculum is fundamentally lacking which does not provide the student with the training, power, and personal victory in Jesus Christ.

—Lewis Sperry Chafer

It is said that a certain guide lived in the deserts of Arabia who never lost his way. He carried with him a homing pigeon with a very fine cord attached to one of its legs. When in doubt as to which path to take, he threw the bird into the air. The pigeon quickly strained at the cord to fly in the direction of home, and thus led the guide accurately to his goal. Because of this unique practice he was known as "the dove man."

So, too, the Holy Spirit, the heavenly Dove, is willing and able to direct us in the narrow way that leads to the more abundant life if in humble self-denial we submit to His unerring supervision.

"I have come a hundred miles," said a minister, "to get some of Mr. Moody's spirit." "You don't want my spirit," was the reply. "What you want is the Spirit of God."

HOME (Also see FAMILY)

Home is where one starts from.

—T. S. Eliot

Where family prayer is daily said,
God's Word is regularly read,
And faith in Christ is never dead,
That is a Christian home.
Where family quarrels are pushed aside
To let the love of God abide
Ere darkness falls on eventide,
That is a Christian home.
Where joy and happiness prevail
In every heart without a fail
And thoughts to God on high set sail,
That is a Christian home.
Where Jesus Christ is Host and Guest,
Through whom we have eternal rest
And in Him are forever blest,
That is a Christian home.

There is no doubt that it is around the family and the home that all the greatest virtues, the most dominating virtues of human society are created, strengthened, and maintained.

—Winston Churchill

A child was given a complex jigsaw puzzle to work. In a short time, the pieces were all put together. A visiting friend was amazed and asked, "How did you do that so fast?" "Oh, you see, there is a picture of Jesus on the other side and I just put that one together." When the Lord Jesus is given His rightful place in the home, the complexities are adjusted.

A newspaper in London had a contest for the best definition of home. The winning definition was "home is where you are treated the best and complain the most."

Home is the place where, when you come there they have to let you in.

—Robert Frost

A young doctor, his wife, and three children couldn't find a house to live in so they had to stay in a hotel.

A friend said to the six-year-old girl, "Too bad you have no home."

"Oh, yes we have a home," she replied promptly, "but no house to put it in."

If there is righteousness in the heart, there will be beauty in the character. If there is beauty in the character, there will be harmony in the home. If there is harmony in the home, there will be order in the nation. When there is order in the nation, there will be peace in the world.

Ironically, John Howard Payne, composer of "Home, Sweet Home," virtually never had a home of his own.

Though he was born in New York City in June 1791, and passed much of his childhood in East Hampton, Long Island, Payne spent most of his years wandering about the world, homeless, and more often than not, penniless. From the bankruptcy of his father while he was a student at Union

College until Payne's death in Tunis, North Africa, where he served as American Consul, his fabulous career casts fiction in the shade.

As an actor, Payne made his debut in 1809 and for months was the rage of New York, Boston, Philadelphia, and then Drury Lane in London. Later he became a playwright, with hits in Paris and London. But because he lacked business ability, many of his varying successes ended in failure.

In 1821 Payne was sent to debtor's prison in England, and was released only after he managed to slip through the guards and sell one of his plays. It was with the profits from this play that he went gaily off to Paris to finish an opera little remembered today—but the music of which is still sung all over the civilized world. That opera was *Clari,* and the hit tune was the ever-remembered "Home, Sweet Home."

Today, the old gray-shingled homestead at East Hampton where Payne spent his boyhood is maintained by the village as a shrine, for it was probably this lowly thatched cottage about which the composer wrote so wistfully while homesick in Paris. To Americans everywhere—as it once was to John Howard Payne—this humble cottage is now cherished as "Home, Sweet Home."

HONESTY (Also see INTEGRITY)

In 1945, just months after World War II had ended, American newspapers reported that occupation forces in Japan had arbitrarily destroyed five atomic cyclotrons. Enraged scientists and public officials called the action "a crime against mankind." They likened the destruction of this valuable research equipment to the burning of a library.

An investigation revealed that the cyclotrons had been destroyed by mistake. What is most interesting, however, is the way the error was handled by the military. According to author M. Hirsh Goldberg, some officials called for a coverup. But General Leslie R. Groves, the officer in charge, issued a statement admitting that the War Department had made an error.

The press was surprised by such honesty and soon lost interest in the story. Later, after the dust had cleared, General Groves concluded, "Honest errors, openly admitted, are sooner forgiven."

When Grover Cleveland was a boy, he insisted on returning the egg that a neighbor's hen daily laid on the Cleveland side of the fence. Honesty and respectability are learned early in life, fitting one for positions of trust later.

A commentary on the times is that the word "honesty" is now preceded by "old-fashioned."

—Larry Walters

Two opposing political candidates argued on a busy street while a crowd of interested spectators listened.

"There are hundreds of ways of making money," one of the campaigners declared, "but only one honest one."

"And what's that?" jeered the other candidate.

"Ah, ha!" rejoined the first. "I thought you wouldn't know."

—*Wall Street Journal*

It is better to be more than you seem, than to seem more than you are.

A fictitious story is told about a racing event staged by the United States and the Soviet Union. Both governments commissioned their best engineers to produce the fastest automobile possible.

After much experimenting and preparation, the important day arrived for the high-speed contest. It finished with the American car winning by inches. This was rather hard for the Russians to swallow, and *Pravda,* their leading newspaper, carried the following report:

"Russia and the U.S. competed in a long-awaited race yesterday afternoon. Both cars broke all former speed records. The Soviets came in second, and the Americans finished next to last."

Make yourself an honest man and then you

may be sure there is one less rascal in the world.

—Thomas Carlyle

Roger Young was a janitor in Charleston, West Virginia. One day he found a billfold on the shelf in a phone booth. He returned it to its owner at once, not realizing that it contained a thousand dollars. When he learned this, he said, "I don't care if it was one dollar or one million. I wouldn't keep it." A similar incident took place in Washington, D.C. when William Taylor found a suede purse on the floor of his taxicab. Looking inside, he saw a lot of money, so he immediately turned it over to the police. They found nearly $42,000 in cash, traveler's checks, and jewelry. The purse belonged to the wife of Edward Cole, retired president of General Motors.

While both Young and Taylor received substantial rewards, that did not motivate their actions. They were simply being honest.

I hope I shall always possess firmness and virtue enough to maintain what I consider the most enviable of all titles: the character of an honest man.

—George Washington

Do the right thing. It will please some people and astonish others.

—Mark Twain

Diogenes, the Greek philosopher, was reported to have been seen recently in Paris. Two French gendarmes approached the lamp-bearing, toga-garbed wise man.

"Diogenes, what are you doing in Paris?"

"Messieurs, I am looking for an honest man."

A few months later he was reported to have appeared in London. Some bobbies there asked him his business in London. The answer was the same: he was still searching for an honest man. Some time later he was reported to have turned up in New York City. Two of the city's finest stopped him in Central Park. "I suppose you are in New York looking for an honest man?" one of the cops asked him.

"I was," replied Diogenes, "but now I'm looking for my lamp."

—*Bits & Pieces*

In the Civil War a farmer boy heard General Robert E. Lee order his troops to attack Gettysburg rather than Harrisburg. The boy hurried with the news to Governor Curtin who said to his officers, "I'd give my right hand to know if that boy is telling the truth." A corporal stepped forward and said, "Sir, I know that lad. It is impossible for him to lie. There is not a drop of false blood in his veins." In fifteen minutes the Union troops were marching into Gettysburg to win their final victory.

Henry Clay was one of America's great statesmen. He had the unfortunate epithet "Compromiser" attached to his name, a label that tended to detract from the genuine integrity of the man. But in the course of events which led to this infamous title, an incident occurred which turned a shaft of brilliant light on his true moral character. Five times he unsuccessfully sought to be president. Bitterly disappointed though he was, he rose above personal ambitions and bent his efforts toward averting the Civil War. Within two years after reelection to the Senate in 1848, he was introducing his famous compromise. During the course of a speech on the compromise, someone taunted him about his unsuccessful quest for the presidency and warned him that if he pursued his trend of thinking, she would never be president. Clay replied in crisp and penetrating words, "I would rather be right than president."

Honesty is still the best policy, but strange to say, some people feel they cannot afford the best.

A man once testified as follows: "For years, when I have bowed in private prayer, a certain incident in my life has slapped me in the face. When I was a young man I bought some hay from a neighbor. It was weighed, and I gave the man an I.O.U. Before the account was settled, however, the farmer, from whom I had made the purchase, died. I went to the administrator and asked if there was anything charged against me. He looked, but found nothing, and so I never paid the debt. The matter has put a cloud on my life for years and hindered my spiritual progress. I am now eighty years of age, and the Lord has spoken to me about this dishonesty. Therefore, the first thing tomorrow morning I am going to the widow and settle that account in full." The man kept his word, and once again his testimony rang clear, and a great load was lifted from his soul.

"One of the striking traits in the character of General Ulysses S. Grant," writes an unknown author, "was his absolute truthfulness. He seemed to have an actual dread of deception. One day while sitting in his bedroom in the White House where he had retired to write a message to Congress, word of an unscheduled visitor was brought in by a servant. An officer, seeing that the Chief of State did not want to be disturbed, said to the attendant, 'Just tell him the President is not in.' Overhearing the remark, General Grant swung around in his chair and cried out, 'Tell him no such thing. I don't lie myself, and I don't want anyone else to do so for me.'"

An honest man is the noblest work of God.
—Alexander Pope

HONOR

As the man who was tarred and feathered said as he ran out of town, "If it weren't for the honor of the thing, I'd just as soon forget it."

HOPE

Who can live without hope?
—Carl Sandburg

There is no medicine like hope, no incentive so great, and no tonic so powerful as expectation of something better tomorrow.
—Orison Sweet Marden

Don't tell me what you will do
When you have time to spare;

Tell me what you did today
To ease a load of care.
Don't tell me what you will give
When your ship comes in from sea;
Tell me what you gave today
A fettered soul to free.
Don't tell me the dream you have
Of conquest still afar;
Don't say what you hope to be
But tell me what you are.
—*Union Church News,*
Lima, Peru

Traditionally there are two schools of thought in Germany. The industrial, practical, northern part of the country has this philosophy: "The situation is serious but not hopeless." In the southern part of Germany, more romantic and perhaps less practical, the philosophy seems to be: "The situation is hopeless but not serious."
—Bruce Larson

Unbelievable as it may seem, it is possible for a person to live up to seventy days without food. It is also possible to exist for nearly ten days without water. And one can live for up to six minutes without air.

But there is one thing it is impossible to live without—hope.

A famous American cardiologist said in his autobiography, "Hope is the medicine I use more than any other. Hope can cure nearly everything." Another doctor commented, "If you lead a person to believe there's no hope, you drive another nail in his coffin."
—Leslie B. Flynn

It looked like Saturday morning TV time at the Van Pelt household. Lucy and Linus were sitting in front of the television set when she said to Linus, "Go get me a glass of water."

Linus looked surprised. "Why should I do anything for you?" he said. "You never do anything for me."

"On your seventy-fifth birthday," Lucy promised, "I'll bake you a cake."

Linus got up, headed for the kitchen, and said, "Life is more pleasant when you have something to look forward to."

Dr. Armand May Nicholi II says, "Psychiatrists have long suspected that hope fosters health, both physical and emotional. An increasing body of medical evidence documents the deleterious effect that depression and hopelessness have on physical health." Dr. Nicholi quotes Freud who as early as 1905 declared that "duration of life can be appreciably shortened by depressive effects."

—Leslie B. Flynn

Years ago a hydroelectric dam was to be built across a valley in Maine. The people in the town were to be relocated and the town itself submerged.

During the time between the initial decision and the completion of the dam, the town, which had once been well kept, fell into disrepair. Why keep it up now?

Explained one resident: "Where there is no faith in the future, there is no work in the present."

—Bits & Pieces

When you say a situation or a person is hopeless, you are slamming the door in the face of God.

—Charles L. Allen

Hope is the major weapon against the suicide impulse.

—Karl Menninger

In an old inn at St. Moritz in Switzerland is an inscription which translated from the German reads, "When you think everything is hopeless, a little ray of light comes from somewhere."

A tourist once asked a native Texan, "Have you lived here all your life?" And the Texan replied, "Nope, not yet."

Bumper sticker: "Since I gave up hope I feel much better."

When Alexander the Great was setting out on one of his campaigns, he was distributing numerous gifts to his friends. In his generosity he had given away nearly all his possessions. "Sir," said one of his friends, "you will have nothing left for yourself." "Oh yes I have," said Alexander, "I still have my hopes."

Things never go so well that one should have no fear nor so ill that one should have no hope.

—Danish proverb

There is one thing which gives radiance to everything. It is the idea of something around the corner.

—G. K. Chesterton

There are three ingredients in the good life: learning, earning, and yearning.

—Christopher Morley

In recounting his experience as a political prisoner in Russia, Alexander Solzhenitsyn tells of a moment when he was on the verge of giving up all hope. He was forced to work twelve hours a day at hard labor while existing on a starvation diet, and he had become gravely ill. The doctors were predicting his death. One afternoon while shoveling sand under a blazing sun, he simply stopped working. He did so even though he knew the guards would beat him severely—perhaps to death. But he felt he just couldn't go on. Then he saw another prisoner, a fellow Christian, moving toward him cautiously. With his cane the man quickly drew a cross in the sand and erased it. In that brief moment Solzhenitsyn felt all the hope of the Gospel flood through his soul. It gave him the courage to endure that difficult day and the months of imprisonment that followed.

Self-made millionaire Eugene Lang greatly changed the lives of a sixth-grade class in East Harlem. Mr. Lang had been asked to speak to a class of fifty-nine sixth-graders. What could he say to inspire these students, most of whom would drop out of school? He wondered how he could get these predominantly black and Puerto Rican children even to look at him. Scrapping his notes, he decided to speak to them from his heart. "Stay in school," he admonished, "and I'll help pay the college tuition of every one of you." At that moment the lives of those students changed. For the first time they had hope. Said one student, "I had something to look forward to, something waiting for me. It was a golden feeling." Nearly ninety percent of that class went on to graduate from high school.

—*Parade* magazine

HOPELESSNESS (Also see LOST)

There are no hopeless situations. There are only people who have grown hopeless about them.

Remove hope from a man and you make him a beast.

—Darnell G. Neister

H. G. Wells said before he died, "This world is at the end of its tether. The end of everything we call life is close at hand."

As Socrates was in his prison cell dying from drinking the hemlock, one of his disciples whispered to him, "Master, will we live again?" Socrates answered, "I hope so, but no man can know for sure."

HORSE RIDING

A riding academy in West Texas advertises that they have something for everyone. For fat people they have fat horses, for skinny people they have skinny horses, for fast people they have fast horses, and for people who have never ridden before they have horses who have never ridden before.

HOSPITALITY

When there is room in the heart, there is room in the house.

—Danish proverb

After three days, both fish and guests begin to smell.

—Danish proverb

Hospitality is the art of making people feel at home when you wish they were at home.

—*Rolling in the Aisles*

HOUSEWIVES

The most creative job in the world involves taste, fashion, decorating, recreation, education, transportation, psychology, romance, cuisine, designing, literature, medicine, handicraft, community relations, pediatrics, geriatrics, entertainment, maintenance, purchasing, direct mail, law, accounting, religion, energy, and management.

Anyone who can handle all those has to be somebody special. She is. She is a homemaker.

—A United Technologies Corporation ad by Richard Kerr

HOUSEWORK

I hate housework! You make the beds, you do the dishes—and six months later you have to start all over again.

—Joan Rivers

HUMAN BODY

Each chromosome contains 20 billion bits of information. That amount of information would equal three billion letters. If there are six letters in an average word, the information in one human chromosome equals about 500 million words. If there are 300 words on a printed page, this would equal two million pages. If the typical books contain 500 pages, a single chromosome contains 4,000 books. Chromosomes carry every bit of information concerning the development of a human being. God programmed every minute detail into every single chromosome.

If you're an adult of average weight, here is what you accomplish in 24 hours:

Your heart beats 103,689 times.
Your blood travels 168,000,000 miles.
You breathe 23,040 times.
You inhale 438 cubic feet of air.
You eat 3 $1/4$ pounds of food.
You drink 2.9 quarts of liquids.
You lose $7/8$ pounds of waste.
You speak 25,000 words, including some unnecessary ones.
You move 750 muscles.
Your nails grow .0000646 inch.
Your hair grows .01714 inch.

You exercise 7,000,000 brain cells.
. . . feel tired?

—Paul Lee Tan

The monetary worth of the average human being has increased by 643 percent during the last few years and possibly much more today. However, I would hold off cashing in just yet. Even with our double-digit inflation you are only worth about $7.28 or so.

The minerals and trace elements that make up the body of humans were only about $.98 in 1970, according to a survey released then. Now with prices the way they are you could get more for your 1.5 pounds of phosphate, nine ounces of potassium, six ounces of sulphur and sodium, one ounce of manganese, and under one ounce of iron, copper, and iodine.

However, if you were to calculate the value of the working chemicals in your body, you might be worth more than $6 million—an appropriate figure for the price of man. Your follicle-stimulating hormone, for example, sells for more than $4 million a gram, and prolactin goes for almost $17 million a gram.

—Patricia S. Voldberg

HUMANISM

The ten most important two-letter words: "If it is to be, it is up to me."

HUMILITY

Humility is the mother, root, nurse, foundation, and center of all other virtues.

—Chrysostom

Humility is a strange thing. The minute you think you've got it, you've lost it.

Humility is the ability to act ashamed when you tell people how wonderful you are.

—Lee Liechansky

The moderator of a Presbyterian church in Melbourne, Australia, gave J. Hudson Taylor a flattering introduction. When the founder of the China Inland Mission stepped into the pulpit, he quietly said, "Dear friends, I am a little servant of an illustrious Master." The late A. W. Tozer was once presented to a congregation in a similar manner, and his response was, "All I can say is, dear God, forgive him for what he said—and forgive me for enjoying it so much!"

—James L. Snyder

John McNeil preached a sermon on humility. After the service, a woman said to him, "Yes, Dr. McNeil, humility is my forte."

Humility is not denying the power you have. It is realizing that the power comes through you, not from you.

—Fred Smith

A young man once received a medal from an organization which used very extravagant language in extolling his accomplishments. Jubilantly the prize winner proudly repeated the words to his mother. Then he asked, "How many great men are there in the world today?" His mother pondered for a while and then wisely said, "One less than you think!"

Alex Haley, the author of *Roots*, had a picture in his office showing a turtle sitting atop a fence. The picture was there to remind him of a lesson he learned long ago: If you see a turtle on a fence post, you know he had some help.

And Alex Hley would say, "Any time I start thinking, Wow, isn't this marvelous what I've done! I look at that picture and remember how this turtle—me—got up on that post."

—Philip B. Osborn

Someone has to give way. There is a rule in sailing that the more maneuverable ship should give way to the less maneuverable craft. I think this is sometimes a good rule to follow in human relationships as well.

—Joyce Brothers

Martin Luther is credited with the following interesting story: Two mountain goats met each other on a narrow ledge just wide enough for one of the animals. On the left was a sheer cliff, and on the right a deep lake. The two face each other. What should they do? They could not back up—that would be too dangerous; they could not turn around, because the ledge was too narrow. Now if the goats had no more sense than some people, they would meet head-on and start butting each other till they fell into the lake below. Luther said that goats have better sense than this. One lay down on the trail and let the other literally walk over him—and both were safe.

Humility is unconscious self-forgetfulness.
—W. H. Griffith Thomas

A famous multimillionaire while attending a dinner, heard a discussion on the subject of prayer. After listening for a while, the man of means exclaimed with a sneer, "Prayer may be all right for some of you, but I don't need it. Everything I have today I've worked hard for, and I've earned it all myself. I didn't ask God for anything." A university president listened politely, then said to the braggart, "There is one thing you don't have that you might pray for." Startled, the millionaire blurted out, "And what might that be?" The educator replied gently, "Sir, you could pray for humility."

Humility is something we should constantly pray for, yet never thank God that we have.
—M. R. De Haan

When someone asked Saint Francis of Assisi why and how he could accomplish so much, he replied: "This may be why. The Lord looked down from heaven upon the earth and said, 'Where can I find the weakest, the littlest, the poorest man on the face of the earth?' Then He saw me and said, 'Now I've found him, and will work through him. He won't be proud of it. He'll see that I am only using him because of his littleness and insignificance.'"
—C. Reuben Anderson

One day John Knox approached the court of Mary, Queen of Scots, and was warned that it might be better to postpone his visit as she was in one of her angriest moods. He continued on his way replying, "Why should I be afraid of a queen when I have just spent four hours with God?"

The humble person does not take offense or fight back. He turns the other cheek to the one who hits him. And yet humility is not cowardice, for humility requires high courage. Humility makes you willing to take a lower place than you deserve, to keep quiet about your merits, to bear slights, insults, and false accusations for a higher purpose. Jesus displayed humility for "when He was reviled, [He] did not revile in return; when He suffered, He did not threaten."
—John Haggai

Humility is not thinking less of yourself than you are. Nor is humility always talking about your faults and shortcomings as compared with everyone else's superiority and achievements. Humility is simply a recognition of the truth about ourselves; and then most often, a forgetfulness of self that allows genuine concern for others and a genuine worship of God.
—S. Craig Glickman

I believe the first test of a truly great man is his humility. I do not mean by humility, doubt of his own power, or hesitation in speaking his opinion. But really great men have a curious under-sense of powerlessness, feeling that the greatness is not in them but through them; that they could not do or be anything else than God made them.
—John Ruskin

Moses spent forty years thinking he was somebody; then he spent forty years on the back side of the desert realizing he was nobody; finally, he spent the last forty years of his life learning what God can do with a nobody!
—D. L. Moody

Humility is not depreciation of ourselves, but appreciation of God.

A haughty lawyer once asked a godly old farmer, "Why don't you hold your head up high the way I do? No one pushes me around. I bow before neither God nor man!" "See that field of grain yonder?" replied the farmer. "Only the empty heads stand up. Those that are well filled always bow low."

It is no great thing to be humble when you are brought low; but to be humble when you are praised is a great and rare achievement.
—Bernard of Clairvaux

Someone quipped, "Someday when I get to be rich and famous, I wonder if I'll be the same sweet, lovable, humble person I am now?"

A man can counterfeit hope, love, faith, and many other graces, but it is very difficult to counterfeit humility.

Someone asked Leonard Bernstein, "What's the most difficult instrument to play?" Immediately he answered, "Second violin."

God has two thrones, one in the highest heavens, the other in the lowliest heart.
—D. L. Moody

People who think they know it all are especially annoying to us who do.

Be wiser than other people if you can; but do not tell them so.
—Philip Chesterfield

Humility is recognizing our limits.

Humility is to make a right estimate of oneself. It is no humility for a man to think less of himself than he ought.
—Charles H. Spurgeon

Sammy Morris, a devoted Christian from Africa, came to America to go to school. Although his pathway to service for Christ was not easy, his difficulties never deterred him. Perhaps this was because he had learned genuine humility. One incident that showed this occurred when he arrived at Taylor University in Upland, Indiana. He was asked by the school's president what room he wanted. Sammy replied, "If there is a room nobody wants, give it to me." Later the president commented, "I turned away, for my eyes were full of tears. I was asking myself whether I was willing to take what nobody else wanted."
—Our Daily Bread

If all people were as anxious to get to the bottom as some are in climbing to the top, they would have no trouble in reaching both places.

Near the entrance to a large hospital in the eastern United States there stands a white marble statue of Christ. On its base are engraved the words, "Come unto Me, all ye that labor and are heavy laden, and I will give you rest." One day a cynical man walked around the statue, viewing it disapprovingly from every angle. A small girl stood and watched him for a time and then she said, "Oh, sir, you cannot see Him that way. You must get very close and fall upon your knees and look up."

H. A. Ironside asked a military captain one day, "How can I be humble?" "Why don't you take your Bible and read it downtown on the sidewalks?" "Do you think it will make me humble?" "At least it will help." So he did. At noon he was hungry and hot, but he didn't stop. He went on reading texts from the Bible until 4:00 P.M. Then he went home and said to himself, "There's not another man in town that would do that."

Humility is a bag into which Christ puts the riches of His grace. The one infallible test of our holiness will be the humility before God and men which marks us. Humility is the bloom and the beauty of holiness. The chief mark of counterfeit holiness is its lack of humility.
—Andrew Murray

In the summer of 1940 the Netherlands had fallen. A surgeon, talking to an elderly Frisian farmer, asked, "And what are we to do now?" The old Christian replied, "Before men we must be as eagles; before God, as worms."

I used to think that God's gifts were on shelves one above the other; and that the taller we grew in Christian character, the easier we could reach them. I now find that God's gifts are on shelves one beneath the other; and that it is not a question of growing taller but of stooping lower; and that we have to go down, always down, to get His best gifts.

—F. B. Meyer

When little Wilhemina was crowned queen of Holland, the happy little girl, too young to realize the gravity of the occasion, with thousands of people cheering her on, was unable to take it all in. Turning to her mother she said, "Mama, do all these people belong to me?" Her mother replied, "No, dear, you belong to all these people!"

Who flies the kite? I, said the boy. I fly the kite. It is my joy. I fly the kite.
Who flies the kite? I, said the wind. I fly the kite. It is my whim. I fly the kite.
Who flies the kite? I, said the string. I'm the thing that flies the kite.
Who flies the kite? I, said the tail. I made the sail. I fly the kite.
Who flies the kite? All are wrong—all are right. All fly the kite!

Let it be repeated, there are two views of one's life. One is that a man's life is his own, to do with as he [or she] pleases; the other is that it belongs to another and . . . that the other to whom it belongs is Christ Himself.

—John R. Mott

Humility is perfect quietness of heart. It is for me to have no trouble; never to be fretted or vexed or irritated or sore or disappointed. It is to expect nothing, to wonder at nothing that is done to me, to feel nothing done against me. It is to be at rest when nobody praises me and when I am blamed or despised. It is to have a blessed home in the Lord where I can go in and shut the door and kneel to my Father in secret and be at peace as in a deep sea of calmness when all around is trouble. It is the fruit of the Lord Jesus Christ's redemptive work on Calvary's cross, manifested in those of His own who are definitely subject to the Holy Spirit.

—Andrew Murray

The humble man feels no jealousy or envy. He can praise God when others are preferred and blessed before him. He can bear to hear others praised while he is forgotten because . . . he has received the spirit of Jesus, who pleased not Himself, and who sought not His own honor.

Therefore, in putting on the Lord Jesus Christ he has put on the heart of compassion, kindness, meekness, longsuffering, and humility.

—Andrew Murray

HUMOR

Sir Thomas More, as he was about to ascend the gallows, said to the master of the Tower, "Help me climb up. I can manage the trip down myself."

The kind of humor I like is the thing that makes me laugh for five seconds and think for ten minutes.

—William Davis

Someone criticized Charles H. Spurgeon for his humor. He said to her, "You should hear what I hold back."

HUSBANDS

Two old friends met. "How's your husband?" said one.
    Her pious friend smiled complacently, "Oh, he's an angel!"
    "You're lucky," said the other. "Mine's still alive."

—Murray Watts

A man's unhappy life ended at age forty-seven. The widow, inconsolable at first, finally got a dog to ease her loneliness. The sorrow mellowed as she became attached to the dog.
    "She's happy because she's gotten back

to her old pattern of living," reported a neighbor. "That dog is a perfect substitute for her poor husband. He's out all day, sleeps all evening, and she feeds him out of cans."

A wife said to her husband, "Did anyone ever tell you that you were witty, intelligent, and handsome?" "No." "Then where did you get that idea?"

A New England farmer once said to his wife, "Wife, I love you so much sometimes it's all I can do to keep from telling you."

Husband: "You are so beautiful and yet so dumb."

Wife: "God made me beautiful so you would marry me, and dumb so I would marry you."

"Do you know someone perfect? Of course, no one of us does."

But then a hand went up.

"Do you mean to say you know of someone perfect?"

"Yes, my wife's first husband."

Husbands were made to be talked to. It helps them concentrate on what they're reading.

HYMNS

Tuberculosis cut short the lives of at least five noted hymn writers: Sarah Flower Adams ("Nearer My God to Thee"), W. B. Bradbury ("He Leadeth Me"), Curtis Kauffman ("Fling Wide the Gates"), Augustus Toplady ("Rock of Ages"), and Philip Doddridge ("O Happy Day").

Toplady was beset by a life-long physical weakness. "He was a fearless preacher, with the courage of a lion, but with a frame as brittle as glass." Tuberculosis cut short his life at the age of thirty-eight.

Isaac Watts was similarly handicapped by physical infirmity. "He was a frail little body, not much above five feet high, a life-long invalid, and much of the time an acute sufferer." When he proposed marriage, the woman refused on account of his frail stature. He remained a life-long bachelor.

Despite his physical frailty, he wrote thousands of hymns including, "Am I a Soldier of the Cross?" "Alas, and Did My Savior Bleed," "When I Survey the Wondrous Cross," "Jesus Shall Reign," "Marching to Zion," and "Joy to the World."

One time Charles Wesley was suffering under some depressing circumstances. While contemplating his troubles, he sat at a desk beside an open window. Suddenly he was startled by a small bird that flew excitedly into his room and hid under the open lapel of the large preacher's coat. Quickly putting his hand over the quivering creature whose fast-beating heart he could see palpitating against his own, he walked to the window and looked out to see if he could discern the object of its terror. There, circling nearby, was a huge hawk. Still holding the bird against his chest and seeing in the action of the fledgling a picture of his own search for refuge in God, Wesley wrote the words that have struck a responsive chord in the souls of thousands of others in times of deep distress. "Jesus, Lover of my soul, let me to thy bosom fly, while the nearer waters roll, while the tempest still is high! Hide me, O my Savior, hide—till the storm of life is past; safe into the haven guide; O receive my soul at last!"

HYPOCHONDRIACS

I never knew my uncle was a hypochondriac until a doctor told him he was in perfect health—and he asked for a second opinion.

—Bob Orben

HYPOCRISY

A man snubbed the local vicar at a cocktail party. "The church is full of hypocrites!"

"Why don't you join?" suggested the vicar. "One more won't make any difference."

—*Rolling in the Aisles*

A professor of ethics at a leading university was attending a convention. He and another teacher of philosophy had lunch at a restaurant and were discussing deep issues of truth and morality. Before they left the table, the professor slipped the silverware into his pocket. Noticing his colleague's puzzled look, he explained, "I just *teach* ethics. I need the spoons."

Lead your life so you wouldn't be ashamed to sell the family parrot to the town gossip.

A farmer once said to a friend, "I have some delicious apples growing in my orchard. If you come over, I'll give you a bushel." He repeated the offer, but his friend never came. Finally he asked, "John, why didn't you accept my offer?" "Well, to tell you the truth," said the other, "I have tasted them. As I went along the road a few weeks ago, I picked one up that had fallen over the wall and frankly, I have never eaten anything so sour!" "Oh," laughed the farmer. "I thought that might be the case. Those apples around the outside were placed there because we have so many boys in the neighborhood. In order to protect my crop, I selected the sourest varieties to plant around the outer edge of my orchard. When the boys tasted these, they gave up stealing, thinking all the fruit was just as bad. However, if you will come with me, you'll find that I grow a very different quality on the inside. You'll really enjoy them. They're as sweet as honey."

Those who judge the church by its worst members make the same mistake when they allow the "sour apple hypocrites" to keep them away from the "orchard of fellowship" they might enjoy with God's saints.

Why condemn the church because all its members aren't fine saints? You don't tear down the hospital because not all the patients recover.

Finding himself desperately in need of money, a man went to the city zoo, hoping to find a job feeding the animals. Although no such opportunity was available, the manager, seeing the size and the strength of the applicant, suddenly got an idea. "You know," he said, "there are a few creatures who attract attention like a gorilla. Unfortunately, ours died yesterday. If we got you a special fur suit, would you be willing to imitate him for a few days?"

The hungry man agreed to try. He was quite successful as he beat his chest, bellowed, and shook the bars of the cage—much to the amusement of visitors who said they had never seen a gorilla with such intelligence.

One day, while swinging on his trapeze, he accidentally lost his grip and landed in the lion's den. The huge beast gave a ferocious roar. Backing away, the impostor realized he couldn't cry for assistance without revealing that he was a fake. He retreated, hoping to crawl back over the fence into his own cage. The lion, however, followed him.

Finally, in desperation, he yelled, "Help!" Immediately the lion said in an undertone, "Shut up, stupid! You'll get us both fired!"

A hypocrite is one who complains there is too much sex and violence on his VCR.

The General Electric Company uses about two million sapphires a year for bearings in their meters and other delicate apparatus. To separate the real from the synthetic they use a cathode ray tube, which, when turned on a tray of stones in a dark room, makes them all glow. But when the ray is turned off, the artificial sapphires continue to glow and are picked from the tray. The real sapphires cannot be seen.

It is also said that under this ray, artificial diamonds turn brown while the genuine stones are unaffected.

The expression "face the music" is said to have originated in Japan. According to the story, one man in the imperial orchestra couldn't play a note. Being a person of great influence and wealth, he had demanded that he be given a place in the group because he wanted to "perform" before the emperor.

The conductor agreed to let him sit in the second row of the orchestra, even though he couldn't read music. He was given a flute, and when a concert would begin, he'd raise the instrument, pucker his lips, and move his fingers. He would go through all the motions of playing, but he never made a sound. This deception continued for two years.

Then a new conductor took over. He told the orchestra that he wanted to audition each player personally. One by one they performed in his presence. Then came the flutist's turn. He was frantic with worry, so he pretended to be sick. However, the doctor who was ordered to examine him declared that he was perfectly well. The conductor insisted that the man appear and demonstrate his skill. Shamefacedly, he had to confess that he was a fake. He was unable to "face the music."

I

IDEAS

An invasion of armies can be resisted, but not an idea whose time has come.
—Victor Hugo

Ideas are very much like children—your own ideas are wonderful.

Don't lose heart if one of your pet ideas is killed. If it's right it will come back to life.

You can't pass a law against an idea. The only way to fight an idea is to show a better one.

Many ideas grow better when transplanted into another mind than the one where they sprang up.
—Oliver Wendell Holmes

Don't hoard ideas. The more you radiate, the more you germinate.

Ideas are capital that bears interest only in the hands of talent.
—Antoine Rivaroli

Irrigate widely but dig your wells deep.
—Kenneth L. Pike

New ideas can be good or bad, just the same as old ones.
—Franklin D. Roosevelt

The man with a new idea is a crank, until the idea succeeds.
—Mark Twain

Fear of ideas makes us impotent and ineffective.
—William O. Douglas

Men possessed with an idea cannot be reasoned with.
—James Anthony Froude

To welcome new ideas, avoid these "killer phrases":
  It's not in the budget.
  Who thought of that?
  We tried that before.
  We're not ready for it yet.
  Not timely.
  Too hard to administer.
  Too theoretical.
  Doesn't conform to our policy.
  Takes too much time.
  Takes too much work.
  Let's wait and see.
  Let's form a committee.
  Has anyone ever tried it?
  What you are saying is . . .

IDLENESS

Never be idle, but either be reading, or writing, or praying, or meditating, or endeavoring something for the public good.
—Thomas á Kempis

He who is busy is bothered by only one devil; he who is lazy is bothered by a thousand.
—Spanish proverb

IDOLATRY

A man's god is that for which he lives, for which he is prepared to give his time, his energy, his money, that which stimulates him and rouses him, excites, and enthuses him.

—D. Martyn Lloyd-Jones

A rabbi was explaining to his pupils how strongly God condemns the worship of idols. One of them asked, "If God so abhors idolatry, why does He not destroy the idols that men worship?" The rabbi replied, "Because some of them, the sun and the moon for example, are an essential part of the fabric of God's economy." After a moment's pause, the student said, "Then why does He not at least destroy those that are not essential?" To which the rabbi answered, "Because it would then appear He was condoning the worship of the idols He did *not* destroy."

—Arthur C. Custance

IF

If you can keep your head when all about you
 Are losing theirs and blaming it on you;
If you can trust yourself when all men doubt you,
 But make allowance for their doubting too;
If you can wait and not be tired by waiting,
 Or, being lied about, don't deal in lies,
Or, being hated, don't give way to hating,
 And yet don't look too good, nor talk too wise;
If you can dream—and not make dreams your master;
 If you can think—and not make thoughts your aim;
If you can meet up with triumph and disaster
 and treat those two impostors just the same;
If you can bear to hear the truth you've spoken
 Twisted by knaves to make a trap for fools,
Or watch the things you gave up your life to broken,
 And stoop and build 'em up with worn out tools;
If you can make one heap of all your winnings
 And risk it on one turn of pitch-and-toss,
And lose, and start again at your beginnings
 And never breathe a word about your loss;
If you can force your heart and nerve and sinew
 To serve your turn long after they are gone,
And so hold on when there is nothing in you
 Except the will which says to them, "Hold on";
If you can talk with crowds and keep your virtue,
 Or walk with kings—nor lose the common touch;
If neither foes nor loving friends can hurt you;
 If all men count with you, but none too much;
If you can fill the unforgiving minute
 With sixty seconds' worth of distance run—
Yours is the earth and everything that's in it,
 and—which is more—you'll be a man, my son!

—Rudyard Kipling

IGNORANCE

Teach your tongue to say, "I do not know."

—A rabbi

To be ignorant of one's ignorance is the malady of ignorance.

—A. A. Alcott

We don't know one millionth of one percent of anything.

—Thomas Edison

Ignorance is an unhappy human condition in which all of us share much too richly.

IMAGINATION

Imagination is more important than knowledge.

—Albert Einstein

Imagination is more than knowledge. It is a preview of life's coming attractions.

—Albert Einstein

IMITATION

Imitation is the tribute that mediocrity pays to genius.

Imitation is the sincerest flattery.
—C. C. Colton

IMMORTALITY

The late first lady Eleanor Roosevelt once wrote in her syndicated column, "Almost every person with whom I have ever talked in my world travels has believed in life after death."

If there is no immortality, I shall hurl myself into the sea.
—Alfred Tennyson

The belief that death is the door to a better life is the oldest, strongest, and most insistent wish of mankind.
—Sigmund Freud

Albert Einstein scorned the idea of immortality. *The New York Times* of April 19, 1955, quotes him as saying, "Neither can I believe that the individual survives the death of his body, although feeble souls harbor such thoughts through fear or religious egotism."

The manuscripts of radio sermons in Britain must be submitted to the Director of Religious Broadcasting before they are broadcast to the people.

The late director, Dr. Welch, in speaking at a conference on evangelism, stated that out of six thousand manuscripts he had read only *one*, as far as he could recall, which dealt with the hope of immortality.

IMPATIENCE

There are two cardinal sins from which all the others spring: one is impatience and the other is laziness.
—Franz Kafka

IMPRESSIONS

First impressions never have a second chance.
—Chuck Swindoll

INCARNATION

An eminent naturalist believed in a "Supreme Being" but found it impossible to believe that the God who had created the wonders of the universe could be known by man.

One day as he was walking in his garden, he came on an ant hill covered with a swarm of ants that seemed greatly agitated as his shadow fell on them. "If only these ants knew how kindly I feel towards them," he thought, "they would not be disturbed at my presence."

Following this line of thought, he found himself wondering if a man would ever communicate his thoughts to ants. "No," he decided. "That is impossible. For a human to teach an ant what he is like, and to convey to them his thoughts, he would have to become an ant." Then, like a flash of lightning came this thought—"That is it exactly; the God of this universe, infinitely high as He is above us in His being and in His thoughts, had to become a man to teach man to know Him, and to know His thoughts."

If one were desiring to communicate with another person concerning business, and the recipient of the news did not understand the letter, nor even the telegram, then the best thing would be that the person sending the news would go to the other person. So it is with God. In order for us to understand God, it is necessary that He come down to our level and reveal Himself.

INDECISION

A man's home was on the border that separated the North and the South during the Civil War. He didn't want to take sides so he wore a Confederate Army jacket and Union Army pants. But he ran into trouble. The Union soldiers shot at his jacket and the Confederates shot him in the pants.

Indecision is fatal. It is better to make a wrong decision than build up a habit of indecision. If you're wallowing in indecision, you certainly can't act—and action is the basis of success.
—Marie Beynon Ray

INDECISION

I used to be indecisive, but now I'm not so sure.

INDIFFERENCE

The opposite of love is not hate—it's indifference.

—Ellie Wiesel

A pastor announced his topic for his sermon as "Ignorance and Indifference." A person in the congregation saw that in the bulletin and leaned to his neighbor and said, "What does that mean?"

He answered, "I don't know and I don't care."

INFLATION

"Inflation is creeping up," a young man said to his friend. "Yesterday I ordered a twenty-five dollar steak in a restaurant and told them to put it on my American Express card . . . and it fit."

—Reader's Digest

There was an old woman who lived in a
    shoe,
Who said, "With inflation, what's a body
    to do?
But I'm not so bad off,
for just down the block,
Is a little old woman
Who lives in a sock."

People used to wait until the price came down before buying something. Now they buy before the price goes up.

By the time a person acquires a nest egg these days, inflation turns it into chicken feed.

INFLUENCE

In the spring of 1894, the Baltimore Orioles came to Boston to play a routine baseball game. But what happened that day was anything but routine.

The Orioles' John McGraw got into a fight with the Boston third baseman. Within minutes all the players from both teams had joined in the brawl. The warfare quickly spread to the grandstands. Among the fans the conflict went from bad to worse. Someone set fire to the stands and the entire ballpark burned to the ground. Not only that, but the fire spread to 107 other Boston buildings as well.

A demonstration was once performed to show that a tiny cork could eventually move a heavy piece of steel. An eight-foot bar was suspended by a very strong wire. Nearby, a small cork hanging by a fine silk thread was swung gently and rhythmically against the metal. At first the large object remained apparently motionless, but after being struck repeatedly for ten minutes, a slight variation could be observed. At the end of half an hour the impact of the cork had transferred enough momentum to the bar to make it swing like a mighty pendulum.

My life shall touch a dozen lives
    before this day is done,
Leave countless marks for good or
    ill ere sets the evening sun.
This is the wish I always wish, the
    prayer I always pray:
Lord, may my life help other lives
    it touches by the way.

If you live with a lame man, you learn to limp.

—Plutarch

He who lives with wolves will learn to howl.

—Italian proverb

Jonathan Edwards, known as a religious and moral man, had at the time of this study, 1,394 descendants from his union with a Christian wife, Sarah. Of them, there were 100 preachers and missionaries, 100 lawyers, 80 public officials, 75 army and navy officers, 65 college professionals, 60 authors of prominence, 60 physicians, 30 judges, 13 college presidents, 3 United States senators, 1 vice-president of the United States, and 295 college graduates, among whom were governors of states and ministers to foreign countries.

But the power of the nuclear family works both ways. Max Jukes was an atheist and an example of ungodly living. From his union sprang 540 known descendants whose record is less impressive—310 died as paupers; 150 were criminals; 100 drunkards; 7 murderers; and more than half of the women were prostitutes. The offspring of Jukes and his wife are a vivid reminder that what can work for good can also produce evil.

—Leonard Ravenhill

Our lives are either sand dunes or sculptures. Our lives are shaped either by influences or by purposes.

—John Gardner

You will be the same person five years from now that you are today except for the people you meet and the books you read.

—Charlie "Tremendous" Jones

INGRATITUDE

A. J. Cronin had an unusual experience in New York City. He took a taxi and once inside he could tell from the driver's expression and the way he slammed the gears that something was wrong. He asked the driver what the trouble was.

"I've got good reason to be sore," he growled. "One of my fares left a wallet in my cab this morning. Nearly three hundred bucks in it! I spent more than an hour trying to trace the guy. Finally I found him at his hotel. He took the wallet without a word and glared at me as though I meant to snitch it."

"He didn't reward you?" Cronin asked.

"Not a cent, and me on my time and gas. But it wasn't the dough I wanted . . ." He fumbled for words, then exploded, "If the guy had only said something."

During World War II, a young army captain was hit by enemy fire while dragging a seriously wounded sergeant to safety. Both were taken to an army hospital. The officer died, but the rescued soldier recovered. The captain's parents, having been informed about the heroism of their son, invited the sergeant to their home for dinner. He accepted the invitation, but when he arrived he was not only late but in a half-intoxicated condition. All the while he was there he acted boorishly, said nothing about the one who had saved his life, wolfed down his food, and left without even saying thanks for their gracious hospitality. As soon as he was gone, the mother burst into tears, exclaiming, "To think that our son had to die for an ungrateful person like that!"

INHERITANCE

Some few years ago a poverty-stricken man in New Jersey opened an old family Bible and found, scattered throughout its pages, five thousand dollars in United States currency. This book had been in his possession for about thirty-five years, for while he was still a young man it was left to him by his aunt, a portion of whose will read: "To my beloved nephew . . . I will and bequeath my family Bible and all it contains, with the residue of my estate after my funeral expenses and just and lawful debts are paid."

INJUSTICE

To do injustice is more disgraceful than to suffer it.

—Plato

During the Great Depression, my father moved to a farm as a tenant. He signed a contract stating that he and the owner would share equally in the proceeds from milk and crops. In the fall, however, the landlord wouldn't give us our share of the money from the wheat crop. Dad's appeals to him accomplished nothing, so he consulted a Christian lawyer.

Reading the fine print in the contract, the lawyer advised my father that he could take no legal action. The landowner was unethical, but he had been clever enough to keep out of trouble. Rather humorously, the lawyer said, "Mr. Vander Lught, you have three choices. You can kill the crook and get yourself in deep trouble. You can cheat him and become like him. Or you can take the wrong and let God take care of you and him."

—Herbert Vander Lught

"Sometimes I would like to ask God why He allows poverty, famine, and injustice when He could do something about it."

"Well—why don't you ask Him?"

"Because I'm afraid God might ask me the same question."

INSTRUCTIONS

I've learned the same thing about my garden that Adam and Eve learned about theirs. It's best to follow the instructions.
—Bob Orben

INSULTS

Never insult an alligator until after you have crossed the river.
—Cordell Hull

The wound of words is worse than the wound of swords.
—Arabic proverb

INSURANCE

An old farmer at an insurance company reported that his barn burned down. He wanted to collect cash totaling two thousand dollars. But the insurance agents said they don't give cash but they would replace the old building with a new one built in the same size and shape. The farmer then said, "If that's your policy, I want to cancel my insurance on my wife."

INTEGRITY (Also see HONESTY)

The supreme quality for a leader is unquestionably integrity. Without it, no real success is possible, no matter whether it is on a section gang, on a football field, in an army, or in an office. If a man's associates find him guilty of phoniness, if they find that he lacks forthright integrity, he will fail. His teachings and actions must agree with each other.
—Dwight D. Eisenhower

Integrity is the integration of one's life around his core values.
—William D. Lawrence

"My boy," said the store owner to his new employee, "wisdom and integrity are essential to the retail business. By 'integrity' I mean if you promise a customer something, you have to keep that promise—even if it means we lose money."

"And what," asked the teenager, "is wisdom."

"That," answered the boss, "is not making any stupid promises."
—Handley Herold

Vision without integrity is not mission— it's manipulation.
—Howard G. Hendricks

INTELLIGENCE

Being intelligent involves being ignorant about those things that are not worth knowing.

Smart is when you believe one half of what you hear. Brilliant is when you know which half to believe.
—*Presbyterian Journal*

INTENTIONS

Mr. Meant To has a comrade,
And his name is Didn't Do;
Have you ever chanced to meet them?
Did they ever call on you?
These two fellows live together
In the house of Never Win;
And I'm told that it is haunted
By the ghost of Might Have Been.

Good intentions will not help a man on his way if he takes the wrong road.

INTEREST

Interesting people are people who are interested.
—*Teen Esteem*

INTERPERSONAL RELATIONS

Ten suggestions for getting along better with people:
1. Guard your tongue. Say less than you think.
2. Make promises sparingly. Keep them faithfully.
3. Never let an opportunity pass to say a kind word.

4. Be interested in others, their pursuits, work, families.
5. Be cheerful. Don't dwell on minor aches and disappointments.
6. Keep an open mind. Discuss but don't argue. Disagree without being disagreeable.
7. Discourage gossip. It's destructive.
8. Be careful of others' feelings.
9. Pay no attention to ill-natured remarks about you. Live so that nobody will believe them.
10. Don't be anxious about getting credit. Just do your best and be patient.

—*Bits & Pieces*

You can handle people more successfully by enlisting their feelings than by convincing their reason.

—Paul P. Parker

If you treat a person as he is, he will stay as he is. But if you treat him as if he were what he ought to be, he will become that bigger and better person.

—Johann von Goethe

INTERPRETATION

Once a country doctor was called in to see a sick girl. Only the girl's sister was with her so the doctor told the sister to give her some quinine. He said, "Give her just a little bit every morning, just about as much as you could put on a dime."

So one day later he got a call from the girl's sister. She said, "Come right away, Doctor. She's about to die."

The doctor hurried out, and when he saw her he said, "It looks like your only trouble is that you have had too much quinine."

Her sister then spoke up and said, "Well, I couldn't find a dime, so I gave her some quinine on two nickels."

INTERPRETERS

The sentence, "The spirit is willing but the flesh is weak," was given to a translation machine to be rendered into Japanese word by word. The result in English was, "There is some good whiskey but the roast beef is mediocre."

Speaking through an interpreter in Japan, Bob Jones once said, "The die is cast." The Japanese interpreter said in Japanese, "Death is thrown away."

INTRODUCTIONS

A preacher whose first language was not English was introduced as a model preacher. Not knowing what "model" meant, he looked it up in the dictionary and found it means "A small imitation of the real thing."

Also the man who introduced him said the speaker was "a warm person." He didn't know what "warm" means so he looked it up in the dictionary and found it means "not so hot."

A preacher from America went to Korea. He said, "I'm tickled to death to be here." The translator didn't know what he meant so he asked the preacher. The translator still didn't understand, so he simply said, "I scratch and scratch until I die."

You're fortunate that I'm speaking tonight because I used to give long speeches, speeches of an hour or an hour and a half. But I had to shorten them because of my throat. Someone threatened to cut it out.

A man gave a glowing introduction of the speaker. When the speaker stood up to speak, he said, "Thank you. That was beautiful. I wish my parents were here. My father would have enjoyed it and my mother would have believed it."

A man was preaching in a jail. He began by saying, "I'm glad to be here, and I'm glad to see all of you here." He didn't realize what he had said so he continued, "I know it took a lot of effort for you to be here." Still he didn't realize what he was saying so he continued, "You have no idea how much better the world will be because you are here."

A man told about a breakfast meeting where he was the speaker. The breakfast was at 7:00 and he arrived at 6:20. A woman was preparing the meal all by herself, so the man, an inexperienced speaker, offered to help. He ended up cracking the eggs and scrambling them.

When it was time for him to speak, he explained what he had done. He said, "If the eggs are no good, it's because my mind was on the message. If the message is no good it's because my mind was on the eggs." He added, "I just hope the eggs are scrambled and not the message."

A famous governor of New York once visited Sing Sing prison. After being shown several of the buildings he was asked to speak to the inmates. He was somewhat embarrassed and did not know exactly how to begin. Finally he said, "My fellow citizens," . . . but then he remembered that prisoners lose their citizenship. Then he said, "My fellow convicts," . . . but that didn't sound right either. So at last he said, "Well, anyhow, I'm glad to see so many of you here!"

At a baptismal service in Pine Cove in 1988 a high school boy was about to be baptized. He said, "I don't want to do this."

Someone said to a speaker, "You are God's sovereign choice for us. All the other speakers we wanted couldn't come."

Eighty percent of life is showing up.
—Woody Allen

A man who survived the Jonestown flood loved to tell about it. Then he died and went to heaven. Michael told him he could tell about the flood, but only once. After that he would have to keep quiet about it. He was delighted with this opportunity to speak to this large audience. Just as he began to speak, Peter turned to him and said, "Just remember that Noah is here."

INVENTIONS

The bathtub was invented in 1850, and the telephone in 1875. Had you lived in 1850, you could have sat in the bathtub for twenty-five years without having the phone ring once.

Elijah McCoy was a black man whose slave parents escaped to Canada where he

was born. Later he went to Detroit where he got a job as an oiler on the railroad.

In those days, machinery had to be shut down frequently and oiled by hand. McCoy invented the lubricating cup, a simple device that made this unnecessary. He also patented more than fifty other inventions dealing with lubricating devices, many of which are still used on railroads and steamships all over the world.

In McCoy's day, no respectable piece of machinery was complete without a McCoy lubricating cup. If it had the cup, it was "the real McCoy."
—Bits & Pieces

IRELAND

"Is it true that if you ask a man from Galway a question, he'll always answer you with another question?"

He said, "Who told you that?"
—Hal Roach

ISOLATION

In the year 1403, one of the wealthiest men in Paris died, leaving his entire estate to his teenage daughter Agnes. She was a beautiful and virtuous young woman, and many men wanted to marry her. But Agnes decided to give up her fortune and become a recluse. To isolate herself from society, she asked to be sealed in a cell within the wall of a church.

The entrance was plastered shut except for one small hole through which food could be passed. She was confined in that small area at eighteen years of age and she remained there until she died at age ninety-eight.

J

JEALOUSY (Also see ENVY)

Eve was so jealous of Adam that when he came home each night she used to count his ribs.
—Rolling in the Aisles

JOY

Always remember to forget the things that made you sad; but never forget to remember the things that made you glad.
—Elbert Hubbard

Charles M. Alexander tells that as a student at the Moody Bible Institute he often wondered how earnest Christians could be so lighthearted. One day when Mr. Moody gathered the students around him for a confidential talk, he noticed that some were wearing exceptionally long faces. Mr. Alexander says, "I was one of them, for I had been studying that sentence in the New Testament which says that for every idle word we shall have to give an account. I was naturally of a lively disposition and always sought to cheer those who were downhearted. But now I thought I had been wrong. Therefore I tried to control my face so that no smile would ever come upon it. That morning Mr. Moody spoke about Matthew 12:36. Looking up with a joyous countenance, he said, 'Young men, do not think this verse means that you shall go around with a long face and never express any happy sentiments. Remember, a cheerful word is not an idle one.'"

Joy is the gigantic secret of the Christian.
—G. K. Chesterton

Many years ago a great earthquake did considerable damage in San Francisco, California. Many buildings were wrecked by the quake and others through fire started by the earth tremors. In the midst of this great tragedy an elderly grandmother was observed sitting in her rocking chair on her front lawn and singing. A passerby asked her how she could be so happy when the earth was cracking up. Her reply was, "I'm rejoicing to see how my God can change things."
—Theodore H. Epp

The best way to cheer yourself up is to cheer someone else up.
—Mark Twain

The German philosopher Friedrich Nietzsche said scornfully about Christians of his day, "I would believe in their salvation if they looked a little more like people who have been saved."

Martin Luther in his later years was gloomy. One day his wife came into his study dressed in black. Martin asked, "Who's dead?" She said, "God is." Martin responded, "My soul, why should you talk like that?" She said, "Because of your gloom."

Wondrous is the strength of cheerfulness and its power of endurance. The cheerful man will do more in the same time, will do it better, and will persevere in it longer, than the sad or sullen.
—Thomas Carlyle

Joy is not the absence of trouble but the presence of Christ.
—William Vander Haven

Joseph Haydn, the great musician, was once asked why his church music was so cheerful, and he replied, "When I think upon God, my heart is so full of joy that the notes dance and leap, as it were, from my pen, and since God has given me a cheerful heart it will be pardoned me that I serve Him with a cheerful spirit."

Shared joy is double joy and shared sorrow is half-sorrow.

A. G. Swinburne, English poet and critic (1837–1909), pictured Christ as a pale Galilean "who made the world grow gray at His breath." Such a description of Jesus Christ is reprehensible and diabolically false.

Christianity is the most encouraging, the most joyous, the least repressive of all the religions of mankind. While it has its sorrows and stern disciplines, the end of it is a resurrection, not a burial—a festival, not a funeral.
—L. P. Jacks

The New Testament is the happiest thing in literature, with the sound of singing in

it everywhere, opening with the choir of angels over Bethlehem and closing with the Hallelujah Chorus of the redeemed.
—Arthur Gossip

The late Gypsy Smith used to say that you could not get a "hallelujah" out of some Christians if you squeezed them through a wringer.

The flag flown from the castle of the heart is to show that the King is in residence there.

Now since I have been converted, I am happier when I am unhappy than I was happy before I was converted.
—John McNeil

The religion that makes a man look sick certainly won't cure the world.
—Phillips Brooks

There are two kinds of people—those who cause happiness wherever they go and those who cause happiness whenever they go.

It's easy enough to be pleasant
　　When life flows by like a song,
But the man worthwhile
　　Is the man who can smile,
When everything goes dead wrong.

Oh, God, thou hast made us for Thyself, and our hearts find no rest until they rest in Thee.
—Augustine

Joy is not a luxury or a mere accessory in the Christian life. It is the sign that we are really living in God's wonderful love, and that love satisfies us.
—Andrew Murray

JUDGMENT

A woman once said to a French Cardinal, "My Lord Cardinal, God does not pay at the end of every week; nevertheless He pays."

Once a young man was drowning. He cried for help and a man passing by the water jumped in and saved the fellow from death. Several years later this same young man had fallen into sin. He had stolen a car and was brought into court.

He was greatly relieved to see the man who saved him from a watery grave sitting as a judge on the bench. "He will save me again, I am sure," he thought.

The trial came to an end and the judge in giving the verdict said, "You are guilty and I must condemn you."

"Oh, but you were the one who saved my life before."

"Young man, one day I was your savior, but now I am your judge. Your day of grace has come to an end."

JUSTICE

In the famous Un-American Activities trial of the Rosenbergs of 1952, they said to the court, "Give us justice. That's all we ask for. That's what we're after." The court said, "No, what you're after is mercy. But this court can't give mercy—only justice. And what you've got is justice."

In the Supreme Court Building in Switzerland is a huge painting by Paul Robert. When he was asked to paint this tremendous mural on the stairway leading up to the Supreme Court offices, he expressed in painting what Samuel Rutherford placed in magnificent words. The title of the painting is Justice Instructing the Judges. In the foreground are all forms of litigation—the wife against the husband, the architect against the builder, and others. Above them stand the Swiss judges. How will they judge the litigation? Robert's answer is this: Justice (no longer blindfolded with her sword vertical as is common) is unblindfolded with her sword pointing downward to a book on which is written "The Word of God."

JUSTIFICATION

After Charles H. Spurgeon had finished preaching a sermon on justification by grace, a man came to him and said, "Oh, sir, I have been praying and I do not think God will forgive me unless I do something to deserve it." Spurgeon replied, "I tell you, sir, if you bring any of your deservings, you shall never have it. God gives away His justification freely; and if you bring anything to pay for it, He will throw it in your face and will not give His justification to you."

A Jewish soldier named Alfred Dreyfus showed such marked ability that in 1891 he was appointed to the general staff of the French Army. Three years later he was arrested, being charged with selling military information to Germany. His trial resulted in dismissal from the army, public degradation, and commitment to the French penal colony on Devil's Island. Due to popular demand Dreyfus was retried in 1899, but was again declared guilty. Because of public dissatisfaction with the result of the trial the president of France pardoned Dreyfus. But the friends of Dreyfus were not satisfied with a mere pardon and in 1906 in a third trial Dreyfus was completely vindicated. He was given the more advanced rank of major and enrolled in the Legion of Honor.

When Alfred Dreyfus was pardoned after the second trial the penalty of the crime of which he was accused was remitted. He was taken from the penal colony on Devil's Island. He came back to his family and friends, but the stigma of being a traitor still rested on him. But when through the third trial he became vindicated and was promoted to the rank of major and enrolled in the Legion of Honor, he was justified before the whole world. He had a standing of perfect righteousness and was given recognition that comes only to those who have served and brought honor to their country.

This is exactly what happens when God justifies the one who believes in Jesus.

Not on my guilty head
    The wrath of God shall fall—
The Lamb has suffered in my stead;
    His blood atones for all.
I seek no other way—
    My soul is satisfied,
To know that God forgives today,
    Because my Savior died.

JUVENILE DELINQUENCY

The place to stop crime is at the high chair and not the electric chair.
—Judge Jonah J. Goldstein

A Harvard University survey shows:

Six out of every ten juvenile delinquents have fathers who drink to excess. Also many of their mothers drink to excess.

Three out of four are permitted by parents to come and go as they please.

Three out of five are from homes where there is discord between parents.

Seven out of ten are from homes where there is no group or family recreation.

Four out of five have parents who take no interest in their children's friends.

Four out of five delinquent boys say their mother was indifferent to them.

Three out of five delinquent boys say their father was indifferent to them.

K

KINDNESS

'Tis better to buy a small bouquet,
    And give to your friend this very day,
Then a bushel of roses white and red,
    To lay on his coffin after he's dead.
—Irish blessing

Kindness is a language the deaf can hear and the dumb can understand.
—Seneca

There is no tranquilizer in the world more effective than a few kind words.

Do you know a soul downhearted
    Needing cheer along life's way?
If you do, then share your gladness,
    Freely speak kind words today.
—Beverly J. Anderson

If someone were to pay you ten cents for every kind word you ever spoke about people, and then take back five cents for every unkind word you ever spoke about people, would you be poor or rich?

Do all the good you can,
in all the ways you can,
in all the places you can,
at all the times you can,
to all the people you can,
as long as ever you can.
—John Wesley

The only people you should try to get even with are those who have helped you.

There has never been an overproduction of kind words.

Kindness always pays but it pays most when you don't do it for pay.

Often the only thing a child can remember about an adult in later years, when he or she is grown, is whether or not that person was kind to him or her.
—Billy Graham

One kind word can warm up three winter months.
—Japanese proverb

The best portion of a good life is little, nameless, unremembered acts of kindness and love.
—William Wordsworth

You can no more have love without kindness than you can have springtime without flowers. The greatest thing a man can do for his heavenly Father is to be kind to some of His other children.
—Guy King

Someone said regarding William Beecher, "You never knew the force of his kindness until you had done him some wrong."

If you confer a benefit, never remember it. If you receive one, never forget it.

A bit of fragrance always clings to the hand that gives you roses.
—Chinese proverb

How far you go in life depends on your being tender with the young, compassionate with the aged, sympathetic with the striving, and tolerant of the weak and the strong. Because someday in life you will have been all of these.
—George Washington Carver

Little acts of kindness—small may be their cost,
Yet when they are wanting—life's best charm is lost.

Kind words soothe and quiet and comfort the hearer. They shame him out of his sour, morose, unkind feelings. We have not yet begun to use kind words in such abundance as they ought to be used.
—Blaise Pascal

Scatter kindness along the way and you will never walk alone.

You can never tell when you do an act
Just what the result will be;
But with every deed you are serving a need,
Though its harvest you may not see.

Kindness is one thing you cannot give away; it always comes back!

When I was young, I admired clever people. Now that I am old, I admire kind people.
—Abraham Joshua Heschel

People are unreasonable, illogical, and self-centered.
    Love them anyway.
If you do good, some will accuse you of selfish motives.
    Do good anyway.
If you succeed, you win false friends and true enemies.
    Succeed anyway.
The good you do today may be forgotten tomorrow.
    Do good anyway.
Honesty and frankness make you vulnerable.
    Be honest anyway.
What takes years to build may be destroyed overnight.
    Build well anyway.

One of the most difficult things to give away is kindness; it is usually returned.

—Cort R. Flint

In *Les Miserables*, Victor Hugo tells the story of Jean Valjean. His only crime was the theft of a loaf of bread to feed his sister's starving children. After serving nineteen years for his crime, he was released. Unable to find work because he had been a convict, he came to the home of a Christian bishop who kindly gave him supper and a place to sleep. Yielding to temptation, however, Valjean stole the bishop's silver plates and slipped out into the night. But he was apprehended and brought back to the scene of the crime. The kind bishop did not want to prosecute the man. Deciding to try to win him to the Lord instead, he told the officers he wanted Valjean to have the silver plates. Turning to the culprit, he said, "And Jean, you forgot to take the candlesticks." The criminal was astounded and the kindness later resulted in his conversion. This brought a deep sense of joy to the compassionate bishop.

—*Our Daily Bread*

There is a beautiful Hebrew legend of two brothers who lived side by side on adjoining lands. One was the head of a large family, the other lived alone. One night, the older brother lay awake and thought, "My brother lives alone; he has not the companionship of wife and children to cheer his heart as I have. While he sleeps, I will carry some of my sheaves into his field."

At the same hour, the younger brother reasoned, "My brother has a large family, and his necessities are greater than mine. As he sleeps I will put some of my sheaves on his side of the field."

Thus, the two brothers went out, each laden with sheaves—and met at the dividing line. There they embraced. Years later, at the very place stood the Jerusalem temple, and on the very spot of their meeting stood the temple's altar.

Always try to be a little kinder than necessary.

—James M. Barrie

Former President William McKinley was once planning to appoint an ambassador to a foreign country. There were two candidates whose qualifications were almost equal, and McKinley searched his mind for some yardstick by which he might measure the true greatness of the men in question. He later confided that the self-centeredness of the one and the magnanimous kindness of the other were the deciding factors in the scale of his judgment. Many years before, when he was still a representative in Congress, McKinley said he had boarded a street car at the rush hour and managed to get the last vacant seat.

An old washer woman entered shortly afterward carrying a heavy basket. She walked the length of the car and stood in the aisle, hardly able to keep her balance as the vehicle swayed from side to side in its race down the tracks. No one offered her a seat. One of the men the President was later to consider was sitting opposite where she was standing. McKinley noticed that he shifted his newspaper in order to avoid seeing her. Mr. McKinley walked down the aisle, took her basket of washing and offered her his seat in the back of the car. The candidate never knew that this little act of selfishness had deprived him of perhaps the crowning honor of his lifetime. For the President later recalled this unkindness and decided to appoint the other man as his ambassador.

"What is good?"
I asked in a musing mood.
Order, said the law court;
Knowledge, said the school;
Truth, said the wise man;
Pleasure, said the fool;
Love, said the maiden;
Beauty, said the dreamer;
Home, said the sage;
Fame, said the soldier;
Equity, said the seer;
Spoke my heart full sadly,
"The answer is not here."
Then within my bosom
Softly this I heard:

KINDNESS

"Each heart holds this secret;
Kindness is the word."
—John Boyle O'Reilly

Stephen Grellet was a French-born Quaker who died in New Jersey in 1855. Grellet would be unknown to the world today except for a few lines that made him immortal. The familiar lines, which have served as an inspiration to so many people, are these:

"I shall pass through this world but once. Any good that I can do, or any kindness that I can show any human being, let me do it now and not defer it. For I shall not pass this way again."

Forget injuries, never forget kindnesses.
—Confucius

A shepherd in India was troubled by his neighbor's dogs, who were killing his sheep. Shepherds usually counter that problem with lawsuits or barbed wire fences or even shotguns, but this man went to work on his neighbors with a better idea. To every neighbor's child he gave a lamb or two as pets, and in due time, when all his neighbors had their own small flocks, they began to tie up their dogs, and that put an end to the problem.
—J. Wallace Hamilton

H. H. Lee said that at one end of the truck terminal where he worked was a coal company with a high fence around it. Nearby was a railroad, and each day several freight trains passed by. Lee often noticed that the owner of the yard, who was a Christian, threw chunks of coal over the fence at various places along the track. One day he asked the man why he did this. With compassion in his voice, he replied, "A poor elderly woman lives across the street, and I know that her old-age pension is inadequate to buy enough coal. After the trains go by, she walks along and picks up the pieces she thinks have fallen from the coal car behind the engine. Her eyesight is failing, and she doesn't realize that diesels have replaced steam locomotives. I don't want to disappoint her, so I just throw some pieces over the fence to help her." That is Christianity in action!

KNOWLEDGE

He who knows not, and knows not that he knows not is a fool; avoid him.
He who knows not and knows that he knows not, is simple; teach him.
He who knows, and knows not that he knows, is asleep; wake him.
He who knows, and knows that he knows, is a wise man; follow him.

I'd rather know a lot of things for certain than to be sure of a lot of things that aren't so.
—Josh Billings

Know what you know, and know that you don't know what you don't know—that is characteristic of one who knows.
—Confucius

A devoted follower of Socrates asked him the best way to acquire knowledge. Socrates responded by leading him to a river and plunging him beneath the surface. The man struggled to free himself, but Socrates kept his head submerged. Finally, after much effort, the man was able to break loose and emerge from the water. Socrates then asked, "When you thought you were drowning, what one thing did you want most of all?" Still gasping for breath, the man exclaimed, "I wanted air!" The philosopher wisely commented, "When you want knowledge as much as you wanted air, then you will get it!" The same is true with our desire for righteousness.

He has learned more and more about less and less so that he knows everything about nothing.

L

LABOR DAY

Tomorrow is Labor Day, I suppose set by an act of Congress. How Congress knew anything about labor is beyond me.
—Will Rogers

LAUGHTER

Laughter is the shortest distance between two people.
—Victor Borge

A retired surgeon said to me on a plane, "I've practiced medicine for fifty-eight years and I've never known a person to die from laughter."
—Roy B. Zuck

The day has never dawned that I couldn't find something to laugh at.
—Flannery O'Connor

We don't stop laughing because we get old. We get old because we stop laughing.

Make it a point to indulge in at least one hearty laugh every day. If nothing funnier comes along, laugh at yourself.

Man is the only creature endowed with laughter. And he is the only creature that deserves to be laughed at.
—Philip Chesterfield

Few people realize that health actually varies according to the amount of laughter. So does recovery. People who laugh actually live longer than those who do not laugh.
—James J. Walsh

The wife of a drunkard once found her husband in a filthy condition, with torn clothes, matted hair, bruised face, asleep in the kitchen, having come home from a drunken revel. She sent for a photographer, had a picture of him in all his wretched appearance, and placed it on the mantel beside another picture taken at the time of his marriage, which showed him handsome and well dressed. When he became sober, he saw the two pictures and awakened to a consciousness of his condition, from which he arose to a better life. The purpose of the Law is not to save people, but to show them their true condition compared with the divine standard.

If laughter could be ordered at the corner drugstore, any doctor would prescribe many laughs every day. A dose of laughter is a combination of stimuli like that of vitamin tablets plus the relaxation of bromides. Laughter is exercise for the diaphragm, which is neglected in most exercises except deep breathing. If you could x-ray yourself when you laugh, you would see astonishing results. Your diaphragm goes down, and your lungs expand. You are taking in more oxygen than usual. A surge of power runs from head to toes.

During the dark days of the Civil War, Abraham Lincoln confided to a friend, "With the fearful strain that is on me night and day, if I did not laugh I should die."

Laughter translates into any language.

Bud Abbott and Lou Costello once took out a hundred thousand dollar insurance policy with Lloyds of London that stipulated payment if any of their audience should die of laughter.
—*The Little, Brown Book of Anecdotes*

LAW

When you are cooking a roast in the oven, if it is done, you try to pick it out with a fork, but find you are unable to do so. This is like the Mosaic law. It is unable to pick us up out of sin.

Then you find that you are able to get the roast out only if you place a pan under the roast and lift it out in this manner. This is grace. It gets under us and lifts us out of the bondage of sin.

The law brings out sin; grace covers it. The law wounds; the Gospel heals. One is a quiver of arrows; the other a cruise of oil.
—D. L. Moody

LAWYER

A jury consists of twelve persons chosen to decide who has the better lawyer.
—Robert Frost

Two farmers began to fight over the ownership of a cow. One began to pull from the head and the other from the tail. While they were doing this, a third came and began to milk the cow. He happened to be a lawyer.
—*Pulpit Helps*

LAYPEOPLE

Leave it only to the ministers, and soon
 the church will die;
Leave it to the womenfolk—the young will
 pass it by.
For the church is all that lifts us from the
 coarse and selfish mob,
And the church that is to prosper needs the
 laymen on the job.
Now, a layman has his business, and a layman has his joys,
But he also has the training of his little girls
 and boys;
And I wonder how he'd like it if there were
 no churches here,
And he had to raise his children in a godless atmosphere.
It's the church's special function to uphold
 the finer things,
To teach that way of living from which all
 that's noble springs;
But the minister can't do it singlehanded
 and alone,
For the laymen of the country are the
 church's buildingstones.
When you see a church that's empty,
 though its doors are open wide.
It's not the church that's dying—it's the
 laymen who have died;
It's not just by song or sermon that the
 church's work is done,
It's the laymen of the country who for God
 must carry on.
—Edgar A. Guest

LAZINESS

A lazy maid was once asked, "Don't you do anything fast?"
 "Yes, I get tired fast."

It is better to be bent by hard work than to be crooked by trying to avoid it.

A lazy, chronically unemployed man was asked, "How are things going?" He said, "Things are tough. I sleep at night fairly well, and in the morning I can make it, but in the afternoons I just toss and turn."

A student once wrote to the famous preacher Henry Ward Beecher, asking him how to obtain "an easy job." Mr. Beecher replied, "If that's your attitude, you'll never amount to anything. You cannot be an editor or become a lawyer or think of entering the ministry. None of these professions is easy. You will have to forget the fields of merchandising and shipping, abhor the practice of politics, and forget about the difficult field of medicine. To be a farmer or even a good soldier, you must study and think. My son, you have come into a hard world. I know of only one easy place in it, and that is in the grave."

The only thing necessary for the triumph of evil is that good men do nothing.
—Edmund Burke

If the Devil catches a man idle, he will set him to work.

God will not do for you what He has given you strength to do for yourself.
—Bob Jones

If you want to kill time, try working it to death.

He who waits to do a great deal of good at once will never do anything.

The Bible promises no loaves to the loafer.

A lot of people who spout so profusely about capital and labor never had any capital and never did any labor.

Some people use Christianity like a bus; they ride on it only when it is going their way.

Easy come, easy go, but not so easy when it's gone.

We'll never leave any footprints in the sands of time by sitting down.

The lazier a man is, the more he is going to do tomorrow.
—Norwegian proverb

Good luck is a lazy man's estimate of a worker's success.

I like the word *indolence*. It makes my laziness seem classy.
—Bern Williams

Poverty of purpose is worse than poverty of purse.

An old mountaineer and his wife were sitting in front of the fireplace one evening just whiling away the time.

After a long silence the wife said: "Jed, I think it's raining. Get up and go outside and see."

The old mountaineer continued to gaze into the fire for a second, sighed, then said, "Aw, Ma, why don't we just call in the dog and see if he's wet."

Be ashamed to find yourself idle.

No one is so tired as the one who does nothing.

There are but a few men who have character enough to live a life of idleness.
—Josh Billings

LEADERSHIP

The best executive is the one who has sense enough to pick good people to do what he wants done, and self-restraint enough to keep from meddling with them while they carry it out.
—Theodore Roosevelt

The real art of management is to attract, retain, and motivate individuals— recognizing their intrinsic differences and lifestyles—and to assist and make possible in every way the achievement of their personal objectives in the accomplishment of our corporate goals.

Management Dimensions, Inc. surveyed 241 business executives and asked what traits make workers succeed. Executives could select more than one trait. The most important trait was enthusiasm—80 percent of the executives listed it. Second was a can-do attitude, with 63 percent listing it.
—*Bits & Pieces*

Management is not being brilliant. Management is being conscientious. Beware the genius manager. Management is doing well a few simple things and doing them well.
—Peter Drucker

A leader has two important characteristics: first, he is going somewhere; second, he is able to persuade other people to go with him.

A good boss is a guy who takes a little more than his share of the blame and a little less than his share of the credit.

A good supervisor, someone once said, is a guy who can step on your toes without messing up your shine.

A company is known by the people it keeps.

The man who gets the most satisfactory results is not always the man with the most brilliant single mind, but rather the man who can best coordinate the brains and talents of his associates.
—W. Alton Jones

Good supervision is the art of getting average people to do superior work.

There is a very obvious dearth of people who seem to be able to supply convincing answers or even to point the direction toward solutions.
—Derek Bok

A man lays the foundation of true greatness when he becomes more concerned with building his character than with expanding his reputation.

He who would be great must be fervent in his prayers, fearless in his principles, firm in his purposes, and faithful in his promises.

—William Arthur Ward

A leader must see the vision, state the mission, and set the tone.

—David Rockefeller

Leadership appears to be the art of getting others to want to do something you are convinced should be done.

—Vance Packard

People cannot be managed. Inventories can be managed, but people must be led.

—H. Ross Perot

To manage is to lead, and to lead others requires that one enlist the emotions of others to share a vision of their own.

—Henry M. Boettinger

A leader is an individual who has an inspiring vision and can get others to buy into it.

—Laurence Smith

Hanging on a wall in former president George Bush's office in the White House were the words: "Think big. Be frank. Fight hard for your position."

Trust your subordinates. You can't expect them to go all out for you if they think you don't believe in them.

Develop a vision. People want to follow someone who knows where he or she is going.

Keep your cool. The best leaders show their mettle under fire.

Encourage risk. Nothing demoralizes the troops like knowing that the slightest failure could jeopardize their entire career.

Be an expert. From boardroom to mail room, everyone had better understand that you know what you're talking about.

Invite dissent. Your people aren't giving you their best if they are afraid to speak up.

Simplify. You need to see the big picture in order to set a course, communicate it, and maintain it.

—Kenneth Labich

One of the marks of true greatness is the ability to develop greatness in others.

—J. C. McCauley

Two qualities make the difference between leaders and men of average performance. They are curiosity and discontent. I have never known an outstanding man who lacked either. And I have never known a man of small achievement who had both.

—Charles H. Brower

The boss drives his men; the leader coaches them.
The boss depends on authority; the leader on goodwill.
The boss inspires fear; the leader inspires enthusiasm.
The boss says "I"; the leader, "we."
The boss fixes the blame for the breakdown; the leader fixes the breakdown.
The boss knows how it is done; the leader shows how.
The boss says "Go"; the leader says "Let's go!"

—H. Gordon Selfridge

No one need aspire to leadership in the work of God who is not willing to pay a price greater than his contemporaries and colleagues are willing to pay. True leadership always exacts a heavy toll on the whole man, and the more effective the leadership is, the higher the price to be paid.

—J. Oswald Sanders

Studies of people in business and industry who have achieved success show that four factors are almost always present. They are:
1. The ability to think.
2. An inner drive and love of work.
3. The capacity to assume responsibility.
4. The ability to lead people.

—*Bits & Pieces*

A leader is a person who is going somewhere—but not going alone. He takes others with him. His ability in setting up situations in which others are willing to follow him and happy to work with him is a precious skill called leadership. This skill is made up of many qualities—thoughtfulness and consideration for others, enthusiasm, the ability to share responsibility with others, and a multitude of other traits. But fundamentally a leader is one who leads, one who has a plan, one who keeps headed toward a goal and a purpose. He has the enthusiasm to keep moving forward in such a way that others gladly go with him.

—Walter MacPeek

Reason and calm judgment are the qualities specially belonging to a leader.

—Tacitus

The speed of the leader determines the rate of the pack.

Do not follow where the path may lead. Go instead where there is no path and leave a trail.

Anyone who influences others is a leader.

—Chuck Swindoll

A leader is an average, everyday person who is highly motivated.

—Theodore Roosevelt

One measure of leadership is the caliber of people who choose to follow you.

—Dennis A. Peer

Leaders need to cultivate two things: a righteous heart and a rhinoceros skin.

—Charles Swindoll

Leadership is calculated risk-taking.

—Ted Ward

The two great laws of life are growth and decay. When things stop growing, they begin to die. This is true of men, businesses, or nations.

—Charles Gow

Leadership consists of character and strategy. If you can't have both, opt for character.

—General Norman Schwarzkopf

Henry Ford had a habit of going to the offices of other executives whenever a problem had to be discussed, rather than have them come to his own office. He did it to save time.

"I've found," he said, "that I can leave the other fellow's office a lot quicker than I can get him to leave mine."

No man will make a great leader who wants to do it all himself, or to get all the credit for doing it.

—Andrew Carnegie

The trouble with being a leader today is that you can't be sure whether people are following you or chasing you.

Tom Peters, coauthor of *In Search of Excellence* and *A Passion for Excellence,* claims exceptional leaders have many traits in common. Prominent among them are:

1. They soak up information, often take notes obsessively, and realize they can learn from anyone, regardless of title or position.
2. They're constantly looking for ways to make things better. They're starving for thousands of tiny improvements. To them, no idea is too small.
3. They delight in the success of others. They never attempt to hog credit. They give credit where credit is due.

The higher you go the more dependent you become on others.

A leader is best when people barely know he exists. . . . When his work is done, his aim fulfilled, they will say, "We did this ourselves."

—Lao-tzu

Frederick the Great sent a messenger to one of his generals: "I send you against the enemy with sixty thousand men." When the troops were counted they numbered only fifty thousand. The general sent a letter of protest and complaint, insisting there must be a mistake. "No," replied Frederick, "there is no mistake. I counted you for ten thousand men."

—David A. MacLennon

Leadership is the discipline of deliberately exerting special influence within a group to move it toward goals of beneficial permanence that fulfill the group's real needs.

—John Haggai

When in charge, ponder. When in trouble, delegate. When in doubt, mumble.

—Lawrence J. Peter

Anne O'Hare McCormick visited Hitler, Mussolini, and Roosevelt and asked all three, "How did you get where you are?"

Mussolini puffed out his chest, as he often did, and replied, "I came!" Hitler got a faraway look in his face and said, "I was sent."

When she asked Roosevelt, he laughed and said, "Well, somebody had to do it!"

Leadership is the ability to inspire other people to work together as a team under your direction in order to attain a common objective.

—Harold Geneen

When Thomas Jefferson presented his credentials as U.S. Minister to France, the French premier remarked, "I see that you have come to replace Benjamin Franklin." "I have come to succeed him," corrected Jefferson. "No one can replace him."

—*Bits & Pieces*

See everything; overlook a lot; deal with a little.

—Pope John XXIII

Common traits exhibited by successful leaders in almost every field are these:

They observe with application. They observe and absorb. They look at everything as though it's the first and last time they'll ever see it.

They know how to listen—really listen. Listening is wanting to hear.

They welcome ideas, urging others to bring their best thinking on a subject. They're open, responsive, sensitive, aware, and encouraging.

They value time highly.

—Whitt N. Schultz

I use not only my own brains but also all I can borrow.

—Woodrow Wilson

When Benno Schmidt Jr. assumed the presidency of Yale University, he expressed some concern regarding the busyness of the job. "If I can't put my feet on the desk and look out the window and think without an agenda, I may be managing Yale, but I won't be leading it."

A research organization polled five hundred executives, asking them what traits they thought were most important in dealing with others. From the information received, five basic "rules" were formulated. They are:

1. Always give your people the credit that is rightfully theirs. To do otherwise is both morally and ethically dishonest.
2. Be courteous. Have genuine consideration for other people's feelings, wishes, and situations.
3. Never tamper with the truth. Never rationalize. What you might like to believe is not necessarily the truth.
4. Be concise in your writing and talking, especially when giving instructions to others.
5. Be generous. Remember that it is the productivity of others that makes possible your executive position.

—*Bits & Pieces*

Qualities essential to effective leadership are boldness, imagination, and strength of character.

—Gail Sheehy

Why are administrators like bananas? They are green when they are taken aboard, they get yellow half way across the gulf, and they get thrown overboard when they start to get soft.

A man applied for a job at a prison as a warden. "Can you handle this job? This is a tough bunch here." He responded, "No problem. If they misbehave, out they go."

It is hard to learn the mind of any mortal, or the heart till he be tried in chief authority. Power shows the man.

—Sophocles

Someone asked General Douglas McArthur, "What is the greatest quality of a leader?" He answered, "Selflessness."

Murphy's Law: If something can go wrong, it will.

Weiler's Law: Nothing is impossible for the person who doesn't have to do it himself.

Chisholm's Law: Anytime things appear to be going better, you have overlooked something.

Finangle's Law: Once a job is fouled up, anything done to improve it makes it worse.

Crane's Law: There is no such thing as a free lunch.

At the University of Santa Clara, California, a researcher conducted a study of fifteen hundred business managers to determine, among other things, what workers value most in a boss. The survey revealed that employees respect a leader who shows competence, has the ability to inspire workers, and is skillful in providing direction. But there was a fourth quality they admired even more—integrity. Above all else, workers wanted a manager whose word is good, a manager who is known for his honesty, a manager whom they could trust.

What kind of people don't make good leaders? A study by a team of psychologists at the University of California found them to be:

Aggressive against people who do not agree with them, or who do not do as they want them to.

Apprehensive that others are scheming against them, or the firm.

Fatalistic in thinking that most workers aren't to be trusted; intolerant of democratic leaders.

Inflexible, believing that there must be no deviation from the course they have set.

Impulsive, preferring action to thinking it over before acting.

Prejudiced against certain social groups, firms, religions, or nations.

—*Bits & Pieces*

LEARNING (Also see EDUCATION)

What we have to learn to do, we learn by doing.

—Aristotle

Learning is a treasure that accompanies its owner everywhere.

—Chinese proverb

Some students drink at the fountain of truth, but others gargle over it. And still others drown in it.

Michelangelo, at ninety, having lost his eyesight, ran his hands over statues in St. Peter's Cathedral and exclaimed, "I am still learning."

Personally I'm always ready to learn, although I do not always like to be taught.

—Winston Churchill

To look at is one thing;
  To see is another.
  To understand is a third.
  To learn from what you understand is still something else.
  But to act on what you learn is what really matters.

Instruction is given the wise by reason; ordinary minds, by experience; the stupid, by necessity; and brutes, by instinct.

—Cicero

LEFT-HANDEDNESS

The members of the Lefthanders International want its members to be accorded the same respect as righthanders and are urging a written "Bill of Lefts" to outline their "rights." They question—

Why do most country road signs read: "Keep Right?"

Why are most TV knobs on the right?

Why is the torch in Lady Liberty's right hand?

Why is a "lefthanded compliment" considered a subtle insult?

Despite society's seeming stereotype of the lefthanded, history has produced overachievers. Alexander the Great, Michelangelo, Queen Victoria, Thomas Edison, Picasso, Babe Ruth, including three recent U.S. presidents: George Bush, Ronald Reagan, and Gerald Ford.

In 1989, President Bush was awarded "Lefthander of the Year" by Lefthanders International. The organization hopes to prove that it is all right to be left and all wrong to be left out.

LIBERALITY

Many years ago two young men were working their way through Stanford University. At one point their money was almost gone, so they decided to engage the great pianist Paderewski for a concert and use the profits for board and tuition. Paderewski's manager asked for a guarantee of two thousand dollars. The students worked hard to promote the concert, but they came up four hundred dollars short. After the performance, they went to the musician, gave him all the money they had raised, and promised to pay the four hundred dollars as soon as they could. It appeared that their college days were over. "No, boys, that won't do," said the pianist. "Take out of this sixteen hundred dollars all your expenses, and keep for each of you 10 percent of all the balance for your work. Let me have the rest."

Years passed. Paderewski became premier of Poland following World War I. Thousands of his countrymen were starving. Only one man could help—the head of the U.S. Food and Relief Bureau. Paderewski's appeal to him brought thousands of tons of food. Later he met the American statesman to thank him. "That's all right," replied Herbert Hoover.

"Besides, you don't remember, but you helped me once when I was a student in college."

LIBERALS

Liberals are always for the inclusion of every possible point of view except those points of view that do not include every possible point of view.

—Stanley Hauerwas

LIFE (Also see PURPOSE IN LIFE)

Fear less, hope more; eat less, chew more; whine less, breathe more; talk less, say more; hate less, love more; and all good things are yours.

—Swedish proverb

Robert Fulghum, in his book *All I Really Need to Know I Learned in Kindergarten*, has written:

1. Share everything.
2. Play fair.
3. Don't hit people.
4. Put things back where you found them.
5. Clean up your own mess.
6. Don't take things that aren't yours.
7. Say you're sorry when you hurt somebody.
8. Wash your hands before you eat.
9. Flush.
10. Warm cookies and cold milk are good for you.
11. Live a balanced life—learn some and think some and draw and paint and sing and dance and play and work every day some.
12. Take a nap every afternoon.
13. When you go out into the world, watch out for traffic, hold hands, and stick together.
14. Be aware of wonder.

A town outside San Francisco has a population of five hundred, but it is surrounded by cemeteries with thousands of graves. At an entrance to the town is a sign, "It's great to be alive."

Life can't give me joy and peace;
    It's up to me to will it.

Life just gives me time and space;
It's up to me to fill it.

The great use of life is to spend it for something that will outlast it.
—William James

A ninety-three-year-old man finally conceded he couldn't live alone. After much thought, he decided he didn't want to live with his daughter. So he went to see a local nursing home.

After one look at a large room where older people sat silently staring into space, he quipped, "Well, one thing's for sure; if I come here, we are going to have to turn this *waiting* room into a *living* room!"

I think of life as a good book. The further you get into it, the more it begins to make sense.
—Harold S. Kusher

The Manchester, New Hampshire, *Union Leader* carried the following paragraph, which appeared first in the *Evangelist* Magazine: "The average man or woman in the United States who has reached seventy years of age has spent his time from birth to that date in this way:

3 years in education
8 years in amusement
6 years in eating
11 years in working
24 years in sleeping
5 $^1/_2$ in washing and dressing
6 years in walking
3 years in conversation
3 years in reading
6 months in church"

Anthony Campolo took a survey of ninety-five-year-olds. He asked them, "If you could live your life over, what would you do differently?" They said two things: "We would reflect more" and "We would do more things that would last beyond our lifetime."

Fear not that your life shall come to an end, but rather that it shall never have a beginning.
—John Henry Newman

Life is a battle (Marcus Aurelius); a hollow bubble (E. V. Cooke); an empty dream (Robert Browning); a walking shadow (Shakespeare); a long tragedy (Isaac Watts); a jest (John Gay); a document to be interpreted (Amiel); a cup of tea (J. M. Barrie); a dusty corridor, shut at both ends (Roy Campbell); a bumper filled by fate (Thomas Blacklock); a smoke that curls (W. E. Henley).

There was a very cautious man
Who never laughed or played.
He never risked, he never tried,
He never sang or prayed!
And when one day he passed away
His insurance was denied,
For since he never really lived,
They claimed he never died!

Twelve Things to Remember

1. The value of time.
2. The success of perseverance.
3. The pleasure of working.
4. The dignity of simplicity.
5. The worth of character.
6. The power of kindness.
7. The influence of example.
8. The obligation of duty.
9. The wisdom of economy.
10. The virtue of patience.
11. The improvement of talent.
12. The joy of originating.
—Marshall Field

A long life may not be good enough, but a good life is long enough.
—Benjamin Franklin

One morning a radio announcer was telling of a special offer for *Life* magazine. He closed by saying, "Enjoy *Life* at half price."

Many people are trying to enjoy life at half price! But it doesn't work.

After the ball hit him on the right temple, a man was taken to the hospital, where x-rays of his head showed nothing. No doubt that's why he failed to duck.

It is interesting to observe some of the estimates men of note have made of life.

Christopher Morley said, "There are ingredients in the good life: learning, earning, and yearning." John Christian said, "Life is the art of drawing without an eraser." Robert Frost said, "Life is tons of discipline." And back in 1958, the *New York Times* quoted Nikita Khrushchev as saying, "Life is short, live it up!"

I like living better and better the older I get. I wish it could go on forever.
—Howard Pyle

As Shakespeare's drama *Macbeth* draws near its close, the central figure is shown in his castle of Dunsinane, surrounded by a few of his officers and soldiers. Macbeth has run his bloodstained course to power, but his sins are catching up with him. He is besieged in his castle. Word is brought to him that Lady Macbeth, who nerved him to his crimes, is dead. Then Macbeth breaks forth into these words:
"Life's but a walking shadow; a poor player,
That struts and frets his hour upon the stage,
And then is heard no more; it is a tale
Told by an idiot, full of sound and fury,
Signifying nothing."

The Vanderbilt University student application form includes the question, "How do you view life: as a journey, a drama, a jungle?"

Not what we gain
But what we gave
Measures the worth
of the lives we live.

The average man lives but seventy-four years. That is approximately 888 months, 3,848 weeks, 27,010 days, 648,240 hours, 38,894,400 minutes and 2,022,508,800 heartbeats.
—Jon Johnston

James A. Knight, in his book *For the Love of Money,* says that, when he was visiting in Bergen, Norway, the guide told him of a family who lived on a small farm located on the top of a mountain outside of Bergen. The rough country and the height made it impossible to use horses, and a two-hour walk was required to reach the farm on top of the mountain from the point where the transportation stopped. But the family was independent. They made essentially everything they needed. The mother would sometimes knit as she climbed up and down the mountain.

An American, after he had seen how hard this life was for this family, asked the mother, "Does it pay to live here and put up with all of this?" She replied, without a moment's hesitation, "Life itself is pay enough."

There are three tenses to a person's life: What he is, what he has become, and what he is becoming.
—Aristotle

Lives of great men all remind us
We can make our lives sublime,
And departing leave behind us
Footprints on the sands of time.
—Longfellow, "Psalm of Life"

Life does not consist in what a person possesses, but in what possesses him.

Is life a living death or a dying life?
—Augustine

Life is definitely uncertain. For instance, Justinian died entering a painted room and Adrian was choked to death by a fly.

The psychologist William Moulton Marston asked three thousand persons, "What do you have to live for?"

He was shocked to find that 94 percent were simply enduring the present while they waited for the future; waited for "something" to happen; waited for children to grow up and leave home; waited for next year; waited for another time to take a long dreamed-about trip; waited for someone to die; waited for tomorrow without realizing that all anyone ever has is today because yesterday is gone and tomorrow never comes.
—Douglas Lurton

LIMITATIONS

As a ship captain was about to embark on a voyage he said, "Woe is me, I'm confined to the oceans of this world."

LISTENING

My wife said I never listen to what she says; at least I think that's what she said.

The most important thing in communication is to hear what isn't being said.
—Peter Drucker

Former Secretary of State Dean Rusk is quoted as having said, "One of the best ways to persuade others is with your ears— by listening to them."

When Lyndon B. Johnson was a senator from Texas, he displayed a sign on his office wall which read, "You ain't learnin' nothin' when you're talkin'."

An aspiring politician asked Oliver Wendell Holmes how to get elected to office. He replied, "To be able to listen to others in a sympathetic manner is, perhaps, the most effective mechanism in the world for getting along with people and tying up their friendship for good."

Good listeners are not only popular everywhere but after a while they know something.
—*Bits & Pieces*

A high school class in music appreciation was asked the difference between listening and hearing. At first there was no response. Finally a hand went up and a youngster offered this wise definition: "Listening is wanting to hear."
—*Bits & Pieces*

God gave us two ears but only one mouth. Some people say that's because He wanted us to spend twice as much time listening as talking. Others claim it's because He knew listening was twice as hard as talking.

I know you believe you understand what you think I said, but I am not sure you realize that what you heard is not what I meant.
—*Teleview*

Skillful listening is the best remedy for loneliness, loquaciousness, and laryngitis.
—William A. Ward

"Do you have trouble hearing?" asked the teacher of a youngster who sat dreamily at his desk. "No, ma'am," replied the boy. "I have trouble listening."

Listening, not imitation, is the sincerest form of flattery
—Joyce Brothers

It's easy to know all the answers if you don't bother to listen to the questions.

When in the company of sensible men, we ought to be doubly cautious of talking too much, lest we lose two good things—their good opinion and our own improvement; for what we have to say we know, but what they have to say we know not.
—Charles Caleb Colton

Paul Tournier, Swiss psychiatrist, was asked one time to share his secret for counseling. He replied, "I don't know how to help people. I simply listen and love and try to provide a safe place where people can come and report on their progress without any judgment."

LITTLE THINGS

For the want of a nail,
  a shoe was lost.
For the want of a shoe,
  the horse was lost.
For the want of a horse,
  a rider was lost.
For the want of a rider,
  a battle was lost.
For the want of a battle.
  a war was lost.
For the want of a war,
  the kingdom was lost.
—Benjamin Franklin

Little things are the hinges on which great results turn.

God is great in great things, but very great in little things.

—Henry Dyer

Our great matters are little to His power; our little matters are great to His love.

—D. L. Moody

LITERATURE

If religious books are not widely circulated in this country, I do not know what is to become of us as a nation. If truth be not diffused, error will be; if God and His Word are not known and received, the Devil and his works will gain the ascendancy; if the evangelical volume does not reach every hamlet, the pages of a corrupt and licentious literature will; if the power of the Gospel is not felt throughout the land, anarchy and misrule, degradation and misery, corruption and darkness, will reign without mitigation or end.

—Daniel Webster

LONELINESS

One of my friends can always tell when he has reached the crisis stage of being lonely—it's when he opens his junk mail and actually reads through it.

—Burton Hillis

Our language has wisely sensed the two sides of being alone. It has created the word "loneliness" to express the pain of being alone. And it has created the word "solitude" to express the glory of being alone.

—Paul Tillich

The great tragedy of life is not hunger or disease, but to feel unwanted.

—Mother Teresa

People are lonely because they build walls instead of bridges.

Loneliness is the first thing God's eye named not good.

—John Milton

Loneliness is a growing problem in our society. A study by the American Council of Life Insurance reported that the most lonely group in America are college students. That's surprising! Next on the list are divorced people, welfare recipients, single mothers, rural students, housewives, and the elderly. To point out how lonely people can be, Chuck Swindoll mentioned an ad in a Kansas newspaper. It read, "I will listen to you talk for 30 minutes without comment for $5.00." Swindoll said, "Sounds like a hoax, doesn't it? But the person was serious. Did anyone call? You bet. It wasn't long before this individual was receiving ten to twenty calls a day. The pain of loneliness was so sharp that some were willing to try anything for a half hour of companionship."

Isadora Duncan, the great ballet dancer who danced before the royalty of Europe and was considered one of the greatest ballet dancers of all time, said, "I have never been alone but that my heart did not ache, my eyes fill with tears, and my hands tremble for a peace and a joy that I never found." She went on to say that in the midst of millions of admirers, she was actually a very lonely woman.

I am sixty-five and I am lonely and have never found peace.

—H. G. Wells

After the death of her husband, Queen Victoria said, "There was no one left to call me Victoria." Even though she was a queen, she knew what it meant to be lonely.

A beautiful young Hollywood star with apparently everything a woman could want, ended her life. In the brief note she left was an incredibly simple explanation—she was unbearably lonely.

LONG-RANGE PLANNING

The undisciplined view is illustrated in a fable by the Russian poet Krylov about a pig who ate his fill of acorns under an oak tree and then started to root around the tree. A crow sitting in the oak tree remarked, "You should not do this. If you lay bare the roots, the tree will wither and die." "Let it die," replied the pig. "Who cares as long as there are acorns?"

LORD'S SUPPER

The Lord's Supper is a link between the Lord's first coming and His second coming.
—Frederic Godet

One day when the Duke of Wellington was at the communion table, an old and extremely poor man took his place beside him. An usher was about to ask him to leave, but the duke, sensing what was going on, grasped the elderly gentleman's hand and whispered, "Do not move, friend, we are all equal here."

LOST (Also see HOPELESSNESS)

One time when Clyde Cook, president of Biola College, La Mirada, California, was in Taipei, he asked a man, "What do you think of Jesus Christ?"

The man responded, "Who is he?"

"You mean you have never heard of Jesus Christ?"

"No."

Dr. Cook then led him to Christ. As the man shook Cook's hand, he said repeatedly in Chinese, "Shi-shi, Shi-shi. Thank you for leading me to Christ."

He was one of the two billion people who have never once heard the name of Christ.

On the side of a wholesale magazine truck was an advertisement of an article in a weekly magazine. The title of the article was "Joe Louis: A Sad Story." How true of many people who have gained wealth and fame—after all this, their life is actually a sad story.

Lady Huntington was trying to lead a man to Christ. To her urgent entreaties he answered, "Oh! It is of no use! I am lost, I am lost."

"Thank God for that!" she said.

"Why?" exclaimed the man in astonishment.

"Because," said Lady Huntington, "Christ came to save the lost. He is just the One who can save you."

To lose your wealth is much
To lose your health is more
To lose your soul is such a loss
As no man can restore.

When Mark Twain was in Berlin, he received an invitation asking him to call upon the Kaiser. "Why, Papa," exclaimed his little daughter, after contemplating the missive for a moment in speechless awe, "if it keeps on this way, there won't be anybody left for you to get acquainted with but God."

One of life's greatest tragedies is to be lost and not realize it. The next greatest is to be lost and know it, but not admit it or do anything about it.

No man ever got lost on a straight road.
—Abraham Lincoln

Life's greatest tragedy is to lose God and not to miss Him.
—F. W. Norwood

The body of a forty-year-old woman was found on the hot sands of the Mojave Desert, fifteen miles northwest of Twenty-Nine Palms, California. As a journalist, she had gone to the desert from Los Angeles seeking material for a feature story. Search for her began when the owner of a desert cabin found a note written by her that said, "I am exhausted and must have water. I do not believe I can last much longer." She had left three dollars to pay for a window she had broken to gain entrance into the cabin, but she found no water there. Apparently she collapsed en route back to her car, which was stuck in the sand two miles away. She died of thirst and exposure just two miles from Surprise Springs, where there was plenty of water.

One day David Garrick, a famous Shakespearean actor, was attracted to a gospel meeting. He was deeply moved to see tears freely coursing down the speaker's face. Suddenly an old woman raised a withered finger at the preacher and said, "Sir, I have heard you plead five times today on various streets of this city and five times I have seen your tears. Why do you weep?" He replied that he couldn't help but cry with concern over the fearful condition of the lost. The preacher was George Whitfield.

—Our Daily Bread

A writer polled several famous people asking them their selection for the saddest word in the English language. T. S. Eliot: "The saddest word in the English language is, of course, 'saddest.'" Oscar Hammerstein II: "but." John D. Pessor quoted Keats: "Forlorn! The very word is like a bell." Karl Menninger, the psychiatrist: "Unloved." Bernard M. Baruch: "Hopeless." Balanchine, the choreographer: "The saddest word in any language is 'vacuum.'" Truman quoted Whittier: "For all sad words of tongue or pen, the saddest are these: 'It might have been!'" Tolstoy: "The saddest word in all languages, which has brought the world to its present condition is 'atheism.'"

Combine all these and we have the picture of the soul out of Christ. He goes on his way to the vacuum of outer darkness, hopeless and forlorn, because having accepted the atheism which exalts himself to the place of God, he refuses to admit that he is loved by God, "but" goes to the saddest extremity of defiance against God.

A young man, twenty-two years of age, traveled to Chicago and registered at the Sherman Hotel. Taking a walk around the business district of the city, he became lost. He did not know the name, location, and appearance of the hotel so he was unable to find it again. So it was necessary to secure another room and he selected one in the Hotel Astor which was next door to the Sherman. Then, unwilling to acknowledge to the authorities that he was lost, for five days he tried to find the place where he had deposited his baggage. Unsuccessful in his attempts, he finally had to appeal to the police as his time was limited and his belongings valuable.

The police soon found his original registration and informed him that for five days he had been living right next door to the place where he had left his baggage. Although so near, he lost five days peace of mind, five days of time, and five days' use of his baggage, all because he would not tell an officer that he was lost.

Your best resolution must wholly be
   waived,
Your highest ambitions be crossed;
You never need think that you'll ever be
   saved,
Till first you have learned that you're lost.

LOVE

Girl: "Do you love me?"
Boy: "Yes, Dear."
Girl: "Would you die for me?"
Boy: "No . . . mine is an undying love."

In describing the first-century Christians to the Roman emperor Hadrian, Aristides said, "They love one another. They never fail to help widows; they save orphans from those who will hurt them. If they have something, they give freely to the man who has nothing; if they see a stranger, they take him home and are happy, as though he were a real brother. They don't consider themselves brothers and sisters in the usual sense, but brothers instead through the Spirit, in God."

It's not how much you do, but how much love you put into what you do that counts.
   —Mother Teresa

We are shaped and fashioned by what we love.
   —Johann von Goethe

Love cures people—both the ones who give it and the ones who receive it.
   —Karl Menninger

Peace is love resting.
Prayer is love keeping tryst.
Sympathy is love tenderly feeling.
Enthusiasm is love burning.
Hope is love expecting.
Patience is love waiting.
Faithfulness is love sticking fast.
Humility is love taking the true pledge.
Modesty is love keeping out of sight.

Soulwinning is love pleading.
Sanctification is love in action.

Love, it has been said, is a form of amnesia during which a woman forgets there are 1,222,978,173 other men in the world.

In vital areas, agreement; in doubtful areas, liberty; in all areas, love.

A Hindu manufacturer told Stanley Jones why he had come to one of his meetings. "Years ago when I was a boy we heckled a missionary preaching in the bazaar—threw tomatoes at him. He wiped off the tomato juice from his face and then after the meeting took us to the sweet shop and bought us sweets. I saw the love of Christ that day, and that's why I'm here."

A young man was condemned by a jury to die. He hated everyone, even his mother. His mother came before the judge and pleaded with him for her son. But the judge could do nothing. He said, "Why don't you let him alone? There's nothing you can do. He doesn't love you." "I know," said the mother, "but I love him."

At a men's retreat a truck driver told about the change Christ had made in his life, and I asked him to think of some specific way in which he was different.

After a pause, he said, "Well, when I find somebody tailgating my truck, I no longer drive on the shoulder of the road to kick up cinders on him." How simple but how profound is this understanding of what it means to love people in relevant and demonstrable ways.

—Bruce Larson

Love is an attitude—love is a prayer,
For a soul in sorrow, a heart in despair.
Love is good wishes for the gain of another,
Love suffers long with the fault of a brother.
Love gives water to a cup that's run dry,
Love reaches low, as it can reach high.
Seeks not her own at expense of another,
Love reaches God when it reaches our brother.

It is said of Abraham Lincoln that he never forgot a kindness, but that he had no room in his mind for the memory of a wrong. There is a morality of memory, and love keeps a list of its creditors but none of its debtors.

—W. Graham Scroggie

Love may not make the world go around, but it sure makes the trip worthwhile.

I not only want to be loved, I want to be *told* that I'm loved.

—George Elliot

Perfect love is . . .
   Slow to suspect—quick to trust
   Slow to condemn—quick to justify
   Slow to offend—quick to defend
   Slow to expose—quick to shield
   Slow to reprimand—quick to forbear
   Slow to demand—quick to give
   Slow to provoke—quick to conciliate
   Slow to hinder—quick to help
   Slow to resent—quick to forgive

You can give without loving, but you cannot love without giving.

Love is a feeling you feel when you have a feeling you've never felt before.

Joy is love's music.
Peace is love's agreement.
Longsuffering is love's endurance.
Kindness is love's service
Goodness is love's deportment.
Faithfulness is love's measure.

—John Haggai

The best gifts are always tied with heartstrings.

Love is like a smile—neither have any value unless given away.

Love cannot be wasted. It makes no difference where it is bestowed, it always brings in big returns.

Love doesn't really make the world go around. It just makes people dizzy so it looks like it.

LOVE

Love is giving all you can.

May I never, never outgrow my love for You.
    —Bernard of Clairvaux

My true love brought me flowers tonight,
And I'm all smiles and song,
I guess I'm doing something right—
Or he's done something wrong!
    —Maureen Cannon

Christian love is . . .
  Silence when your words would hurt,
  Patience when your neighbor's curt.
  Deafness when the scandal flows,
  Thoughtfulness for another's woes.
  Promptness when a stern duty calls,
  Courage when misfortune falls.

A noted doctor has listed several emotions that produce disease in human beings—fear, frustration, rage, resentment, hatred, envy, and jealousy. He says the only antidote that can save people from being destroyed by these powerful forces is love.

A man was complaining to a missionary about missions in Africa. "How can you go to Africa and preach to them about love when there is so much injustice in your own country?" he demanded.

The mission leader's answer was classic. "We don't go in and preach to them about love. We go in and love them."

A man who was a tyrant insisted that his wife arise early in the morning to prepare his breakfast. He was very demanding with regard to her care of the house, required a strict accounting of the money spent on groceries, clothes for the children, etc. Then he died. Later she married a man who was the opposite, loving, tender, considerate, unselfish. One day she was going through some of the effects of her first husband and found a list of all the things he had required her to do. Then to her amazement, she realized she was doing all those things for her present husband without being required to do them. She was doing them voluntarily because she loved him.

The work of the Menninger Clinic is organized around love. "From the top psychiatrist down to the electricians and caregivers, all contacts with patients must manifest love." And it was "love unlimited." The result was that hospitalization time was cut in half. There was a woman who for three years sat in her rocking chair and never said a word to anyone. The doctor called a nurse and said, "Mary, I'm giving you Mrs. Brown as your patient. All I'm asking you to do is to love her till she gets well." The nurse tried it. She got a rocking chair of the same kind as Mrs. Brown's, sat alongside her, and loved her morning, noon, and night. The third day the patient spoke and in a week she was out of her shell—and well.

A teenage girl, returning from an early date, found her mother still sitting up reading. "Mom," she said, sprawling in a chair, "how do you tell if you're really in love?"

Her mother smiled, walked over to the desk, pulled a weathered clipping out of the drawer, and handed it to her daughter. It read: "True love is like two deep rivers that meet and merge, intertwining completely into one, then flowing on together. The joys, happiness, and sorrows of each become the joys, happiness, and sorrows of the other. True love cannot be hurried, but once unselfishly rooted, it will grow forever."

It's wondrous what a hug can do.
  A hug can cheer you when you're blue.
A hug can say, "I love you so"
  Or "I hate to see you go."
A hug is "Welcome back again,"
  And "great to see you! Where've you been?"
A hug can soothe a small child's pain,
  And bring a rainbow after rain.
A hug, there's just no doubt about it—
  We scarcely could survive without it!
A hug delights and warms and charms,
  It must be why God gave us arms.
Hugs are great for fathers and mothers,
  Sweet for sisters, swell for brothers.
And chances are your favorite aunts
  Love them more than potted plants.

Kittens crave them, puppies love them,
  Heads of states are not above them.
A hug can break the language barrier,
  And make travel so much merrier.
No need to fret about your store of 'em,
  The more you give, the more there's
    more of 'em.
So stretch those arms without delay
  And give someone a hug today!

In Dostoyevsky's *Crime and Punishment,* the central character, Raskolnikov, finally confessed his crime and was sent to Siberia. Sonya, the girl who loved him, followed voluntarily and found a job in a town nearest his work camp. At first, Raskolnikov was bitter about his exile and contemptuous of everyone, including Sonya. But the day came when her unflagging love and humble service melted his heart, and he loved her in return. Dostoyevsky writes, "They were renewed by love; the heart of each held infinite resources of life for the heart of the other. They had another seven years to wait, and what terrible suffering and infinite happiness before them! But he had risen again, and he knew it and felt it in his being, while she—she lived only in his life. Seven years, *only* seven years!"

One day a young man left home and denounced his father and mother. He wanted nothing to do with them. But years later he felt led to return home, so he wrote a letter to his mother asking forgiveness. "Mom, if you will let me come home, then hang a white handkerchief on the clothesline in the backyard." The train passes near the rear of their house, and he said that, as he passed by, if the handkerchief were there, he would know she would let him come home.

But to his amazement, as he passed by in the train, there was not a white handkerchief on the line, but a number of white sheets hung out. How great was the love of that mother for her son. And how great is God's love for the lost sinner.

In January 1981, Colombian rebels kidnapped Chet Bitterman, shot him, and left his body in a hijacked bus.

But in April 1982, as a demonstration of international good will, the churches and civic groups of Bitterman's native area, Lancaster County, Pennsylvania, gave an ambulance to the State of Meta in Colombia, where the young linguist was killed.

Bitterman's parents traveled to Colombia for the presentation of the ambulance. At the ceremony his mother explained, "We are able to do this because God has taken the hatred from our hearts."

When Alexander the Great became a world conqueror, he decided to have his portrait painted in oils. The finest artist in the realm was called to produce a masterpiece. When he arrived at Alexander's court, the renowned general requested that the portrait be a full-face pose instead of a profile. This filled the artist with great distress, for one side of Alexander's face was hideously disfigured by a long scar—the result of a battle wound. After studying his subject for some time, the painter came up with a happy solution. First he seated Alexander at a table; then, placing the General's elbow on it, he asked him to cup his chin in his hand. As a final thoughtful gesture, the artist adjusted Alexander's fingers so that they covered his unsightly scar. Then he went to work with paint and brushes and produced a flattering likeness of the General.

In much the same way, Christian love will overlook or seek to minimize the faults and shortcomings of others.

LOVING-KINDNESS

"Johnnie, what do you think loving-kindness means?" asked a Christian mother.

After thinking a few moments, scratching his head, the boy replied, "Well, when I ask for a piece of bread and butter and you give it to me, that's kindness. But you know Mom, when you put jam on it, that's loving-kindness."

LOYALTY

A wounded soldier of Napoleon was given no anesthetic and when those operating on him were probing for the bullet, he remarked, "Be careful, because a little deeper and you will strike my heart, and the emperor is there."

LUCK

If we could cross poison ivy with four-leaf clovers, we'd all have a rash of good luck.

Someone asked the French writer Jean Corteau if he believed in luck. "Certainly," he said, "how else do you explain the success of those you don't like?"

LUTHERANS

Three Lutheran pastors were invited by a Catholic priest to attend mass one Sunday at his church. They arrived a bit late. All the pews were filled and they had to stand in the back of the church.

The priest noticed them as he began the mass and he whispered to one of the altar boys, "Get three chairs for our Lutheran friends."

The altar boy didn't hear, so the priest spoke a bit louder, motioning to the rear of the congregation, "Three chairs for the Lutherans."

Dutifully, the boy arose, stepped to the altar rail and loudly proclaimed to the congregation, "Three cheers for the Lutherans!"

—*Bits & Pieces*

LYING

A man was being baptized in a remote village, high in the mountains. Before his conversion, he had been an outrageous liar, and the villagers were skeptical of this sudden change of heart. The missionary doused him in the freezing waters of a mountain river and the man emerged shivering.

"Is it cold?" the missionary asked anxiously.

"No, it's fine," said the man.

"Dunk him again, Pastor," shouted a villager, "he's still a liar!"

—Murray Watts

A preacher was weaving in and out of traffic, as if he were drunk. A policeman stopped him and said, "Preacher, you are weaving as if you are drunk." The preacher responded, "Oh, I wouldn't do that." Then the policeman asked, "What is that bottle in the brown bag?" He reached in and grabbed the bottle and smelled it. He said, "Preacher, that is wine." The preacher then said, "It is? How wonderful! The Lord has done it again."

A good liar needs a good memory.

—Arabic proverb

According to an ancient Chinese story, a young boy and his mother lived alone on a meager income. One day the child found a purse at the market. He hurried home to show his mother what he had found.

When they emptied the purse, fifteen coins fell out. His mother insisted that he go back to the market, find the owner, and return the purse. However, the owner, seeing an opportunity to make a profit off the young boy, claimed there had been thirty coins in the purse.

A judge listened to the dispute and ruled that since the purse the man had lost contained thirty coins, and this one had only fifteen, it couldn't possibly be his. Further, he explained, since no one had reported a lost purse with fifteen coins in it, he gave the purse and its contents to the finder.

Mary Jones hurriedly parked her car, climbed out, and raced into the butcher shop. She arrived at the door just as the owner was locking up. "I need a roasting chicken," she said. The butcher quickly put his last chicken on the scale and said, "It's two pounds and four ounces." "Do you have a larger one?" she asked. The butcher went to the cooler and returned with the same chicken. He placed it on the scale and said, "This one weighs three pounds." After pausing a moment, Mary said, "I think I'll take them both."

He has three hats: one to wear on his head; one that he tosses in the ring; and the one he talks through.

—Hal Roach

"A lie is an abomination unto the Lord and an ever present help in time of trouble," said a little girl in Sunday school.

A lie is a coward's way of trying to get out of trouble.

A boy explained what an alibi was in this way: "An alibi is when you prove you were at a prayer meeting when you weren't to show you weren't in somebody's cash register when you were."

A lie that is all of a lie can be met with and fought outright. But a lie that is partly the truth is a harder matter to fight.

—Tennpon

Those who are given to white lies soon become color blind.

A twelve-year-old boy was a key witness in a crucial lawsuit. One of the lawyers had put him through a rigorous cross-examination and had been unable to shake his clear, damaging testimony. In a stern voice, the lawyer said, "Your father has been telling you how to testify, hasn't he?" "Yes," said the boy. "Now," said the lawyer, with smug satisfaction, "just tell us what your father told you to say." "Well," replied the boy, "Father told me that the lawyers may try to tangle me, but if I would just be careful and tell the truth, I could say the same thing every time."

"Catchin' any?" the bystander asked the fisherman.

"Caught forty bass out here yesterday."

"Say, do you know who I am?"

"No," said the fisherman, "can't say as I do."

"Well I'm the county fish and game warden."

The fisherman thought for a moment, then said, "Say, do you know who I am?"

"No," said the officer.

"Well, I'm the biggest liar in eastern Indiana."

Famous American Fibs

The check is in the mail.

I'll start my diet tomorrow.

We service what we sell.

Give me your number and the doctor will call you right back.

Money cheerfully refunded.

One size fits all.

This offer limited to the first one hundred people who call in.

Your luggage isn't lost, it's only misplaced.

Leave your résumé and we'll keep it on file.

This hurts me more than it hurts you.

I just need five minutes of your time.

Your table will be ready in a few minutes.

Open wide, it won't hurt a bit.

Let's have lunch sometime.

It's not the money, it's the principle.

—*Bits & Pieces*

According to a UPI news item, the Metropolitan Insurance Company received some unusual explanations for accidents from its automobile policyholders. The following are just a few: "An invisible car came out of nowhere, struck my car, and vanished." "The other car collided with mine without warning of its intention." "I had been driving my car for forty years when I fell asleep at the wheel and had an accident." "As I reached an intersection, a hedge sprang up, obscuring my vision." "I pulled away from the side of the road, glanced at my mother-in-law, and headed over an embankment." "The pedestrian had no idea which way to go, so I ran over him." "The telephone pole was approaching fast. I attempted to swerve out of its path when it struck my front end." "The guy was all over the road. I had to swerve a number of times before I hit him." "The indirect cause of this accident was a little guy in a small car with a big mouth."

M

MAN—FINITENESS OF

MacNeile Dixon, in his *Gifford Lectures*, depicts a fly crawling across Raphael's masterpiece in the Vatican. How much can it know about the picture? It knows something, of course. It knows there are smooth places and rough; that some pigments are brighter than others. But it has no overall view of the painting or the goal of the painter, not because there is something wrong with the mural, but because of the fly's limited vision.

MARRIAGE

A girl said to a boy, "The man I marry must be brave as a lion, but not forward; handsome as Apollo, but not conceited; wise as Solomon, but meek as a lamb; a man who is kind to every woman, but loves only me."

The boy said, "How lucky we met!"

Eve was so jealous of Adam that when he came home each night she used to count his ribs.

—*Rolling in the Aisles*

First man: "I proposed to a girl and would have married her if it hadn't been for something she said."

Second man: "What was that?"

First man: "No."

—Murray Watts

Marriage is like a castle under siege; those within want to get out, those outside want to get in.

—Arabic proverb

First year of marriage: "Sugar dumpling, I'm really worried about my baby girl. You've got a bad sniffle and there's no telling about these things with all the strep going around. I'm putting you in the hospital this afternoon for a general checkup and a good rest. I know the food's lousy but I'll be bringing your meal in from Rozzini's. I already have it all arranged with the floor superintendent."

Second year: "Listen darling, I don't like the sound of that cough. I've called Doc Miller to rush over here. Now you go to bed like a good girl, just for Poppa."

Third year: "Maybe you had better lie down, honey. Nothing like a little rest when you feel lousy. I'll bring you some soup."

Fourth year: "Now look, dear, be sensible. After you've fed the kids and got the dishes done and the floor finished, you better lie down."

Fifth year: "Why don't you take a couple of aspirin?"

Sixth year: "I wish you'd just gargle or something instead of sitting around barking like a seal all evening."

Seventh year: "For Pete's sake, stop sneezing! Are you trying to give me pneumonia?"

A bridegroom of forty was chided because he had married a woman of twenty. He answered, "It's not as bad as it seems. When she looks at me she feels ten years older, and when I look at her I feel ten years younger. So really, we're both thirty."

It takes two to make a marriage a success and only one a failure.

—Viscount Samuel Herbert

Ten Keys to a Successful Marriage

Talk with each other.

Tell each other "I love you."

Touch each other.

Tantalize each other.

Tolerate each other.

Trust each other.

Treat each other.

Treasure each other.

Thank each other.

Track with each other.

—Kenneth Kilinski

A woman said to a marriage counselor, "I married looking for an ideal. But I got an ordeal and now I want a new deal."

In the words of a philosopher, "Marriage is a high sea for which no compass has yet been invented." He's wrong.

A judge in a divorce case asked the husband, "Will you tell the court what passed between you and your wife during your big argument that caused you to seek this separation?"

"I will," said the husband. "It was a rolling pin, six plates, and a frying pan!"

Love is blind—marriage is the eye-opener.

The most disillusioned women are those who married because they were tired of working.

A man who gives in when he is wrong is wise. A man who gives in when he is right is married.

Love is blind and marriage is an institution. Therefore, marriage is an institution for the blind.

Let the wife make the husband glad to come home, and let him make her sorry to see him leave.

—Martin Luther

Sign on a cash register operated by a cashier in a supermarket: "Just married: Count your change twice."

—Bits & Pieces

If a man has enough horse sense to treat his wife like a thoroughbred, she will never turn into an old nag.

A woman who had been married seventy years filed for divorce. The judge asked, "Why?" She said, "Enough is enough."

A woman went up to a man and said, "You look like my fourth husband!" He asked, "How many husbands have you had?" She answered, "Three."

Arnold Olson, in a lecture before a conference in Jerusalem, told of a time when he returned from his first trip to the Orient. His wife came to the Minneapolis airport to meet him. When she got there, she was surprised to find their pastor and some other elders from the congregation in front of the flight information board. The pastor offered an explanation, "We've come to see how you two greet one another when your husband returns from his journey."

When Winston Churchill was prime minister of Great Britain, his marriage was considered one of the best examples in England of true loyalty and love. Often, when he gave a speech in the House of Commons, he would not begin until he had received a sign from her.

Later in his life, someone interviewed Mr. Churchill and asked, "If you could live again, what would you want to be?"

With a twinkle in his eye, Churchill replied, "Mrs. Churchill's next husband."

What a benediction on a marriage! And what a monumental compliment for one's wife.

—Mark Littleton

In Burlington, Vermont, a tombstone has the epitaph indicating that beneath it lies the remains of a woman who was married to her husband for fifty years and hoped for a better life.

My young daughters had returned from a marriage ceremony and were playing "wedding." When the oldest, who was the minister, said, "Do you take this man for richer or poorer?" the bride replied firmly, "For richer."

—Reader's Digest

She didn't want to marry him for his money, but it was the only way she could get it.

The Earl of Shaftesbury once said, "If the pope had been married, he would soon discover that he was not infallible."

After due deliberation,
And much consideration,
I have had an inclination,
To make you my relation.
So if you'll meet me at the station,
With the preacher's cooperation,
We will form a combination,
That will increase the population.
Yours, in desperation,
Temptation.

One day a brother and sister were fussing and eventually it began to emerge into a fight. Just then the mother came in and demanded that they stop.

The girl then explained, "Oh Mama, we're not fighting. We're just pretending we are married."

When William Jennings Bryan went to call on the father of his prospective wife to seek the hand of his daughter in marriage, knowing the strong religious feeling of the father, he thought to strengthen his case by quoting the proverb of Solomon: "Whoso findeth a wife findeth a good thing" (Prov. 18:22).

To his surprise the father replied with a citation from the apostle Paul to the effect that he that marrieth doeth well, but that he that marrieth not doeth better. The young suitor was for a moment confused. Then with a happy inspiration he replied that Paul had no wife and Solomon had seven hundred, and Solomon, therefore, ought to be the better judge as to marriage.
—C. Reuben Anderson

Matrimony is the only state that allows a woman to work eighteen hours a day.

Some men marry poor women to settle down, and others marry rich ones to settle up.

Marriage is like a violin. After the beautiful music is over, the strings are still attached.

Don't ever question your wife's judgment. After all, she married you.

If you do housework at two hundred dollars a week, that's domestic service. If you do it for nothing, that's matrimony.

Courtship makes a man spoon, but it's matrimony which makes him fork over.

Socrates once advised a young man, "By all means get married. If you get a good wife you will be happy. If you get a bad one, you'll become a philosopher!"

The young couple sat in the romantic moonlight, hands clasped, and looked into each other's eyes. He asked cautiously, "If I proposed, would you say yes to me?"

She was even more cautious. "If you knew I'd say yes, would you propose?"

Two teenagers were talking. Doris inquired, "When is your sister thinking of getting married?" Frank exclaimed, "Constantly!"

The wife who gives back to her husband the woman he married stands a more than even chance of getting back the man she married.
—John D. Jess

Whenever a man opens a car door for his wife, you know either the car is new or the wife is new.

When Mr. and Mrs. Henry Ford celebrated their golden wedding anniversary, a reporter asked them, "To what do you attribute your fifty years of successful married life?" "The formula is the same one I've used in making cars," said Ford. "Just stick to one model!"

A successful marriage required falling in love many times, always with the same person.
—Mignon McLaughlin

Keep your eyes wide open before marriage, half shut afterward.
—Benjamin Franklin

A city mayor and his wife met a man whom she used to date. The man was a construction engineer. The mayor said, "Just think. If you'd married him, you'd be the wife of a construction engineer."

She replied, "No. You got it wrong. If I had married him, *he* would be the mayor."

When you marry him, love him.
After you marry him, study him.
When he is sad, cheer him.
When he is noble, praise him.
If he is jealous, cure him.
If he is honest, honor him.
When he is angry, ignore him.
If he is secretive, trust him.
When he deserves it, kiss him.
If he is generous, appreciate him.
When he is talkative, listen to him.
Let him think how well you understand him
But never let him know you manage him!

When Albert Einstein and his wife were being interviewed on the occasion of their golden anniversary, they were asked the routine question, "To what do you attribute the success of your marriage?"

Einstein replied, "When we first got married, we made a pact. It was this. That in our life together I would make all the big decisions and she would make all the little decisions. And we have kept to it for fifty years. That, I think, is the reason for the success of our marriage." Then he looked up and added, "The strange thing is that in fifty years there hasn't yet been one big decision."

My two neighbors were having coffee. "You know," said one, "I was telling my husband that even after twenty years of marriage your husband is still a gentleman. I always see him get out of the car, walk around to your side and open the door for you."

"Well," said her friend, "what you don't know is that every time he does it, he says he is going to have that blasted door handle fixed tomorrow if it's the last thing he does."

—Reader's Digest

A young man was in love with two women and could not decide which of them to marry. Finally, he went to a marriage counselor. When asked to describe his two loves, he noted that one was a great poet and the other made great pancakes. "Oh," said the counselor, "I see what the problem is. You can't decide whether to marry for batter or verse."

—Karan F. Minick

MARTYRDOM

One of the old martyrs said to his persecutors as they were leading him to his death, "You take a life from me that I cannot keep, and bestow a life upon me that I cannot lose."

—D. L. Moody

Bishop Hugh Latimer was martyred in 1555. After being sentenced to death for his convictions, he wrote an open letter in which he declared, "Let us consider all the dear friends of God, how they have gone after the example of our Savior, Jesus Christ; whose footsteps let us also follow, even to the gallows if God's will be so." A short time later he and his friend Nicholas Ridley were tied to a stake. As the leaping flames began to touch their bodies, Latimer called out, "Be of good cheer, Brother Ridley, and play the man; we shall this day light such a candle by God's grace in England as I trust shall never be put out!"

The cruel Roman emperor Diocletian was bitterly persecuting the church. Actors on the stage often included in their routine a parody on baptism, the Lord's Supper, and other items of the Christian faith. An entertainer named Genesius, who had been reared in a Christian home, was doing a pantomime on baptism one day when suddenly the arrow of conviction pierced his heart. To the amazement of the crowd and the consternation of the emperor who was seated in a box near the stage, Genesius cried out, "I want to receive the grace of Christ that I may be born again and be set free from the sins which have been my ruin!" Turning fearlessly toward Diocletian, he said, "Illustrious Emperor, and all of you who have laughed loudly at this parody, believe me, Christ is the true King!" The enraged emperor demanded a slow and tortuous death for the actor, and Genesius died a noble witness for Christ.

Polycarp, a disciple of the apostle John, was burned at the stake in Smyrna in A.D. 155. He had been a Christian for eighty-six years. When the proconsul told him to deny his faith, Polycarp answered, "Eighty-six years I have served Him, and He has done me no harm. Why should I forsake Him now?"

The proconsul then threatened to cast him in with the wild beasts, but Polycarp answered, "Call them!" He was then warned that he might be burned at the stake. Even that failed to move him. He responded, "You threaten me with fire which burns only for a moment, but you are ignorant of the fire of eternal punishment, reserved for the ungodly."

These are Polycarp's final words: "O Father of Thy beloved and blessed Son, Jesus Christ! I bless Thee that Thou hast counted me worthy of this day, and of this hour, to receive my portion in the number of the martyrs, in the cup of Christ."

When the cruel Bonner told John Ardly of the pain connected with burning at the stake, the condemned Christian replied, "If I had as many lives as I have hairs on my head, I would lose them all in the fire, before I would lose Christ!"

According to David Barrett, 41 million Christians have been martyred, with 26 million Christians martyred after 1900.

A workman tells of a young officer attached to the court of Galerius. He was deeply impressed by the courage of the martyrs at Nicomedeia. He went to the Christians and asked them the secret of their courage. He was instructed in the Christian faith. On the next occasion when Christians were examined, he stepped forward and asked Galerius to add his name to theirs. "Are you mad?" demanded Galerius. "Do you wish to throw away your life?" "I am not mad," was the answer. "I was mad once but am now in my right mind." And so he died.

—William Barclay

John Huss, the Bohemian reformer, was burned at the stake in 1415. Before his accusers lit the fire, they placed on his head a crown of paper with painted devils on it. He answered this mockery by saying, "My Lord, Jesus Christ, for my sake, wore a crown of thorns; why should I not then, for His sake, wear this light crown, be it ever so ignominious? Truly I will do it willingly." After the wood was stacked up to Huss's neck, the Duke of Bavaria asked him to renounce his preaching. Trusting completely in God's Word, Huss replied, "In the truth of the Gospel which I preached, I die willingly and joyfully today." Huss died while singing, "Jesus Christ, the Son of the living God, have mercy on me."

When Chrysosyom was brought before the Roman emperor, the emperor threatened him with banishment if he remained a Christian. Chrysostom replied, "Thou canst not banish me for this world is my Father's house." "But I will slay thee," said the emperor. "Nay, thou canst not," said the noble champion of the faith, "for my life is hid with Christ in God." "I will take away thy treasures." "Nay, but thou canst not for my treasure is in heaven and my heart is there." "But I will drive thee away from man and thou shalt have no friend left." "Nay, thou canst not for I have a friend in heaven from whom thou canst not separate me. I defy thee; for there is nothing that thou canst do to hurt me."

Arthur Tylee, who was murdered by the Indians of Brazil, on his return to the field for the last time was warned by a cousin, "These Indians may kill you."

He replied, "Suppose they do?"

"But, " she said, "you are going to give up your life?"

He replied, "I have nothing to do with how long I shall live. I am in the will of God. If He sees fit to let me live to complete the language and to present the Lord Jesus and His power to save, I shall be happy. If not, His will be done. A grace often speaks louder than a life."

MATERIALISM (Also see POSSESSIONS and WEALTH)

If you don't get everything you want, think of all the things you don't get that you don't want.

The best things in life aren't things.

—Art Buchwald

We have been so anxious to give our children what we didn't have that we have neglected to give them what we did have.

Theirs is an endless road, a hopeless maze, who seek goods before they seek God.

—Bernard of Clairvaux

Materialism may be called "affluenza."

—Mrs. Ray Stedman

Many people are buying things they don't need with money they don't have to impress people they don't like.

When Alexander the Great conquered a city, all the loot was in the valley before him. A soldier said to him, "Sir, what more can you ask for?" Alexander said, "But it doesn't last."

A king said to his sage, "How can I be happy?" The sage said, "Find the happiest person in your kingdom and wear his shirt." So the king sent his courier throughout the kingdom and he found the happiest man. The courier told the king, "I've found the happiest man, but he didn't even own a shirt."

Don't try to have it all. Where would you put it?

There are three classes of people: the Haves, the Have-Nots, and the Have-Not-Paid-For-What-They-Haves.
—Earl Wilson

Yussiff, the Terrible Turk, was a 350-pound wrestler who two generations ago won the European wrestling championship and then came to this country seeking other continents to conquer. Here he found a wrestler named Strangler Lewis, who was the American champ. Yussiff promptly challenged him to a contest for the world championship.

When the two wrestlers met, the Strangler found his great potent weapon—that of winding his mighty arm around his opponent's neck and pressing his bulging biceps on his Adam's apple until he collapsed from lack of oxygen—useless. The Turk's neck was so huge he could not get his arm around it. Lewis tried hard to strangle Yussiff but he simply would not cooperate. Lewis weighed only 200 pounds and with his one weapon gone he was helpless. The Turk tossed the American champ around like a volleyball and won the bout.

Yussiff won not only the crown, but along with that he received something of more practical value and much more to his liking—a purse of five thousand dollars, his share of the gate receipts. Yussiff loved money and he loved to possess it in its most tangible form, so he demanded his pay in U.S. gold, which he crammed into a money belt and strapped around his huge equator. Thus attired in glory and gold he sailed on the *S.S. Burgoyne.*

Part way across the Atlantic, the Burgoyne sank. Yussiff went over the side with his gold still clasped around his body. The added weight was too much for even the Terrible Turk to keep afloat and before the sailors in the lifeboats could reach him, he plunged to the bottom like an anvil and was never seen again.

Years ago, when W. E. Sangster visited the United States, someone asked him what impressed him most about our country. He said, "You seem to have more of everything than anyone else. You have more cars, more televisions, more refrigerators, more of everything. In fact, I've noticed that you also have more books on how to be happy than anybody else."

If a nation values anything more than freedom, it will lose its freedom; and the irony of it is that if it is the comfort of money that it values more, it will lose that too.
—Somerset Vaughn

If you have something you can't do without, you don't own it; it owns you.
—Albert Schweitzer

In capitalism, man exploits man. In communism, it's the exact opposite.
—John Galbraith

In this world there are only two tragedies. One is not getting what we want, and the other is getting it.
—Oscar Wilde

We rich men covet our happiness to lie in the little superfluities, not in necessities.
—Plutarch

The more of heaven there is in our lives, the less of earth we shall covet.

There is no doubt you can't take it with you. You can't even keep it while you're here.

In a Soviet prison camp, Solzhenitsyn discovered that "the meaning of earthly existence lies not, as we have grown used to thinking, in prospering, but . . . in the development of the soul." Perhaps this is why he spends much of his time writing in a small cabin furnished only with the barest necessities.

—*Our Daily Bread*

Bumper sticker: He who dies with the most toys wins.

Just because people are better off doesn't mean they are better. A Christian in a Cadillac is no more precious in the sight of God than a believer on a bicycle.

—Michael Guido

E. Stanley Jones, in his book *Growing Spiritually,* talks about a fictional person who lived out a fantasy life. All he had to do was think of it and (poof!) it happened. So this man, in a moment of time, sticks his hands in his pockets and leans back and imagines a mansion and (poof!) he has a fifteen bedroom mansion, three stories with servants instantly available to wait upon his every need.

Why, a place like that needs several fine cars. So he again closes his eyes and imagines the driveway full of the finest wheels money can buy. And (poof!) there are several of the best vehicles instantly brought before his mind's eye. He is free to drive them himself or sit way back in the limousine with that mafia glass wrapped around the rear, and have the chauffeur drive him wherever he wishes.

There's no other place to travel so he comes back home and wishes for a sumptuous meal and (poof!) there's a meal in front of him with all of its mouth-watering aromas and beauty—which he eats alone. And yet . . . there was something more he needed to find happiness.

Finally, he grows so terribly bored and unchallenged that he whispers to one of the attendants, "I want to get out of this. I want to create some things again. I'd rather be in hell that be here." To which one of the servants replies quietly, "Where do you think you are?"

I recently heard of a young woman who said to a real estate agent, "Why do I need a home? I was born in a hospital, educated in a college, engaged in a car, married in a hotel. I live out of a delicatessen and paper bags. I spend my mornings on the golf course, my afternoons at the bridge table, and my evenings at the movies. When I die, I'm going to be buried at the undertaker's. All I need is a garage."

—Jack D. Spiro

On the Shetland Islands off the northern coast of Scotland, a man spent five years constructing a sixty-two-foot yacht that weighed 126 tons. On the day of its launching, he invited a local band to play, and most of the townspeople came out to help him celebrate his achievement. He planned to start a voyage around the world as soon as the boat was launched. As the band played and the customary bottle was smashed across the bow, the ship was lowered into the water. But it didn't float! It immediately sank to the bottom of the harbor. And with it went a lifetime of savings and five years of hard work.

A newspaper carried this article: I read, "A young man once found a five-dollar bill in the street. From that time on, he never lifted his eyes when walking. In the course of years, he accumulated 29,516 buttons, 54,172 pins, 12 cents, a bent back, and a miserly disposition. He lost the glory of the sunlight, the sheen of the stars, the smiles of friends, tree blossoms in the spring, the blue skies, and the entire joy of living."

Many people today look to this earth for satisfaction, pleasure, wealth, and happiness, and have never looked to Jesus Christ for eternal life.

A man walked down a street in Atlanta and came to a furrier shop. He stopped to look at a leopard skin that had been made into a coat. He gazed at the fur and thought about the price. "O cat," he said, "you were better off before you were worth so much."

An old rabbinic tale records the concern of a man of God for a young friend who was becoming worldly and materialistic. The rabbi invited him into his study and led him to the window.

"What do you see?" he asked. There was a playground next door.

"I see children playing."

Then the rabbi took a little hand mirror out of his pocket and held it before the visitor's face. "Tell me what you see now?"

"I see myself," he said, wondering what was going on.

"Isn't it strange," the rabbi asked, "that when a little silver gets between yourself and others, you see only yourself?"

MATHEMATICS

Three Indian squaws were going to have babies. One was going to have hers born on a buffalo skin, another on a cow hide, and the third on a hippopotamus hide. When the children were born, it was discovered that the squaw with the hippopotamus hide had twins while the other had only one son each.

Moral: The squaw of the hippopotamus is equal to the sons of the squaw of the other two hides.

MATURITY

Maturity is the ability to control anger and settle differences without violence or destruction.

Maturity is patience. It is the willingness to pass up immediate pleasure in favor of the long-term gain.

Maturity is perseverance, the ability to sweat out a project or a situation in spite of heavy opposition and discouraging setbacks.

Maturity is the capacity to face unpleasantness and frustration, discomfort and defeat, without complaint or collapse.

Maturity is humility. It is being big enough to say "I was wrong." And, when right, the mature person need not experience the satisfaction of saying, "I told you so."

Maturity is the ability to make a decision and stand by it. The immature spend their lives exploring endless possibilities; then they do nothing.

Maturity means dependability, keeping one's word, coming through in a crisis. The immature are masters of alibi. They are disorganized. Their lives are a maze of broken promises, former friends, unfinished business, and good intentions that somehow never materialize.

Maturity is the art of living in peace with that which we cannot change, the courage to change that which should be changed, and the wisdom to know the difference.

—Ann Landers

Maturity is:
- the ability to stick with a job until it is finished.
- the ability to do a job without being supervised.
- the ability to carry money without spending it.
- the ability to bear an injustice without wanting to get even.

—Abigail Van Buren

A sign of maturity is when you go from a thick skin and a hard heart to a tough skin and a soft heart.

—Chuck Swindoll

MEALS

Football player's wife: "I hate it when my husband calls leftovers 'replays.'"

TV executive's wife: "My husband calls them 'reruns.'"

Mortician's wife: "Be grateful. My husband refers to them as 'remains.'"

MEASUREMENTS

Foot: the length of Charlemagne's foot, modified in 1305 to be thirty-six barleycorns laid end to end.

Inch: the width across the knuckle on King Edgar's thumb, or, obviously, three barleycorns.

Yard: the reach from King Henry I's nose to his royal fingertips, a distance also twice as long as a cubit.

MEASUREMENTS

Cubit: the length of the arm from elbow to fingertip.

Mile: one thousand double steps of a Roman legionary. Later, Queen Bess added more feet so the mile would equal eight furlongs.

Furlong: the length of a furrow a team of oxen could plow before resting.

Acre: the amount of land a yoke of oxen could plow in one day.

Fathom: the span of a seaman's outstretched arms; 880 fathoms make a mile.

The metric system, on the other hand, uses the meter, defined precisely as 1,650,763.73 wavelengths of orange-red light emitted by the krypton-86 atom, or originally one-ten-millionth the length of the longitude from the North Pole to the equator. The meter is exactly 39.37 inches—or, that is, some 118 barleycorns.

—*National Geographic* News Service

MEDICINE

In 1980 the World Health Organization announced that vaccinations had finally wiped out the dreaded disease smallpox from the face of the earth. It had been almost three hundred years since a little-known slave in Boston, Massachusetts, told a Puritan minister how Africans would take a drop of liquid from a smallpox sore and put it into a cut on a healthy person's arm. The person sometimes got slightly ill but seldom got smallpox. Modern inoculation was born.

MEDIOCRITY

Only the mediocre are always at their best.
—Jean Girandoux

Mediocrity is climbing molehills without sweating.
—Icelandic proverb

A small motel in Clarendon, a small west Texas town, is named "It'll Do Motel."

The greatest heresy is mild religion.
—Elton Trueblood

MEEKNESS

A boy was once asked, "Who are the meek?" He thought for a moment and then answered, "They are the people who give soft answers to hard questions."

In Greek antiquities is the story of a young soldier who wrote to his sweetheart concerning a gift he longed to present to her: a silver stallion. "He is the most magnificent animal I have ever seen," related the soldier, "but he responds obediently to the slightest command. . . . He allows his master to direct him to his full potential. He is truly a meek horse."
—Gerald Mann

MEMORIES

Memories are a gift of God so we can enjoy the roses in December.

Things aren't what they used to be and probably never were.

MEMORY

A rookie salesman said to a top salesman, "How can you remember names so well?"

He answered, "I took the Dick Carnegie course."

The faintest ink is more lasting than the strongest memory.
—Chinese proverb

Scientists tell us that the human mind can store as many as six hundred memories a second in a lifetime of seventy-five years with the slightest strain. That works out to 1,419,120,000,000 memories! When memory becomes flabby, lack of mental exercise (more than advancing years) is usually the reason.

To live in the hearts of those we leave behind us is not to die.
—Thomas Campbell

Lincoln attributed his excellent memory to a lifelong habit of reading outloud. "When I read aloud, two senses catch the idea: first I see what I read; second I hear it, and therefore I can remember it better."

A woman came down to the River Styx to be ferried across to the region of departed spirits. Charon, the ferryman, reminded her that it was a privilege to drink of the waters of the Lethe and thus forget the life she was leaving. This seemed to be a wonderful idea and she said, "I will forget how I have suffered." "And," added Charon, "remember, too, that you will forget how you have rejoiced." She said, "I will forget my failures." The old ferryman added, "And also your victories." She continued, "I will forget how I have been hated." "And also how you have been loved," added Charon. So, when she considered the whole matter, she decided not to drink the Lethe potion, but retain her memory even of the bad that she might not forget the good.

—Gerald Kennedy

Three men in Canada invented Trivial Pursuit. The game sold widely, and they made millions of dollars. When one of them was interviewed as to why the game was successful, he answered, "People are buying memories."

MENNONITES

At a Mennonite school boys and girls sat separately in chapel, with the girls on one side and the boys on the other. One day the boys were singing, "Oh to be over yonder." The girls were singing, "Why do you wait, dear brothers?"

MENTAL HEALTH

There are three main areas of importance to every human being. They are *identity*, recognition as a person; *stimulation*, the need for change as escape from boredom; and *security*, the opposite of anxiety.

—Earl Nightingale

MENTORING

In ancient mythology, before he left for Troy, Odysseus (the forever-after symbol of the eternal quest of man) gave his son, Telemachus, into the care of Mentor, whom he charged with looking after the household and attending to Telmachius's educational needs. Thus "mentor" has become a term that speaks of closeness and kindness in education.

MERCY

One night in 1935, Fiorello H. La Guardia, mayor of New York, showed up in a night court in the poorest ward of the city. He dismissed the judge for the evening and took over the bench. One case involved an elderly woman who was caught stealing bread to feed her grandchildren. La Guardia said, "I've got to punish you ten dollars or ten days in jail."

As he spoke, he threw ten dollars into his hat. He then fined everyone in the court fifty cents for living in a city "where a person has to steal bread so that her grandchildren can eat." The hat was passed around and the woman left the courtroom with her fine paid and an additional $47.50.

An ancient Saxon chronicle tells of a king in whose country a rebellion developed. This king set out with an army to quell the insurrection. Soon things were in control again, with the rebel army defeated. The king, who had made his headquarters in one of the castles of that distant province, placed a candle in the archway over its entrance. Lighting the candle, he then announced that if all who were in rebellion against him would surrender and take an oath of loyalty while the candle was still burning, they would be spared. Here is clemency, but only for the life of the candle.

—Walter K. Price

METRIC SYSTEM

Here is a sampling of how the metric system would affect some of our most popular slogans and proverbs:

"A kilogram of flesh."

"A 30.48 centimeter-long hot dog."

"Kilogram for kilogram, he's the best."

"I'd walk 1,609 kilometers for a Camel."

"A miss is as good as 1,609 kilometers."

"It hit me like 907 kilograms of bricks!"

"He missed by 1,609 kilometers."

"Peter Piper picked 8.81 liters of pickled peppers."

"Give him 2.54 centimeters and he'll take 1,609 kilometers."

"28,350 grams of prevention are worth 453,592 grams of cure."

MIDDLE AGE (Also see AGE and OLD AGE)

The prime of life is that fleeting time between green and overripe.
—Cullen Hightower

Middle age is the time of life when work begins to be a lot less fun and fun begins to be a lot more work.
—Farmers' Almanac

You've reached middle age when all you exercise is caution.

A man has reached middle age when the girl he winks at thinks he has something in his eye.

The period between adolescence and old age is when you have to take care of yourself.

Years ago, I remember listening to Arthur Godfrey do a radio ad for a cure-all medicine. The ad went, "At last, hope for middle age." Godfrey paused and said, "I've got hope. What I need is help."
—Fred Smith

Middle age is the metallic age: you have gold in your teeth, silver in your hair, and lead in your pants.

Life may begin at forty, but everything else begins to wear out, fall out, or spread out.

The big five of middle age are baldness, bifocals, bridgework, bulges, and bunions.

MILLENNIUM

A lad inquired of his father, "What is the millennium?" Answer: "Don't you know what a millennium is? It's just about like a centennial, only it's got more legs."
—K. A. Carlson

MIND

The mind is like the stomach. It is not how much you put into it that counts, but how much it digests.

MINISTRY

"Do you know what the formula is for blessing in ministry?" Lehman Strauss asked Warren Wiersbe many years ago. "It is to simply preach, pray, and plug away!"

A friend of Leighton Ford said to him, "Ministry is what we leave in our tracks as we follow the Lord."

Someone asked Robert G. Lee, "What is your secret in the ministry?" He answered, "Love the people and preach the Word."

Ministry without emotion is like motherhood without the tenderness of affection.
—Chuck Swindoll

When evangelist D. L. Moody was preaching in Birmingham, England, in 1875, the noted Congregational theologian and preacher R. W. Dale cooperated in the campaign. After listening to Moody preach and seeing the blessings, Dale wrote in his denomination's magazine, "I told Mr. Moody that the work was most plainly of God, for I could see no real relation between him and what he had done. He laughed cheerily, and said he would be very sorry if it were otherwise."
—A. W. W. Dale

An old minister in Scotland was nearing the end of a long ministry in an obscure parish. He felt disappointment about the results of his work because he could point to no seemingly clear-cut conversions. He was telling his disappointment to a distinguished minister whose work had appeared so fruitful.

The famous preacher listened till the old man had finished. Then he said, "Do you remember a young woman who used to worship in your church some twenty years ago?" When he had described her, the minister said, "Yes, I remember her. She came for quite a while, but she never joined the church." "Well," replied the great man, "that young woman had a younger brother who was rapidly becoming a drunkard. She would come home from church and talk to him about your sermons until he finally changed his habits. That young man was myself."

—Ralph W. Sockman

MIRACLES

Voltaire said that if he and one thousand men in Paris saw a miracle before their very eyes he would rather disbelieve his eyes and the eyes of the one thousand than to believe in the miracles.

A pastor was once talking to an agnostic and was trying to convince him and convert him to Christ. "Speaking of miracles," the pastor said, "if a man jumped out of a ten-story building and did not die, would that not be a miracle?" "No," said the agnostic, "it would only be an accident."

"Then what if he jumped out the second time and he didn't die. Wouldn't you say that would be a miracle?"

"No, that would be a coincidence."

"Then what if the third time? Wouldn't that be one?"

"No, that's just a habit!"

MISERY

The secret of being miserable is to have the leisure to think about whether you are happy or not.

—George Bernard Shaw

How to Be Perfectly Miserable

1. Think about yourself.
2. Talk about yourself.
3. Use "I" as much as possible.
4. Mirror yourself continually in the opinion of others.
5. Listen greedily to what people say about you.
6. Expect to be appreciated.
7. Be suspicious.
8. Be jealous and envious.
9. Be sensitive to slights.
10. Never forgive a criticism.
11. Trust nobody but yourself.
12. Insist on consideration and respect.
13. Demand agreement with your own views of everything.
14. Sulk if people are not grateful to you for favors shown them.
15. Never forget a service you may have rendered.
16. Be on the lookout for a good time for yourself.
17. Shirk your duties if you can.
18. Do as little as possible for others.
19. Love yourself supremely.
20. Be selfish.

The recipe is guaranteed to be infallible.

—*Gospel Herald*

MISSIONS

In World War II, Winston Churchill pleaded with the American people over the radio for help. "Give us the tools and we will finish the job."

The Spirit of Christ is the spirit of missions, and the nearer we get to Him the more intensely missionary we must become.

—Henry Martyn

Recently a cannibal complained that since the ecumenical movement had taken over, all missionaries taste the same.

—*Farmers' Almanac*

"But I have never felt any compelling call to give my life for missionary service," the young man told the conference speaker. "Are you sure you are within calling distance?" was the disquieting reply.

John Warr, an eighteenth-century apprentice shoemaker, was determined to be a faithful witness for Christ. Another apprentice was hired, and John repeatedly talked to him about spiritual things. That new worker, however, didn't want to be bothered. Then one day he was caught exchanging a counterfeit shilling for a good one. In his guilty humiliation he asked John for help and prayer. Through the faithful witness of John Warr, that man put his faith in Christ and developed into a committed disciple.

The young apprentice was William Carey, who later became a remarkably fruitful missionary to India. Carey's life and ministry had a tremendous influence on the cause of outreach in modern times.

I Was Not Called

"I cannot go," I hear you say. "It's not my
  work;
I was not called. Too bad so many die that
  way,
Without a hope, without a God,
But here at home I have to stay."
But then I hear my Savior say, "It was my
  work to die for you.
In Heav'n I did not please to stay.
I came to earth not for a few,
But all should know I am the Way."
"I cannot go," I hear you say. "My child is
  small
And he needs all the world can give him
  today.
It would not do to be so cruel
To one who cannot choose his way."
And then I hear my Father say, "I gave My
  Son,
My only One, to give the world the only
  Way.
He suffered all upon the cross.
Can you do less for Me today?"
"I cannot go," I hear you say. "It takes so
  much
Of strength and grace. I have no talents to
  display,
My faith is weak; right here I'll stay.
The smart and strong go far away."
I hear my Lord and Master say, "Have you
  not read
Within My Word, 'Ye are vessels made of
  clay?'
I choose the weak to give My strength.
Let all who will serve Me today."

A certain rich man did not approve of
foreign missions. One Sunday at church,
when the offering was being received, the
usher approached the millionaire and held
out his plate. The millionaire shook his
head. "I never give to missions," he
whispered.

"Then take something out of the plate,
Sir," said the usher softly. "The money is
for the heathen."

It is reported that a missionary lady was telling the story of her work in China. When
she finished, a little girl came forward and
gave her twelve pennies. "Please," she said,
"I have been saving these pennies and now
I want them to be missionaries in China."
How happy the missionary was to receive
the offering from its wholehearted giver.
Months went by and finally a letter came
for the little girl which read, "With your
twelve pennies I bought twelve Gospels of
John. I gave one to each of my class of Chinese girls. They read the wonderful story in
their own little books, and today all twelve
gave their hearts to Christ. What a splendid
investment you made."

In encouraging young men to come out as
missionaries, do use the greatest caution.
One strongheaded, conscientiously
obstinate man would ruin us. Humble,
quiet, persevering men; men of decent
accomplishments and some natural
aptitude to acquire a language; men of
amiable yielding temper, willing to take the
lowest place, to be least of all, and the
servant of all; men who enjoy closet
religion and live near to God and are
willing to suffer all things for Christ's sake
without being proud of it.

—Ann Judson

When asked, "What equipment does one
need in order to be a missionary?"
J. Hudson Taylor answered as follows: "A
life yielded to God, a restful trust in Him
to supply your needs, a willingness to take
a lowly place, adaptability toward circumstances, steadfastness in discouragement, love for prayer and the study of
God's Word, some experience and blessing in the Lord's work at home."

T. S. McCullough, father of Jim
McCullough, martyred by the Auca Indians, prayed, "Lord, let me live long enough
to see these Auca Indians saved so I can
see them in heaven and wrap my arms
around them for they love my Savior."

It was a Jew who brought the Gospel to
Rome; a Roman who took it to France; a
Frenchman who took it to Scandinavia; a
Scotsman who evangelized Ireland; and an
Irishman who in turn made the missionary
conquest of Scotland.

In the Great Commission:
Matthew emphasizes authority.
Mark emphasizes universality.
Luke emphasizes order of procedure.
John emphasizes spiritual qualifications and demands.

What is 750,000 miles long, reaches around the earth thirty times, and grows twenty miles longer each day? Answer: The line of people who are without Christ.

C. T. Studd, England's most famed athlete and member of the fabled Cambridge Seven a century ago, who forsook fortune and notoriety to toil for Christ on several continents of missionary service, had an overpowering vision. He said, "If Jesus Christ be God and died for me, then no sacrifice can be too great for me to make for Him."

—Edward Kuhlman

The missionary statesman Woodward, when asked about the past of missions and the future and what should be done, said, "Hats off to yesterday and coats off to tomorrow."

Today nine of every ten people in the world are lost.

Of these nine, six of ten have never heard a clear presentation of the Gospel.

Of these six, three of ten have no one near them to tell them about Christ.

Consider the world as if it were shrunk down to a community of 1,000 persons:
In our town of 1,000—
180 of us live high on a hill called the developed world.
820 of us live in the rocky bottom called the rest of the world.
The fortunate 180 on the hill have 80 percent of the wealth of the whole town, over half of all the rooms in town with over two rooms per person, 85 percent of all the automobiles, 80 percent of all the TV sets, 93 percent of all the telephones, and an average income of $5,000 per person per year.
The not-so-fortunate 820 people on the bottom get by on only $700 per person per year, many of them on less than $75. They average five persons to a room.

How does the fortunate group of hill-dwellers use its incredible wealth? Well, as a group they spend less than 1 percent of their income to aid the lower land. In the United States, for example, of every $100 earned:
$18.30 goes for food.
$6.60 is spent on recreation and amusement.
$5.80 buys clothes.
$2.40 buys alcohol.
$1.50 buys tobacco.
$1.30 is given for religious and charitable uses, and only a small part of that goes outside the U.S.

I wonder how the villagers on the crowded plain—a third of whose people are suffering from malnutrition—feel about the folks on the hill?

—Paul Brand and Philip Yancey

The first message at the birth of Christ was a missionary message (Luke 2:10).

The first prayer Christ taught was a missionary prayer (Matt. 6:10).

The first disciple, Andrew, was a missionary (John 1:41).

The first message of the risen Lord was a missionary message (John 20:17).

The first command of the risen Lord to His disciples was a missionary command (John 21:21).

The first apostolic sermon was a missionary sermon (Acts 2:17–39).

The greatest reason for Christian love was a missionary reason (John 13:35).

The first coming of Christ was a missionary work (Luke 6:18–21).

The second coming of Christ is to be hastened by missionary work (Matt. 24:14).

Our Savior's last wish on earth was a missionary wish (Matt. 28:19).

And the last wish of the departing Savior should be the first wish of His waiting people.

—*Christian Beacon*

In the early part of the nineteenth century the elders of a small church in Scotland met with their aged pastor and urged him to retire. They complained that there had not been a single conversion in the church in a year. "There was one," he told them, "The wee lad Bobbie."

They remembered, then. Not only had the boy confessed Christ as his Lord and Savior but a few months later, at a missionary meeting, had done an outstanding thing. When the offering plate was passed, Bobbie asked the usher to place the plate on the floor. The, removing his shoes, the lad stepped on it and said, "I give myself to missionary service. It is all I have."

Wee Bobbie became known and revered the world over by those who love the Lord as the gifted missionary to Africa, Robert Moffat. If any brighter light ever shone in the dark continent, it would be Moffatt's son-in-law, David Livingstone.

—E. Schuyler English

Whose I am is more important than who I am.
Who I am is more important than what I do.
What I do is more important than where I do it.

—Don Hillis

There's no greater joy than giving out of gratitude rather than out of hope for return favors.

In Paris a woman who was poor and blind was seen placing twenty-seven francs in the offering plate.

"But you cannot afford so much," observed a friend.

"Oh, yes I can," she said, "I asked my fellow straw workers how much they spend for oil in their lamps each year. 'Twenty-seven francs,' they told me. So that is how much I save by being blind. I need no lamp, so I give it to shed light in the darkness of heathen lands."

There were two boys in the Taylor family. The older said he must make a name for the family, and so he turned his face toward Parliament and fame. The younger decided to give his life to the service of Christ, and so he turned his face toward China and duty. J. Hudson Taylor, the missionary, died, beloved and known on every continent. "But when I looked in the encyclopedia to see what the other son had done," one person said, "I found these words, 'The brother of Hudson Taylor.'"

Tertullian, arrested for his faith, stood before the judge and said, "Sir, the majority in every village [in North Africa] are followers of Jesus Christ."

A missionary in Africa was once asked if he really liked what he was doing. His response was shocking. "Do I like this work?" he said. "No, my wife and I do not like dirt. We have reasonably refined sensibilities. We do not like crawling into vile huts through goat refuse . . . But is a man to do nothing for Christ he does not like? God pity him, if not. Liking or disliking has nothing to do with it. We have orders to 'go' and we go. Love constrains us."

Each year 30 million people die in the world.
Each day 82,000.
Each hour 3,400.
Each minute 57.
That's almost one every time the clock ticks!

The least promising lad in a lady's class was a raggedly dressed boy named Bob. The superintendent secured a new suit of clothes for him. After three Sundays Bob was missing. The teacher visited him to discover that his new clothes were torn and dirty. The superintendent gave him a second new suit. He returned to Sunday school. After attending twice, his place was empty again. Once more the teacher learned that the second suit had gone the same way as the first. Discouraged, she told the superintendent she must give him up. "Please don't do that," urged the superintendent. "I'll give him a third suit if he promises to attend regularly." Bob did promise. He did attend regularly. He became an earnest Christian, joined the church, became a teacher, studied for the ministry. He became Robert Morrison, honored missionary to China, who translated the Bible into the Chinese language and opened the gate to millions in that country.

A very hospitable Christian family very often entertained missionaries on furlough. The small boy in the family noticed how well the missionaries were treated, and what luxuries they had when they came.

One day someone asked Johnny what he wanted to be when he grew up, and he quickly replied, "I want to be a missionary home on furlough!"

If the Lord is coming soon, is this not a very practical motive for greater missionary effort? I know of no other motive that has been so stimulating to myself.

—J. Hudson Taylor

At an international gathering of young people in New York City, a young American asked a girl from Burma what was the religious belief of the majority of the Burmese. The young woman informed him that it was Buddhism. The American said quite casually, "Oh well, that doesn't matter; all religions are the same anyway."

The Burmese girl looked directly at the young man and said, "If you had lived in my country you would not say that. I have seen what centuries of superstition, fear, and indifference to social problems have done for my people. We need the truth and uplift of Christianity. When I became a Christian, it cost me something. If your religion had cost you more, you might be more aware of its superiority. My country needs Christ."

If ten men are carrying a log—nine of them on the little end and one of them on the heavy end—and you want to help, on which end will you lift?

—Borden of Yale

A young artist painted the picture of a forlorn woman and a child out in a storm. The picture had such an effect on him personally that he put aside his palette and brush and said, "I must go to the lost instead of painting them." He prepared for the ministry and for some time worked in the city's slums. At length he said, "I must go to that part of the world where people seem to be helplessly lost."

That young artist became the famous missionary Bishop Tucker of Uganda, Africa.

One billion seconds have passed since Jesus was born, and in the next ten years one and a half billion people will be born.

When David Livingstone's body was taken back to England, crowds thronged the streets to pay tribute to the noble missionary. An elderly man among them was heard to sob aloud, and people wondered at his deep grief. It was revealed that he and Livingstone had been friends in their youth, and, as an ambitious young man he had scorned Livingstone's choice to give his life for Christ in Africa. With a life of selfish interest behind him, the man saw with regret who had made the wiser choice, and he cried out, "I put the emphasis on the wrong word."

—*Christian Digest*

The vitality of a church may be measured by its interest in the evangelization of the world.

—A. T. Pierson

The message of Robert Moffat which turned the steps of David Livingstone to missionary service in Africa still holds true in many parts of the world today. "Many a morning from my porch in Africa, I have seen the smoke of a thousand villages, whose people are without Christ, without God, and without hope in the world."

MISTAKES

A zoo built a special eight-foot-high enclosure for its newly acquired kangaroo, but the next morning the animal was found hopping around outside. The director of the zoo increased the height of the fence to fifteen feet, but the kangaroo escaped again. Puzzled, the director had the height increased to thirty feet; but, much to his dismay, the kangaroo was still able to escape.

Watching the director build higher and higher fences, a giraffe asked the kangaroo, "How high do you think they'll build the fence?"

"I don't know," said the kangaroo. "Maybe a thousand feet if they keep leaving the gate unlocked!"

—*Today in the Word*

The greatest mistake you can make is to be constantly fearful you will make one.

—*Teen Esteem*

He who never made a mistake never made anything.

The man who makes a mistake and neglects to correct it makes another mistake.

Forget failures. Forget everything except what you are going to do now and do it. Today is your lucky day.

—William Durant

Do not ask for perfection in all you do, but for the wisdom not to repeat mistakes.

—Brenda Sloat

There are two kinds of people who make mistakes: those who won't admit them and those who call them experience.

Experience is the name everyone gives to their mistakes.

—Oscar Wilde

A man must be big enough to admit his mistakes, smart enough to profit from them, and strong enough to correct them.

Several years ago a young Frenchman captured the attention of the world by walking a tightrope between the towers of New York City's World Trade Center 1,350 feet above the ground. A few months later, however, while practicing on a relatively low wire in St. Petersburg, Florida, he fell thirty feet and was injured. As he lay waiting for help, he reportedly beat his fist on the ground, saying, "I can't believe it! I can't believe it! I never fall!" Perhaps he lost his concentration because he was working at a low level where the risk did not seem very great.

At ceremonies commemorating the hundredth anniversary of Harry S. Truman's birth, Clark M. Clifford, who was White House counsel during the Truman administration, was reminiscing. Clifford recalled being at a White House banquet one night when one of the guests turned to the woman seated next to him.

"Did I get your name correctly?" he asked. "Is your name Post?"

"Yes, it is." the woman replied.

"Is it Emily Post?"

"Yes," she replied.

"Are you the world-renowned authority on manners?" the man asked.

"Yes," Mrs. Post said. "Why do you ask?"

"Because," said the man, "you have just eaten my salad."

—*Bits & Pieces*

The wise man studies others so that he can learn from their mistakes and at their expense.

There are two kinds of people who should never say "Oops:" dentists and magicians.

A woman going over her offspring's brand-new checking account noted the following entries: "Rent, $350"; "Electricity, $63.47"; "Phone, $41.82"; and ESP, $45.76. What's ESP?" asked the puzzled mother.

"Error Some Place," replied the young banking whiz.

There are three kinds of people: those who can count, and those who can't.

One good thing about being wrong is the joy it brings to others.

A real leader will make mistakes. The man who never makes mistakes never does anything. I would rather make a hundred mistakes and accomplish something than to make no mistakes and accomplish nothing. Mistakes are not sins. Man always has and always will err. God allows him to blunder again and again in order to teach him and keep him humble.

—Oswald J. Smith

He never seems to make the same mistakes twice, but it seems to me he has made them all once.

I beseech you, in the bowels of Christ, think it possible you may be mistaken.

—Oliver Cromwell

Errors should be reasons for growth not excuses for discouragement.

The Six Mistakes of Man

1. The delusion that personal gain is made by crushing others.
2. The tendency to worry about things that cannot be changed or corrected.
3. Insisting that a thing is impossible because we cannot accomplish it.
4. Refusing to set aside trivial differences.
5. Neglecting development and refinement of the mind, and not acquiring the habit of reading and studying.
6. Attempting to compel others to believe and live as we do.

—Cicero

A man had to get off the train at 3:00 A.M. so he said to the conductor, "Here's ten dollars. Please wake me in time. You'll have to fight to get me awake."

However, the conductor didn't wake him. The man was mad and then jumped off the train.

Another passenger said, "I never saw a man so mad in my life, did you?" the conductor said, "Yes. You should have seen the man I put off at 3 A.M.!"

No man ever became great or good except through many and great mistakes.

—William Gladstone

An irate employee went to the paymaster's window and laid down his pay envelope. Carefully counting the money, he looked the paymaster in the eye and said, "Twenty dollars short."

The paymaster picked up the envelope and turned to the record sheet to check the amount due. Smiling broadly, he came back to the window. "Last week we overpaid you twenty dollars," he explained. "You didn't complain then."

"An occasional mistake I can overlook," replied the angry employee, "but not two in a row!"

The better a man is, the more mistakes he will make, for the more new things he will try. I would never promote into a top-level job a man who was not making mistakes. . . . otherwise he is sure to be mediocre.

—Peter Drucker

No man ever became great or good except through many and great mistakes.

—William Gladstone

Men will always be making mistakes if they are striving for things.

—Johann von Goethe

MODERATION

Moderation in temper is always a virtue, but moderation in principle is always a vice.

—Thomas Paine

MONEY

George W. Truett, long-time pastor of First Baptist Church, Dallas, Texas, was invited to dinner in the home of a wealthy man in Texas. After the meal, the host led him to a place where they could get a good view of the surrounding area.

Pointing to oil wells punctuating the landscape, he boasted, "Twenty-five years ago I had nothing. Now, as far as you can see, it's all mine." Looking in the opposite direction at his sprawling fields of grain, he said, "That's all mine." Turning east toward huge herds of cattle, he bragged, "They're all mine." Then, pointing to the west and a beautiful forest, he exclaimed, "That too is all mine." He paused, expecting Truett to compliment him on his great success.

Truett, however, placing a hand on the man's shoulder and pointing heavenward, simply said, "How much do you have in that direction?" The man hung his head and confessed, "I never thought of that." Although that wealthy Texan had succeeded in making money, he had failed to prepare for eternity.

A teacher of second-graders said, "I'll give this five dollar bill to the student who can tell me who is the greatest person in the world." One child said, "It's George Washington." "No, he's great, but not the greatest." Another said, "Abraham Lincoln." "No, he's great, but not the greatest." Others suggested John F. Kennedy, Martin Luther King, etc. A Jewish boy in the class raised his hand and said "Jesus Christ." The teacher gave the child the five dollar bill, but said, "How is it that you, a Jewish boy, said 'Jesus?'" He said, "In my heart it is Moses, but business is business."

Money is in some respects like fire; it is a very excellent servant, but a terrible master.
—P. T. Barnum

A Rothschild had died. Outside his house stood a poor Jew sobbing in heart-breaking fashion. A servant, taking pity on the man, came out to console him. "Why do you weep so?" he asked. "After all, you are not a relative."

"That's why I'm crying," came the swift reply.

Just about the time you think you can make both ends meet, somebody moves the ends.
—Penny Penner

Money is a wonderful thing, but it's possible to pay too high a price for it.
—Mark Hambourg

A robber said to me, "Your money or your life." I paused, then said, "I'll have to think it over."
—Jack Benny

A man's treatment of money is the most decisive test of his character—how he makes it and how he spends it.
—James Moffat

At age 65 Sophie Tucker said,
"A girl up to age 18 needs good parents. From age 18 to 35 she needs good looks. From age 35 to 55 she needs a good job. After age 55 she needs cash."

Money, like prestige, sought directly is almost never gained. It must come as a by-product of some worthwhile objective or result that is sought and achieved for its own sake.
—Robert Townsend

Money is an article which may be used as a universal passport everywhere except heaven, and as a universal provider for everything except happiness.
—*The Wall Street Journal*

That money talks I'll not deny,
I heard it once, it said "Good-bye."
—Richard Simmons

Life is so tragic for the person who has plenty to live on, but nothing to live for.

If a person gets his attitude toward money straightened out, then almost all other areas of his life will be straightened out.
—Billy Graham

Get to know two things about a man—how he earns his money and how he spends it—and you have the clue to his character, for you have a searchlight that shows up the innermost recesses of his soul. You know all you need to know about his standards, his motives, his driving desires, and his real religion.
—Robert J. McCracken

Bertha Adams was seventy-one years old. She died alone in West Palm Beach, Florida, on Easter Sunday, 1976. The coroner's report read: "Cause of death . . . malnutrition." After wasting away to fifty pounds she could no longer stay alive. When the state authorities made their preliminary investigation of her place, they found a veritable "pigpen . . . the biggest mess you can imagine." One seasoned inspector declared he had never seen a dwelling in greater disarray. The pitiable woman had begged food from neighbors and gotten what clothes she had from the Salvation Army. From all appearances, she was a penniless recluse—a pitiful and forgotten widow. But such was not the case.

Amid the jumble of her unclean, disheveled belongings, two keys were found which led officials to safe deposit boxes at two different local banks. The discovery was absolutely unbelievable. The first box contained over 700 stock certificates, plus hundreds of other valuable certificates, bonds, and solid financial securities, and cash amounting to nearly $200,000. The second box had more currency—$600,000. Adding the net worth of both boxes, the woman had well over a million dollars. Bertha Adams's hoarding was tragic, and her death was an unusually grim testimony to the shriveled focus on her life. Her great wealth did her no good whatsoever. Its proper use could have meant good health for her and many others.

The perpetual saver always lives in poverty.
—Danish proverb

To get his wealth he spent his health
And then with might and main
He turned around and spent his wealth
To get his health again.

So George Washington never told a lie? Then why is his picture on a bill that isn't even worth a dollar?

Money is like sea water. The more you drink, the thirstier you get.
—Roman proverb

A young person asked an old millionaire, "Which is better, wealth or youth?" The millionaire replied, "Ask any old millionaire."

Money can buy:
   a bed, but not sleep,
   books, but not brains,
   food, but not appetite,
   finery, but not beauty,
   a house, but not a home,
   medicine, but not health,
   luxuries, but not culture,
   amusement, but not happiness,
   companions, but not friends,
   flattery, but not respect.

As little Jimmy's uncle was about to leave after a visit, he placed a crisp new dollar bill in his nephew's hand, saying, "Be careful how you spend this, Jimmy. You know the old proverb, 'A fool and his money are soon parted.'" To this the lad replied, "I'll remember what you said, Uncle Bill. But thanks anyway for parting with it!"
—Our Daily Bread

Out of this life I shall never take
Things of silver and gold I make.
All that I cherish and hoard away
After I leave, on earth must stay.
Though I have toiled for a painting rare
To hang on my wall, I must leave it there.
Though I call it mine and boast of its worth
I must give it up when I quit the earth.
All that I gather and all that I keep,
I must leave behind when I fall asleep.
And I often wonder what I shall own
in that other life, when I pass alone.
What shall they find and what shall they see
In the soul that answers the call for me?
Shall the Great Judge learn, when my task
   is through
that the spirit had gathered some riches too?
Or shall at the last it be mine to find
That all I had worked for I'd left behind?
—Edgar A. Guest

You can't win. If you run after money, you're materialistic. If you don't get it, you're a loser. If you get it and keep it, you're a miser. If you don't try to get it, you lack ambition. If you get it and spend it, you're a spendthrift. If you still have it after a lifetime of work, you're a fool who never got any fun out of life.
—Bits & Pieces

Some boys and girls were discussing what they wanted to be when they grew up. When it was Jimmy's turn to speak, he didn't mention one of the more common professions like doctor, lawyer, policeman, and fireman. What he wanted to be was a philanthropist. When the other kids asked him why, he replied, "Because I heard they are the guys who have all the money."

A rabbi was awakened one night by a sound in the house and asked, "Who's there?" A voice from the shadows replied, "A burglar." "What are you looking for?" asked the rabbi, and the voice replied, "Money." The rabbi said, "Wait, I'll get up and help you!"

When a noted scientist rejected an offer of a large sum of money to lecture, he revealed his values by explaining, "I cannot afford to waste time making money."

Some things in the world are far more important than wealth; one of them is the ability to enjoy simple things.

—Dale Carnegie

Millionaire John D. Rockefeller said, "I have made many millions, but they have brought me no happiness. I would barter them all for the days I sat on an office stool in Cleveland and counted myself rich on three dollars a week." Broken in health, he employed an armed guard.

The care of 200 million bucks is too great a load for any brain or back to bear. It is enough to kill anyone. There is no pleasure in it.

—W. H. Vanderbilt

The real measure of our wealth is how much we'd be worth if we lost all our money.

—John Henry Jowett

Benjamin Franklin, oldest member of the Constitutional Convention, addressing the matter of Congressional salaries, said, "Two passions have powerful influence on the affairs of men: the love of power and the love of money."

A retiree from New Jersey had moved south with his life savings of $11,300.

When he went to deposit it in a Florida bank, the envelope in which he had placed it was missing. A thorough search of his new home failed to uncover the money. By the time he realized what had happened, the envelope was being bulldozed into a huge pit at the county dump. He knew he had no chance of recovering the money. Neighbors and friends reported that they found the poor man in a state of total dejection.

A miser, who never stopped worrying about the safety of his possessions, sold all his property and converted it into a huge lump of gold. This he buried in a hole in the ground near his garden wall, and every morning he went to visit it and gloat over the size of it.

The miser's strange behavior aroused the curiosity of the town thief. Spying on the rich man from some bushes, the thief saw him place the lump of gold back in the hole and cover it up. As soon as the miser's back was turned, the thief went to the spot, dug up the gold, and took it away.

The next morning, when the miser went to gloat over his treasure, he found nothing but an empty hole. He wept and tore his hair, and so loud were his lamentations that a neighbor came running to see what was the trouble. As soon as he had learned the cause of it, he said comfortingly, "You are foolish to distress yourself over something that was buried in the earth. Take a stone and put it in the hole, and think that it is your lump of gold. You were never meant to use it anyway. Therefore, it will do you just as much good to fondle a lump of granite as a lump of gold."

This fable by Aesop has a very significant moral for every Christian: "The true value of money is not in its possession but in its use."

Wesley lived on twenty-eight pounds a year. "When some money comes my way, I soon give it away, lest it find a place in my heart."

They call it take-home pay because there is no other place you can afford to go with it.

Let us all be happy and live within our means, even if we have to borrow money to do it.

—Artemus Ward

When a person loves earthly things so much that he can't get along without them, he opens himself to much suffering, both physical and mental. Some people, for example, have taken foolish risks to keep their riches intact. They have died rushing into burning houses or they were killed because they stubbornly resisted armed robbers. Apparently they felt that without their material possessions life would not be worthwhile. Others, when forced to part with their wealth, have been thrown into agonizing despair, even to the point of suicide. In 1975, six armed gunmen broke into the deposit boxes in a London bank and stole valuables worth more than $7 million. One lady, whose jewelry was appraised at $500,000, wailed, "Everything I had was in there. My whole life was in that box." What a sad commentary on her values!

A man's wife helped him become a millionaire. "She must be a wonderful woman." "She is, I'd like you to meet her." "I'd like to. What were you before you met her?" "A multimillionaire."

The British ship Britannia was wrecked off the coast of Brazil. Stored in the hold were many kegs filled with Spanish gold coins. The crew, hoping to save them, started to carry the barrels on deck. But the vessel was breaking up so fast that they had to abandon their efforts and rush for the lifeboats. Just before the last one pushed off, a young midshipman was sent back to see if anyone had been left behind. To his surprise, a man sat on the deck with a hatchet by his side. He had broken open a few kegs and was heaping the gold up around him. "What are you doing?" shouted the sailor. "Don't you know this ship is going to pieces?" "It may go down," said the man, "but I've lived in poverty all my life, and I'm determined to die rich."

A Mafia leader had an elaborate funeral, including a gold casket. And when his casket was taken out of the funeral home at the end of the service, someone said, "Man, that's the way to live."

The three sons of a lawyer, a doctor, and a minister, respectively, were talking about how much money their fathers made.

The lawyer's son said, "My father goes into court on a case and often comes home with as much as fifteen hundred dollars."

The doctor's son said, "My father performs an operation and earns as much as two thousand dollars for it."

The minister's son, determined not to be outdone, said, "That's nothing. My father preaches for fifteen minutes on Sunday morning, and it takes four men to carry the money."

The difference in the case of the minister is that the money is for God's service and not for self.

An aged Christian mother heard one of her sons describe his brother's sudden rise to wealth. When he finished telling of his brother's money, luxurious home, and new cars, he declared, "Bill is certainly getting on in the world."

The mother looked at her son, then asked sorrowfully, "Which world?"

Sign in the window of a store: "Use our new easy credit plan—100% down, nothing to pay each month."

One of the world's most successful door-to-door sales approaches: "Madam, let me show you a little item your neighbors said you couldn't afford. . . ."

One reason so many people are extravagant these days is that there are a thousand ways to spend money and only one way to save it.

Teach your kids the value of money—borrow from them.

Some years ago a newspaper offered a prize for the best definition of money. Out of the hundreds who competed, the winner submitted the following: "Money is a universal provider for everything but happiness and a passport to everywhere but heaven."

Virtue is not given by money, but from virtue comes money and every other good of man.

—Plato

If the rich could hire other people to die for them, the poor could make a wonderful living.

—Yiddish proverb

Wealth is not the standard of worth. Some people put cash before character.

—Billy Sunday

People of means often act the meanest.

MORALS

There is no tragedy as tragic as combining high mentality with low morality.

Keep away from places where people say to you, "I didn't expect to see you here."

Whenever you face a decision, you have three choices: Do what you please, do what others do, or do what is right.

Two things fill my heart with awe and never-ceasing wonder: the starry heavens above me and the moral imperative within me.

—Immanuel Kant

Television commentator Andy Rooney once announced his revulsion at the perverse sexual conduct increasingly evident in our culture. But pressure from special interest groups that promote immoral lifestyles coerced him to apologize.

To educate a man in mind and not in morals is to educate a menace to society.

—Theodore Roosevelt

Of all the dispositions and habits which lead to political prosperity, religion and morality are indispensable supports. . . .

And let us with caution indulge the supposition that morality can be maintained without religion. . . . Reasons and experience both forbid us to expect that national morality can prevail in exclusion of religious principle.

—George Washington

Society cannot exist unless a controlling power upon will and appetite be placed somewhere, and the less of it there is within, the more there must be without.

—Edmund Burke

MOTHERS

Thomas Edison's tribute to his mother:

I did not have my mother long, but she cast over me a good influence that lasted all my life. The good effects of her early training I can never lose. If it had not been for her appreciation and her faith in me at a critical time in my experience, I would never likely have become an inventor. I was always a careless boy, and with a mother of different mental caliber, I would have turned out badly. But her firmness, her sweetness, her goodness, were potent powers to keep me on the right path. My mother was the making of me. The memory of her will always be a blessing to me.

M is for the million things she gave me;
O is only that she's growing old;
T is for the tears she shed to save me;
H is for her heart of purest gold;
E is for her eyes with lovelight shining;
R is for right and right she'll always be.
Put them all together, they spell "Mother," the name that means all the world to me.

Because I Loved My Mother

When I was just a little child
  I loved my mother so,
I liked to touch what she had touched,
  And always tried to know
The things she loved the best of all,
  So I could love them too.
I made a secret list of them,
  Although she never knew.
And now, although I am grown, I love
  My heavenly Father so,

That like a little child again
  I humbly seek to know
The things which are the most dear to Him
  So I may love them too.
And thus draw closer to the heart
  Of the Lord my mother knew.

The newest development in manufacturing is robotics. Robots put in endless hours, function in different environments, never seem to run down, cost very little to maintain, and do it all without praise, personal attention, or stroking. Actually, robotics are nothing new. They used to be called mothers.

Behind every great man is his mother:
  Mrs Morse: "Sam, stop tapping your fingers on the table. It's driving me crazy!"
  Mrs. Lindbergh: "Charles, can't you do anything by yourself?"
  Mrs. Washington: "George never did have a head for money."
  Mrs. Armstrong: "Neil has no more business taking flying lessons than the man on the moon."

                 —Reader's Digest

Men want to improve only the world, but mothers want to improve their whole family. That's a much harder task.
                —Harriet Freezer

No man is poor who has a godly mother.
                —Abraham Lincoln

One godly mother is worth a hundred clergy.

My mother was one of the most beautiful women I have ever seen.
                —Eleanor Roosevelt

Mothers Who Made History

The mother of George Washington taught her son the biblical ideals of political and social morality which Washington kept before the nation throughout his life. Family prayers were held twice a day with regular readings from the Scriptures.

The mother of Ferdinand Foch, the great general of World War II, taught him to put his faith in God and to pray. As a result his men said of him, "General Foch is a man of prayer, a prophet whom God inspires." Throughout his life he continued the prayer habits he learned in his mother's home.

James A. Garfield's mother was an earnest Christian who taught her children that "the fear of the Lord is the beginning of wisdom." A widow with four children, she not only managed her farm, but built with her own hands a log house which was also used as a church. There she taught her own children as well as others the Scriptures.

The mother of England's famous William E. Gladstone led her son to faith in God when he was nine. He chose as his life's motto: "In practice, the great thing is that the life of God may be the supreme habit of my soul." He also wrote, "All I think, all I write, all I am is based on the divinity of Jesus Christ, the central hope of our poor wayward race."

Oliver Cromwell's mother taught him the simple truths of Scripture and he chose as his favorite verse, "I can do all things through Christ which strengtheneth me."

The mother of Dwight L. Moody struggled against poverty on a New England farm. A widow with many problems, she taught her son the importance of eternal values. At seventeen, Moody accepted Christ and a few years later dedicated his life for service.

The mother of William Penn so impressed him with the importance of faith in Christ that he took as his life text, "This is the victory, even our faith which overcometh the world."

Sir Isaac Newton's mother prayed with and for her son every day of her life. It was the grief of her deathbed that she left a son of seven years at the mercy of a rough world. But Newton said, "I was born in a home of godliness and was dedicated to God in my infancy."

                —Harry Albus

Lunch-Box Recipe

An apple for his missing tooth!
  A sandwich for his size!
And lettuce for his clear young skin;
  A carrot for his eyes.

A meat to make him swagger,
   And a sweet to make him sing . . .
A lunch box for a boy in school
   Is not a simple thing.
So much of love and wisdom
   Must be packed inside, unbidden—
The love completely visible,
   The wisdom wisely hidden.
           —Mary Elizabeth Counselman

The washer breaks, the stew gets burned,
And Junior catches cold;
Then Sister tears her brand new dress . . .
You try hard not to scold . . .
You head for bed to nurse your head,
And hope to leave it all,
And that's the very time, of course,
The preacher seems to call!
The dinner's late and Daddy shouts,
"Where did you hide my shirt?"
You cut your finger on a knife,
And boy, does it hurt!
At last you tumble into bed,
Your vision strangely blurred,
You lift your heart to heaven,
But you wonder if God heard.
Ah, God is in His heaven!
He saw what just transpired:
He placed another star upon
The crown that you inspired!
He knows your every heartache . . .
He sees your deep despair,
And in His way He keeps you,
And loves your every hair!
The woman is His buffet
For every wind that blows:
She has a special portion
Of His grace . . . and how it glows!
           —Sarah Jane Tomlinson

I look at him and think of her;
   So many years ago
She held him close, sang lullabies,
   And rocked him to and fro.
Her loving prayers, her tenderness
   Hopes, cares, and sacrifice
Produced a man who seems to be
   All virtue and no vice.
One plainly sees her honesty
   In his clear eyes of blue
Her sweetness is reflected in
   His every action too.

In him she realized her dreams
   Then gave him to another
Yes, I'm the lucky girl, and oh!
   So grateful to his mother!

How to Bake a Cake

Light oven; get out utensils and ingredients. Remove blocks and toy autos from table. Grease pan, crack nuts.

Measure two cups of flour; remove Johnny's hands from flour; wash flour off him. Remeasure flour.

Put flour, baking powder, and salt in sifter. Get dustpan and brush up pieces of bowl Johnny knocked on floor. Get another bowl. Answer doorbell.

Return to kitchen. Remove Johnny's hands from bowl. Wash Johnny. Answer phone. Return. Remove one-fourth inch salt from greased pan. Look for Johnny. Grease another pan. Answer telephone.

Return to kitchen and find Johnny. Remove his hands from bowl. Take up greased pan and find layer of nutshell in it. Head for Johnny who flees, knocking bowl off table.

Wash kitchen floor, tables, walls, dishes. Call baker. Lie down.

A Mother's Prayer

I wash the dirt from little feet, and as I wash, I pray, "Lord, keep them ever pure and true to walk the narrow way."

I wash the dirt from little hands, and earnestly I ask, "Lord, may they ever yielded be to do the humblest task."

I wash the dirt from little knees, and pray, "Lord, may they be the place where victories are won and orders sought from Thee."

I scrub the clothes that soil so soon and pray, "Lord, may her dress throughout eternal ages be Thy robe of righteousness."

E'er many hours shall pass, I know I'll wash these hands again, and there'll be dirt upon her dress before the day shall end. But as she journeys on through life and learns of pain and want, Lord keep her precious little heart cleansed from all sin and stain. For soap and water cannot reach where Thou alone canst see. Her hands and feet, these I can wash . . . But Lord, I trust her heart to Thee!

My mother was a saintly woman. I owe everything to her.

—Lyndon B. Johnson

Year after year my mother drove into us, "I expect you always to be first, not second, or third, but first."

—Christian Barnard

My mother always seemed to me like a fairy princess: a radiant being possessed of limitless riches and power. She shone for me like the evening star. I loved her dearly.

—Winston Churchill

Not once can I recall from my earliest recollections hearing mother lift her voice in anger. She did not deliver lectures but guided us by her example. Mother gave balance to the home and led us into a rich spiritual life.

—Marian Anderson

When I was a child my mother said to me, "If you become a soldier, you'll be a general. If you become a monk, you'll end up as the Pope." Instead I became a painter and wound up as Picasso.

—Pablo Picasso

In spite of the squalor in which we were forced to live, she kept Sidney (a brother) and me off the streets and made us feel we were not the ordinary product of poverty but unique and distinguished.

—Charlie Chaplin

MOTHERS-IN-LAW

What is the penalty for bigamy?
Two mothers-in-law.

When a man's mother-in-law died, he was asked by the undertaker, "Do you want her cremated, buried, or embalmed?" He replied without hesitation, "All three. Don't take any chances."

MOTIVATION

Don't drive your horse with the whip—use the oat bag.

—Russian proverb

There is only one way under high heaven to get anybody to do anything. Did you ever stop to think of that? Yes, just one way. And that is by making the other person want to do it.

—Dale Carnegie

Why, I wonder, don't we use the same common sense when trying to change people that we use when trying to change dogs? Why don't we use meat instead of a whip? Why don't we use praise instead of condemnation? Let's praise even the slightest improvement. That inspires the other fellow to keep on improving.

—Dale Carnegie

The greatest talent of all is the ability to get others to use their talents fully.

Seventy psychologists were asked, "What is the most essential thing for a supervisor to know about human nature?" Two-thirds said that motivation and an understanding of what makes people think, feel, and act as they do is uppermost.

Few leaders in history have been able to stimulate men to action as Napoleon could. The secret of his leadership was simple. He first determined what his men wanted most, then did all in his power to help them get it.

A coach is a man who is smart enough to get his team keyed up and dumb enough to think it makes a difference.

—Eugene McCarthy

MUSIC

"The sole purpose of all music is to bring praise to God," Sebastian Bach said.

At the top of all his music he wrote the initials "J.J.," which are the Latin abbreviations for "Jesus, help me," and at the bottom of all his music he wrote the initials "SDG," which stands for "Sola Dei Gloria" ("Only to God Be the Glory").

He who despises music, as do all the fanatics, does not please me. Music is a gift of God, not a gift of men. . . . After theology, I accord to music the highest place and greatest honor.

—Martin Luther

Next to the Word of God music deserves the highest praise. The gift of language combined with the gift of song was given to man that he should proclaim the Word of God through music.

—Martin Luther

An old Jewish legend says that after God had created the world He called the angels to Himself and asked them what they thought of it. One of them said, "The only thing lacking is the sound of praise to the Creator." So God created music, and it was heard in the whisper of the wind and in the song of the birds. He also gave man the gift of song.

—*Our Daily Bread*

N

NEEDS

Christian psychiatrists say people have seven basic needs: Significance, Security, Acceptance, Love, Praise, Discipline, and the Lord!

As long as I have a want, I have a reason for living. Satisfaction is death.

—George Bernard Shaw

NEUROSES

A normal person is one who thinks two plus two are four and accepts it.

A psychotic person is one who thinks two plus two are five and believes it.

A neurotic person is one who thinks two plus two are four and it bothers him.

NEW BIRTH

Dear Abby:

"Please explain in simple, pool-hall language what it means to be born again." B. H. Carlton.

She answered, "That means they have accepted Jesus Christ as their Savior and have put their faith and trust in Him."

A man noticed one morning that his name was in the death column of the newspaper. In indignation he called the newspaper office and asked them why they put his name in the obituary column. The man on the other side of the line said, "Just a second. I'll go see about it." He came back and said, "Yes, you are right. We have made a mistake. But don't worry. In the paper tomorrow we will put your name in the birth column."

When we are saved our name is put out of the death column of the dead in sin, to the birth column of those who have been born again.

Once an Indian came to America and wanted to become a citizen of our country. First he said, "I will change my name." But he was still an Indian. Then he renounced his form of dress, but he was still an Indian. Then he learned the language of America, but he still wasn't an American citizen.

The only way he could be a true American was to have been born in America. So with the sinner. He can become a citizen of the heavenly family, a child of God, only by being born into it by faith in Jesus Christ.

NEW YEAR

Jonathan Edwards (1703–1758) made five resolutions in his youth.

1. Live with all my might while I do live (he died at 55).
2. Never lose one moment of time, but improve it in the most profitable way possible.
3. Never do anything I should despise or think meanly of in another.
4. Never do anything out of revenge.
5. Never do anything which I should be afraid to do if it were the last hour of my life.

Dear Master, for this coming year
just one request I bring:

I do not pray for happiness,
 Or any earthly thing—
I do not ask to understand
 The way Thou leadest me,
But this I ask: Teach me to do
 The thing that pleaseth Thee.
I want to know Thy guiding voice,
 To walk with Thee each day.
Dear Master, make me swift to hear
 And ready to obey.
And thus the year I now begin
 A happy year will be—
If I am seeking just to do
 The thing that pleaseth Thee.

Another year is dawning: Dear Father, let
 it be,
In working or in waiting, another year with
 Thee;
Another year of progress, another year of
 praise,
Another year of proving Thy presence all
 the days.
Another year of mercies, of faithfulness
 and grace,
Another year of gladness in the shining of
 Thy face;
Another year of leaning upon Thy loving
 breast.
Another year of trusting, of quiet, happy rest.
Another year of service, of witness for Thy
 love;
Another year of training for holier work
 above.
Another year is dawning: Dear Father, let
 it be,
On earth or else in heaven, another year
 for Thee.
 —Francis Ridley Havergal

During the coming year, may you have . . .
 Enough happiness to keep you sweet;
 Enough trials to keep you strong;
 Enough sorrow to keep you human;
 Enough hope to keep you happy;
 Enough failure to keep you humble;
 Enough success to keep you eager;
 Enough friends to give you comfort;
 Enough faith and courage in yourself,
  your business, and your country to
  banish your depression;
 Enough money to meet your needs;

Enough determination to make each day
 a better day than yesterday.
 —Everett Melton Garrett

I know not what awaits me
 As dawns another year;
The path untrod I cannot see,
 Yet knows my heart no fear!
I know not whether long or short
 My pilgrimage will be—
But I'll daily praise my God in song
 For all His love for me.
With joy I greet the year—
 It cannot bring me ill
Since Christ my Lord is ever near,
 My soul with peace to fill!

Recipe for a Happy New Year
I will:
 Like Enoch—walk in daily fellowship with my Heavenly Father.
 Like Abraham—trust implicitly in my God.
 Like Job—be patient under all circumstances.
 Like Joseph—turn my back on all seductive advances.
 Like Moses—choose to suffer rather than enjoy the pleasures of sin.
 Like Caleb and Joshua—refuse to be discouraged because of numbers.
 Like Gideon—advance, even though my friends are few.
 Like David—lift up my eyes to the hills from which comes my help.
 Like Jehoshaphat—prepare my heart to seek the Lord.
 Like Daniel—commune with God at all times and in all places.
 Like Andrew—strive to lead others to Christ.
 Like Stephen—manifest a forgiving spirit toward all who seek my hurt.
 Like Paul—forget those things that are behind and press forward.
 —Adapted from *Gospel-Lite*

NEW YEAR'S RESOLUTIONS
Fifty-five percent of Americans keep their New Year's resolutions for one month, 40 percent for six months, and 19 percent for two years.

NEW YORK

An executive was notified that he was being transferred from a Midwest office to New York. His small daughter, having lived all her short life where they were, was very unhappy about the move.

The night before the moving vans came she was saying her prayers. She went through the usual, "God bless Mommy and Daddy," then added, "I guess I'd better tell you, too, God, that this is good-bye. I won't be able to pray to you anymore—we're moving to New York."

—Bits & Pieces

NUTRITION

If you drop a slice of bread with jelly on it, it always lands jelly-side down. It's God's way of telling you that you shouldn't snack between meals.

—Bits & Pieces

I'm all for yogurt, tofu, wheat germ, fish oil, and all those other good, healthy, nutritional things. But please, not while I'm eating.

—Bob Orben

An older man told a friend he didn't like natural foods marked as having no preservatives, no artificial coloring, no additives, no starch, no sugar, no salt, no cholesterol, no fat. "Why not?" his friend asked. The older man answered, "Because at my age I need all the preservatives I can get."

O

OBEDIENCE

A missionary translator was struggling to find a word for obedience, but couldn't. One day he called his dog to him, and the dog came running. A national said, "Your dog was all ear." That gave the translator the word he needed for obedience—"to be all ear."

Only those who obey can believe and only those who believe can obey.

—Dietrich Bonhoeffer

God uses broken things: broken soil and broken clouds to produce grain; broken grain to produce bread; broken bread to feed our bodies. He wants our stubbornness broken into humble obedience.

—The Vance Havner Quote Book

A little girl asked her girlfriend if she could go on a picnic with her. "Just a minute. I'll go ask my mother." When she came back she told her that her mother told her she couldn't go. The other little girl then said, "Aw, you probably didn't talk hard enough. Don't let your mother go at that. Go beg her some and then she'll probably let you go."

"Oh, no," she answered. "When my mother says 'no' she doesn't change her mind. She knows what's best for me, so I'll do what she says."

How much Christians should be like that—willing to take what God says, realizing that He knows what's best for us.

The Lord had a job for me,
  But I had so much to do.
I said, "You'll get somebody else,
  Or wait'll I get through."
I don't know how the Lord made out,
  No doubt He got along,
But I felt kind of sneaking like,
  I knew I'd done God wrong.
One day I needed the Lord,
  Needed Him right away;
But He never answered me at all,
  And I could hear Him say,
Down in my accusing heart:
  "Child of Mine, I've got too much to do
You get somebody else
  Or wait'll I get through!"
Now when the Lord has a job for me
  I never try to shirk.
I drop what I have on my hands
  And do the Lord's good work.
And my affairs can run along
  Or wait'll I get through,
For nobody else can do the work
  That God's marked out for you!

An aviation cadet on a practice flight was suddenly stricken with blindness. Frantically, he contacted the control tower and told of his desperate plight. His commanding officer radioed back, "Don't be afraid, just do what I tell you!" After being advised to keep circling the field until all was clear for a landing, the sightless pilot was instructed to begin losing altitude. As the aircraft approached the runway, the officer's voice called out encouragingly, "You're coming in right on target!" The cadet, giving unquestioning obedience to his commander, brought the plane down safely.

—*Our Daily Bread*

Abraham Lincoln once told of a farmer who was trying to teach his son how to plow a straight furrow. After the horse had been hitched up and everything was ready, he told the boy to keep his eye on some object at the other end of the field and plow straight toward it. "Do you see that cow lying down over there?" he asked. "Keep your eye on her and plow straight ahead." The boy started plowing and the father went about his chores. When he returned a little later to see what progress had been made he was shocked to find, instead of the straight line, something that looked more like a question mark. The boy had obeyed his instructions. The trouble was—the cow had moved.

Nothing will ever be attempted if all possible objections must first be overcome.
—Samuel Johnson

OBSERVATION

A farmer couldn't tell his two horses apart, so he tried cutting the tail off of one horse. This didn't work because it grew right back. Then he cut the mane off the other horse. This didn't work either because it grew right back. Finally he measured them and found that the white horse was two inches taller than the black horse.
—*Elberton Star*

You can do a lot of observing by just watching.
—Yogi Berra

OBSTACLES

Advice columnist Abigail Van Buren illustrated man's ability to overcome obstacles when she wrote:

—Cripple him, and you have a Sir Walter Scott.

—Lock him in a prison cell, and you have a John Bunyan.

—Bury him in the snows of Valley Forge, and you have a George Washington.

—Afflict him with asthma as a child, and you have a Theodore Roosevelt.

—Make him play second fiddle in an obscure South American orchestra, and you have a Toscanini.

—Deny her the ability to see, hear, and speak, and you have a Helen Keller.

There is an old legend of a benevolent king who had his men place a great heavy stone on a certain roadway over which all his subjects would have to travel. He then hid himself to see who would try to remove the stone. No one stopped to try to remove the stone, but all worked their way around it, loudly blaming the king for not keeping the roadway clear. Finally, a poor peasant farmer on his way to town with a load of vegetables which he hoped to sell in the marketplace came to the blocked roadway. He laid down his load and with considerable effort and loss of time managed to move the great stone to the side of the roadway. Then, turning to leave, he spied a purse which had been under the stone. He opened the purse and found it to be filled with pieces of gold, with a note from the king indicating that it was all to be the property of the one who would remove the stone.
—C. Reuben Anderson

Clarence Jones had plowed around a large rock in one of his fields for years. He had broken several plowshares and a cultivator on it and had grown rather morbid about the rock.

After breaking another plowshare one fall, and remembering all the trouble the rock had caused him through the years, he finally determined to do something about it.

When he put his crowbar under the rock,

he was surprised to discover that it was only six inches thick and that he could break it up easily. As he was carting it away he had to smile, remembering all the trouble the rock had caused him and how easily it would have been to have fixed it sooner.

Obstacles are those frightening things you see when you take your eyes off the goal.

OFFERINGS

A family was driving home from church. They were complaining, "The sermon was dry." "The people were unfriendly." "The music was bad,"

The boy said, "I didn't think it was so bad. After all, we got in for only one dollar."

A pastor took an offering for a building fund drive. He connected electric wires to each pew with buttons in the pulpit.

"How many will give $1,000?"

Then he pushed the first button and all in the first row jumped up.

Then he asked, "How many will give $500?"

He pushed the second button and all in the second row jumped up. And he continued this on until the last row. "How many will give $5?"

No one jumped. The pastor wondered what was wrong. He pushed and pushed the button. Then he went back to the pew and there were several electrocuted Scotsmen lying on the pew.

The minister asked, "Is there anyone in the congregation who wants a prayer said for their failings?" "Yes," came an answer from a man in the front row. "I'm a spendthrift. I throw money around recklesslike." "Very well," said the minister. "We will join in prayer for the brother here—just after the collection plate has been passed around."

One Sunday morning the preacher took the offering in church and when the ushers began to pass the plates, he himself put in a quarter. The offering was not very large that day and the preacher's son who was very observant said, "Daddy, maybe you would have gotten more out if you had put more in!"

A man, looking for a place to stay, had a hard time finding a hotel with a vacancy. Finally he came to a hotel that had only one room. "But," the clerk informed him, "this room has not been used for a very long time. It seems to have a bit of mystery attached to it. People will even leave the hotel from that room in the wee hours of the night. They claim it has ghosts in it, and they hear strange noises and rattling of chains, etc."

"Oh, well," the man said in an unconcerned manner, "that's okay. I need a place to stay so I'll take it." Then he went up to the room, got ready for bed, and sure enough, he began to hear the strange noises and chains rattling. Then he saw ghosts come into the room. However, the unfrightened man, hesitating for a moment, then said, "Will the ushers please come forward." At that moment, the ghosts immediately departed, and he was never troubled with ghosts again!

A minister was speaking just before the offering was to be taken. He encouraged the congregation to give, speaking with forcefulness and to some length until one arose and said, "See here, preacher, I thought you said the water of life was free." The minister replied, "It sure is, brother, but it sure does cost a lot to get it piped up to all of you."

A preacher announced from the pulpit that a brother had neglected to lock the door of his chicken house the night before with the result that most of his fowls were missing.

"I have my suspicions who stole those chickens," the preacher said, "and I also believe that such a low-down person isn't likely to put money in the collection plate that will now be passed." The result was a record-breaking collection.

An old preacher used to say, "Bring three books with you to church: the Bible, a hymn book, and your pocketbook."

OLD AGE (Also see AGE and MIDDLE AGE)

If I'd known I was going to live this long,
I'd have taken better care of myself.
—Mickey Mantle

"Your age, please?" asked the census taker.
"Well," said the woman, "let me figure it out. I was 18 when I was married and my husband was 30. He is now 60, or twice as old as he was then, so I am now 36."

More people would live to a ripe old age if they weren't too busy providing for it.

Do not resent growing old. Many are denied the privilege.

How do I know my youth is all spent?
Well, my get up and go has got up and went.
But in spite of it all, I am able to grin
When I think of the places my get up has been.
Old age is golden, so I've heard it said.
But sometimes I wonder as I get into bed.
With my ears in a drawer, my teeth in a cup,
My eyes on the table, until I wake up.
Ere sleep dims my eyes, I say to myself,
Is there anything else I should put on the shelf?
And I'm happy to say as I close my door
My friends are the same, or perhaps even more.
When I was young my slippers were red,
I could kick up my heels up over my head.
When I grew older, my slippers were blue,
But still I could dance the whole night through.
Now that I'm old, my slippers are black,
I walk to the store and puff my way back.
The reason I know my youth is all spent,
My get up and go has got up and went.
But I really don't mind,
When I think with a grin
Of all of the places my get up has been.

In a seminar for senior citizens, a person asked a geriatrics specialist, "When do the signs of old age begin?" The doctor thought for a moment and then answered, "At conception."

Just a line to say I'm living,
That I'm not among the dead.
Though I'm getting more forgetful
And more mixed up in the head.
For sometimes I can't remember
When I stand at the foot of the stair,
If I must go up for something
Or if I've just come down from there.
And before the fridge so often
My poor mind is filled with doubt,
Have I just put food away, or
Have I come to take it out?
And there're times when it's dark out,
With my night cap on my head
I don't know if I'm retiring
Or just getting out of bed.
So if it's my turn to write you
There's no need of getting sore,
I may think that I have written
And don't want to be a bore.
Remember—I do love you,
And I wish that you were here;
But now it's really mail time
So I must say, "Good-bye, dear."
There I stood beside the mailbox,
With a face so very red.
Instead of mailing you my letter,
I had opened it instead!
—Rose Mary Hogan

People grow old only by deserting their sense of mission and values.
—Mary Kampleman

You stop growing when you stop learning.
—Henry Ford

In the early church there was a saying that a man should not be made a bishop until he was fifty because then he would be beyond the disorders of youth.

Agatha Christie once said of her husband, "I married an archaeologist because the older I grow, the more he appreciates me."

H. A. Ironside prayed, "Oh, God, keep me from becoming a foolish old man. Help me end well."

A retired professor in his nineties is still publishing significant works. He has trouble walking, but, as he said, "It is better to die from the feet up than the head down."

We have always needed old people to keep things from going too fast and young people to keep them from going too slow. Youth has fire and age has light and we need them both.
— *The Vance Havner Quote Book*

Why is it when you're seven, today is forever and tomorrow never, but when you're seventy, tomorrow is yesterday before you knew it was today.
— Sue Jane Purcell

Everyone wants to live long, but no one wants to be called old.
— Icelandic proverb

Henri Nouwen, a Catholic priest, asked the question, "Is my growing old making me any closer to Christ? Am I only getting older or am I getting more godly?"

Don't think of yourself as growing old. Just think of yourself as getting one day closer to Medicare.

Amos Alonzo Stagg was the founder of football. When Stagg reached age 102, a newsman took his photo at a nursing home. As the newsman got ready to leave, he said, "I hope I can come back next year and take your photo when you're 103." Stagg said, "You look pretty healthy to me. I think you'll make it."

A friend of Daniel Auber engaged him in conversation as they descended the grand stairway at the opera. "My friend, we're all getting older, aren't we?" he observed. Auber sighed, "Well, there's no help for it. Aging seems to be the only way to live a long time."
— *The Little, Brown Anecdote Book*

Beethoven composed some of his most glorious musical works toward the end of his life when he was completely deaf. Milton wrote some of his most magnificent poetry during his last years of blindness.

The world would have been greatly impoverished had there been no Beethoven's Ninth Symphony and no *Paradise Lost*.
— J. Oswald Sanders

The young and the old have all the answers. Those in between are stuck with the questions.
— *Bits & Pieces*

Prayer for Older People

Lord, Thou knowest I am growing older. Keep me from the idea that I must express myself on every subject. Release me from the craving to meddle in everyone's affairs. Keep my tongue from the recital of endless details of the past which do not interest others. Seal my lips when I am inclined to tell of my aches and pains. They are increasing with the years, and my love to speak of them grows sweeter as time goes by. Teach me the glorious lesson that occasionally I may be wrong. Make me thoughtful but not interfering, helpful but not bossy. With my vast store of wisdom and experience it does seem a pity not to use it all, but Thou knowest Lord, that I want a few friends left at the end. So help me to pray more, say less. And beyond all this, let me continue to flourish spiritually and bring forth fruit to Thy glory even in old age. Amen!

Lord Beaconsfield, British statesman and novelist, summed up his philosophy of life in these words, "Youth is a mistake, manhood a struggle, and old age a regret."

Wrinkles should merely show where smiles have been.
— Mark Twain

When John Wesley was an old man, striking testimony was borne to the radiance of his personality. "Wherever he went he diffused a portion of his own felicity. In him old age appeared delightful, like an evening without a cloud. And it was impossible to observe him without wishing, 'May my latter end be like him!'"

A nationwide "Older Americans" survey conducted by the Colonial Penn Group among two hundred customers over the age of one hundred revealed that material possessions were low on the list of what they considered the most valuable contributors to the quality of life.

Most of them believed children, friends, and relatives to be life's most precious possessions. When asked what they miss most about the good old days, personal relationships top the list, with good health and mobility following close behind. Material possessions were rarely mentioned.

—*Bits & Pieces*

My false teeth fit me dandy,
My hearing aid's just fine,
My glasses come in handy—
But I sure do miss my mind.

How can I be over the hill when I never made it to the top?
—Mrs. O. E. Anderson

Look at the bright side: No matter how old you are, you're younger than you'll ever be again.
—Bob Orben

An old body may house a young mind. When Alexander Graham Bell reached the age of seventy-five, a friend commented, "The most remarkable thing about Dr. Bell is that he is younger in mind that most men half his age. Mentally he seems to have discovered a fountain of youth which keeps him perennially alert and vigorous." Bell followed three rules of study: observe, remember, and compare—principles which belong to a youthful outlook on life.
—Leslie B. Flynn

When Henry Longfellow was well along in years, his head as white as snow but his cheeks as red as a rose, an ardent admirer asked him how it was that he was able to keep so vigorous and write so beautifully.

Pointing to a blooming apple tree nearby, he replied, "That apple tree is very old, but I never saw prettier blossoms on it than those it now bears. The tree grows a little new wood every year, and I suppose it is out of that new wood that those blossoms come. Like the apple tree, I try to grow a little new wood every year."

Benjamin Ririe retired as a missionary with the China Inland Mission at the age of seventy. When he was eighty and found time hanging on his hands, he decided to learn New Testament Greek, because he had lacked the opportunity when he was younger. Ririe became proficient in reading the Greek New Testament.

At ninety, he attended a refresher course in Greek at a Toronto seminary. When he was one hundred, he was present at a meeting at which I was speaking. In his pocket was a small, well-worn Greek lexicon he used to brush up his language skill as he traveled on the subway to and from the meeting.
—J. Oswald Sanders

My middle name is Wendell; I'm named after Wendell P. Loveless, who was associated for many years with the Moody Bible Institute in Chicago, especially with the radio station WMBI. He lived into his nineties and was alert to the very end. During one of our visits with him, he told me and my wife, "I don't go out much now because my parents won't let me—Mother Nature and Father Time!"
—Warren W. Wiersbe

Miguel Cervantes wrote *Don Quixote* when he was almost seventy years old. John Milton wrote *Paradise Regained* when he was sixty-three. Noah Webster wrote his monumental dictionary at seventy. Socrates gave his wise philosophies at seventy. Ignace Paderewski still gave concerts before large audiences at seventy-nine. William Gladstone still presented a powerful figure in political circles at eighty. Clara Barton founded the American Red Cross at fifty-nine. Benjamin Franklin helped to frame the U.S. Constitution at eighty-one. Benjamin Disraeli became prime minister of England for the second time at seventy.

Johann von Goethe completed *Faust* at eighty-two. Thomas Edison worked busily in his lab at eighty-three. Alfred Tennyson published his memorable poem, *Crossing the Bar*, at eighty-three. Guiseppe Verdi composed *Othello* at seventy-three, *Falstaff* in his seventies, and *Te Deum* at eighty-five. Michelangelo was in his late eighties when he painted some of his masterpieces. Arturo Toscanini conducted an orchestra at eighty-seven. Grandma Moses did many of her paintings after ninety. The Earl of Halsburg was ninety when he began preparing a twenty-volume revision of English law. Galileo made his greatest discovery when he was seventy-three. At sixty-nine, Hudson Taylor was still vigorously working on the mission field, opening up new territories in Indochina.

Old age occurs the moment you realize there isn't something wonderful about to happen around the corner. In some people this occurs very soon; in others, not at all.

The advantage age has over youth is that youth knows nothing about being old, whereas the old know all about being young.

—*Bits & Pieces*

Dan Rather said to a man who is 106, "What's your secret to a long life?" He rocked for a long time and then finally said, "Keep breathing."

There are three stages to life: youth, middle age, and "You're looking good."

The first sign of old age is when you hear snap, crackle, and pop and it isn't your cereal.

Old age is that time of life when you know all the answers and nobody asks you the questions.

When I was in the sixth grade, an elderly lady in the community visited our one-room schoolhouse to help us prepare for a Christmas program. She was energetic but quite wrinkled. After she left, one of the students said, "Boy, I never want to get that old!" The teacher, who overheard him, asked, "So you want to die young?" The youngster said, "No." To which the teacher responded, "Well, it is going to be one or the other."

—Herbert Vander Lugt

At age twenty, we worry about what others think of us. At forty, we don't care what they think of us. At sixty, we discover they haven't been thinking about us at all.

—Jack Falson

Life really isn't fair. You eat properly, exercise and take good care of yourself for sixty years—and what's your reward? Old age!

To me, old age is always fifteen years older than I am.

—Bernard Baruch

Never regret growing old; many are denied that privilege.

Age is a matter of mind. If you don't mind, it doesn't matter.

Henry Ford, who lived to eighty-four, was asked late in life how he got so much done. He said, "I never stand up when I can sit down; and I never sit down when I can lie down."

When Konrad Adenauer, still chancellor, was approaching the age of ninety, he succumbed to a heavy cold. His personal physician, unable to be of very much help, had to put up with Adenauer's impatience. "I'm not a magician," protested the harassed doctor. "I can't make you young again."

"I haven't asked you to," retorted the chancellor. "All I want is to go on getting older."

—*The Little, Brown Anecdote Book*

Old age is when everything finally begins to click, including your joints, knees, etc. It's when everything that works, hurts.

Old age is when you look forward to a dull evening. Or it's when you get out of the shower and you're glad the mirror is fogged up. It's when your back goes out more often than you do.

How do I know my youth has been spent?
Because my get-up-and-go got up and went!
But in spite of all that I am able to grin
When I think where my get-up-and-go has been.

"Old Age is golden," I've heard it said,
But sometimes I wonder when I go to bed;
I put my ears in a drawer, my teeth in a cup,
My eyes on a table, until I wake up.
E're sleep dims my eyes, I say to myself
Is there anything else I should lay on the shelf?

You know you're getting old when . . .
   resisting temptation is not as hard as recognizing it.
   you know your way around, but you don't feel like going.
   you go into a record store and expect to see records.
   you're seven around the neck, thirty-eight around the waist, and 126 around the golf course.

—Jim Murray

Everything is farther away than it used to be. It is even twice as far to the corner and they have added a hill.

I have given up running for the bus; it leaves earlier than it used to.

It seems to me that they are making the stairs steeper than in the old days. And have you noticed the smaller print they use in the newspapers?

There is no sense in asking anyone to read aloud anymore, as everybody speaks in such a low voice I can hardly hear them.

The material in dresses is so skimpy now, especially around the hips and waist, that it is almost impossible to reach one's shoelaces. And the sizes don't run the way they used to. The 12s and 14s are so much smaller.

Even people are changing. They are so much younger than they used to be when I was their age. On the other hand, people my own age are so much older than I am.

I ran into an old classmate the other day and she has aged so much that she didn't recognize me.

I got to thinking about the poor dear while I was combing my hair this morning and in doing so I glanced at my own reflection. Really now, they don't even make good mirrors like they used to.

OPPORTUNITIES

We are faced with great opportunities brilliantly disguised as impossible situations.
—Chuck Swindoll

If we haven't the best, we can make the best of what we have.

A wise man will make more opportunities than he finds.
—Francis Bacon

Do what you can, with what you have, where you are.
—Theodore Roosevelt

Opportunity seldom knocks at your door. It now leaves an 800 number.

Recognize your responsibilities and you will see your opportunities.
—William Arthur Ward

When asked the secret of her joy and serenity, a grand, elderly woman replied, "I make the most of what comes and the least of what goes."

Gentlemen, we are surrounded by insurmountable opportunities.
—Pogo

Luck is what happens when preparation meets opportunity.
—Elmer Letterman

The Chinese call luck opportunity, and they say it knocks every day at your door. Some people hear it; some do not. It's not enough to hear opportunity knock. You must let him in, greet him, make friends, and work together.

—Bernard Gittelson

In the days before modern harbors, a ship had to wait for the flood tide before it could make it to the port. The term for this situation in Latin was *ob portu*, that is, a ship standing over against a port, waiting for the moment when it could ride the turn of the tide to harbor.

The English word *opportunity* is derived from this original meaning. The captain and the crew were ready and waiting for it, that one moment, for they knew that if they missed it, they would have to wait for another tide to come in.

—*Bits & Pieces*

Results are obtained by exploiting opportunities, not by solving problems. All one can hope to get by solving problems is to restore normalcy.

—Peter Drucker

William Jennings Bryan gave an outstanding speech at the Democratic convention as the third time presidential candidate. Someone said, "That was an excellent message." Bryan replied, "I made use of an opportunity." Then he added, "That's about all we do in life: use or abuse our opportunities."

Opportunity is missed by most people because it is dressed in overalls and looks like work.

—Thomas Edison

OPTIMISM (Also see PESSIMISM)

When Goliath went to the Israelites, the soldiers all thought, "He's so big, we can never kill him." But David looked at him and thought, "He's so big, I can't miss."

Two bumper stickers express an optimistic outlook: "Onward through the fog" and "On with the dream."

A mayor, who was very proud of his city, was asked how the recession had affected it. He answered, "We don't have a recession here, but I will admit we are having the worst boom in many years."

Be so strong that nothing can disturb your peace of mind. Talk health, happiness, and prosperity to every person you meet. Make all your friends feel there is something in them. Look at the sunny side of everything. Think only of the best, work only for the best, and expect only the best. Be as enthusiastic about the success of others as you are about your own. Forget the mistakes of the past and press on to the greater achievements of the future. Give everyone a smile. Spend so much time improving yourself that you have no time left to criticize others. Be too big for worry and too noble for anger.

—Christian D. Larsen

When British Methodist preacher William Sangster learned that he had progressive muscular atrophy and could not get well, he made four resolutions and kept them to the end: (1) I will never complain; (2) I will keep the home bright; (3) I will count my blessings; (4) I will try to turn it to gain.

—Warren W. Wiersbe

A classic example of optimism is the seventy-year-old couple who bought some real estate and took out a thirty-year loan.

A man stopped to watch a Little League baseball game. He asked one of the youngsters what the score was.

"We're behind eighteen to nothing," was the answer.

"Well," said the man, "I must say you don't look discouraged."

"Discouraged?" the boy said, puzzled. "Why should we be discouraged? We haven't come to bat yet."

An optimist is a lady who puts her shoes on when the preacher says, "And now in conclusion."

Things turn out best for the people who make the best of the way things turn out.

I'm an optimist, but I'm an optimist who carries a raincoat.

—Sir Harold Wilson

The habit of looking on the best side of every event is worth more than a thousand pounds a year.

—Samuel Johnson

I'm not entirely an optimist who believes that the best will happen—and I'm not entirely a pessimist who believes that the worst will happen. You might say I'm a pessoptimist. I believe that the best will happen—but it won't be good enough.

A man had lost a leg in an accident and when he was picked up and discovered what had actually happened, he said to those around him, "Thank God it was the leg with the arthritis."

A pessimist says the rain will make mud; the optimist says it will lay the dust. The optimist says, "I am better today"; the pessimist says, "I was worse yesterday." The optimist says, "I'm glad I'm alive"; the pessimist says, "I'm sorry I must die." The optimist discovers some good even in evil; the pessimist finds some evil even in good.

If we can learn anything from reading history, it is that the optimists and enthusiasts have been right much more often than the pessimists and critics. For example, in 1899, Charles H. Deuell, Director of the U.S. Patent Office, wrote, "Everything that can be invented has been invented." In 1905 Grover Cleveland said, "Sensible and responsible women do not want to vote." Robert Millikan, Nobel Prize recipient in physics in 1923, said, "There is no likelihood man can ever tap the power of the atom." Lloyd Kelvin, president of the Royal Society, said in 1895, "Heavier than air flying machines are impossible." And in 1921, someone remarked, "Babe Ruth made a big mistake when he gave up pitching."

The pessimist sees only the dark side of the clouds and moans; the philosopher sees both the dark and bright side of the clouds and shrugs; and the optimist doesn't even see the clouds—he is walking on them.

—Leslie B. Flynn

The doormat to the pessimist is a welcome mat to the optimist.

—William Arthur Ward

An optimist is a man who undertakes a seemingly impossible task in a spirit of immeasurable enthusiasm, unbounded determination, unbelievable excitement, indestructible confidence, uncompromising thoroughness, and indefatigable persistence . . . with understandable success.

—William Arthur Ward

If you laugh at your troubles, there'll always be enough to laugh at.

An optimist is a man who, finding himself in hot water, decides he needs a bath anyway.

I figure there's no use in being too particular. I don't care which side my bread is buttered on. I always eat both sides anyway.

—Will Rogers

To an optimist, an alarm clock's ring is an invitation to opportunity, adventure, and service.

The optimist recognizes a responsibility in every crisis; the pessimist sees a crisis in every responsibility.

To the optimist, all doors have handles and hinges; to the pessimist, all doors have locks and latches.

—William Arthur Ward

I am a short-term pessimist and a long-term optimist.

—Kenneth L. Kantzer

The pessimist majors in mistakes, misfortunes, and misery; the optimist accentuates assets, abundance, and advantages.

OPTOMETRIST

Sign in an optometrist's office: "If you don't see what you're looking for, you've come to the right place."

—*Farmer's Almanac*

ORDER

Most people believe in law and order as long as they can lay down the law and give the orders.

One of the advantages of being disorderly is that one is constantly making exciting discoveries.

—A. A. Milne

A man hurt his finger when he was downtown. He asked someone where to go for help. So he went to the building and there were two doors marked "Physical" and "Mental." He went in the "Physical" door. Inside that were two doors marked "Bone" and "Muscle." He went in the "Bone" door. Inside that were two doors: "Surgery" and "Therapy." He went in the "Surgery" door. Inside that were two other doors: "Major" and "Minor." He went in the door marked "Minor," and he was outside.

Someone said, "Did they help you in there?"

"No, but that's the most organized place I've ever seen."

ORDINATION

Ordination is the laying of empty hands on empty heads.

—Charles H. Spurgeon
(who was never ordained)

P

PAIN

God whispers to us in our joys, speaks to us in our difficulties, and shouts to us in our pain.

—C. S. Lewis

Pain is God's megaphone to rouse a deaf world.

—C. S. Lewis

PANIC

On a recent visit to Chad, Charles McCordic Jr. gave an illustration of panic. He had placed a hen on some duck's eggs. When the little ones hatched, the hen mothered them as any good mother would. They followed her about, pecking when she pecked and doing all the things expected of good little chicks. But one day they went near the pond, and the little ones took out across the water. Mother hen panicked. She ran back and forth on the bank clucking her frustration. "Don't you know you can't do that? Chicks don't swim, only dumb ducks do that!" But God had put something else into those babies and that was why they had webbed feet!

The photographer for a national magazine was assigned to get photos of a great forest fire. Smoke at the scene hampered him, and he asked his home office to hire a plane. Arrangements were made, and he was told to go at once to a nearby airport, where the plane would be waiting.

When he arrived at the airport, a plane was warming up near the runway. He jumped in with his equipment and yelled, "Let's go! Let's go!" The pilot swung the plane into the wind, and they soon were in the air.

"Fly over the north side of the fire," yelled the photographer, "and make three or four low level passes."

"Why?" asked the pilot.

"Because I'm going to take pictures," cried the photographer. "I'm a photographer and photographers take pictures!"

After a pause the pilot said, "You mean you're not the flight instructor?"

—*Bits & Pieces*

PARADOXES

To conquer we must surrender (Matt. 5:39; 1 Cor. 15:57).

To live, we must die (John 12:23, 25).

To save life, we must lose it (Matt. 10:39; Luke 17:33).

To get, we must give (Prov. 11:23, 25).

To reign, we must serve (Luke 12:42–44).

To be wise, we must become fools (1 Cor. 3:18).

To be exalted, we must become humble (Matt. 18:4; 23:12).

To be first, we must be last (Mark 9:35; Matt. 20:26).

We must be humble in order to be exalted.
We must take up our yoke in order to find peace and rest.
We must work in order to be stronger.
We must surrender in order to win.
We must die in order to live.
We must give in order to receive.

PARENTING

If you know his father and grandfather, you can trust his son.

—Moroccan proverb

We never know the love of a parent until we become parents ourselves.

—Henry Ward Beecher

There are only two lasting bequests we can hope to give our children. One of those is roots, the other is wings.

—Hodding Carter

One way to curb delinquency is to take parents off the street at night.

—Morrie Gallant

The trouble with being a parent is that by the time you're experienced, you're unemployable.

We are so busy giving our children what we never had that we forget to give them what we did have.

—James Dobson

Success in Parenting

You can use most any measure
When you're speaking of success.
You can measure it in fancy home,
Expensive car or dress.
But the measure of your real success
Is the one you cannot spend.

It's the way your kids describe you
When talking to a friend.

—Martin Buxbaum

Sound really does travel slower than light. The advice parents give to their eighteen-year-olds doesn't reach them until they're about forty.

—Bob Orben

When it comes to clothes, I never argue when our kids come back from the store with something that's garish, outlandish, bizarre, in bad taste, and an affront to all normal sensibilities. I just say I like it. They take it back the next morning.

—Bob Orben

Parents who do not carry out their duty of instruction by example fail to assume their responsibility in a manner which is detrimental to our Christian society and increases the need for teaching by organized religion. If we have an enduring Christian nation, we must strive to reduce crime. The plain and simple maxims of the Bible contain the essential rules which should govern human conduct.

—J. Edgar Hoover

Between the child and God stands the parent: a separating wall or a connecting link.

PASSION

When a businessman in Pennsylvania was asked what he looks for in hiring employees, the first thing he mentioned was "passion."

PASTORING

The perfect pastor has been described as one who preaches exactly twenty minutes and then sits down. He condemns sin but never hurts anyone's feelings. He labors from 8 A.M. to 10 P.M. in every kind of work, from preaching to custodial service. He makes sixty dollars a week, wears good clothes, buys good books regularly, has a nice family, drives a good car, and gives thirty dollars a week to the church. He also stands ready to contribute to every good work that comes along. The ideal pastor is twenty-six years old and has been preaching for thirty years. He is at once tall and short, thin and heavyset, and handsome. He has one brown eye and one blue; his hair is parted in the middle with left side dark and straight and the right side brown and wavy. He has a burning desire to work with teenagers and spends all his time with older folks. He smiles all the time with a straight face because he has a sense of humor that keeps him seriously dedicated to his work. He makes fifteen calls a day on church members, spends all his time evangelizing the unchurched, and is never out of his office!

If the pastor of the smallest church in North Carolina became the president of the United States, he'd be stepping down.
—Vance Havner

If I accept the call, I must have a two-month vacation and the privilege of taking an occasional lecture tour. My lecture on "Over the Wall in a Basket" is worth two drachmas of any man's money!
    Sincerely yours,
    Paul

Pastoring a church combines all the features of crossing the Grand Canyon on a tightrope, lunching with Gargantua, and chasing a rainbow. A pastor needs the sprint of the Boy Who Stood on the Burning Deck, the intestinal fortitude of Hercules, and the courage of David meeting Goliath. Doing the most important job of the country, he must tackle the tasks of Superman, and while doing it, he is considered a legitimate target for indiscriminate rock heaving.
    To state the situation a little more elegantly and scripturally: the pastor needs the power of the Spirit, the love of God, and the grace, wisdom, and patience of Christ, to carry on with his great work.

Dear Pastoral Search Committee,
    This pastoral search chain letter is meant to bring you just the right man to serve as your pastor. Unlike other chain letters it does not cost money. Just send a copy of this letter to six other churches that

are tired of their ministers; then bundle up your pastor and send him to the church at the top of the list. In six weeks, you will receive 16,436 ministers delivered directly to you. One of them should be a dandy.
    P.S. But beware . . . do not break the chain. One church did and they got their old preacher back.

How to Get Rid of a Pastor

1. Look him straight in the eye and say "amen," and he'll preach himself to death.
2. Give him a living wage. He's been on a starvation salary for so long that he'll eat himself to death.
3. Brag about all his good points to him, and he'll work himself to death.
4. Go to him and tell him you want to help in the church, and he'll have a heart attack and die.
5. Have the church unite together in prayer for him and really get behind him and help him, and then a bigger church will call him from you.

Dear Brethren:
    Doubtless you will remember the invitation you extended to me to come over to Macedonia and help the people in that section. You will pardon me for saying that I'm somewhat surprised that you should expect a man of my standing in the church to seriously consider a call on such meager information. There are a number of things I should like to learn before giving my decision, and I would appreciate your dropping me a line, addressed to Troas.
    No mention was made of a salary I was to receive. While it is true that I am not preaching for money, there is the certainty that these things must be taken into account. I have been through a long and expensive course of training; in fact, I may say with reasonable pride that I am a Sanhedrin man! The day is past when you can expect a man to rush into a field without some idea of the support he is about to receive. Kindly give the word to the good brethren to get together and see what you can do in the way of support.
    You have told me nothing about

Macedonia beyond the implication that the place needs help. What are the social advantages? Is the church well organized?

I recently had a fine offer to return to Damascus at an increase of salary, and I am told that I made a very favorable impression on the church at Jerusalem. You might mention these facts.

For recommendations you can write to Rev. S. Peter, D.D., Jerusalem, Palestine. I will say that I am a first-class mixer and especially strong in argumentative preaching.

—Paul

If he is young, he lacks experience; if he is gray, he is too old; if he has five or six children, he has too many; if he has none, he is setting a bad example.

If his wife sings in the choir, she is being forward; if she does not, she is not interested in her husband's work.

If he speaks from notes, he has canned sermons and is dry; if he is extemporaneous, he is too deep.

If he spends too much time in study, he neglects his people; if he visits, he is a gadabout.

If he is attentive to the poor, he is playing to the grandstand; if to the wealthy, he is trying to be an aristocrat.

If he suggests improvement for the church, he is a dictator; if he makes no suggestions, he is a figurehead.

If he uses too many illustrations, he neglects the Bible; if not enough, he is not clear.

If he condemns wrong, he is cranky; if he does not, he is a compromiser.

If he preaches an hour, he is windy; if less, he is lazy.

If he preaches the truth, he is offensive; if not, he is a hypocrite.

If he fails to please everybody, he has no convictions.

If he preaches tithing, he is a money-grabber; if he does not, he is failing to develop his people.

If he receives a large salary, he is mercenary; if a small salary, it proves he is not worth much.

If he preaches all the time, the people get tired of hearing the man; if he invites guest preachers, he is shirking his responsibility. Yes! They say the preacher has an easy time.

The ministry of a pastor is like a full moon—it brings light to many darkened souls, but also causes many dogs to bark.

A pastor left the pastorate after twenty years. He decided to become a funeral director. Somebody asked him, "Why did you do that?"

He answered, "Well, I spent about twelve years trying to straighten out John. He never did get straightened out. I spent fourteen months trying to straighten out the marriage of the Smith's, and it never did get straightened out. I spent three years trying to straighten out Susan, and she never did get straightened out. Now when I straighten them out, they stay straight."

Gentlemen: Understanding your pulpit is vacant, I should like to apply for the position. I have many qualifications. I've been a preacher with much success and also some success as a writer. Some say I'm a good organizer. I've been a leader most places I've been.

I'm over 50 years of age. I have never preached in one place for more than three years. In some places I have left town after my work caused riots and disturbances. I must admit I have been in jail three or four times, but not because of any real wrongdoing.

My health is not too good, though I still get a great deal done. The churches I have preached in have been small, though located in several large cities.

I've not gotten along well with religious leaders in towns where I have preached. In fact, some have threatened me and even attacked me physically. I am not too good at keeping records. I have been known to forget whom I have baptized.

However, if you can use me, I shall do my best for you.

The board member looked over the committee. "Well, what do you think? Shall we call him?"

The good church folks were aghast. Call

an unhealthy, trouble-making, absent-minded ex-jailbird? Was the board member crazy? Who signed the application? Who had such colossal nerve?

The board member eyed them all keenly before he answered. "It's signed, 'The Apostle Paul.'"

If the pastor is young, they say he lacks experience; if his hair is gray, then he's too old for the young people.

If he has five or six children, he has too many; if he has no children, then he's setting a bad example.

If he preaches from notes, he has canned sermons and is too dry; if his messages are extemporaneous, he is not deep.

If he is attentive to the poor people in the church, they claim he is playing to the grandstand; if he pays attention to the wealthy, he is trying to be an aristocrat.

If he uses too many illustrations, he neglects the Bible; if he doesn't use enough illustrations, he isn't clear.

If he condemns wrong, he's cranky; if he doesn't preach against sin, he's a compromiser.

If he preaches the truth, he's offensive; if he doesn't preach the truth, then he's a hypocrite.

If he preaches tithing, he's a moneygrabber; if he doesn't preach scriptural giving, he is failing to develop his people.

If he drives an old car, he shames his congregation; if he drives a new car, then he is setting his affection on earthly things.

If he preaches all the time, the people get tired of hearing one man; if he invites guest speakers, he's shirking his responsibility.

If he receives a large salary, he's mercenary; if he receives only a small salary, well—it proves he isn't worth much anyway.

—Richard DeHaan

PATIENCE (Also see ENDURANCE)

There are three qualifications for missionaries: patience, patience, patience.

—J. Hudson Taylor

One moment of patience may ward off a great disaster; one moment of impatience may ruin a whole life.

—*Bits & Pieces*

No one treated Lincoln with more contempt than did Edwin Stanton, who denounced Lincoln's policies and called him a "low cunning clown." Stanton had nicknamed him "the original gorilla" and said that explorer Paul Du Chaillu was a fool to wander about in Africa trying to capture a gorilla when he could have found one so easily in Springfield, Missouri. Lincoln said nothing in reply. In fact, he made Stanton his war minister because Stanton was the best man for the job. He treated him with every courtesy. The years wore on.

The night came when an assassin's bullet struck down Lincoln in a theater. In a room off to the side where Lincoln's body was taken, stood Stanton that night. As he looked down on the silent, rugged face of the president, Stanton said through his tears, "There lies the greatest ruler of men the world has ever seen." The patience of love had conquered in the end.

—*Illustrations for Biblical Preaching*

In his book *Five Musts of the Christian Life*, F. B. Meyer told about a conversation he had with several believers in the home of William Wilberforce. As they were talking about the difficulties of living as a Christian, a minister, well advanced in years, arose and confessed that he was somewhat "short-fused." He recalled a time he was trying to control the students in a Sunday school class who were unusually boisterous. His patience was stretched to the breaking point. In fact, he was just about ready to blow his top when he felt inclined to pray, "Lord, give me Your patience, for mine is giving out." In a moment, his spirit was calmed. He therefore decided right then to draw on the Lord's strength in every difficult situation.

One telephone operator turned to another and said, "He's a patient man. I was flustered and gave him a wrong number four times, and he said so kindly, 'You gave me the wrong number four times, operator. Try once again.' I'd like to meet that man." And the other inquired, "What is his number?" When she was told, she said, "I know him, he's my pastor." Then said the other, "I'm going to hear him preach."

A Quaker farmer had a stubborn mule. Most farmers would get impatient and strike the mule to get them to go. But the Quaker's religion kept him from that. One day he said to his mule, "Thou knowest I can't kick or hit thee because of my religion. Thou knowest I must be patient. But what thou don't knowest is that I can sell thee to an Episcopalian."

The secret of patience is doing something else in the meantime.

He who can have patience can have what he will.

—Benjamin Franklin

Regardless of how much patience we have, we would prefer never to use any of it.

—James T. O'Brien

Simply wait on Him. So doing, we should be directed, supplied, protected, corrected, and rewarded.

—Vance Havner

Patience is something you admire greatly in the driver behind you, but not in the one ahead of you.

Patience is the necessary ingredient for genius.

PEACE

Sometimes God calms the storm, and sometimes He lets the storm rage and calms His child.

—Donna Wallis

A West Coast doctor took an informal poll among his patients to find out what wish each would make if his wish were granted. The tally was very interesting. Eighty-seven percent said that peace of mind was their paramount goal.

"What is peace?" A little boy answered, "Peace is when you feel all smooth inside."

On Admiral Perry's first boat cruise, before he was an admiral, he was scared stiff. He put his arms around the mast for three days. He wouldn't eat, and he wouldn't let go. The Scottish captain went out to see him. "Laddie, do you think the ship will sink?" "Yes." "Why don't you let go and prove it?"

Perry said later that his most exhilarating experience in life was when he gradually let go inch by inch and stepped back.

A submarine was on patrol during wartime and had to remain submerged overnight. When it resurfaced the next day, a friend on another ship radioed the captain, "How did you fare in that terrible storm last night?" Surprised, the officer exclaimed, "What storm? We didn't know there was one!"

Although the ocean surface had been whipped into huge waves by high winds, the vessel was not affected because the waters below were calm and tranquil.

R. J. Campbell went to see a lady who was dying in Brighton, England. He found her to be a person of means and education but ignorant of Christ and the plan of salvation. She knew Christ only as a great Teacher but nothing at all of redemption through Him. Her life story was one of sadness, stained with sorrow and sin. In the course of the conversation she sighed and said, "Oh that it were possible for some great strong friend to take my conscience as though it were his own that I may have a little peace!"

Remember the little boy who got into an argument with some boys twice his size? They thought he was crazy when he drew a line in the dirt and dared them to cross over. When they did, the little boy just smiled and said, "Now you're on my side."

—Bits & Pieces

In acceptance lieth peace
  O my heart be still;

Let thy restless worries cease
   And accept His will.
Though this test be not thy choice;
   It is His—therefore rejoice.
In His plan there cannot be
   Aught to make thee sad:
If this is His choice for Thee,
   Take it and be glad.
Make from it some lovely thing
   To the glory of Thy King.
Cease from sighs and murmuring,
   Sing His loving grace,
This thing means thy furthering
   To a wealthy place.
From thy fears He'll give release,
   In acceptance lieth peace.

In 1555 Nicholas Ridley was burned at the stake because of his witness for Christ. On the night before Ridley's execution, his brother offered to remain with him in the prison chamber to be of assistance and comfort. Nicholas declined the offer and replied that he meant to go to bed and sleep as quietly as ever he did in his life. Because he knew the peace of God, he could rest in the strength of the everlasting arms of his Lord to meet his need.

—Our Daily Bread

On a rough ocean crossing Mr. Jones became terribly seasick. At an especially rough time, a kindly steward patted Jones on the shoulder and said, "I know, sir, that it seems awful. But remember, no man ever died of seasickness." Mr. Jones lifted his green countenance to the steward's concerned face and replied, "Man, don't say that! It's only the wonderful hope of dying that keeps me alive."

God did not create hurry.

—Finnish proverb

During World War II in London there was a blitz bombing at night. The people stayed each night in underground protection. But one Christian lady just stayed at home and slept through all the bombing. When asked about it, she said, "Well, my God neither slumbers nor sleeps, and there's no need for both of us to stay awake!"

In 1873 a successful businessman lost all his material possessions in the great Chicago fire. This did not trouble him too much for he had set his affection on "things above." However, just a few weeks later, when his wife and children were on board the "Ville du Havre" to visit France, their ship was rammed by an English vessel and sank within two hours, claiming the lives of 226 people. Although his wife survived, all four of their children perished in the icy waters. While en route to Europe to join his wife, the man was given the tragic news and later shown the spot in the mid-Atlantic where the shipwreck occurred. Although heartsick with grief, Mr. Spafford suddenly felt an inrush of supernatural peace and comfort as he looked to the Lord for strength. With tears streaming down his face, he picked up a pen to record his feelings, and from his well-blest heart flowed these thrilling words, "When peace like a river attendeth my way, when sorrows like sea billows roll; whatever my lot, Thou hast taught me to say, 'It is well, it is well with my soul!'"

The sultan of Brunei, with an estimated fortune of $25 billion, is the richest man in the world. The basic source of his wealth are the rich Serio oil fields in Brunei.

The sultan—educated in Britain—owns the world's largest palace, a variety of airplanes, fleets of cars, and some of the world's top hotels, among them the Beverly Hills Hotel in California. He lives a life of opulent luxury. He knows that he is the target of burglars, kidnappers, terrorists, against whom he must be constantly guarded. He owns several private houses and hotels in and around London and makes it a point to move from one to the other without divulging his schedule to more than a few trusted intimates.

What he cannot purchase is what he treasures most—peace of mind.

A Japanese soldier by the name of Oneda had not heard that World War II was over. He continued to fight on a small island in the Philippines. People tried all kinds of ways to let him know that the war was over.

They dropped flyers and tried other ways to communicate to him. He said, "I will not stop fighting unless my captain personally tells me to quit." So they went back to Japan and found his captain and took him to the Philippines to tell the soldier. Then thirty years after the war was over, in 1974, he said, "I will now stop fighting because the last thing my captain told me was to fight to the end." Someone then asked him, "Has anything good happened to you in these thirty years?" He said, "No, nothing good has happened in these thirty years."

Nothing good happens when we are fighting and not at peace.

Peace rules the day when Christ rules the heart.

PEOPLE

People need people. Laurie was about three when she requested my aid in getting undressed. I was downstairs and she was upstairs. "You know how to undress yourself," I reminded her.

"Yes," she explained, "but sometimes people need people anyway, even if they know how to do things for themselves."

As I slowly lowered the newspaper, a strong feeling came over me, a mixture of delight, anger, and pride; delight in the realization that what I had just heard had crystallized many stray thoughts on interpersonal behavior; anger because Laurie stated so effortlessly what I had been struggling with for months; and pride because, after all, she is my daughter.

—William C. Schutz

You must live with people to know their problems, and live with God in order to solve them.

—Peter T. Forsyth

PERFECTION

Perfectionists are those who take great pains and give them to others.

There is scarcely anybody who is absolutely good for nothing, and hardly anybody good at everything.

—Philip Chesterfield

The trouble with a lot of us is we each want to be human, but we're expecting everybody else to be perfect.

Nothing would be done at all if a man waited until he could do it so well that no one would find fault with it.

—John Henry Newman

Michelangelo was once putting what appeared to be the finishing touches on a sculpture when a friend dropped by for a visit. Days later, the friend dropped by again and was surprised to find the artist still working on the same statue.

The statue looked the same to the friend as it had days earlier, so he said, "You haven't been working on this statue all this time, have you?"

"I have," said Michelangelo. "I've been busy retouching this part and polishing that part; I've softened this feature and brought out that muscle; I've given more expression to the lips and more energy to that arm."

"But all those things are so insignificant," said the friend. "they're mere trifles."

"That may be so," replied Michelangelo, "but trifles make perfection, and perfection is no trifle."

—*Bits & Pieces*

PERSECUTION

"That doctor," said the hypochondriac, "he says there's nothing wrong with me—he just doesn't like me personally. He says I have a persecution complex. That's a lie—he says that only because he hates me."

The Turks, having tortured and slain the parent of a little Armenian girl before her eyes, turned to the child and said, "Will you renounce your faith in Jesus and live?" She replied, "I will not." "Then to the dogs!" She was thrown into a kennel of savage and famished dogs and left there. The next morning they came and looked in and saw the little girl on her knees praying and beside her the largest and most savage of all the dogs, snapping at every dog that ventured near, thus protecting the child. The men ran away terrified, crying out, "There is a God here; there is a God here."

PERSEVERANCE

Day after day Columbus entered these words in the log of the Santa Maria: "This day we sailed on."

Alexander the Great was asked how he had conquered the world. He replied, "By not wavering."

If all of this world falls from the truth, I will stand!
—Athanasius, at the Council of Nicea

Eustace, if after my removal anyone should think it worthwhile to write my life, I will give you a criterion. If he gives me credit for being a plodder, he will describe me justly. Anything beyond this will be too much. I can plod.
—William Carey

Shortly after the turn of the century a young man in Missouri enrolled in the State Teachers College in Warrenburg to get an education. He was a poor lad who could not afford to live in town, so he commuted three miles each day by horseback in order to attend classes. He had only one good suit. His coat was too thin. He tried out for the football team and was rejected.

In spite of his obvious pluck and courage, the young student was developing a deep-seated inferiority complex. His mother urged him to do something that would demonstrate his real potential, so he tried public speaking. Unfortunately, he failed at that too. At this stage in his life, everything the young man did ended in failure.

Yet Dale Carnegie kept on and eventually became the best known teacher of public speaking in history. The lad who had failed at speaking became the personal manager of radio's celebrated newscaster and author Lowell Thomas and developed a course of instruction on "How to Win Friends and Influence People" that made him a millionaire.
—James M. Boice

Two Frogs in Cream

Two frogs fell into a can of cream,
    Or so I've heard it told;
The sides of the can were shiny and steep,
    The cream was deep and cold.
"O what's the use?" croaked Number One.
    "It is fate, no help's around.
Good-bye my friends! Good-bye sad world!"
    And weeping still, he drowned.
But Number Two, of sterner stuff,
    Dog-paddled in surprise,
Then while he wiped his creamy face
    And dried his creamy eyes,
"I'll swim awhile, at least," he said—
    Or so I've heard it said;
"It really wouldn't help the world
    If one more frog were dead."
An hour or two he kicked and swam,
    Not once he stopped to mutter,
But kicked and kicked and swam and kicked,
    Then hopped out, via butter!
—T. C. Hamlet

On March 15, 1915, the British Navy attacked the Turks at the Dardanelles. There was a terrific naval barrage from the guns on the shore. Three ships had been sunk, and finally, at noon, the British Navy withdrew never to take that point during the engagement. What they didn't know was that the Turks had only sixty seconds of ammunition left and at that very moment were preparing to surrender. Had the British Navy been persistent and continued to press the battle, they would have taken the Dardanelles, split the enemy forces, closed the war years earlier, and saved millions of lives.

Let me tell you the secret that has led me to my goal. My strength lies solely in my tenacity.
—Louis Pasteur

Heroism consists of hanging on one minute longer.
—Norwegian proverb

William Carey spent over forty years in Burma and India and when asked to explain his astonishing accomplishments, he simply answered, "Perseverance."

Winston Churchill was asked to give a commencement address. He was introduced, and he stood up and said firmly, "Never quit!" and he sat down. This was probably the shortest commencement address in history.

Although he had only an elementary education, by the time he was in his teens, he could read the Bible in six languages. He later became professor of Oriental Languages at Fort William College in Calcutta and his press at Serampore provided Scriptures in over forty languages and dialects for more than 300 million people.

His name? William Carey, "father of modern missions."

His secret? He was a plodder.

I hold a doctrine to which I owe much, indeed, but all the little I ever had, namely, that with *ordinary* talent and *extraordinary* perseverance, all things are attainable.

—T. F. Baxter

A child once said to his mother, "You never speak ill of any one. I think you would have something good to say of the Devil."

"Well," she said, "imitate his perseverance."

—D. L. Moody

The Romans came to the cliffs of Dover. They first were repulsed and sent back home. When they came again the Saxons were on the cliffs looking down, far outnumbering the Romans. But the Romans landed and, taking all their supplies ashore, turned with one dramatic and decisive event that carried the day. They set fire to their wooden ships and pushed them back out into the English Channel to burn to the waterline and to sink. Then with great resolve they unsheathed their swords and turned to march with forceful resolution into the face of the battle. The Saxons fled. Such persistence, such total commitment was unimaginable. The day was won for the Romans by default.

—Mack R. Douglas

PERSISTENCE

Energy and persistence conquer all things.

—Benjamin Franklin

Pay as little attention to discouragement as possible. Plow ahead as a steamer does, rough or smooth, rain or shine. To carry your cargo and make port is the point.

If Columbus had turned back, no one would have blamed him. No one would have remembered him either.

He who gives up when he is behind is cowardly. He who gives up when he is ahead is foolish.

—William Arthur Ward

Never give in. Never, never, never, never. In nothing great or small, large or petty— never give in except to convictions of honor and good sense.

—Winston Churchill

No one would ever have crossed the ocean if he could have gotten off the ship in the storm.

—Charles F. Kettering

A lad saw a want ad in a small Massachusetts paper asking for a young man to assist the office manager of a brokerage house in Boston. Applications were to be mailed to Box 1720 in Boston. The young man wrote the best letter of application he knew how. When no reply came, he wrote a second letter. Still no reply. Though discouraged, he did not quit. He rewrote his letter, changing the wording, improving the construction. Still he received no reply from his third letter.

The lad knew that success required persistence. So he took a train to Boston, went directly to the post office and asked, "Who rents Box 1720?" The clerk replied that to give out such information was against the law.

The boy hunted for Box 1720, then waited hours until someone came. He followed the person to one of Boston's largest brokerage houses. When the manager heard his story, he said, "My young friend, you are just the type we are looking for. The job is yours." Thus began the career of Roger Babson, one of America's illustrious statisticians.

Keep on going and the chances are you will stumble on something, perhaps when you are least expecting it. I have never heard of anyone stumbling on something sitting down.
—Charles F. Kettering

Don't Quit

When things go wrong, as they sometimes
will,
When the road you're trudging seems all
uphill,
When the funds are low and the debts are
high,
And when you want to smile, but you have
to sigh,
When care is pressing you down a bit—
Rest if you must, but don't you quit.
Life is queer with its twists and turns,
As everyone of us sometimes learns,
And many a failure turns about
When he might have won though he stuck
it out.
Don't give up, though the pace seems slow—
You may succeed with another blow.
Often the goal is nearer than
It seems to a faint and faltering man;
Often the struggler has given up
When he might have captured the victor's
cup
And he learned too late, when the night's
slipped down
How close he was to the golden crown.
Success is failure turned inside out—
The silver tint of the clouds of doubt,
And you never can tell how close you are,
It may be near when it seems afar;
So stick to the fight when you're hardest
hit—
It's when things seem worst that you
mustn't quit.

The bulldog's nose is slanted upward so that it can breath while it holds on.

Nothing in this world can take the place of persistence. Talent will not; nothing is more common than unsuccessful men with talent. Genius will not; unrewarded genius is almost a proverb. Education will not; the world is full of educated derelicts. Persistence and determination alone are omnipotent. The slogan "press on" has solved and always will solve the problems of the human race.
—Calvin Coolidge

The English writer Samuel Crowther once wrote an article in which he examined the traits of many successful people.

"The only common trait that can be discovered among them," he wrote, "has to do with the capacity for sustained work in an emergency. Someone has said that the chief difference between a big man and a little man is that the little man quits when he is tired and sleepy, while that is the very time the big man presses on harder than ever."

Along the same lines, another author wrote, "The longer I live the more deeply I am convinced that the difference between one person and another, between the weak and the powerful, the great and insignificant, is energy—invisible determination. This quality will do anything that has to be done in the world; and no talents, no circumstances, no opportunities, will make one a successful person without it."
—*Bits & Pieces*

Some men give up their designs when they have almost reached the goal; while others, on the contrary, obtain a victory by exerting, at the last moment, more vigorous efforts than ever before.
—Herodotus

PERSPECTIVE

The angle from which we view things makes a big difference. Lord Chesterfield once pointed out that a horse looks much like a horse from ground level, but if you look at one from the top, a horse looks much like a violin.

PERSUASION

To be persuasive, we must be believable; to be believable, we must be credible; to be credible, we must be truthful.
—Edward R. Murrow

You cannot antagonize and persuade at the same time.

PESSIMISM

A pessimist is someone who complains about the noise when opportunity knocks.

A pessimist is one who has swallowed an egg; he's afraid to move for fear it would break and afraid to sit still for fear the thing will hatch.
—E. D. Solomon

A pessimist is one who no's too much.
—Franklin Krook

The pessimist is severe on others, and severe on himself. The optimist is generous on others and generous on himself. The realist is generous on others and severe on himself.

An optimist is one who thinks we now have the best of all worlds; a pessimist is one who fears the optimist may be right.

An optimist goes to the window every morning and says, "Good morning, God." The pessimist goes to the window and says, "Good God, morning!"

The pessimist's epitaph: "Just what I might have expected."

PHILOSOPHY

A little philosophy inclines men's minds to atheism, but depth in philosophy brings men's minds about to religion.
—Francis Bacon

Philosophy proved a washout to me.
—Bertrand Russell

PIETY

At the funeral of Jeremy Taylor (1613–1667) it was said that he "had devotion enough for a cloister and learning enough for a university."

Unite the pair so long disjoin'd,
Knowledge and vital piety.
—Charles Wesley

PILGRIMS

A fugitive is one who is running from home;
A vagabond is one who has no home;
A stranger is one away from home;
And a pilgrim is on his way home.

PLAGIARISM

A sermon that is all work and no plagiarism is no good.

There was an old preacher named Spurgy
Who didn't like our liturgy
But his sermons were fine
So I preached them as mine
And so did the rest of the clergy.

Plagiarism is stealing a ride on someone else's train of thought.
—Russell E. Curran

Plagiarism is taking something from one man and making it worse.
—George Moore

Plagiarism is the highest form of compliment and the lowest form of larceny.

A plagiarist is an educated pickpocket and a literary body-snatcher.

When people are free to do as they please they usually imitate each other.
—Eric Hoffer

When someone asked Charles Lamb where he got the material for one of his essays, he said he had milked three hundred cows for it, but the butter was his own.

PLANNING

An engineer was confined to his bed because his lower limbs were paralyzed from a serious accident. Because of his reputation for great skill he was asked to design and prepare the blueprints for a great suspension bridge. After many months his plans were completed and placed in the hands of those who were to be in charge of the construction of the bridge. After many more months the bridge construction was completed. The engineer was brought on his bed to the scene of the beautiful bridge spanning the wide river. As he watched for the first time, the cars sped over the bridge, and as he looked at the blueprints which he held in his hands, the tears began to fill his eyes, and he cried out, "It's just like the plan; it's just like the plan."

—C. Reuben Anderson

My company has a plan for the next one hundred years, but my church hasn't given a thought to what it will do next year.

—A. Weyerhauser

I have thought that a man of tolerable ambitions may work great changes, if he first forms a good plan and makes the execution of that same plan his whole study and business.

—Benjamin Franklin

If you do not think about the future, you cannot have one.

—John Galsworthy

Plans are nothing. Planning is everything.

—Dwight Eisenhower

During the Napoleonic Wars, a count was captured who had been spying for Napoleon's enemy. He was interrogated and refused to give out any information. Consequently, the count was sentenced to the guillotine. With this head on the chopping block, the blade was released. When it was halfway down, the count cried, "I'll tell! I'll tell you all you want to know!"

Moral: Don't hatchet your count before he chickens.

When the French marshal Louis Lyautey announced that he wished to plant a tree, his gardener responded that the tree would not reach a full growth for more than a hundred years. "In that case," Lyautey replied, "we have no time to lose. We must start planting this afternoon."

Make no little plans; they have no magic to stir men's blood.

—Daniel Burnham

Refrain from calculating on the quality of

juvenile poultry prior to the completion of the entire process of incubation. In other words, don't count your chickens before they hatch.

PLEASING CHRIST

Several years ago a young minister was called to be the pastor of a rather large church. He was asked how he thought that he, a young man with little experience, would be able to please so many men and women. He replied, "I am not going there to please one thousand people, but to please One."

POISE

Poise is the ability to be at ease inconspicuously.

POLICE

When Lyndon B. Johnson was president of the United States, he went to church one Sunday morning accompanied by the Secret Service and motorcycle police. After the service he was approached by a small boy who asked him, "Are you the guy who came with the police?"

He replied, "Yes, sonny, I am."

"Well, you'd better duck out the back door," the lad said, "they're still out there waiting for you."

—A. L. "Kirk" Kirkpatrick

POLITENESS

A man walked to a newsstand to buy a paper. He thanked the proprietor politely, but the proprietor didn't even acknowledge his greeting. A friend observed, "He's a sullen fellow." The first man replied, "Oh, he's that way every night." His amazed friend asked, "Then why do you continue to be so polite to him?" Answered the man, "Why should I let him decide how I am going to act?"

—Leslie B. Flynn

POLITICS (Also see ELECTIONS)

A politician who had changed his views rather radically was congratulated by a colleague, who said, "I'm glad you've seen the light."

"I didn't see the light," came the reply. "I felt the heat."

The politician is my shepherd, I'm in want,
He maketh me to lie down on park benches
He leadeth me beside the still factories,
He disturbeth my soul.
Yea, though I walk through the valley of
the shadow of depression and recession,
I anticipate no recovery, for he is with me.
He prepareth a reduction in my salary in
the presence of my enemies,
He anointed my small income with great
losses.
My expenses runneth over.
Surely unemployment and poverty shall
follow me all the days of my life
And I shall dwell in a mortgaged house
forever.

Too bad the only people who know how to run the country are busy driving cabs and cutting hair.

—George Burns

At a college job fair, a man bumped into one of his school's guidance counselors. "I can't seem to find a career that intrigues me," he said.

"What are your interests?" he asked.

"I like to take things apart," the man said, "but I hate putting them back together."

"Son," replied the adviser, "you ought to consider politics."

Political speeches are like the horns of a steer . . . a point here and a point there . . . with a lot of bull in between.

POPULATION

If all the people of the world were brought together into one place, they could stand, without touching anyone else, in less than two hundred square miles.

It took until 1820 for the world's population to reach its first billion. It took one hundred years after that for a second billion (1930). A third billion came thirty-five years later (1965), a fourth billion sixteen years later (1981), and the world's population reached five billion five years later (1986). In seventy years the world's population, it is estimated, may reach sixteen billion.

POSITIVENESS

Some years ago a shoe manufacturer ran an ad on slippers. The headline under the picture of the slippers read: "Keeps feet from getting cold." The ad was a flop. Then the ad manager changed the headline to read: "Keeps feet warm and comfortable." Sales picked up immediately.

POSSESSIONS (Also see MATERIALISM)

In the David Livingstone museum near Glasgow, Scotland, there stands a stained-glass window given by the United Free Church of Scotland in 1932. Its inscription is taken from the pioneer missionary's diary. It reads simply, "I will place no value on anything I have or possess, except in relation to the kingdom of Christ."

—Edward L. Hayes

When we look at what we want and then compare it with what we have, we will be unhappy. When we think of what we deserve, rather than of what we have, we will thank God.

POTENTIAL

If we love people, we will see them as God intends them to be.

—Russian author

Antonio, a sculptor, chipped away at a stone and could do nothing with it. So he tossed it away. Later Michelangelo took it and carved one of the greatest statues of all times, the statue of David. He saw the potential in the stone.

Treat a man as he appears to be, and you make him worse. But treat a man as if he already were what he potentially could be, and you make him what he should be.

—Johann von Goethe

A rooster took his hens to see some ostrich eggs, and said, "I just want you to see what can be done."

A woman was dusting an old marble stone continually in the workshop of Gutzon Borglum. Then one day the sculptor made a bust of Lincoln. The woman said, "Is that

Mr. Lincoln?" "Yes." "How did you know that Lincoln was in that piece of marble?"

Diamonds in the Rough

A diamond in the rough
is a diamond sure enough,
For, before it ever sparkled,
It was made of diamond stuff.
Of course, someone must find it
Or it never will be found;
And then, someone must grind it,
Or it never will be ground!
But when it's found
And when it's ground,
And when it's burnished bright,
That diamond's everlasting
Flashing out its radiant light.
O Christian, please whoe'er you be,
Don't say you've done enough,
That worst man on the street may be
A diamond in the rough.

There is no greater burden than a potential.
—Charlie Brown

Treat a man as he appears to be, and you make him worse. But treat a man as if he already were what he potentially could be, and you make him what he should be.

POVERTY

In the October 14, 1980 issue of the *Tyler Morning Telegraph* was an article about Maddalena Borella, who lived in the village of Gorduno, Switzerland. Local children feared the eighty-eight-year-old Maddalena, and called her a witch. She never washed and never changed her clothes. She slept on a straw mat on the floor of a dirty, dilapidated hut. When she collapsed in the middle of the road one day, doctors said that she was weak because of malnutrition—she had been eating one meager meal per day. Maddalena was hospitalized, then placed in a home for the aged. She died shortly thereafter.

Officials sealed Maddalena's hut, then began to search for her only relative, a nephew who was living in the United States. Once the nephew was located, the authorities inspected the aunt's tiny home to see what, if anything, was of value. To their amazement they found a bank savings book showing that Maddalena had $312,000 in her account. They also found a key to a safety deposit box which, when opened, was discovered to hold gold coins worth one and a quarter million dollars!
—Don Anderson

It's no disgrace to be poor, but it can be inconvenient.
—Danish proverb

Poverty is a state of mind often induced by looking at a neighbor's new car.

Luigi Coneglio died after having lived seventy years in poverty. Most of these years he begged, and his outstretched hand became his trademark. Then they found his body in a filthy tenement after it had lain dead for three days amid dirty rags and papers yellowed with age.

Just another dead pauper it was thought. But in the attic of his squalid living quarters were forty-seven violins, one of them a costly Stradivarius.

POWER

Nearly all men can stand adversity, but if you want to test a man's character, give him power.

Nothing will divide the church so much as the love of power.
—Chrysostom

Power corrupts, and absolute power corrupts absolutely.
—Lord Acton in a letter to Bishop Mandell Creighton in 1887

When visiting the Niagara Falls, a man inquired of a bystander, "What's that house down there?" "The powerhouse. From it wires go to all the houses giving them the needed electricity." "Where does all that power come from?" "Well Lake Erie is 169 feet below Lake Ontario. The fall of the water provides the power. If they were the same level, there would be no power."

PRACTICE

All good maxims have been written; it only remains to put them into practice.

—Blaise Pascal

Dallas Green, former manager of the New York Yankees, had this motto on the wall of the clubhouse at the winter training center in Fort Lauderdale, Florida: "The will to win is not worth a nickel unless you have the will to practice."

PRAISE

He who merits praise he never receives is better off than he who receives praise he never merits.

Praise is boasting about what you enjoy.

—C. S. Lewis

We protest against unjust criticism, but we accept unearned applause.

—Jose Narosky

The hardest thing for a speaker to remember is not to nod his head in agreement when the toastmaster praises him.

—"Doc" Blakely

He who seeks only for applause from without has all his happiness in another's keeping.

—Goldsmith

PRAYER

Years ago an old lady had no money to buy food. She prayed, "Dear Lord, please send me a side of bacon and a sack of corn meal." Over and over again she prayed the same prayer aloud. One of the town's unscrupulous citizens decided to play a trick on her. He dropped a side of bacon and a sack of corn meal down her chimney. It landed in front of her as she knelt in prayer.

Jumping to her feet, she exclaimed, "Oh, Lord! You've answered my prayer!" Then she went all over town telling everyone the good news.

This was too much for the scoundrel who dropped the food down her chimney. He ridiculed her publicly and told her that God didn't answer her prayer; he did. The old lady replied, "Well, the Devil may have brought it, but it was the Lord who sent it!"

—*Paper Pulpit*

In the spring of 1994, *The Dallas Morning News* surveyed 1,011 adults in far north Texas counties about their religious beliefs and practices. Eighty-seven percent of the respondents said they believe prayer gets results, with slightly more women (93%) than men (80%) believing in prayer.

I often question why we spend so much time in our church prayer meetings praying for sick Christians who, if they die—and they will eventually—will go to be with Jesus, but we spend almost no time praying for the sinners who, when they die, will go to a Christless eternity.

—Evelyn Christenson

During the Spanish-American War, Clara Barton was overseeing the work of the Red Cross in Cuba. One day Colonel Theodore Roosevelt came to her, wanting to buy food for his sick and wounded Rough Riders. But she refused to sell him any.

Roosevelt was perplexed. His men needed the help and he was prepared to pay out of his own funds. When he asked someone why he could not buy the supplies, he was told, "Colonel, just ask for it!" A smile broke over Roosevelt's face. Now he understood—the provisions were not for sale. All he had to do was simply ask and they would be given freely.

A little girl was fishing with her dad. She waited awhile. Then after getting no nibbles, she said, "I quit." Her dad asked, "Why?" She answered, "I can't seem to get waited on."

Now I lay me down to sleep
I pray the Lord nobody wakes me up.
If I should die before I wake
I wouldn't be surprised.

—Betty Rollin

I asked for health that I might do greater things;
I was given infirmity that I might do better things.

293

I asked God for strength that I might achieve;
I was made weak that I might learn to obey.
I asked for riches that I might be happy;
I was given poverty that I might be wise.
I asked for power and the praise of men;
I was given weakness to sense my need of God.
I asked for all things that I might enjoy life;
I was given life that I might enjoy all things.
I got nothing I asked for but everything I hoped for;
In spite of myself, my prayers were answered—
I am among all men most richly blest.

Walk softly, speak tenderly, and pray fervently.

—T. J. Bach

Mary, Queen of Scots, said she feared the prayers of John Knox more than the efforts of ten thousand soldiers.

I have so much to do today that I must set apart more time than usual to pray.

—Martin Luther

In Africa each Christian native in a certain tribe had a secret separate place where he prayed. A path which led to his place of prayer off in a distance in the jungle was cleared by each native for his own use. Whenever he was neglecting his prayer life, all that was needed to bring his attention to this fact was the simple statement, "I see there's grass on your prayer trail."

Satan trembles when he sees the weakest saint upon his knees.

—William Cowper

A little boy was always asking God for things when he prayed. He said, "God, gimme this; gimme that." But when he was through, his mother said, "Son, don't ask God for so many things; just report for duty."

Begin the day with God, kneel down to Him in prayer.
Lift up your heart to see His abode and seek His love to share.

Open the Book of God and read a portion there,
That it may hallow all your thoughts and sweeten all your care.
Go through the day with God, e'en though you may not see,
Where'er you are, at home, abroad, He is still near to thee.
Converse in mind with God, your spirit heavenward raise;
Acknowledge every good bestowed and offer grateful praise.
Conclude your day with God, your sins to Him confess;
Trust in the Lord's atoning blood and plead His righteousness.
Lie down at night with God, who gives His servants sleep;
And when you tread the vale of death, He'll safely guard and keep.

It was the custom of John Fletcher of Madeley, England, never to meet a Christian without saying, "Friend, do I meet you praying?" This unusual salutation reminded the person that his life should be an unbroken expression of prayer and fellowship with God.

—*Our Daily Bread*

Dring the lunch hour, the president of a large factory wanted to talk to his company's manager about an urgent matter, but the manager's secretary said, "He cannot be disturbed for he is in conference—as he is everyday at this time." "But," said the impatient official, "tell him the president wants to see him." She firmly replied, "I have strict orders, sir, not to disturb him while he is in conference." Angrily the man brushed the secretary aside and opened the door to the manager's private office. After one quick look he backed out, gently closed the door, and said, "I'm sorry! Is this a daily occurrence?" "Yes, everyday he spends fifteen minutes in such a conference." The president had found the manager on his knees before his open Bible.

An ancient legend tells of a monarch who hired some people to make tapestries and garments for him. Among the workers was a young child who was selected because he was especially skilled at weaving. The king gave the silk and the patterns to the employees with the strict instructions to seek his aid immediately if any difficulties arose.

The boy, left to work by himself, made quiet and steady progress while the others were distressed by their many failures. One day they gathered around the youngster and inquired, "Why are you so happy and successful while we are always having trouble? Either our silk becomes tangled or our weaving varies from the pattern." "Don't you remember the words of the king when he told us to send for him whenever it was necessary?" asked the lad. "We finally did ask for his assistance," replied the others, "but by then things were so snarled that now it will take days to unravel our mistakes." "Didn't you notice how often I called for him?" he inquired. "Yes, but he's very busy, and we thought you were wrong in disturbing him so frequently." "Well," replied the little weaver, "I just took him at his word, and he was always happy to help me!"

I used to ask God to help me. Then I asked if I might help Him. I ended up asking Him to do His work through me.

—J. Hudson Taylor

Two men in a boat were caught in a sudden squall. While the one earnestly prayed for a deliverance, the other frantically rowed to reach safety. Soon the latter touched bottom with one of the oars. With a sigh of relief he turned to his comrade and said, "You can quit praying now, we're almost to land."

A fisherman who was out of fellowship with the Lord was at sea with his godless companions when a storm came up and threatened to sink their ship. His friends begged him to pray; but he demurred, saying, "It's been a long time since I've done that or even entered a church." At their insistence, however, he finally cried out, "O Lord, I haven't asked anything of You for fifteen years, and if You help us now and bring us safely to land, I promise I won't bother you again for another fifteen!"

—*Prairie Overcomer*

In the town of Port Hope, Canada, there stands a monument, not for the leading citizen who just died, but for a poor, unselfish working man who gave most of his life and energy to help those who could not repay him.

Joseph Scriven was born in Dublin in 1820. In his youth, he had the prospect of a great citizen with high ideals and great aspirations. He was engaged to a beautiful young woman who had promised to share his dreams, but on the eve of their wedding her body was pulled from a pond into which she had accidentally fallen and drowned.

Young Scriven never overcame the shock. Although a college graduate and ready to embark on a brilliant career, he began to wander to try to forget his sorrow. His wanderings took him to Canada where he spent the last forty-one of his sixty-six years. He became a very devout Christian. His beliefs led him to do servile labor for poor widows and sick people. He often served for no wages.

It was not known that Mr. Scriven had any poetic gifts until a short time before his death. A friend, who was sitting with him in an illness, discovered a poem he had written to his mother in a time of sorrow, not intending that anyone should see it. His poem was later set to music and has become a much-loved gospel song. It is said to be the first song that many missionaries teach their converts. In polls taken to determine the popularity of hymns and gospel songs, his poem set to music is always near the top. What was his poem?

What a friend we have in Jesus,
All our sins and griefs to bear.
What a privilege to carry
Everything to God in prayer.
Oh, what peace we often forfeit,
Oh what needless pain we bear,
All because we do not carry,
Everything to God in prayer.
—*The Cross and the Crown*

A boy quoted the Westminster Confession Shorter Catechism, "Man's chief end is to glorify God and to annoy Him forever."

To talk with God
No breath is lost
Talk on!
To walk with God
No strength is lost
Walk on!
To wait on God
No time is lost
Wait on!

It is not lost time to wait on God.
—J. Hudson Taylor

Sin will keep prayer away, or else prayer will keep sin away.

A man once asked a lifeguard, "How can you hear a person drowning when all these people are making this noise on the beach—talking, yelling, whistling, etc.?"

The lifeguard said, "I've been at this job for twenty years and I haven't let one person go on in distress. My ears are turned toward those in distress."

Too often our prayers are never geared toward asking for something definite. When a boy asks his father for something, he doesn't beat around the bush about it, but he comes right out and asks for it. We need to be like that in our praying. Ask for something definite.

When you pray, pray as though everything depended on God. When you work, work as though everything depended on you.

A steward came to the presiding elder and asked for a preacher. "How big a man do you want?" asked the elder. "I do not care much about his size," said the steward. "But I want him to be tall enough to reach heaven when he is on his knees."

A little boy in New York walked in a large bank past the policeman, the teller, the vice-president, and went right up to the president and spoke to him, while others stood outside, looking at a sign, "No Admittance." The boy could speak to the president because he was his father.

An atheist owned a brewery. A local church prayed earnestly that God would somehow do away with the brewery. One day the brewery was struck by lightning and was destroyed. The atheist sued the church. But the church said they took no responsibility for the act. The judge said, "This is the strangest case I've ever seen. An atheist believes in answered prayer, and a church takes no responsibility for prayer."

In prayer, it is better to have a heart without words than words without heart.
—John Bunyan

There is no greater threat to our devotion to Christ than our service for Christ.
—Oswald Chambers

A clergyman, walking on the public highway, observed a poor man breaking stones, and kneeling so that he could do it more effectually. Passing him and saluting him, he remarked, "Ah, John, I wish I could break the stony hearts of my hearers as easily as you are breaking those stones."

"Perhaps, Pastor," he said, "You do not work on your knees."

A little girl said to her mother, "Mommy, I'm not going to say 'Amen' to my prayers anymore. I'm going to say 'RSVP.'"

Whenever the Nenney family was able to get all the members of the family together at the same time for a breakfast they took turns saying, "grace." Finally it came to Dale's turn. Outside was gloomy and overcast, without a prospect of sunshine anywhere. Yet when he prayed, Dale said, "Thank you dear God, for my family, for this good food, and thank you God for this beautiful morning. Amen." Dale's mother, thinking that perhaps he was getting a little bit perfunctory in his prayers, pointed out the window at the fog and gloom and said, "Dale, what on earth are you doing, thanking God for a beautiful morning on a

day like this?" Dale thoughtfully replied, "Mother, never judge a day by its weather!"
—Melvin E. Wheatley Jr.

These forty years have not seen the sun rise in China without my father kneeling in prayer.
—Howard Taylor,
son of J. Hudson Taylor

Secret, fervent, believing prayer lies at the root of all personal godliness.
—William Carey

Prayer is a radical conversation of all our mental processes because in prayer we move away from ourselves, our worries, preoccupations, and self-gratification— and direct all that we recognize as ours to God in the simple trust that through his love all will be made new.

When man works, man works. When man prays, God works.
—Pat Johnson

If a small child receives a check, the check is perfectly valid, but the child does not know how to write his name. His parents show him how to endorse the check with his "X," and then one of them signs his own name. Without the parent's signature, it is doubtful that the check would be cashed. This illustrates crudely what we mean by offering prayer in the name of Jesus. We have signed our names, so to speak, to some promise in the Bible. The Lord Jesus comes along and signs His Name, too, and that opens the treasures of heaven to us.

A girl prayed, "Lord, I am not going to pray for myself today; I'm going to pray for others." But at the end of her prayer she added, "And give my mother a handsome son-in-law."

Sam Walter Fause wrote a little poem about prayer illustrating the importance of fervency in a rather comical way. Some men were arguing about the right positions to pray and so he put these thoughts in this bit of poetry.

"The proper way for men to pray," said Deacon Lemuel Keys, "and the only proper attitude is down upon his knees." "No, I should say the way to pray," said Reverend Dr. Wise, "is standing upright with outstretched arms and rapt and upturned eyes." "Oh, no, no, no," said Elmer Slow, "such posture is too proud. A man should pray with eyes fast closed and head contritely bowed." "It seems to me his hand should be austerely clasped in front, with both thumbs pointing toward the ground," said Reverend Dr. Blunt. "Last year I fell in Hitchkin's well headfirst," said Cyrus Brown, "both my heels were sticking up and my head was pointing down. And I made a prayer right then and there, the best prayer I ever said. The prayingest prayer I ever prayed was a standing on my head."

A Christian widow in Scotland had difficulty providing food and clothing for her children, but she trusted the Lord and lovingly taught them to put their confidence in Him.

One day her purse was empty and the pantry was depleted. Only a handful of flour remained in the big barrel. The mother reached down into the container to scrape up the last bit of flour to make some bread for her hungry little ones. As she bent over the barrel, her faith began to waver and she could hold back the tears no longer. Her little son Robbie heard her sobs and began tugging at her dress until she lifted her head and looked into his questioning eyes. In his Scottish dialect he asked, "Mither, what are ye weepin' aboot? Dinna God hear ye scrapin' the bottom o' the barrel?"

A Roman emperor was parading through the streets of the imperial city in a victory celebration. Tall legionnaires lined the route to keep back the cheering masses. At one place along the way was a platform on which the royal family was sitting. As the emperor approached, his youngest son, who was just a little boy, jumped down, burrowed through the crowd, and tried to run out to meet him. "You can't do that," said one of the guards as he scooped up the lad. "Don't you know who's in that chariot? That's the emperor!" Quickly the youngster replied, "He may be your emperor, but he's my father!"

Albert Thorwaldsen, famous Danish sculptor, sculpted his Kristus, a statue of Christ, which now stands in the Copenhagen Cathedral.

When he finished molding the plastic clay for the statue, he went home, leaving the clay to dry and harden. But during the night, a dense mist rolled in from the sea. When the sculptor returned to his studio the following morning, he thought the masterpiece had been ruined. The majestic head of Kristus, which had been gazing heavenward, now faced downward. The hands of the clay figure, which had been held aloft as though to bless, were now stretched forward in an inviting way.

Gazing on the altered statue, Thorwaldsen suddenly realized that this was the way the figure ought to be. "If you want to see the face of Kristus," the sculptor exclaimed, "you must get down on your knees."

An elderly gentleman passed his granddaughter's room one night and overheard her repeating the alphabet in an oddly reverent way. "What on earth are you up to?" he asked.

"I'm saying my prayers," explained the little girl. "But I can't think of exactly the right words tonight, so I'm just saying all the letters. God will put them together for me, because He knows what I'm thinking."

When we pray, the Lord expects us to have a hoe in hand.

A minister was talking to a woman on an airplane flight. The flight got very bumpy. The woman said, "You're a minister. Can't you do something about this storm?"

He said, "Yes, I'm a minister. But I'm in sales, not in management."

A little boy who had been begging his father for favors all day came once more into his daddy's office. "What do you want this time?" asked the weary parent. "I don't want anything," was the astonishing reply, "I just want to be with you."
—*The Vance Havner Quote Book*

Samuel Zwemer wrote forty-seven books (twelve of which were in joint authorship) and several tracts. One tract entitled "Do You Pray?" was written in Cairo and became so well known there that people began to use this as a title and he would be pointed out on the street with the words, "There goes, 'Do You Pray?'"
—J. Christy Wilson

Forgive us for thinking that prayer is a waste of time and help us to see that without prayer our work is a waste of time.
—Peter Marshall

A coach said to the team chaplain, "Lead us in a few words of silent prayer."

Dear Lord,
Help me to live this day quietly, easily;
To lean upon Thy great strength trustfully, restfully;
To wait for the unfolding of Thy will patiently, serenely;
To meet others peacefully, joyously;
To face tomorrow confidently, courageously.

I can take my telescope and look millions of miles into space but I can go away to my room and in prayer get nearer to God in heaven than I can when assisted by all the telescopes of earth.
—Sir Isaac Newton

A woman said to G. Campbell Morgan, "Oh, I could never take my little problems to God. I wouldn't want to bother him with those. I take only the big problems to God."

He answered, "Are any problems big to God?"

Prayer is our highest privilege, our gravest responsibility, and greatest power God has put into our hands.
—*The Kneeling Christian*

A Pastor's Wish for God's People

May a dying Savior's love inspire you (2 Cor. 5:14).

May a risen Savior's power preserve you (Phil. 3:19).

May an ascended Savior's blessing enrich you (Eph. 4:8).

May a constant Savior's ministry aid you (Heb. 7:24–25).

May a living Savior's word sanctify you (Eph. 5:25–26).

May a seated Savior's acceptance rest you (Heb. 10:10–14).

May a faithful Savior's grace empower you (2 Cor. 12:93).

May a present Savior's presence cheer you (Isa. 41:10).

May a holy Savior's indwelling mold you (Gal. 2:20).

May a joyful Savior's joy strengthen you (John 15:11).

May a powerful Savior's Spirit use you (Acts 1:8).

May a loving Savior's yoke couple you (Matt. 11:29).

May a perfect Savior's example allure you (John 13:15).

May a coming Savior's return attract you (Rev. 22:12).

May Christ Himself be all in all to you (Col. 3:11).

Prayer and helplessness are inseparable. Only the one who is helpless can truly pray. Your helplessness is your best prayer. It calls from your heart to the heart of God with greater effect than all your uttered pleas.

—O. Hallesby

Do not pray for easy lives. Pray to be a stronger person. Do not pray for tasks equal to your powers, but pray for powers equal to your tasks.

—Phillips Brooks

Let inward prayer be your last act before you fall asleep and the first act when you awake. And in time you will find as did Brother Lawrence, that "those who have the gift of the Holy Spirit go forward even in sleep."

—Thomas Kelly

A couple of girls were walking to school one morning when it suddenly dawned on them that unless they really hurried they were going to be late. One of them suggested that they stop and pray that they wouldn't be tardy. "No," the other replied, "let's pray while we run as fast as we can."

A youngster was asked by his pastor, "Son, do you pray every day?" "Not every day," was his response, "some days I don't want anything."

Bill Moyers, who was an ordained Baptist minister during the time he was President Lyndon Johnson's press secretary, was saying grace at a White House dinner one evening. Johnson was seated at the other end of the table and was having trouble hearing. "Speak up," he said, "I can't hear you."

"I wasn't talking to you," replied Moyers.

If I wished to humble anyone, I would ask him about his prayer life.

The agnostic H. G. Wells became angry when he prayed and didn't get what he wanted. While taking an accounting exam for which he was not prepared, he desperately pleaded with the Lord to "balance his books." When the figures didn't add up properly, he said, "All right, Mr. God, You won't ever catch me praying again!" And he never did.

Men generally pray in public in inverse proportion to their private prayers. If they pray a great deal in private, they are apt to be rather short in public prayer. If they pray very little in private, they are in danger of being more lengthy.

—D. L. Moody

A wealthy lady was traveling on a train with her little boy and a pet dog. A nurse was in charge of the child, and the rich woman sat in front of them holding her dog and reading a book. Soon the youngster was whining and complaining because he wanted something. "Nurse," said the woman, "how many times have I told you to let Billy have whatever he wants." The nurse replied, "Yes, ma'am." A few minutes later Billy was crying loudly and the mother impatiently said, "Didn't I tell you to let Billy have whatever he wants?" The nurse replied, "Yes, ma'am, you did, and there was a big ugly wasp playing on the window. Billy wanted it, so he got it!"

Prayer is not overcoming God's reluctance but cooperating with His willingness.
—Richard C. Trench

Wally Howard asked people in a retirement home, "What do you find the most difficult thing to do here?" He was surprised with the answer, "To find time to read the Bible and pray."

Pray, always pray; the Holy Spirit pleads
Within thee all thy daily, hourly needs.
Pray, always pray; beneath sin's heaviest load
Prayer sees the blood from Jesus' side that flowed.
Pray, always pray; though weary, faint, and alone,
Prayer nestles by the Father's sheltering throne.
Pray, always pray; amid the world's turmoil,
Prayer keeps the heart at rest, and nerves for toil.
Pray, always pray; if joys thy pathway throng,
Prayer strikes the harp, and sings the angel's song.
Pray, always pray; if loved ones pass the veil,
Prayer drinks with them of springs that cannot fail.
All earthly things with earth shall fade away;
Prayer grasps eternity; pray, always pray.
—E. H. Bickersteth

A young boy, ready for bed, interrupted a family gathering in the living room. "I'm going to say my prayers now. Anybody want anything?"

Anna Marx, daughter of Karl Marx, said, "I was told by my father not to believe in God. But somewhere I ran across a prayer. I don't know its source [Then she quoted the Lord's Prayer.] If there is a God like that, I could believe in Him."

Praise is our being occupied with our blessings, prayer is being occupied with our need, and worship is our being occupied with the Lord Himself, the Blesser.

A Baptist preacher prayed this brief invocation at the Texas legislature on January 11, 1989: "Our Father, please read our lips. We need help. Amen."

If we grow wiser and more learned in our intercourse with wise and learned persons, how much more will we gain in our inner life by communing with God in prayer.
—Ulrich Zwingli

The secret of being a saint is being a saint in secret.

When Hudson Taylor was asked if he ever prayed without any consciousness of joy, he replied, "Often. Sometimes I pray on with my heart feeling like wood; often, too, the most wonderful answers have come when prayer has been a real effort of faith without any joy whatever."

Abraham Lincoln, during the Civil War, once said, "I have been driven many times to my knees by the overwhelming conviction that I had nowhere else to go. My own wisdom and that of all about me seemed insufficient for the day."

There's no weapon half so mighty,
As the intercessors bear;
Not a greater field of service
Than the ministry of prayer.

Daniel chose rather to spend the night in a lion's den than go through the day without prayer.

A boy wanted a baby brother. His dad told him the way to get things is to pray for them. So the boy prayed for a baby brother. But after a couple of weeks no baby came, so he quit praying. Nine months later his father said his mother would give birth to a baby. Later, the father showed the boy twin boys. "Aren't you glad you prayed as you did?" The boy answered, "Yes, but aren't you glad I stopped when I did?"

God's promises show his heart; your prayers show yours.

Let prayer be the key of the morning and the bolt of the evening.

—Matthew Henry

Prayer will make a man cease from sin, or sin will entice a man to cease from prayer.

Prayer is a shield to the soul, a sacrifice to God, and a scourge for Satan.

Oh, I wish that God had not given me what I prayed for! It was not so good as I thought.

—Johanna Spyri in *Heidi*

A child of God can see more on his knees than can a philosopher on his tiptoes.

Speech is that which distinguishes men from animals, but prayer distinguishes the children of God from the children of this world. Speech we use to communicate our thoughts to each other, but prayer is the speech used by the believer to commune with God.

A lot of kneeling keeps us in good standing.

A sweating woodchopper who wasn't doing too well was urged to stop and sharpen his ax. He snorted, "It's tough enough now getting this job done without taking time to grind an ax." Take time for prayer!

To be miserable—
   Look within.
To be distracted—
   Look around.
To be happy—
   Look up.

James Gilmour, pioneer missionary to Mongolia, was a man of prayer. He had the habit in his writing of never using a blotter. He made it a rule when he got to the bottom of any page to wait until the ink dried and spend the time in prayer. That kind of habit drives prayer right into all the chinks and corners of our lives like the mortar that holds the building stones together.

A Moment in the Morning

A moment in the morning ere the cares of
   the day begin,
Ere the heart's wide door is open for the
   world to enter in;
Oh then alone with Jesus, in silence of the
   morn,
In heavenly sweet communion let your
   happy day be born;
In the quietude that blesses with a prelude
   of repose,
Let your soul be soothed and softened as
   the dew revives the rose.

A Scottish Presbyterian pastor prayed long prayers in lofty language that only heaven could understand. A woman in the chair tugged on his frocked tail and said, "Just call Him Father and ask Him for something."

Isaac Bashevis Singer, the storyteller whose tales of Polish ghettos and immigrant Jews in America have charmed readers for three generations, once explained his attitude toward prayer.

"Whenever I'm in trouble, I pray. And since I'm always in trouble, there is not a day when I don't pray. The belief that man can do what he wants, without God, is as far from me as the North Pole."

Sign in a post office: "Don't lift with your back; lift with your knees."

Do you wonder how your brother
Has a life that's ever been
One of victory and triumph?
Why, he's been alone with Him.
Does your life blaze out in brightness
Or is it growing dim?
You can fill your lamp most surely,
If you'll get alone with Him.

It is not how much you're doing
It is not your zeal and vim
That wins the souls for Jesus;
It's time spent alone with Him.

It is not the arithmetic of our prayers, how many they are; nor the rhetoric of our prayers, how eloquent they are; nor the geometry of our prayers, how long they be; nor the music of our prayers, how sweet our voice may be; nor the logic of our prayers, how argumentative they may be; nor the method of our prayers, how orderly they may be—which God cares for. Fervency of spirit is that which availeth much.

—William Low

God knows our needs before we ask. Then, what is prayer for? Not to inform Him, nor to move Him, unwilling to have mercy, as if like some proud prince He required a certain amount of recognition of His greatness as the price of His favors. Prayer fits our own hearts by conscious need, true desire and dependence to receive the gifts which He is ever willing to give, but which we are not always fit to receive. As St. Augustine has it, the empty vessel is by prayer carried to the full fountain.

—Alexander Maclaren

When J. Hudson Taylor went to China, he made the voyage on a sailing ship. As it neared the channel between the southern Malay Peninsula and the island of Sumatra, the missionary heard an urgent knock on his stateroom door. He opened it and there stood the captain of the ship.

"Mr. Taylor," he said, "we have no wind. We are drifting toward an island where the people are heathen, and I fear they are cannibals."

"What can I do?" asked Taylor.

"I understand that you believe in God. I want you to pray for wind."

"All right, Captain, I will, but you must set the sail."

"Why, that's ridiculous! There's not even the slightest breeze. Besides, the sailors will think I'm crazy."

Nevertheless, the captain finally agreed.

Forty-five minutes later he returned and found the missionary still on his knees. "You can stop praying now," said the captain. "We've got more wind than we know what to do with!"

In the Near East camels are taught to kneel by a certain word being spoken to them when a heavy load is placed on their backs so that they are forced to bend down because of the heavy weight. This is done a number of times so that eventually they kneel when just the word is spoken though there be no load on them.

Sometimes Christians have to learn in the same manner to kneel. It takes some heavy loads to force us to our knees.

In the unpublished writings of Miss Ruth Paxton was found a list of her "Prayer Check" by which she tested her own prayer life. (1) Has my prayer life been powerless because of some besetting sin? (2) Has it been hindered by haste, irregularity, insufficient preparation? (3) Have I had such power with God that I have had real power with people? (4) Has my prayer life been limited to my own life or am I an intercessor after God's own heart? (5) Has my prayer life been starved, or have I, through meditation on the Word, let the Lord teach me to pray? (6) Has my prayer life been joyless—more of a duty than a privilege? (7) Has my prayer life been sacrificial—has it cost me anything in time and energy?

Last night my little boy confessed to me
    Some childish wrong;
And kneeling at my knee
    He prayed with tears;
"Dear God, make me a man,
    Like Daddy—wise and strong;
I know you can."
Then while he slept
    I knelt beside his bed,
Confessed my sins,
    And prayed with low-bowed head;
"O God, make me a child,
    Like my child here—
Pure, guileless,
    Trusting Thee with faith sincere."

Old Mrs. Cobley used to visit Leicester Infirmary with flowers. One day a young doctor met her coming out of a ward, and in a frolicsome mood, asked, "Well, Mrs. Cobley, I suppose you have been telling these people that God hears prayer?" "Yes, sir," she answered. "My Father always hears His people when they cry." "I am very glad to hear it," he replied, "for I am very hard up this morning. Do you think that if I asked your Father for a five-pound note, He would give it to me?" That was a bit of a poser; for "yes" or "no" would have been equally wrong; but at last she said, "Suppose you were introduced to the Prince of Wales today, sir, do you think that the first day you know him, you could ask him for a five-pound note?" "No, I suppose I would need to wait until I got to know him better." "Yes," finished the old lady in triumph, "and you will need to know my Father better before you can ask Him for five-pound notes."

—Guy H. King

Who is there so full that he wants nothing? Let none cease his praying but he who needs nothing and let none cease his praising who hath anything. Is not the mercy we want worth asking? Is not the mercy we have worth acknowledging? No Christian has so little from him but there is ground for praise nor has so much but there is need of prayer.

—Venning

Lord, what a change, within us one short hour
Spent in Thy presence, will avail to make!
What heavy burdens from our bosoms take!
What parched grounds refresh as with a shower!
We kneel, and all around us seems to lower;
We rise, and all the distant and the near
Stands forth in sunny outline, brave and clear!
We kneel, how weak!
We rise, how full of power!
Why therefore should we do ourselves this wrong,
Or others—that we are not always strong,
That we are overborne with care,

That we should ever weak or heartless be,
Anxious or troubled, when with us is prayer,
And joy and strength and courage are with Thee?

Be Lord,
within me to strengthen me,
without me to guard me,
over me to shelter me,
beneath me to establish me,
before me to guide me,
after me to forward me,
round me to secure me.

—Lancelot Andrews

A boy was overheard saying his nightly prayers: "Please God, make Boulder the capital of Colorado." When he had said "Amen," his mother asked, "Why did you ask that?" "Because," he explained, "that's what I put down on my exam paper today."

Much that perplexes us in our Christian experience is but the answer to our own prayers.

We pray for patience and God sends us tribulation, for tribulation works patience (Rom. 5:3–5).

We pray for submission and God sends suffering, for we learn obedience by the things we suffer (Heb. 5:8).

We pray for unselfishness and God gives us opportunities to sacrifice ourselves by thinking of the needs of others (Phil. 2:4).

We pray for victory and the things of the world swoop down on us in a storm of temptation, for this is the victory that overcomes the world (1 John 5:4).

We pray for strength and humility and some messenger of Satan torments us until we cry for its removal (2 Cor. 12:7).

We pray for love and God sends suffering and puts us with unlovely people and lets them say things that fray the nerves, for love suffers long and is kind (1 Cor. 13:4–8).

A happy Christian met an Irish peddler and exclaimed, "It's a grand thing to be saved!"

"Aye," said the peddler, "It is, but I know something better than that."

"Better than being saved?" asked the other. "What can you in your position possibly know that is better than that?"

"The companionship of the Man who saved me," was the unexpected reply.

Trouble and perplexity drive me to prayer, and prayer drives away perplexity and trouble.

—Philipp Melancthon

Satan may build a wall about us, but he can't put a roof over us to keep us from praying to God.

—J. Hudson Taylor

Without time for prayer, nothing can be accomplished.

—W. Graham Scroggie

A man in Ireland who came in contact with a Bible colporteur, at first repulsed him. Finally he persuaded him to take a Bible and later said, "I read a wee bit out of the New Testament every day, and I pray to God every night and every morning." When asked if it helped him to read God's Word and to pray he answered, "Indeed it does. When I go to do anything wrong, I just say to myself, 'Pat, you'll be talking to God tonight!' That keeps me from doing it."

Someone spoke this searching word at Edinburgh in 1910: "We have lost the eternal youthfulness of Christianity and have aged into calculating manhood. We seldom pray for the extraordinary, the limitless, the glorious. We seldom pray with any confidence, for any good to the realization of which we cannot imagine away. And yet, we suppose ourselves to believe in an Infinite Father."

The spectacle of a nation praying is more awe-inspiring than the explosion of an atomic bomb. The force of prayer is greater than any possible combination of man-made or man-controlled powers, because prayer is man's greatest means of tapping the infinite resources of God. Invoking by prayer the mercy and might of God is our most efficacious means of guaranteeing peace and security for the harassed and helpless people of the earth.

—J. Edgar Hoover

A military cadet who had just been saved by Christ was in his room pouring out thanksgiving for pardoned sin. A heavy knock sounded on the door and before the cadet could get to his feet, a colonel entered.

"What," he said, "do you pray? I gave that up long ago. I have all I want so there's nothing to ask God for."

"Well, sir," replied the cadet, "you must have a lot to thank Him for!"

A test of faith is whether you are surprised when your prayers are answered.

Begin the day with God,
    Kneel down to Him in prayer,
Lift up thine heart to His abode,
    And seek His love to share.
Open the book of God,
    And read a portion there,
That may hallow all thy thoughts,
    And sweeten all they care.
Go through the day with God;
    Whate'er thy work may be;
Whate'er thou art, at home, abroad,
    He still is near to thee.
Converse in thy mind with God;
    Thy spirit heavenward raise,
Acknowledge every good bestowed,
    And offer grateful praise.
Conclude the day with God;
    Thy sins to Him confess,
Trust in the Lord's atoning blood,
    And plead His righteousness.

PREACHING

Some ministers would make good martyrs: they are so dry they would burn well.

—Charles H. Spurgeon

The vicar stepped into the pulpit and opened up the Bible in front of him with a flourish.

"What does that mean, Daddy?" said the little boy in the front row.

"It means that he's going to tell us important things about the Bible."

Then the vicar took out a sheaf of notes and laid them carefully on the lectern.

"What does that mean, Daddy?"

"That means he is going to explain all the things in the Bible story."

Then the vicar took off his watch and put it on the side of the pulpit.

"What does that mean, Daddy?"

"That means absolutely nothing at all."

—Murray Watts

A preacher in Cornwall puzzled his congregation by choosing the following text for his harvest message: "One of them that stood by drew his sword, and smote the servant of the high priest, and struck off his ear" (Mark 14:47). When asked afterwards why he had not picked a more suitable text, he replied, "No, this is a good one. Don't you see? First the blade and then the ear."

A vicar was on holiday when his house was flooded. All his sermons were kept in the basement, and the first question he asked his son, who had gone in to investigate the damage, was, "Are my sermons wet?"

"No, Dad," the son replied. "They are as dry as ever."

—*Rolling in the Aisles*

The preacher who can't broaden or deepen his sermons usually lengthens them.

When a man preaches to men, I want him to make it a personal matter, a personal matter, a personal matter.

—Daniel Webster

A gray-haired old woman, long a member of her community and church, shook hands with the minister after the service on Sunday morning. "That was a wonderful sermon," she told him. "Everything you said applies to someone I know."

A pastor asked George Burns, of all people, how to interest people in his sermons. He answered, "Have a good beginning and a good ending, and have them close together."

Preach not because you have to say something but because you have something to say.

—Archbishop Whatley

A sermon is no sermon in which I cannot hear the heartbeat.

—Henry Longfellow

No man preaches his sermon well to others if he does not first preach it to his own heart.

—John Owen

To make a speech immortal you don't have to make it everlasting.

Some preachers think their duty is to comfort the afflicted and to afflict the comforted.

A church member said of her minister, "Six days of the week he is invisible and on the seventh he is incomprehensible."

A minister said to his wife, "Do you think I put enough fire into my sermons?" She said, "To tell the truth, I don't think you put enough of your sermons into the fire."

To love to preach is one thing; to love to whom you preach is quite another.

—D. Martin Lloyd-Jones

How good we are as preachers depends—not altogether, but (make no mistake!) primarily—on how good we are as men.

—John Knox

Three common lies:
1. The check is in the mail.
2. I'm from the government; I'm here to help.
3. I'll be brief.

If you preach to hurting hearts, you will never want for a congregation; there is one in every pew.

—Joseph Parker

After all our preparation, general and specific, for the conduct of public worship and for preaching, our dependence for real success is on the Spirit of God.

—John A. Broadus

A young man asked Charles H. Spurgeon, "Why don't I get results from my preaching?"

Spurgeon answered, "You must preach for a *verdict*."

A bishop gave a masterful oration that drew the ecstatic applause of the people when he finished. He then noticed that Francis de Sales was in the congregation, and he asked the spiritual leader what he thought of the sermon. After a long silence, St. Francis replied, "You pleased all but one."

—Donald Coggan

The new preacher's car broke down just after the morning service. On Monday morning he drove it to the town's one garage for repairs.

"I hope you'll go a little easy on the cost," he told the mechanic. "After all, I'm just a poor preacher."

"I know it," came the reply. "I heard you preach yesterday."

When Joseph Parker, the brilliant biblical preacher of City Temple, London, preached at a farewell service for G. Campbell Morgan, he affirmed out of his years of devotion to the Scriptures: "You may depend on one thing—the only ministry that will last, and be as fresh at the end as it was at the beginning, is a biblical and an expository one. Mere anecdotes, whether possible or impossible—most of them are impossible—fail, and in the long run exhaust themselves, but the Word of the Lord abideth forever."

An elder said to his pastor, "Every Monday morning I see you coming from the YMCA. What do you do there?"

"Our ministerium meets there."

"What do you do there?"

"We exchange sermons from each other so that we don't have to prepare sermons."

"How is it that you get rooked every time?"

Someone asked Spurgeon, "What should you do when your people get sleepy?" He answered, "Put pins in the preacher!"

Henry David Thoreau was reportedly unimpressed by telegraph wires which had been strung across the New England sky to speed news from New York to Boston. After a friend had glowingly described the rapidity and clarity with which a message could be sent, Thoreau raised a simple but crucial question, "What if we have nothing to say?"

The man of God must have something to say!

If God calls you to be a minister, don't stoop to become a king.

—Charles H. Spurgeon

Carved on a pulpit: "If you haven't struck oil in twenty minutes, quit boring."

"Why do actors seem to have no difficulty in making an impression on their audiences?" was the question asked by the then Archbishop of Canterbury to Thomas Betterton (1635–1710). The famous actor replied, "Actors speak of things imaginary as if they were real, while you preachers too often speak of things real as if they were imaginary."

A reporter once said to George Bernard Shaw, "You have a marvelous gift for oratory. How did you develop it?"

Shaw replied, "I learned to speak as men learn to skate or cycle, by doggedly making a fool of myself until I got used to it."

The Devil will let a preacher prepare a sermon if it will keep him from preparing himself.

—Vance Havner

I often dream that I'm called on to preach, but I can't find my outline.

—Martin Luther

After the Bishop of Lichfield spoke of the necessity of studying the Word, a vicar told the bishop that he could not believe his doctrine. "Often when I am in the vestry I do not know what I am going to talk about; but I go into the pulpit and preach and think nothing of it." The bishop replied, "And you are quite right in thinking nothing of it, for your church wardens have told me that they share your opinion."

—Charles H. Spurgeon

A preacher stood up and said, "I have so much to say, I don't know where to begin." A little boy stood up and said, "Could you begin somewhere near the end?"

I value a sermon not by the approbation of men, or of the ability manifest in it, but by the effect produced in comforting the saint and awakening the sinner.

—Charles H. Spurgeon

When you shoot over their heads, all you prove is that you are a poor aim.

One evening a Christian was walking home from a church service when he stopped to talk to a fellow member who had missed the meeting. The absentee asked him, "Is the sermon done?" "No," came the reply, "the sermon is preached but it remains to be done."

Illustrations in a sermon are like windows, but a sermon should not be all windows. A good story helps, but I have heard sermons that were built several stories too high!

—*The Vance Havner Quote Book*

Several years ago *The British Weekly* published this provocative letter.
Dear Sir:
It seems ministers feel their sermons are very important and spend a great deal of time preparing them. I have been attending church quite regularly for thirty years and I have probably heard three thousand of them. To my consternation, I discovered that I cannot remember a single sermon. I wonder if a minister's time might be more profitably spent on something else?

For weeks a storm of editorial responses ensued, which finally ended with this letter.
Dear Sir:
I have been married thirty years. During that time I have eaten 32,850 meals—mostly my wife's cooking. I cannot remember the menu of a single meal. And yet . . . I have the distinct impression that without them, I would have starved to death long ago.

—John Schletewitz

Luther's advice to a young preacher:
Stand up cheerfully.
Speak out manfully.
Leave off speedily.

—D. L. Moody

After an outstanding man attended the men's Bible class, he was asked for a comment on the lesson. He replied that it was like the peace and mercy of God.

"Yes," he continued, "it was like the peace of God because it passed all understanding, and like His mercy because I thought it would endure forever."

It is not skillfully composed discourse, nor the mode of delivery, nor well-practiced eloquence that produces conviction, but the communication of divine power.

—Origen

The test of a preacher is that his congregation goes away saying not "What a lovely sermon!" but "I will do something."

—Francis de Sales

A lady called a Presbyterian minister and said, "My mother is very sick. Please come over quick."
"But lady, you're a Baptist. Why don't you call your preacher?"
"Well, my mother has a contagious disease and I don't want our preacher to get it."

Ted Fix, a Dallas Theological Seminary graduate and evangelist, was holding meetings in Cambridge, Massachusetts. A shabby man came up afterwards and said, "I don't believe a word you said—but I believe you believe it."

307

W. H. Griffith Thomas's advice to young preachers was: "Think yourself empty, read yourself full, write yourself clear, pray yourself keen—then enter the pulpit and let yourself go!"

John Wesley was so desirous of using the language of his people that he frequently read his sermons to the serving maid to see if she understood what he was saying.

God gives us the message, but He does so through a messenger who has been impacted by the truth.

—Phillips Brooks

A minister was called to a church of seven hundred and on his first Sunday someone asked him how he hoped to please seven hundred people. He wisely replied, "I don't. I have come to please only One."

"Why is it you have so many conversions and I never seem to have any?" a young preacher asked Spurgeon. "You do not expect to have conversations every time you preach, do you?" Spurgeon asked. "No, certainly I don't expect anything like that," he replied. "Then that is just the reason you don't have them. I aim for conversions and expect to have them every time I preach."

John Bunyan told of an incident which took place at the close of one of his sermons. A man said, "Mr. Bunyan, what a beautiful sermon you gave us this morning." "You are too late," said Bunyan, "the Devil told me that before I came out of the pulpit."

A child said, "My dad's a doctor. I can be sick for nothing." Another said, "My dad is a lawyer. I can be bad for nothing." A third lad responded, "My dad is a preacher. I can be good for nothing."

"How did you like Mr. Spurgeon?" someone asked of a friend who had just returned from hearing the famous preacher.

The reply was, "I forgot to investigate Mr. Spurgeon; my attention was drawn so closely to the Savior of whom he was preaching."

The true way to get rid of the boniness of a sermon is not by leaving out the skeleton, but by clothing it with flesh.

—Phillips Brooks

Charles H. Spurgeon once told of a man who preached so well and lived so badly that when he was in the pulpit everybody said he ought never to come out again, and when he was out of it they declared that he ought never to enter it again.

"You," said Demosthenes to his great rival orator, Aeschilus, "make them say, 'How well he speaks!' I make them say, 'Let us march against Philip.'"

The average man's idea of a good sermon is one that goes over his head—and hits one of his neighbors.

The story is told of a preacher who was often referring to the unction of the Lord. Someone chided him about this and said, "Just what do you mean by unction?"

"Well," he replied, "I don't know if I can tell you exactly what it is but I can sure tell you what it ain't."

The Scottish preacher Alexander Whyte met a person one Sunday who said to him, "Dr. Whyte, you preached today as if you had come straight from the presence of God." Whyte replied, "Perhaps I did."

—*Our Daily Bread*

A curate went to his vicar and showed him his very early attempt at preaching. He had it all written out, as a lot of Anglicans do, and he handed it to his vicar and said, "Will it do?" Somewhat unkindly, the vicar replied, "Will it do what?"

I preach as though Christ were crucified yesterday, rose from the dead today, and is coming back to earth again tomorrow!

—Martin Luther

Each time you go into the pulpit, go as if it were your first time, and your best time, and your last time.

—Vance Havner

"Would you do anything different if you had to live your life over again?" a reporter asked Billy Graham. The reply: "Yes, I would have studied more and spoken less. At least three times more than I had done."

Donald Grey Barnhouse said, "If I had only three years to serve the Lord, I would spend two of them studying and preparing."

A preacher's throne is the pulpit; he stands in Christ's stead; his message is the Word of God; around him are immortal souls; the Savior, unseen, is beside him; the Holy Spirit broods over the congregation; angels gaze upon the scene, and heaven and hell await the issue. What associations, and what vast responsibility!

—Matthew Simpson

When a young man was preaching, an older pastor was there. After the sermon, the young preacher asked the older man what he thought. The man said it was pretty good except for three things.

"You read your sermon."
"Oh, I shouldn't do that."
"You didn't read it very well."
"I'll need to work on it."
"It wasn't worth reading."

C. S. Lewis told Frank Gaebelein of a preacher who said that people "would be in danger of severe eschatological consequences." C. S. Lewis asked the preacher after the service, "Do you mean they will be in danger of hell?"
"Yes."
"Then why didn't you say so?"

One highly successful pastor reports that as a young preacher he preached in the usual abstract, flowery, oratorical style, over the heads not only of the children but also of the grownups, as younger preachers are tempted to do. One day a faithful elder said to him, "You preach well, Pastor, but you will never move this congregation until your sermons go with them into their homes." The pastor changed his ways. Each sermon now pointed out to his hearers how to apply the truth of the text in their daily life at home. He learned to invent stories to do that. That, he reported, changed his congregation. It is well known that Richard Baxter changed his parish by going from home to home, showing his people how to have effective daily devotions.

A young minister fresh from college said to W. L. Watkinson, that master of satire, "You know, Dr. Watkinson, preaching does not take anything out of me." "No," said Watkinson, "and therefore it puts nothing into anyone else!"

When a country minister asked Henry Ward Beecher what to do when an audience went to sleep on a hot Sunday afternoon, Beecher replied, "Have an usher get a sharp stick and prod the preacher!"

Genius is not essential to good preaching, but a live man is.

—Austin Phelps

I preached as never sure to preach again
The message of a dying man to dying men.
—Richard Baxter

Preach any Christ but a crucified Christ and you will not draw people for long.
—R. A. Torrey

In many churches a mild-mannered man is preaching to mild-mannered people telling them to be mild.

You're not called to preach if you're not called to study.

After all our preparation, general and special, for the conduct of public worship and for preaching, our dependence for real success is on the Spirit of God.
—John A. Broadus

Sermons come out of a man's life. Good preaching depends more on what a man is in himself than on academic preparation, accumulated reading, or the experience of years.
—Edward L. R. Elson

Martin Luther said preaching made his knees knock.

I preached in a little church not long ago, and while I was waiting to preach, I looked over and saw a fire extinguisher on the side of the pulpit. Strangest thing I'd ever seen! But the more I thought about it, the more appropriate it seemed because if a fire is going to start anywhere it's likely to start in the pulpit. If it doesn't start there, you can forget about the rest of it.

—William Hinson

The message for tomorrow evening is rich. You will give it as something that has helped you, won't you? Otherwise it is just an interesting little Bible study. The great thing is to give what has strengthened you and kindled your own soul. Then it is sure to kindle others.

—Amy Carmichael

A young preacher having trouble in his congregation came to me about it. I told him about my experience when I was a boy. When I would go to the barn at night to feed the horse or the cow, I would light a lantern and carry it with me. When I would open the barn door and step in, two things would happen: The rats would scurry and run for cover, and the birds which were roosting on the rafters would begin to sing. Light had those two very different effects. And when the Word of God is preached, you will see the rats run for cover and the birds begin to sing.

—J. Vernon McGee

A prominent preacher was delayed in getting to a meeting. Seeing this, Satan got there first and told the people he was the substitute. He opened the pulpit Bible, read a text, and proceeded to preach. The scheduled preacher finally arrived, recognized Satan in the pulpit, and was amazed to hear him declaring evangelical truth. After the meeting he said to the Devil, "Weren't you afraid to preach the truth of God's Word, lest it weaken your own kingdom?" Satan smiled and replied, "My preaching won't change anybody's life.

You see, I can speak the right words, but I don't have any unction."

—Warren W. Wiersbe

An old American Indian attended a church service one Sunday morning. The preacher's message lacked real spiritual food, so he did a lot of shouting and pulpit pounding to cover up his lack of preparation. In fact, as is sometimes said, he "preached up quite a storm." After the service someone asked the Indian, who was a Christian, what he thought of the minister's message. Thinking for a moment, he summed up his opinion in six words: "High wind. Big thunder. No rain."

A pastor who was remarkable in the first period of his ministry for a boisterous mode of preaching, suddenly changed his whole manner in the pulpit and adopted a mild and dispassionate mode of delivery. When asked about the change, he replied, "When I was young I thought it was thunder that killed people; but when I grew older and wiser I discovered that it was the lightning. So I determined to thunder less and lighten more."

I want to begin preachin' you today about the parable of the Good Samaritan who commenced to go down from Jerusalem to Jericho, but he fell among thieves and they left him for dead. And lo and behold the Queen of Sheba came by in her chariot, in her high class silver-spoked wheels, but before she could help him, here came Elijah in his chariot and he challenged her to a drag race. And off they went in a cloud of exhaust fumes, and great, I say great, was the smell thereof. The Good Samaritan was worried 'cause the Queen of Sheba was not a good driver, so he got down on the floor of the chariot and after a few yards he wanted to see where he was, so he lifted up his head, and just as he did they passed under a juniper tree and his hair caught in the limbs, and there he was dangling between heaven and earth, forty days and forty nights. And the ravens brought him food, locusts, and wild honey. Then his wife Delilah came along and cut his hair.

And some of it fell on stony ground, and some of it fell on good ground, and some of it fell among thorns. Then the Good Samaritan picked himself up and started walkin' down the road and he came to a fork in the road and he didn't know which way to go so he took the broad smooth path that headed down. And he ran into a little boy trying to kill a giant with a slingshot and he knew he didn't want none of that.

So he got down on his knees before the burning bush and he said, "Lord, if there is one thing you can give me, give me wisdom to know which decision I should make." He told him to go back to the fork in the road and go the other way. So he went back and took the straight path that led to the narrow gate. And he came into a cloud that was just about the size of a mustard seed. And out of that cloud, I say out of that cloud, it rained forty days and forty nights. And the whole earth was flooded, so he built himself an ark. Then he heard a voice saying, "Adam, Adam, where are you?" And he said, "Here I am, send me." Then the animals on the ark cast lots to see who should be thrown overboard. And the Good Samaritan won the toss. And he chose to be thrown overboard. And when he was thrown into the water, a great big fish ate him and after three days and three nights, he spit him up on the shore, and great, I say great, was the mess thereof.

Then the Samaritan began to walk down the road and he got hungry. An' he saw a man tearing down barns and buildin' bigger barns. And he tried to buy some food from him, five loaves and two fishes with thirty pieces of silver. But the rich young ruler told him, "Go hang yourself." And he came upon a crowd of people of about five thousand, just countin' the men. And he climbed up into a sycamore tree to see what he could see, and someone yelled up at him, "Come down and eat with me." And he said, "I can't. I just took a wife." And while he was up in that sycamore tree he looked out into the far distance and he saw the leaning tower of Babel, and on top of that tower there was Jezebel with her coat of many colors. And he cried out, "Throw her down!" And they threw her down. And he cried out again, "Throw her down!" Seventy times seven they threw her down. And the fragments they collected were twelve baskets full. Now the question I want to ask you, dearly beloved brethren, is "Whose wife will she be in the judgment?"

A young minister in a college town was embarrassed by the thought of criticism in his cultured congregation. Seeking counsel from his father, an old and wise minister, he said, "Dad, I'm hampered in my ministry here. If I cite something from geology, there is a professor of science right there before me. If I use an illustration from Roman mythology, another professor is ready to trip me up for my little inaccuracy. If I mention something in English literature that pleases me, I'm cowed by the presence of the learned man who teaches that subject. What shall I do?"

The sagacious old man replied, "Don't be discouraged, son. Preach the Gospel. They probably know little of that."

PREDESTINATION

A group of theologians were discussing predestination and free will. When the argument became heated, the dissidents split into two groups. One man, unable to make up his mind which group to join, slipped into the predestination crowd. Challenged as to why he was there, he said, "I came of my own free will." The group retorted, "Free will. You can't join us!" He retreated to the opposing group and met the same challenge. "I was sent here," he answered honestly. "Get out!" they stormed. "You can't join us unless you come of your own free will." And the confused Christian was out in the cold.

—Leslie B. Flynn

PREDICAMENTS

A woman rushed to the camera counter and gasped, "My husband slipped off the ladder and is hanging from the eaves with his hands. Please hurry!" "What can I do?" asked the clerk. "Sell me a roll of film as quickly as you can" was the answer. "My camera is empty!"

PREJUDICE

Prejudice is self-inflicted blindness.

Prejudice is being down on what you're not up on.

Prejudice is a great time saver. It enables one to form opinions without bothering to get the facts.

PREPARATION

Someone asked H. A. Ironside, "Why should I get a seminary education? You didn't and you're a great preacher." Ironside responded, "God does bless some who don't have an education, but He doesn't bless those who have an opportunity for education but don't take advantage of it."

My father, John Roach Straton, had a reputation as a defender of the faith. A young man had come to him and said, "I want to preach." Questioning him, my father discovered that he had not finished high school, much less college or seminary. So his advice was to complete all three. The fellow replied, "But I believe that God will fill my mouth." Father responded, "Yes, God will fill your mouth if you fill your head first."

—Hillyer H. Straton

Dig the well before you are thirsty.
—Chinese proverb

When the chief of a New England town's voluntary fire department was asked what was the first thing they did when called to extinguish a fire, he said, "The first thing we do is drench the premises with water, knock out the windows, and chop up the furniture."

"What's the second thing you do?"

"The second thing we do," added the chief, "is to make absolutely certain we are at the right address."

—*Accent on Youth*

If you give me ten minutes to chop down a tree, I'll spend my first two minutes sharpening my ax.

—C. S. Lewis

I will study and get ready, then maybe my chance will come.

—Abraham Lincoln

Some people are making such thorough preparation for rainy days that they aren't enjoying today's sunshine.

Nelaton was a skilled and highly esteemed French surgeon. Once he said that if he had only four minutes to perform a life-saving operation, he would take at least one minute to assess the best way to do it.

PRESIDENTS

In America anyone can grow up to be president. That's just the chance we all take.
—Adlai E. Stevenson

During World War II a young navy pilot made an air strike against the Japanese-held Chichi Jima Island. His plane was struck by anti-aircraft fire, and he had to bail out over the Pacific. Another pilot spotted his chute just as it hit the water and radioed his position. Within minutes, the submarine USS *Finback* surfaced and rescued the flyer. Safely on board, he silently thanked God for sparing his life. That young pilot was George Bush, the man who became the forty-first president of the United States.

PRESSURE

It does not matter how great the pressure is, it matters only where the pressure lies—whether it comes between you and God, or whether it presses you closer to His heart.

—J. Hudson Taylor

You will never be the person you can be if pressure, tension, and discipline are taken out of your life.

—James G. Bildey

PRIDE (Also see BOASTING)

I read a fable about a dog who loved to chase other animals. He bragged about his great running skill and said he could catch anything. Well, it wasn't long until his boastful claims were put to the test by a

rabbit. With ease the little creature outran his barking pursuer. The other animals, watching with glee, began to laugh. The dog excused himself, however, by saying, "You forget, folks, that I was only running for fun. He was running for his life!"
—Richard W. De Haan

A man was asked why he so often talked to himself. He replied, "Well, sir, you see it's this way. I like to talk to an intelligent person and I like to hear an intelligent person talk."

A conceited person never really gets anywhere—because he thinks he's already there.
—Hal Roach

He who falls in love with himself will have no rivals.
—Hal Roach

Your halo only has to slip a few inches to become a noose.

An egotist is a self-made man who worships his creator.

A mother whale said to her baby whale, "When you get to the surface and start to blow, that's when you get harpooned."

Paul Dixon, president of Cedarville College, was successful and sensed he was filled with pride. He told his pastor about his problem with pride when a young man. His pastor just laughed at him and then said in all seriousness, "What makes you think you have reason to be proud?" He then added, "I'll tell you what you should realize is the cause of pride." "What's that?" Dixon asked. "Imagination."

Sometime when you're feeling important,
Sometime when your ego's in bloom,
Sometime when you take it for granted
That you're the best qualified in the room.
Sometime when you think you're going
Would leave an unfillable hole,
Just follow this simple direction
And see how it humbles your soul.

Take a bucket and fill it with water.
Put your hand in it up to the wrist.
Take it out and the hole that's remaining
Is a measure of how you'll be missed.
You may splash all you wish as you enter.
You may stir up the water, galore,
But stop—in just a minute
It looks much the same as before.
Now the moral of this little lesson
Is to try to improve and not worsen.
Be proud of yourself, but remember—
There is no indispensable person.

Some people are willing to serve God but only as His consultant.

The essential vice, the utmost evil, is pride. Unchastity, anger, greed, and drunkenness are mere flea biters in comparison. It was through Pride that the Devil became the Devil. Pride leads to every other vice. It is the complete anti-God state of mind. . . . As long as you are proud you cannot know God. A proud man is always looking down on things and people. And, of course, as long as you are looking down, you cannot see something that is above you.
—C. S. Lewis

The human body is very sensitive. Pat a man on the back and his head swells.

Do you wish people to speak well of you? Then do not speak at all of yourself.

A top-ranking British official once entertained a haughty and sophisticated lady in his home. By mistake his assistant asked her to sit on the left of her host rather than in the place of honor at his right hand. The visitor was offended and became very indignant. Turning to the general she said, "I suppose you have real difficulty in getting your aide-de-camp to seat your guests properly at the table." "Oh, not at all," came the reply. "I have found that those who matter don't mind, and those who mind don't matter!"

The bigger a man's head becomes, the easier it is to fill his shoes.

A proud man is one who waits for a vacancy in the Trinity.

—Mark Twain

He who sings his own praises is always a soloist.

There's one thing to be said about the egotist—he doesn't talk much about other people.

There are only two classes of people: those who say to God, "Thy will be done," and those to whom God finally says, "Thy will be done."

—C. S. Lewis

A pompous boor was loudly telling his companion and the world about his accomplishments.

"I tell you, I started with nothing," he proclaimed. "I am completely self-made."

A sad little man could no longer stand it. "I sympathize with you, friend," he said quietly. "I'm no good at those do-it-yourself projects either."

It isn't the things we know that get us into trouble. It's the things we know for sure that do.

The person who knows everything has a lot to learn.

My sermon today is on humility, and in my opinion, it's one of the finest pieces ever written.

Bumper sticker: "I'm back by popular demand."

Pride has its built-in hazard, as illustrated in the fable of the two ducks and the frog. These best of friends had to leave their home pond when it began to dry up. The ducks knew they could easily fly to another location. To transport their friend the frog, they decided to fly with a stick between their two bills, with the frog hanging on the stick with its mouth. A farmer, looking up from his field at the flying trio, remarked, "Well, isn't that a clever idea. I wonder who thought of that." The frog said, "I did." He learned the hard way that pride goeth before a fall.

—Leslie B. Flynn

Jumbo the elephant and Flick the flea were longtime friends. They often walked and chatted together.

One day they were walking along a backcountry road when they came to a flimsy wooden bridge that spanned a deep gorge. They walked across side by side, the little bridge swaying and creaking under the weight of the elephant. When they were across, the flea asked his big friend, "Did you notice how we shook that bridge?"

When you sing your own praise, you always get the tune too high.

Don't brag; it isn't the whistle that pulls the train.

An egotist is an "I" specialist.

None are so empty as those who are full of themselves.

—Benjamin Whichcote

When small men cast long shadows, it is a sign that the sun is setting.

The greatest of all faults is to imagine you have none.

While still a young man, Henry Morehouse conducted evangelistic services in Canada. He was quite distressed when there were little outward results. He had seen many some to Christ in the United States and Great Britain, but in Canada he seemed to meet only with defeat. Day and night he was on his knees searching his heart and crying, "Oh God, why is there no revival? Why is there no seeming movement of the Holy Spirit?" The next day as he walked along the street he saw a large sign on which appeared these words: "Come to hear Henry Morehouse, the most famous of all British preachers!" "Ah," he said to himself, "now I have found the reason!"

He went at once to the campaign committee and said, "Brethren, I see how you have advertised me as the greatest of this and the greatest of that! No wonder the Holy Spirit cannot work! He is grieved and quenched because you haven't magnified the Lord Jesus Christ."

Make sure it is God's trumpet you are blowing. If it is only yours, it won't wake the dead; it will simply disturb the neighbors.

—Major Ian Thomas

The greatest sin in the ministry is pride.

—J. Vernon McGee

A man who had a high opinion of himself stepped on a coin-operated scale that dispensed a card, giving his weight and comments about his personality. After reading the card, he handed it to his wife and said, "Here, look at this!" She took it and read aloud, "You are dynamic, a born leader, handsome, and much admired by women for your personality." Giving a second look, she added, "Hmmmm . . . I see it got your weight wrong too!"

—Our Daily Bread

While walking along the water's edge one day, Oliver Wendell Holmes met a small child. After they had strolled down the beach for a short distance, she announced, "I must go home now." As she was leaving, he remarked, "When your mother asks you where you've been, tell her you've been walking with Oliver Wendell Holmes!" The sweet youngster replied, "And when your folks ask you where you've been, tell them you have been walking with Mary Susanna Brown." In Christ there are no "big shots" and no "favored ones."

The head begins to swell when the mind stops growing.

It is a sign that your reputation is small and shrinking if your tongue must praise you.

—Mathew Hale

"Pali, this bull has killed me." So said Jose Cubero, one of Spain's most brilliant matadors, before he lost consciousness and died.

Only twenty-one years old, he had been enjoying a spectacular career. However, in this 1985 bullfight, Jose made a tragic mistake. He thrust his sword a final time into the bleeding, delirious bull, which then collapsed. Considering the struggle finished, Jose turned to the crowd to acknowledge the applause.

The bull, however, was not dead. It rose and lunged at the unsuspecting matador, its horn piercing his back and puncturing his heart.

Just when we think we've finished off pride, just when we turn to accept the congratulations of the crowd, pride stabs us in the back. We should never consider pride dead before we are.

—Craig Brian Larson

He who thinks he can find in himself the means of doing without others is much mistaken; but he who thinks that others cannot do without him is still more mistaken.

—La Rochefoucauld

"Thank you for that message, Pastor."

"Don't thank me. Thank the Lord."

"I thought of that, but it wasn't quite that good."

In the summer of 1986, two ships collided in the Black Sea, causing a tragic loss of life. The news of the disaster was further darkened, however, when an investigation revealed the cause of the accident which hurled hundreds of passengers into the icy waters. The tragedy was not traced to some major problem like a breakdown in radar or thick fog. The blame was attributed to human stubbornness. Each captain was aware of the other's presence. Both could have taken evasive action to avert the collision. But according to the news reports, neither wanted to give way to the other. It seems that each was too proud to yield and make the first move. By the time they saw the error of their ways, it was too late.

—Our Daily Bread

The man who does as he pleases is seldom pleased with what he does.

When Napoleon set out to conquer Russia at the head of the Grand Army of Europe, someone reminded him that "man proposes but God disposes." The conqueror of Europe replied, "I am he that both proposes and disposes."

The secretary of Ray Stedman, former pastor in Palo Alto, California, had a sign in her office that said, "I've come to accept two truths: (1) There is one God, and (2) You ain't Him."

More irksome than the person who exalts himself is someone who agrees with you when you describe your faults.
—William Walden

Mohamed Ali, when he was Cassius Clay, was on a plane. A flight attendant said, "Please fasten your seatbelt." He responded in pride, "Superman don't need no seatbelt." She responded, "Superman don't need no airplane either."

Nothing's as hard to do gracefully as getting down off your high horse.
—*Soundings*

George Allen wrote a book entitled *Presidents Who Have Known Me*.

Five things I keep meekly hid
"Myself" and "I"
And "Mine" and "My"
And what "I did and said."

He who sings his own praises is seldom asked for an encore.

Temper is what gets most of us into trouble. Pride is what keeps us there.

At one time the newspaper cartoonist H. T. Webster amused himself by sending telegrams to twenty of his acquaintances, selected at random. Each message contained the one word, "Congratulations!" So far as Webster knew, not one of them had done anything in particular on which he might be complimented. But each of the twenty took the message as a matter of course and wrote him a letter of thanks. Each had assumed that he had done something worthy of a congratulatory telegram!

You can have no greater sign of a confirmed pride than when you think you are humble enough.

No man is wise enough, nor good enough, to be trusted with unlimited power.
—Charles Caleb Cotton

God has humbled Himself, but man is still proud.
—Augustine

The man who has an exalted opinion of himself is usually a poor judge of human nature.

A man wrapped up in himself makes a small package.

No man is great in the eyes of his butler.

Talk to a man about himself and he will listen for hours.
—Benjamin Disraeli

Every time he looks in the mirror he takes a bow.

The Devil has no fault to find with people who are satisfied with themselves.

Few can tell what they know without also showing what they don't know.

Good breeding consists in concealing how much we think of ourselves and how little we think of the other person.
—Mark Twain

A man is never as good as he says he is or as bad as others say he is.

The quickest way to take the starch out of a man who is always blaming himself is to agree with him.

Be big enough to admit and admire the abilities of people who are better than you are.

The worker who has a right to boast doesn't have to.

Far better a sinner who knows he is a sinner than a saint who knows he is a saint.

No man can give the impression at the same time that he is clever and that Jesus Christ is Lord.

—James Dewey

Nothing is more to me than myself.

—Max Stirner

An egotist is a person who thinks that if he hadn't been born people would ask why not.

—E. Pangborne

An insurance company pictured the Titanic sailing straight for the iceberg which many years ago sank that luxury liner. States the advertisement, "They called her the 'Millionaire's Special.' Four city blocks long, eleven stories high, powered by triple propellers, protected by the latest, most ingenious devices, luxurious and beautiful beyond words, she caught the fancy of the world. On April 10, 1912, she slipped out of Southampton on her maiden voyage to New York. Less than five days later, she went down in 12,000 feet of icy water, 300 feet of her hull ripped open by a massive iceberg. Actually the Titanic was more than a ship. She was a symbol of man's power. Majestic! Colossal! Unsinkable! But when the 'unsinkable' sank, something went down with it. No one would ever again feel the same confidence in man's strength."

He who falls in love with himself will have no rivals.

—Benjamin Franklin

An egotist is a person of low taste who is more interested in himself than in me.

—Ambrose Pierce

I had dinner with a relation who, when thanks were offered for the food, said, "I bow my head before no one, neither God or man. I've made my own way by myself."

—E. Schuyler English

One of Socrates' disciples asked the master, "Why is it, sir, that you tell all who want to become your disciple to look into this pond and tell you what he sees?"

The sage answered, "That is very simple, my friend. I am ready to accept all those who tell me they see the fish swimming around. But those who see only their own image mirrored in the water are in love with their ego. I have no use for them."

Out of the night that covers me,
  Black as the pit from pole to pole,
I think whatever gods may be,
  For my unconquerable soul.
In the full clutch of circumstance
  I have not winced nor cried aloud.
Under the bludgeoning of chance
  My head's bloody, but unbowed.
Beyond this place of wrath and tears
  Looms but the horror of the shade,
And yet the menace of the years
  Finds and shall find me unafraid.
It matter not how strait the gate,
  How charged with punishments the scroll
I am the master of my fate,
  I am the captain of my soul.
  —William Ernest Henley, *Invictus*

The family was discussing a domineering and extremely self-centered maiden aunt. Mother, exasperated by Aunt Ella's latest demand, said, "What Ella needs is to experience some *real* trouble, such as losing someone she loves very much."

Grandma, who had been listening, remarked quietly, "True child, true. But you can't cry at your own funeral."

PRIORITIES

When Charles E. Hummell was going into the ministry, a businessman gave him an excellent piece of advice. "Be careful that the urgent doesn't crowd out the important."

—*The Tyranny of the Urgent*

PRISON

A socialite wanted to have a book written about her family. Much to her horror she discovered that one of her grandfathers had been electrocuted in the Sing Sing prison. Since she was ashamed of that and wanted that fact hidden, the following statement appeared in the book: "One of her grandfathers occupied a chair of applied electricity in one of America's best known institutions. He was very much attached to his position and literally died in the harness."

PROBLEMS

With me, a change of trouble is as good as a vacation.

—David Lloyd George

It's really not so bad to have a few problems. The only people who don't are in the cemetery.

"The hardest thing about milking cows," observed a farmer, "is that they never stay milked."

Yard by yard, life is hard. Inch by inch, life's a cinch.

A man of character finds a special attractiveness in difficulty, since it is only by coming to grips with difficulty that he can recognize his potentialities.

—Charles de Gaulle

I think I see light at the end of the tunnel. I only hope it's not a locomotive.

Life is like a grindstone. Whether it grinds you down or polishes you up depends on the stuff you're made of.

No one can hold two watermelons in one hand.

—Afghanistan proverb

Wendell Wilkie said, "What a man needs to get ahead is a powerful enemy." Edmund Burke said, "Our antagonist is our helper. He that wrestles with it strengthens our muscles and sharpens our skills."

Apparently human nature must have something to push against and something to wrestle with. I suppose this is the hopeful thing about handicaps. We all have them in some form. Handicaps are the hard things we wrestle with and push against.

—J. Wallace Hamilton

Each problem has hidden in it an opportunity so powerful that it literally dwarfs the problem. The greatest success stories were created by people who recognized a problem and turned it into an opportunity.

—Joseph Sugarman

A man and his wife were taking a bus trip through the mountains, and the bus broke down right in front of a backwoods grocery store. The woman there apparently had seldom been anywhere else.

The wife said, "I don't believe she knows what's going on in the world outside."

Her husband replied, "Well, don't tell her. I wouldn't want the poor soul to know. Let her die in peace."

I may not know all the answers, but I at least know where to get them.

—Henry Ford

In Greek mythology Gordius, a peasant, became king of Phrygia in Asia Minor. He used to tie the ox yoke to his chariot, both of which he dedicated to Zeus. If someone could untie the difficult knot, he would become ruler of all of Asia. No one could do it, but Alexander the Great cut the knot with his sword, an unusual solution. So the phrase "cut the Gordian knot" means solving a difficult problem in an unusual way.

Sam Moore, former president of Thomas Nelson Publishers, had a sign on his office door, "Bring me your solutions, not your problems."

—Ted Engstrom

PROCRASTINATION

Always put off until tomorrow what you shouldn't do at all.

—Farmer's Almanac

Procrastination is the thief of time, but more so, it is the thief of souls.

The more you leave to chance, the less chance there is for you.

The things you'll do tomorrow are the things you would have done today if you had thought about them yesterday.

One of the greatest labor-saving inventions of today is tomorrow.
—Vincent T. Foss

In Guatemala, the Chequel Indians always answer the questions asked of them by saying "No." Then they think about it for a while before answering "Yes."

The best way to kill time is to get busy and work it to death.

Joe's chronically late for everything. His ancestors came over on the Juneflower.

It takes more to plow a field than merely turning it over in your mind.

God promised forgiveness to your repentance, but He has not promised tomorrow to your procrastination.

The future is that time when you'll wish that you'd done what you aren't doing now.

In my second year at Biola Bible College I and several students went every Sunday morning to one of the missions on skid row.

After the service one Sunday morning, I was talking with a man about his soul. He knew the way of salvation. He knew practically every verse I showed him. In fact, he said he wanted to be saved, but he didn't want to then. I pleaded with that man for an hour and a half to turn to Christ now that he had the opportunity, but he would not yield to Christ. He himself even told me of incidents in which men were suddenly taken by death. I told him he was preaching his own sermon, and that that could happen to him too. But he put it off,

and in despair I left the man who continued to say, "Not now. Not now." What a tragedy that many are the same way today. They intend to be saved, but "not now."
—Roy B. Zuck

Colonel Rahl, the Hessian commander at Trenton, was playing cards when a courier brought a message stating that General George Washington was crossing the Delaware River. Rahl put the letter in his pocket and didn't bother to read it until the game was finished. Then, realizing the seriousness of the situation, he hurriedly tried to rally his men to meet the coming attack, but his procrastination was his undoing. He and many of his men were killed, and the rest of the regiment was captured.

Tomorrow is the excuse of the lazy and the refuge of the incompetent.
—Nolbett Quayle

Learn right at the outset not to play with the spoon before you take the medicine. Putting off an easy thing makes it hard, and putting off a hard one makes it impossible.
—George Horace Lorimer

"Tomorrow," he promised his conscience;
  "tomorrow I mean to believe;
Tomorrow I'll think as I ought to;
  tomorrow my Savior receive;
Tomorrow I'll conquer the habits that
  hold one from heaven away."
But ever his conscience repeated one
  word, and only one: "Today."
Tomorrow, tomorrow, tomorrow—thus
  day after day it went on;
Tomorrow, tomorrow, tomorrow—till
  youth like a vision was gone:
Till age and his passions had written
  the message of fate on his brow;
And forth from the shadows came Death,
  with the pitiless syllable, "Now!"

When the ship *Stephen Whitney* struck on an Irish cliff and clung there for a few moments, all the passengers who leaped instantly onto the rock were saved. Those who lingered were swept off by the returning wave and engulfed forever.

PROCRASTINATION

If you should wake one dreadful day,
Before His throne and hear Him say,
"I am the Way you did not take,
Although I died once for your sake;
I am the Truth you did not heed;
You were so sure you had no need;
I am the Light you would not see
Now darkness for eternity!"
You cannot say, "I did not know:"
He plainly wrote and told you so.
And if you would not read His Word,
That Word still stands, "Thus saith the
    Lord!"
                    —Martha Snell Nicholson

Suppose you are in the army and you are out on the battlefield raiding the enemy and on the way back to your trench you get hit. Bill Smith stops long enough to pick you up and carry you back to the trenches, and while doing so he gets two bullets in the back. You are both taken to the hospital and later you both are won back from the very verge of death. Two months later the doctor comes along helping a poor fellow who limps badly and moves with evident difficulty. They stop at your bedside and the doctor says, "I want to introduce you to Mr. Smith, the man who risked his life to save you." And you fold your arms and say, "I don't know whether I want to make his acquaintance today or not. I'll think it over." No, you wouldn't say that. You would grip him by the hand and try to tell him something of the gratitude you felt.

PRODIGAL SON

They were talking about the Prodigal Son in the class at Sunday school when the teacher asked, "Was anyone sorry when the Prodigal Son returned?"

After a bit of soul-searching, one little boy said, "The fatted calf."

PROGRESS

Three words on the grave of a guide who died while climbing the Alps: "He died climbing."

David Livingstone's motto was, "Any-where, provided it is forward."

All man has learned in the last decades is how to go faster, work less, spend more, and die quicker.
                    —Construction Digest

"I'm glad you're making progress," the psychiatrist said to a patient of his. "Progress? You call that progress? Six months ago I was Napoleon, now I'm nobody."

PROMISES

The promises of God are certain but they do not all mature in days.
                    —A. J. Gordon

J. Hudson Taylor started a bank account for the China Inland Mission in Brighton, England. On the application where he was asked to designate his assets, he wrote, "Ten pounds and the promises of God."

Every promise is built upon four pillars: God's justice and holiness, which will not suffer Him to deceive; He grace or goodness, which will not suffer Him to forget; His truth, which will not suffer Him to change; and His power, which makes Him able to accomplish.
                    —H. G. Salter

A pastor visited an old man who was held fast to his chair by rheumatism, but he had his Bible open in front of him. The minister noticed the word "Proved" was written continually in the margin. The dear man had taken God's Word and written his own experience in the margin. Beside each promise as he found it come true in his own life, he had written "Proved."

If asked when you can deliver something, ask for time to think. Build in a margin of safety. Name a date. Then deliver it earlier than you promised.

The world is divided into two classes of people: the few people who make good on their promises (even if they don't promise as much) and the many who don't. Get in column A and stay there. You'll be very valuable wherever you are.
                    —Bits & Pieces

PROOFS

Adelina Patti, the great singer, instructed her home post office to forward her mail to a post office in a small French village. There she planned to pick it up.

"Any mail for Adelina Patti?" she inquired of the postmaster to whom she was a stranger.

"Yes," said the postmaster, "but have you anything to identify yourself with?"

She presented a visiting card which the postmaster said was insufficient evidence.

"What can I do?" she mused. Then a brilliant idea came to her. She began to sing! In a few moments the post office was filled with people listening in wonderment to her rapturous voice. As she concluded her song she asked the postmaster, "Are you satisfied now that I am Adelina Patti?"

"Abundantly satisfied!" said he apologetically. "Only Adelina Patti could sing as you have sung," he said as he gave her her bundle of mail.

PROPHECY

It is difficult to prophesy, particularly with regard to the future.

—Chinese proverb

PROVIDENCE (See GOD—PROVIDENCE OF)

PROVISIONS

To make ends meet, put the Lord between them.

—T. J. Bach

I have always lived from hand to mouth but it has been the Lord's hand and my mouth.

—Samuel Zwermer

PSYCHIATRY

Hello, welcome to the Psychiatric Hotline.

If you are obsessive-compulsive, please press 1 repeatedly.

If you are codependent, please ask someone to press 2.

If you have multiple personalities, please press 3, 4, 5, and 6.

If you are paranoid-delusional, we know who you are and what you want. Just stay on the line so we can trace the call.

If you are schizophrenic, listen carefully and a little voice will tell you which number to press.

If you are manic-depressive, it doesn't matter which number you press; no one will answer.

Sign outside a psychiatrist's office: "Guaranteed satisfaction or your mania back."

PSYCHOLOGY

Others worship at the shrine of education, but what about all the educated fools? A woman with a master's degree in psychology said to her boyfriend with a Ph.D., "I hope you won't mind, but I'm feeling a little schizophrenic today." "That's all right," he replied, "that makes four of us!"

PUBLIC RELATIONS

Public relations is the fine art of making sure that something is no sooner done than said.

—Bob Orben

PUNCTUALITY

A new employee was habitually late. Finally, the foreman called him in. "Don't you know what time we go to work here?" he shouted. "No, sir," was the reply, "I haven't been able to figure it out yet because the rest of you are already here."

PUNISHMENT

He who does not punish evil commands it to be done.

—Leonardo da Vinci

PURITY (Also see HOLINESS)

At fifteen, I prayed, "God keep me pure in money, morals, and motives."

—Philip Howard

One day a young minister was being escorted through a coal mine. At the entrance of one of the dim passageways, he spied a beautiful white flower growing out of the black earth. "How can it blossom in such purity and radiance in this dirty mine?" the preacher asked. "Throw some coal dust on it and see for yourself," his guide replied. When he did, he was surprised that the fine,

black particles slid right off the snowy pet-
als, leaving the plant just as lovely and un-
stained as before. Its surface was so smooth
that the grit and grime could not adhere to
it.

—*Our Daily Bread*

PURPOSE IN LIFE (Also see LIFE)

Since World War II, an Austrian psychiatrist, Victor Frankl, has written extensively
on the relation of the meaning of life to
the whole structure of personality. He
claims that the need to find meaning in life
is more basic to a human being than pleasure or power or anything else. The thesis
he repeats again and again is that if a person has a "why" to live, he can endure almost any "how." But if that dimension of
"why" is lacking, then the whole structure
of one's life eventually collapses.

This insight into the importance of
meaning was developed by Frankl during
the years he spent as a Jewish prisoner in a
German concentration camp. Life there
was unbelievably harsh and brutal. The
prisoners were forced to work long hours
and were barely given enough food, clothing, and shelter to survive. As the months
unfolded, Frankl began to note that some
prisoners soon collapsed under the pressure and gave up and died, while others
under the same conditions continued to
hope and managed to stay alive.

Using the tools of his psychiatric training, he would talk in the evening to scores
of fellow inmates about this, and he found
a pattern beginning to emerge. Those prisoners who had something to live for, an
objective that gave a sense of meaning to
their lives, were the ones who tended to
mobilize their strength and survive.

Their objectives varied widely. One
prisoner had a retarded child back home
and had a great desire to get back and take
care of the child. Another had a girlfriend
he expected to marry as soon as the war
was over. Frankl himself had begun a book
and had a fierce desire to survive and finish it and get it published.

Q

QUALITY

Quality is never an accident; it is always
the result of high intention, sincere effort,
intelligent direction, and skillful execution;
it represents the wise choice of many
alternatives.

An elderly gentleman worked as a carpenter with diligence and great precision. He
explained why he spent so much time on
each project. "I learned long ago that speed
should always be secondary to quality
workmanship. Years from now when I'm
gone and people inspect what I'm building today, no one will ask, 'How long did
this project take him?' Instead, they'll ask,
'Who made this?'"

It is not the length but the nature of our
service for Christ which counts for eternity.
Consider two young men whose lives were
very brief. David Brainerd, who brought
hundreds of American Indians to Christ,
died at age twenty-four. Robert Murray
McCheyne, through whom countless lives
were transformed in Scotland, died at age
twenty-nine. What was their secret?

From Brainerd's diary: "How sweet it
is to be the Lord's, to be sensibly devoted
to Him! I have less desire to live for the
pleasures of this world, but rather to be a
pilgrim, and to imitate the life, labors, and
sufferings of Paul."

From McCheyne's memoirs: "It is my
truest happiness to live entirely for the
glory of Christ. Not my preaching nor my
influence, but the work of God through me
to the glory of Christ."

—*The Pilgrim*

QUESTIONS

Asking dumb questions is easier than cor-
recting dumb mistakes.

Learning usually passes through three
stages. In the beginning you learn the right
answers. In the second stage you learn the
right questions. In the third and final stage

you learn which questions are worth asking.

—*Bits & Pieces*

Charles Steinmetz, called "the wizard of General Electric," said, "There are no foolish questions, and no man becomes a fool until he has stopped asking questions."

He who asks a question is a fool for a minute. He who asks no questions is a fool for a lifetime.

When an animal doesn't have anything to do, it goes to sleep. When humans have nothing to do, they ask questions.

—Bernard Lonergan

QUESTIONABLE PRACTICES

"Everything is permissible for me—but not everything is beneficial" (1 Cor. 6:12). Question 1: Is it helpful—physically, spiritually, and mentally?

"Everything is permissible for me—but I will not be mastered by anything" (1 Cor. 6:12). Question 2: Does it bring me under its power?

"Therefore, if what I eat causes my brother to fall into sin, I will never eat meat again, so that I will not cause him to fall" (1 Cor. 8:13). Question 3: Does it hurt others?

"So whether you eat or drink or whatever you do, do it all for the glory of God" (1 Cor. 10:31). Question 4: Does it glorify God?

—Jerry Bridges

R

RAPTURE (Also see SECOND COMING)

Do you know why the dead must rise first? Because they have farther to go.

—W. R. Riley

A man in Louisiana called to the attention of his non-Christian friend the word "Maranatha" on a bumper sticker. "What's that mean?" "The Lord is coming." "Ah, I don't believe that!" "Well, He's not coming for you."

A woman lost her husband to death. She knew that she would see him again. And this assurance was confirmed when she returned home after the funeral. She found a sign that her husband had used: "Gone out, back soon." That spoke to her of the fact of the rapture.

READING

Reading Christians are growing Christians. When Christians cease to read, they cease to grow.

—John Wesley

I cannot live without books.

—Thomas Jefferson

No man can be called friendless who has God and the companionship of good books.

—Elizabeth Barrett Browning

Happy is he who has laid up in his youth and held fast in all fortune, a genuine and passionate love for reading.

—Rufus Choate

The reading which counts is the reading which, in making a man think, stirs and exercises and polishes the edge of his mind.

—Leon Gutterman

At a dinner party in Paris when Benjamin Franklin was one of the distinguished guests, the Abbe Raynal asked, "What kind of man deserves the most pity?"

Franklin answered, "A lonesome man on a rainy day who does not know how to read."

He who no longer reads should get out of the ministry.

—John Wesley

When you sell a man a book you don't just sell him twelve ounces of paper and ink and glue—you sell him a whole new life.

—Christopher Morley

READING

After three days without reading, talk becomes flavorless.

—Chinese proverb

Reading is to the mind what exercise is to the body.

—Joseph Addison

The only real use of books is to make a person think for himself. If a book will not set one to thinking, it is not worth shelf room.

—Aleph Bey

Resolve to edge in a little reading each day. If you gain but fifteen minutes a day, it will make itself felt at the end of the year.

—Horace Mann

REAL ESTATE

Unobstructed view: No trees.
Awaiting your imaginative touch: Sparse interior decor.
Handyman's dream: Owner's nightmare.
Central to everything: Noisy location.
Easy commuting: Remote from everything.
Country kitchen: No dining room.
Needs finishing touches: Needs roof.
All services available: Nothing hooked up.
On the paved road: Fronts on a major highway.
Secluded: No road in.

REASON

He who will not reason is a bigot.
He who cannot reason is a fool.
He who does not reason is a slave.

REBELLION

Louis Blanc, French socialist and historian, said shortly before his execution, "When I was an infant, I rebelled against my nurse. When I was a child, I rebelled against my teachers. When I was a young man, I rebelled against my mother and father. When I reached a mature age, I rebelled against the state. When I die, if there is a heaven and a God, I'll rebel against them!"

RECONCILIATION

In one of his little books on the New Testament, A. M. Hunter describes the picture at Catterick Camp in Yorkshire, which shows a signaler lying dead in no-man's land. He had been sent out to repair a cable which had been broken by shell fire. And there he lies, cold in death, but with his task accomplished, for in his stiffened hands he holds the broken ends together. Beneath the picture is the one word "Through." So too, by his once-for-all death on Calvary, Christ has brought God and man together in reconciliation and fellowship. Moreover, by his living presence at God's right hand, he lives to make that death a potent reality in every worshiper.

—John Wood

A husband and wife became estranged and decided to separate. They moved away and lived in different parts of the country. The husband happened to return to the city on business and went out to the cemetery to the grave of their only son. Standing by the grave he heard a step behind him. When he turned, he saw his estranged wife. The initial impulse of both was to turn away. But they had a common interest in that grave, and instead of turning away they clasped hands over the grave of their son and were reconciled. They were reconciled by death.

—Clarence E. Macartney

REDEMPTION

A woman phoned her bank to arrange for the disposal of a one-thousand-dollar bond.

"Is the bond for redemption or conversion?" a clerk inquired.

There was a long pause. Then the woman asked, "Am I talking to the First National Bank or the First Baptist Church?"

When Dr. Howard Kelley of Johns Hopkins University was going on a walk, he got rather thirsty. Seeing an old farmhouse, he went to the door and asked the girl who answered if her parents were home. She said no. He then asked if he could have a drink of water. She said she would have to pipe it uphill. She offered to let him come in and have some milk though. He did, and then went on his way. Weeks later he operated on a girl on the operating table and she was this same little girl.

The hospital and doctor's bills soon came to the family and they had no idea how they could pay them. However, they looked down at the bottom of the bill and read these words: "Paid in full by two glasses of milk."

REJECTION

In 1830 George Wilson was sentenced in Philadelphia to be hanged for murder. Andrew Jackson, the president, pardoned him, but when the jailer presented the pardon, Wilson refused it. The sheriff had to know whether Wilson should hang or not, so the matter came before the United States Supreme Court. No such point of law had ever been raised before.

Chief Justice Marshall gave the following decision: "A pardon is a paper, the value of which depends upon its acceptance by the person implicated. It is hardly to be supposed that one under sentence of death would refuse to accept a pardon, but if it is refused, it is no pardon. George Wilson must hang." And he was hanged.

He could not have been more than five, and he was a pathetic little figure as he carried a valise down the front steps of his home. Around the block he trudged, and around again. In fact, he kept walking around the block until it got dark and a policeman stopped him. "What's the idea?" the officer asked. "Runnin' away," explained the boy sadly. "Look," said the officer, "I've had my eye on you and you've been doing nothing but walking around the block. Do you call that running away?" "Well, what do you want me to do?" cried the boy tearfully. "I ain't allowed to cross the street alone."

And that is just what happened when Adam fell. Ever since then mankind has been running away—but God has arranged it so that man cannot run from his fears; man cannot run away from his frustrations; man cannot run away from sin and its fruits; man cannot run away from death; man cannot run away from himself. There is only one refuge—the cross.

RELATIONSHIPS

Three men were marooned on an island. Suddenly a genie appeared and said, "What would you like to have? Any wish is yours."

One man said, "I miss my family in L.A." Whoosh—and he was gone. Another said, "I miss by brokerage in Boston. I wish I were back at my desk. I wish I were at work." Whoosh—and he was gone.

Then the third man said, "I'm lonely. I wish my friends were back here."

RELATIVES

Friends are always welcome; relatives are by appointment only.

RELIGIONS

Projected: If the world were a town of 1,000 people it would include 564 Asians, 210 Europeans, 86 Africans, 80 South Americans, and 60 North Americans. Its religions: 300 Christians, 175 Muslims, 128 Hindus, 55 Buddhists, and 47 animists, according to Development Innovations and Networks.

—Pulse

REMEMBERING

Always remember to forget,
The things that made you sad.
But never forget to remember
The things that made you glad.
Always remember to forget
The friends that proved untrue.
But don't forget to remember
Those that have stuck by you.
Always remember to forget
The troubles that passed away.
But never forget to remember
The blessings that come each day.

REPENTANCE

A Sunday school teacher asked a class what the word "repentance" means. A little boy put up his hand and said, "It is being sorry for your sins." A little girl also raised her hand and said, "It is being sorry enough to quit."

A schoolgirl was saved and someone asked her, "What were you before?" She said, "A sinner." The she was asked, "What are you now?" She answered, "A sinner." They asked, "What's the difference?"

She answered, "I was a sinner running after sin. But now I'm a sinner running from sin."

REPUTATION

The easiest thing to get, but the most difficult thing to get rid of, is a bad reputation.
—*Teen Esteem*

Reputation is precious, but character is priceless.

RESENTMENT

A visitor, leaning on a fence, was watching an old farmer plowing with a mule which didn't seem to know which way to go. The visitor commented, "I hope you don't think I'm telling you how to run your business, but you could save yourself a lot of time and energy if you'd say 'Giddyap' and 'Whoa' to your mule instead of just pulling and tugging on those reins."

The farmer, drawing a hankie from his pocket and wiping his forehead, answered, "You're right. But this animal stepped on my toe five years ago, and I haven't spoken to him since."
—Leslie B. Flynn

RESOLUTIONS

Resolved, never to do anything which I would be afraid to do if it were the last hour of my life.
—Jonathan Edwards

RESPECT

Your job gives you authority. Your behavior earns you respect.
—Irwin Federman

RESPONSIBILITY
Whose Job Is It?

This is a story about four people named Everybody, Somebody, Anybody, and Nobody. There was an important job to be done and Everybody was sure Somebody would do it. Anybody could have done it, but Nobody did it.

Somebody got angry about that, because it was Everybody's job. Everybody thought Anybody could do it but Nobody realized that Everybody wouldn't do it. It ended up that Everybody blamed Somebody when Nobody did what Anybody could have done.

People need responsibility. They resist assuming it, but they can't get along without it.
—John Steinbeck

The thing that keeps your feet on the ground is the responsibility placed on your shoulders.
—Jack Moffitt

A youth was questioning a lonely old man. "What is life's heaviest burden?" he asked. The old fellow answered sadly, "To have nothing to carry."
—*Bits & Pieces*

Let me do the thing that ought to be done,
When it ought to be done,
As it ought to be done,
Whether I like to do it or not.

REST

According to a Greek legend, in ancient Athens a man noticed the great storyteller Aesop playing childish games with some little boys. He laughed and jeered at Aesop, asking him why he wasted his time in such frivolous activity.

Aesop responded by picking up a bow, loosening its string, and placing it on the ground. Then he said to the critical Athenian, "Now answer the riddle, if you can. Tell us what the unstrung bow implies."

The man looked at it for several moments but had no idea what point Aesop was trying to make. Aesop explained, "If you keep a bow always bent, it will break eventually; but if you let it go slack, it will be more fit for use when you want it."

People are also like that. That's why we all need to take time to rest.

RESTITUTION

After F. E. Marsh preached on restitution, a young man came to him and said,

"Pastor, you have put me in a bad fix. I've stolen from my employer, and I'm ashamed to tell him about it. You see, I'm a boat builder, and the man I work for is an unbeliever. I have often talked to him about Christ, but he only laughs at me. In my work, expensive copper nails are used because they won't rust in water. I've been taking some of them home for a boat I am building in my backyard. I'm afraid if I tell my boss what I've done and offer to pay for them, he'll think I'm a hypocrite, and I'll never be able to reach him for Christ."

Later when the man saw the preacher again, he exclaimed, "Pastor, I've settled that matter and I'm so relieved." "What happened when you told your boss?" asked the minister. "Oh, he looked at me intently and said, 'George, I've always thought you were a hypocrite, but now I'm not so sure. Maybe there's something to your Christianity after all. Any religion that makes a man admit he's been stealing a few copper nails and offer to settle for them must be worth having.'"

—*Our Daily Bread*

RESTRAINT

Liberty exists in proportion to restraint.
—Daniel Webster

RESURRECTION

When that great Christian and scientist Sir Michael Faraday was dying, some journalists questioned him as to his speculations for a life after death. "Speculations!" said he, "I know nothing about speculations. I'm resting on certainties. 'I know that my Redeemer liveth,' and because He lives, I shall live also."

—*Gospel Trumpet*

Road repairs were being made on one of the main highways in the mountains of Pennsylvania. At the point where the construction began there were two signs. One read: "Travel at Your Own Risk"; the other: "Road Closed Beyond the Cemetery." But spiritually the road is not closed beyond the cemetery. Rather, there are two roads beyond the grave—one to life everlasting through faith in the Lord Jesus Christ; the other to spiritual death.

A little lad was gazing intently at the picture in the art store window: the store was displaying a notable picture of the crucifixion. A gentleman approached, stopped, and looked. The boy, seeing his interest, said, "That's Jesus." The man made no reply, and the lad continued, "Them's Roman soldiers." And, after a moment, "They killed Him."

"Where did you learn that?" asked the man.

"In the Mission Sunday school," was the reply.

The man turned and walked thoughtfully away. He had not gone far when he heard a youthful voice calling, "Say, Mister," and quickly the little street lad caught up with him. "Say, Mister," he repeated, "I wanted to tell you that He rose again."

A German princess on her deathbed ordered that her grave be covered with a great granite slab, that around it should be placed solid blocks of stone, the whole be fastened together with clamps of iron, and that on the stone should be cut these words: "This burial place, purchased to all eternity, must never be opened."

It happened that a little acorn was buried in the process of covering the grave. During the months that followed, the seed sprouted, and the tender shoot found its way up through the crevice between two of the stones. Years passed and the small shoot grew into a sapling, then a huge oak tree. It burst asunder the clamps of iron binding the stones and pushed aside the rocks that were never to be moved.

"Father declared he was going to buy a new plot in the cemetery, a plot all for himself. 'And I will buy one on a corner,' he added triumphantly, 'where I can get out.'"

—Clarence Day

A very learned man once said to a little child who believed in the Lord Jesus, "My poor little girl, you don't know whom you believe in. There have been many christs. In which of them do you believe?" "I know which one I believe in," replied the child. "I believe in the Christ who rose from the dead."

Asoka, once emperor of India, distributed Buddha's ashes, in minute portions, to eighty-four thousand shrines all over India! Buddhism is centered around the worship of the ashes of the dead founder. Christianity centers around its living Lord!

A wounded soldier, knowing he was going to die, took his Bible out of his pocket and placed his finger on John 11:25. As the blood ran down his finger it caused his finger to stick to the page of his Bible at that verse when he died. How true for the Christian. "I am the resurrection and the life!"

One day during the French revolution, a man said to a bishop, "The Christian religion—what is it? It would be easy to start a religion like that."

"Oh, yes. One would only have to get crucified and rise again the third day."

Easter is a time of new life. That which was dead now lives. Darkness is gone. A warm sun shines. Life has a new meaning.

Easter dates back originally to the spring festival in honor of Eastra, the Teutonic goddess of light and spring. As early as the eighth century the name was transferred by the Anglo-Saxons to the Christian festival designed to celebrate the resurrection of Christ.

Today we are privileged to celebrate Easter because of Jesus' victory over sin and death and hell.

Christianity begins where religion ends—with the resurrection of Christ.

An old Greek legend tells how the Sphinx at Thebes, which had the body of a lion and the upper part of a woman, lay crouched on the top of a rock on the highway and propounded to all travelers a riddle. Those who failed to solve the riddle were slain by the Sphinx. None yet had been able to answer it. But when Oedipus came to the Sphinx

and was asked the question, "What creature walks in the morning on four feet, at noon upon two, and the evening on three?" Oedipus replied, "Man, who in childhood creeps on hands and knees, in manhood walks erect, and in old age goes with the aid of a staff." The Sphinx, mortified at the solution of her riddle, cast herself down from the rock and perished. So for ages on the highway of human life crouched the cruel sphinx of death, propounding to all travelers its unsolvable and unanswerable enigma. No one was able to answer; death reigned. But Christ solved the riddle and overturned the sphinx from her rock.

RETIREMENT

Early to bed and early to rise,
Till I make enough to do otherwise.

"Now that I'm retired I can finish my book." "I didn't know you were writing a book." "I'm not. I'm reading it."

I have no problem with retirement. I'd much rather be put out to pasture than under it.

—Bob Orben

Retirement is twice as much husband on half as much income.

Retirement really doesn't change our lives that much. The biggest difference is that all those things you never had the time to do now become all those things you don't have the money to do.

—Bob Orben

REVELATION

An old Christian gentleman who was known for his optimistic outlook was asked the secret of his triumphant attitude. He replied, "I've read the last book of the Bible, so I know how the story ends. I'm on the winning side."

REVENGE

Forgiveness is better than revenge, for forgiveness is the sign of a gentle nature, but revenge is the sign of a savage nature.

—Epictetus

REVIVAL

Due to reports of successful revivals by the late Gypsy Smith, he was asked to explain the best method to start a revival. He answered, "Lock yourself in a private room. Take a piece of chalk and mark a circle on the floor, get down on your knees inside the circle and pray God to start a revival inside this circle. When this prayer is answered, the revival will be on."

If all the sleeping folk will wake up—and all the lukewarm folk will fire up—and all the dishonest folk will confess up—and all the disgruntled folk will sweeten up—and the discouraged folk will look up—and all the estranged folk will make up—and all the gossipers will shut up—and all the dry bones will shake up—and all the true soldiers will stand up—and all the church members will pray up—then you will have a revival.

REWARDS

A young man once studied violin under a world-renowned master. Eventually the time came for his first recital. Following each selection, despite the cheers of the crowd, the performer seemed dissatisfied. Even after the last number, with the shouts louder than ever, the talented violinist stood watching an old man in the balcony. Finally the elderly one smiled and nodded in approval. Immediately the young man relaxed and beamed with happiness. The applause of the crowd had meant nothing to him until he had first won the hearty approval of his famous teacher. So, too, the Christian must do all he does looking for God's approval and in that be rewarded.

Let the task be the reward.

—Peter Drucker

RIDICULE

Abuse is the weapon of the vulgar.

—S. G. Goodrich

Ridicule is the first and last argument of fools.

—C. Simmons

RIGHT

It takes less time to do a thing right than it does to explain why you did it wrong.

—Henry Longfellow

I care not if God is on my side. My constant hope and prayer is that I may be found on God's side.

—Abraham Lincoln

It is better to be despised for the right than praised for the wrong.

Always do right. This will gratify some people, and astonish the rest.

—Mark Twain

RIGHTEOUSNESS

A man who claimed to be a citizen of the United States and also of England was arrested in Brazil and tried, court-martialed, and condemned to die. The British and American representatives did all they could to save his life but their plans failed, and the Brazilian government said, "He has violated the law and we are going to execute him."

The day came for his execution. He stood out in the open field, and the soldiers of the government were ready with their guns; and just before the time to shoot, out came the representative of the English government and the representative of the United States. They walked out and this prisoner was wrapped around with the English flag and then with the American flag. Those two men stood back and said, "If you fire on this man, you fire on the English and the American armies and the English and the American navies. He is covered with the flags of these governments." The executioners lowered their guns.

RISK

You cannot discover new oceans unless you have the courage to lose sight of the shore.

If no one ever took risks, Michelangelo would have painted the Sistine floor.

—Neil Simon

Sometimes you must go out on a limb. That's where the fruit is.

RUMORS

"I hear you made a million dollars in oil in Texas."

"No. In the first place it wasn't Texas; it was Kentucky. In the second place it wasn't oil; it was coal. Also it wasn't a million dollars; it was two million. And it wasn't me; it was my brother. Finally it wasn't that he made two million; he lost it!"

RUTS

Getting back on the right track usually involves getting out of a rut.

Each September in northern Manitoba, the temperature drops and rain freezes. This causes ruts in the dirt roads. A sign by the road reads, "Choose your rut carefully. You'll be in it for the next 60 miles."

S

SACRIFICE

Late in the fifteenth century, two young woodcarving apprentices in France confided to each other their desire to study painting. But this plan would take money, and both Hans and Albrecht were poor.

Finally though, they had a solution. One would work and earn money while the other studied. Then, when the lucky one became rich and famous, he in turn could help the other. They tossed a coin and Albrecht won.

So while Albrecht went to Venice, Hans worked as a blacksmith. As quickly as he received his wages, he forwarded money to his friend.

The months stretched into years—and at last Albrecht returned to his native land, an independent master. Now it was his turn to help Hans.

The two men met in joyous reunion, but when Albrecht looked at his friend, tears welled in his eyes. Only then did he discover the extent of Hans's sacrifice. The many years of heavy labor in the blacksmith shop had calloused and bruised Hans's sensitive hands. His fingers could never handle a painter's brush.

In humble gratitude to Hans for his years of sacrifice, the artist, the great Albrecht Durer, painted a portrait of the workworn hands that had labored so faithfully so that he might develop his talent. He presented this painting of praying hands to his devoted friend.

Today this masterpiece, a symbol of friendship and sacrifice, is familiar to millions of people throughout the world.

If Jesus Christ be God and died for me, then no sacrifice can be too great for me to make for Him.

—C. T. Studd

The queen of Sweden sold her jewels to provide her people with hospitals and orphanages. One day she visited a convalescent home she had helped provide for. When tears of gratitude from a bedridden woman fell on the royal hand, the queen exclaimed, "God is sending me back my jewels again."

In a Japanese seashore village over a hundred years ago, an earthquake startled the villagers one autumn evening. But, being accustomed to earthquakes, they soon went back to their activities. Above the village on a high plain, an old farmer was watching from his house. He looked at the sea, and the water appeared dark and acted strangely, moving against the wind, running away from the land. The old man knew what it meant. His one thought was to warn the people in the village.

He called to his grandson, "Bring me a torch! Make haste!" In the fields behind him lay his great crop of rice. Piled in stacks ready for the market, it was worth a fortune. The old man hurried out with his torch. In a moment the dry stalks were blazing. Then the big bell pealed from the temple below: "Fire!"

Back from the beach, away from the strange sea, up the steep side of the cliff, came the people of the village. They were trying to save the crops of their rich neighbor. "He's mad!" they said.

As they reached the plain, the old man shouted back at the top of his voice, "Look!" At the edge of the horizon, they saw a long, lean, dim line—a line that thickened as they gazed. That line was the sea, rising like a high wall and coming swiftly. Then came a shock, heavier than thunder. The great swell struck the shore with a weight that sent a shudder through the hills and tore their homes to match sticks. It drew back, roaring. Then it struck again, and again, and yet again. Once more it struck and ebbed; then it returned to its place.

On the plain no word was spoken. Then the voice of the old man was heard, saying gently, "That is why I set fire to the rice." He stood among them almost as poor as the poorest, for his wealth was gone—but he had saved four hundred lives by his sacrifice.

—Lafcadio Hearn

Some folks say there is nothing they wouldn't do for the Lord; that nothing is too good for the Lord; or there is nothing in their lives He cannot have; and nothing is about what the Lord gets.

SAINTS

"Daddy, what are saints?" the youngster
  asked.
And I paused before making my reply.
"Do we know any saints right here on
  earth.
Or do they all live with God in the sky?"
We entered the church of God just then,
As the morning sun shone bright and fair
Through the stained glass windows, wide
  and high,
And the reverent figures painted there.
"These are all saints, my son," I said,
And his face took on a rapture new.
"Oh, I know what saints are now, Dad;
They are the people God's light shines
  through."

—Jack Gormley

SALARIES

Everybody should be paid what he or she is worth, no matter how big a cut they'll have to take.

SALESMANSHIP

Queen to king: "It doesn't matter if the salesman convinced you—we just don't need aluminum siding on our castle."

SALVATION

A preacher and an unconverted manufacturer of soaps met on the street. Sneering, the latter exclaimed, "The gospel you preach can't be very good, for there are still a lot of wicked people." The preacher was silent until they passed a child making mud pies. The tot was smeared from head to toe with dirt. Pointing to the youngster the preacher said, "George, your product can't be very effective, for there is still a lot of filth in the world." "Oh, but my soap cleans only those to whom it is applied," replied the manufacturer. "Exactly!" exclaimed the preacher. The man was caught in his own trap.

Phillips Brooks was once asked, "Is it necessary to have a personal experience of Christ to be a Christian?" The great New England preacher paused and then made this reply. "My friend, a personal experience of Christ is Christianity."

There was a shop girl in Chicago a few years ago; one day she could not have bought a dollar's worth of anything; the next day she could buy a thousand dollars worth of anything she wanted. What made the difference? She married a rich husband. She had accepted him and, of course, all he had became hers. And so you can have everything, if only you will receive Christ.

—D. L. Moody

During the early years of missionary activity in China, the members of one family accepted Christ as Savior, but the youngest, a little boy, didn't. Later, he came to his father and said he wanted to receive the Savior and live for Him. The father felt the boy was not old enough to understand what he was doing, so the father explained what it meant to receive Christ. He told him that following Christ would not always be easy. The boy gave this touching reply: "God has promised to carry the lambs in His arms. I am only a little boy. It will be easier for Jesus to carry me."

The late venerable and godly Dr. Archibald Alexander of Princeton had been a preacher of Christ for sixty years and a professor of divinity for forty. On his deathbed he was heard to say to a friend, "All my theology is reduced to this narrow compass—Jesus Christ came into the world to save sinners."

—Charles H. Spurgeon

Years ago Billy Graham was preaching in Scotland. Some reporters were making fun of "Preacher Graham." An older man replied, "He's saying we are all sinners. It's not hard to believe that."

"And he's saying that Christ died for us." And then that statement which he voiced pricked his heart, and he realized that he needed Christ as his Savior and he accepted Him.

An unsaved man talked with a soulwinner about how to be saved because he was deeply convicted about his sin. When he asked the Christian what he could do to be saved, the Christian said he was too late.

"Too late! What do you mean? You mean I'm too late to be saved?"

"No, you're just too late to do anything yourself. Christ has already done it all."

A group of boy scouts went hiking and when they were returning, a couple of the fellows said they knew a short-cut back to camp. Later one of these two fellows said he knew an even shorter way. But the other boy thought it best to stay on the one he was on. So they separated. But when evening came, the boy who went on the newest trail didn't return. Even the search party didn't find him that night nor the next two days.

Later the father drove out of his way up to the camp after work every day and climbed into the mountains hunting for his boy. It was one of the most pathetic sounds to hear that father calling out that boy's name somewhere there in the mountains. But the boy was never found.

Similarly, Jesus is searching and calling for lost sinners.

In one of J. Wilbur Chapman's meetings, a man gave the following testimony: "I got off at the Pennsylvania Depot one day as a tramp, and for a year I begged on the streets for a living. One day I touched a man on the shoulder and said, 'Mister, please give me a dime.' As soon as I saw his face, I recognized my father. 'Father, don't you know me?' I asked. Throwing his arms around me, he cried, 'I have found you; all I have is yours.' Men, think of it, that I a tramp, stood begging my father for ten cents, when for eighteen years he had been looking for me, to give me all he was worth."

No Condemnation

No condemnation can be brought
    Against the sons of God;
Christ hath for them a cleansing wrought,
    And washed them in His blood.
They are righteous in what He's done,
    And evermore will be;
They stand complete in Christ the Son,
    From condemnation free.
Justice demanded all the debt,
    Of Christ in whom it laid;
Just as the time the Savior set,
    The debt He came and paid.
If Jesus had not paid the debt,
    Or suffered all the pain,
He ne'er had been at freedom set,
    He ne'er had rose again.
But when we see the Savior rise,
    Triumphant from the dead,
Our hopes ascend above the skies,
    With our victorious Head.

—Samuel Bernard

Jesus was born, that I might be born twice. He became poor, that I might possess wealth.

He became homeless, that I might have mansions.

He was stripped, that I always should have clothes.

He was forsaken, that I always should have friends.

He was bound, that I might have perfect liberty.

He was sad, that I might have full joy.

He descended, that I should be lifted up.

He became a servant, that I might be a son forever.

He was hungry, that I should always have food.

He was made sin, that I should share His righteousness.

He died, that I should never taste eternal death.

He will come down, that I might go up.

All of this—that He might display in me the riches of His grace and be the companion of God in the heavenlies.

It is not easy to be a Christian, but it is easy to start.

—J. Alexander Findlay

There used to be a quaint and really beautiful custom in the Orient that, when a man paid a personal debt, his creditor would nail the canceled bill over his door, so that all might see that his debt was paid.

Helen Keller, deaf, dumb, and blind, was taken to Phillips Brooks for spiritual instruction. In the simplest of terms the great preacher told the girl about Jesus. As she heard the Gospel, her face lit up and she spelled out in the hand of the preacher-teacher, "I knew all the time there must be one like that, but I didn't know His name."

An English earl visited the Fiji Islands. Being an infidel, he critically remarked to an elderly chief, "You're a great leader, but it's a pity you've been taken in by those foreign missionaries. They only want to get rich through you. No one believes the Bible anymore. People are tired of the threadbare story of Christ dying on a cross for the sins of mankind. They know better now. I'm sorry you've been so foolish as to accept their story." The old chief's eyes flashed as he answered, "See that great rock over there? On it we smashed the heads of our victims. Notice the furnace next to it? In that oven we formerly roasted the bodies of our enemies. If it hadn't been for those good missionaries and the love of Jesus that changed us from cannibals into Christians, you'd never leave this place alive! You'd better thank the Lord for the Gospel; otherwise we'd be feasting on you. If it weren't for the Bible, you'd now be our supper!"

Christ came to pay a debt he didn't owe because we owed a debt we couldn't pay.

An Indian told a missionary that he believed in Jesus Christ and meant to give Him his love some day. A native helper turned to him and said, "If you and I were walking through the jungle and came face to face with a tiger, if I placed myself in front of you and said, 'Run, brother, for your life!' would you love me?"

"Yes, surely."

"When, some day?"

The native saw the power of the friend's argument and said, "I will give myself to Him now."

In Belgium, on one of the most important bridges, there stands the bronze statues which represent the mutual love and affection of a father and his son who won the hearts of their countrymen.

However, because of political offense, both were condemned to die by the blade of the axe. Great difficulty arose though when the government couldn't find anyone to be the executioner, since the two were so popular with the people.

Then, a strange proposition was made— one would have his life spared if he would behead the other. The proposal was accepted since each saw that in so doing at least one life might be spared. The son wanted his father to be saved so that he himself could die happily. But, after much persuasion, the son consented to perform the ghastly deed, since the parent reminded him how his own years were so few. On the day of the event, anxious throngs jammed the courtyard as the two were led from the prison. The scene was grim, with the scaffolds built around a huge wooden block. Slowly, the aging man placed his head on the cold block and awaited the fatal blow. Then the son, pale-faced and with a wild look, seized the axe and lifted it with trembling hand. But, just as he started to bring it down, he threw it to the side and placed his head next to that of his father and shouted, "No, we die together!"

In response to the demands of the people, the government ordered the immediate release of the two and later, through the years, sculptors made memorials in bronze to their honor.

During the seventeenth century, Oliver Cromwell, Lord Protector of England, sentenced a soldier to be shot for his crimes. The execution was to take place at the ringing of the evening curfew bell. However, the bell did not sound. The soldier's fiancée had climbed into the belfry and clung to the great clapper of the bell to prevent it from striking. When she was summoned by Cromwell to account for her actions, she wept as she showed him her bruised and bleeding hands. Cromwell's heart was touched and he said, "Your lover shall live because of your sacrifice. Curfew shall not ring tonight!"

—*Our Daily Bread*

A newly married couple had invited members of their two families to a Sunday dinner. The guests were seated around the table. All desired to be at their best. As the rich brown gravy was being passed, one young lady accidentally tipped the bowl with a resultant large brown spot on the immaculately clean linen tablecloth. The hostess quickly and skillfully scraped up the gravy and spread a napkin over the spot and the meal went on. The napkin did not take away the spot; it merely covered it so the dinner could go on. To the unfortunate young woman who had spilled the gravy the white napkin was a constant reminder of her accident. So the Old Testament sacrifices covered the sins of the Israelites but were a constant reminder of sin. The day after the dinner the tablecloth was washed

and the spot taken away. So by the sacrifice of Christ, believers are washed from their sins in His blood (Rev. 1:5). There is no napkin to remind of sin.

A banker said to a Christian, "Do you mean to say that, without my paying a cent or making any recompense, I can expect God to have mercy on me? Do you say I can be saved merely by trusting Jesus Christ? How absurd! If I am to be saved, I must accomplish it by my own efforts."

"Well," the Christian said, "suppose someone should come to you in great need and want to borrow some money. Who would have the right to make the terms and conditions on which the money would be loaned, you or the borrower?"

"Why, I would, of course. He would have to meet my conditions before he could get the money," said the banker.

"Exactly, and this is your position. You are the poor, lost, sinner and God is the banker. So who has the right to make the terms and conditions on which you can come to Him—you or Him?"

In South Texas a little home in the country burned down, and before the neighbors could rescue the family all were burned to death except one little girl, nine or ten years of age, and she was badly burned on one side of her face and body. After a few days the neighbors consulted and sent little Mary to the Buckner Orphans Home in Dallas. They advised the head of that home when little Mary would come, on what train, and there Dr. Buckner was waiting for her, of course. When she got off the train, her eyes were red from weeping, and she seemed intuitively to know that he was her protector, and she started toward him saying, "Is this Mr. Buckner?" He said, "Yes, and is this little Mary?" And then she came and laid her head against his knee and sobbed with indescribable emotion, and looked up at last with that little burned face and said, "You will have to be my papa and mama both." He said, "I will, the best I can Mary." Then she went into the home and was looked after along with hundreds of other children.

I have been there time and time again and preached to them, and I have seen them come out to greet him when he would return to them after an absence. The little tots come down the avenue and vie with one another as they swing around him, each wishing to kiss him first. Along in that group one day came the little burned-faced Mary and the little children kissed him, but little Mary stood off, several feet away and looked across her shoulder watching the whole affair, sobbing like her heart would break. And when those little ones had kissed the good man, he looked across at her and said, "Mary, why don't you come over and kiss me?" That was entirely too much for her and she sobbed aloud, and then he went over and touched her little chin and lifted it up and said, "I do not quite understand you, Mary. Why didn't you come to kiss me?" And she had difficulty in speaking and when she did speak she said, "O Papa Buckner, I could not ask you to kiss me, I am so ugly. After I got burned I am so ugly I just could not ask you to kiss me, but if you will just love me like you love the other children and tell me you love me, then you need not kiss me at all." He pushed all those other children away and took up little Mary in his arms and kissed the burned cheek again and again and said, "Mary, you are just as beautiful to Papa Buckner as are any of the rest."
—George W. Truett

Ole Bull, the world's most noted violinist, was always wandering about. One day he became lost in the interminable forests. In the dark of the night he stumbled against a log hut, the home of a hermit. The old man took him in, fed him, and warmed him; after the supper they sat in front of a blazing fireplace, and the old hermit picked up some crude tunes on his screechy, battered violin. Ole Bull said to the hermit, "Do you think I could play on that?" "I don't think so; it took me years to learn," the old hermit replied. Ole Bull said, "Let me try it."

He took the old marred violin and drew the bow across the strings and suddenly the hermit's hut was filled with wonderful music; and, according to the story, the hermit sobbed like a child.

We are battered instruments; life's strings have been snapped; life's bow has been bent. Yet, if we will let Him take us and touch us, from this old battered, broken, shattered, marred instrument, He will bring forth music fit for the angels.

Longfellow could take a worthless sheet of paper, write a poem on it, and make it worth six thousand dollars. That's genius.

Rockefeller could sign his name to a piece of paper and make it worth millions. That's capital.

Uncle Sam can take gold, stamp an eagle on it, and make it worth dollars. That's money.

A craftsman can take material that's worth only five dollars and make an article worth fifty dollars. That's skill.

An artist can take a fifty cent piece of canvas, paint a picture on it, and make it worth a thousand dollars. That's art.

But God—and only God—can take a life, sinful and without joy, wash it in the blood of Christ, put His Spirit in it, and make it a blessing to humanity. That's salvation!

Nicolas II, czar of Russia, had the habit of disguising himself and visiting his military outposts for the purpose of evaluating them. In one of his outposts was a young man whose father had enlisted him in the military with the hope of putting some discipline and direction into his life. However, army life served as fuel that fed the fires of the wild life he lived.

One of this young soldier's weaknesses was gambling. It so happened that he was also the bookkeeper at his particular outpost. As his gambling debts grew, he found it necessary to pilfer some of the outpost's funds to pay his debts. Instead of hitting it rich, however, he continued to go deeper into debt to the outpost's treasury.

One night he decided to add up all the debts and see how much he owed. When he saw the immense debt, he decided to commit suicide. He took out his gun and wrote across the ledger, "So great a debt. Who can pay?" As he contemplated suicide, he dozed off to sleep.

Czar Nicolas II was inspecting the outpost that night, disguised as an officer of low rank. Seeing a light burning in the bookkeeper's shack, he went to investigate.

Inside the shack he saw the man with the gun in his lap and the writing on the ledger. Immediately he understood the situation.

When the soldier awoke from his sleep, he put the gun to his head. For a moment he stared at the ledger and read these words, "So great a debt. Who can pay?" underneath those words were these, "Paid in full, Czar Nicolas II!"

There came to my father's house a young man who had been brought to Christ a few months before. One day he was out in our garden talking to me. While we chatted, he stooped down and took a leaf from a nasturtium plant, put it on his hand, and said to me, "Did you ever see anything so beautiful?" As I looked I saw all the veins and the exquisite beauty of the leaf. Then he said, "Do you know, I never saw how beautiful that leaf was until six months ago, when I gave myself to Christ."

—G. Campbell Morgan

At the close of the War between the States, a party of Federal cavalrymen were riding alone along a road toward Richmond one day when a poor fellow, weak and emaciated and in ragged remnants of a Confederate uniform, came out of the bushes on one side and attracted their attention by begging hoarsely for bread. He said he had been starving in the woods for a number of weeks and subsisting only on the few berries and roots he could find. They suggested he go into Richmond with them and get what he needed. He demurred, saying that he was a deserter from the Confederate army, and he did not dare show himself lest he be arrested and confined to prison, or possibly even shot for desertion in time of war. They looked at him in amazement and asked, "Have you not heard the news?" "What news?" he anxiously inquired. "Why, the Confederacy no longer exists. General Lee surrendered to General Grant over a week ago and peace is made." "Oh!" he exclaimed, "peace is made and I have been starving in the woods because I didn't know it."

In a certain village a man sold wood to his neighbors, always taking advantage of them by cutting his logs a few inches under the required four feet. One day the report was circulated that the woodchopper had been converted. Nobody believed it for they all declared that he was beyond being reached.

One man, however, slipped quietly out of the grocery store where the conversation was being discussed. He soon came running back in excitement and shouted, "It's so! He has been!" They all asked, "How do you know?" "Well, I . . . measured the wood he cut yesterday, and it's a good four feet long!" That convinced the crowd.

A missionary took the Gospel to an old pearl diver, but he didn't respond. He said if the Gospel is free, it's worth nothing, and he didn't want it. Later because of the missionary's continual kindness and hospitality to the national, he brought a pearl to the missionary and said he wanted to give it to him. Then the national went on to tell him the story behind the pearl.

His son one day was pearl diving and he put a pearl in his bag. Then as he reached for another pearl and started to come up, he went down a little way and seemed to lose his strength. Later he came up but water was in his lungs and he died. "I want you to have this pearl."

The missionary said, "This is just like salvation. You are giving me this pearl. It is free yet it is worth very much."

As a result, the man accepted Christ.

Charlotte Elliot came to Caesar Milan and asked how she could become a Christian. The old man replied, "My dear, it is very simple. You have only to come to Jesus." And she said to him, "But I am a very great sinner, will He take me just as I am?" "Yes, He will take you just as you are, and no other way." And then she said, "If He will take me just as I am, then I will come," and she went home to her room, sat down at her desk, and wrote the beautiful words of the gospel song:

"Just as I am without one plea,
O Lamb of God, I come, I come."

A godless workman was carrying freight up a gangplank to a steamer. Accidentally jostled by another, he fell into the water between the wharf and the boat. His last utterance was a horrible oath! He did not surface, but after some time he was rescued and brought to shore, apparently drowned. The strenuous efforts put forth to resuscitate him were finally successful. With his first breath he cried out, "Praise God, I'm saved!" "Yes, you were almost gone," someone replied. "Oh," he said, "I don't mean from drowning; I mean saved inside! The Lord has taken my sin away."

Then he told them that when he felt himself being sucked under the waves, he thought the end had come. In his mind's eye he saw himself as a boy, kneeling again at his mother's knee as she poured out her earnest prayers for him. His sin, high as a mountain, rose up before him, and in desperation he cried out to the Lord to save his poor soul. In that moment he realized forgiveness and cleansing. He then had lapsed into unconsciousness. However, when he regained his senses, he knew that the great transaction had been accomplished; and so he praised God with his first breath!

—*Alliance Weekly*

SANCTIFICATION

In justification we are declared righteous, that in sanctification we may become righteous. Justification is what God does for us, while sanctification is what God does in us. Justification puts us into a right relationship to God, while sanctification exhibits the fruit of that relationship.

—William Evans

As soon as you do not desire to become better, then you have ceased to be good.

—Bernard of Clairvaux

SATAN

The Devil never kicks a dead horse.

—Charles H. Spurgeon

A missionary in Africa says there are three beasts that lie in wait for their prey: the lion, the leopard, and the hyena. The hyena does not devour, but attacks only the vital organs and quickly leaves after eating a few meager mouthfuls. The leopard too does not eat its prey, but desires only its blood. The lion, however, completely devours its helpless victim, leaving not a single portion. What a perfect picture of Satan, the destroyer of souls.

Two little six-year-olds struggled with the problem of demythologizing the demonic when they were heard arguing about the existence of the Devil. One little boy said, "Oh, there isn't any Devil." The other little boy who was very upset by this said, "What do you mean, there isn't any Devil? It talks about him all the way through the Bible." The first little boy said in a very knowing way, "Oh, that's a lot of nonsense you know. Just like Santa Claus, the Devil turns out to be your daddy."

—John Warwick Montgomery

On a marquee of a theater in Omaha, Nebraska, a man was dressed as a devil because a movie about Satan was showing. The man was dressed in red, had a long tail, pitchfork, and horns. A girl and her mother were walking along the street, and when the girl saw the man dressed that way, she said in a scared way to her mother, "What's that?" Her mother said, "Oh, don't be afraid. That's only the Devil."

Some years ago I was standing before the cage of a wildcat in the zoo of one of our large cities. As I stood there wondering just what good purpose a wildcat might serve, an attendant entered the cage through a door on the opposite side. He had nothing in his hands but a broom. Carefully closing the door, he proceeded to sweep the floor of the cage.

The shivers went down my spine as I

saw him in there alone with that wildcat. So far as I could tell he had no weapon with which to protect himself in case of attack. But he seemed not to be afraid in the least and went about his work.

In spite of his composure, I supposed that when he got to where the cat lay he would treat him with the utmost respect, but nothing of the kind. When he got near the beast, he gave him a shove with the broom to make him get out of the way. The wildcat made no response except a disapproving hiss, after which he lay down in another corner of the cage.

"You certainly are a brave man," I said to the attendant.

"No, I ain't brave," the man answered, continuing to sweep.

"Well then," said I, "that cat must be tame."

"No," he answered again, "he ain't tame."

"Well," I said again, "if you are not brave and that cat is not tame, then I cannot understand why he does not attack you."

The man chuckled. "Mister," he said, "he's old—and he ain't got no teeth."

—Carl Armerding

SATISFACTION

I've never been satisfied with anything we've ever built. I've felt that dissatisfaction is the basis of progress. When we become satisfied in business, we become obsolete.

—J. Willard Marriott Sr.

No artist is totally satisfied with his work. The Danish sculptor Bertel Thorvaldsen was asked, "Which is your greatest statue?" "The next one," he replied. Chopin, it is said, would walk the floor, chewing his quill pen to pieces and tearing up his half finished scores. Why? Not because he couldn't compose music good enough for the people but because it wasn't good enough for Chopin.

SCHOOL

College professor: "I will not begin today's lecture until the room settles down."

College freshman: "Why don't you go home and sleep it off?"

A mother had a hard time getting her son to go to school. He responded, "Nobody likes me at school. The teachers don't like me and the kids don't either. The superintendent wants to transfer me, the bus driver hates me, the school board wants me to drop out, and the custodians have it in for me. I just don't want to go to school."

The mother insisted, "You've got to go. You're healthy, you've got a lot to learn. You're a leader. Besides you're forty-nine years old, and you are the principal."

I remember the story of the school boy who had done no work whatever and was trying to pass an examination from a junior school to a more senior school. He found himself faced with questions, no one of which reminded him of anything; so he wrote across his answer book, "God knows, I don't," and as the examination was in December, he finished off "Merry Christmas." His answer book eventually returned from the examiners marked "God passed; you didn't. Happy New Year."

—C. Northcote Parkinson

While the late Dr. Charles W. Eliot was the active head of Harvard University, someone asked why that noble institution had acquired a reputation as the nation's greatest storehouse of knowledge.

"I'm sure I don't know," responded the good doctor, his old eyes twinkling merrily, "unless it's because the freshmen bring us so much of it, and the seniors take so little away."

Little Herman went to his first day of school, and when he came home, his mother asked, "What did you learn today?" Herman said, "I learned to write." "Oh," she said, "to think my little Herman on his first day of school learned to write. What did you write?" "How should I know?" replied Herman. "I haven't learned to read yet."

—Charles A. McClain Jr.

At the University of Kentucky a student wrote a paper on Othello in literature. He got an A and the professor wrote on the paper, "Please see me." The student thought he would get a scholarship from the professor or some ego-building praise.

The professor sat on his desk and lit his pipe. "That was an excellent paper."

"Thank you."

"That exceeded the normal work of an undergraduate."

"You think so?"

"Tell me, do you belong to such and such a fraternity?"

"Yes." (The student sensed that the professor was on to something).

"Do they still have that file in that fraternity with past exams and papers?"

"Yes," the student had to admit.

"Did you copy that paper?"

"Yes."

Then the student asked, "Tell me, why did you give me an A?"

The professor responded, "I wrote that paper, but I got a C on it, and I always felt it was worth an A."

SCIENCE

Science without religion is lame; religion without science is blind.

—Albert Einstein

I cannot believe that God plays dice with the universe.

—Albert Einstein

In my front yard are six huge oak trees that must be over one hundred years old. As I look at them, I realize that the leaves must have barrels of fresh water each day to stay green. As a retired engineer, I know that no pump ever devised or designed by man could force that amount of water through the dense wooden trunk of these trees. Yet God causes their roots to gather all the water these trees need. To do this, these roots must exert a working pressure of more than three thousand pounds per square foot just to move the water up to the leaves—not considering the resistance of the wood in the tree trunk. That is just another of God's miracles that occur every day unnoticed.

—T. C. Roddy Jr.

SECOND COMING (Also see RAPTURE)

One day, while visiting a home for mentally handicapped children operated by a Christian friend, Joseph Stowell, president of Moody Bible Institute, noticed the tiny handprints of children covering the window. Stowell remarked about them to his friend.

"Oh, those," he replied. "The children here love Jesus, and they are so eager for Him to return that they lean against the windows as they look up to the sky."

The war was over and the boys began to return. Excitement ran high in many families. One little girl was anxious to see her brother who had been gone for over three years. Everyday she wondered if today was the day he would arrive.

"You may wear your new white dress and stockings, but please do be careful. Bob will be home today." It seemed like a long wait to little Mary. She began to feel hungry and decided to have a little lunch. As she was eating cookies and a cup of chocolate, she accidentally upset the cup and spilled the contents over her beautiful dress. She quickly ran upstairs and then into the clothes closet. At just this moment the big brother arrived. He soon called out, "Mary, Mary. Where are you?" Finally they found her, hiding in the closet, where she was crying and sobbing. "What are you doing here?" they asked her. "Oh, Bob, I'm so ashamed. My dress is all dirty, and I wanted to be clean when you came home."

At the height of World War II, Dietrich Bonhoeffer was imprisoned for taking a stand against Hitler. Yet he continued to urge fellow believers to resist Nazi tyranny. A group of Christians, believing that Hitler was the Antichrist, asked Bonhoeffer, "Why do you expose yourself to all this danger? Jesus will return any day, and all your work and suffering will be for nothing." Bonhoeffer replied, "If Jesus returns tomorrow, then tomorrow I'll rest from my labor. But today I have work to do. I must continue the struggle until it's finished."

The early believers were not looking for something to happen, they were looking for Someone to come. Looking for the train to arrive is one thing, but looking for someone we love to come on that train is another matter.

—*The Vance Havner Quote Book*

Arno C. Gaebelein referred to his longing for Jesus' second coming as "the home-sickness of the new life." Someone else put it this way, "Blessed are the homesick, for they shall be called home."

Mrs. Dave Bartlett, TEAM missionary in Japan, taught missionary children in the third grade. One day she was teaching about Jesus' return, and the same day another class had a drama of a Bible event for which a man was dressed in Bible clothes. A third-grader walked out of class, saw the man dressed in Bible attire, and ran back into the classroom and yelled to the class, "Here he is now!"

Plan as though Christ were not coming for ten years. Live as though He were coming in ten seconds.

Francis of Assisi, hoeing in his garden, was asked, "What would you do if you knew Christ were coming back today?" He answered, "I would keep right on hoeing."

The royal parents of Princess Victoria felt that she should be told early in life that someday she might become the queen of England. So they instructed her governess, who was a countess, to make this known to her. She in turn inserted in the girl's history textbook a listing of the Hanoverian kings. At the end of the column she had written the name "Victoria." The governess watched closely as the princess studied her lesson. When Victoria read down the page and came to her own name, she looked up and said, "Can it really be that I may become the queen of England?" The countess replied,

"Yes, in all possibility you will." After a pause, the princess said thoughtfully, "Then I will be good." From then on she began to apply herself with all her ability, realizing that someday she would sit on the throne.

A man was visiting a certain school and made a promise to the pupils that he would give a prize to the one whose desk was found in the very best order when he returned. He gave no indication, however, when he might come back. Shortly after he left, a little girl, noted for her disorderly habits, announced that she meant to win the prize. Her schoolmates jeered and laughed at her, saying, "Why, Mary, your desk is always out of order. It's never cleaned up." "Oh," she replied, "but starting right now, I'm going to clean it up the first of every week." Someone questioned, "Just supposing he comes at the end of the week?" "Well then," Mary answered, "I'll clean it up every morning." "What if he comes at the end of the day?" another asked. At that suggestion, Mary was silent for a moment. Then, with her face lighting up, she said, "I know what I'll do, I'll just keep it clean all the time!"

Frederic Farrar was a personal friend of Queen Victoria of England. On one occasion he told of a conversation he had with her Majesty after she had heard one of her chaplains preach on Christ's second coming. She said, "Oh, Dean Farrar, how I wish that the Lord would come during my lifetime!" When he asked why she desired this, her countenance brightened, and with deep emotion she replied, "Because I would love to lay my crown at His blessed feet in reverent adoration."

A Christian doctor was suddenly taken home to be with the Lord. His wife, who was frail and sickly, was heartbroken over her loss. But then as she turned to the Lord for comfort, she was strengthened and felt a sense of peace. To express her new confidence in the Lord and the fact that she knew she would see her husband again, she posted in her living room door a sign her husband always displayed when he left his office for a while. It read, "Gone out—Back soon."

Both the Old and the New Testaments are filled with promises of the second coming of Christ. There are 1,845 references to it in the Old Testament, and a total of seventeen Old Testament books give it prominence.

Of the 260 chapters in the entire New Testament, there are 318 references to the Second Coming, or one out of thirty verses. Twenty-three of the twenty-seven New Testament books refer to this great event. The four missing books include three which are single-chapter letters written to individual persons on a particular subject, and the fourth is Galatians which does imply Christ's coming again.

For every prophecy on the first coming of Christ, there are eight on Christ's second coming.

—Paul Lee Tan

Robert Murray McCheyne of Scotland was hosting a ministers' meeting in his home. In a lull in the conversation he asked the ministers individually, "Do you think Jesus will come tonight?" All said, "No, I think not." After going the rounds and receiving the same answer, McCheyne solemnly repeated, "Therefore be ye also ready; for in such an hour as ye think not the Son of man cometh" (Matt. 24:44).

—Leslie B. Flynn

Dr. John Gill was asked to speak in a series of meetings in the First Presbyterian Church in Dallas. Entering the pastor's study, he said to Dr. William Anderson, "Do you love His appearing?" "Well, I've had no time for it because I've been studying His first coming." "Well, I just wondered if you love His appearing," Dr. Gill said and walked out. That got Dr. Anderson to thinking and actually revolutionized his life and preaching.

One day a traveler in Switzerland discovered a beautiful but secluded estate on the shores of a tranquil lake. Knocking at the garden gate, he was met by an aged caretaker who cordially asked him to come in. The guardian seemed glad to see another person and eagerly showed him around the garden. "How long have you been here?" the tourist asked. "A very long time," he replied. "And how often has your master returned?" "Four times." "When was he here last?" "Many years ago. I am almost always alone—it's very seldom that even a stranger visits me." "Yet you have the garden in such perfect order," said the traveler, "and everything is flourishing as if you were expecting your master tomorrow." "No, sir," exclaimed the caretaker, "I have it fixed as if he were coming today!"

Hachi, a Japanese dog, would accompany his master to the railroad station every morning. And every evening Hachi would be back to greet his friend, tail wagging, as his master arrived home from work.

One night, however, the dog's master did not return. He had traveled to another city that day and while there, he died. Hachi, unable to comprehend the situation, continued to go to the railroad station every evening, and faithfully and patiently waited for at least an hour for his master's return. He then turned and sadly trotted home. This he did every evening—for over ten years.

Hachi's faithfulness so impressed the Japanese people that the government erected a statue of the dog on the spot where he had so patiently waited—and then sent statuettes to all the schools in what was then the Japanese Empire.

At the beginning of World War II, when 200,000 Japanese troops forced General Douglas MacArthur, commander of the U.S. forces, to withdraw from the Philippine Islands, he promised the discouraged Filipinos and Americans, "I shall return."

In February 1945, troops under MacArthur's command did return to Bataan. They forced the Japanese to surrender and freed the surviving Americans and Filipinos. MacArthur kept his promise to return.

It seems to me impossible to retain in any recognizable form our belief in the divinity to Christ and the truth of the Christian revelation while abandoning, or even persistently neglecting, the promised and threatened return of Christ.

—C. S. Lewis

A shoeshine man named Sam worked in a building that put him in contact with many students of theology. Sam loved the Lord and listened intently as the young men would discuss and debate their positions. Two men especially interested Sam. These men had different opinions on the book of Revelation. Day after day, Sam listened to eloquent and often passionate discussions in defense of the various views. One day, in the middle of a debate between the two men, one jokingly looked at Sam and said, "Sam, what do you think all these things in the book of Revelation mean?" With a smile on his face, Sam looked up and said simply, "Jesus is gonna win."

The Sultan Mohammed Ibn Daud ruled Iran during that nation's so-called "Golden Age." He extended the frontiers of his country through conquest and expansion, accumulating great wealth in the process. Following Daud's death it was believed that he would rise from his tomb, mount his horse, and lead his subjects to new conquests and glory. This belief is so strong that in the centuries since his death a thoroughbred charger has been kept in readiness before his tomb in the Mosque of Kuchan. Followers still wait for the day when the dead leader will arise and resume his reign.

—*Today in the Word*

The sailors on a Scottish fishing vessel were returning home after many days at sea. As they neared the shore, they gazed eagerly toward the dock where a group of their loved ones had gathered. The skipper looked through his binoculars and identified some of them: "I see Bill's Mary, and there is Tom's Margaret, and David's Anne." One man became concerned because his wife was not there. Later, he left the boat with a heavy heart and hurried up the hill to his cottage. As he opened the door, she ran to meet him saying, "I have been waiting for you!" He replied with a gentle rebuke, "Yes, but the other men's wives were *watching* for them."

SECRETARIES

I have a very simple and straightforward approach to work. The difficult I do myself. The impossible I give to my secretary.

—Bob Orben

A successful man is one who has a wife to tell him what to do and a secretary who does it.

SECRETS

Three of the most difficult things to do in life are to keep a secret, forget an injury, and make good use of leisure time.

—*Bits & Pieces*

There are two kinds of secrets: those too good to keep and those not worth repeating.

Most of us can keep a secret. It's the people we tell it to who can't.

Three may keep a secret if two of them are dead.

—Benjamin Franklin

A secret is something you tell one person at a time.

SECURITY

Security is our nearness to God, not our distance from danger.

—Kenneth R. Hendren

Roland Hill, a Welsh preacher, used to like to quote John 5:24. He would say, "He who hears my word and believes Him who sent Me, hath eternal life. H-a-t-h; that spells 'we've got it.'"

When the San Francisco Golden Gate Bridge was under construction, several workmen lost their lives by falling from precariously high positions. The work was proceeding much too slowly till someone hit on the idea of building a net under the construction area. Then any workman who fell would not tumble to his death, but be caught by the net.

So a giant safety net of stout cord was made and swung under the construction work (the first time in the history of major construction that such a net was used). The cost was reportedly about $100,000. The work then proceeded at a much faster rate because the workmen knew that if they did slip, their lives would be spared. They could work without the dread of uncertainty.

—Leslie B. Flynn

In a sermon Juan Carlos Ortiz spoke of a conversation with a circus trapeze artist. The performer admitted the net underneath was there to keep them from breaking their necks.

Then he added, "The net also keeps us from falling. Imagine there is no net. We would be so nervous that we would be more likely to miss and fall. If there wasn't a net, we would not dare to do some of the things we do. But because there is a net, we dare to make two turns, and once I made three turns—thanks to the net!"

Ortiz makes this observation: "We have security in God. When we are sure in His arms, we dare to attempt big things for God. We dare to be holy. We dare to be obedient. We dare, because we know the eternal arms of God will hold us if we fall."

—Vernon Luchies

More secure is no one ever
Than the loved ones of the Savior—
Not yon star on high abiding
Nor the bird in home-nest hiding.
God His own doth tend and nourish,
In His holy courts they flourish,
Like a father kind He spares them,
in His loving arms He bears them.
Neither life nor death can ever
From the Lord His children sever,
For His love and deep compassion
Comforts them in tribulation.
Little flock, to joy then yield thee!
Jacob's God will ever shield thee;

Rest secure with this Defender—
At His will all foes surrender.
What He takes or what he gives us
Shows the Father's love so precious;
We may trust His purpose wholly
'Tis His children's welfare solely.

SELF

As I look back on my life, I see it as one long obstacle course with myself as the main obstacle.

—Jack Paar

There are two sins of man that are bred in the bone and that continually come out in the flesh. One is self-dependence and the other is self-exultation.

—Charles H. Spurgeon

The goal of life is not to gain freedom but to find your master.

—P. T. Forsythe

I've conquered an empire but I've not been able to conquer myself.

—Peter the Great

Scott Peck, author of *The Road Less Traveled*, stated that after twenty years of psychotherapy he found that people who try to fulfill themselves at the expense of others lose everything and are unfulfilled.

Man is trying to make something for himself rather than something of himself.

—Jascha Heifetz

To be enslaved to oneself is the heaviest of all servitudes.

—Seneca

SELF-CONFIDENCE

Self-confidence is the first requisite to great undertakings.

—Samuel Johnson

SELF-CONTROL

Hold tight rein over three T's—thought, temper, and tongue—and you will have few regrets.

—*Teen Esteem*

SELF-CONTROL

The man who masters himself is free.
—Epictetus

Men are qualified for civil liberties in exact proportion to their disposition to put moral chains on their own appetites.
—Edmund Burke

Society cannot exist unless a controlling power on will and appetite be placed somewhere, and the less of it there is within, the more there must be without.
—Edmund Burke

Choose rather to punish your appetites than be punished by them.
—Magnus Maximus

The Christian philosophy is a philosophy of self-denial, self-control, and self-restraint.

The satanic philosophy is a philosophy of "live as you please," "have what you want," "don't let anyone tell you what to do," and "it's your life, you have a right to live it."
—Bob Jones

Most powerful is he who has himself in his own power.
—Seneca

Self-mastery is the essence of heroism.
—Ralph Waldo Emerson

SELF-DENIAL

It is when we forget ourselves that we do things that are remembered.

Socrates said, "Know yourself." Marcus Aurelius said, "Control yourself." Other orient sages said, "Give yourself." Jesus said, "Deny yourself."

Michelangelo was asked why he always wore a miner's cap when he painted. His reply was that he never wanted a shadow of himself to fall on his canvas.

SELF-DISCIPLINE

No horse gets anywhere until harnessed. No steam or gas ever drives anything until confined. No life ever grows great until it is focused, dedicated, and disciplined.
—Harry Emerson Fosdick

In reading about the lives of great men, I found that the first victory they won was over themselves . . . self-discipline with all of them came first.
—Harry S. Truman

SELF-ESTEEM

Educator and comedian Sam Levinson was standing with a group of men who seemed to tower above him.

Someone asked, "Sam, don't you feel strange surrounded by so many tall people?"

He replied, "Yes, I do. I feel like a dime among a lot of pennies!"

A psychiatrist said to Ziggy, "You have low self-esteem, but don't let it bother you because it's common among losers."

The most deadly of all possible sins is the mutilation of a child's spirit.
—Erik Erikson

A recent Harris poll showed that over 90 percent of the people polled would change their lives dramatically if they could, and in most cases they ranked such intangibles as self-respect, affection, and acceptance higher than status, money, and power. They don't like the way they live now, but they don't know how to change.
—Warren Bennis

Lack of something to feel important about is almost the greatest tragedy a person may have.
—Arthur E. Morgan

Little Maria Taft was asked who she was. She said, "My great-grandfather was president of the United States, my grandfather was a United States senator from Ohio, my father is the United States ambassador to Ireland, and I'm a Brownie."

Everybody must be somebody to somebody to be anybody.

Every once in a while ask yourself, "Based on my own work each day, would I hire myself?"

SELFISHNESS

A peevish old fellow boarded a train, occupied the best seat, and then tried to reserve another seat for himself by placing his luggage on it. Just before the crowded vehicle started, a teenage boy came running up and jumped aboard. "This car is full," said the man irritably; "that seat next to me is reserved for a friend of mine who has put his bag there." The youth paid no attention but sat down saying, "All right, I'll stay here until he comes." He placed the suitcase on his knee while the elderly man glared at him in vain. Of course, the "friend" didn't appear, and soon the train began to move. As it glided past the platform, the young fellow tossed the bag through the open window remarking, "Apparently your friend has missed the train. We mustn't let him lose his luggage too!"

A church had a sign in front: "Jesus Only." One night a storm blew out the first three letters and left "Us Only." Too many churches have come to that.

—Vance Havner

Two friends decided they would each have filet of sole for their evening meal in the restaurant. After a few minutes the waiter came back with their order. Two pieces of fish, a large and a small, were on the same platter. So one of the men proceeded to serve his friend. Placing the small piece on a plate, he handed it across the table. "Well you certainly do have the nerve!" exclaimed the other. "What is troubling you, old fellow?" asked the other. "Look what you've done. You've given me the little piece and kept the big one for yourself," he answered. "How would you have done it?" asked his friend. "If I were serving, I'd have given YOU the big piece." "Well," replied the other man, "I've got it, haven't I? What are you kicking about?" At that, they both laughed.

—Our Daily Bread

Patrick Henry shouted, "Give me liberty or give me death."

The next generation shouted, "Give me liberty."

The present generation shouts, "Give me."

People who live for self never succeed in satisfying self or anybody else.

—Trumbull

No man can live happily who regards himself alone, who turns everything to his own advantage. You must live for others, if you wish to live for yourself.

—Bits & Pieces

Character is like chiseling a statue; one has to knock off huge chunks of selfishness, which requires self-discipline. Only then does character begin to emerge.

—Bits & Pieces

SELFLESSNESS

When General Douglas MacArthur was asked, "What is the greatest quality of a leader?" he answered, "Selflessness."

In 1928 Time magazine encouraged Will Rogers to run for president. When someone asked him, "What is your business?" he answered, "Everybody's."

SELF-REALIZATION

Roland Hayes, a famous singer, was scheduled to sing before the king and queen of England. Before the appointed time, he received a telegram from his mother which had just five words: "Roland, remember who you are."

SELLING

A young man got a job as a salesman with a large insurance company. He was ambitious and applied himself eagerly to the task of learning all the techniques of selling. Yet, despite the fact that he worked hard at it, sales were few and far between. This went on for several weeks before the sales manager finally called him in. "Son," he said, "I'm afraid you just weren't cut out to be a salesman. You just don't seem to be able to sell."

The young man was surprised. "Oh, that's not it," he said. "I'm selling all right. It's just that people aren't buying."

SEPARATION

Three men were caught smuggling Bibles into Russia. They were Jerry Falwell, Oral Roberts, and Bob Jones. The official asked them, "Do you have any last words?"

Jerry Falwell said, "I love America; I'll be glad to die for my country."

Oral Roberts said, "Something good is going to happen to me today."

Bob Jones responded, "Hang me separately from these two scoundrels."

Attachment to Christ is the only secret of detachment from the world.
—A. J. Gordon

In Kentucky the electricity used over a wide area is generated from the power furnished by the Kentucky River. One night the power failed. All lights were out—no electricity. The engineers tested the power plant but could find nothing wrong with the turbines; they still operated. But still there was no electricity. Hours later a man discovered at the top of the building a black snake which had crawled onto the building and across the wires and had been electrocuted; but its body was still short-circuiting the current.

Christians need to be constantly on the alert lest some "black snake" come wriggling its way into their lives and cause a leakage of power.

Some people were ready one day to go into a coal mine just to look around. Among them was a woman wearing a white dress. The people told her she couldn't go in with that dress. She insisted she could but they said she couldn't. Then she went to the foreman and asked him if she could go in. He said, "Why, yes, you can go in, but I can't guarantee your dress will be white when you come out."

A pastor asked his young people in a catechism class, "What is religion?" A boy immediately replied, "Religion shows us the things we must not do."

You are supposed to have your boat in the water and not water in the boat. Christians are in the world, but are not to be of it.

A lady had a canary that could sing beautifully. She kept it in a cage, and one day she thought she would put it outside. So she hung the cage, in which was the bird, on a tree outside. It sang just as beautifully for a while, but after awhile it began to lose its song and to sound like the other birds. Concerned, the lady took it to the "bird doctor." He said, "Lady, there's not a thing wrong with your bird. The only trouble is that it has been outside too long."

A girl caught her hand in a vase. She couldn't get her hand out, and her parents didn't want to break the vase so the doctor was called. He worked for three hours but couldn't get her hand out. He finally said the only way to get her hand out was to break the vase. The father hated to do that so he asked the daughter to relax her hand once more and to try once again to get her hand out.

"But Daddy," she said, "I can't relax my hand. If I do I'll drop the penny I'm holding on to."

Two men were out in a boat fishing one day. Everything was going along well with one of them. He caught a long string of fish before the other man even had one.

The lucky one said to his friend, "I bet I know what is the matter—your hook is dirty."

The other man thought to himself, "How could it be dirty when it's been in the water for hours?"

But the other man persisted and said, "Pull up your line and see."

So he pulled up his line and exclaimed, "See, I told you so. It's clean."

"No, it isn't," said his friend. "See this piece of weed? That's your dirt. Remove that and you will catch fish."

"Why, that's not dirt."

The friend replied, "It may not be dirt to you, but it's still dirt to the fish."

SERIOUSNESS

Human affairs are not worthy of much seriousness, and yet one must take them seriously.

—Plato

SERVICE

Teach us, good Lord, to serve Thee as Thou deservest:
To give and not to count the cost;
To fight and not to heed the wounds;
To toil and not to seek for rest;
To labor and not ask for any reward
Save that of knowing that we do Thy will.

—Ignatius Loyola

If you do it because no one else will, it's a job.
If you are doing it to serve the Lord, it's a ministry.
If you do it just enough to get by, it's a job.
If you do it to the best of your ability, it's a ministry.
If you quit because someone criticized you, it was a job.
If you keep serving, it's a ministry.
If you quit because no one praised you, it was a job.
If you do it because you think it needs to be done, it's a ministry.

It is hard to get excited about a job.
It's almost impossible not to get excited about a ministry.
Average churches are filled with many people, doing many jobs.
Great churches are filled with many people who are involved in ministry.
If your concern is just success, it's a job.
If your concern is faithfulness to God, it's a ministry.
People may say, "Well done," when you do your job.
The Lord will say, "Well done," when you complete your ministry.

—*Bethany Beach Newsletter*

All of God's great men have been weak men who did great things for God because they reckoned on His being with them; they counted on His faithfulness.

—J. Hudson Taylor

You can tell whether you are becoming a servant by how you act when people treat you like one.

—Gordon MacDonald

It is high time we change the ideal of success for the ideal of service.

—Albert Einstein

God always uses the man closest to Him.

—D. L. Moody

At the close of life, the question will not be how much have you got, but how much have you given. Not how much have you won, but how much have you done. Not how much have you saved, but how much have you sacrificed. Not how much were you honored, but how much have you served.

—Nathan C. Schaeffer

Do what you can where you are with what you have.

Do not pray for tasks equal to your powers. Pray for powers that are equal to your tasks.

—Phillips Brooks

How often do we attempt work for God to the limit of our incompetency, rather than the limit of God's omnipotence?

—J. Hudson Taylor

Opportunity with ability make responsibility.

—Bishop Hunt

A Christian worker is good; a worker for Christ is better; but Christ, in a worker, working out His will through Him, is best of all.

The service we render for others is really the rent we pay for our room on this earth.

—Wilfred Grenfell

A talented young minister's wife was sitting in the pew one Sunday nervously twisting her handkerchief as she waited to sing a solo. An elderly lady who was deaf wrote her a note asking her what was wrong. The paper was returned with this reply, "I'm afraid of what people will think." The little slip came back with the words, "Sing to God!"

There is no greater threat to our devotion to Christ than our service for Christ.
— Oswald Chambers

Dawson Trotman once said to LeRoy Eims, "Don't be so busy in the kingdom that you don't have time for the King."

Let us do little things as though they were great, because of the majesty of Jesus Christ who does them in us and who lives our life; and do the greatest things as though they were little and easy, because of His omnipotence.
— Blaise Pascal

Be ashamed to die until you have done something for humanity.
— General Douglas MacArthur

In a modest little grave sight in Connecticut, Fanny Crosby is buried with a small gravestone. On it are the words, "She hath done what she could."

I'm willing to be a servant; I just don't want to be treated like one.

Never allow the thought "I am of no use where I am." You are certainly of no use where you're not.
— Oswald Chambers

Moses was busy with his flock at Horeb.
Gideon was busy threshing wheat by the winepress.
Saul was busy searching for his father's lost sheep.
David was busy caring for his father's sheep.
Elisha was busy plowing with twelve yoke of oxen.
Nehemiah was busy bearing the king's wine cup.
Amos was busy following the flock.
James and John were busy mending their nets.

Matthew was busy collecting taxes.
Saul was busy persecuting the friends of Jesus.

Edwin M. Stanton ran roughshod over Abraham Lincoln in a law case and later was very vindictive. But when Lincoln became president, he invited him to be his Secretary of War. When Stanton learned of this, he was overwhelmed. With tear-filled eyes, he accepted the honor. "Tell him," he said to the messenger, "that such magnanimity will make me work with him as man was never served before!"

The great violinist Nicolo Paganini willed his marvelous violin to Genoa—the city of his birth—but only on the condition that the instrument never be played. It was an unfortunate condition, for it is a peculiarity of wood that as long as it is used and handled, it shows little wear. As soon as it is discarded, it begins to decay.

The exquisite, mellow-toned violin has become worm-eaten in its beautiful case, valueless except as a relic. The moldering instrument is a reminder that a life withdrawn from all service to others loses its meaning.
— Bits & Pieces

In a remote district of Wales a baby boy lay dangerously ill. The widowed mother walked five miles in the night and through drenching rain to get a doctor. The doctor hesitated about making the trip. "Would it pay?" he questioned. He would receive no money, and besides, if the child's life were saved, he would grow up, no doubt, to become only a poor laborer. But love for humanity and professional duty conquered, and the little life was saved.

Years after, when this same child— Lloyd George—became prime minister of England, the doctor said, "I never dreamed that in saving the life of that child on the farm hearth, I was saving the life of the greatest man in Wales!"

A young woman gave her life to Christ as a missionary. Many thought she was incapable of the hard work and rugged strain of missionary life. However, she went to the mission field and gave her life unflinchingly to the service of the Lord and her people. Having died years later in the service of her Lord, she was buried and a short epitaph was placed at her grave. It said, "She did what she couldn't." What a testimony of a life given to God!

At a railroad station is a man whose job it is to sit and open and close a gate at a certain time when he is signaled. Often someone complains and criticizes him for shutting the gate when he did. When asked how he could work there when there was all that criticism, he answered, "See that man up there? When he signals for me to shut the gate, I shut it regardless of what others say, because he's the one I work for and who gives me my pay."

There are three types of Christians who respond to the call of service: (1) rowboat Christians—they have to be pushed wherever they go; (2) sailboat Christians—they always go with the wind; and (3) steamboat Christians—they make up their mind where they ought to go and go there regardless of wind or weather.

Michelangelo once entered the studio of his student Raphael and, viewing one of his landscapes, Michelangelo took a piece of chalk and wrote across it, "Amplius!" (Larger!). Raphael's perspective was too small.

The anniversaries of my birth are not important. What is important is that I've tried to lead a meaningful life. Someone much wiser than I once said, "Life begins when you begin to serve." Well, I've had that opportunity to serve, and I'm especially happy in this work. Maybe because it is service.
—Ronald Reagan

On a cold winter day in 1827 a young university student went to the city of Weimar to visit Johann von Goethe, the noted author. He hoped to interview the great man and to hear from him some weighty words of counsel.

Although the student had no appointment, the famous man of letters received him cordially. The student respectfully requested an autograph and in those days, in addition to the signature, a few wise sentiments were appreciated.

Goethe thought for a moment, and then wrote, "Let each person sweep in front of his own door, and then the whole world will be clean."

Each person doing his best, linked to other persons exerting their best efforts, can accomplish great things.
—John R. Brahham

Joyce Parfet tells of hearing a minister put together in his sermons these two popular phrases of the day: "What in the world are you doing?" and the somewhat flippant exclamation, "For heaven's sake!" He suggested that every Christian should respond to this question five times, emphasizing progressively a different portion of these combined expressions, as follows:

"*What* in the world are you doing for heaven's sake?"

"What *in the world* are you doing for heaven's sake?"

"What in the world are *you* doing for heaven's sake?"

"What in the world are you *doing* for heaven's sake?"

"What in the world are you doing for *heaven's* sake?"

An executive died and went to heaven. There he found all former executives separated into two groups—the failures in one hall and the successful in the other.

Around mealtime he entered the hall of those who failed and was surprised to find the occupants thin and hungry-looking. When the angels began to serve dinner, large platters of delicious food were placed at the table, but before anyone was seated, another angel came along and strapped a long iron spoon to each executive's arm. The long handle of the spoon was fastened to the wrists and biceps, making it impossible to bend the arm. As a result none was able to lift the spoon to his mouth. Walking over to the hall of those who had succeeded, he was surprised to find them well fed and healthy. Dinner was already on the table and an angel had just finished strapping the long iron spoons to the arms of the diners. Each executive then dipped his spoon into the food and fed the man seated across from him.

—*Bits & Pieces*

People talk of the sacrifice I have made in spending so much of my life in Africa. Can that be called a sacrifice which simply pays back a small part of the great debt we owe God? Is anything a sacrifice when it brings its own blessed reward in healthful activity, consciousness of doing good, peace of mind, and a bright hope of a glorious destiny hereafter? Away with such a thought. It's not sacrifice—it's a privilege!

—David Livingstone

Some years ago a break in the electric circuit occurred just as King George was about to deliver his radio address at the London Disarmament Conference. A humble workman caught the loose ends in his hands and bridged the gap, becoming for a time a part of the circuit. He didn't create the power by which the king's message was transmitted. He only closed the circuit so that it could flow. But through him the king's will was done.

God is not looking for more stars; He's looking for more servants.

—Howard G. Hendricks

An elderly widow, restricted in her activities, was eager to serve Christ. After praying about the matter, she decided that although she could not do much walking around to distribute tracts or witness, she was able to play the piano. The next day she placed this small ad in the *Oakland Tribune*: "Pianist will play hymns by phone daily for those who are sick and despondent—the service is free." The notice included the number to dial. When people called, she would immediately inquire, "What hymn would you like to hear?" Within a few months she had played for several hundred depressed and lonely individuals. Frequently they would pour out their hearts to her, and she was able to help and encourage them. Later she testified, "That service became the most rewarding thing I ever did in my life."

SICKNESS

A German went to a doctor and learned he was in poor health. The doctor said he had three months to live. The doctor advised him to marry a Norwegian and move to Wisconsin. "Will that help?" "No, but it will seem longer."

SILENCE

Silence is said to be golden, but it can sometimes be pretty yellow.

It often shows a fine command of language to refrain from using it.

SIMPLICITY

We must simplify, simplify, simplify.

—Henry David Thoreau

Twinkle, twinkle little star,
How I wonder what you are,
Up above the world so high,
Like a diamond in the sky.
Scintillate, scintillate, globule vivific,
Vain would I fathom thy nature specific;
Loftily poised in the other capricious
Strongly resembling a gem carbonaceous.

SIN

One reason sin flourishes is that it's treated like a cream puff instead of a rattlesnake.

—Billy Sunday

A man said to R. A. Torrey, "I'm an upright man. What do you have against me?" Torrey replied solemnly, "I charge you, Sir, with treason against the King of heaven."

The essence of sin is the refusal to recognize that we are accountable to God at all.

—Oswald Chambers

The doctrine of original sin is the one philosophy empirically validated by thirty-five hundred years of human history.

—G. K. Chesterton

When sin drives, shame sits in the back seat.
—Swedish proverb

It's the little things that irritate. It doesn't hurt to sit on a mountain top, but it does hurt to sit on a tack!

Like ripples on a tranquil pond
    That reach the farthest shore,
Our sins affect those close to us,
    And many, many more.

The Roman Emperor Valentinian made this memorable deathbed statement, "Amongst all my conquests this is the only one that now comforts me. I have overcome my worst enemy, my own sinful heart."
—Leslie B. Flynn

The truth is that the world is as it is because individually we are as we are.
—Canon Dick Shepherd

Sow an act, reap a habit,
Sow a habit, reap a character,
Sow a character, reap a destiny.
—Reade

Little sins are what hinder. You don't stumble over a house, but you do over a pebble.

There is no greater evil than good perverted.

A preacher announced that there are eighty-six kinds of sin. The following week he was besieged with requests for the list.

We are all like the moon. We all have a dark side we want no one else to see.
—Mark Twain

Those who would feign serve Him best are most conscious of sin within.

Men know what is good, but do what is bad.
—Socrates

Right is always right, even if everyone is against it.

And wrong is always wrong, even if everyone is for it.
—William Penn

Man calls sin an accident, God calls it an abomination.
Man calls sin a blunder, God calls it blindness.
Man calls sin a chance, God calls it a choice.
Man calls sin a defect, God calls it a disease.
Man calls sin an error, God calls it enmity.
Man calls sin fascination, God calls it a fatality.
Man calls sin infirmity, God calls it iniquity.
Man calls sin luxury, God calls it lawlessness.
Man calls sin a trifle, God calls it tragedy.
Man calls sin a mistake, God calls it madness.
Man calls sin a weakness, God calls it willfulness.

C. T. Studd, the great missionary pioneer, was sharing a room with a colleague on one of their journeys. The young man awoke before daybreak to discover C. T. huddled in the corner of the room, wrapped in a blanket, poring over his well-thumbed Bible in the light of a sputtering candle.
"What are you doing?" he inquired.
C. T. replied, "I couldn't sleep because I felt I had something wrong in my relationship with the Lord, and so I have been reading through the New Testament to check on His commands to me in case I have been disobedient."

Mahatma Gandhi said there are seven sins in the world.
1. Wealth without work.
2. Pleasure without conscience.
3. Commerce without morality.
4. Science without humanity.
5. Worship without sacrifice.
6. Politics without principle.
7. Knowledge without character.

Dear Abby: I have long been a student of the Bible, but I cannot find a list of the seven deadly sins anywhere, and I am too embarrassed to ask my pastor. Please tell me where I can find them. —Midwest Christian.

Dear Christian: The seven deadly sins are not listed as such in any Bible. They can be found in the writing of St. Thomas Aquinas. They are: envy, greed, lust, gluttony, sloth, pride, and anger.

When I was a small boy in Boston, one requirement for admission to the police force was that the man must be six feet tall. Only a six-footer could get in the force— not 5' 11" or not even 5' 11 $\frac{1}{2}$". He might just as well be only 5' 5" tall as 5' 11 $\frac{1}{2}$" tall so far as getting on the police force is concerned. If he comes short, it doesn't make any difference how far short he comes; he is still rejected.

—William H. Houghton

In *A View from the Zoo,* Gary Richmond, a former zookeeper wrote, "Raccoons go through a glandular change at about twenty-four months. After that they often attack their owners. Since a thirty-pound raccoon can be equal to a one hundred-pound dog in a scrap, I felt compelled to mention the change coming to a pet raccoon owned by a young friend of mine, Julie. She listened politely as I explained the coming danger. I'll never forget her answer.

"'It will be different for me . . . ' And she smiled as she added, 'Bandit wouldn't hurt me, he just wouldn't.'

"Three months later Julie underwent plastic surgery for facial lacerations when her adult raccoon attacked her for no apparent reason. Bandit was released into the world."

Sin, too, often comes dressed in an adorable guise, and as we play with it, it is easy to say, "It will be different for me."

An old deacon who frequently led the prayer meetings would often conclude his petitions with the words, "O Lord, clean all the cobwebs out of my life!" Finally a man who lived next door to him could stand it no longer for he knew that he was a self-seeking, carnal Christian. So one Wednesday night when the old fellow ended in his usual manner, his neighbor jumped to his feet and shouted, "Don't do it Lord! Don't do it! Make him kill the spider!"

Someone asked Charles Darwin, "Is there any way in which man differs from animals?" He thought and said, "Man is the only creature that blushes." When Mark Twain heard that he said, "Yes, and man is the only creature with reason to blush."

The Italian painter Leonardo da Vinci wandered the streets of Milan, Italy, staring intently at one passerby, then another.

He had been painting *The Last Supper* on the walls of a convent church and had sketched the outline. Now he was seeking the right men to pose for Christ and the different disciples.

Seeing a strong young man who had a benign expression on his face, he thought he would be good for posing for the apostle John. The man consented to his request for this posing.

A few years passed. He found men to pose for each of the disciples, but he needed someone for Judas. Then one night he saw a man who seemed appropriate as a model for Judas. Then man agreed to pose as "one of the disciples." After that, the painting was finally completed.

The man who had posed for Judas looked at the painting, his dark face turning pale. He said, "You painted me before. Don't you remember me?" "No." "When I first came to Milan I was your model for John. During the years I have lived in sin."

A friend who lives in a forested area found his home overrun with mice—too many to exterminate with traps. So he bought a few boxes of D-Con and distributed them around the house. That night he couldn't believe his ears; below him was a feeding frenzy.

In the morning he checked the box and found it licked clean.

Just to make sure the plan worked, he bought and placed another box. Again, the mice went for the flavored poison.

But the tasty and popular nighttime snack did its deadly work. In the days that followed, all was quiet. What the mice thought was good was actually deadly.

—Craig Brian Larson

Sin arises when things that are a minor good are pursued as though they were the most important goals in life. If money or affection or power are sought in disproportionate, obsessive ways, then sin occurs. And that sin is magnified when for these lesser goals we fail to pursue the highest good and the finest goals.

So when we ask ourselves why, in a given situation, we committed a sin, the answer is usually one of two things. Either we wanted to obtain something we didn't have, or we feared losing something we had.

—Augustine

No sin is small. It is against an infinite God and may have consequences immeasurable. No grain of sand is small in the mechanism of a watch.

—J. Hudson Taylor

The *St. Petersburg Times* carried a news item about a hungry thief who grabbed some sausages in a meat market, only to find they were part of a string forty-five feet long. Tripping over them, he was hindered in his getaway, and the police found him collapsed in a tangle of fresh sausages. Ironically the very loot this culprit tried to take became the loop that trapped him.

He who sins for profit shall not profit by his sins.

—D. L. Moody

A little boy said, "Sins of commission are the sins we commit, and the sins of omission are those we meant to commit but forgot."

In 1799 the American ship *Nancy* was captured by a British cutter in the Caribbean. The officers were arrested and charged with carrying contraband. However, before they reached port they managed to toss the incriminating papers overboard and forge some new ones.

As the exciting trial drew toward the end, it was evident that all of the crew would be released because of the lack of evidence. The papers produced did not list any contraband. But just before the judge raised his gavel to acquit them, another British ship brought in a harpooned shark.

When the shark was slit open, the original papers of the *Nancy* were found lodged in its insides. The papers were rushed to the trial and arrived just in time for a conviction.

Evangelist Wilbur Chapman told of a preacher friend who delivered a powerful sermon on the subject of sin. After the service, one of the church officers confronted the minister in his study and offered what he thought was some needed counsel. "Pastor," he said, "we don't want you to talk as openly as you do about man's guilt and corruption, because if our boys and girls hear you discussing that subject they will more easily become sinners. Call it a mistake, if you will, but do not speak so plainly about sin." The pastor removed a small bottle from the shelf behind his desk. Showing it to the man, he said, "You see this label? It says 'Strychnine,' and underneath in bold red letters is the word 'poison.' What you are asking me to do would be like changing this label. Suppose I write over it 'Essence of Peppermint.' Someone who doesn't know the danger might use it and become very ill. The milder the label, the more dangerous the poison!"

If you find yourself loving any pleasure above prayer, any book better than the Bible, any house more than the house of God, any table better than the Lord's, or any person more than Christ, take alarm.

—Thomas Guthrie

A boy walked across the United States. At the end of his escapade, newspaper reporters were there to publicize such a spectacular event. One person asked him what gave him the most difficulty. "The rivers?" "No, I always managed to find a

353

bridge or a shallow place to wade across." "The need of shelter?" "No, I could always find shelter." "What then gave you the most difficulty?" "The sand in my shoes." So-called little sins can often be the greatest problems.

Sin is character; sins are conduct.
Sin is the center; sins are the circumference.
Sin is the source of which sins are the secretion.
Sin is the root; sins are the fruit.
Sin is the producer, sins the product.
Sin is the old nature; sins its manifestations.
Sin is the sire; sins his offspring.
Sin is one single act; sins many sinful acts.
Sin is what we are; sins what we have done.
Sin is the fountain; sins its flow.

A corpse, of course, would not feel a four-pound weight placed on its chest. Neither would it feel a four-hundred-pound weight on its chest. So it is with people who do not think they are sinners or need Christ. They can't feel sin's weight because they are dead in trespasses and sins.

A cork placed on top of the water will float on the surface. If it is pressed down ten feet or fifty feet or even one hundred feet below the surface and then released, it will rise again. But if it is pressed down two hundred feet below the surface, it can't rise. The cork will collapse because the pressure is so great.

So it is with people who sink to the depths of sin. The greater the depth, the less probability of their ever rising again.

A scorpion asked a beaver to take him across the river on his back. "Are you insane?" asked the beaver. "While I'm swimming you'll sting me and then I'll drown."

"Oh, come now," laughed the scorpion. "Why would I string you? Then I'd drown too. Come on. Be logical."

"That makes sense," said the beaver. "Hop on and off we'll go." The scorpion climbed on the beaver's back, but halfway across the river he gave the poor trusting beaver a mighty sting. As they both sank to the bottom, the beaver asked, "Why did you do such a wicked thing? You said yourself there would be no logic in your stinging me. Why then did you do it?"

"Logic has nothing to do with it," sighed the scorpion. "It's just my nature."

In and around Ohinemutu, New Zealand, the crust of the earth is so thin that a jet of steam will burst forth if a walking stick is thrust through it. The veneer that is over the old Adamic nature in the heart of a human being is so thin that anything can pierce it, and then symptoms of the volcanic fires of sin in the heart will manifest themselves.

We have all sinned . . . some in serious, some in trivial things; some from deliberate intention, some by chance impulse, or because we are led away by the wickedness of others; some of us have not stood strongly enough by good resolutions and have lost our innocence against our will though still clinging to it; and, not only have we done wrong, but we shall go on doing wrong to the very end of life.

—Seneca

Some sins we have committed, some we have contemplated, some we have desired, some we have encouraged; in the case of some we are innocent only because we did not succeed.

—Seneca

There are some things we should never ever get used to.

A man consulted a doctor. "I've been misbehaving, Doc, and my conscience is troubling me," he complained.

"And you want something that will strengthen your will power?" asked the doctor.

"Well, no," the man said. "I was thinking of something that would weaken my conscience."

A man in Alexander's army was accused of a crime. He was brought in to see

Alexander personally. "Are you guilty?" "Yes." "What's your name?" "Alexander." "What?! Change your conduct or change your name!"

The rule that governs my life is this: Anything that dims my vision of Christ or takes away my taste for Bible study or cramps my prayer life or makes Christian work difficult is wrong for me, and I must, as a Christian, turn away from it.
—J. Wilbur Chapman

A broadcasting company in Finland conducted a contest to find how many synonyms people could think of. First place went to a contestant who came up with 747 synonyms for drunkenness. A man in prison was awarded second place for sending in 678 words for the same thing. He also won a prize for thinking of 170 synonyms for stealing. Another man knew 203 words for lying.
—*Our Daily Bread*

A prisoner was breaking stones on the road in back of a prison when a preacher approached and asked him how he was getting along. The prisoner responded, "Well, Parson, I sure have come to the conclusion that breaking stones is like breaking God's law: you can break God's law but you can't get rid of it. I am breaking these stones day after day, but they are stones just the same and they are still here—I can't get rid of them."

Sin is like a river which begins in a quiet spring and ends in a stormy sea.

There is a great difference between sin dwelling and reigning in us. It dwells in every believer, but reigns in the unbeliever.
—D. L. Moody

The loose character generally winds up in a tight place.

The trouble with little sins is that they don't stay little.

Sir James, the discoverer of chloroform, was asked, "What's the greatest discovery you ever made?" He answered, "That I am a sinner."

Pennsylvania Dutch sayings:
"As you make your bed, so you must lie in it."
"If you go barefoot, don't plant thorns."
"After your fling, watch for the sting."
"As we make it, so we have it."

Sins are like car headlights. The other fellow's are always more glaring than our own.

Good ends do not make bad actions lawful, yet bad ends make good actions lawful.
—D. L. Moody

In a museum in Athens, Greece, is a strange sight in one of the rear rooms—two bodies fastened close together by a heavy chain. The bodies and the chains have petrified and become like stone.
Long ago, the courts sentenced a criminal to die by being chained to a dead man's body. Those petrified bodies in the Athens Museum had been chained together; a living man had been chained to a dead body. When he died, the two bodies were buried together.

Joseph Cook, a famous preacher in Boston, was invited to represent Christianity at the Parliament of World Religions. When he was asked to speak, he got up and said, "Is there any one who can cleanse the bloody hands of Lady Macbeth?" Of course no other religion could offer an answer. Then he told of the only One who can cleanse from sin.

It is precisely when you consider the best in a man that you see there is in each of us a core of pride or self-centeredness which corrupts out best achievements and blights our best experiences. It comes out in jealousy which spoils our friendships, in the vanity we feel when we have done something pretty good, in the easy conversion of love into lust, in the meanness which makes us depreciate the efforts of other people, in the distortion of our own self-interest, in our fondness for flattery and our resentment of blame, in our self-assertive profession of fine ideals which we never begin to practice.

—Malcolm Muggeridge

An evangelist tells this story. "I asked a girl of fourteen at the close of a Sunday afternoon service, 'Do you know how many sins you have?' 'No,' she replied, 'I have never thought about it.' 'Well, suppose we try to find out. Do you think you have committed three sins a day—one of thought, one of word, and one of deed?' 'Oh, I expect lots more than that,' she said immediately. 'Well then, how many would that be for a year?' 'Probably more than a thousand a year,' she replied. 'As you are now fourteen, how many sins would that make in all?' 'Fourteen thousand!' she said under her breath. 'Jenny,' I said, 'that's all I want to say to you today. Fourteen thousand sins, think of that!'"

When you pick up an apple with a worm hole in it, you are inclined to think that a worm crawled to the surface of the apple, liked it, and bored the hole from the outside. But this is not generally the case. Rather, a worm lays an egg in an apple blossom and the egg is hatched in the core of the apple. The hole that you see indicates that the worm has bored its way out from within.

Sin breaks fellowship with God. A little girl committed a certain offense, and when her mother discovered it she began to question her daughter. Immediately the child lost her smile and a cloud darkened her face as she said, "Mother, I don't feel like talking."

So it is with us when our fellowship with God is broken by sin in our lives. We do not feel like talking to Him. If you do not feel like praying, it is probably a good indication that you should start praying immediately.

—Billy Graham

A boy was dressing to go out for the evening. He queried his mother, who was in the adjoining room, "Mother, is this shirt dirty?"

Without so much as looking she replied, "Yes, it's dirty; put on a clean one." When he had dressed, he entered his mother's room and asked her how she knew the shirt was not clean when she had not looked at it.

"If it had been clean," she replied, "you would have known and not asked me. Remember, if it's doubtful, it's dirty."

In the sixteenth century Juan Nepomucen, a cabin boy of Panfile Narvaez' Fleet who was afflicted with smallpox, escaped ashore on the coast of Mexico and caused the deaths of three million Indians by infecting them with smallpox. Dreadful as it was, it doesn't compare with the infection of sin transmitted by Adam to the whole human race.

An army marched through a certain country, and the commander-in-chief ordered that there should be no plundering; no one must touch a bunch of grapes in going through the vineyards, or he would die for his disobedience. One soldier, tempted by a bunch of grapes, plucked it and began to eat it. He was brought before the captain who declared that the law must be carried out and the thief must die. He was taken out to die; and though he knew his head would be cut off, he went on eating the grapes as he walked along. A comrade wondered about this; but the condemned man answered that no one ought to grudge him his grapes for they cost him dear enough.

Two brothers lived terrible lives and were dissolute. They had a terrible reputation in the town. Then one of them died. The living brother said to the pastor, "I'd like for you to have the funeral and to refer to him as a saint." The pastor said, "I can't do that." "I wish you would. If you will, I will give the church fifty thousand dollars." "Well, maybe I should think about it. I'll call you back." He called back and said, "I'll do it." At the funeral he said, "He was a scoundrel, a wild dissolute person. We all know the reputation of the brothers. And compared to his brother, he was a saint."

SINCERITY

In a Peanuts cartoon, Charlie Brown said, "Why do we always lose when we are so sincere?"

SKILL

A small factory had to stop operations when an essential piece of machinery broke down. No one could get the machine operating. An outside expert was finally called in. The fellow looked over the situation for a moment, then took a hammer and gently tapped the machine at a certain spot. It began running again immediately and continued to run as if nothing had ever been wrong.

When the expert submitted his bill for one hundred dollars, the plant supervisor hit the ceiling and demanded an itemized bill. The bill the man submitted was as follows: For hitting the machine, $1. For knowing where to hit, $99.

—*Bits & Pieces*

SLEEPING

A professor stopped in the middle of his lecture and said, "If all students who sleep during my lectures were placed end to end, they would be more comfortable."

Long sleepers (nine hours or more) are likely to be anxious, mildly depressed, chronic complainers about minor aches and pains, and not very sure of themselves. Short sleepers (six hours or less) are likely to be energetic, ambitious, decisive, socially adept, and satisfied with life. These are characteristics of males studied in psychological tests at the sleep laboratory of Boston State Hospital.

—*Science Digest*

People who say they sleep like a baby usually don't have one.

Getting up in the morning is a matter of mind over mattress.

SMILE

A smile is such a little thing
To have such a vital worth;
Sad faces it dispels at sight,
It makes the darkest places bright
And changes gloom to mirth.
A smile is such a passing thing
To bring such lasting pleasure;
It eases up the load of care
And rids the soul of dark despair
No one its worth can measure.
—Ben L. Byer

Nothing on earth can smile but man. Gems may flash reflected light, but what is a diamond flash compared with an eye-flash and a mind-flash? A smile is a light in the window of the face by which the heart signifies it is at home and waiting.

—Henry Ward Beecher

A smile can add a great deal to one's face value.

A smile is worth a million dollars but it doesn't cost a cent.

SMOKING

"I am not much of a mathematician," said the cigarette, "but I can add to a man's nervous trouble. I can subtract from his physical energy. I can multiply his aches and pains. I can divide his mental powers. I take interest from his work and discount his chances for success."

If you smoke, you won't go to hell, but you'll smell like you've been there.

A young man entered the tobacco shop in the plush hotel and asked for a pack of cigarettes. "What kind?" asked the clerk. "Any kind," replied the man. "King size or regular?" "King." "Filter tip or plain?" "Plain." "Mentholated or straight?" "Mentholated." "Crushproof box or softpack?" "Never mind," said the man. "I think I just broke the habit."

A professor in Switzerland warned her class to beware of polls and pollsters. "They can get any answer they want with loaded questions," she warned. She cited the case of Swiss voters who replied "No," when asked if they approved of smoking while praying. "The vote turned to 'Yes' when the same people were asked if they approved of praying while smoking," she told the class.

SOLITUDE

Conversation enriches the understanding, but solitude is the school of genius.
—Edward Gibbon

SONSHIP

During World War II, Brigadier General Theodore Roosevelt Jr. was waiting at an airport for a plane.

A sailor stepped to a ticket window and asked for a seat on the same plane explaining, "I want to see my mother; I ain't got much time."

The indifferent young woman at the ticket window was not impressed. "There's a war on, you know," she replied curtly.

At this point, Roosevelt, who had overheard the conversation, stepped to the window and told her to give the sailor his seat. A friend spoke in surprise, "Teddy, aren't you in a hurry too?" "It's a matter of rank," came the reply. "I'm only a general; he's a son!"
—Charles R. Diffee

SORROW

Shared sorrow is half sorrow.
—Danish proverb

Believe me, every man has his secret sorrows which the world knows not; and oftentimes we call a man cold when he is only sad.
—Henry W. Longfellow

An elderly Chinese philosopher was approached by a young woman who was grief stricken because of the loss of her only son. "I will be able to help you," he assured her, "if you will bring me some mustard seed, but it must be obtained at a home where there has never been any sorrow." Eagerly the woman started her search. In every place she visited, however, there had been trials and loss of loved ones. Returning, she exclaimed, "How selfish I

have been! Sorrow is common to all." "Ah," said the elderly sage, "you have now learned a valuable lesson and acquired a wealth of wisdom which not only has eased your own grief but also has prepared you to sympathize with others."

A sign on the side of a garage in southern Georgia read, "We can mend everything but a broken heart."

SOULWINNING

Two friends met and, after a chat, one said to the other, "Come and have a round of golf on Sunday morning."

"Oh, no. I have to attend church."

"Well," replied his friend, "I do not know what your religion is, but you keep it to yourself. I have asked you to play golf half-a-dozen times, but you have never invited me to your church."

I have always felt that wherever doctors could go to save men's bodies, I could go to save their souls.
—D. L. Moody

Dean Hart once sat at the same table with a Roman Catholic priest. During the conversation, the Dean said, "Father, if I believed as you do that I could pray people out of a suffering hell and purgatory, I would spend all my time on my knees, getting them out." The priest answered, "And if I believed as you do, that once a man is in hell he can never get out, I would wear out shoe leather urging, constraining, compelling men and women to get saved now!"

Everyone knows of Heinz, of the "fifty-seven varieties," but few know of his zeal as a soulwinner. At a revival meeting one day, the minister turned to him and said, "You are a Christian man; why aren't you up and at it?" He went home in anger and went to bed, but he could not sleep. At four o'clock in the morning he prayed that God would make him a power in his work, and then went to sleep. At the next meeting of bank presidents which he attended shortly afterward, he turned to the man next to him and spoke to him about Christ. His friend looked at him in amazement and said, "I've wondered many times why you never spoke to me about it if you really believed in Christ." That man was the first of 267 people Heinz won to Christ after that time.

O Lord, give me souls, or take my soul!
—George Whitefield

Praying Hyde, a missionary in India, pleaded, "Father, give me these souls or I die."

SPEAKING

Public speaking is like drilling for oil; if you don't strike it in three minutes, stop boring!
—George Jessel

When they booked the main speaker, they told him money was no object. So he's not getting any.

I would rather people said, "Why has he stopped speaking?" than "Why doesn't he?"
—Lord Maveroft

If you want to be a truly successful speaker, advises J. Oliver Crom, president of Dale Carnegie and Associates, remember three Key E's: Increase your *expertise* on your subject; be *eager* to share your knowledge; and generate *excitement* by the manner in which you present your speech.

A reporter once said to George Bernard Shaw, "You have a marvelous gift for oratory. How did you develop it?"
Shaw replied, "I learned to speak as men learn to skate or cycle, by doggedly making a fool of myself until I got used to it."

It seems the frailest of all weapons, for what is a word? It is only a puff of air, a vibration trembling in the atmosphere for a moment and then disappearing. . . . (Yet) though it be a weapon of air, the word is stronger than the sword of the warrior.
—James Stalker

Three rules of banquet speaking: To be seen one must stand up; to be heard one must speak up; to be appreciated one must sit down.

The young minister was giving his first after-dinner speech before a large audience. He was extremely nervous. Before long he gave up.
"My dear friends," he told his listeners, "when I came here this evening only God and I knew what I planned to say to you; now only God knows!"

Some speakers are like some gamblers— they don't have sense enough to quit while they're ahead.

There are three difficult things to do:
1. To climb a wall when it's leaning toward you.
2. To kiss a woman when she's leaning away from you.
3. To know what to speak on in chapel.
I have never tried to climb a wall when it's leaning away from me. But several times (pause) I have tried to know what to speak on in chapel.

It isn't easy being a program chairman. Let's face it, speakers are a lot like mushrooms. You never know if you're getting a bad one until it's too late.
—Bob Orben

I love a finished speaker
Yes indeed I do
I don't mean one who's polished
I just mean one who's through.

What you cannot say briefly you do not know.
—Danish proverb

As Henry VIII said to one of his wives, "I won't keep you long."

A speaker had difficulty with the loud-speaker system. Finally the audio man handed him a note: "We've found what the trouble is. There's a screw loose in the speaker."

A boy with rather mediocre talents was anxious to become a public speaker. "Do you think," he asked his instructor, "that if I were to fill my mouth with pebbles and practice enunciation as Demosthenes did, that it would improve my delivery?"

"Well," said the candid instructor, "if what I have heard is a fair sample, I would suggest that you use Portland cement."

Your audience has better things to do than listen to you. So prove to them they are wrong.

—Mark Lee

Take a lesson from the land of Demosthenes.

Fill your mouth with marbles and make a speech.

Every time you give a speech thereafter, put one less marble in your mouth. By the time you lose all your marbles, you'll be a great orator.

—*Bits & Pieces*

How much it adds to human grief
That witty speech is often brief.
How true it is—and what a pity
That lengthy talks are seldom witty.

Lyndon B. Johnson said in a speech, "Al Smith was addressing a crowd when a heckler yelled, 'Tell 'em what's on your mind, Al. It won't take long.' Smith grinned, pointed to the man, and shouted, 'Stand up, pardner, and I'll tell 'em what's on both our minds. It won't take any longer.'"

The only way to stay awake during the after-dinner speech is to make it.

When Cicero spoke, people said, "How well he spoke."

When Demosthenes spoke, people said, "Let's march."

A student chauffeured his science professor to meetings where he gave his speeches. After the speeches the people would applaud. One day the student said, "That must be great." The teacher responded, "Yes, it is. You've heard it fifty times now. You know it well. Why don't we exchange places next time."

So they did, and the student did well and the people applauded. After the speech the master of ceremonies said, "Let's have a time of questions." Someone in the back stood and asked a complicated question about one of his scientific formulas. The student said, "I'm surprised. You asked a simple question that even my chauffeur can answer."

The late Yale professor and lecturer William Lyon Phelps once said he got credit for only one-fourth of his after-dinner speeches. "Every time I accept an invitation to speak, I really make four addresses. First is the speech I prepare in advance. That is pretty good. Second is the speech I really make. Third is the speech I make on the way home, which is the best of all; and fourth is the speech the newspapers the next morning say I made, which bears no relation to any of the others."

—*Bits & Pieces*

Three things matter in a speech: who says it, how he says it, and what he says.

—Lord Morley

All public speaking of real merit is characterized by nervousness.

—Cicero

My wife says to me that two things are wrong with my speeches. One, I depart from my topic. Two, I return to my topic.

—Henry King Stanford

A man's brain is a strange mechanism. It starts working the minute we are born and quits the moment we get up to make a speech.

A man spoke at a Yale University alumni dinner. He gave a brilliant address. He spoke thirty minutes on the letter Y (Youth), one-half hour on A (Achievement), thirty minutes on L (Leadership), and one-half hour on the E (Excellence).

Afterward a man was crying. The

speaker asked him what it was about his message that touched him so. He said, "I'm so happy."

"Why?"

"I'm so glad this isn't the alumni dinner of the Massachusetts Institute of Technology!"

Care not for the reward of your speaking but simply and with undivided mind for the truth of your speaking.

—Thomas Carlyle

Woodrow Wilson was once asked to speak. Before accepting the invitation he said, "When do you want me to speak? If you want me to speak five minutes, I will be ready in a month. If you want me to speak fifteen minutes, I will be ready next week; but if you want me to speak an hour, I can speak right now."

SPECIFICS

You get better results when you ask for specific results. If you ask for a 10 percent cut in the cost of supplies, you may get it. If you just ask employees to watch out for waste in the use of supplies, nothing is likely to change.

SPIRITUAL DEVELOPMENT

1. I deliberately place myself daily before God to allow Him to use me as He wills (Rom. 12:1–2).
2. Ask God at a specific time daily to reveal His strategy and will for me that day.
3. Set and achieve a goal for personal spiritual development through reading one significant book per week.
4. Isolate a known point of weakness (spiritually), and work on it with the help of the Holy Spirit to correct and improve this weakness.
5. Make a study of several Bible people who are good examples—and seek deliberately to emulate them in their strong points.
6. Set up a measuring device to check spiritual development (quantitatively) and measure regularly.

—Ted Engstrom

SPIRITUALITY

An electrician converted a gas stove to electricity, but he did not have time to adjust it. He had to do it the next day. So he took a piece of cardboard and wrote on it, "Converted but not adjusted."

It's possible to be straight as a gun barrel in orthodoxy, but empty as a gun barrel in spirituality.

SPORTSMANSHIP

The trouble with being a good sport is that you have to lose in order to prove it.

It takes a good man to win without boasting and lose without murmuring.

STANDARDS

I'd push people back to their typewriters and drawing tables, telling them, "You can do better; you have to do better." And they'd do better. Good people respond to high standards.

—Shephard Kurnit

The reasons some people require so much of others is that they require so little of themselves.

STATISTICS

He uses statistics as a drunken man uses lampposts—for support rather than for illumination.

—Andrew Lang

STEALING

A young man who swept the floors in a bank after working hours found a small pack of bills which had somehow fallen under a counter. He took the money home and thought long and hard about whether he should keep it, for his family was in dire need and the extra cash would come in handy. The next morning, however, he returned the currency. "Tell me," said the banker, "what kept you honest? We never could have traced the loss or pinned the blame on you." "Well, Mr. Brown," said the young man, "I'm a Christian and God would know about it! Besides, I would have a troubled conscience, and I decided I just didn't want to live with a thief."

STEWARDSHIP

A beggar asked a gift from one who appeared to be a wealthy lady. She gave him a coin saying, "This is more than God has ever given me." "Oh, lady," said the beggar, "everything you have has been bestowed by the Lord." "True," said the lady, "but God has not given it to me, it remained His all the time; He only loaned it to me to distribute to others."

STRIFE

Two ladies in a train coach were arguing about the window. One claimed she would die of heatstroke unless it was opened. The other insisted she would die of pneumonia if it wasn't kept closed. The ladies called the conductor who was at a loss to solve the problem. It was then that the stranger sitting with them in the coach spoke up. "First, open the window. That will kill one. Then close it. That will kill the other. Then we'll have peace."

—Leslie B. Flynn

STUDYING

If I had only three remaining years of ministry, I would spend two of them studying.
—Donald Grey Barnhouse

The more we study,
    the more we know.
The more we know,
    the more we forget.
The more we forget,
    the less we know.
The less we know,
    the less we forget.
The less we forget,
    the more we know.
So why study?

A Quaker said to a preacher who was a fox hunter, "If I were a fox and wanted to hide from thee, I'd hide where you'd not find me."

"And where's that?" asked the preacher.
"In your study."

SUBMISSION

Horatio Nelson, the great British admiral, always treated his vanquished opponents with the greatest kindness and courtesy. After one of his naval victories, the defeated admiral was brought aboard Nelson's flagship and onto Nelson's quarterdeck. Knowing Nelson's reputation for courtesy and thinking to trade on it, he advanced across the quarterdeck with arms outstretched as if he were advancing to shake hands with an equal. Nelson's hand remained by his side. "Your sword first," he said, "and then your hand."

SUBSTITUTION

A judge was surprised to see his son brought into his court. His son was guilty of speeding. The judge pronounced him guilty and announced the fine. Then he dismissed the court, went down to his son, and paid the fine. "But no judge can do that." Yes, but a father can.

Franciszek Gajowniczek was a Nazi prisoner in Auschwitz when a fellow inmate escaped. The standard discipline when anyone escaped was to select ten men at random and place them in a cell where they were left to starve to death. When Gajowniczek heard his name read, he sobbed, "My wife and my children." At that moment a Franciscan priest and fellow inmate named Koble stepped forward and said, "I will die in his place. I have no wife or children." The commandant granted his request.

Since that time Gajowniczek has gone back every year to Auschwitz on August 14 to remember the man who died for him that day in 1941. And in his yard he has placed a plaque to honor this priest and to remind others of his great sacrifice.

In the marketplace of Rotterdam, Holland, stood for many years an old corner house known as "The House of a Thousand Terrors."

During the sixteenth century, the Dutch people rose in revolt against the cruel King Philip II of Spain. Philip sent a great army under the Duke of Alva to suppress the rebellion. Rotterdam held out for a long time but finally capitulated.

From house to house the victors went,

searching out citizens and then killing them in their houses. A group of men, women, and children were hiding in a corner house when they heard soldiers approaching. A thousand terrors gripped their hearts. Then a young man had an idea. He took a goat in the house, killed it, and with a broom swept the blood under the doorway out into the street.

The soldiers reached the house and began to batter down the door. Noticing the blood coming out from under the door, one soldier said, "Come away, the work is already done. Look at the blood beneath the door." And the people inside the house escaped.

—Paul Lee Tan

A tornado swept through western Pennsylvania and in a matter of seconds turned lovely rural towns into disaster areas. Homes, businesses, and lives were shattered.

One of the poignant scenes was that of a man on some steps sobbing softly. Behind him was a pile of rubble that once was his home. His tears, he explained, were not from loss of grief, but of gratitude. His young son had miraculously been spared.

A neighbor, driving the boy home, had seen the tornado coming, stopped the car, pushed the boy into a ditch, and covered him with his own body. The neighbor lost his life in the storm, but the boy survived.

—Edward H. Morgan

In Stroudburg, Pennsylvania, is the grave of a certain Civil War soldier. The stone bears the date of his birth and death, plus these words: "Abraham Lincoln's Substitute." In the woe and anguish of the war, realizing that thousands were falling on the field of battle, President Lincoln chose to honor one particular soldier as his substitute—making him a symbol, as it were, of the fact that those who perished in the battle were dying that others might live!

A mother was crossing a prairie with her baby in her arms. As she journeyed along, she saw in the distance a dark cloud of smoke, gradually increasing in size until it grew to immense proportions. She knew it was a prairie fire. She saw that she could not possibly escape the flames; the fire was traveling with lightning-like speed. So she prepared for the inevitable. As the fiery billows rolled like a seething mass across the prairie, she kneeled down, dug a hole, and laid her baby in the hole. As the roaring flames approached, she threw herself across the hole in the ground. In a moment it was all over. Later her charred body was found over the spot, but the baby was alive. She gave herself for the baby. Her sacrifice saved the baby from a fiery death.

Christ took our hell so that we might take His heaven.

—Donald Grey Barnhouse

SUBSTITUTING

"I'm substituting for the pastor today. It's something like a pane in the window being out and a cardboard in its place."

After the service, a lady said to the preacher, "You were no substitute; you were a real pain."

SUCCESS (Also see FAILURE)

Success is living in such a way that you are using what God has given you—your intellect, abilities, and energy—to reach the purpose that he intends for your life.

—Kathi Hudson

The most important single ingredient in the formula of success is knowing how to get along with people.

—Theodore Roosevelt

The average man has five senses: touch, taste, sight, smell, and hearing. The successful man has two more: horse and common.

If you're successful, don't crow. If you're defeated, don't croak.

—Samuel Chadwick

The dictionary is the only place where success comes before work.

Behind every successful man there's a woman who's surprised.

The success of tomorrow depends on the work of today.

Don't aim for success. Just do what you love and believe, and it will come naturally.
—David Frost

If you can meet success and failure and treat them both as imposters, then you are a balanced man, my son.
—Rudyard Kipling

The difference between a successful person and others is not a lack of strength, nor a lack of knowledge, but rather a lack of will.

If people are happy in their work—exerting themselves to the full extent of their limitations and capabilities and enjoying it—they're successful.

There is a four-word formula for success that applies equally well to organizations and individuals—*make yourself more useful.*

The secret of success is to do the common things uncommonly well.
—John D. Rockefeller Jr.

I would rather fail in the cause that someday will triumph than triumph in a cause that will someday fail.
—Woodrow Wilson

There are no victories at bargain prices.
—Dwight D. Eisenhower

Success depends on the proper functioning of the glands, especially the sweat glands.

If at first you don't succeed, you're probably not related to the boss.

The success of a great person is doing what others will not do.

Success is for those energetic enough to work for it, hopeful enough to look for it, patient enough to wait for it, brave enough to seize it, and strong enough to hold it.

One of the biggest troubles with success is that its recipe is about the same as that for a nervous breakdown.

John Kenneth Galbraith in *Economics, Peace and Laughter* discussed Eisenhower's success as a leader: "His rule was to keep one eye on the Germans, one eye on his generals, and both ears bent toward Washington."

The common idea that success spoils people by making them vain, egotistic, and self-complacent is erroneous; on the contrary, it makes them, for the most part, humble, tolerant, and kind. Failure makes people bitter and cruel.
—Somerset Maugham

A success without a struggle challenges nobody.
—Homer Dowdy

Success in life is a matter not so much of talent as of concentration and perseverance.
—C. W. Wendte

Most people who succeed in the face of seemingly impossible conditions are people who simply don't know how to quit.
—Robert H. Schuller

If at first you *do* succeed, try something harder.

There's just one discouraging thing about the rules of success: They won't work unless you do!

The best way to succeed in life is to act on the advice we give others.

If at first you don't succeed, so much for skydiving.

Success is measured not so much by the position that one has reached in life as by the obstacles he has overcome while trying to succeed.
—Booker T. Washington

To do a common thing uncommonly well brings success.

—Henry John Heinz

Science says that success is relative. The more success . . . the more relatives.

Someone asked the French writer Jean Costeau if he believed in luck. "Certainly," he said, "How else do you explain the success of those you don't like?"

Success is not a matter of pure luck. It is mainly a matter of, first, work; second, work; third, work—with, of course, a plentiful mixture of brains, foresight, and imagination.

—B. C. Forbes

Striving for success without hard work is like trying to harvest where you haven't planted.

—David Bly

The Lord gave us two ends—one to sit on and the other to think on. Success depends on which one we use the most.

—Ann Landers

Behind every successful man is an exhausted woman.

People rarely succeed at anything unless they have fun doing it.

A successful person is one who went ahead and did the thing the rest of us never quite got around to.

Whatever you are by nature, keep to it; never desert your line of talent. Be what nature intended you for and you will succeed.

—Sydney Smith

Success consists not of getting but of doing.

There is no success without honor; no happiness without a clear conscience; no use in living at all if only for one's self.

—Robert Waters

The man who gets ahead is the one who does more than is necessary—and keeps on doing it.

For every*one* who can handle prosperity there are one hundred who can handle adversity.

—Thomas Carlyle

Success cannot evolve without the element of failure present. It is not failure which shapes lives but what is done about failure.

—F. C. Ellenburg

Success is getting what you want; happiness is wanting what you get.

Happiness comes when you find out what you like to do better than anything else and do it so well that people will come to you and pay you to do it.

—Samuel Graflin

The road to success runs uphill, so don't expect to break any speed records.

Success equals effort plus vision.

You can fear yourself to failure, or you can fire yourself to success.

Many successful people today were failures yesterday, who never gave up.

Success comes to those who have the character to continue when all seems lost.

A successful man is one who lets God control his mind, his body, and his pocketbook.

Hard work is the easiest bridge to cross over to success.

If there is any one secret of success, it lies in the ability to get the other person's point of view and see things from his angle as well as your own.

—Henry Ford

The following definition of success was written in 1904 by Bessie Anderson Stanley from Lincoln, Kansas. She was paid $250 for this prize-winning essay. "He has achieved success who lived well, laughed often and loved much; who has enjoyed the trust of pure women, the respect of intelligent men and the love of little children; who has filled his niche, and accomplished his task; who has left the world better than he found it, whether by an improved poppy, a perfect poem, or a rescued soul; who has never lacked appreciation of earth's beauty, or failed to express it; who has always looked for the best in others and given them the best he had; whose life was an inspiration; whose memory was a benediction."

—Ann Landers

Toward the end of his long and productive life a wise man was once asked what advice he had for young men just starting out on life's journey. This was his answer:

Belong to something bigger than yourself.

Work with others toward a common goal. Do your part.

Take pride in doing your job well.

Work hard to make your ideas take shape in reality.

Help build something of lasting value.

Some ingredients of success: to be able to carry money without spending it; to be able to bear an injustice without retaliating; to be able to keep on the job until it is finished; to be able to do one's duty even when one is not being watched; to be able to accept criticism without letting it whip you.

—*Bits & Pieces*

Marie Ray, a psychiatrist, says that most great people become great because of their struggles with some disability or because of responsibilities too great for their own powers. "No one succeeds without a handicap," she said. "No one succeeds in spite of a handicap. When anyone succeeds, it's because of a handicap."

Does a bird need to theorize about building its nest or boast of it when built? All good work is essentially done that way—

without hesitation, without difficulty, without boasting.

—John Ruskin

When the late Edward Cole was president of General Motors he was asked, "What makes you different from other men—why have you succeeded over thousands of others to the top job at G.M.?" He thought for a moment and replied, "I love problems!"

—Ted Engstrom

At a dinner party, a woman said to Lord Northcliffe, "It is really quite surprising— Thackeray awoke one morning and found himself famous!" "When that morning dawned," Lord Northcliffe answered, "Thackeray had been writing eight hours a day for fifteen years! No, madam, the man who wakes up and finds himself famous hasn't been asleep!"

Industrial psychologists, seeking the reason why some people move up faster than others, found that the supervision of most workers depends upon the amount of supervision they require. People who see needs and supply them without being told or ordered are the ones who succeed.

—*Bits & Pieces*

After actor/director Michael Douglas had been in five blockbuster films, his father, actor Kirk Douglas, wrote him a note. It said, "Michael, I'm more proud of how you *handle* success than I am of your success."

—*Bits & Pieces*

The Winner—is always part of the answer;
The Loser—is always part of the problem;
The Winner—says, "Let me do it for you";
The Loser—says "That's not my job";
The Winner—sees an answer for every problem;
The Loser—sees a problem for every answer;
The Winner—sees a green near every sand trap;
The Loser—sees two or three sand traps near every green;

The Winner—says "It may be difficult but it's possible";
The Loser—says, "It may be possible but it's too difficult."

I believe that a human being can do a lot himself to shape his life. For me, the most important thing is to work hard when I work and acquire all possible knowledge in my line of work . . . and then learn how to relax in between.

—Lauritz Melchior

Men give me some credit for genius. All the genius I have lies in this: When I have a subject at hand, I study it profoundly. Day and night it is before me. I explore it in all its bearings. My mind becomes pervaded with it. Then the efforts that I make are what people are pleased to call the fruits of genius. It is the fruit of labor and thought!

—Alexander Hamilton

Actress Helen Hayes said her mother drew a distinction between achievement and success. Her mother advised her that "achievement is the knowledge that you have studied and worked hard and done the best that is in you. Success is being praised by others, and that's nice too, but not as important or satisfying. Always aim for achievement and forget about success."

The Ladder of Success

0% — I won't.
10% — I can't.
20% — I don't know how.
30% — I wish I could.
40% — I could.
50% — I think I might.
60% — I might.
70% — I think I can.
80% — I can.
90% — I will.
100% — I did.

Some of the world's most successful financiers met in 1923 at the Edgewater Beach Hotel in Chicago.

Present were the president of the largest independent steel company, the president of the largest utility company, the greatest wheat speculator, the president of the New York Stock Exchange, a member of the cabinet of the President of the United States, the greatest "bear" on Wall Street, the president of the Bank of International Settlements, and the head of the world's greatest monopoly. These eight men together controlled more wealth than the United States Treasury.

Success stories of these men had been featured in magazines and books for many years. Charles Schwab, president of the steel company, lived the last years of his life on borrowed money and died broke. Arthur Cutten, the greatest speculator, died abroad, insolvent. Richard Whitney, president of the New York Stock Exchange, served a term in the Sing Sing Prison. Albert Fall, member of the President's Cabinet, was pardoned from prison to die at home. Jessie Livermore, the greatest "bear" on Wall Street, Leon Fraser, president of the Bank of International Settlements, and Ivan Krueger, head of the world's largest monopoly, all committed suicide. Seven of the eight "successful" men ended their lives in tragedy and sorrow.

By his mid-thirties, Winston Churchill was by far the most successful politician of his age in Britain. His career had been like a brilliant meteor blazing across the sky. The son of a notorious politician, he had achieved fame as a reporter and author whose chief subject matter was his own military adventures. Elected to Parliament at the tender age of twenty-five, he entered the Cabinet at thirty-one, and at the outbreak of World War I, was Lord of the Admiralty and part of the War Cabinet. Intelligent, hardworking, eloquent, single-minded, ambitious—the world lay at his feet. But Churchill's world revolved around him as the sun. He was more interested in himself and his own ideas than in anything else, and his peers were reluctant to trust him.

Then in 1915, his world collapsed. A military expedition at Gallipoli for which he was held responsible (critics still debate the validity of the charge) turned into a bloody debacle. He was forced to resign from the Cabinet, and his long years in the political wilderness, with intermittent respites, began. One biography gives this period of his life a fascinating title, "The Rise to Failure."

In the crucible of failure, Churchill forged some new qualities which became instrumental in his success as the great Allied leader during World War II. But until he refocused his life, he was a brilliant failure. Achievement in itself can never be the mark of excellence or greatness.

—Gary Inrig

SUFFERING

The child of God is often called to suffer because there is nothing that will convince onlookers of the reality and power of true religion as suffering will do, when it is borne with Christian fortitude.

—F. B. Meyer

Don't be like the boy during World War II who said, "I wouldn't mind going to war and being a hero if I knew I wouldn't get hurt."

—Mack R. Douglas

It is doubtful God can use any man greatly until He has hurt him deeply.

—A. W. Tozer

Some knees bend only under the load of a heavy heart; some eyes are opened only after the head is bowed.

—William Arthur Ward

It is possible to escape a multitude of trouble by living an insignificant life.

—John Henry Jewett

Margaret Sangster Phippen wrote that in the mid-1950's her father, British minister W. E. Sangster, began to notice some uneasiness in his throat and a dragging in his leg. When he went to the doctor, he found he had an incurable disease that caused progressive muscular atrophy. His muscles would gradually waste away, his voice would fail, his throat would soon become unable to swallow.

Sangster threw himself into his work in British home missions, figuring he could still write and he would have even more time for prayer. "Let me stay in the struggle, Lord," he pleaded. "I don't mind if I can no longer be a general, but give me just a regiment to lead." He wrote articles and books, and helped organize prayer cells throughout England. "I'm only in the kindergarten of suffering," he told people who pitied him.

Gradually Sangster's legs became useless. His voice went completely. But he could still hold a pen, shakily. On Easter morning, just a few weeks before he died, he wrote a letter to his daughter. In it, he said, "It is terrible to wake up on Easter morning and have no voice with which to shout, 'He is risen!'—but it would be still more terrible to have a voice and not want to shout."

—Vernon Grounds

William Sangster, well-known British pastor, was told he had progressive muscular atrophy and could not get well. He made the following resolutions and stuck by them to the day he died.

1. I will never complain.
2. I will keep the home bright.
3. I will count my blessings.
4. I will try to turn it to good.

A family in India were the first in their village to turn to Christ. Shortly after their conversion, everybody said, "The gods will go against you. You're going to be cursed."

They were a little concerned about this. And then their child got sick. When the child got sick, everyone said, "See, the gods have punished you! See what has happened!"

The family went to church and said, "Please pray for us. Our child is sick; the people are saying this is a punishment for becoming Christians."

The church prayed earnestly, but the child got worse and finally died.

When they had the funeral, the first Christian funeral in the village, the people of the village heard the hope of the resurrection and their eyes were opened and many people came to Christ.

SUICIDES

Ernest Hemingway was an infantryman and ambulance driver in World War I, a war correspondent in the Spanish Civil War and World War II. In peacetime he was an avid sportsman, hunting big game in Africa and fishing off the coasts of Key West and Cuba. He traveled extensively. His novels hit the bestseller lists time after time. In winning the Pulitzer Prize in 1953 and the Nobel Prize for Literature in 1954, he established a place for himself as one of the greatest American authors of all time. By most standards, he had it all, but it must not have been enough. Discouraged and despondent, he shot himself in a cabin in Idaho in 1961.

The number of people who commit suicide after experiencing the fame or fortune of worldly success is astonishing. Multimillionaire George Vanderbilt killed himself by jumping from a hotel window. Lester Hunt, twice governor of Wyoming before being elected to the U.S. Senate, ended his own life. Actress Marilyn Monroe, writer Ernest Hemingway, and athlete Tony Lazzeri represent a host of highly influential and popular people who became so disenchanted with earthly success that they took their own lives.

What's the use of worrying?
     It never was worthwhile,
So, pack up your troubles
     In your old kit-bag
And smile, smile, smile.

Those words, written by British vaudeville actor George Powell, were set to a cheerful melody by his piano-playing brother Felix. It earned them $60,000.

Yet one day years later, Felix sat down at a piano and played his well-known melody "Smile, Smile, Smile." Then he went into a room where he was all alone and shot and killed himself.

—*Our Daily Bread*

SUNDAY SCHOOL

"Our teacher is like the deep sea diver," a teenager exclaimed.

"How's that?"

"He dives deep into the truth, stays under a while, and comes up dry."

A small boy: "Why don't you come to my Sunday school?"

Another small boy: "Cause I belong to another abomination."

"I shall now illustrate what I have in mind," said the teacher as she erased the board.

The prayer meeting is the indicator of the present vitality of a church, but the Sunday school is the outline of what church will be tomorrow.

—J. B. Chapman

SURGERY

I got the bill for my surgery. Now I know why those doctors were wearing masks.

—James H. Boren

SURPRISES

While she was enjoying a transatlantic ocean trip, Billie Burke, the famous actress, noticed that a gentleman at the next table was suffering from a bad cold.

"Are you uncomfortable?" she asked sympathetically. The man nodded.

"I'll tell you what to do for it," she offered. "Go back to your stateroom and drink lots of orange juice. Take two aspirins. Cover yourself with all the blankets you can find. Sweat the cold out. I know just what I'm talking about. I'm Billie Burke from Hollywood."

The man smiled warmly and introduced himself in return. "Thanks," he said, "I'm Dr. Mayo of the Mayo Clinic."

—*Bits & Pieces*

SWEARING

A Quaker, backing up his car, bumped into the vehicle behind him. The driver jumped out and called him several very insulting names. When he ran out of names the Quaker said, "If you offer a man something and he refuses it, to whom does it belong?"

Taken by surprise at the unexpected question, the other driver replied, "To the one who originally offered it, I suppose."

"We agree," smiled the Quaker. "The abuse and ugly names you offer me I refuse to accept."

T

TACT

Tact is making a point without making an enemy.

The more right you are, the more careful you should be to express your opinion tactfully. The other fellow never likes to be proven wrong.

—John Luther

A schoolboy defined tact in this way: "The thing that if it's there, nobody notices it, but if it isn't there, everybody notices it."

Cultivate tact for it is the mark of culture . . . the lubricant of human relations, softening contacts and minimizing friction.

—Baltasar Gracian

The new minister's family was presented with a pie baked by one of the congregation who was a rather poor cook. The pie was inedible, so the minister's wife threw it onto the garbage.

The preacher was faced with the problem of thanking the lady, while at the same time being truthful. After much thought he sent the following note: "Dear Mrs. Jones: Thank you for being so kind and thoughtful. I can assure you that a pie like yours never lasts long at our house!"

Why is it that those who have something to say can't say it, while those who have nothing to say keep saying it?

Tact is telling someone where to go and doing it so nicely that he looks forward to going there.

Tact is the art of building a fire under people without making their blood boil.

TALKING

A verbose and extremely boring man said to the philosopher Plato, "I hope I'm not boring you?" Plato smiled ingeniously. "Oh, no," he said, "I wasn't listening."

A family was entertaining some friends for dinner. The hostess, anxious to show that they upheld Christian standards in their own home, asked her five-year-old son to say grace. There was an awkward pause, followed by a reassuring word from the boy's mother. "Well, darling, just say what Daddy said at breakfast this morning." Obediently the boy repeated, "Oh God, we've got those awful people coming for dinner tonight."

—*Rolling in the Aisles*

Flies cannot enter the mouth that is closed.

—Moroccan proverb

The world may be much happier if men were as fully able to keep silence as they are able to speak.

—Baruch Spinoza

The tongue is the only tool that becomes sharper with use.

There is nothing so annoying as to have two people go right on talking when you're interrupting.

—Mark Twain

Dr. John Abernathy was renowned for his dislike of idle chatter. With this in mind, a young lady once entered his surgery and, without a word, held out an injured finger for examination. The doctor dressed the wound in silence. The woman returned a few days later. "Better?" asked Abernathy. "Better," replied the patient. Subsequent calls passed in much the same manner. On her final visit the woman held out her finger, now free of bandages. "Well?" inquired the doctor. "Well," she replied. "Upon my word, madam," exclaimed Abernethy, "you are the most rational woman I have ever met."

—*The Little, Brown Book of Anecdotes*

People with sharp tongues often end up cutting their own throats.

A physician says that yawning is caused by an oversupply of fresh air. That may be so, but it can also be caused by an oversupply of hot air.

Keep your words soft and sweet. You never know when you may have to eat them.

Good words cost no more than bad.

Smooth words make smooth ways.

A word hurts more than a wound.

Soft words win bad hearts.

Better is a good word in time than two afterward.

A spoken word is an arrow let fly.

There once was a man of verbosity
Who loved words with savage ferocity;
   Waxing profound,
   He fell to the ground
Knocked out by his own pomposity.
       —M. Venita Victoria

Astronaut Michael Collins, speaking at a banquet, quoted the estimate that the average man speaks 25,000 words a day and the average woman 30,000. Then he added, "Unfortunately, when I come home each day I've already spoken my 25,000 and my wife hasn't started her 30,000."

According to statisticians the average person spends at least one-fifth of his or her life talking. Ordinarily, in a single day enough words are used to fill a fifty-page book. In one year's time the average person's words would fill 132 books, each containing four hundred pages.
       —Paul Lee Tan

After all is said and done, more is said than done.

A fool tells what he will do; a boaster tells what he has done; a wise man does it and says nothing.

What Men and Women Talk About

Men and women don't necessarily want to discuss the same subjects, according to a poll of one thousand adults by Bruskin Associates.

The leading discussion subject for men was news events talked about by 71 percent of respondents in the previous week, followed by work (68 percent).

Women, on the other hand, talked about food (76 percent), and health (72 percent).

Men were far more likely to have talked about sports (65 percent to women's 42 percent); women were more likely to have discussed personal problems (52 percent to men's 40 percent).

But many subjects—television, money, and celebrities, for example—were discussed about the same amount by either sex. And neither men nor women talked much about sex (men, 2 percent; women, 0.8 percent).

If you want to save face, try keeping the lower end of it closed.

One reason a dog has so many friends is that it spends more time wagging its tail than wagging its tongue.

There are two types of people who say very little—the quiet ones and the gabby ones.

A flow of words does not mean a flow of wisdom.
       —Rosalind Ferguson

A bore talks mostly in the first person, a gossip in the third, and a good conversationalist in the second.

A slip of the foot you may soon recover from, but a slip of the tongue you may never get over.

If something will go without saying, let it.

Keeping your mouth shut can keep a lot of ignorance from leaking out.

A carpenter said it: "The best rule for talking is the same as for carpentering—measure twice, then saw once."

A lot of people don't have much to say, and that's fine. The trouble with some of them is you have to listen a long time to find out.

—*Bits & Pieces*

God gave man a mouth that closes and ears that don't; which should tell us something!

Socrates said to his student, "I must teach you two things: how to hold your tongue, and how to use it."

Lord, fill my mouth with worthwhile stuff, and nudge me when I've said enough.

A wise owl lived in an oak,
The more he saw the less he spoke;
The less he spoke the more he heard.
Why can't we be like that old bird?

Talking or writing that is too long is generally the result of thinking that wasn't long enough.

A careless work
    May kindle strife;
A cruel word
    May wreck a life;
A bitter word
    May hate instill;
A brutal word
    May smite and kill;
A gracious word
    May smooth the way;
A joyous word
    May light the way
A timely word
    May lessen stress;
A loving word
    May heal and bless.

It takes two years for a baby to learn to talk, but it takes fifty years for a person to learn to keep his mouth shut.

The slanderous tongue kills three: the slandered, the slanderer, and him who listens to the slanderer.

—Talmud

Some people are like buttons—always popping off at the wrong time.

I'm careful of the words I speak,
I keep them soft and sweet.
I never know from day to day
Which ones I'll have to eat.

Talking and eloquence are not the same: to speak, and to speak well, are two things. A fool may talk, but a wise man speaks.

—Ben Johnson

The word that lies nearest the heart comes first to the lips.

—Norwegian proverb

The fellow with the smallest mind is usually the one most willing to give someone else a piece of it.

A lot of people who wouldn't talk with full mouths will go around talking with empty heads.

If your lips would keep from slips,
    Five things observe with care:
Of whom you speak, to whom you speak,
    And how, and when, and where.

—William Norris

An intellectual is someone who takes more words than necessary to tell more than he knows.

—Dwight D. Eisenhower

The Devil is the accuser of the brethren, so let him do all the dirty work.

—H. A. Ironside

Men may doubt what you say, but they will believe what you do.

The boneless tongue, so small and weak, can crush and kill.

—Unknown Greek writer

The thing most frequently opened by mistake is the human mouth.

Once a woman gossiped to the preacher about what people said about him. The preacher replied, "That's not half of what I know about myself."

The secret of being a bore is to tell everything.

—Voltaire

What is the difference between a fool and a mirror? A mirror reflects without speaking, while a fool speaks without reflecting.

There is no wholly satisfactory substitute for brains, but silence does pretty well.

I will chide no brother in the world but myself, against whom I know most fault.

—Shakespeare

As a vessel is known by the sound whether it be cracked or not, so men are proved by their speeches, whether they be wise or foolish.

—Demosthenes

Talk is cheap because the supply exceeds the demand.

The trouble with the guy who talks too fast is that he often says something he hasn't thought of yet.

These thoughts were discovered inscribed on the walls of an ancient Persian temple:

"Do not say all you know, for he who says all he knows often says more than he knows.

"Do not tell all you hear, for he who tells all he hears often tells more than he hears."

Former president Calvin Coolidge was known as a man of few words. Once, at a White House dinner, a woman approached Coolidge and said, "Mr. President, I have a bet with a friend that I can get you to say at least three words." Coolidge looked at her and said, "You lose."

The best way to get the last word is to apologize.

Several ladies were visiting at a minister's home. As he entered the room, he heard them speaking in low voices of an absent friend.

"She's very odd," said one.

"Yes, very singular indeed," said another.

"Do you know, she often does so and so," said another mentioning certain things to her discredit.

The minister asked who it was. When told, he said, "Oh, yes, she is odd; she's remarkably singular. Why, would you believe it," he added in a low voice, "she was never heard to speak ill of any absent friend!"

Better to remain silent and be thought a fool than to speak out and remove all doubt.

—Abraham Lincoln

A woman said to John Wesley, "I think I know what my talent is." "What is it?" "To speak my mind." Wesley replied, "I don't think God would mind if you bury that talent."

There is nothing wrong with having nothing to say—unless you insist on saying it.

They say it's not smart not to believe more than half of what you hear. But which half?

Franklin D. Roosevelt started his career as a lawyer in New York. One of the first cases he was retained to represent was a particularly difficult civil suit. The opposing lawyer, a notable orator, did well in his pleadings before the jury. However, he made one big mistake; he talked on and on for hours. Roosevelt, noticing the inattention of the jury, decided on his strategy. When his turn came to sum up his client's side of the case, he merely said, "Gentlemen, you have heard the evidence. You have also listened to my distinguished colleague, a brilliant orator. If you believe him, and disbelieve the evidence, you will have to decide in his favor. That's all I have to say."

Within five minutes the jury returned. It had ruled in favor of Roosevelt's client.

—*Bits & Pieces*

TARDINESS

Better late than never, but never late is better!

TARDINESS

Better three hours too soon than one minute too late.

—Shakespeare

TAXES

A tax collector has what it takes to take what you've got.

—*Farmer's Almanac*

Our founding fathers objected to taxation without representation. They should see it today with representation.

It seems a little ridiculous now, but this country was originally founded as a protest against taxation.

Tax his cow,
  tax his goat,
Tax his pants,
  tax his coat,
Tax his crops,
  tax his work,
Tax his tie,
  tax his shirt,
Tax his chew,
  tax his smoke,
Teach him taxes
  are no joke.
Tax his tractor,
  tax his mule,
Teach him taxes
  are a rule.
Tax his oil,
  tax his gas,
Tax his notes,
  tax his cash,
Tax him good
  and let him know—
After taxes
  he has no dough.
If he hollers,
  tax him more.
Tax him till
  he's good and sore
Tax his coffin
  tax his grave,
Tax the sod
  in which he lays.
Put these words
  upon his tomb:

"Taxes drove me
  to my doom."
And after he's gone
  he can't relax,
They'll still be after
  inheritance tax.

TEACHING

Give me a fish and I eat for a day. Teach me to fish and I eat for life.

—Chinese proverb

There is nothing more inspiring than having a mind unfold before you. Let people teach who have a calling. It is never just a job.

—Abraham Kaplan

The object of teaching is to enable those taught to get along without a teacher.

In every man there is something of which I may learn of him, and in that he is my teacher.

—Ralph Waldo Emerson

A teacher affects eternity; he can never tell where his influence ends.

—Henry Brooks Adams

A teacher in a Denver Sunday school convention wrote on the convention evaluation sheet, "I've been learning far more than I can put into practice. Should I continue coming?"

The church is not a gallery for the exhibition of eminent Christians, but a school for the education of imperfect ones.

—Henry Ward Beecher

Those who can do, do.
Those who can't do, teach.
Those who can't teach, teach others to teach.

A witty student spoke of the dull and uninteresting teaching of his school teacher. "Why," he exclaimed, "it took Sir William Ramsay sixteen years to discover helium; the Curies thirty years to find radium; and yet in five minutes she produces tedium."

A Yale University president some years ago gave this advice to a former president of Ohio State University: "Always be kind to your A and B students. Someday one of them will return to your campus as a good professor. And also be kind to your C students. Someday one of them will return and build you a two-million-dollar science laboratory."

—Bits & Pieces

I am not willing that this discussion should close without mention of the value of a true teacher. Give me a log, with only a simple bench, Mark Hopkins (president of Williams College) on one end and I on the other, and you may have all the buildings, apparatus, and libraries without him.

—William Bartlett

Thomas Carlyle once received a letter from a young man with these words: "Mr. Carlyle, I wish to be a teacher. Will you tell me the secret of successful teaching?" Carlyle wrote back, "Be what you would have your pupils be. All other teaching is unblessed mockery."

TEAMWORK

Coming together is a beginning; keeping together is progress; working together is success.

—Henry Ford

A group becomes a team when each member is sure enough of himself and his contribution to praise the skills of the others.

—Norman G. Shidle

TEENAGERS

Teen Code

Don't let your parents down.
They brought you up.
Be humble enough to obey.
You might give orders some day.
Choose companions with care.
You become what they are.
Guard your thoughts.
What you think, you are.
Choose only a date who
would make a good mate.
Be master of your habits,
or they will master you.
Don't be a showoff when you drive.
Drive with safety and arrive.
Don't let the crowd pressure you.
Stand for something or you'll fall for anything.

Father to teenage son: "Mind if I use the car tonight? I'm taking your mother out and I'd like to impress her!"

Notice to teenagers: If you are tired of being hassled by unreasonable parents, now is the time for action! Leave home and pay your own way while you still know everything.

A Gallup survey asked 48,000 teenagers, "What influences teenagers most?" Their answers were these:

Friends	87%
Home	51%
School	45%
Music	41%
Television	32%
Religion	13%

My wife keeps saying that our teenager eats like a horse. I only wish he did. Oats we can afford.

—Bob Orben

TELEVISION

The average child between the ages of two and eleven views television 27.3 hours each week. By the time a person is sixteen, he or she has watched more than 20,000 hours of television, including 200,000 acts of violence, 50,000 of which are murders.

—Paul Simon

I find television very educating. Every time somebody turns on the set I go into the other room and read a book.

—Groucho Marx

Don't tell me that kids aren't influenced by television. I asked my son where he'd like to spend his next vacation, and he said, "Fantasy Island." I said, "And how would you get there?" He said, "The Love Boat."

I said, "And how would you pay for it?"
He said, "Father Knows Best."

—Bob Orben

There would be fewer problems with children if they had to chop wood to keep the TV set going.

TEMPTATION

A mother told her boy not to go swimming. However, when he came into the house his mother noticed that his hair and bathing trunks were wet.

"Johnnie," his mother scolded, "I told you not to go swimming."

"I couldn't help it, Mom," he defended himself. "The water looked so good."

"But why did you take your trunks with you?"

"Just in case I was tempted."

No one can be delivered from temptation unless he has firmly determined to do the best he can to keep out of it.

—John Ruskin

Temptation is to see the tempter standing outside the back door of your heart. Sin is to unlock that door so that he may have his desire. Victory is to open wide the front door of your heart, inviting the Savior to enter and give you strength to bar tight the back door.

—E. Schuyler English

You cannot play with the animal in you without becoming wholly animal, play with falsehood without forfeiting your right to truth, play with cruelty without losing your sensitivity of mind. He who wants to keep his garden tidy doesn't reserve a spot for weeds.

Former president James Garfield faced the opportunity to make a lot of money but by unscrupulous means. Someone said to him, "No one will ever know."

He responded, "But President Garfield will know, and I have to sleep with him."

Traveling is one of the Devil's special opportunities for tempting us. Seek always to know the mind of God before you do anything, but even more so before going on a trip. Don't needlessly expose yourself and give the Devil an opportunity to ensnare you.

—George Mueller

A small boy was being cared for by a nursemaid. When he saw a beautiful vase in a china cabinet, he wanted it. When he was refused, he began crying, screaming, and kicking. His mother, hearing the fuss, came into the room to find out what the problem was. Picking up her child, she said to him, "What do you want, darling?" He pointed to the vase, so she gave it to him. But that didn't satisfy him, and soon he began crying again. "Now what does my little darling want?" the mother asked. "I want—I want," said the boy between sobs, and then he blurted out, "I want anything I'm not supposed to have!"

—*Our Daily Bread*

To be tempted is not to sin. The strongest attacks are made on the strongest forts.

—D. L. Moody

An exasperated motorist parked his car in a no-parking zone in London and attached the following message to the windshield: "I have circled this block twenty times. I have an appointment to keep. Forgive us our trespasses."

When the owner of the car returned, he found this reply attached to his own note: "I've circled this block for twenty years. If I don't give you a ticket, I lose my job. Lead us not into temptation."

Years ago as a young Christian I battled the tobacco habit. Again and again I threw my pipe and cigarettes away, but always where I could find them again—"just in case!" I learned from that not to put our temptations where they can taunt us—just so we can prove how strong we are. As one has so aptly said, "To pray against temptations, and yet rush into occasions, is to thrust your fingers into the fire, and then pray they may not be burnt."

—John O. Jess

Mark Antony was known as the "silver-throated orator of Rome." He was a brilliant statesman, magnificent in battle, courageous, and strong. And he was handsome. As far as personal qualities are concerned, he could have become a world ruler. But he had the very vulnerable and fatal flaw of moral weakness, so much so that on one occasion his personal tutor shouted into his face, "Oh, Marcus, oh, colossal child! Able to conquer the world, but unable to resist a temptation."

—Chuck Swindoll

Unless we have within us that which is above us, we shall soon yield to that which is about us.

Fervency in prayer by the power of the Holy Spirit is a good preservative against thoughts rushing in. Flies never settle on a boiling pot.

—D. L. Moody

Temptation can never come in such form, as to make it safe or profitable to yield.

Opportunity knocks only once, but temptation bangs on the door for years.

In a poll taken by *Leadership* magazine five hundred pastors were asked, "What is your greatest temptation?"

The number-one temptation was illicit sex, and the second was the temptation to quit the ministry.

Temptation is the Devil whistling at the keyhole; sinning is opening at the door and letting him in.

—Billy Sunday

The enemy will wait forty years, if necessary, to set a trap for you.

—Joe Aldrich

I can resist everything except temptation.

—Oscar Wilde

Be cautious. Opportunity does the knocking for temptation too.

—M. Batt

Temptations are like bums. Treat one nice and he'll return with his friends.

Many of the world's most attractive temptations are like some television commercials: frequently deceptive and frightfully costly.

—William Arthur Ward

A shopkeeper in Brighton, England, had in the little room behind his shop a portrait of F. W. Robertson, an Anglican clergyman. Whenever in his business he was tempted to trickery or meanness, he would hurry into the back room and look at the picture. "And then, sir, I felt that it was impossible for me to do it." With those pure eyes upon him he could not sin.

A boy was much helped by Bishop Hamline, who said, "When in trouble, my boy, kneel down and ask God's help; but never climb over the fence into the Devil's ground, and then kneel down and ask for help. Pray from God's side of the fence."

No one is so good that he is immune from temptation. We will never be entirely free from it. . . . There is no order so holy, no place so secret where there will be no temptation.

—Thomas á Kempis

Temptation can bring a service to us. It may be a burden, but it can bring us humility and teach us good lessons. All of the saints experienced more than their share of trials and temptations, and they grew as a result.

—J. Oswald Sanders

Some ducks once found a good feeding place in the reeds that grew on the edge of a quiet stream in South Africa. A group of boys soon laid a plan to catch them. They began by placing pumpkins in the water and letting the river carry them down to where the ducks were swimming. At first the birds were nervous and flew away, but soon they decided there was no harm in permitting the pumpkins to float among them. Then came the second part of the plan. Each boy scooped out the inside of

TEMPTATION

one of the pumpkins and made two small holes to see through. Then placing the hollow globes over their heads, they quietly slipped into the river. Allowing only the orange decoys to show above the waterline, they moved slowly toward their victims. Suddenly they grasped the ducks' legs under the water and captured their unsuspecting prey.

In much the same way the Devil sends his deceptive "pumpkins" of temptations down the river of life. At first we think we can live with them and experience no harm; then, often when it's too late, we find ourselves in the clutches of some fatal sin or habit.

An overweight business associate of mine decided it was time to shed some excess pounds. He took his new diet seriously, even changing his driving route to avoid his favorite bakery. One morning, however, he arrived at work carrying a big gigantic coffee cake.

"This is a very special coffee cake," he explained. "I accidentally drove by the bakery this morning and there in the window were a host of warm goodies. I felt this was no accident so I prayed, 'Lord, if you want me to have one of those delicious coffee cakes, let me have a parking place directly in front of the bakery.'

"And sure enough," he continued, "the eighth time around the block, there it was!"
—Jim Grant

Temptations, unlike opportunities, will always give you second chances.
—O. A. Battista

I can resist everything except temptation.
—Oscar Wilde

TENSION

This is the age
Of the half-read page
And the quick hash
And the mad dash
The bright night
With the nerves tight
The plane hop
With the brief stop

The lamp tan
In a short span
The Big Shot
In a good spot
And the brain strain
And the heart pain
And the cat naps
Till the spring snaps
And the fun's done.
—Virginia Brasier,
Saturday Evening Post, May 28, 1949

TESTIMONY

A train plunged into a river over an opened drawbridge, and eighteen people died. The bridge engineer said he put up the red flag, warning the train in sufficient time to stop. The train engineer said the flag was white, and therefore he felt the bridge was there and it was safe to cross. The flag was examined, and it was red, but it had faded. Thus at a distance it appeared white.

Our faded testimony can misdirect others to cause them to sin.

TEXAS

Two kids were talking. One a Texan; one, not. The Texan said, "My ancestors came over on the Mayflower." The non-Texan said, "That's nothing. When my folks came over, the immigration laws were more strict."

A Texan was bragging to a New Yorker about how big everything is in Texas. The New Yorker, however, pointed out that he knew Texas had nothing like Niagara Falls. The man from Texas thought for a second and then replied, "That's true, but we have a plumber who can fix it."

A Texan said to a person from Connecticut, "You can stay on a train all day and all night and tomorrow, and still be in Texas."

"Oh, we have a train like that in Connecticut."

THANKFULNESS (Also see GRATITUDE)

I'm a Christian, but sometimes I forget to thank God for the things that haven't happened. Not this year. I'm grateful for the accidents I wasn't involved in, the illnesses that never developed, and the times I could have been mugged, but wasn't. I'm thankful my house didn't burn down when I left the iron on for five hours. I'm thankful that when we left the garage door up all night, nothing was taken. Sometimes I forget to thank God for electricity, but this Thanksgiving I'll make a point of it. I'm also thankful for indoor plumbing, anesthetics . . . Ever since my daughter nearly sheared her fingertip in the bathroom door, I'm thankful for every uneventful day. I'm thankful for my small son's paraphrase of Psalm 100: "Enter into His gates on Thanksgiving." I'm glad I have Someone to thank.

—Jessica Shaver

Thanks to God for my Redeemer,
Thanks for all Thou dost provide!
Thanks for times not but a mem'ry,
Thanks for Jesus by my side!
Thanks for pleasant, balmy springtime,
Thanks for dark and dreary fall!
Thanks for tears by now forgotten,
Thanks for peace within my soul!
Thanks for prayers that Thou hast answered,
Thanks for what Thou does deny!
Thanks for storms that I have weathered,
Thanks for all Thou dost supply!
Thanks for pain, and thanks for pleasure,
Thanks for comfort in despair!
Thanks for grace that none can measure,
Thanks for love beyond compare!
Thanks for roses by the wayside,
Thanks for thorns their stems contain!
Thanks for home and thanks for fireside,
Thanks for hope, that sweet refrain!
Thanks for joy and thanks for sorrow,
Thanks for heavenly peace with Thee!
Thanks for hope in the tomorrow,
Thanks thro' all eternity!

—Swedish hymn

A four-year-old boy said he was thankful for his glasses. "Why?" someone asked him. "Because it keeps the boys from hitting me—and the girls from kissing me."

One day on the streets of London Charles H. Spurgeon was robbed. When he arrived home and told his tale, he said, "Well, thank the Lord anyway."

His wife countered, "Thank the Lord that somebody stole your money?"

"No, my dear," answered her husband. Then he began to enumerate some reasons why he was thankful. "First, I'm thankful the robber just took my money, not my life. Secondly, I'm thankful I had left most of our money home and he didn't really rob me of much. Thirdly, I'm thankful to God that I was not the robber."

O precious Father, as we bow
Before Thy throne today—
We count the many blessings
Thou hast showered on our way.
The comfort of our humble homes,
Our health and happiness,
The strength provided for each day
To meet the strain and stress.
We thank Thee for thy precious Son
Who brought salvation free,
And for this mighty land of ours—
A land of liberty!
So Lord, help us give Thee thanks
For all that we hold dear—
Not only on Thanksgiving Day,
But each day of the year!

The words "Think and Thank" are inscribed in many of the Cromwellian churches in England.

As two men were walking through a field one day, they spotted an enraged bull. Instantly they darted toward the nearest fence. The storming bull followed in hot pursuit, and it was soon apparent they wouldn't make it. Terrified, the one shouted to the other, "Put up a prayer, John. We're in for it!" John answered, "'I can't. I've never made a public prayer in my life." "But you must now!" implored his companion. "The bull is catching up to us." "All right," panted John, "I'll say the only prayer I know, the one my father used to repeat at the table: 'O Lord, for what we are about to receive, make us truly thankful.'"

In old Anglo-Saxon, to be "thankful" meant to be "thinkful." Thinking of one's blessings should stir one to gratitude.

A man was walking home with his sack lunch. His shoelace came untied and he stooped over and put his sack down on the sidewalk. A dog came along and ran off with his lunch. The man replied, "Thank God, I still have my appetite."

I hate ingratitude more in man than lying, vainness, babbling, drunkenness, or any taint of voice, whose strong corruption inhabits our frail blood.

—Shakespeare

O Thou who hast given us so much, mercifully grant us one more thing—a grateful heart.

—George Herbert

Mark Tidd of Webster, New York, describes an experience from his college days. "An old man showed up at the back door of the house we were renting. Opening the door a few cautious inches, we saw his eyes were glassy and his furrowed face glistened with silver stubble. He clutched a wicker basket holding a few unappealing vegetables. He bid us a good morning and offered his produce for sale. We were uneasy enough that we made a quick purchase to alleviate both our pity and our fear.

"To our chagrin, he returned the next week, introducing himself as Mr. Roth, the man who lived in the shack down the road. As our fears subsided, we got close enough to realize it wasn't alcohol but cataracts that marbleized his eyes. On subsequent visits, he would shuffle in, wearing two mismatched right shoes, and pull out a harmonica. With glazed eyes set on future glory, he'd puff out old gospel tunes between conversations about vegetables and religion.

"On one visit, he exclaimed, 'The Lord is so good! I came out of my shack this morning and found a bag full of shoes and clothing on my porch.'

'That's wonderful, Mr. Roth!' we said. 'We're so happy for you.'

'You know what's even more wonderful?' he asked. 'Just yesterday I met some people who could use them.'"

—*Leadership* journal

There is a legend of a man who found the barn where Satan kept his seeds ready to be sown in the human heart, and on finding the seeds of discouragement more numerous than others, learned that those seeds could be made to grow almost anywhere. When Satan was questioned he reluctantly admitted that there was one place in which he could never get them to thrive. "And where is that?" asked the man. Satan replied sadly, "In the heart of a grateful man."

If anyone would tell you the shortest, surest way to happiness and all perfection, he must tell you to make it a rule to yourself to thank and praise God for everything that happens to you. For it is certain that whatever seeming calamity happens to you, if you thank and praise God for it, you turn it into a blessing.

—William Law

A missionary in China was living a defeated life. Everything seemed to be touched with sadness, and although he prayed for months for victory over depression and discouragement, his condition remained the same. He finally determined to leave his work and go to an interior station where he could pray and seek victory over his morbid state. When he reached the new place, he was entertained in the home of a fellow missionary. The first thing he saw on the wall was a motto which read, "Try thanksgiving!" The words gripped his heart and he thought within himself, "Have I been praying all this time and not praising?" He stopped and began to give thanks, and immediately his heart was uplifted.

A good king in Spain known as Alfonso XIX learned that the boys who served in his court were forgetting to pray before their meals. So he decided to teach them a lesson. He gave a banquet and invited them to attend. Midway through the dinner a ragged beggar came in, sat down, and began eating ravenously. When he was finished, he went out without saying a word. "That ungrateful wretch ought to be whipped," shouted the boys. "He ate the king's food and never showed gratitude." Quietly the king rose to his feet, and silence fell over the group. "Daily you have taken the rich blessings of life from the hand of your heavenly Father," said the king. "You've enjoyed His sunshine, breathed His air, eaten His food He has provided, and you have not bothered to say 'thank you' for any of them. You are more ungrateful than that beggar."

—*Our Daily Bread*

Tom Hale, longtime missionary doctor to Nepal, says in his book *Don't Let the Goats Eat the Loquat Trees:* "The concept of disinterested love is totally foreign to Nepalis because their primary motive for good works is to acquire merit that will benefit them in the next life. Most of our patients have no sense of gratitude for our services; instead, they expect that we be grateful to them for providing us an opportunity to gain merit for ourselves. This is why 'Thank you' is so rarely heard in Nepal; in fact, the Nepali language has no word for it. It's just as well. We wouldn't last long here if we had come to receive thanks."

Mission worker Sam Hadley said, "The night I was converted, I went out and looked up at stars and thanked God for their beauty. I had not seen them for ten years. A drunkard never looks up."

In a sermon at Immanuel Presbyterian Church in Los Angeles, Gary Wilburn said, "In 1636, amid the darkness of the Thirty Years War, a German pastor, Martin Rinkart, is said to have buried five thousand of his parishioners in one year, an average of fifteen a day. His parish was ravaged by war, death, and economic disaster. In the heart of that darkness, with the cries of fear outside his window, he sat down and wrote this table grace for his children:

"Now thank we all our God
With hearts and hands and voices
Who wonderous things hath done
In whom His world rejoices
Who, from our mother's arms
Hath led us on our way

With countless gifts of love
And still is ours today."

Scottish minister Alexander Whyte was known for his uplifting prayers in the pulpit. He always found something for which to be grateful. One Sunday morning the weather was so gloomy that one church member thought to himself, "Certainly the preacher won't think of anything for which to thank God on a wretched day like this." Much to his surprise, however, Whyte began by praying, 'We thank Thee, O God, that it is not always like this."

THANKSGIVING DAY

This proclamation was made by Governor Bradford in 1623, three years after the Pilgrims settled at Plymouth:

To all ye Pilgrims:

Inasmuch as the great Father has given us this year an abundant harvest of Indian corn, wheat, peas, beans, squashes, and garden vegetables, and has made the forests to abound with game and the sea with fish and clams, and inasmuch as he has protected us from the raids of the savages, has spared us from pestilence and disease, has granted us freedom to worship God according to the dictates of our own conscience; now I, your magistrate, do proclaim that all ye Pilgrims, with your wives and ye little ones, do gather at ye meeting house, on ye hill, between the hours of 9 and 12 in the day time, on Thursday, November ye 29th, of the year of our Lord one thousand six hundred and twenty-three, and the third year since ye Pilgrims landed on ye Plymouth Rock, there to listen to ye pastor and render thanksgiving to ye Almighty God for all His blessings.

President George Washington made this national Thanksgiving proclamation in 1789:

Whereas it is the duty of all nations to acknowledge the providence of almighty God, to obey His will, to be grateful for His benefits, and humbly to implore His protection, aid, and favors . . .

Now, therefore, I do recommend and assign Thursday, the 26th day of November next, to be devoted by the people of the United States to the service of that great and glorious Being, who is the benefient Author of all the good that was, and is, or that will be; that we may all then unite in rendering unto Him our sincere and humble thanks for His kind care and protection of the people of this country, and for all the great and various favors which He has been pleased to confer upon us.

How to Observe Thanksgiving

Count your blessings instead of crosses;
Count your gain instead of losses.
Count your joys instead of woes;
Count your friends instead of foes.
Count your smiles instead of tears;
Count your courage instead of fears.
Count your full years instead of lean;
Count your kind deeds instead of mean.
Count your health instead of wealth;
Count on God instead of yourself!

THINKING

To act is easy; to think is hard.
—Johann von Goethe

You are what you think—not what you think you are.

Think as a man who acts, and act as a man who thinks.

The most important things in life are the thoughts you choose to frame.
—Marcus Aurelius

Life is simply a matter of concentration: you are what you set out to be. You are a composite of the things you say, the books you read, the thoughts you think, the company you keep, and the things you desire to become.
—B. C. Forbes

Use your brains; it's the little things in life that count.

What we think about when we are free to think about what we will—that is what we are or soon will become.
—A. W. Tozer

The happiness of your life depends on the character of your thoughts.
—Marcus Aurelius

Thinking is the hardest work there is, which is probably the reason so few engage in it.
—Henry Ford

A person is what he thinks about all day.
—Ralph Waldo Emerson

You are not what you think you are. What you think, you are.

Only 5 percent of the people think.
Only 15 percent think they think.
The other 80 percent would rather die than think.
—George Bernard Shaw

TIME

Time is the wisest of all counselors.

Know the value of time; snatch, seize, and enjoy every minute of it.
—Philip Chesterfield

Time flies; but remember, you are the navigator.

You will never *find* time for anything. If you want time you must *make* it.
—Charles Burton

Everything comes to those who hustle while they wait.
—Thomas A. Edison

Most Americans spend six months of their lives sitting at traffic lights, contends a time management expert. Michael Fortino, president of Priority Management Pittsburgh, Inc., bases that and other estimates on his firm's year-long research.

The study indicates that the average person in the United States spends one year searching for misplaced objects (eyeglasses, keys, etc.), six years eating, and eight months opening junk mail. We spend five years waiting in line—at banks, stores, theaters, sports events, the post office, etc.

—*Have a Good Day!*

If you have a time and place for everything and do everything in its time and place, you will not only accomplish more but have more leisure than those who are always hurrying as if vainly attempting to overtake what has been lost.

—Tyron Edwards

If we live seventy-five years, this is how we would normally spend it:

Activity	Percentage of Your Time
23 years sleeping	31
19 years working	25
9 years watching TV or other amusements	12
7.5 years in dressing and personal care	10
6 years eating	8
6 years traveling	8
.5 year worshiping and praying	0.7

—Mark Porter

Time is God's gift to mortal man.
It is that fleeting little span
Between our birth and heaven's door,
Where we begin God's ever more
When time is o'er.
How then, should we our time employ?
In service or in passing joy?
Can we afford to throw away
And squander time in passing play—
O men of clay?

—*Neighbor*

Time is what we want the most but what we use the worst.

—William Penn

Counting time is not nearly so important as making time count.
I have only just a minute
Just sixty seconds in it;
Forced upon me—can't refuse it,

Didn't seek it, didn't choose it
I must suffer if I lose it,
Give account if I abuse it;
Just a tiny little minute
But eternity is in it.

What we love to do we find time to do.

—John Spaulding

Time flies even when you aren't having fun.

A small town operator received a call each day for the correct time. One day she asked the caller why he phoned each day for the time.

"I have to know the exact time," he explained, "so I can blow the town whistle right at noon."

"My goodness," the operator gasped. "I always set my clock by your whistle."

—Lowell Nusbaum

I defeated the Austrians because they never learned the value of five minutes.

—Napoleon

When as a child I laughed and wept,
Time crept.
When as a youth I dreamed and talked,
Time walked.
When I became a full-grown man,
Time ran.
And later as I older grew,
Time flew.
Soon I shall find while traveling on,
Time gone.

Oh, how precious is time; and how guilty it makes me feel when I think I have trifled away and misimproved it or neglected to fill up each part of it with duty to the utmost of my ability and capacity.

—David Brainerd, who died at age 29

I wasted time; now time doth waste me.

—William Shakespeare

The less one has to do, the less time one finds to do it in.

Somebody once thought it would be a

wonderful thing if every day of our lives each of us had $1,440 in the bank that we had to spend before the end of the day—none of it could be carried over to the following day.

Each of us does have 1,440 minutes every day. Could they be spent in a better way?

—*Bits & Pieces*

Take time to work—it is the price of success.

Take time to think—it is the source of power.

Take time to play—it is the secret of youth.

Take time to read—it is the foundation of knowledge.

Take time to worship—it is the highway of reverence.

Take time to help and enjoy friends—it is the source of happiness.

Take time to love—it is the one sacrament of life.

Take time to dream—it hitches the soul to the stars.

Take time to laugh—it is the music of the soul.

Take time to pray—it helps bring Christ near.

No time for God,
What fools we are to clutter up
And leave without heart's gate
The Lord of life, and life itself—
Our God.
No time for God?
As soon to say, no time
To eat or sleep or love or die.
Take time for God
Or you will dwarf your soul.
And when the angel death
Comes knocking at your door,
A poor misshapen thing you'll be
To step into eternity.
No time for God?
Some day you'll lay aside
This mortal self and make your way
To worlds unknown
And when you meet Him face to face
Will He—should He—
Have time for you?

—Trott

An emissary from a learned society came to invite Jean Agassiz, Harvard professor of zoology, to address its members. Agassiz refused on the grounds that lectures of this sort took up too much time that should be devoted to research and writing. The man persisted, saying that they were prepared to pay handsomely for the talk. "That's no inducement to me," Agassiz replied. "I can't afford to waste my time making money."

—*The Little, Brown Anecdote Book*

John Erskine, the well-known author, professor, and lecturer, once wrote that he learned the most valuable lesson of his life when he was fourteen. His piano teacher asked him how much he practiced and how long at a stretch. The boy replied that he practiced for an hour or more at a time.

"Don't do that," warned the teacher. "When you grow up, time won't come in long stretches. Practice in minutes, whenever you can find them—five or ten minutes before school, after lunch, between chores. Spread the practice throughout the day, and music will become part of your life."

Erskine stated that the observance of this advice enabled him to live a comparatively complete life as a creative writer, outside his regular duties as an instructor. He wrote most of *Helen of Troy,* his most famous work, on streetcars while commuting between his home and the university.

At an annual Trooping of the Colors ceremony in England, Queen Elizabeth rode horseback from Buckingham Palace down the Mall to take the salute of the second battalion of Scots Guards. She reached the parade ground just as the Horse Guards' clock boomed out the hour of 11 A.M. However, a BBC commentator informed millions of people that the Queen was two minutes and ten seconds late. The truth was—the clock had been prevented from striking the hour at the correct time in order to perpetuate the myth that the Queen was always on time. Reporters traced down the clock expert who had climbed into the clock tower and held back a three-foot-wide governing wheel till the exact moment when the queen's horse stepped onto the parade ground. He confessed he had done the same thing at every Trooping of the Colors during her reign. Most years she was just a few seconds late, but one year he had courageously made time stand still for four minutes.

Time management consultant Antonio Herrera asked the participants in a seminar, "If we had to buy time, would there be any difference in how we would spend it? Would the days of our lives be used more wisely?" He asked, "What if you had to pay in advance one hundred dollars an hour for the time allotted to you? Would you waste it?" The answer should be obvious.

TIREDNESS

Our fatigue is often caused not by work, but by worry, frustration, and resentment.
—Dale Carnegie

"How far down do you want to sit?" asked the usher.

"All the way," answered the little old lady. "I'm very tired."

The population of this country is 220 million, 84 million over sixty years of age, which leaves 136 million to do the work. People under twenty years of age total 95 million, which leave 41 million to do the work.

There are 22 million who are employed by the government, which leaves 19 million to do the work. Four million are in the Armed Forces, which leaves 15 million to do the work. Deduct 14,800,000, the number in state and city offices, leaving 200,000 to do the work. There are 188,000 in hospitals, insane asylums, etc., so that leaves 12,000 to do the work.

Now it may interest you to know that there are 11,998 people in jail, so that leaves just 2 people to carry the load. That's you and me—and brother I'm getting tired of doing everything myself.

TITANIC

When Mrs. Albert Calwell came aboard at Southampton, she had asked a deck hand,

"Is this ship really nonsinkable?"

"Lady," he answered, "God Himself could not sink this ship."

On the evening of April 15, 1912, during its first trip from England to New York City, what was called an unsinkable seagoing vessel struck an iceberg and began to go down. That ship was the *Titanic*. The tragedy happened about 1,600 miles northeast of New York City in the heart of the Atlantic Ocean. The iceberg tore a 300-foot gash in the ship's hull. Unfortunately, there were lifeboats for less than half of the 2,200 passengers. Two-and-one-half hours after the impact, nearly 1,500 people went to a watery grave. Most of the survivors were women and children.

That horrible night there were men who scrambled and sought to save themselves, caring nothing of others. But there were also those who willingly stepped aside to let others be saved, knowing they would die. Fathers kissed their wives and children good-bye. Friends embraced for the last time and separated, knowing they would not see each other again on this earth. Many willingly paid the ultimate sacrifice for their friends—death.

An insurance company pictured the Titanic sailing straight for the iceberg which many years ago sank that great luxury liner. The advertisement read, "They called her the 'Millionaire's Special.' Four city blocks long, eleven stories high, powered by triple propellers, protected by the latest, most ingenious devices, luxurious and beautiful beyond words, she caught the fancy of the world.

"On April 10, 1912, she slipped out of Southampton on her maiden voyage to New York. Less than five days later, she went down in 12,000 feet of icy water, 300 feet of her hull ripped open by a massive iceberg. Actually the Titanic was more than a ship. She was a symbol of man's power. Majestic! Colossal! Unsinkable! But when the 'unsinkable' sank, something went down with it. No one would ever again feel the same confidence in man's strength."

What a perfect illustration this is of all

of human society. Proud, modern civilization—heedless of the claims of Christ—is rushing headlong toward destruction.

TITHING

A man came to visit his pastor and said, "Pastor, my tithe is becoming a problem to me. When I was only a fifty-dollar-a-week ribbon clerk, it wasn't much trouble to drop five dollars in the offering plate; but now that I've gotten a large income I can't spare the large amount of tithe that would be my portion now. I wonder if you could help me with this problem?"

The pastor replied, "Bill, I appreciate your candidness in coming to me. Let's pray about it." And he prayed along this line, "Lord, Bill's tithe is a problem to him because he is making so much money. Lord, give him business reverses, reduce his income so his tithe won't be a problem."

The man interrupted and said, "Hold on, Pastor, I don't think my tithe will be a problem anymore!"

—Morris Chalfant

TODDLER'S CREED

If I want it, it's mine.
If I give it to you and change my mind later, it's mine.
If I can take it away from you, it's mine.
If I had it a little while ago, it's mine.
If it's mine, it will never belong to anyone else, no matter what.
If we are building something together, all the pieces are mine.
If it looks just like mine, it is mine.

—*Creators Syndicate*

TOLERANCE

Tolerance is the virtue of people who don't believe in anything anymore.

—G. K. Chesterton

TOMORROW

It is tomorrow that fills men with dread. God is there already. All the tomorrows of our life have to pass Him before they can get to us.

—F. B. Meyer

TONGUE TWISTER

The most difficult tongue-twister is said to be, "The sixth sick sheik's sixth sheep is sick."

—*Farmer's Almanac*

TRADITION

Tradition is the living faith of those now dead. Traditionalism is the dead faith of those now living.

TRAFFIC

Despite the fact that computer speeds are measured in nanoseconds and picoseconds—one billionth and one trillionth of a second, respectively—the smallest interval of time known to man is that which occurs between the traffic light turning green and the driver behind you blowing his horn.

—Johnny Carson

TRAGEDY

The wise learn from tragedy; the foolish merely repeat it.

—Michael Novak

TRAVELING

"I understand you're not going to Rome this summer," said one woman to another.

"That was last year," said the other. "This year we're not going to London."

—*Bits & Pieces*

The following are things you hate to hear when you are traveling:

"I thought you were listening when he was giving us directions."

"It isn't on the map."

"Still glad we took the scenic back roads?"

"Folks, in my forty-two years of piloting, I've never seen anything like this."

"According to your policy, a 'masked holdup' is an Act of God."

"I've never seen a rash like that in my life."

"You'll have to share your cabin."

"Didn't you know this is our monsoon season?"

"What reservation?"

"We believe we found part of your suitcase."

"Here are some candles and matches."

"This is not your passport."

"In your money, that converts to—hold onto your hat . . ."

"No, the man you gave your bags to does not work here."

"Hey, Joe, you'll never guess where these folks think they are."

"Of course I can hear the boiler room over the phone. Now how may I help you, sir?"

—David Brenner

TRILLION

If you stack thousand-dollar bills, one on another, when you have a stack which is three inches high, you have a million dollars.

If you continue to stack them up to 250 feet high, you have a billion dollars.

If you continue to stack them up to a height of forty-seven miles, you have a trillion dollars.

The amount to pay off our national debt would be a stack of thousand-dollar bills almost 188 miles high.

—Henry C. Jones

If you began to count dollar bills at the rate of one a second, it would take you "only" 11.57 *days* to count to one million dollars. At the same rate, it would take you 31.69 *years* to count to one billion dollars. And at the same dollar a second rate, it would take you 31,688.09 *years* to count to one trillion dollars. The current national debt is more than three and one-half times that much.

TROUBLES (Also see DIFFICULTIES)

It isn't what happens; it's how you deal with it that's important.

—*Teen Esteem*

A life freed from all obstacles and difficulties would reduce all possibilities and powers to zero.

—Zig Ziglar

The second law of spiritual thermodynamics: the greater the heat, the greater the expansion.

Colonel Bill Kehler's son Tim was a strong Christian and had a bright future. He was attending the Air Force Academy in Colorado when he was killed in bombing practice.

"Why Tim?" asked a young man, himself disabled in a car accident. Kehler replied, "Why *not* Tim?"

J. Hudson Taylor was talking to a young missionary about to start work in China. "Look at this," Taylor said as he brought his fist down hard on the table, knocking over the tea cups and spilling their contents. As he gazed at the startled young man, Taylor said, "When you begin your work, you will be buffeted in numerous ways. The trials will be like blows. Remember, those blows will only bring out what is in you."

Lord, sometimes You have to:
. . . break, so You can rebuild
. . . wound, so You can heal
. . . let me walk in darkness,
    so that I see Your light
. . . let me be confused,
    so I seek Your truth
. . . let me feel emptiness,
    so You can fill me
. . . let me feel lonely, so I
    can see what a friend You are
. . . let me learn the hard things,
    so I can be a gentle teacher
. . . let me be void of feelings,
    so I must walk by faith
. . . take away my future plans,
    to teach me to live one day at a time
. . . show me the futility of life,
    so I will see that everything is loss
    compared to the surpassing value
    of knowing Christ Jesus my Lord.

—Sue Knepp

People are a lot like tea bags; they don't know their own strength until they get into hot water.

—*Farmer's Almanac*

Life is hard—but God is good.

Life is unpredictable—but God is sovereign.

Life is unfair—but God is just.
Life is short—but God is eternal.
—Mary Farrar

If you pray for rain, be prepared to deal with some mud.

Things turn out best for the people who make the best of the way things turn out.
—Art Linkletter

Everything is needful that He sends.
Nothing is needful that He withholds.
—John Newton

I do not know what may befall
    Of sunshine or of rain;
I do not know what may be mine,
    Of pleasure and of pain;
But this I know—my Savior knows,
    And whatsoe'er it be,
Still I can trust His love to give
    What will be best for me.

I'll say this for adversity—people seem to be able to stand it, and that's more than I can say for prosperity.
—Kim Hubbard

Even a blind hen finds a grain occasionally.
—Finnish proverb

If you should find your house on fire, go up and warm yourself by it.
—Spanish proverb

Life is mostly faith and bubble,
Two things stand like stone,
Kindness in another's trouble,
Courage in your own.
—Adam Lindsay Gordon

Thomas Edison's warehouse was burning. After the fire, he gathered his workers and said, "We are going to rebuild. Because you can always build opportunity out of tragedy."

Great men rise above adversity and attain new heights of achievement by turning tribulations into triumphs, failures into fortunes, setbacks into successes, obstacles into opportunities, and burdens into blessings. They refuse to be hampered by handicaps, dismayed by discouragements, overcome by opponents, defeated by disappointments, or destroyed by disasters.
—William Arthur Ward

God hath not promised
    Skies always blue,
Flower-strewn pathways
    All our lives through.
God hath not promised
    Sun without rain,
Joy without sorrow,
    Peace without pain.
God hath not promised
    We shall not know
Toil and temptation,
    Trouble and woe.
He hath not told us
    We shall not bear
Many a burden,
    Many a care.
But God hath promised
    Strength for the day,
Rest for the laborer,
    Light for the way,
Grace for the trials,
    Help from above,
Unfailing sympathy,
    Undying love.

Smooth seas do not make skillful sailors.
—African proverb

The harder the conflict, the more glorious the triumph. When we obtain too cheap, we esteem too lightly; it is dearness only that gives everything its value. I love the man who can smile in trouble, who can gather strength from distress and grow brave by reflection.
—Thomas Paine

Thomas Edison's manufacturing facilities in West Orange, New Jersey, were heavily damaged by fire one night in December 1914. Edison lost almost $1 million worth of equipment and the records of much of his work.

The next morning, walking about the charred embers of his hopes and dreams, the sixty-seven-year-old inventor said, "There is a value in disaster. All our mistakes are burned up. Now we can start anew."

—Alan Loy McGinnis

The measure of a man is the way he bears up under misfortune.

—Plutarch

Two young boys were raised in the home of an alcoholic father. As young men, they each went their own way. Years later, a psychologist who was analyzing what drunkenness does to children in the home searched out these two men. One had turned out to be like his father, a hopeless alcoholic. The other had turned out to be a teetotaler. The counselor asked the first man, "Why did you become an alcoholic?" And the second, "Why did you become a teetotaler?" And they both gave the same identical answer in these words, "What else could you expect when you had a father like mine?"

A woman was driving home one evening when she noticed that a huge truck was right behind her. Thinking it was too close, she stepped on the gas. But the truck stayed right behind her. By this time she had panicked, so she drove up to a gas station and leaped out of the car, screaming. The truck driver pulled in right behind her, jumped out of his truck, ran to her car, and opened the back door. There, crouched behind her seat, was a hunted rapist. The truck driver, from his high vantage point, had seen him. He was pursuing the woman, not to harm her, but to keep her from being hurt or killed.

A little girl about four years old was traveling one day on a train. In childish glee she romped up and down the aisle, completely free from care and worry. Suddenly the train entered a long, dark tunnel. The youngster was terrified until she heard her mother call to her. Like a bird that flies to its nest, she found comfort and reassurance in her mother's loving arms. So too, we may go through dismal tunnels of trial that strike fear into our hearts, but the Lord knows all about our anxieties.

In a storm at sea, apparent disaster was ahead. Robert Louis Stevenson's son was on board. He went to the pilot's cabin and started to ask if something could be done about the bad situation. Just then the pilot turned and smiled. Stevenson's son went back to the men and said, "I have good news." "What do you mean?" they asked. "I've just seen the pilot's face, and that's enough."

In *A View from the Zoo,* Gary Richmond tells about the birth of a giraffe: "The first thing to emerge are the baby giraffe's front hooves and head. A few minutes later the plucky newborn calf is hurled forth, falls ten feet, and lands on its back. Within seconds, he rolls to an upright position with his legs tucked under his body. From this position he considers the world for the first time and shakes off the last vestiges of the birthing fluid from his eyes and ears.

"The mother giraffe lowers her head long enough to take a quick look. Then she positions herself directly over her calf. She waits for about a minute, and then she does the most unreasonable thing. She swings her long, pendulous leg outward and kicks her baby, so that it is sent sprawling head over heels.

"When it doesn't get up, the violent process is repeated over and over again. The struggle to rise is momentous. As the baby calf grows tired, the mother kicks it again to stimulate its efforts. . . . Finally, the calf stands for the first time on its wobbly legs. Then the mother giraffe does the most remarkable thing. She kicks it off its feet again. Why? She wants it to remember how it got up. In the world, baby giraffes must be able to get up as quickly as possible in order to stay with the herd, where there is safety. Lions, hyenas, leopards, and wild hunting dogs all enjoy young giraffes, and they'd get it, too, if the mother didn't teach her calf to get up quickly and get with it. . . .

"I've thought about the birth of the giraffe many times. I can see its parallel in my own life. There have been many times when it seemed that I had just stood up after a trial, only to be knocked down again by the next. It was God helping me to remember how it was that I got up, urging me always to walk with him, in his shadow, under his care."

Georgi Vins is another person who made the best out of life's worst. A pastor of a small Russian Baptist church, he was exiled to the United States because of his Christian faith. But Georgi Vins had first spent eight years sleeping on a grimy concrete floor next to an open toilet and subsisting on barley extract, tea, and soup in a Russian prison.

While locked deep in the bowels of a Siberian compound, he wrote a diary of his stay titled *Testament from Prison.* The book contains not one description of prison cruelty, inhumane conditions, or palpable misery that pervades most writings smuggled out of Russian labor camps. Instead, Vins describes the beauty of the Siberian winters, his joy at receiving letters from his wife, his love for Russia, and intimate conversations with God. Except for the title, the book could have been written by a free man living in a penthouse overlooking the Black Sea.

—Paul W. Powell

You know, I used to try to take each day as it came. That is, I would live one day at a time. My philosophy, however, has changed! Now I'm down to a half a day at a time.

—Snoopy

First: He brought me here;
   It is by His will that I am in this strait place
   In that will I rest.
Next: He will keep me here in His love,
   and give me
   grace in this trial to behave as His child.
Then: He will make the trial a blessing,
   teaching me
   the lessons He intends me to learn and working
   in me the grace He means to bestow.

Last: In his good time He can bring me out again—how
   and when, He knows.
Say: I am here—
   1) By His appointment.
   2) In His keeping.
   3) Under His training.
   4) For His time.

—Paul W. Powell

An eastern monarch once charged his wise men to invent an aphorism which would be true and appropriate at all times and in all situations. Their answer was, "And this, too, shall pass away."

Trouble is only opportunity in work clothes.

—Henry J. Kaiser

As long as you keep your face toward the light, the shadow will fall behind you.

Man's extremity is God's opportunity.

It's good to know that, when we think we are at the end of our rope, God is at the other end.

Are You Able?
Able to suffer without complaining,
To be misunderstood without explaining?
Able to endure without breaking,
To be forsaken without forsaking?
Able to give without receiving,
Able to ask without commanding,
To love despite misunderstanding?
Able to turn to the Lord for guarding;
Able to wait for His own rewarding?
A clay pot in the sun will always be a clay
   pot. It has to go through the white heat
   of the furnace to become porcelain.

—Mildred White Stouven

Everyone is either coming out of a storm, in a storm, or headed for a storm.

—H. Beecher Hicks Jr.

If it is true in anything, it is especially true of divine things, that what costs little is worth little.

—J. Hudson Taylor

It doesn't matter, really, how great the pressure is; it only matters where the pressure lies. See that it never comes between you and the Lord—then, the more it presses you, it presses you closer to Him.

Difficulties provide a platform on which the Lord can display His power.
—J. Hudson Taylor

Nothing lasts forever, not even your troubles.
—Arnold H. Gleason

God does not comfort us that we may be comforted but that we may be comforters.
—Alexander Nowell

Storms make oaks take deeper root.
—George Herbert

You gain strength, courage, and confidence by every experience in which you really stop to look fear in the face. You are able to say to yourself, "I lived through this horror. I can take the next thing that comes along."
—Eleanor Roosevelt

Life is full of disappointments. Nothing ever comes off except buttons.

The north wind made the Vikings.
—Norwegian proverb

The Christian life is a series of troughs and peaks.
—Peter Marshall

There is no education like adversity.
—Benjamin Disraeli

God gives us burdens, and He also gives us shoulders.
—Yiddish proverb

Many men owe the grandeur of their lives to their tremendous difficulties.
—Charles H. Spurgeon

He who has a "why" to live for can bear almost any "how."

Things turn out best for the people who make the best of the way things turn out.

Crises—like sudden rainstorms—can help or hinder, enrich or engulf, depending on whether or not we have properly prepared for them.
—William Arthur Ward

Christians should be like the teakettle: sing even though we are up to our necks in hot water.

Our heavenly Father never takes anything from His children unless He means to give them something better.
—George Mueller

Affliction comes to the believer not to make him sad, but sober; not to make him sorry, but wise. Even as the plow enriches the field so that the seed is multiplied a thousandfold, so affliction should magnify our joy and increase our spiritual harvest.
—Henry Ward Beecher

Arthur Gossip, a Scottish preacher from the early 1900s, lost his wife suddenly. Upon his return to the pulpit following her death, he preached "When Life Tumbles In, What Then?" In that message, Gossip announced that he did not understand this life of ours. But still less could he understand how people facing loss could abandon the Christian faith. "Abandon it for what!" he exclaimed. Speaking from the darkest storm of life, he concluded, "You people in the sunshine may believe the faith, but we in the shadow *must* believe it. We have nothing else."
—Daniel T. Hans

A little boy was leading his youngest sister up a steep mountain path. The climbing was difficult, for there were many rocks in the way. Finally, the little girl, exasperated by the hard climb, said to her brother, "This isn't a path at all. It's rocky and bumpy." "Sure," her brother replied, "but the bumps are what you climb on."
—*Our Daily Bread*

He Maketh No Mistakes

My Father's way may twist and turn,
    My heart may throb and ache.
But in my soul I'm glad I know,
    He maketh no mistake.
My cherished plans may go astray,
    My hopes may fade away,
But still I'll trust my Lord to lead,
    For he doth know the way.
Tho' night be dark and it may seem
    That day will never break,
I'll pin my faith, my all in Him,
    He maketh no mistake.
There's so much I cannot see,
    My eyesight far too dim,
But come what may, I'll simply trust
    And leave it all to Him.
For bye and bye the mist will lift,
    And plain it all He'll make.
Through all the way, tho' dark to me,
    He maketh not one mistake!

A young marine was huddled in a foxhole with bullets whizzing overhead and shells bursting all around. He had received no mail for weeks, so he was delighted to be handed a letter even in such imminent danger. Quickly ripping open the envelope, he burst out laughing as he read this message from a business establishment in his hometown: "Your account is seven days overdue. If the balance of $25 is not paid in seven days, you will be in serious trouble!"

The Scriptures often exhort us to be filled with godly virtues—which means what? How do we know if we are "full of goodness" (Rom. 15:14), for example?

Think a moment about a water-saturated sponge. If we push down with our finger even slightly, water runs out onto the table. We immediately know what fills the interior pockets of the sponge.

The same is true of ourselves. We can tell what fills us on the inside by what comes out under pressure.

—Robert Schmidgall

A Christian man was walking with John Wesley one day and rehearsing his many troubles, saying that he did not know what to do. As they approached a stone fence over which a cow was looking, Wesley asked, "Why is that cow looking over the wall? I'll tell you—because he can't look through it! That is what you must do with your troubles—look over them!"

The noblest souls are the most tempted. The Devil is a sportsman and likes big game. He makes the deadliest assaults on the richest natures, the finest minds, the noblest spirits.

—John L. Lawrence

We are safer in a storm with God than anywhere else without Him.

—Jeremy Taylor

Difficulty is sand thrown on the tracks to keep you from skidding.

The only difference between stumbling blocks and stepping stones is the way you use them.

Men think God is destroying them because he is tuning them. The violinist screws up the key till the tense cord sounds the concert pitch; but it is not to break it, but to use it tunefully, that he stretches the string upon the musical rock.

—Henry Ward Beecher

Every loss is meant to be filled up by His presence; every sorrow is meant to make His fellowship more to us.

—Andrew Murray

On his sick bed Martin Luther said between groans, "These pains and troubles here are like the type which printers set; as they look now, we have to read them backwards and they seem to have no meaning or sense to them. But up yonder, when the Lord prints us off in the life to come, we shall find they make brave reading."

A little boy made a boat and eagerly ran to the water to sail it. After a few minutes of pleasure, he became frantic when it suddenly drifted beyond his reach. His distressed cry for help was answered by an older youth. Picking up some pebbles, his new-found friend began tossing them directly at his treasured craft—or so it appeared. As the youngster watched, all hope of retrieving his boat faded from his heart. But then he noticed something. Instead of hitting the tiny vessel, each stone fell beyond it creating a wave that moved it toward the shore. By carefully aiming each throw, the youth was able to get the floating toy back within reach. What joy filled the little fellow as he grasped his treasure.

It is the roughness of the grindstone that sharpens the axe. It is the storm that hardens the fiber of the oak. It is the workday and not the holiday that makes muscle.

Do not ask God to give you a light burden; ask Him to give you a strong shoulder to carry a heavy burden.

—Bob Jones

It has been said that the Christian life is certainly not a bed of roses, but in one sense of the word it is because, when one lies on a bed of roses, there is not only the fragrance of the roses which arises but also there are the thorns.

Track star Wilma Rudolph won three gold medals in the 1960 Olympics, but to get there she had to overcome enormous hurdles. Stricken with scarlet fever at the age of four, she lost the use of her left leg and had to learn to walk again when she was seven.

Years ago a dear saint of God penned these interesting lines: "In the days before passenger trains were equipped with lights, I was traveling by rail to a distant city. Our route was through several tunnels; consequently, at times the cars would be enveloped in deep darkness. Beside me sat a sympathetic Englishman. We were enjoying a pleasant conversation when we started into a long underground mountain pass, and it became pitch black in our coach. My companion, a Christian, had traveled that way many times before. Reassuringly he said, 'Cheer up, my friend,

we're not in a sack—there's a 'ole at the other end!' I never forgot his words. They cheered me later in many of the dark passages of life."

Jesus, the great Physician
Took my good health away
He gave me pain and suffering
That someday I could say:
Thank you, Lord Jesus,
For sending these trials my way;
Now I know your grace is sufficient
To cover me day by day!
Of course, I ask the questions:
Why? Why me? Why now?
Strange that it would take these things
To work perfection out.
But if through trials
I'm perfect in the end—
Send me your trials,
My Savior, and my Friend.
Lord, I know you're only
Making me a man,
And for that reason
I need not understand.
I just trust you
And the things you've spoken of;
For you have proven to me
That you're a God of love.
Lord, I know this suffering
Was not sent for my faults;
But that through this weakness
Power would result!
Oh, bless you, Jesus,
For giving me this light!
I know you have a blessing
O'er the hill, out of my sight.
I know you have a blessing
O'er the hill, out of my sight.

—Les Zartman

My diet consists mostly of hasty pudding, boiled corn, and bread baked in ashes, and sometimes a little meat and butter. My lodging is a little heap of straw, laid upon some boards. . . . My work is exceedingly hard and difficult. I travel on foot a mile and a half in the worst of roads almost daily, and back again; for I live so far from my Indians. . . . These and many other uncomfortable circumstances attend me; and yet my spiritual conflicts and distresses so far exceed all these, that I scarce think of them, but feel as if I were entertained in the most sumptuous manner.

—David Brainerd

A little girl was walking in a garden when she noticed a particularly beautiful flower. The child admired its beauty and enjoyed its fragrance. "How lovely!" she exclaimed. As she gazed on it, her eyes followed the stem down to the soil in which it grew. "What a shame!" she cried. "This flower is too pretty to be planted in such dirt!" So she pulled up the plant by its roots and ran to the water faucet to wash away the clinging soil. It wasn't long until the flower wilted and the plant began to die. The gardener saw what she had done and scolded her. "You have destroyed my finest plant," he said. "But I didn't like it in that dirt," whimpered the child. The gardener replied, "I chose that spot and collected and mixed the soil because I knew that only there it would come to maturity."

The Sequoia trees of California tower as much as 300 feet above the ground. Strangely, these giants have unusually shallow root systems that reach out in all directions to capture the greatest amount of surface moisture. Seldom will you see a redwood standing alone, because high winds would quickly uproot it. That's why they grow in clusters. Their intertwining roots provide support for one another against the storms.

One day at a time, with its failures and fears,
With its hurts and mistakes, with its weakness and tears
With its portion of pain and its burden of care;
One day at a time we must meet and must bear.
One day at a time—but the day is so long,
And the heart is not brave and the soul is not strong.
O Thou pitiful Christ, be Thou near all the way;
Give courage and patience and strength for the day.

Swift cometh His answer, so clear and so sweet;
"Yea, I will be with thee, thy troubles to meet;
I will not forget thee, nor fail thee, nor grieve;
I will not forsake thee; I never will leave."
Nor yesterday's load we are called on to bear,
Nor the morrow's uncertain and shadowy care;
Why should we look forward or back with dismay?
Our needs, as our mercies, are but for the day.

—Annie Johnson Flint

Christian, when thy way seems darkest,
    When thine eyes with tears are dim,
Straight to God thy Father hast'ning,
    Tell thy troubles all to Him.
Not to human ear confiding
    Thy sad tale of grief and care,
But before thy Father kneeling,
    Pour out all thy sorrows there.
Sympathy of friends may cheer thee,
    When the fierce, wild storms have burst,
But God only can console thee
    When it breaks upon thee first.
Go with words or tears of silence,
    Only lay thee at His feet;
Thou shalt prove how great His pity,
    And His tenderness how sweet.
Far too well thy Savior loves thee
    To allow thy life to be
One long, calm, unbroken summer,
    One unruffled, stormless sea.
He would have thee fondly nestling
    Closer to His loving breast;
He would have that world seem brighter,
    Where alone is perfect rest.
Through His wise and loving purpose
    Clearly yet thou may'st not see,
Still believe with faith unshaken,
    All will work for good to thee.
Therefore, when thy way is gloomy
    And thine eyes with tears are dim,
Straight to God thy Father hast'ning,
    Tell thy sorrows all to Him.

The difference in the musical tone of a violin depends mostly on the quality of the wood it is made of, even more than how it is made. The best violin maker in the world cannot make a good instrument from poor material.

A famous violinist always made his own instruments because he wanted to choose a special kind of wood. He shunned the forest but went instead to the mountains. There at the top of a cliff exposed to all the storms he obtained his trees. He knew the severe weather conditions toughened the wood and produced a quality of grain and resiliency that could be developed in no other way. In fact, he used only the wood from the side of the tree facing the wind! Thus, too, by the storms of adversity, does our loving Father prepare in us the music of heaven.

A customer asked a shopkeeper, "What makes this set of china so much more expensive than the other?" "It has had more done to it," was the reply. "You see, it has been put through the kiln twice. Look, the flowers are on a yellow band. In the cheaper one, they are on a white background. The costly china had to be put through the fire once to get the basic yellow and the second time to get the design on it."

If we are going through a deep trial that seems to be lasting far too long or has been repeated too often, the Heavenly Father may be developing some aspect of our character.

One by one He took them from me,
　　All the things I valued most,
Until I was empty handed;
　　Every glittering toy was lost.
And I walked earth's highways, grieving,
　　In my rags and poverty,
Till I heard His voice inviting,
　　"Lift your empty hands to Me!"
So I held my hands toward heaven,
　　And He filled them with a store
Of His own transcendent riches,
　　Till they could contain no more.
And at last I comprehended
　　With my stupid mind and dull
That God could not pour His riches
　　Into hands already full!
　　　　　　—Martha Snell Nicholson

A gifted young man in London began preparing for the ministry. Having surrendered his life to Christ, he wanted to be fully used by the Lord. Before his ordination, he was required to preach a trial sermon before a select group of clergymen. The tenseness of the situation made him nervous, especially when he saw his beautiful fiancée in the audience. In his anxiety he lost his train of thought and failed to be approved. His rejection by the examining board was a stunning disappointment, and his grief was increased when the young lady broke their engagement because he had done so poorly. He fought a terrible battle with depression. After pouring out his complaint before God, he felt the burden lifted as he realized that the Lord was working out a blessed plan for his life. He was deeply impressed with Romans 8:28 and experienced peace in his soul.

Taking the test again, he was ordained to the ministry. Later the profound preaching of G. Campbell Morgan moved the masses by its biblical depth and heartwarming appeal. He authored a good number of Bible commentaries and other books, and at his death he left a legacy of sermons that still stir the hearts of people whenever they are read. The crisis he survived by God's grace made him a spiritual giant.

A cowboy was once asked, "What important thing have you learned from your experience on the range?"

"The Herefords taught me one of life's most important lessons," he replied. "We used to breed cattle for a living, but the winter storms would take an awful toll. Again and again after a severe storm we would find most of our stock piled up against the fences, dead. They would turn their backs on the icy blasts and slowly drift downward twenty miles until the fences stopped them. There they just piled up and died.

"But the Herefords were different. They would head straight into the wind and slowly walk the other way until they came to the upper boundary fence, where they stood still facing the storm. We always found them alive and well. They saved themselves by facing the storm!"

Take a piece of wax, a piece of meat, some sand, some clay, and some shavings, put them on the fire and see how they react. Each of them is being acted on by the same agent, yet . . . the wax melts, the meat fries, the sand dries up, the clay hardens, the shavings blaze.

Just so . . . under identical influence of circumstances and environment one person is made better and stronger, another weaker, while another withers away.

—*The Vineland Voice*

The old sea captain was quizzing a young naval student. "What steps would you take if a sudden storm came up on the starboard?"

"I'd throw out an anchor, sir."

"What would you do if another storm sprang up aft?"

"I'd throw out another anchor, sir."

"But what if a third storm sprang up forward?"

"I'd throw out another anchor, captain."

"Just a minute, son," said the captain. "Where in the world are you getting all these anchors?"

"From the same place you're getting all your storms."

Dan Crawford had the difficult task of following in the steps of David Livingstone, the missionary who gave his life in ministering the Word of God in Africa. Crawford didn't have the imposing personality of his famous predecessor, so at first he had trouble winning the loyalty of the tribal people. Even his church back home wasn't sure he could carry on the work. With God's help, however, he did a magnificent job. When he died, a well-worn copy of the New Testament was found in his pocket. A poem, evidently his own, handwritten on the inside cover, revealed the secret of his success:

I cannot do it alone!
The waves dash fast and high;
The fog comes chilling around,
And the light goes out in the sky.

But I know that we two shall win in the end—
Jesus and I.
Coward, and wayward, and weak,
I change with the changing sky,
Today so strong and brave,
Tomorrow too weak to fly;
But—He never gives in! So we two shall win—
Jesus and I!

The hymn writer George Neumark was afflicted with blindness in his later years. This infirmity was just one more trial in a life already filled with sorrow and distress. While still a young man, he had been reduced to deep poverty and was down to his last penny. Yet his trust in God did not fail, for he found great strength in the promise of Psalm 55:22, "Cast thy burden upon the Lord, and He shall sustain thee." He prayed most earnestly for the Savior's direction and consolation. The answer came in the form of an unexpected appointment as tutor for the family of a rich judge. Relieved and delighted, he was prompted to compose one of his best-known hymns, "If Thou But Suffer God to Guide Thee." He said he had penned it to thank the Lord for His sustaining grace. Later Johann Sebastian Bach saw such beauty in the hymn that he used it as the basis for a cantata, and Mendelssohn included it in his oratorio "Saint Paul."

There is a legend about a grandfather clock that stood in a corner for three generations, faithfully ticking off the minutes, hours, and days—its means of operation was a heavy weight suspended by a double chain. One of its new owners, believing that an old clock should not bear such a load, released the weight. Immediately the ticking stopped. According to the legend, the clock asked, "Why did you do that?" The owner replied, "I wanted to lighten your burden." "Please put my weight back," replied the clock. "That is what keeps me going."

—John D. Jess

There is a beautiful figure in one of Wordsworth's poems of a bird that is swept from Norway by a storm. It battles against the storm with desperate effort, eager to wing back to Norway. But all is vain, so at last he yields, thinking the gale will carry it to its death—but the gale carries it to sunny England with its green meadows and forest glades.

In the winter the mountains are covered with snow and its seems as though they will remain white forever. However, as spring comes, the sun shines on the snow-capped peaks and melts off the snow. The snow then flows off into streams, thus providing water power and supply for man. It has in this way become a blessing to others.

A medieval man of God went on a journey. All he owned were a scroll, a candle, and a cock. The scroll he read and loved, the candle provided him light, the cock crowed to awaken him in the morning.

One evening he arrived in a small town. He asked hospitality from home after home but was rudely refused both food and lodging.

"God in His mercy and justice does all things well," said the believing man. He found protection from the wind in the clump of high bushes, tethered his cock nearby and, with praise in his heart, began to read his scroll.

A sudden gust of wind blew out his light, and the good man found himself without the means to relight his candle.

"God in His mercy and justice does all things well," said the trusting man. And he prepared to lie down to sleep. Suddenly a fox snapped out of the darkness, and the life of his cock was gone.

"God in His mercy and justice does all things well," said the godly man, yet with sorrow. And he lay down and slept.

In the morning, the light awakened him. He gathered his book to his heart and walked back to the unfriendly village.

To his horror, he saw that the robbers had come in the night. The village had been plundered and burned. The villagers had been murdered.

The man of God remembered. Had he been granted hospitality, he too would have died; and had his light shone or his cock crowed, the robbers would have been led to him.

"God in His mercy and justice does all things well," said the godly man. And in the light of day, he read his scroll and praised God.

Glancing out of my picture window, I was impressed by an interesting sight. A robin was busily flitting about in the rain, stopping only momentarily to sing his lovely, trilling song. Unlike the other birds, this fine-feathered creature wasn't seeking shelter from the downpour, but was delighting himself in the shower. He knew that much valuable food was being made available by the rain, for the worms he sought would be near the surface and more plentiful in the dampened sod. As I watched, I thought of the torrents of trial and testing that come into our lives as Christians. We too should never try to hide from them, but rather rejoice in the spiritual benefits God wants us to derive from these experiences.

—Russell Spray

Years ago the captain of an ocean liner took his young daughter along on his run from Liverpool, England, to New York City. One night when all the passengers were asleep, the huge vessel ran into some violent weather. The wind came sweeping over the water, and mighty swells rolled across the bow of the ship. All movable objects were being tossed about, and everyone soon sensed the imminent danger. Many sprang from their berths in alarm and began to dress. The captain's little girl, eight years old, was awakened and cried out, "What's the matter?" When told about the storm, she asked, "Is my father steering the ship?" Being assured that he was, she put her head on her pillow, and in spite of the howling gale and crashing waves she was soon fast asleep.

A man was walking down a city street unaware that the broken end of a high voltage wire was lying across the pavement just

397

ahead of him. A workman saw the man approaching the wire. Unable to warn him by voice because of the surrounding noise, the workman picked up a stone and threw it at him. It struck him on the chest and this caused the man to stop and look up. Thus he saw the danger he was in just a moment before he was about to step on the wire. With tears streaming down his face he thanked the man who threw the stone for saving his life. How often the Lord has to use some such measure to spare us from the unseen dangers that surround us.

"You smell delightfully fragrant," said the Gravel Walk to the bed of Chamomile flowers under the window.

"We have been trodden on," replied the Chamomiles.

"Treading on me produces no sweetness," said the Gravel Walk.

"Our natures are different," answered the Chamomiles. "Gravel walks become only the harder by being trodden upon; but the affect on our own selves is that, if pressed and bruised when the dew is upon us, we give forth the sweet smell you now delight in."

"Very delightful," replied the Gravel Walk.

One day a naturalist, out in his garden, observed a most unusually large and beautiful butterfly, fluttering as though in great distress; it seemed to be caught as though it could not release itself. The naturalist, thinking to release the precious thing, took hold of the wings and set it free. It flew but a few feet and fell to the ground dead.

He picked up the poor thing, took it into his laboratory, and put it under a magnifying glass to discover the cause of its death. There he found the life-blood flowing from the tiny arteries of its wings. Nature had fastened it to its chrysalis and was allowing it to flutter and flutter so that its wings might grow strong. It was the muscle-developing process that nature was giving it so that it might have an unusual range among the flowers and gardens. If it had only fluttered long enough, the butterfly would have come forth ready for the wide range; but release ended the beautiful dream.

Martin Wells Knapp was once undergoing a severe trial, and in his secret devotions he asked God to remove his trial. As he waited before the Lord, the vision of a rough piece of marble rose before him with a sculptor grinding and chiseling. Watching the dust and chips fill the air, he noticed a beautiful image begin to appear in the marble. The Lord spoke to him and said, "Son, you are that block of marble. I have an image in my mind, and I desire to produce in your character, and I will do so if you will stand the grinding; but I will stop now if you so desire." Knapp broke down and said, "Lord, continue the chiseling and grinding."

The cupola of that world-famous structure, Saint Paul's Cathedral in London, was painted by Sir James Thornhill, who was compelled to do his work while standing on a swinging scaffold far above the pavement. One day when he had finished a detail on which he had spend hours of painstaking effort, he stopped to inspect his artistry. Slowly he began moving backward in order to get a better view. A man working with him suddenly became aware that one more backward step would result in a fatal fall. To startle Thornhill with a shout might also make him topple from the scaffold. Quick as a flash he took a brush and made a sweeping stroke across the exquisite work Thornhill was admiring. Greatly disturbed, the artist rushed forward with a cry of anger and dismay. After his companion explained his strange action, however, the great artist burst into expressions of gratitude.

Passengers were seated on a plane at the Washington Airport, ready to take off for New York, when an enormous storm suddenly came up. Great clouds appeared and the sky became dark and sinister. In a matter of minutes a high wind came over the Potomac River, and great sheets of rain beat against the windows of the plane. The plane, which was at the end of the runway, actually rocked from the force of the wind. The soft, drawling, Texas-like voice of the pilot came on. "Ladies and Gentlemen," he said, "there's a storm center directly above the airport and we are getting the brunt of it. We cannot take off in this storm. We are going to wait it out. Our report," he continued, "is that this storm will pass in about forty-five minutes. So you people who have business engagements in New York which you are fretting about may just as well sit back and relax, because we're not going to New York for a while yet. Meanwhile," he went on, "I'm going to bring the plane into the wind so you will be more comfortable. Don't worry about anything." And then he added this bit of philosophy: "All storms ultimately pass."

Phyllis Walk of Colorado Springs, Colorado, was traveling a back road in Colorado when she came on a large herd of sheep. She stopped and turned off the engine while waiting for them to pass. But instead of passing they encircled the car as if it were part of the geography.

She rolled down the window and yelled, "Hey, you guys, give me a break and let me through!"

Sounding the horn didn't work. The sheep just bleated back. She grew more and more frustrated. She had meant the back road to be a short cut. "Listen," she said, "I could starve here!"

"Baaahh!"

At last their shepherd came along. "Your mistake was stopping," he said, smiling at her. "Sheep are like troubles. Show them you mean to go forward, and they'll move aside."

Driving away, she thought a little bit about the philosopher-shepherd. He had a point. All her yelling and beeping and fretting hadn't impressed the sheep. Only her moving forward showed them she meant business.

—Charles R. Diffee

I've found that it is not good to talk about your troubles. Eighty percent of the people who hear them don't care and the other twenty percent are glad you're having trouble.

—Tommy Lasorda

A man in a large eastern city wrote to the local newspaper to report that the country is in far worse shape than most people suspect. His evidence: "Everytime I call Dial-a-Prayer, I get a busy signal."

—Bits & Pieces

An elder was known for his counseling ministry, but not so much for his example. They had a little quip about him. They said, "In solving problems, he is quite a whiz—when the trouble is yours instead of his."

TRUST

A New York City businessman decided to avoid a twenty dollar service charge by replacing the bulb in a seven-foot fluorescent light himself. He managed to smuggle a new tube into his office, but then faced the problem of how to dispose of the old tube. He recalled that a construction site near the subway stop in Brooklyn had a large waste receptacle. He decided to deposit the tube there.

After work that evening the man got on the subway holding the white tube vertically with one end resting on the floor. As the train became crowded, other passengers took hold of the tube, assuming it was a hand rail.

By the time the man reached his stop, he had devised another plan. He simply removed his hand, leaving the other passengers to continue holding the tube, and got off the subway.

If the train came to a sudden stop, those passengers would have learned that their "anchor" was not secure.

I believe in the sun even when it's not shining,
I believe in love even when I'm alone.
I believe in God even when He's silent.

Stonewall Jackson and his sister were crossing a treacherous torrent just below the mighty Niagara Falls. The current so rocked and tossed the boat that the woman became terrified. Jackson took her firmly by the arm and turning to one of the two boatmen, said, "How often have you crossed here before?" "Continually, sir, for the past twelve years." "Did you ever meet with an accident?" "Never, sir." "Never capsized and lost a life?" "Nothing of the kind, sir." Turning to his sister, Jackson reassuringly replied, "You heard what the boatman said. Unless you think you can row better than he does, just sit still and trust him as I do."

—*Our Daily Bread*

An elderly woman in West Virginia had never ridden in an airplane. Her grandson finally persuaded her to take an air flight. With fear and trepidation, she agreed.

After a short flight, the plane landed. As she deplaned, the grandson asked cheerily, "How did you like the flight, Grandma?" "Well," she unenthusiastically replied, "I went up in the plane, but I never let my weight down during the whole flight."

That fearful, distrustful grandma is like many of God's children. In all His greatness, we too often neglect to rest completely in His all powerful hands.

If sorrow makes us shed tears, faith in the promise of God makes us dry them.

—Augustine

Sure, it takes a lot of courage
    To put things in God's hands—
To give ourselves completely,
    Our lives, our hopes, our plans;
To follow where He leads us
    And make His will our own—
But all it takes is foolishness
    To go the way alone!

When you have nothing left but God, then you become aware that God is enough.

—Rayden

There is no conceivable situation in which it is not safe to trust God.

—J. Oswald Sanders

Trust in God—but tie your camel tight.

—Persian proverb

The men who trust God are the men who can be trusted.

If I really, really trust Him,
    Shall I ever fret?
If I really do expect Him,
    Can I e'er forget?
If by faith I really see Him,
    Shall I doubt His aid?
If I really, really love Him,
    Can I be afraid?

A man reportedly said, "I'm not the least bit afraid of thieves breaking into my house. I've got the place rigged so if I hear a burglar, I touch a button that sends an electric current to explode the dynamite in my cellar. That would blow the burglar sky high!"

—Leslie, B. Flynn

In what are you trusting? Trust in yourself and you are doomed to disappointment.

Trust in your friends and they will die and leave you.

Trust in money and you may have it taken from you.

Trust in reputation and some slanderous tongue may blast it.

But trust in God and you will never be confounded in time or eternity.

Trust the past to the mercy of God, the present to His love, and the future to His providence.

—Augustine

Never be afraid to trust an unknown future to a known God.

—Corrie Ten Boom

A man was traveling along in a car when he saw a poor fellow standing at the side of the road, carrying a large and heavy sack. He offered him a lift, and the man got in the car but kept the sack on his shoulder. The driver said, "Why don't you put that sack down?" The man replied, "Well, sir, I'm so grateful you are carrying me I don't think it is fair to ask you to carry my sack as well!"

—Alan Redpath

A television program preceding the Winter Olympics featured blind skiers being trained for slalom skiing, impossible as that sounds. Paired with sighted skiers, the blind skiers were taught on the flats how to make right and left turns. When that was mastered, they were taken to the slalom slope, where their sighted partners skied beside them shouting, "Left!" and "Right!" As they obeyed the commands, they were able to negotiate the course and cross the finish line, depending solely on the sighted skiers' word. It was either complete trust or catastrophe.

—Robert W. Sutton

A father, seeing three small children playing atop a high fence, feared that they would fall; and so he cried, "Come, jump into my arms!" Two of them promptly did so. The other hesitated. Why did the third child react more slowly? The father explained, "The first two obeyed immediately because they were my own children. They knew me and therefore trusted me." So, too, those who truly know and love the Lord never resist His good leading.

So I go on not knowing,
I would not if I might;
I'd rather walk with God in the dark
Than to walk alone in the light;
I had rather walk with Him by faith
Than to walk alone by sight.

When nothing whereon to lean remains,
  When strongholds crumble to dust;
When nothing is sure but that God still
  reigns,
  That is just the time to trust.
'Tis better to walk by faith than sight,
  In this path of yours and mine;
And the pitch-black night, when there's no
  light,
  Is the time for our faith to shine.

A fellow wrote to a mail-order house: "Please send me the engine you show on page 878, and if it's any good, I'll send you a check."

A week later he received the reply: "Please send the check. If it's any good, we'll send you the engine."

His Way Is Perfect

'Tis far, far better to let Him choose
  The way that we should take,
If only we leave our life with Him,
  He will provide without mistake.
We, in our blindness, would never choose
  A pathway dark and rough,
And so would never find in Him,
  "The God who is enough."
In disappointment, trouble, and pain,
  We turn to God without dismay
And prove how wonderful, good and wise,
  Is God's own perfect way.

Years ago the English steamer *Stella* was wrecked on a rocky coast. Twelve women were put in a lifeboat, but the boisterous sea immediately carried it away. Having no oars, they were at the mercy of the winds and the waves, and they spent a fearful night being tossed about by the raging tempest. They probably would have lost hope if it had not been for the spiritual stamina of one of the women, Margaret Williams, who was well known for her work in sacred oratorios. Calmly she prayed aloud for divine protection. Then, urging her companions to put their trust in the Lord, she encouraged them by singing hymns of comfort. Throughout the dark hours her voice rang out across the water. Early the next morning a small craft came searching for survivors. The man at the helm would have missed the women in the fog if he had not heard Miss Williams singing the selection from *Elijah*, "Oh, rest in the Lord, wait patiently for Him!" Steering in the direction of her strong voice, he soon spotted the drifting lifeboat. While many others were lost that night, those trusting few were rescued.

To do Thy will is more than praise,
  As words are less than deeds;
And simple trust can find Thy ways
  We miss with chart of creeds.
Our Friend, our Brother, and our Lord,
  What may thy service be?
Nor name, nor form, nor ritual word,
  But simply following Thee
  —J. G. Whittier

401

Oliver Cromwell's secretary was dispatched to the continent on some important business. He stayed one night at a seaport town and tossed on his bed, unable to sleep.

According to an old custom, a servant slept in his room and on this occasion slept soundly enough. The secretary at length wakened the man, who asked how it was that his master could not rest.

"I am so afraid something will go wrong with the embassage," was the reply.

"Master," said the valet, "may I ask a question or two?"

"To be sure."

"Did God rule the world before we were born?"

"Most assuredly he did."

"And will He rule it again after we are dead?"

"Certainly He will."

"Then, master, why not let Him rule the present too?"

The secretary's faith was stirred, peace was the result, and in a few minutes both he and his servant were sound asleep.

A distressed believer once said to a Christian counselor, "It's hard for me to trust God when everything looks dark." The man replied, "Well, brother, if you can't trust someone when he's out of your sight, he isn't worth much. So, too, if you can't trust God in the dark, you really don't consider Him trustworthy." Then pointing to a baby chick that had just taken refuge beneath a large hen, he added, "See that little chick hiding under the wing of its mother? As long as it's there, it can't see anything, but it's still protected and secure." Opening his Bible to Psalm 91, the counselor continued, "Notice it doesn't say 'under His wings shalt thou *see*,' but 'under His wings shalt thou *trust*.'"

A drugstore in Galveston, Texas, was in existence for twenty years. The owners decided to have an anniversary celebration. They put all their filled prescriptions—all one million of them—all over the wall. Over them they put a sign with the words, "Trusted—One Million Times."

God has been and can be trusted many more times than that.

TRUTH

Unless we love the truth we cannot know it.

—Blaise Pascal

Truth is stranger than fiction, but only because fiction is limited to possibilities.

—Mark Twain

Our minds possess by nature an insatiable desire to know the truth.

—Cicero

It is not hard to find the truth. What is hard is not to run away from it once you have found it.

—Etienne Gilson

No man should be angry at what is true.

—Plato

We can easily forgive a child who is afraid of the dark; the real tragedy of life is when men are afraid of the light.

—Plato

The fewer the voices on the side of truth, the more distinct and strong must be your own.

—Channing

A preacher made the mistake on Saturday afternoon of showing two boys the Bible lesson he was planing too read Sunday morning. When he turned his back, the boys glued the pages together. Next morning, the preacher read at the bottom of one page, "And Noah when he was 120 years old, took unto himself a wife who was," and then, turning the page, "300 cubits long, 50 cubits wide, and 30 cubits high, built of gopher wood and pitched within and without with pitch." Puzzled, he paused. Then he read it again. And again he paused, nonplused. Looking up, he said, "Beloved, I have read the Bible through many, many times, but this is the first time I have ever read this. But I believe the Bible to be true from cover to cover. So I accept it as proof that we are fearfully and wonderfully made!"

TWO NATURES

Suppose a farmer put duck eggs under a chicken. Then after they were hatched, the ducks followed the hen. But then a thunderstorm came and the ducks delayed behind in a puddle of water. But the hen did not like water and so she could not understand why the ducks stayed behind in the puddle.

Why did the ducks like water and the hen not? Because ducks have duck nature and hens have hen nature.

In a particular nation two competing factions were fighting for control of the country. Eventually, with the help of an outside army, one faction won the war and assumed control of the nation's government. But the losing side did not stop fighting. They simply changed their tactics to guerrilla warfare and continued to fight. In fact, they were so successful that the country supplying the outside help could not withdraw its troops.

So it is with the Christian. Satan has been defeated and the reign of sin overthrown. But our sinful natures resort to a sort of guerrilla warfare to lead us into sin. This results in the struggle between the Spirit and our sinful natures.

U

UNBELIEF

Two fishermen were driving along a highway when they came to a crossroad with a "Closed" sign blocking the main road. They noticed fresh tire tracks leading around the sign, so they decided to follow the tracks and disregard the sign. They had gone some three miles when the road ended at a broken bridge. The only thing to do was to turn around, and on passing the road block again they observed this inscription

on the reverse side of the sign: "It was really closed, wasn't it."

During the Franco-German War of 1870–71, two unexploded shells were found near a house. The homeowner cleaned them up and put them on display near his fireplace. A few weeks later he showed these interesting objects to a visitor. His friend, an expert in munitions, suddenly had a horrible thought. "What if they're still loaded?" After quickly examining the shells, he exclaimed, "Get them away from the fire immediately! They're as deadly as the day they were made!" Without realizing it, the homeowner had been living in grave peril.

UNITED STATES

James Russell Lowell was once asked by Francois Guizot, "How long do you think the American Republic will endure?" Lowell had no trouble with the answer: "So long as the ideas of its founding fathers continue to be dominant."

We have been recipients of the choicest bounties of heaven . . . but we have forgotten God . . . intoxicated with unbroken success, we have become too self-sufficient to feel the necessity of redeeming and preserving grace, too proud to pray to the God who made us.

—Abraham Lincoln

Our greatest danger is not from invasion by foreign armies. Our dangers are that we may commit suicide from within by compliance with evil. Or by public tolerance of scandalous behavior. . . . These evils have defeated nations many times in human history.

—J. Edgar Hoover

In his book *The Decline and Fall of the Roman Empire* Edward Gibbon discussed five reasons for the fall of that empire:

1. The rapid increase of divorce; the undermining of the dignity and sanctity of the home, which is the basis of human society.
2. Higher and higher taxes and the

spending of public monies for free bread and circuses for the people.

3. The mad craze for pleasure, sports becoming every year more exciting and more brutal.
4. The building of gigantic armaments, when the real enemy was within— the decadence of the people.
5. The decay of religion—faith fading into mere formalism; losing touch with life and becoming impotent to guide the people.

Many of these same things are evident in the United States today.

UNITY

You may tie the tails of a cat and a dog together by a rope and have union, but you surely don't have unity!

The reason mountain climbers are roped together is to keep the sane ones from going home.

Has it ever occurred to you that one hundred pianos all tuned to the same fork are automatically tuned to each other? They are of one accord by being tuned, not to each other, but to another standard to which each one must individually bow. So one hundred worshipers (meeting) together, each one looking away to Christ, are in heart nearer to each other than they could possibly be were they to become "unity" conscious and turn their eyes away from God to strive for closer fellowship.

—A. W. Tozer

If two agree on everything, one of them is not needed.

V

VACATIONS

Nothing arrives more slowly and passes more quickly than a vacation.

A family vacation is one where you arrive with five bags, four kids, and seven I-thought-you-packed-its.

—Ivern Ball

"Don't you ever take a vacation?"

"I can't get away."

"Why not? Can't the company do without you?"

"Yes, they can. But I don't want them to find out."

Every now and then go away, have a little relaxation. For when you come back to your work, your judgment will be surer, since to remain constantly at work, you lose power of judgment. Go some distance away because then the work appears smaller, and more of it can be taken in at a glance, and a lack of harmony or proportion is more readily seen.

—Leonardo da Vinci

Spend your vacation in your own backyard, and your friends will know the kind of person you are: sensitive, introspective, home-loving, and broke.

A Scottish vacation is staying home and letting your mind wander.

VALENTINE'S DAY

According to legend, Valentine's Day takes it name from a young Christian who once lived in ancient Rome. Like so many of the early Christians, Valentine had been imprisoned because of his faith. Often and longingly he thought of his loved ones and wanted to assure them of his well-being and his love.

Beyond his cell window and beyond reach, grew a cluster of violets. He picked some heart-shaped leaves and pierced them to spell the words, "Remember your Valentine," then set them off by a friendly dove. On the next day and the next, he sent more messages that simply said, "I love you." In this way the valentine had its beginning. On Valentine's Day, people of all ages remember those they love by sending valentine cards.

VALUES

Try not to become a person of success but rather a person of value.
—Albert Einstein

Some people know the price of everything, but the value of nothing.
—Warren W. Wiersbe

Not everything that counts can be counted. Not everything that can be counted counts.
—Charles Garfield

VARIETY

Variety may be the spice of life, but monotony brings home the groceries.

VENGEANCE

Two motorcyclists in a truckstop restaurant tried to irritate a driver who was sitting alone. When one of them dumped the trucker's food on the floor, the man quietly got up and left. The tough fellows remarked to the waitress, "He sure isn't much of a man."

She paused as she looked out the window. "He isn't much of a driver either," she answered. "He just ran his rig over two motorcycles on his way out."

When a pony kicked a little boy in Kansas, his father decided to take quick revenge. He gave the animal a swift kick in return.

The result was disappointing. The man suffered two broken toes. Then he found that his son had not been injured after all. Neither was the pony.

Revenge is the poor delight of little minds.
—Juvenal

To return evil for good is devilish.
To return good for good is human.
To return good for evil is godlike.
—Spanish proverb

People usually get at odds with each other whenever they try to get even.

VICTORY

When the Greeks defeated the Persians at the Battle of Marathon in 490 B.C., Pheidippides, a swift runner, raced twenty-five miles to Athens to give the news of victory. When he arrived exhausted, he gasped, "Rejoice, we conquer," and fell to the ground, dead.

I would rather fail in a cause that I know some day will triumph than to triumph in a cause that I know some day will fail.

Martin Luther was once asked how he overcame the Devil. He replied, "Well, when he comes knocking on the door of my heart, and asked, 'Who lives here?' the Lord Jesus goes to the door and says, 'Martin Luther used to live here but he has moved out. Now I live here!' The Devil, seeing the nailprints in My hands and My pierced side, takes flight immediately."

In every defeat are the seeds of victory, and in every victory are the seeds of defeat.
—Walter Mondale

The British preacher Guy King stood on a railroad platform waiting for his train. Before it arrived, another train pulled into the station. On board was a football team returning home from a game in a distant city. As the players got off, a boy who had been eagerly waiting rushed up to one of them and asked the score of the game. As soon as he heard, he dashed off to join his friends, calling out, "We've won! We've won!" Mr. King, who had been watching the lad, observes, "Now really, how much had he done to gain the victory? What did he have to do with the struggle on the football field?" The boy had identified so closely with the team that he could rejoice in the successful outcome of the game.

In the War of 1861 a timid supporter said to Abraham Lincoln that he hoped the Lord would be on the side of the North. Lincoln replied, "About that I am not at all concerned; but only that we should be on the side of the Lord."

When Felix of Nola was hotly pursued by murderers, he took refuge in a cave, and instantly over the rift the spiders wove their webs. Seeing this, the murderers passed by. Then said the saint, "Where God is not, a wall is but a spider's web; where God is, a spider's web is as a wall."

The story is told of a pilot who, when flying one day, heard a gnawing noise in the fuselage of his plane. He looked and saw it was a rat. He knew that a rodent was not made to withstand high altitudes, so he soared high in the sky as high as he could go. After being up at that altitude for a number of minutes, he landed. He looked and saw that the rat was dead.

The only way a Christian can defeat his enemy, Satan, is by rising spiritually in his Christian life.

An Indian said a black dog lived in his heart, but when Christ became his Saviour a big white dog came to live in his heart, and two dogs were then fighting all the time.

After the meeting someone approached him and inquired, "Which dog wins, the white one or the black one?"

The Indian replied, "The one I feed the most."

The Devil found defeat in victory at the cross; the Christian finds victory in defeat at the cross.

When British field marshal Bernard Montgomery defeated the German field marshal Erwin Rommel in the desert of North Africa in World War II, many thought this would be the end of the war. But Winston Churchill said, "This is not the beginning of the end, but the end of the beginning."

There are no victories at bargain prices.
—Dwight D. Eisenhower

Victory at all cost, victory in spite of all terror, victory however long and hard the road may be; for without victory there is no survival.
—Winston Churchill,
May 13, 1940

VIRTUE

If you could understand virtue, observe the conduct of virtuous men.
—Aristotle

Wisdom is knowing what to do; skill is knowing how to do it; and virtue is doing it.
—David Starr Jordan

VISION

A vision without a task is but a dream; a task without a vision is drudgery; a vision and a task is the hope of the world.
—A church in Sussex, England,
around 1730

No institution can survive without a vision to pull it forward.

The bravest are surely those who have the clearest vision of what is before them, glory and danger alike, and yet, notwithstanding go out to meet it.
—Thucydides

Soon after the completion of Disney World someone said, "Isn't it too bad that Walt Disney didn't live to see this?" Mike Vance, creative director of Disney Studios, replied, "He did see it. That's why it's here."

Vision is seeing the invisible.
—Jonathan Swift

Don't be pushed by your problems; be led by your dreams.

If I have seen further than you . . . it is by standing on the shoulders of giants.
—Sir Isaac Newton

Helen Keller was asked, "What is the greatest calamity?" She answered, "To have eyes and not see."

He who knows only one's generation is a child.

The man who has vision and no task is a dreamer. The man who has a task and no vision is a drudge. The man who has task and a vision is a giant.

VOTING

In 1654 one vote gave Oliver Cromwell control of England.

In 1649 one vote caused Charles I of England to be executed.

In 1776 one vote gave America the English language instead of the German language.

In 1839 one vote elected Marcus Morton governor of the state of Massachusetts.

In 1845 one vote brought Texas into the Union.

In 1868 one vote saved President Andrew Johnson from impeachment.

In 1875 one vote changed France from a monarchy to a republic.

In 1876 one vote gave Rutherford B. Hayes the presidency of the United States.

In 1923 one vote gave Adolf Hitler leadership of the Nazi Party.

In 1941 one vote preserved the selective service system just twelve weeks before the Japanese attack on Pearl harbor.

In 1960 Richard Nixon lost the presidential election to John F. Kennedy by less than one vote per precinct in the United States.

W

WARS

When General Dobey, British commander of Malta during World War I, was stationed in the Holy Land in 1916, an aide approached him and said, "Sir, this is a funny war we're fighting. The Muslims won't fight on Fridays, the Jews won't fight on Saturdays, and the Christians won't fight on Sundays."

With Solomonlike wisdom, Dobey replied, "Well, if you can find four other world religions that refuse to fight on Monday, Tuesday, Wednesday, or Thursday, because of their holy days, you have solved the problem of world peace."

From 2,678 wars in the twelfth century, the total increased to 13,835 in the first quarter of this century. Wilbur M. Smith estimated that "up to the close of the nineteenth-century . . . 14 billion people have been killed in the wars of the human race."

From 1496 B.C. to A.D. 1861, the world knew 3,130 years of war and 227 years of peace. In the last four hundred years European nations have signed more than eight thousand peace treaties. In this century 37.5 million died in World War I, and 45.4 million died in World War II. In the Vietnam conflict 57,605 U.S. lives were lost and 304,000 U.S. military personnel were injured.

WARNINGS

A man who lived on Long Island was able one day to satisfy a lifelong ambition by purchasing for himself a very fine barometer. When the instrument arrived at his home, he was extremely disappointed to find that the indicating needle seemed to be stuck, pointing to the sector marked "Hurricane." After shaking the barometer very vigorously several times, its new owner sat down and wrote a scorching letter to the store from which he had purchased the instrument. The following morning on the way to his office in New York, he mailed the letter. That evening he returned to Long Island to find not only the barometer missing, but his house also. The barometer's needle had been right— there was a hurricane!

—E. Schuyler English

WEAKNESSES

The first step toward growing up is learning to like ourselves. More than half the hospital beds are filled with people who haven't been able to come to terms with themselves. Granted, it isn't always easy to do, because it involves taking a good look at our weaknesses as well as our strengths. Few of us like to do that, but there is nothing wrong with having deficiencies. It's what we do about them that counts. Better expend our energies improving, rather than deploring. To work at overcoming weaknesses and reinforcing strengths is the way we grow.

—Doris Dickelman

Winston Churchill once referred to his opponents in the British Parliament as those who were "decided only to be undecided, resolved to be irresolute, adamant for drift, solid for fluidity, all-powerful to be impotent."

—Edward L. Hayes

WEALTH (Also see MATERIALISM)

Perhaps the most famous gold strike in American history occurred in January 1848 when a man named John Marshall found gold at Sutter's Mill in northern California. The find set off a gold rush that reached a frenzied pitch and even attracted prospectors from Europe—but it ruined Marshall and John Sutter, the man who owned the land where gold lay for the taking. Sutter's land was overrun by gold seekers, his cattle were stolen, and he was driven into bankruptcy. Marshall died penniless. Although both men had access to untold riches, neither one possessed them.

—*Today in the Word*

In 1917 the British liner *Laurentic* was sunk in one hundred fifty feet of water by a German submarine. This ship carried the largest treasure that any ship up to that time had ever carried. It was loaded with 3,211 gold bars worth twenty-five million dollars.

Because of the shallow water and the amount of treasure, the British Navy kept drivers going down into the hulk for many years. Diving in those days was not what it is now, and often operations had to stop because of a storm. Seldom could a diver stay down longer than one hour at a time. But the project was very successful, for the divers were able to recover all but 154 gold bars. The cost of the program was only a half a million dollars.

Those remaining 154 gold bars are still there. The Navy gave up because the cost of recovery was more than the treasure is worth. For all practical purposes, the treasure in the *Laurentic* is exhausted. This is typical of all human treasure.

Why snatch at wealth
And hoard and stock it?

Your shroud, you know,
Will have no pocket!

—Barbara Elizabeth Gluck

In the opening pages of Russell H. Conwell's inspirational classic, *Acres of Diamonds,* the well-known preacher and educator tells a story he learned from an old Arab guide in Persia. It is the story of a rich man named Ali Hafed, who was content with his riches until he learned about diamonds. He had never thought about diamonds before—he did not even know about them. But now he began to aspire to the kind of wealth they would bring. Eventually, he left home in pursuit of them. Over a period of years, Hafed used up his money in searching and at last died a poor man on the shores of the Bay of Barcelona. Meanwhile, back in Persia, the man who had purchased Hafed's farm found an unusual pebble in the brook where the former owner had often watered his cattle. It turned out to be a diamond. Soon more were discovered. In this way, said Conwell's guide, the world-famous Golconda mines developed, from which have been taken many of the most famous jewels of the crowned heads of Europe.

—James M. Boice

If you want to feel rich, just count up all the things you have that money cannot buy.

—Daniel Webster

A wealthy industrialist leaped from the ninth-story room of a Chicago hotel leaving behind this note: "I am worth ten million dollars as men judge things, but I am so poor in spirit that I cannot live any longer. Something is terribly wrong with life." He was right. Something was terribly wrong with his life—because he had been born only once.

WEATHER

It's so cold here that two politicians were seen with their hands in their *own* pockets.

WEDDINGS

Apart from other blessings
That formal wedding means

Is the chance to see your daughter
In something else but jeans.
　　　　　　—Rosemarie Williams

When he requests my daughter's hand
In marriage, I won't block it.
I only hope he takes the hand
That's always in my pocket.
　　　　　　—Roger W. Dana

Many women marry men just like their father, which may explain why many mothers cry at weddings.

"Will you stand with us at our wedding?"
　"Why? Won't there be enough chairs for us to sit?"

Henry Moorhouse always enjoyed preaching on John 3:16. When he came to the word "whoever," he would emphasize its all-inclusiveness. That term, he would point out, makes it clear that everyone and anyone who trusts Christ will be saved.

He said he was glad the word "whoever" appeared in John 3:16 instead of the name Henry Moorhouse, because if that name were there he could not be sure it meant him. He would then explain how he arrived at that conclusion.

"I once bought a typewriter that was shipped mistakenly to another man named Henry Moorhouse at a different address. If John 3:16 had said that God loved Henry Moorhouse, I could have thought it meant the other Henry Moorhouse. But since it says 'whoever,' there can be no mistake!"

WILL OF GOD

When he was crossing the Irish Channel one dark starless night, F. B. Meyer stood on the deck by the captain and asked him, "How do you know Holyhead Harbor on so dark a night as this?" He said, "You see those three lights? Those three must line up behind each other as one, and when we see them so united we know the exact position of the harbor's mouth."

When we want to know God's will, three things must always concur: the inward impulse, the Word of God, and the trend of circumstances.

An individual's highest fulfillment, greatest happiness, and widest usefulness are to be found in living in harmony with His will.
　　　　　　—John D. Rockefeller Jr.

The question is not whether we know the will of God but whether we are willing to do the will of God. If so, God will then make His will clear to us.

A Sunday school teacher asked her pupils how they thought the angels of heaven do the will of God. The first child replied, "They do it immediately"; the second, "Diligently"; third, "They do it always"; fourth, "With all their hearts." Then a small child arose and said, "They do it without asking any questions."

The will of God will never lead you where the grace of God cannot keep you.

If you are not willing to be used by God, ask God to make you willing to be willing.
　　　　　　—F. B. Meyer

Most people don't want to know the will of God in order to do it; they seem to want to know it just in order to consider it!
　　　　　　—William L. Pettingill

There is only one way to bring peace to the heart, joy to the mind, and beauty to the life; it is to accept and do the will of God.

　　　　　　—William Barclay

An old Scottish woman traveled around the countryside selling housewares. Whenever she came to a fork in the road, she would throw a straw into the air; and when it dropped to the ground, she would proceed in the direction it indicated. The residents of the area knew her strange custom, but one day a friend saw her tossing the straw several times before choosing the path she would take. He inquired, "Why did you do that more than once?"

"Oh, it kept pointing to the road on the left." she replied, "and I wanted to go the other way because it looks so much smoother." She had continued casting her straw to the wind until it fell in the direction she wanted.

A dear old lady once prayed, "Lord, we're afraid of our wills. If we follow our own inclinations we fear the consequences. Teach us Thy will!"

A young woman was talking to an evangelist about total commitment to God. "I don't dare give myself wholly to the Lord," she said. "I'm afraid He'll send me to the mission field, where I'd be miserable."

The evangelist replied, "Suppose that some cold, snowy morning a small bird came half-frozen, pecking at your window. Imagine that the helpless little creature would let you take it in and feed it, thereby putting itself entirely under your control. Tell me, what would you do? Would you grip it in your hand and crush it? Or would you give it shelter, warmth, and care?" Immediately the young woman's eyes brightened as she saw the application.

—Our Daily Bread

In September 1952, David Young and I were attending our college's camp at Catalina Island. We went hiking one sunny, hot afternoon to the top of a ridge of mountains. We were thirsty and didn't have any water with us, so we were glad to see a beautiful, blue lake in the valley a few hundred yards below us. We hiked down the mountain very fast to get a drink, but when we got to the bottom of the hill and walked to the lake, the whole shore was muddy and hundreds of green slimy frogs jumped into the water. We saw that it wasn't such good water after all; it was very muddy. So we went without our drink.

Sometimes we see something that looks so good that we believe it must be God's plan for us. But it is not always what it seems to be. We need the guidance of the Spirit to show us if it is really God's plan for us.

—Roy B. Zuck

George Mueller of Bristol, England, was an example to all believers of the life of faith, as he trusted God for the care of hundreds of children in his orphanages. His walk with God was also marked by his ability to discern the will of God, "in matters," as he used to say, "both trivial and important."

When asked about this he replied, "I seek at the beginning to get my heart into such a state that it has no will of its own in regard to a given matter. Nine-tenths of the difficulties are overcome when our hearts are ready to do the Lord's will, whatever it may be. When one is in this state, it is usually but a little way to the knowledge of what His will is."

—The Pilgrim

WILLS

When a will is read, heirs listen with probated breath.

—Farmers' Digest

Where there's a will, I want to be in it.

WISDOM

Automaker Henry Ford asked electrical genius Charlie Steinmetz to build the generators for his factory. One day the generators ground to a halt, and the repairman couldn't find the problem. In desperation, Ford called Steinmetz, who tinkered with the machines for a few hours and then threw the switch. Sure enough, the generators whirred to life—but Ford received a bill for ten thousand dollars from Steinmetz. Flabbergasted, the tightfisted carmaker inquired why the bill was so high.

Steinmetz sent his reply: for tinkering with the generators, $10; for knowing where to tinker, $9,900. Ford paid the bill.

He who knows not, and knows not that he knows not, is a fool, shun him;

He who knows not, and knows that he knows not, is a child, teach him.

He who knows, and knows not that he knows, is asleep, wake him;

He who knows, and knows that he knows is wise, follow him.

An old mountaineer from West Virginia was celebrated for his wisdom. "Uncle Zed," a young man asked, "how did you get so wise?"

"Weren't hard," said the old man. "I've got good judgment. Good judgment comes from experience. And experience—well, that comes from having bad judgment."

—*Bits & Pieces*

Wisdom only comes with experience and experience only comes with time.

The art of being wise if the art of knowing what to overlook.

—William James

Scripture nowhere condemns the acquisition of knowledge. It is the wisdom of this world, not its knowledge, that is foolishness with God.

—H. A. Ironside

Many persons might have attained to wisdom had they not assumed they had already possessed it.

—Seneca

Don't sail out farther than you can row back.

—Danish proverb

Many of us spend half our time wishing for things we could have if we didn't spend half our time wishing.

—Alexander Woollcott

A student in Columbia University was under the impression that he had been assured by the institution that he would be taught wisdom. Feeling that the university had failed him in the matter, he filed suit against it for eight thousand dollars.

The Superior Court dismissed the case; and the Appellate Division of the Superior Court ruled that the suit had been properly dismissed.

The presiding judge Sidney Goldmann of the three-man appellate court declared, "These charges were set in a frame of intemperate, if not scurrilous, accusations. We agree with the trial judge that wisdom is not a subject that can be taught and that no rational person would accept such a claim made by any man or institution."

The difference between a smart man and a wise man is that a smart man knows what to say and a wise man knows whether to say it or not.

—Frank M. Garafda

Wise men learn more from fools than fools learn from the wise.

—Marcus Cato
(the Elder)

Common sense in an uncommon degree is what the world calls wisdom.

—Samuel Coleridge

No man is wise enough by himself.

—Plautus

Here's to the man who is wisest and best.
Here's to the man who with judgment is
    blest.
Here's to the man who's as smart as can
    be—
I mean the man who agrees with me.

WITNESSING

Preach the gospel at all times. If necessary, use words.

—Francis of Assisi

Bishop John Tanner used to test chaplains by saying, "If I had two minutes to live, how would you tell me to get to heaven?" If they couldn't tell him in two minutes, he knew they couldn't tell him in two hours.

T. J. Bach was converted while a student in Copenhagen, Denmark. Walking down the street on a Sunday afternoon, he noticed a young man crossing the street to give him a tract. Bach crushed the tract in his hand, muttering that people should mind their own business. The young man did not respond but instead turned aside to pray, as tears began to run down his cheeks. Noticing the man's tears, Bach thought, "He has given his money to buy the tract. He has given his time to distribute it. And now he has given his heart in prayer for me." The young man's compassion toward Bach's crude behavior brought deep conviction. Half an hour later in his room, Bach pasted the tract together. Before he finished reading it, he was down on his knees, asking God for forgiveness.

—Leslie B. Flynn

A Christian baroness, living in the highlands of Nairobi, Kenya, told of a young national who was employed as her houseboy. After three months he asked the baroness to give him a letter of reference to a friendly sheik some miles away. The baroness, not wishing the houseboy to leave just when he had learned the routine of the household, offered to increase his pay. The lad replied that he was not leaving for higher pay. Rather, he had decided he would either become a Christian or a Mohammedan. This was why he had come to work for the baroness for three months. He had wished to see how Christians acted. Now he wanted to work for three months for the sheik to observe the ways of the Mohammedans. Then he would decide which way of life he would follow. The baroness was stunned as she recalled her many blemishes in her dealings with the houseboy. She could only exclaim, "Why didn't you tell me at the beginning!"

—Leslie B. Flynn

Mark J. Goodger made it a weekly practice to hand out tracts from door to door. One day in South Carolina he stopped at a house and rang the bell. Because he heard sounds inside, he knew someone was home; so he kept ringing, even though no one came. Finally a man appeared, took the tract he offered, and rudely slammed the door in his face. A week later, Goodger returned to the same house. This time the man answered almost immediately. Inviting him in, he asked him to come to the attic. There he saw a sturdy rope dangling from the rafters with a box below it. The man said, "Friend, when you rang my bell last week, my head

was in that noose. I was ready to jump! But you were so persistent that I decided to go down and see who it was. After receiving your tract, I read it because its title interested me, and through it God spoke to me. Instead of jumping off that box, I knelt beside it and gave my heart to the Lord." How thankful Goodger was that he had been diligent in his witnessing! Without that leaflet the man would have gone into eternity unsaved.

A barber felt he must testify for the Lord; so when his first customer came in, he tilted him back in the chair, vigorously stropped his razor, and suddenly asked, "Are you ready to die?" In horror the man bolted out the door. The barber's misguided enthusiasm lost him his customer.

—M. R. De Haan

A young minister, returning to his home late one evening after conducting a service some miles distant, entered a crowded bus, having his Bible under his arm. Some of the passengers, rough fellows, poked fun at the young man, and one of them shouted at him in a derisive way, "Say, Mister, how far is it to heaven?"

The minister turned to face his antagonist and, in soft-spoken tones and with gracious manner, replied, "It is only one step, Sir. Will you not let me show you the way?"

The story is told of a man who was teaching his wife how to drive the car. He got her in the driver's seat and said, "Now just turn the hickey over, pull on the jigger, push down on the jimcrack, then press down on the do-dad with your foot and pull the thingamabob at the same time. When it starts, push down on the dofunny and yank the uptiddy and then let up on the foot dingus, put your other foot on the hickey-madoodle and don't forget to push down on the hootenanny. See?"

That reminds us of the way some people explain the Bible. Let us be clear and explicit in our teaching and preaching— especially in explaining the Way of Life; for so much depends on it.

—Christian Victory

On one occasion John Vassar, a great soul-winner, was going from house to house distributing tracts and talking with people about their souls. One woman who heard about this strange man and what he was doing said, "If he comes to my house, he will get the door slammed in his face." Without knowing that this woman had made such a statement, Mr. Vassar rang her doorbell the next day. When she saw that he was the man who had been described to her, she slammed the door in his face. John Vassar sat down on her doorstep and sang:

But drops of grief can ne'er repay
The debt of love I owe,
Here Lord I give myself away;
'Tis all that I can do.

The woman heard the earnest verse as he sang and was convicted. She opened the door and called Mr. Vassar in, who led her to Jesus Christ.

Publius Aristides, a second-century Athenian philosopher, was asked to report on the Christians of that day. Here is part of his letter:

"The Christians, O King, know and believe in God, the Maker of heaven and earth. They walk in all humility and kindness, and falsehood is not found among them. They observe scrupulously the commandment of their Messiah; every morning, and at all times, on account of the goodness of God toward them, they praise and laud Him, and over their meals they render Him thanks. On account of them, there flows forth much beauty in the world."

—Edward H. Morgan

WIVES

A man is a person who, if a woman says, "Never mind, I'll do it myself," lets her.

A woman is a person who, if she says to a man, "Never mind, I'll do it myself," and he lets her, gets mad.

A man is a person who, if a woman says to him, "Never mind, I'll do it myself," and he lets her and she gets mad, he says, "Now what are you mad about?"

A woman is a person who, if she says to a man, "Never mind, I'll do it myself," and he lets her, and she gets mad and he says, "Now what are you mad about?" says, "If you don't know, I'm not going to tell you."

—Katherine S. Beamer

I really don't understand my wife sometimes. She insisted on buying a new bathing suit before we went on vacation just because her old one had a hole in the knee.

WOMEN

"What's the greatest water power know to man?"

"A woman's tears."

In her childhood, a woman wants love and protection.

In her teen years, a woman wants excitement.

In her 20s, a woman wants romance.

In her 30s, a woman wants appreciation.

In her 40s, a woman wants sympathy.

In her 50s, a woman wants cash.

WONDERMENT

A little girl was riding on a train for the first time with her mother. She was looking through the window with eyes opened wide in wonder. She would say, "Look, Mama, cows! Look, Mama, horses! Oh, Mama, houses!" Being a bit embarrassed, the mother turned to those sitting nearby and said, "My daughter still thinks that everything is wonderful."

A passenger on a long train trip was so enthralled by the journey that every few moments he was heard to say, "Wonderful!" The passing scenery, the faces of the fellow passengers, even the smallest details elicited from him glad expressions of keen enjoyment. Finally one traveler, overcome by curiosity, asked him, "How is it that while the rest of us are worn out with this monotonous trip, you are having the time of your life and you keep saying, 'Wonderful!' " He answered, "Until a few days ago, I was a blind man. A great doctor has just given me my sight and what is ordinary to the rest of you is 'out of this world' to me."

—*The Best of Vance Havner*

WORDS

In 1675, Sir Christopher Wren laid the first stone on what was to be his masterpiece, St. Paul's Cathedral in London. For thirty-five years he labored on the massive project, and in 1710 he presented it for inspection to his sovereign, Queen Anne. England's grand monarch pronounced it "artificial," "amusing," and "awful." Sir Christopher was delighted.

For in 1710, the word "artificial" meant artful, "amusing" meant amazing, and "awful" meant "full of awe," "awe-inspiring."

The six most important words are "I admit I made a mistake." The five most important words are "You did a good job." The four most important words are "What is your opinion?" The three most important words are "If you please." The two most important words are "Thank you." The least important word is "I."

—David Weiss

Have you ever considered the awesome power of the spoken word? For instance:
    Waiter: What'll you have for dessert?
    First Diner: Nothing for me.
    Second Diner: I'm stuffed.
    Third Dinner: Couldn't eat another bite.
    Waiter: It comes with the dinner.
    First Diner: Ice cream.
    Second Diner: Pecan pie.
    Third Diner: Chocolate layer cake.

WORK

We the unwilling
led by the unknowing
are doing the impossible
for the ungrateful.
We have done so much
for so long with so little,
we are now qualified
to do anything
with nothing!

God put me on earth to accomplish a certain number of things. Right now I am so far behind I will never die.

Thank God every morning when you get up that you have something to do that day which must be done whether you like it or not. Being required to work, and doing so to the best of your ability, will breed in you self-control, diligence, contentment, and a hundred other virtues which the idle never know.

—Charles Kingsley

Luck may sometimes help; work always helps.

—*Teen Esteem*

Do more than belong, participate.
Do more than care, help.
Do more than believe, practice.
Do more than be fair, be kind.
Do more than forgive, forget.
Do more than dream, work.

—William Arthur Ward

The secret of happiness is not in doing what one likes to do, but in liking what one has to do.

Work done grudgingly is servitude.
Work done willingly is service.
Work done lovingly is a sacrament.

Nothing is work unless you would rather be doing something else.

—William James

When you work, work hard. When you play, play hard.

—Theodore Roosevelt

I had to learn the difference between planning to do God's work and being willing to work at God's plan.

—William P. Andrews

A hard-working Irishman, asking for a well-deserved raise, was put off by his boss who was known to be the town skinflint. "Pat," he said, "you really don't work as hard as you say. And I can prove it to you. There are 365 days in a year. You sleep eight hours every day, totaling 122 days. Subtracted from 365, that leaves 243. You also have eight hours every day for recreation and taking care of your family, which makes another 122 days. That leaves a balance of 121 days. Then, too, there are 52 Sundays; deducting these leaves 69 days. As you know, our office is closed every Saturday afternoon, giving 52 half-holidays or 26 more days that you do not work. This leaves a balance of only 43 days. However, we allow you one hour for lunch, which over the year makes 16 days, leaving 27 days. We give you two weeks vacation; that leaves only 13 days. Also, there are 12 legal holidays, leaving only one day; and if you add up all your coffee breaks, you will see that you probably owe me money!" Poor Pat, not having heard the old adage, "Figures don't lie, but liars can figure," hastily retreated to his workbench, fearing he might not even get his regular paycheck.

God never goes to the lazy or the idle when He needs someone for His service. When God wants a worker, He calls a worker. When He has work to be done, He goes to those who are already at work. When God wants a great servant, He calls a busy person. Scripture and history attest this truth.

Moses was busy with his flock at Horeb.

Gideon was busy threshing wheat by the winepress.

Saul was busy searching for his father's lost beasts.

David was busy caring for his father's sheep.

Elisha was busy plowing with twelve yoke of oxen.

Nehemiah was busy bearing the king's wine cup.

Amos was busy following the flock.

Peter and Andrew were busy casting a net into the sea.

James and John were busy mending their nets.

Matthew was busy collecting customs.

Saul was busy persecuting the friends of Jesus.

William Carey was busy mending and making shoes.

We do not attach ourselves lastingly to anything that does not cost us care, labor, or longing.

—Honoré de Balzac

A fellow applied for a job at a grocery store. "I'm interested in filling the vacancy left by the one who left."

"I'm sorry, but when he left, he didn't leave a vacancy."

Work is the only pleasure. It is only work that keeps me alive and makes life worth living. I was happier when doing a mechanic's job.

—Henry Ford

Mankind will be in a sorry way when men look for satisfaction outside their work instead of in their daily tasks—in a job well done. It's a low form of happiness that is pursued only after working hours. Without work, life is drudgery, dull.

—William Feather

I've been a dead weight many years
  Around the church's neck;
I've let the others carry me
  And always pay the check.
I've had my name upon the rolls
  For years and years gone by;
I've criticized and grumbled too,
  Nothing could satisfy.
I've been a dead weight long enough
  Upon the church's back;
Beginning now, I'm going to take
  A wholly different track.
I'm going to pray and pay and work
  And carry loads instead;
And not have others carry me
  Like people do the dead.

I am a great believer in luck, and I find the harder I work, the more I have of it.

—Stephen Leacock

To be active in God's work is one thing; to be effective in God's work is another.

It is a mark of intelligence, no matter what you are doing, to have a good time doing it.

People develop character by earning things, not by getting them for nothing.

—John Luther

A sitting crow starves.

—Icelandic proverb

God gives every bird its food but does not drop it into the nest.

—Danish proverb

People who believe that the dead never come back to life should be here at quitting time.

The most miserable man in the world is the one who has no work to dedicate himself to.
—Nelson Boswell

Blessed is he who has found his work; let him ask no other blessedness. He has a work, a life-purpose; he has found it and will follow it. Labor is life; from the inmost heart of the worker rises his God-given force, the sacred, celestial life-essence breathed into him by Almighty God.

—Thomas Carlyle

If you observe a really happy man, you will find him building a boat, writing a symphony, educating his son, growing double dahlias in his garden, or looking for dinosaur eggs in the Gobi desert. He will not be searching for happiness as if it were a collar button that has rolled under the radiator. He will have become aware that he is happy in the course of living twenty-four crowded hours of the day.

—W. Beran Wolfe

If you would succeed, love your work.

A veterinarian in Oklahoma lived in a little town called Sasakwa. Everybody liked him. He was a grand vet. Since they didn't have enough people to hold all of the offices in the town, they decided they'd run him for sheriff and he was elected. He was a very good sheriff, as he was a very good veterinarian. One night quite late a telephone caller said to his wife, "Could we speak to your husband?" And she said, trying to be quite proper, "In what capacity do you need my husband? Do you need him as a veterinarian or as a sheriff?" There was a long pause. The response was, "Both. We can't get our dog's mouth open and there's a burglar's leg in it."

R. G. LeTourneau was once asked, "When should a child start work?" He gave the startling reply, "I would say about the age of three. Now don't misunderstand, I am not in favor of the sweatshop or child labor that deprives a youngster of his education or the pleasure of carefree hours, nor do I approve of anything that breaks down his health or stunts his development. But there's one thing sure: if one does not learn to work as a child, he will never do much when he grows up. I probably sawed as much wood as a boy and shoveled as much sand at the foundry in my early teens as the next fellow, and it never hurt me. In fact, I don't know what it means to lose a day through sickness. I think that almost without exception the ones who get things done are those who learned to work as children. We need to teach our youngsters the dignity of labor and the pleasure of accomplishment. They must be made to understand that only by determined effort do we create things worthwhile. Not only does work keep us from mischief, but the more we sweat and toil, the bigger kick we get out of our labors."

For any sorrow there is only one medicine, better and more reliable than all the drugs in the world: work.

—Ferenc Molnár

Adam Clark is reported to have spent forty years writing his commentary on the Scriptures. Noah Webster labored thirty-six years forming his dictionary; in fact, he crossed the ocean twice to gather material needed to make the book absolutely accurate. John Milton rose at four o'clock every morning in order to have sufficient hours to compose and rewrite his poetry, which stands among the best of the world's literature. Edward Gibbon spent twenty-six years on his book *The Decline and Fall of the Roman Empire,* but it towers as a monument to careful research and untiring dedication to his task. Bryant rewrote one of his poetic masterpieces a hundred times before it was published, just to attain complete beauty and perfection of expression. These men enjoyed what they were doing, and each one threw all his energy into his effort no matter how difficult the job.

Folks who never do any more than they are paid for, never get paid for any more than they do.

—Elbert Hubbard

Work is the true elixir of life. The busiest man is the happiest man. Excellence in any art of profession is attained only by hard and persistent work.

—Sir Theodore Martin

It has been my observation that most people get ahead during the time that others waste.

—Henry Ford

Some people dream of worthy accomplishments while others stay awake and do them.

God gives us the nuts, but he does not crack them.

—German proverb

The three great essentials to achieve anything worthwhile are, first, hard work; second, stick-to-itiveness; three, common sense.

—Thomas Edison

The highest reward for a person's toil is not what they get for it, but what they become by it.

—John Ruskin

Do a little more each day than you think you possibly can.

—Lowell Thomas

I never did a day's work in my life. It was all fun.

—Thomas Edison

Achievement seldom exceeds effort.

—Mortimer Adler

Let me . . . remind you that it is only by working with an energy which is almost superhuman and which looks to uninterested spectators like insanity that we can accomplish anything worth the achievement. Work is the keystone of a perfect life. Work and trust in God.

—Woodrow Wilson

The real essence of work is concentration.

Sign in the counseling office at a San Diego High School: If you think school is boring, wait until you sit around an unemployment office.

The most creative people I know, and some of the happiest, are those who constantly mix business and pleasure.

—Hugh Downs

There are four main bones in every organization:

The wishbones: Wishing somebody would do something about the problem.

The jawbones: Doing all the talking but very little else.

The knucklebones: Those who knock everything.

The backbones: Those who carry the brunt of the load and do most of the work.

A painter went to paint and the only place to park his car was at a "No Parking" sign. He put a sign on his car that read, "Painter working inside." When he came out, another sign was on the car. It said, "Sorry, policeman working outside."

Thomas Edison sent the following recommendations to a youth assembly that requested a message from him:

1. Always be interested in whatever you undertake.

2. Don't mind the clock, but keep at it, and let nature indicate the necessity of rest.

3. Failures, so called, are the fingerposts pointing out the right direction to those who are willing to learn.

4. Hard work and a genuine interest in everything that makes for human progress will make men and women

more valuable and acceptable to themselves and to the world.

—*Bits & Pieces*

"What do you work at?" "At intervals."

Of all the unhappy people in the world, the unhappiest are those who have not found something that they want to do.

The highest reward for man's toil is not what he gets for it, but what he becomes by it.

—John Ruskin

Sign on a church outdoor bulletin board in a small Pennsylvania town: Pray for a good harvest, but keep on hoeing.

One of the greatest pleasures in life consists of being paid handsomely for doing what you would be doing anyway, without pay.

Whether our work be pleasant or unpleasant depends less upon the work itself—provided it be honest—than upon our attitude toward it. Let us strive to regard our work as our best friend in the world, and the chances are that our work will become friendly to us. It isn't our position, but our disposition toward our position that counts.

—B. C. Forbes

My grandfather once told me that there are two kinds of people: those who do the work and those who take the credit. He told me to try to be in the first group; there was less competition there.

—Indira Gandhi

You can tell when you're on the right track—it's usually uphill.

Work harder. Millions on welfare depend on you.

If I were to suggest a general rule for happiness, I would say, "Work a little harder; work a little longer; work!"

—Frederick H. Ecker

If you work at this office long enough, you either become an institution or get committed to one.

One hitchhiker complained to the other: "That's right, just sit there and let me work my finger to the bone."

There are few, if any, jobs in which ability alone is sufficient. Needed also are loyalty, sincerity, enthusiasm, and cooperation.

The main satisfactions of life come through hard work which one enjoys.

—George W. Eliot

It is not enough just to put your shoulder to the wheel; you must remember to push.

Don't learn the tricks of the trade—learn the trade.

God gives us the ingredients for our daily bread, but he expects us to do the baking.

—William Arthur Ward

A worker who does only what he has to is a slave. One who willingly does more than is required of him is truly a free man.

Eventually everything degenerates to work.

—Peter Drucker

There's no labor a man can do that's undignified—if he does it right.

—Bill Cosby

Trust in God, but keep rowing to the shore.

—Russian proverb

God gives no linen, but only flax to spin.

—German proverb

A man who works with his hands is a laborer. A man who works with his hands and his brain is a craftsman. A man who works with his hands and his brains and his heart is an artist.

—Louis Nizer

Work keeps us from three evils: boredom, vice, and need.

—Voltaire

Most of the world's useful work is done by people who are pressed for time, or are tired, or don't feel well.

—Douglas Smithall Freeman

Nobody ever lost his shirt with his sleeves rolled up.

There's no such thing as a perfect job. In any position you'll find some duties which, if they aren't onerous immediately, eventually will be. Success depends not merely on how well you do the things you enjoy, but how conscientiously you perform those duties you don't.

—John Luther

The British poet John Masefield inspired his countrymen on many occasions. When he was asked what it was that inspired him to do his work, he replied with this little four-line verse by an unknown author:

Sitting still and wishing
Makes no person great.
The good Lord sends the fishing
But you must dig the bait.

—Nelson Boswell

If you are rich, work.
If you are burdened with seemingly unfair responsibilities, work.
If you are happy, continue to work.
Idleness gives room for doubts and fears.
If sorrow overwhelms you and loved ones seem not true, work.
If disappointments come, work.
If faith falters and reason fails, just work.
When dreams are shattered and hopes seem dead,
Work, work as if your life were in peril;
It really is.
No matter what ails you, work.
Work faithfully and work with faith.
Work is the greatest material remedy available.
Work will cure both mental and physical afflictions.

—Nelson Boswell

John Wesley traveled 250,000 miles on horseback, averaging twenty miles a day for forty years; preached four thousand sermons, produced four hundred books, knew ten languages. At eighty-three he was annoyed that he could not write more than fifteen hours a day without hurting his eyes, and at eighty-six he was ashamed he could not preach more than twice a day. He complained in his diary that there was an increasing tendency to lie in bed until 5:30 in the morning.

—*Arkansas Baptist*

A high-powered businessman from Milan, Italy, arrived at a government agency in Rome after lunch to transact an urgent matter before taking a late afternoon flight back to Milan. On arriving at the agency, he found the office deserted except for a janitor.

"What's going on here?" asked the businessman. "Don't they work in the afternoon?"

"No, signor, you have got it wrong," replied the janitor. "It is in the morning they don't work. In the afternoon, they don't come."

—*Bits & Pieces*

A little girl was told by her mother that she was in the world to do good for others. The little girl replied, "And what are the *others* in the world for?'

WORKS VERSUS FAITH

Andrew Bonar said that in the highlands of Scotland sheep occasionally wander off among the rocky crags and get themselves trapped on dangerous ledges. Attracted by the sweet grass on the mountainside, they leap down one to twelve feet to get to it. But they can't get back up. A shepherd will allow the helpless animal to remain there for days until it becomes so weak it's unable to stand up. Finally he ties a rope around his waist and goes over the cliff to the rocky shelf and rescues the one that has strayed. Someone asked Bonar, "Why doesn't the shepherd go down right away?" "Ah," came the reply, "sheep are so foolish that they would dash right over the precipice and be killed if the herdsmen didn't wait until their strength is nearly gone."

A wealthy religious man had in his employ an old gardener, a true believer, who tried to show his boss the emptiness of mere religion without Christ. There was one tree on the rich man's estate that never bore any fruit. However, one day as the owner was walking in his orchard, he saw some beautiful apples hanging on it. Imagine his surprise, especially when he went to pick some, and found them to be tied on. The gardener by this simple procedure wanted to point out to his employer the difference between real Christianity and pious sham. Religion without Christ is like a barren tree on which the fruit is merely "tied on."

In a cartoon, some Pharisees are arguing with Jesus about salvation. They said to Him, "We get our salvation the old-fashioned way; we earn it."

A young Italian boy knocked at the door of an artist's studio in Rome. When it was opened, he exclaimed, "Please, madam, will you give me the master's brush?" The painter had died, and the boy, longing to be an artist, wished for the great man's touch. The lady placed the requested item in the youth's hand, saying, "This is his brush; try it, my boy." With a flush of earnestness on his face, he made a supreme effort but soon found that he could paint no better with it than with his own. The lady then said, "Remember, my child, you cannot imitate the great master unless you have his spirit."

An ordinary working man was about to lose one eye because of a serious infection in it, and he needed an operation. He went to an eye specialist who examined his eye and said, "Yes, I believe I can perform the operation that will give you your sight." "What is your fee?" the man asked. "My fee is always 'so much' for that operation," the doctor said, mentioning several hundred dollars. "Why, Doctor, I could never pay a sum like that, but I'll tell you what I can do. I can pay half that much by paying a small amount each week." "But I can't do that," the surgeon said. "I have a standard to maintain in my profession, and I have to charge a regular fee for this operation, and therefore I cannot lower the fee; but there is nothing to stop me from doing it for nothing."

When one breaks the speed limit, the policeman doesn't ask him how well he did at his driving the day or week before. He just gives him a ticket for the thing he did wrong.

God doesn't refrain from punishing the sins of the sinner just because he has been good the biggest part of the time. The penalty for sin must be paid.

If I could preach justification to be bought or to be had by walking a hundred miles or by some torture, who would not seek it? But when it is offered freely, men turn away. . . . What poor ideas men have of the value of Christ's gospel if they think they can buy it!

—Charles H. Spurgeon

A young preacher named John Nelson was talking to a rather self-righteous friend. The man exclaimed, "I do not need your Savior! I'm all right. I'll take my chance in the life I've lived. I think God will not be too hard on me." Nelson answered this boasting by saying, "Friend, if you got to heaven there would be discord. The song they sing in heaven is, 'Worthy is the Lamb that was slain.' If you got to heaven, you would be singing, 'Worthy am I because my own good life fitted me for heaven.' And an angel would throw you over the wall."

Once a girl found at her back fence an old tin can with a fuzzy tail tied to it. She tugged and tugged on it and out came a stiff dead cat. Into the kitchen she dragged it, flies and all, yelling, "Mommy! Mommy!"

"Yes, what is it?"

"Mommy, somebody just threw away a perfectly good cat."

Yes, it was perfectly good except it was

dead. There is only one thing wrong with self-righteous people. They are dead in trespasses and sins.

A man is rowing a boat on a river just above a dreadful cataract. The current begins to bear him downward; the spectators on the banks give him up for lost. "He is gone!" they all exclaim. But in another moment a rope is thrown out toward the wretched man; it strikes the water near the boat. Now how does the case stand? Do all the spectators call on him to row, to row stronger, to try harder to reach the shore? No, they eagerly cried, "Drop your oars! Give up your desperate attempt!"

So also the sinner's hope lies not in struggling to save himself, but in ceasing to struggle.

One of the great American naval vessels destroyed in World War II was the Wasp. Not until it became apparent that the flames had spread beyond hope of control was the order finally given to abandon ship. A surviving officer, Lieutenant Bodell, later said, "I climbed down the cargo net and dropped off into the water. Then I saw my first sign of panic, because some of those 'green kids' had no trust in their lifejackets, and instead of getting clear of the ship, were clinging to its plates by their fingertips—the worst thing you can do."

A poor, untidy man walked into a little drugstore one evening and said to the druggist, "Please, mister, do you have anything for a bad cold?" The druggist, of course, started to work by his rules and he asked, "Do you have your prescription with you?" The man answered, "No, I ain't got no prescription with me, but I've brought my cold with me."

This is just the way God wants sinners to come to Him. Do not try to bring a prescription.

WORLDLINESS

The great albatross flies around the world several times in the course of its life. These birds can stand being buffeted by ocean gales for days, but they become seasick if they stand on the deck of a moving ship.

Christians can face buffeting by life so long as they remember that they are in the world but not of it. When they become a part of this world, they lose their Christian joy and power, because they are out of the element for which God created them.

He who marries the spirit of the age today will be a widower tomorrow.

—William Inge

A small girl thoughtfully watched her mother working among the plants in their colorful garden. Suddenly she said, "I know why the flowers grow, Mom. They're so pretty they want to get out of the dirt!"

Similarly, even though Christians have their roots here on earth, they should not cling to this world. Having been beautified by grace, they should focus their attention on heavenly things.

Whatever weakens your reason, impairs the tenderness of your conscience, obscures your sense of God, or takes off the relish of spiritual things—whatever increases the authority of your body over your mind—that thing to you is sin.

—John Wesley

A popular tavern moved to another part of the city, leaving the "Ole Inn" vacant. A certain congregation rented the vacated tavern for a few months while remodeling and adding recreation rooms and pool halls to their church. The bar was changed to a pulpit, and temporary pews were installed. The tavern owner, however, had forgotten to take his parrot along, so the bird still sat in his cage in the corner. On Sunday morning the preacher took his place and the parrot squawked, "Say, look here! We have a new bartender!" and when the choir entered, he added, "and a new floor show." But when the members began to come in, the parrot croaked, "Aark! but the same customers—the same old crowd!"

If you find yourself loving any pleasure above prayer, any book better than the Bible, any house more than the house of

God, any table better that the Lord's Table, or any person more than Christ . . . take alarm.

—Thomas Guthrie

When some boys caught two chirping baby linnets, they decided to teach these birds to sing by putting them in a small cage and hanging it next to the cage of a pet canary. The canary, of course, sang beautifully, so the boys thought if the linnets were close to it, they too would become good songbirds. Several weeks went by with no apparent results. Then one day the youngsters were startled by a strange noise coming from the canary's cage. "Listen," one of them said, "the canary is cheeping like a linnet."

—H. A. Ironside

Several years ago our family visited Niagara Falls. It was spring, and ice was rushing down the river. As I viewed the large blocks of ice flowing toward the falls, I could see that there were carcasses of dead fish embedded in the ice. Gulls by the score were riding down the river feeding on the fish. As they came to the brink of the falls, their wings would go out and they would escape from the falls.

I watched one gull which seemed to delay and wondered when it would leave. It was engrossed in the carcass of a fish, and when it finally came to the brink of the falls, out went its powerful wings. The bird flapped and flapped and even lifted the ice out of the water, and I thought it would escape. But it had delayed too long so that its claws had frozen into the ice. The weight of the ice was too great, and the gull plunged into the abyss.

—George Sweeting

Worldliness is what any particular culture does to make sin look normal and righteousness look strange.

—David Wells

The dearest idol I have known,
Whate'er that idol be
Help me to tear it from Thy throne,
And worship only Thee.

—William Cowper

WORRY

"Why can't you sleep?" a wife asked her husband, as he paced the floor at 3 A.M. "Honey, I borrowed a thousand dollars from Sam next door, and I have to pay him back tomorrow," the husband replied. "I just don't have the money," he said wringing his hands. The man's wife jumped out of bed and flung open the bedroom window. "Sam! Sam!" she shouted. After a few minutes the groggy neighbor opened his window. "What is it?" he mumbled. "You know the thousand dollars my husband owes you? He doesn't have it," the woman yelled. Turning to her husband, she said, "Now, you go to sleep and let *him* pace the floor."

Most of today's worries are like puddles; tomorrow they will have evaporated.

—*Teen Esteem*

Life is very simple. The first thing to remember about life is—don't worry about it. Really, there are only two things to worry about; either you're successful or you're not successful. If you're successful, there's nothing to worry about. If you're not successful, there are only two things to worry about. Your health is good or you are sick if your health is good, there's nothing to worry about. If your health is bad, there are only two things to worry about: either you're going to live or you're not going to live. If you live there's nothing to worry about, and if you don't live, you have only two things to worry about. Either you're going to heaven or you're not going to heaven. If you are going to heaven, there's nothing to worry about, and if you go to the other place, you'll be so busy shaking hands with all your old friends, you won't have time to worry.

—Milton Berle

To carry worry to bed is to sleep with a pack on your back.

—*Teen Esteem*

If you do the best and the most you can today, don't worry about tomorrow.

—B. C. Forbes

You don't get ulcers from what you eat. You get them from what's eating you.

—Vicki Baum

How to Worry Scientifically

1. Never worry over rumors or what "they" say. First get the facts.
2. Know definitely your worry problem. Write it down. Face it.
3. Worry about only one problem at a time.
4. Set a definite day, afternoon, or night for worrying.
5. Never worry in bed, in the dining room, living room, or at church.
6. Select an air-conditioned room. Lean back in an easy chair.
7. Set a time limit. If you must go beyond it, give yourself credit for time-and-a-half.
8. Never worry with a frowning face. Smile, sing, or whistle.
9. Never worry when you are tired, sick, angry, or depressed.
10. Never worry while working, playing, visiting, shopping, or gossiping.
11. There are two times never to worry—when you can help the situation and when you cannot.
12. Never worry alone. Take it to the Lord and leave it there (Prov. 3:5–6).

We have only two things to worry about. One is that things will never get back to normal. The second is that they already have.

What parents think children worry about:
1. Nuclear war.
2. Terrorism.
3. Being kidnapped.
4. Possible divorce of parents.

What children worry about:
1. Grades at school.
2. Having friends.
3. Being teased or bullied.
4. Being embarrassed.

—*Work and Family Newsletter*

Worry is wasting today's time to clutter up tomorrow's opportunities with yesterday's trouble.

Worry often gives a small thing a big shadow.

—Swedish proverb

Worry is the interest paid by those who borrow trouble.

—G. W. Lyon

In Stonewall, Texas, at a ceremony recognizing highway beautification, President Lyndon B. Johnson told his audience he was feeling fine because he had followed the advice of an old woman who once said, "When I walks, I walks slowly. When I sits, I sits loosely. And when I feel worry comin' on, I just goes to sleep."

If I don't have something to worry about, I worry!

Most of our worries are reruns.

Said the robin to the sparrow,
"I really do not know
Why it is these human beings
Rush about and worry so."
Said the sparrow to the robin,
"I think that it must be
That they have no Heavenly Father,
Such as cares for you and me."

Sign over a chaplain's door: "If you have worries, come in and let's talk them over. If not, come in and tell us how you do it."

A man was worrying all the time about everything. He was a chronic worrier. Then one day his friends saw him whistling. "Can that be our friend? No, it can't be. Yes it is." They asked him, "What happened?" He said, "I'm paying a man to do my worrying for me." "You mean you aren't worrying anymore?" "No. Whenever I'm inclined to worry, I just let him do it." "How much do you pay him?" "Two thousand dollars a week." "Wow! How can you afford that?" "I can't. But that's his worry."

I've joined the new Don't Worry Club,
And now I hold my breath
I'm so afraid I'll worry
That I'm worried half to death.

—R. Lofton Hudson

WORRY

Statisticians at the University of Wisconsin have studied the things human beings worry about. They found that the average individual's worries can be divided into four headings: First, there are the things that never happened, which constitute 40 percent of the worries. Second, there are things over and past that couldn't be changed by all the worry in the world, and they are another 30 percent of the total. Third, there are petty worries and needless worries, which are 22 percent. Fourth, there are legitimate worries, and these are only 8 percent of the whole.

A Chinese man said he could write the biography of every American in three words: Hurry, Worry, Bury.

In 1871 a young man, a medical student, was a worrier. Then one day he read twenty-one words that changed his life. Later he founded the Johns Hopkins University and was the Regis Professor of Medicine at Oxford University. The twenty-one words were written by Thomas Carlyle: "Our main business is not to see what dimly lies at a distant, but to do what clearly lies at hand." The man was Sir William Oscar.

There is only one way to happiness and that is to cease worrying about things beyond the power of our will.
—Epictetus

Today is the tomorrow you worried about yesterday. Was it worth it?

Worry does not empty tomorrow of its sorrows; it empties today of its strength.
—Corrie Ten Boom

Worry is like a rocking chair. It gives you something to do but doesn't get you anywhere.

"I tried counting sheep, like you advised me," a clothing manufacturer told his partner, "but I couldn't get to sleep anyway. I counted thousands of sheep. Then, before I realized what I was doing I sheared them, combed the wool, spun it into cloth and made the cloth into suits. But I lost twenty dollars on each suit—and for the rest of the night I lay awake worrying."

You can't change the past, but you ruin a perfectly good present by worrying about the future.

I am an old man and have had many troubles, most of which never happened.
—Mark Twain

Worry produces doubt in a threefold direction: (1) God's love is doubted. Worry implies that He cares little for His blood-washed children. (2) God's wisdom is doubted. Worry indicates that He is not able to plan for His own, that He does not know what is best for them who belong to Him. (3) God's power is doubted. Worry says His grace is not sufficient for our needs.
—Herbert Lockyer

Don't worry about tomorrow. Remember, God is already there.

Don't tell me worry doesn't help. I know better. Things I worry about don't happen.

Worry is the interest we pay on trouble before it is due.
—Dan Cresten

Worry distorts our thinking, disrupts our work, disquiets our soul, disturbs our body, disfigures our face. It destroys our friends, demoralizes our life, defeats our faith, and debilitates our energy.
—William Arthur Ward

Tranquilizers have done wonders for dealing with the stresses and strains of modern life. For the first time in history, people aren't having nervous breakdowns. What they're having is calm breakdowns.
—Bob Orben

An old man was asked what had robbed him of joy the most in his lifetime. He replied, "Things that never happened."

A chicken-hearted knight had to go on a long journey so he tried to anticipate all problems. He carried a sword and armor in case he met someone unfriendly, a large jar of ointment for sunburn and poison ivy, an axe for chopping firewood, a tent, blankets, pots and pans, and oats for his horse. He then rode off—clanking, gurgling, thudding, and tinkling. He was a moving junk pile. When he was halfway across a dilapidated bridge, the boards gave way and he and his horse fell into the river and drowned. He had forgotten to pack a life preserver.

The moral of the story is that when we overburden ourselves with the anticipation of trouble, Fate is laughing her head off. She can provide us with troubles we could never have foreseen in our wildest dreams.

—Martin Buxbaum

WORSHIP

Worship is the overflow of the heart that asks nothing of God.

—Carl Armerding

A small boy was taken to a church worship service for his first time. Seeing a board on the wall with names, he asked his mother about it. She said, "That's the plaque with names of people who died in the service." Surprised, he asked her, "Was it the 9:30 or 11:00 service?"

To worship is to quicken the conscience by the holiness of God, to feed the mind with the truth of God, to purge the imagination by the beauty of God, to open the heart to the love of God, to devote the will to the purpose of God.

—William Temple

When a monarch of the British Empire is crowned, the Archbishop of Canterbury holds the crown in front of the one seated on the throne. Holding the crown, he speaks in one direction to the audience in Westminster Abbey, "I present to you Elizabeth of Windsor. Will you do her homage?" The people respond, "We will." Then he addresses another part of the audience in another direction with the same

question and the same response, and then to a third part. Only then does he crown the monarch.

The basic human needs are work, play, love, and worship.

—Richard C. Cabat

Worship is a love affair; it is making love to God.

—J. Vernon McGee

The dearest idol I have known,
Whatever that idol be;
Help me to tear it from Thy throne
And worship only Thee.

—William Cowper

If Socrates would enter the room, we should rise and do him honor. But if Jesus Christ came into the room, we should fall on our knees and worship Him.

—Napoleon

We slander God by our eagerness to serve God without knowing Him.

—J. Oswald Chambers

As a boy Lewis Sperry Chafer woke up every morning to the sound of his mother singing a hymn in the kitchen. She always sang the same one:

When morning guilds the skies,
My heart awakening cries,
May Jesus Christ be praised!
Alike at work or prayer
To Jesus I repair,
may Jesus Christ be praised!

Worship isn't crawling through a small hole to some theological wonderland. It is falling back upon God and finding that He is everywhere and anywhere you can fall.

—Kenneth C. Wilson

When Robert Kennedy visited the Amazon, he conversed with a Brazilian Indian, who had recently come to Christ but was not known to Kennedy, through a translator. "What do you most like to do?" Kennedy expected an answer like "hunting with bows and arrows" or "canoeing."

The Indian answered, "Being occupied with God."

Kennedy said, "Ask him again. Something may be lost in translation." But the Indian gave the same answer. This was an excellent definition of true worship.

WRITING

When something can be read without effort, great effort has gone into its writing.
—Enrique Jardiel Poncela

"We're not illiterate; we pick up all our trash."

One owl to another: "I can never remember when to use *who* and when to use *whom.*"
—Ray Rothco

The forcible writer stands boldly behind his words with his experience. He does not make books out of books, but he has been there in person.
—Henry David Thoreau

A ten-year-old boy was struggling through a book that was rather difficult for him. His uncle asked him if he was a "slow reader." He answered, "No, I'm a fast reader—it's just that the author of this book was a slow writer!"

If I had more time I would have written more briefly.
—Cicero

Why is a good writer like a criminal? Because they both like short sentences.
—Richard Crusta

A worker asked for a pay raise and got this note back from his supervisor.

"Because of the fluctuational predisposition of your position's productive capacity as juxtaposed to standard norms, it would be momentarily injudicious to advocate your requested increment."

The puzzled worker went to the supervisor and said, "If this is about my pay raise, I don't get it."

"That's right," said the supervisor.

"He is such a great preacher; has he written any books?"

"Yes, he plans to publish them posthumously."

"Well, I hope it will be soon!"

I hate to write, but I love to have written.
—Robert Louis Stevenson

"What bothers you most about the people you interview?" someone asked Phil Donahue. Without hesitation he answered, "People who float a battleship of words around a tugboat of thoughts."

Writing is like baking a cake for the people I love.
—Belva Plain

I love being a writer; the only thing I can't stand is the paperwork.
—Peter DeVries

Getting started is the hard part of writing. It's like opening a bottle of olives. You get the first olive out of the bottle and the rest come out easily.

There is nothing in the world that should not be expressed in such a way that an affectionate seven-year-old boy can see and understand it.
—Leo Tolstoy

Put it before them briefly, so they will read it, clearly so they will appreciate it, picturesquely so they will remember it, and above all, accurately so they will be guided by its light.
—Joseph Pulitzer

Never try to impress people with the profundity of your thought or by the obscurity of your language. Whatever has been thoroughly thought through can be stated simply.

A few years ago a young copywriter was trying to write an ad for a new kind of soap. Here is what he came up with: "The alkaline element and fats in this product are blended in such a way as to secure the highest quality of saponification, along with a specific gravity that keeps it on top of the water, relieving the bather of the trouble and annoyance of fishing around for it at the bottom of the tub during his ablutions."

A more experienced writer later said the same thing in two words: "It floats."

—*Bits & Pieces*

Novelist Sinclair Lewis was supposed to deliver an hour-long lecture to a group of college students who planned to be writers. Lewis opened his talk with a question:

"How many of you really intend to be writers?"

All hands went up.

"In that case," said Lewis, "my advice to you is to go home and write."

With that, he left.

—*Bits & Pieces*

Sherwood Anderson's first publishers, recognizing his potential, arranged to send him a weekly check in the hope that, relieved of financial pressure, he would write more freely. After a few weeks, however, Anderson took his latest check back to the office. "It's no use," he explained. "I find it impossible to work with security staring me in the face."

—*The Little, Brown Anecdote Book*

If you would not be forgotten as soon as you are dead, either write things worth reading or do things worth writing.

—Benjamin Franklin

Sooner or later a busy man learns to write things down. It's the best way to capture things we are apt to forget. "The strongest memory," says an old proverb, "is weaker than the palest ink."

An overconscientious journalist was admonished by his editor, "Never write anything unless you are absolutely certain that it is true, and when you are not sure, say so very specifically."

The next story he turned in was a masterpiece of hedging. It read as follows: "It is rumored that a party was given yesterday by several reputed ladies. It was said that Mrs. Smith was the hostess and all the alleged guests were local people. Mrs. Smith claims to be the wife of Mr. Joseph Smith, who purports to be the president of the supposed First National Bank."

—*Speak the Language of Success*

Someone in the congregation sent a note to the pulpit. The note read, "Bill Jones having gone to sea, his wife desires the prayers of the congregation for his safety." The preacher was somewhat nearsighted and he did not observe the punctuation. He read the notice but he read it in this way, "Bill Jones, having gone to see his wife, desires the prayers of the congregation for his safety!"

Writing a book is an adventure. To begin with, it is a toy and an amusement. Then it becomes a mistress, then it becomes a master, then it becomes a tyrant. The last phase is that just as you are about to be reconciled to your servitude, you kill the monster and fling him out to the public.

—Winston Churchill

Y

YOUTH

Euripides described the hippies of his day, the girls from Sparta, like this: "No Spartan girl could ever live clean even if she wanted. They are always out on the street in scanty outfits, making a great display of naked limbs . . . Abominable's the word. It is little wonder Sparta is hardly famous for chaste women."

Our youth now love luxury. They have bad manners, contempt for authority, disrespect for older people. Children nowadays are tyrants. They no longer rise when their elders enter the room, they contradict their parents, chatter before company, gobble their food, and tyrannize their teachers.

—Socrates

Things I Wish I Had Known
Before I Was Twenty-One

That a man's habits are mighty hard to change after he is twenty-one.

That a harvest depends on the seeds sown.

That things worthwhile require time, patience, and work.

That you cannot get something for nothing.

The value of absolute truthfulness.

The folly of not taking other people's advice.

That what my mother wanted me to do was right.

That dad wasn't an old fogey after all.

More of the helpful and inspiring messages of the Bible.

The greatness of the opportunity and joy of serving a fellowman.

That Jesus Christ wants to be my Savior and Friend.

The error of youth is to believe intelligence is a substitute for experience, while the error of age is to believe that experience is a substitute for intelligence.

—Lyman Bryson

Alexander the Great was a young man when he conquered the world and wept for more worlds to conquer. Napoleon was only thirty-five when he was made Emperor of France. Thomas Jefferson was less than thirty when he was elected to the Senate, which had to suspend its rules in order that the youthful statesman might be seated. Nathan Hale was only twenty-one when he uttered the famous sentence, "All I regret is that I have but one life to give for my country." William Cullen Bryant was only nineteen when he wrote *Thanatopsis*. The average age of the Pilgrim fathers was twenty-six. Joan of Arc was only sixteen when she lead France to victory.

Horace Greeley was the champion speller of his school at the age of four.

Evangeline Booth preached her first sermon to a congregation of mops and brooms at five.

Robert Louis Stevenson said, "Hush! I'm telling myself a story," at age six.

Kit Carson was a dead shot with a rifle at age eight.

James Talcott, eminent New York merchant, earned his first dollar in a business deal at age ten.

John Hays Hammond, famous engineer, was panning for gold in Nevada at age eleven.

John Paul Jones was a sailor at seventeen.

Mozart reproduced and played the score of Allegri's *Miserere* after hearing it once, at age fourteen.

Hugo Grotius, father of international law, was a Latin scholar at nine, a university student at twelve, a lawyer at fifteen, a historian at twenty, and an international jurist at twenty-one.

McCormick invented the reaper at age twenty-three.

Isaac Newton formulated the law of gravitation at age twenty-four.

Charles Dickens began his *Pickwick Papers* at twenty-four and wrote *Oliver Twist* at twenty-five.

Benjamin Franklin wrote *Poor Richard's Almanac* at twenty-six.

Thomas Jefferson drafted the Declaration of Independence at age thirty-three.

—Howard Harris

You're young only once, but you can be immature indefinitely.

—Oscar Wilde

Young men are fitter to invent than to judge, fitter for execution than for counsel, fitter for new projects than for settled business.

—Francis Bacon

Z

ZEAL

In a wealthy residential section of Richmond, Virginia, some new owners complained that the singing of a small Christian church nearby disturbed them. A petition to be presented to the city council was circulated.

The solicitors brought it for signing to a Jewish resident. He read it and said, "Gentlemen, I cannot sign it. If I believed as do these Christians that my Messiah had come, I would shout it from the housetops and on every street of Richmond, and nobody could stop me."

John Milton got up at four o'clock every morning to work on *Paradise Lost*. William Cullen Bryant rewrote *Thanatopsis* ninety-five times. Noah Webster worked thirty-six years to produce the first edition of his dictionary. Many business executives put in ten or twelve hours a day, six or even seven days a week—not always because they have to, but because they are enthusiastic about their work.

A little girl saw a sign in a church meeting hall and was crying. It read, "The zeal of Thy house hath consumed me." An elder asked why she was crying. "I'm afraid of the zeal." He answered, "Don't worry little girl; there's no zeal in this place."

The seventeenth-century English pastor Richard Baxter said he preached with great intensity because he saw himself as a dying man ministering to dying people. He always spoke as if he were preaching his last sermon and as if his listeners were hearing their last message. And what a schedule he maintained for fifty years! On each Monday and Tuesday he spent seven hours instructing the children of the parish, not omitting even one. On Wednesday he went from house to house to make sure the material needs of the widows, the aged, and the infirm were met. During the rest of the week he prepared his sermons and wrote books—a total of 160 volumes. As a result of his ministry, the town of Kidderminster was transformed. It had been a place full of sexual immorality and other vices, but it became a village in which almost every household honored God, read the Bible, and prayed. Baxter's consuming zeal had paid off.

Dwight Morrow once wrote to his son, "The world is divided into people who do things and people who get the credit. Try if you can to belong to the first class. There's far less competition."

Wake up, sing up, preach up, pray up, pay up, stay up, and never give up or let up, or back up, or shut up, until the cause of Christ in the church and the world is built up.
—Woodland Christian Church,
Kansas City, Missouri

Which Are You?
An attender or an absenter?
A pillar or a sleeper?
A wing or a weight?
A power or a problem?
A promoter or a provoker?
A giver or a getter?
A goer or a gadder?
A doer or a deadhead?
A booster or a bucker?
A supporter or a sponger?
A soldier or a slacker?
A worker or a worrier?
A lighter or a leaner?
A friend or a faultfinder?
A helper or a hinderer?

Taking the line of least resistance makes rivers and men crooked.

If a man stands up and cheers for a football team in a stadium, he is called a "fan." But if he stands and cheers with conviction for the cause of Jesus Christ, he is labeled a "fanatic."

The church needs:
More tithes and fewer drives;
More action and less faction;
More workers and fewer shirkers;
More backers and fewer slackers;
More praying and less straying.

My greatest loss—to lose my soul.
My greatest gain—Christ my Savior.
My greatest object—to glorify God.
My greatest crown—to win souls for Christ.
My greatest joy—God's salvation.

My greatest inheritance—heaven and its glory.

My greatest victory—over death through Christ.

My greatest neglect—so great a salvation.

My greatest crime—to reject Christ.

My greatest bargain—to lose all to win Christ.

My greatest profit—godliness now and forever.

My greatest peace—passes all understanding.

My greatest knowledge—to know God and Christ.

INDEX

INDEX

NOTES

NOTES

NOTES

NOTES

NOTES

NOTES

NOTES

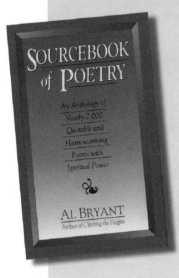

Sourcebook of Poetry

Al Bryant, compiler

A comprehensive collection of nearly two thousand poems, including the inspirational works of modern poets such as Martha Snell Nicholson, Margaret Clarkson, Oswald J. Smith, Edwin Markham, and Grace Noll Crowell.

Thoroughly indexed by subject, title, author, and first line, *Sourcebook of Poetry* is a standard reference work for sermon preparation or inspirational talks. Devotional readers will appreciate the wide variety of though-provoking and heart-warming works in this anthology.

AL BRYANT was editor-in-chief of Zondervan Publishing House for more than twenty-six years and has also served as Managing Editor of Word Books and as Director of Publications for Kregel Publications. As a leading devotional compiler, his more than fifty books have sold over two and half million copies. In addition to his Sermon Outline Series, his other titles include *Day by Day with C. H. Spurgeon, Climbing the Heights,* and *New Every Morning.*

Available from your local bookseller or

kregel
PUBLICATIONS

P.O. Box 2607 • Grand Rapids, MI 49501